Church of England Record Society

Volume 3

THE EARLY LETTERS OF BISHOP RICHARD HURD

1739–1762

Richard Hurd is best known to ecclesiastical historians as one of George III's favourite bishops who was offered, and declined, the archbishopric of Canterbury. These letters, therefore, illuminate the early career of one of the most prominent clerics of the late eighteenth century. The letters begin in 1739, just after Hurd had graduated B.A. at Emmanuel College, Cambridge. They chart his gradual climb up the ladder of ecclesiastical preferment, through his time as a Fellow at Emmanuel and end with him settled in the comfortable country rectory of Thurcaston in Leicestershire. Hurd had a wide circle of correspondents. He became a close friend of William Warburton, Bishop of Gloucester, perhaps the most prominent controversialist of the period. He was also a member of a literary circle which included the poets Thomas Gray and William Mason. Indeed, Hurd himself is well-known to students of English literature as the author of *Letters on Chivalry and Romance* and as a significant figure among the so-called 'pre-romantics'. Hurd's letters reveal the full range of his interests, from theology and university politics, through literature, to painting and sculpture. This edition, therefore, not only tells us about Hurd's early life and career, but also provides a valuable insight into the social life of the Anglican clergy in the eighteenth century.

THE EARLY LETTERS OF BISHOP RICHARD HURD

1739–1762

EDITED BY

Sarah Brewer

THE BOYDELL PRESS

CHURCH OF ENGLAND RECORD SOCIETY

First published 1995

A Church of England Record Society publication
Published by The Boydell Press
an imprint of Boydell & Brewer Ltd
PO Box 9, Woodbridge, Suffolk IP12 3DF, UK
and of Boydell & Brewer Inc.
PO Box 41026, Rochester, NY 14604–4126, USA

ISBN 0 85115 653 3

ISSN 1351–3087

British Library Cataloguing-in-Publication Data
A catalogue record for this book is available
from the British Library

Library of Congress Catalog Card Number: 93–12853

The paper used in this publication meets the minimum requirements of American National Standard for Information Sciences – Permanence of Paper for Printed Library Materials, ANSI Z39.48–1984

Printed in Great Britain by
St Edmundsbury Press Ltd, Bury St Edmunds, Suffolk

CONTENTS

For Beatrice

ACKNOWLEDGMENTS

This edition would have been impossible without the help and co-operation of those libraries and individuals who own manuscript copies of Hurd's letters, to all of whom I am most grateful. The letters in this volume are published by permission of Dr Vincent Giroud, Curator of Modern Books and Papers, and Dr Stephen Parks, Curator of the James Marshall and Marie-Louise Osborn Collection, the Beinecke Rare Book and Manuscript Library, Yale University; the Bodleian Library, Oxford; the Borthwick Institute of Historical Research, York; The Reverend D.F. Brewin, Rector of Thurcaston; the British Library; the Folger Shakespeare Library; Leicestershire Record Office; the National Library of Wales; Norfolk Record Office; Staffordshire Record Office; and the Bishop of Worcester. I am particularly grateful to the late Miss Beth and Miss Philippa Patteson and to Major and Mrs H. Bradshaw, the present owners of the Macro Letter-Book, for allowing me to consult the original.

I have also received invaluable assistance from a large number of archivists and librarians both in Britain and the United States, particularly those at Norfolk Record Office, Shropshire Record Office, Staffordshire Record Office and York Minster Library. The Librarian and administrative staff at Hartlebury Castle have always been especially welcoming. Much of my research was done in Cambridge, and I am grateful to the Archivist and library staff at St John's College and at the University Library (particularly those of the Rare Books Department), and above all at Emmanuel College, where all staff have been consistently helpful over many years.

It is now almost seventeen years since I began work on Hurd's correspondence, and during that time I have incurred many scholarly debts. Among those who assisted me with inquiries and provided information, I am particularly grateful to Dr Ben Benedikz, Graham Cartwright, Professor Donald Eddy, Dr Howard Erskine-Hill, the late Dr Peter Hunter Blair, Professor Michael J. Marcuse, Professor Geoffrey Shepherd, Dr Frank Stubbings, Dr Marcus Walsh, and Professor James T. Boulton, who first suggested that I work on Hurd and then supervised the thesis which was the basis of this edition. For many years Geoff Ferres helped to sustain me with his belief that the project would finally be completed. But my greatest debt is to my parents, for their constant support and encouragement and to my husband, Stephen Taylor, without whose advice and determination this project would never have been completed.

SMB
Reading
November 1992

List of Cue-Titles and Abbreviations

Alum. Cantab.	*Alumni Cantabrigienses. A Biographical List of all Known Students, Graduates and Holders of Office at the University of Cambridge, From the Earliest Times to 1900*, compiled by John Venn and J.A. Venn, 10 vols., Cambridge, 1922–54.
Alum. Oxon.	*Alumni Oxonienses: The Members of the University of Oxford, 1500–1714: Their Parentage, Birthplace, and Year of Birth, with a Record of their Degrees*, ed. Joseph Foster, 4 vols., Oxford, 1891–12.
	Alumni Oxonienses: The Members of the University of Oxford, 1715–1886: Their Parentage, Birthplace, and Year of Birth, with a Record of their Degrees, 4 vols., Oxford, 1888.
Annals	Charles Henry Cooper, *Annals of Cambridge*, 5 vols., Cambridge, 1842–1908.
Beinecke	The Beinecke Rare Book and Manuscript Library, Yale University.
B.L.	British Library.
Bowyer, *Paper-Stock Ledger*	William Bowyer, *Paper-Stock Ledger 1717–73*, 3 vols., Bodleian Library, Ms. Don. b. 4.
Boyce, *Benevolent Man*	Benjamin Boyce, *The Benevolent Man. A Life of Ralph Allen of Bath*, Cambridge, Massachusetts, 1967.
D.N.B.	*Dictionary of National Biography*.
Draper, *Mason*	John W. Draper, *William Mason. A Study in Eighteenth-Century Culture*, New York, 1924.
Discourse	Richard Hurd, *A Discourse, By Way of General Preface to the Quarto Edition of Bishop Warburton's Works, Containing some Account of the Life, Writings, and Character of the Author*, 1794.
Evans, *Warburton and the Warburtonians*	A.W. Evans, *Warburton and the Warburtonians. A Study of Some Eighteenth-Century Controversies*, Oxford, 1932.
Folger	The Folger Shakespeare Library, Washington, D.C.
Gaskell, *First Editions of Mason*	Philip Gaskell, *The First Editions of William Mason*, Cambridge Bibliographical Society Monograph No. 1, 1951.
Gent. Mag.	*Gentleman's Magazine*.
Gray, *Correspondence*	*Correspondence of Thomas Gray*, ed. Paget Toynbee and Leonard Whibley, 3 vols., Oxford, 1935, reprinted with Corrections and Additions by H.W. Starr, 1971.
H.C.	Hartlebury Castle.
Hurd-Mason Corr.	*The Correspondence of Richard Hurd & William Mason, and Letters of Richard Hurd to Thomas Gray*, ed. E.H. Pearce and L. Whibley, Cambridge, 1932.
Illusts.	John Nichols, *Illustrations of the Literary History of the Eighteenth Century*, 8 vols., 1817–58.

Kippis, *Biographia Britannica*	*Biographia Britannica: or, the Lives of the Most Eminent Persons who have flourished in Great Britain and Ireland*, Second Edition, ed. Andrew Kippis, 5 vols., 1778–93.
Lit. Anecs.	John Nichols, *Literary Anecdotes of the Eighteenth Century; comprizing Biographical Memoirs of William Bowyer, Printer . . . and Biographical Anecdotes of a Considerable Number of Eminent Writers and Ingenious Artists*, 9 vols., 1812–16.
Lond. Mag.	*London Magazine*.
M.L.R.	*Modern Language Review*.
Memoirs	Francis Kilvert, *Memoirs of the Life and Writings of the Right Rev. Richard Hurd, D.D., Lord Bishop of Worcester; With a Selection from his Correspondence and other Unpublished Papers*, 1860.
N.C.B.E.L.	*The New Cambridge Bibliography of English Literature*, ed. George Watson, vol. 2, 1660–1800, Cambridge, 1971.
N.L.W.	National Library of Wales
N.U.C.	*National Union Catalog*.
O.E.D.	*Oxford English Dictionary*.
Prelate	[William Warburton and Richard Hurd] *Letters from a Late Eminent Prelate to One of His Friends*, Kidderminster, [1808].
R.O.	Record Office
Scott-Mayor, *Admissions to St John's*	R.F. Scott and J.E.B. Mayor, *Admissions to the College of St John the Evangelist in the University of Cambridge*, 3 vols., Cambridge, 1882–1931.
Straus, *Dodsley*	Ralph Straus, *Robert Dodsley. Poet, Publisher & Playwright*, 1910.
Walpole, *Correspondence*	*The Yale Edition of Horace Walpole's Correspondence*, ed. W.S. Lewis, 48 vols., New Haven, 1937–83.
Wordsworth, *Scholae Academicae*	Christopher Wordsworth, *Scholae Academicae: Some Account of the Studies of the English Universities in the Eighteenth Century*, Cambridge, 1877.

Biography of Richard Hurd (1720–1808)

Richard Hurd was born on 13 January 1720 at Congreve in the parish of Penkridge, Staffordshire. He was the second son of three children of John and Hannah Hurd, "plain, honest & good people".[1] John Hurd, "a very respectable yeoman", rented a farm in Congreve and later a larger area of land in Pendeford, midway between Brewood and Wolverhampton. His last move was to Brewood, where he died on 27 November 1755, aged 70. Hannah Hurd died on 27 February 1773, aged 88.

Hurd's elder brother John (born in 1715) became a farmer at Hatton Grange in Shropshire. He married in 1752, but died without issue in 1792. Thomas, the youngest son, was born in Pendeford in 1725. He became a draper in Birmingham, and in 1748 married Mary Marston: their second son, Richard, became companion, secretary and diocesan registrar to Hurd whilst he was Bishop of Worcester.

Little is known of Richard Hurd's early life, but by his own account, he was educated at a "good Grammar school at Brewood", first under "the reverend Mr Hillman, & upon his death, under his successor, the reverend Mr Budworth". Both, he said, were "well qualified for their office, & both very kind to him".[2] Budworth had been Master of a school at Rugeley, also in Staffordshire, and apparently continued there for two years after his new appointment, while the schoolhouse at Brewood was being repaired. Hurd was therefore sent to Rugeley on Budworth's succeeding Hillman, and returned to Brewood with him, when work on the school was completed. Budworth, he said, "understood Greek & Latin well, & had a true tast of the best writers in those languages. He was, besides, a polite well-bred man, & singularly attentive to the *manners* in every sense of the word, of his scholars. He had a warm sense of virtue & religion, & enforced both with a natural & taking eloquence."[3] The syllabus taught by Budworth incorporated classical grammar, translation of Latin and Greek texts (with particular emphasis on Ovid and Virgil), and "natural philosophy". On Saturday portions of "Mr Nelson's Festivals" were read out, and in Lent the boys studied their catechism. All comedies were disapproved of, and Budworth's pupils were never allowed to go and see one. But they were allowed to go and see "a well-written" tragedy; afterwards, however, they had to prepare "remarks on the principal characters" on which Budworth would then examine them.[4]

On 3 October 1733 Hurd was admitted to Emmanuel College, Cambridge, but did not go up to the university until 1735 when he matriculated.[5] He entered the college

1 *Dates of some occurrences in my own life*, MS HC, p. 1, printed (with some excisions) in *The Correspondence of Richard Hurd & William Mason*, ed. Ernest H. Pearce and Leonard Whibley, Cambridge, 1932, p. xxvi.

2 *Ibid.*

3 *Dates*, MS HC, pp. 2–3.

4 *Gentleman's Magazine*, August 1792, pp. 685–6.

5 *Admissions 1719–1797*, COL. 3. 2; *Alumni Cantabrigienses. A Biographical List of all Known*

as a sizar, the lowest rank of undergraduate, but improved his standing by winning a Thorpe exhibition, and the Sudbury Cup in 1738. Under the Thorpe benefaction he received £15 paid half yearly in arrears. He held his scholarship from early 1738 until the end of 1741, during which time he was also required to give a speech (24 November 1740) for which he was paid 10s.[6] The Sudbury Cup or Plate was awarded each year to a student of the college "at ye time of his taking ye Degree of B. of Arts [i.e. within that academic year] as shall be adjudg'd by ye Mastr & four Senr. Fellows of ye Foundation of ye sd College, or ye Mastr & any two of ye sd four Senr. Fellows to be ye most worthy of ye year for his Piety, Learning & Parts".[7] Hurd won the plate in 1738, although by this time it seems to have been the convention that a sum of £6 should be paid to the undergraduate concerned, rather than a cup awarded.[8]

As an undergraduate, Hurd records that "he was happy in receiving the countenance, & in being permitted to attend the Lectures, of that excellent Tutor, Mr Henry Hubbard, although he had been admitted under another person [Nathaniel Smalley]". His letters give some indication of his studies, his reading, for instance, of "Homer & Burgesdicius" (To Potter, 15 April 1739), and his application to "Reasoning, & Philosophy". (To Potter, 2 December 1739). Undergraduate studies were devoted largely to the study of mathematics, logic, Latin and Greek. A useful source of information on syllabus, Daniel Waterland's *Advice to a Young Student*, 1730, stipulates that undergraduates should spend their mornings in studying "Philosophy" (which comprehended "Mathematics, Geography, Astronomy, Chronology, and other Parts of Physicks; besides Logick, Ethicks, and Metaphysicks"), their afternoons in studying the Classics, and should devote Sundays and holidays to the study of Divinity.[9]

Hurd remained a sizar at Emmanuel until January 1739, when he was made a pensioner, as a necessary preliminary to taking his B.A. degree.[10] Examiners came to the college later that month, and in the first week of February he is listed as "in Batchrs: Coms: Sat Diner" [3 February]. On 4 April he was elected a Whichcot Scholar,[11] and from then on commenced his studies for an M.A. These were of a similar kind to those set out for the B.A., but Hurd's letters reveal a diversifying of interests and reasonable freedom to pursue them.

Soon after his graduating, Hurd made the acquaintance of Edward Macro, son of Cox and Mary Macro (see Biographies), who was admitted to the college on 5 June 1739.[12] His introduction into the Macro family was to provide him with his first living. For the present, however, he remained at Emmanuel until on 5 December 1741 his name was "turn'd".[13] He returned home to his family in Staffordshire then until March of the following year. In the interim, his name was kept on the college

Students, Graduates and Holders of Office at the University of Cambridge, From the Earliest Times to 1900, compiled by John Venn and J.A. Venn, 10 vols., Cambridge, 1922–54; the *Commons Accounts Book*, STE. 15. 9, at Emmanuel indicates that Hurd was in residence during December 1735, and thereafter.

6 *Thorpe Exhibition*, SCH. 1. 17.

7 *Terms of Benefactions (Sudbury)*, SCH. 1. 19.

8 *Whichcot and Sudbury Gift 1719–1765*, SCH. 1. 11.

9 [Daniel Waterland], *Advice to a Young Student. With a Method of Study for the Four First Years*, 1730, pp. 7–8, 12.

10 *Commons Accounts Book*, STE. 15. 9.

11 *Emmanuel College Order Book*, COL. 14. 2.

12 *Emmanuel College Register*, COL. 9. 1. (A).

13 *Commons Accounts Book*, STE. 15. 8.

books. By February of 1742, the Macros had found Hurd a living, but were faced with the difficulty of his not being old enough to go into orders. The problem was circumvented by using another Emmanuel friend, Robert Hudson, to take on the living (Reymerston in Norfolk) as rector, nominating Hurd as his curate. (To Potter, 15 April 1742). With this title, Hurd was ordained deacon on 13 June in St Paul's Cathedral by Joseph Butler, Bishop of Bristol and Dean of St Paul's, on letters dismissory from Dr Gooch, the Bishop of Norwich.[14] Hudson was instituted to Reymerston on 30 June.

Hurd's connections with Emmanuel had not yet, of course, been severed, and in July 1742, at Commencement, he was made an M.A. In the same month a fellowship became potentially vacant by the nomination of Nathaniel Smalley, one of the senior Fellows, to a college living. The usual convention in filling a vacancy was to select a candidate from the same county as the departing Fellow; Smalley was from a Staffordshire family and Hurd, therefore, was an obvious choice to replace him. He was approached by the Master and the two college tutors whilst up at Cambridge to take his degree, but could not immediately make up his mind. For some time he was under the impression that Cox Macro wished him not to accept the fellowship, but when this was clarified, probably late in the year, Hurd, with his patron's encouragement, accepted it, and on 7 December 1742 was officially elected.[15] (To Potter, 27 January 1743). The curacy was handed over to Robert Potter, younger brother of John, and also a graduate of Emmanuel.

Hurd remained at Emmanuel for the next fourteen years. He was moderately active in the college: as Librarian from 1746 to 1756,[16] as Steward from 1748 to 1749, as Sub-lecturer from 1743 to 1744, Lecturer and Hebrew Lecturer from 1747 to 1748, and Dean and Greek Lecturer from 1748 to 1749.[17] He had no duties as tutor to the undergraduates (with the exception of Sir Edward and Fisher Littleton from Staffordshire), but their numbers were small and from 1739 only two Fellows were chosen as tutors for the majority of students. He was, however, curate of St Andrew the Less, Cambridge, a title in the gift of Emmanuel, and held in conjunction with his fellowship.

During these years Hurd established friendships which were to endure for and colour the rest of his life, and a reputation as an acute and subtle critic. He made the acquaintance of William Mason and Thomas Gray, the former of whom became one of his closest friends, and is the recipient of some of his more affectionate letters. He consolidated his friendship with Edward Macro and his family and extended his acquaintance outside Emmanuel, forming friendships with a number of St John's men, amongst them, Thomas Balguy, William Samuel Powell, Samuel Ogden, and William Ludlam.[19] At Emmanuel Hurd's closest connection other than Macro was Sir Edward Littleton. Littleton was admitted to Emmanuel on 30 April 1744;[20] he had been a pupil of William Budworth, and clearly at his instigation chose to apply to Emmanuel

14 *Dates*, pp. 3–4; *Hurd-Mason Correspondence*, p. xxvi.
15 *Order Book*, COL. 14. 2.
16 *Steward's Accounts Book 1744–1759*, STE. 1. 5.
17 *Order Book*, COL. 14. 2.
18 *Commons Accounts Book*, STE. 15. 8.
19 No evidence, however, has been found to suggest that any body of correspondence between Hurd and these friends ever existed, with the exception of the Balguy correspondence.
20 *Admissions 1719–1797*, COL. 3.2.

where it was arranged that Hurd should act as his tutor. The connection between the two men developed into friendship, the apparent disparity in their social and intellectual standing enhancing what was in essence a typical eighteenth century "patron-client" relationship. Littleton injected an element of aristocratic sophistication into Hurd's relatively restricted social circle, and Hurd more than fulfilled expectations as a "client", rapidly finding success as an author respected for his scholarship and critical acumen.

The first work published by Hurd was the anonymous *Remarks on a late Book. Entitled, An Enquiry into the Rejection of the Christian Miracles by the Heathens*, dated 1746 and advertised for sale in December. (To Macro, 5 January 1747). It aroused little interest outside Cambridge circles, although it did elicit a reply from William Weston, the author of the *Enquiry*, against whom Hurd had written. Two years then elapsed before his next publication which was indirectly to alter the course of his career. The work concerned was an edition of Horace's *Ars Poetica* which had initially been prepared, with a commentary and notes, for the benefit of Sir Edward Littleton, to whom the volume is inscribed. The edition was modelled on William Warburton's editing of Pope's *Dunciad*, and in acknowledgment of his influence, Hurd concluded his Introduction with a complimentary flourish paying tribute to a "great author", the "illustrious *friend* and *commentator* of Mr. POPE."[21] As a further courtesy, he sent Warburton a copy of the book and so provided an opportunity for opening a correspondence which lasted until the latter's death in 1779.

The direct consequences of Hurd's acquaintance and growing friendship with Warburton were a recommendation to the Bishop of London which secured him a Whitehall Preachership, and an introduction to Ralph Allen of Prior Park. There were 24 Whitehall Preachers, 12 each from Oxford and Cambridge, who were appointed to preach, in rotation, at the Royal Chapel at Whitehall. The office had been specifically instituted to bring promising young men before the King with a view to their promotion to higher offices in the Church. Hurd's selection, therefore, in 1750, augured well for more substantial preferments in the future. His introduction to Ralph Allen was equally propitious.[22] By the 1750s Allen was solidly established as a man of business and philanthropist. His system of cross-posts brought him in a large income, as did the Combe Down quarries which he owned and had developed. He was known to Princess Amelia, and had found favour with two servants of the crown, General Wade and Sir Robert Walpole. He himself was a patron of William Pitt, and among literary friends had numbered Pope, and now counted Fielding, Richardson, Richard Graves and George Lyttelton. Others of the circle at Prior Park had been drawn there as friends of Warburton. Some of these, for instance Charles Yorke and William Murray, later 1st Earl of Mansfield, were in positions of influence which were to make them valuable friends and allies. Warburton also made Prior Park his home having married Gertrude Tucker, the niece of Ralph Allen, in 1746. The two men formed a powerful combination, Allen's wealth and connections in both literary and political spheres complementing Warburton's intellectual prowess and ambitious energy. Inclusion within their circle was a privilege of some distinction to a young man with aspirations. Hurd had been introduced to Allen by March 1751, when he met him in

[21] *Q. Horatii Flacci Ars Poetica. Epistola ad Pisones. With an English Commentary and Notes*, 1749, p. xv.

[22] For a detailed biography of Ralph Allen, see Benjamin Boyce, *The Benevolent Man. A Life of Ralph Allen of Bath*, Cambridge, Massachusetts, 1967.

company with Henry Fielding. (To Balguy, 19 March 1751). He may have visited Prior Park later that year, but a gap in the correspondence between 21 May 1751 and 18 June 1752 makes this difficult to verify. However, in June 1752 he was proposing a visit for later that summer (To Littleton, 18 June 1752), and in October he apparently stayed there for two or three weeks.

By the early 1750s Hurd's position as a Fellow of a Cambridge college and Whitehall Preacher, and his connections at Prior Park, seemed certain to assure him advantageous preferment. Nevertheless, his life at Cambridge continued very much on an even tenor and allowed him ample time to continue writing. His friendship with Warburton, the Macros and Sir Edward Littleton gave him occasional reason to leave Cambridge during the vacation, but otherwise, apart from visits to London to preach, he remained in college. He was also at this time involved in university politics. The major dispute of 1750 and 1751 centred on the implementation of new disciplinary regulations in the university, which had been strongly resisted, and arising from this, a controversy over the right to appeal from the Vice-Chancellor's Court in university cases involving disciplinary offences. The right of appeal was allowed in non-disciplinary cases, but many members of the university believed it should be extended beyond this. (To Balguy, 19 March 1751, n.8). Hurd's involvement in the dispute may have been affected by his relationship with Balguy, who was active in opposition to the university authorities, and the fact that Emmanuel was a stronghold of opposition. A list apparently giving the names of those who formed the Association of M.A.s established to fight for the right of appeal, has been preserved at Emmanuel.[23] It shows that Emmanuel and St John's had most members (8 and 7), and also reveals how many of those involved were friends of Hurd. William Powell, Balguy, Philip Allen, and William Ludlam are named from St John's; William Dalton of St Catherine's, Thomas Nevile at Jesus, and William Mason at Pembroke are also on the list. At Emmanuel James Bickham (who was very active), and James Devey were members and friends of Hurd. Both sides in the dispute published pamphlets and Hurd contributed his support by writing, anonymously, *The Opinion of an Eminent Lawyer, concerning the Right of Appeal from the Vice-Chancellor of Cambridge, to the Senate*, three editions of which were published in 1751. However, his enthusiasm waned when no immediate solution was reached, and although he kept in touch with the chief litigants as the matter was taken to arbitration, his active support diminished.

Political interests had not prevented Hurd from maintaining his profile as an author. In May 1751 he published an annotated edition of Horace's *Epistola ad Augustum*, a companion volume to his edition of the *Ars Poetica*. The idea, if it had not already occurred to him, had been pressed by Warburton, who possessed manuscript notes of Pope's Imitation of the epistle, which he communicated to Hurd in 1749. (To Balguy, 18 August 1749). Following this publication, his activities for more than a year remain a matter of conjecture due to the gap in his correspondence.[24] But in July 1752 he appeared in the public eye once more, preaching the Assize sermon in Norwich. The appointment was probably made by Francis Longe, the patron of Reymerston, nephew of the Macros, and High Sheriff for Norwich that year. At his request the sermon was published. In 1753, Hurd preached another sermon thought worthy of publication, this time in Cambridge, at the annual meeting of children

[23] *Documents concerning the Ansell Case*, COL. 9. 28.

[24] Some information may, however, be obtained from Warburton's letters in *Letters from a Late Eminent Prelate to One of His Friends*, Kidderminster, [1808].

educated at charity schools. During the same year, he reissued his editions of Horace with two dissertations on dramatic poetry and poetical imitation appended.

The mid 1750s were marked for Hurd by the death of his father on 27 November 1755; the publication in the same year of his defence of Warburton, *On the Delicacy of Friendship. A Seventh Dissertation*, for which he has subsequently been severely criticized; and his leaving Cambridge. His father's lingering illness and death affected Hurd not only at the time but for many months after, haunting him with the sense of his own physical vulnerability. On 7 August 1756, for instance, he wrote to Mason from Brighthelmston where he was trying a "Sea Regimen". "I dare not promise myself too much from it", he said, ". . . It is enough if I can but palliate a disorder which comes, like all our woe, by inheritance". Such sombre thoughts seem also to have informed Hurd's decision to leave Cambridge which he associated with the congenial pleasures of literary companionship, for a country living and the life of a parish priest. By 1756 he had become one of the senior Fellows at Emmanuel and had, moreover, sufficient contacts outside Cambridge to have some hope of gaining further preferments once he commenced his career in the Church. When Thurcaston in Leicestershire fell vacant by the death of the previous incumbent, the living, one of the richest in the gift of the college, was clearly worth Hurd's consideration. It was offered first to Henry Hubbard, a more senior Fellow; he declined it, and Hurd took it. His nomination to the rectory is recorded on 8 November 1756,[25] but he stayed on as a Fellow at Emmanuel for the remainder of the academic year. In fact he did not leave Cambridge permanently for Leicestershire until the spring of 1758, having been instituted on 16 February and inducted on 25 March the previous year.

The intervening twelve months in Cambridge were productive for Hurd. First, in May 1757, he published *Remarks on Mr David Hume's Essay on the Natural History of Religion* on which he had collaborated with Warburton. (To Mason, 15 May 1757). At the same time he was working on a new edition of his Horace, which was to be supplemented by *A Letter to Mr Mason: On the Marks of Imitation*. The latter was published separately and as a further dissertation added to his Horace, now in its third edition. It concludes with Hurd's reflections on the pleasures of his years of friendship with Mason, years associated with the "innocent" amusements afforded by poetry. And with regret he looks to his approaching departure from Cambridge, and a return to "less pleasing, perhaps, but more useful studies."[26] Hurd left Emmanuel in November 1757, but then spent nearly three months at Prior Park and in London, arranging the publication of what was to become *Moral and Political Dialogues*, a volume he had been at work upon, on and off, since early 1755. (To Mason, 31 October 1755, n.1). The *Dialogues* were originally expected to appear in 1758, but their publication was delayed until 1759.

Much of 1758 was spent by Hurd improving the rectory at Thurcaston, and establishing himself and a curate in the house. (To Mason, 13 August 1758). Once the initial discomforts had been removed, he found his "retirement" an agreeable one. The living provided a substantial income, and his accounts books and papers indicate that he managed it competently.[27] His life in the country was relatively solitary and his chief pleasures were his books and garden. Whereas at Reymerston he was on friendly terms with his neighbours, the Grigsons and Sharpins, at Thurcaston Hurd

25 *Order Book*, COL. 14. 2.

26 *A Letter to Mr Mason: On the Marks of Imitation*, 1757, p. 75.

27 Leics. RO, DE1416/60, 61, 73, 83, 85, 86.

apparently remained aloof and relied for company on visits from Littleton, Warburton, and his Cambridge friends. Joseph Cradock was amongst the latter, although not an intimate member of Hurd's immediate circle, and in his *Memoirs* recorded his recollections of life at Thurcaston. The quietness of Hurd's existence and the application with which he addressed himself to his studies are particularly clearly illustrated. Amongst his memories was that of an occasion when he accompanied Hurd on a Sunday to his parish church. After the service Hurd asked him his opinion of the "discourse".

> "You are to speak freely;" said he. I told him, that "I thought it was good, but I did not consider it as his own; for it rather appeared to me that it was given from a printed book." "You are right," replied he; "it was one of Bourdaloue's, and I had only the French volume before me, with many marks and alterations. This is a good practice to obtain the language, and I consider this sermon, on the prospect of Death, as particularly suited to such an audience, and let me recommend to you to make such experiments; for, in a retired place, it will become your duty to read something instructive, perhaps, on a Sunday evening, to your own family."[28]

Hurd read widely and deeply. New publications such as *Tristram Shandy*, *La Nouvelle Héloïse*, and Clarendon's *Life*, were sent up from London or Leicester, and he worked too on the Classics and French and Italian texts. The thoroughness of his application is again illustrated by Cradock who recalled that Hurd used to give him the "key of his closet in the parlour, which contained letters and criticisms, from Warburton, and others of the most learned of his acquaintance; and required that I should make remarks, and sometimes take extracts from them."[29] One product of these months of uninterrupted study was *Letters on Chivalry and Romance*, published in May 1762, and an immediate and popular success. Hurd's enthusiasm for his subject had been fuelled by an interest in the historical origins of feudalism, but the main drive of the *Letters* is their affirmation of the power of the imagination, and the justification of the realms into which it can lead us. The impetus behind his asseveration came from his reading of the Italian renaissance poets and Spenser's *Faerie Queene*, but his own solitude, concentrating awareness of the nature and necessity of inner resources, may have contributed to the emphasis he gives to the power of the individual imagination.

Having published *Letters on Chivalry and Romance* Hurd turned again to writing dialogues, this time on the "Uses of Foreign Travel". He was finishing these in February 1763, but they were not printed till December, and were published in January 1764.[30] Meanwhile he took the responsibilities of his parish seriously. In January 1763, in reply to an invitation from Littleton, he explained that he could on no account leave Thurcaston at that moment since the recent severe weather had made a "perfect Hospital" of his parish, and if he could, he would not choose to leave his parishioners. Some absences were, however, required, since in 1760 he had been made chaplain to Warburton, newly created Bishop of Gloucester, and was therefore obliged to accompany him on visitations. This arrangement, of course, enabling the two men to meet for business as well as pleasure, gave mutual satisfaction. Even more satisfactory from a financial point of view, was the offer of the sinecure rectory of

28 Joseph Cradock, *Literary and Miscellaneous Memoirs*, 4 vols., 1828, pp. 177–8.
29 *Ibid.*, p. 178.
30 *Prelate*, p. 252; 'Extracts from the Destroyed Letters of Richard Hurd to William Mason', ed. James Nankivell, *Modern Language Review*, xlv. (1950) 158.

Folkton in Yorkshire, made by the Lord Chancellor (the Earl of Northington) on the recommendation of Ralph Allen, in September 1762.[31]

The most important appointment for Hurd in the 1760s was his election to the Preachership of Lincoln's Inn, although he resisted nomination for a year before submitting to pressure from Charles Yorke and Warburton. The previous vacancy had occurred in 1761 on the resignation of Warburton, who advocated the appointment of Hurd then as his successor. Charles Yorke supported his candidacy but, on investigation, discovered that the majority of the Benchers had given a promise of their vote to Thomas Ashton. (To Yorke, 1 March 1761). Ashton was elected in April 1761 and held the post till June 1765. However, already in April 1763 he was severely ill and it was clear by 1764 that the Preachership would soon again be vacant. From June 1764 onwards, Yorke tried to persuade Hurd to stand for election, but found him resolutely against the proposition. In the summer of the following year he finally disclosed the true reason for his withstanding nomination.

> The plain truth is, I understood from many quarters that the real reason, why the Bench would not be brought, by your sollicitations for me, to second your intention at that time, was, *That they would not have it thought that the Bp of Gloucester had forced a preacher upon them.* This is generally known, or at least believed. To cloke their refusal to You, they pretended they were engaged. I need not say to You, that I have been obliged by the B.G. in every way up to the height of what any man can be obliged to another; & your own sense of honour will, I am sure, prevent mine in suggesting that, under these circumstances, it is not possible for me, & cannot be grateful to me, to accept their favour.[32]

This objection of Hurd's having come to light, was in a short time overcome, and he was elected Preacher in November 1765.

The Preachership entitled its incumbent to chambers and board in Lincoln's Inn, with the requirement that he should preach each Sunday in term.[33] It was permitted, and not unusual, for the Preacher to appoint an assistant to stand in for him, a licence which Hurd occasionally adopted. Nevertheless in the course of the following six or seven years he spent long periods living in Lincoln's Inn and devoted much of his time to writing sermons both there and at Thurcaston. Life in the country appears to have become increasingly agreeable to him, and his garden at Thurcaston was a particular pleasure. His letters refer often to the tranquillity of his life and indicate a determined acceptance of his lot. In June 1765 he wrote to Mason,

> This dry weather has made sad havock with my Clumps. But, as you know I have little passion for *Shrubs*, this does not affect me. The best is, my forest trees thrive well. Besides this, my walk is *sanded*, & proceeds in so easy & sinuous a trace to *Latebrae dulces*, that I am quite satisfied with it. You laugh at this foolery, but in earnest I neither wish to live, or die, in a pleasanter scene. It is enough that it affords me an asylum from what is called Company, & the world. I pity you at York, while I have these painted fields, & green trees about me, & golden suns rolling thro' cloudless skies over my head.[34]

31 *Dates*, p. 5; *Hurd-Mason Correspondence*, p. xxvii.

32 MS BL, Add. 35637, RH to Charles Yorke, 16 June 1765.

33 *The Records of the Honorable Society of Lincoln's Inn. The Black Books Vol. III. From A.D. 1660 to A.D. 1775*, Lincoln's Inn, 1899, pp. xxiii, 34, 315–6.

34 RH to Mason, 7 June 1765, MS HC, excerpt made by Richard Hurd, nephew, found between flyleaf and back cover of *Poems by William Mason*, M.A., 1764; *M.L.R.*, xlv. (1950) 160.

Later in 1769, he wrote to Balguy in mild admonition of what appear to have been the grumblings of thwarted ambition.

> and are there no objects of desire or means of activity but deaneries and bishoprics? Are there no books to read or to write? Is there no such thing as conversation or amusement?
> – Or, to be grave,
> Have we no friend to serve, or soul to save?
> Will not all this keep a divine from sinking into insipidity and disgust?[35]

Although he may have been able to take advantage of his connections to lead a more social life in London, Hurd seems to have chosen not to do so. He remarks both to Mason and to Balguy that though "stationed in the centre of the metropolis", he is "as much a stranger to what is passing in it" as if he were living in "Pekin, or at Thurcaston".[36] He continued to maintain a distance from society even as he received further preferment and was obliged to move more into the world. It was not, in fact, until the early 1770s, when his presence at court became acceptable and even sought after, that he seems to have found any real enjoyment in the company of others than his close friends.

Hurd's continuing rise in the Church was first marked by his appointment as Archdeacon of Gloucester, a preferment that Warburton, as Bishop of Gloucester, had been anxious to secure for him, not least because it would give them a further chance to meet when Hurd made his yearly visitations of the diocese. The appointment was made in 1767 and brought him an extra £200 p.a. In the following year Warburton again singled Hurd out by choosing him to open the Warburton Lecture, founded in that year, under the trusteeship of Lord Mansfield, Charles Yorke, and Sir Eardley Wilmot. The foundation, for which Warburton set aside £500, was established "for the purpose of reading a Lecture at Lincoln's Inn, in the form of a Course of Sermons, to prove the Truth of Revealed Religion in general, and of the Christian in particular, from the Completion of the Prophecies in the Old and New Testament, which relate to the Christian Church, especially to the Apostacy of Papal Rome".[37] Hurd attracted large congregations to Lincoln's Inn to hear his sermons, of which he gave twelve over a period of about three years.[38] The series was subsequently published in 1772, reissued in a second edition in the same year and had reached a fourth edition by 1776. The Warburton Lecture focused attention on Hurd, and his performance as Lecturer found him favour and friends at court. Public recognition of his abilities came in 1774 when, on the translation of Brownlow North to the see of Worcester, Hurd was created Bishop of Lichfield and Coventry. He was consecrated on 12 February 1775.[39]

For the rest of his life Hurd was to be a staunch supporter of King and court. In 1776 he was introduced into the Royal Family as Preceptor to the Prince of Wales and his brother Frederick. This appointment was followed by that of the Clerkship of the Closet, a position made vacant by the death of the Bishop of Winchester. At the same

35 Francis Kilvert, *Memoirs of the Life and Writings of the Right Rev. Richard Hurd, D.D., Lord Bishop of Worcester; With a Selection from his Correspondence and other Unpublished Papers*, 1860, p. 106.

36 RH to Balguy, 3 December 1770, MS Beinecke; *Memoirs*, p. 108.

37 A.W. Evans, *Warburton and the Warburtonians. A Study in some Eighteenth-Century Controversies*, 1932, p. 261.

38 RH gave his fifth lecture on 21 January 1770 (*Hurd-Mason Correspondence*, p. 72); he gave his tenth on 1 December 1771 (*Memoirs*, p. 111).

39 *Handbook of British Chronology*, ed. Sir F. Maurice Powicke and E.B. Gryde, second edn., 1961.

time in 1781 he was offered and accepted the see of Worcester, vacated by Brownlow North who became the new Bishop of Winchester. The confirmation at Bow church took place on 30 June 1781 and on 7 July Hurd came to Hartlebury Castle, seat of the Bishop of Worcester.[40] Only two years later the King again wished to promote him.

> Had the offer of the Archbishoprick from his Majesty, with many gracious expressions, & pressed to accept it; but humbly begged leave to decline it, as a charge not suited to his temper & talents, & much too heavy for him to sustain, especially in these times.[41]

Hurd's own account of the 1780s onwards dwells frequently on his connection with the Royal Family: his confirmation of the young Prince Edward and Princess Augusta; his preaching before the King; the King's illness; presents from the King and a Royal visit to Hartlebury. Scattered amongst these references are notes of improvements made to the library which he had had built on to Hartlebury, some details of publications, and with increasing frequency the dates of the deaths of his friends and family.

During the previous decade Hurd had published not only his sermons on the study of the prophecies, but also three volumes of sermons preached at Lincoln's Inn (the third published in 1780), and an edition of Cowley. Several other of his works were reissued in new editions, and he published two individual sermons, a charge, and (possibly) the poem Discord: A Satire.[42] The 1780s were not remarkable for new publications but in 1788 Hurd produced his edition of the works of Warburton, handsomely printed in seven quarto volumes. This was his last major publication. The Discourse which prefaces the *Works* was published separately in 1794, and *Letters from a Late Eminent Prelate* was printed in 1795, although it was held for publication until after Hurd's death.

In the very last years of his life many of Hurd's entries in *Dates of some occurrences in my own life* were of diocesan duties he was able to undertake, and those he had to delegate. On 25 July 1804 he wrote:

> . . . held an Ordination in Hartlebury Chapel – 3D. [deacons] 5 P. [priests] – the last I can expect to undertake.[43]

His last record occurs on 23 April 1808 when he granted a commission to the Bishop of Chester to consecrate a new chapel and burial ground within his diocese. By 28 May 1808 he was dead. Hurd had acted as Bishop of Worcester for nearly 27 years, longer than any Bishop of that see since the Reformation. He was buried on 10 June in the graveyard of the parish church at Hartlebury.

40 *Dates*, insert opposite p. 6.

41 *Ibid.*, p. 7.

42 The Cambridge University Library attributes this poem to RH; no other corroborative evidence has been found.

43 *Dates*, p. 20.

BIOGRAPHIES OF CORRESPONDENTS

Thomas Balguy (1716–1795)

Thomas Balguy was born on 27 September 1716 at Lamesley, county Durham, where his father, John Balguy, later to become Vicar of Northallerton and prebendary of South Grantham in the diocese of Salisbury, was then a curate.[1] He was educated at the Free School in Ripon, Yorkshire,[2] and on 28 May 1734 was admitted to St John's College, Cambridge,[3] where his father and grandfather had been before him. In 1738 he took the degree of B.A. and in 1741 he became an M.A. (7 July) and was elected to a Platt Fellowship (17 March).[4]

By the time Balguy came to Cambridge, his father had begun to make a name for himself, first in defending Bishop Hoadly in the Bangorian controversy, and then in his vindication of the theological standpoint adopted by Dr Samuel Clarke against that of Francis Hutcheson. Although John Balguy died on 21 September 1748 his connection with Hoadly, in particular, was to prove useful to his son. Before his death, however, he was able to promote Thomas's career, having several livings in his gift as a prebendary of Salisbury.[5] The first of these to become available for his son, was the living of North Stoke in the diocese of Lincoln, which fell vacant by the death of the previous incumbent, Thomas Day, at some time in 1740.[6] Balguy was unable to take the living immediately having yet to be ordained, but clearly his father had earmarked the rectory for him. The evidence suggests that the right of presentation lapsed before Balguy was able to take deacon's and priest's orders, which he did on 21 September and 21 December 1740. Then, by what must have been a previous agreement, the Archbishop of Canterbury, who now had the right to present, collated Balguy on 9 April 1741.[7] Subsequently, in 1746, another living, Hagworthingham, in the gift of

1 For John Balguy, see *D.N.B.*; *Biographia Britannica: or, the Lives of the Most Eminent Persons who have flourished in Great Britain and Ireland*, Second Edition, ed. Andrew Kippis, 5 vols., 1778–93; Hugh David Jones, *John Balguy. An English Moralist of the 18th Century*, Leipzig, 1907 (Falckenbergs Abhandlungen 2).

2 Robert Forsyth Scott and John E.B. Mayor, *Admissions to the College of St John the Evangelist in the University of Cambridge*, 3 vols., Cambridge, 1882–1931, ii (Part 3). 451.

3 *Ibid.*

4 No record of the date of Balguy's B.A. degree has been found either at St John's College or in the University Archive; his M.A. is recorded in the University Grace Book (C.U.L., Grace Book iota, p. 521). For his election to a Platt Fellowship, see Thomas Baker, *History of the College of St John the Evangelist*, ed. John E.B. Mayor, 2 vols., Cambridge, 1869, i. 305; St John's Bursary, *Platt's Foundation 1675, &c.*, SB9.8.

5 *Biog. Brit.*, i. 550.

6 Lambeth Palace Library, *Act Book of the Archbishop of Canterbury*, 1734–1750, VB 1/8, p. 173. The Act Book makes clear that the living was vacant by the death of [Thomas] Day, but no records of the date of his death have been found.

7 *Ibid.*

the Bishop of Ely,[8] became vacant and was also offered to Thomas. This living was of greater value than North Stoke, estimated at £95 (North Stoke was valued at £55),[9] and in order to hold the two livings together, Balguy had to petition the Archbishop of Canterbury for a dispensation. In the interim he resigned North Stoke and was instituted to Hagworthingham on 26 July 1746.[10] His dispensation was granted on 21 November 1746,[11] and he was reinstituted to North Stoke, which was once more in the gift of his father, on 16 December 1746.[12]

With his two livings, Balguy also acted as chaplain to Bishop Hoadly,[13] and in 1748 was collated (31 May) and installed (16 July) as prebendary of Norton Episcopi in Lincoln cathedral.[14] At Cambridge, he had been appointed Deputy Public Orator under James Tunstall in 1743,[15] and was made assistant tutor to William Samuel Powell at St John's.[16] According to the *Admissions to St John's* he read lectures in Moral Philosophy and the Evidences of Natural and Revealed Religion at the College for sixteen years.[17] In 1758 he took the degree of D.D.[18]

Only a little is known of Balguy's personal life at this time. He was a friend of Thomas Gray and William Mason, and from 1757 onwards is mentioned fairly frequently, though usually passingly, in their correspondence. Gray speaks revealingly of him in a letter of 11 August 1758:

> as to Uncle B: pray do him justice. he stay'd indeed to preach the Commencement-Sermon, but he assured me (in secret) it was an old one, & had not one word in it *to the purpose*. the very next morning he set out for Winchester, & I do really think him much improved since he had his residence there, freer & more open, & his heart less set upon the Mammon of unrighteousness.[19]

Some further documentation of Balguy's life is given in a group of letters addressed to him by Warburton, and dating from 1750.[20] The two men met through Hurd after Warburton had expressly asked that they might be introduced.[21] His stated reason for wishing to know Balguy better was that he was "no stranger to his excellent character" and counted himself unfortunate not to be of his acquaintance. Balguy's

8 John Ecton, *Thesaurus Rerum Ecclesiasticarum: Being an Account of the Valuations of all the Ecclesiastical Benefices in the Several Dioceses in England and Wales . . . To which are added the Names of the Patrons to the several Benefices: and the Dedications of the Churches*, 1742, p. 255.

9 *Act Book*, 1734–50, p. 315.

10 Lincs. RO, *Subscription Book VII*, p. 580.

11 *Act Book*, 1734–50, p. 315.

12 Lincs. RO, Presentation Deed 110–43; *Subscription Book VII*, p. 585.

13 *Act Book*, 1734–50, p. 315.

14 John Le Neve, *Fasti Ecclesiae Anglicanae, or A Calendar of the Principal Ecclesiastical Dignitaries in England and Wales*, Corrected and Continued by T. Duffus Hardy, 3 vols., Oxford, 1854, ii. 196.

15 Scott-Mayor, *Admissions to St John's*, ii. 452.

16 *Ibid.*, p. 451.

17 *Ibid.*

18 St John's Bursary, *Long Book*, 1752–58, DS1.3 (June 1758).

19 *Correspondence of Thomas Gray*, ed. Paget Toynbee and Leonard Whibley. With Corrections and Additions by H.W. Starr, 3 vols., Oxford, 1935, reprinted with corrections, 1971, Letter 275.

20 The Harry Ransom Humanities Research Center, The University of Texas at Austin. Two volumes of copies of letters from Warburton to Balguy have been preserved. The originals were dated 1750–59, and 1760–75.

21 *Prelate*, p. 50.

familiarity with university politics also appears to have attracted Warburton, who was much interested in Cambridge affairs, and though not educated at the university, had been made an M.A. on the King's visit in 1728. But not least amongst Balguy's merits was what Samuel Parr refers to as "Habits of the most exact and enlarged Thinking", a style "equally pure, elegant, and nervous", and "solid Learning".[22] Evidence of Balguy's learning is apparent in Warburton's replies to his letters, as is the similar inclination of their interests. Yet despite this affinity and Warburton's undoubted wish to see Balguy in easy circumstances, he does not seem to have been able to promote his career as he did Hurd's; and Balguy's next preferment was obtained by Bishop Hoadly.

On 1 November 1757 Hoadly collated Balguy to the 11th prebendal stall in Winchester cathedral.[23] Thus began his long connection with Winchester, which was consolidated by his appointment as Archdeacon on 23 July 1759.[24] Balguy, however, maintained his connection with St John's up to the beginning of 1760. Warburton (who had a low opinion of Hoadly as a patron) had insisted that being appointed a prebendary was no reason to leave college,[25] and even when Balguy became Archdeacon he advocated giving up his "employment" in college, but keeping his "Chambers" in case he should "stumble upon some noble pupil who may pay for all".[26] The Platt Fellowship which Balguy had held since 1741 was vacated by him in 1748.[27] No records exist to indicate that he was elected to another fellowship, which suggests that he continued to lecture in the college but without a Fellow's stipend. From 1758 onwards he divided his time largely between Cambridge and Winchester. Hurd notes in a letter of 6 September 1759 that Balguy was intending to settle at Winchester "next Spring" and looks forward to seeing him in his "own Prebendal house". Later in a letter of 26 July 1761, he wishes him a "long & happy enjoyment of your new house & agreable situation". In the same letter he sends his compliments to Miss [Sarah] Drake, a cousin of Balguy's who came to live with him and manage his household and is commemorated on a ledger stone in the nave of Winchester cathedral.[28]

For the remainder of Balguy's life, Winchester was his base, and his final preferment was to the vicarage of Alton in Hampshire by the presentation of the Dean and Chapter of Winchester.[29] He was instituted on 19 September 1771 and ceded his Lincolnshire benefices, retaining Alton, the archdeaconry and the two prebends. Winchester, however, was not always entirely agreeable to him. According to a letter from Warburton to Hurd of February 1767, Balguy was intending to spend the rest of the winter in London, "so that, if it agreed with him, he would spend every winter there". Apparently he had been lately afflicted with asthma and found the air of

22 *Tracts by Warburton, and a Warburtonian; not admitted into the Collections of their Respective Works*, [ed. Samuel Parr], 1789, p. 183.

23 *John Le Neve, Fasti Ecclesiae Anglicanae 1541–1857. III Canterbury, Rochester and Winchester Dioceses*. Compiled by Joyce M. Horn, 1974, p. 105.

24 *Ibid.*, p. 87.

25 Warburton Correspondence, University of Texas at Austin, Warburton to Balguy, 11 February 1758.

26 *Ibid.*, 16 September [1759].

27 Baker, *History of St John's*, i. 306.

28 G.H. Blore, 'An Archdeacon of the 18th Century. Thomas Balguy, D.D., 1716–1795', *Winchester Cathedral Record*, no. 20, 1951, p. 21.

29 Scott-Mayor, *Admissions to St John's*, ii. 452.

Winchester "too sharp for him".[30] Other references in correspondence suggest that Balguy spent some weeks each year taking the waters, usually at Bath, and visiting his friends in various parts of the country, as well as making his archidiaconal visitations on a regular basis, with a diligence and thoroughness that seem to have characterised most of his activities.

It was not until his removal to Winchester that Balguy began to publish. His first publication was *A Sermon preached at Lambeth Chapel, on the Consecration of The Right Rev. Jonathan Shipley, D.D. Lord Bishop of Landaff, February 12, 1769*.[31] Further sermons and discourses followed in the 1770s and 1780s, although by the late 1780s Balguy's eyesight was beginning to fail. His reputation by this time was such that in 1781 the King offered him the see of Gloucester. In a letter to Lord North, the King expressed the opinion that Balguy was "the first Man in point of reputation in the Republic of Letters of either University".[32] He believed Balguy would accept the bishopric, but said that if he did refuse it, "I know the offer will do credit and no other person can think it a dishonor to be called upon after so superior a Man". In fact Balguy did decline the bishopric, on the grounds of his poor and deteriorating health, though with a full sense of the honour done him. He acknowledged his gratitude in the dedication to his *Discourses on Various Subjects*, (1785), and Bishop Hallifax who was nominated to the see on Balguy's declining it, printed in his turn, a dedication to Balguy in recognition of his superior merit and the grounds on which he had been obliged to remain in retirement.[33]

Thomas Balguy died at Winchester on 19 January 1795 and was buried in the cathedral on 26 January, with a tablet commemorating his life.[34]

30 *Prelate*, p. 290.

31 Scott-Mayor records two consecration sermons preached by Balguy in 1769, one at the consecration of Dr Shute Barrington, and the other at the consecration of Jonathan Shipley. No other reference to a sermon preached for Barrington has, however, been found, and Scott-Mayor appears to have confused the dates of the two consecrations, giving 12 February 1769 as the date of Barrington's consecration as Bishop of Landaff, when it was in fact the occasion of Shipley's consecration to the same bishopric.
Two anonymous works of an earlier date have also been attributed to Thomas Balguy. *An Inquiry concerning Faith*, published in 1744, is tentatively catalogued under the authorship of Thomas Balguy by St John's College Library, Cambridge; and the British Library suggests Balguy as the author of *Letters concerning Confessions of Faith, And Subscriptions to Articles of Religion in Protestant Churches; Occasioned by Perusal of the Confessional*, dated 1768. RH, however, in a letter of 13 September 1768 suggests that Balguy's *Sermon* was indeed his first publication: "Your sermon will certainly suit the occasion very well, and will do you credit from the press, provided you do not retouch and correct too much. I know the anxieties of you late adventurers . . ." (*Memoirs*, p. 103).

32 *The Correspondence of King George the Third from 1760 to December 1783*, ed. Sir John Fortescue, 6 vols., 1927–8, Vol. V, Letter 3371, 14 July 1781.

33 Samuel Hallifax, *A Charge delivered to the Clergy at the Primary Visitation of the Diocese of Durham, in the Year MDCCLI; By the Right Reverend Father in God Joseph Butler, LL.D. Then Lord Bishop of that Diocese. The Second Edition. With a Preface, . . . By Samuel, Lord Bishop of Gloucester*, 1786.

34 Scott-Mayor, *Admissions to St John's*, ii. 452.

James Devey (1680–1754)

James Devey was born in 1680, the son of Henry and Margaret "Deavy" of Pattingham, Staffordshire.[1] At a rather later age than was usual, he was sent to Oxford and matriculated at Pembroke College on 13 May 1700.[2] He was made a B.A. on 7 March 1704[3] and by 1706 had been ordained. In July of that year he was presented to the rectory of Kemberton, Shropshire, and was instituted on 3 August.[4] No further preferment seems to have come his way until 1724, when the much more valuable living of Beckbury in the same county became vacant and was secured by him.[5] The two villages of Kemberton and Beckbury lie about four miles apart and in the eighteenth century were joined by a road which passed through Hatton, where Hurd's elder brother John leased a farm from 1736.[6] This connection may account for Hurd's first meeting with Devey in the late 1730s. It seems likely that the reference to the "Parson of the Parish" in Hurd's letter to Potter dated 7 August 1739 is a reference to Devey, and certainly by 1741 when the extant correspondence opens, Hurd and Devey seem to know each other very well.

Hurd's friendship with Devey was reinforced by his acquaintance with his son, also James, who was sent to Emmanuel a few years after Hurd. The younger James (who tended to spell his surname "Devie") was admitted to Emmanuel on 2 March 1741 and was elected a Fellow in 1747.[7] The following year he was ordained deacon and became an M.A.;[8] but he chose to remain in college till 1766 when he accepted the Emmanuel living of Stanground in Huntingdonshire.[9] Hurd knew James Devie well and he remained on the fringe of the Macro-Hurd-Littleton circle for many years;[10] their friendship, however, seems less significant than Hurd's early relationship with his father. The latter's generosity of friendship is indicated in Hurd's letters to him. He was willing to listen sympathetically, to question and to encourage Hurd in his earliest attempts at critical analysis, and was constantly interested in all that concerned the younger man.

The last surviving letter from Hurd to James Devey, senior, was written in 1747. Devey lived seven years longer, dying in 1754; but their correspondence may not have continued with any frequency up to that date. There is no mention of his death in the letters of 1754.

1 *Pattingham Parish Register 1559–1812*, Staffordshire Parish Records Society, ed. H.R. Thomas, Stafford, 1934.

2 *Alumni Oxonienses: The Members of the University of Oxford, 1500–1714: Their Parentage, Birthplace, and Year of Birth, with a Record of their Degrees. Being the Matriculation Register of the University*, [ed.] Joseph Foster, 4 vols., 1891–92.

3 *Ibid.*

4 'Institutions of Shropshire Incumbents', *Transactions of the Shropshire Archaeological and Natural History Society*, Fourth Series, Shrewsbury, v. (1915) 185–208.

5 *Diocese of Hereford, Institutions (AD 1539–1900)*, ed. A.T. Bannister, Hereford, 1923; John Ecton, *Thesaurus Rerum Ecclesiasticarum*, 1742, pp. 103, 226.

6 Shrops. RO, Kenyon-Slaney Collection, Hatton rentals 1952/44. John Hurd leased "Bishops Farm".

7 *Emmanuel College Register*, COL. 9. 1(A); *Order Book*, COL. 14.2.

8 *Alum. Cantab.*; *College Register*, COL. 9. 1(A).

9 *Order Book*, COL. 14. 2.

10 References to Devie and letters from him occur in the Littleton correspondence, Staffs. RO, D1413/2; in the *Macro Letter-book*; and in the Macro correspondence, BL, Add. 32556, 32557.

Sir Edward Littleton (1727–1812)

Edward Littleton was born in 1727, the eldest son of Frances (née Whitehall) and Fisher Littleton of Pipe Ridware, Staffordshire.[1] His parents owned a few hundred acres of land in Staffordshire, but from 1738 Edward was the acknowledged heir to the title and wealth of his uncle, Sir Edward Littleton, third baronet of Pillaton Hall, also in Staffordshire.[2] The Littleton family can be traced back to the thirteenth century when they held lands in Worcestershire. Subsequently, they moved to Staffordshire and by the time the fourth baronet had inherited the Pillaton estates in 1742, the Littletons had been established landowners there for some 350 years.[3] Their estate covered 5,500 acres and the family was of considerable standing in the area, previous generations having represented the county in the capacity of sheriff, deputy lieutenant and member of parliament. Sir Edward also took on these responsibilities in later life, and in addition built up the estate to 8,500 acres. At his death in 1812, his income was sufficient to qualify him as a great landlord, though bringing him only into the lower ranks of the landed aristocracy.[4]

Edward was the eldest of four children. He had a brother (frequently mentioned by Hurd) named Fisher, born in 1728; and two sisters, Ann, who died as an infant, and Frances, probably born about 1730, though no record of her baptism has been found.[5] Both Edward and Fisher came into their inheritances very young. The elder Fisher died in May 1740, leaving the Pipe Ridware lands to his second son; his brother died in January 1742, leaving his estates to Edward. On the death of his uncle the latter was put under the guardianship of a group of family friends and relations until he should reach the age of twenty-one. One of these was his mother, another was Samuel Hill, who is often mentioned in Hurd's letters to Littleton, and there was also Walter Gough of Perry Hall and a John Biddulph of Cannock. The three latter all came from long-established, and Tory, Staffordshire families.

Up to the time of coming into his inheritance, Littleton had been attending the Free Grammar School in Brewood, run by William Budworth, schoolmaster also to the young Richard Hurd. But during 1742 he was taken away from Brewood and sent to Winchester. His name does not appear in the "Long Rolls" of old members, although this may be because he attended the school for less than a year.[6] By July 1743 he had been despatched back to Brewood and Budworth, leaving his mother with bills for fees (paid to Mr Speed, the usher), for music lessons (from the organist and music master, Mr Kent) and for the conveyance of his "Things" to and from Winchester.[7] Budworth taught Littleton again then from the end of July 1743 till

1 *Pipe Ridware Parish Register*, Staffordshire Parish Register Society, ed. F.J. Wrottesley, Exeter, 1905.

2 Will of Sir Edward Littleton, 3rd Bart., 8 August 1738, Staffs. RO, Ex D260/M/T/5/107.

3 Kathleen Wain, *The Financial Affairs of Sir Edward Littleton, 4th Baronet, Landowner of the Teddesley Estate in Staffordshire, 1742–1812*, Liverpool Ph.D thesis, 1975, p. 5. Two copies of Wain's thesis have been consulted, the page numberings of which were at variance. References are to copy 7510 WAI.

4 *Ibid.*, pp. 38, 1–2.

5 *Pipe Ridware Parish Register.*

6 *Winchester Long Rolls 1723–1812*, ed. Clifford W. Holgate and Herbert Chitty, Winchester, 1904.

7 Mrs Littleton to Sir Edward Littleton, Private Accompt, Staffs. RO, Ex D260/M/T/5/107.

about December of that year. By the following April Sir Edward had been accepted as an undergraduate at Emmanuel College, Cambridge, and on 30 April 1744 he was formally admitted.[8] Hurd was appointed to be his tutor; he was his first pupil and the only one for some years to come.

For the next three and a half years Littleton spent about six or seven months a year in college[9] and seems, from contemporary comment, to have been a diligent and intelligent pupil. His style of life was more luxurious than that of the pensioners and sizars (the majority of the undergraduates; Littleton had been admitted as a "nobleman"). He had rooms to himself instead of sharing a room; he had wine with his meals on a fairly regular basis (most people drank beer);[10] and in addition he was exempt by statute from the degree exercises which other students could not evade.[11] Allowing for these advantages arising from his rank, Littleton led a sedate and scholarly life at Cambridge and his continuing interest in education is demonstrated in Hurd's letters. These give information on new publications; advice on the best "method of prosecuting [his] Studies" in "*Classics*, *History*, *Ethics*, and *Divinity*" when he left university;[12] and accounts of Fisher Littleton's progress at Emmanuel about which Edward was concerned.

It was during Littleton's career at Cambridge, in 1745, that Britain was invaded by Charles Edward, the Young Pretender. Littleton was at home at the time and raised a company of men to form part of a Staffordshire regiment.[13] This and a number of other regiments were created to make up for the absence of a large part of the British army which was then stationed on the continent. When the regiment was ready, the men were marched to Chester which was heavily garrisoned in expectation of the rebel army marching to Wales, an area of the country strongly sympathetic to the Jacobite cause. There the troops remained from November 1745 till the following spring. The rebels in the event did not trouble them, but turned towards London and then retreated, so that neither Littleton nor his men were ever seriously threatened. Littleton himself was able to obtain his discharge from the army in February and returned to college in April 1746.[14]

From April to September 1746 Sir Edward worked steadily at Emmanuel, and over the next calendar year spent about another eight or nine months studying in college. By 1748, however, he was being drawn away from the university both by outside interests and by business. He visited Emmanuel on several occasions for a number of weeks in that year, but on 16 November 1748 had his name taken off the college books.[15]

From 1748 to 1752 Sir Edward divided his time between London and Staffordshire. But in May 1752 he married Frances Horton, the daughter of Christopher Horton of Catton Hall, Derbyshire, and from then on spent a considerable part of each year at

8 *Emmanuel College Register*, COL. 9. 1. (A).
9 *Commons Accounts Book*, STE. 15. 9.
10 *Ibid.*; *Commons Accounts Book*, STE. 15.8.
11 D.A. Winstanley, *Unreformed Cambridge. A Study of Certain Aspects of the University in the Eighteenth Century*, Cambridge, 1935, pp. 79–81; *Statuta Academiae Cantabrigiensis*, Cambridge, 1785, pp. 307–8.
12 To Littleton, 7 November 1753.
13 Wain, p. 8; To Littleton, 24 November 1745.
14 *Commons Accounts Book*, STE. 15. 9.
15 *Ibid.*

various fashionable spas.[16] Lady Littleton's health was apparently poor and the Littletons were constantly in search of a cure for her ailments. They visited Bath regularly, but also patronised Bristol and Tunbridge Wells, where Frances died in 1781. There were other spas in the north, and of these the Littletons usually chose to go to Buxton, Harrogate and Scarborough. After 1781 Sir Edward confined his visits to Bath and Buxton.

The Littletons continued to visit London also, particularly during the (winter) season, though they only took a lease on a house from 1769.[17] Having decided to arrange permanent accommodation, they settled on a house in Upper Brook Street, near Hyde Park and Grosvenor Square, one of the most fashionable areas in London.

Sir Edward was drawn to the capital not only for social reasons but by one of his most passionate interests: the collecting of paintings, prints and contemporary sculpture. Even as a young man in the late 1740s he had begun to collect portrait prints (a number of them on Hurd's behalf) and in 1748 had already commissioned paintings for himself from a popular artist, Samuel Scott (1710?–1772).[18] He often apparently consulted Hurd on the merits of less well-known painters, but his chief adviser was Edward Macro. The two men probably met at Emmanuel in the summer of 1744 when their careers at the university briefly coincided. After this date though Macro no longer had any connection with the college, they inevitably met through their mutual friend, Hurd. By the later 1740s they had become close friends, and remained so until Macro's death. Macro had a reputation for good taste and considerable knowledge of the art world; Littleton shared his interest and had enough money to be able to build up a fairly substantial art collection. From the beginning he was interested in contemporary art as well as paintings by seventeenth century Italian and Flemish masters which were widely collected in the mid eighteenth century. He commissioned paintings by Scott, by Benjamin Wilson, Gainsborough, William Hoare, and Benjamin Ferrers.[19] He also did business with Hogarth, through Hurd.[20] The most important work that he commissioned, however, was a series of portrait busts, executed by Michael Rysbrack (1694–1770). It was becoming fashionable to furnish studies with the busts of famous men, and Rysbrack was, with the exception of Roubiliac, the sculptor most often patronised for such work. Edward Littleton ordered a set of twelve busts: three "Philosophers" (Bacon, Locke and Newton); three divines (Isaac Barrow, Samuel Clarke and William Warburton); three poets (Milton, Pope and Shakespeare); and three "Historians" (Lord Clarendon, Walter Raleigh and Littleton's own ancestor, Thomas Littleton).[21]

On the whole Littleton's collection of paintings was of a conventional cast and like many of his contemporaries he believed that there were more original paintings on the market, than was actually the case. The pictures that Hurd mentions, said to be by Ruysdael, Trevisani, Rubens, Rembrandt, Berghem, and Hondecoeter are unlikely all to have been genuine, but with the exception of the Rubens and Rembrandt they are

16 Marriage Settlement of Sir Edward Littleton and Frances Horton, 14 April 1752, Staffs RO, D260/M/T/5/129; Sir Edward and Lady Littleton's travels are documented in the ledgers kept by Littleton from 1752–1808, Staffs RO, D260/ME/116–9a.

17 Wain, p. 17.

18 To Littleton, 14 October 1748; Macro Letter-book, Littleton to Macro, 18 September 1749.

19 Wain, p. 20.

20 To Littleton, 29 May 1757.

21 *Macro Letter-book*, Littleton to Macro, 5 October 1755.

typical of what was generally available and collected. Rubens and Rembrandt were much less popular, but were beginning to be more collected after 1750. Littleton's collecting interests show his taste to have been to some extent independent of prevailing fashions.

During the late 1740s and 1750s Sir Edward also began to consider building a new house on his estate. There were both practical and fashionable reasons for doing this. The old family house was still inhabited by his aunt and was said to be in a state of "disrepair";[22] and, at the same time, many other noblemen were embarking on new building. Sir Edward seems to have begun planning for a new house in 1745, when Mrs Littleton paid for his bed to be taken to Teddesley.[23] Teddesley Coppice was a piece of woodland lying a mile or two north of Pipe Ridware, with a house of the same name nearby. It was here that Littleton stayed whilst planning the layout of grounds and arranging for the building of the house itself. Definite plans to build were afoot by January 1747, and in the early 1750s Sir Edward consulted with James Gibbs who helped him to fix upon the plot of ground on which Teddesley Hall was to be built.[24] However, it was only after Littleton married in 1752 that a particular plan was settled on.

The next few years were spent building a farm, which was nearly complete in 1754;[25] laying out the garden and building its walls; and refining the plans for the house. In June 1759 the Hall was actually begun.[26] By 5 July the foundations had been laid and by the summer of 1760 the builders had "advanced higher than to the Top of the Parlour Windows".[27] Littleton was now employing William Baker, an architect and builder from Cheshire. Baker (1705–1771) was well known for his building in Staffordshire, Shropshire, Derbyshire and Cheshire, and was brought to Littleton's notice in the mid 1750s when he worked for his wife's family, the Hortons of Catton Hall, Derbyshire. Both there and at Patshull in Staffordshire he had followed Gibbs who was first consulted and designed the original house plans.[28] The body of the house was built of brick which was then faced with stone. This work was undertaken by Charles Cope Trubshaw (1715–1772) who had an extensive business as a sculptor and master mason in Staffordshire.[29] The house was probably completed about 1765.

Once settled in the new Hall, Littleton was able to devote more time to improving his estate, to fox-hunting (another great passion of his),[30] and to participating in local and national politics. He served in six successive Parliaments from 1784 to 1812, but

22 *Penkridge Church Register 1575–1735*, Staffordshire Parish Register Society, ed. Norman W. Tildesley, 1945–46, Introduction, p. [ii].

23 Private Accompt, Staffs. RO, Ex D260/M/T/5/107.

24 *Macro Letter-book*, Littleton to Macro, 28 October 1750; RH to Littleton, 1 July 1752.

25 *Ibid.*, Littleton to Macro, 12 July 1754.

26 *Ibid.*, Littleton to Macro, 25 June 1759. This is a much later date than that given in the *Victoria County History of Staffordshire*, v.184; it is, however, based on conclusive evidence obtained from the *Macro Letter-book*.

27 *Macro Letter-book*, Littleton to Macro, 25 June 1759; 4 July 1760. RH to Littleton, 5 July 1759.

28 Arthur Oswald, 'William Baker of Audlem, Architect', *Collections for a History of Staffordshire*, Staffordshire Record Society, 1950–51, pp. [107]–35; Andor Gomme, 'Catton Hall Derbyshire', *The Country Seat. Studies in the History of the British Country House*, ed. Howard Colvin and John Harris, 1970, pp. 157–63; *A Biographical Dictionary of British Architects 1600–1840*, ed. Colvin, 1978.

29 Oswald, 'William Baker', p. 126; *Dictionary of British Architects*.

30 M.W. Farr, 'Sir Edward Littleton's Fox-Hunting Diary 1774–89', *Collections for a History of Staffordshire*, Fourth Series, Vol. 6, Staffordshire Record Society, 1970, pp. 136–70.

appears to have voted only once, in support of Pitt, on the King's illness in 1788.[31] He did, however, introduce several county improvement bills into Parliament.[32] On a county level Sir Edward played a more substantial part, acting as deputy lieutenant of the county, and as sheriff from 1762 to 1763. He is chiefly notable, though, for his encouragement of and contribution to the building of the Staffordshire and Worcestershire, and the Thames and Severn canals.[33] He supported their development both locally and in London, and was an active member of the committee of both the companies responsible for their construction.

Littleton also carried out extensive agricultural improvements on his estate, organising more efficient irrigation and drainage systems and developing better breeds of cattle and sheep.[34] He took a strong interest in the welfare of his tenants, building new houses for labourers, providing them with cowhouses and ponds, and generally ensuring that they should be fully able to provide for themselves on their own plots of land.[35]

The preoccupations and activities of these years distracted Littleton from his earlier interests in art and literature. He did not abandon all interest in the arts, but it is obvious from the nature of Hurd's letters to him, that his interest in literature, certainly, became less intense. He was more keen to continue collecting pictures and sculpture (particularly by Rysbrack) but was deprived of his agent and advisor by the death of Edward Macro in 1766, and this was followed soon after by the death of Rysbrack in 1770. After this date Littleton's connections with the London art world became increasingly tenuous, and his active collecting gradually ceased.

The alteration of the pattern of Sir Edward's life seems not to have affected his friendship with Hurd. By the 1760s their relationship had mellowed into the easy intimacy of long habit and shared interests. Hurd was by this time a well established author and successful churchman; this decreased the gap in social standing which always, to an extent, divided the two men, and clearly enhanced their friendship. They remained in contact until Hurd's death in 1808.

Littleton, like Ralph Allen, the model of Fielding's Squire Allworthy in *Tom Jones*, seems to have represented to his friends many of the characteristics of the figure of the "good man". Something of this is conveyed in Thomas Nevile's imitation of Horace's Epistola XVII which is addressed to Littleton.

> What tho', beyond the promise of your years,
> In all you do, maturest thought appears,
> Tho' blest with manners, sure the Great to please,
> A polish, soften'd by a native ease,
> Scorn not, accomplish'd in whate'er degree,
> To take th'opinion of a friend, ev'n me.
> Say, art thou one, who shuns the tinsel'd sights
> Of liv'ry'd lords, or frantic fools at WHITE'S,
> Who sighs for solitude, when fashion calls
> To Routs, to Revels, or to Birth-night Balls?

31 Josiah C. Wedgwood, 'Staffordshire Parliamentary History, from the Earliest Times to the Present Day, Volume III (1780–1841)', *Collections for a History of Staffordshire*, William Salt Archaeological Society, 1933; Wain, p. 11.

32 Wain, p. 11.

33 *Ibid.*, p. 322ff.

34 *Ibid.*, pp. 394, 26ff.

35 *Ibid.*, pp. 393, 34ff.

Hence then; from Town to *** remove;
Rear the proud pile, or weave the mazy grove,
Or o'er vast Tracts bid thick'ning forests rise,
Till a new Studley spread before our eyes.
Or would you quit Retirement to be great?
Go! mix with patriots, and reform the state;
Till ev'ry plunderer in place be known,
And not a sycophant be near the throne.[36]

This early literary comment on his character is matched by an equally warm description of him in old age. He appears virtually undisguised in a novel by Mary Barker, a Staffordshire woman who was amongst his acquaintance in the county.

> Sir Edwin was a man of very singular character. He possessed a large fortune, kept an hospitable house, was irreproachably just, and studied the happiness and comfort of all his dependents; but he was temperate, generous without ostentation, liberal without profusion, and wise without affectation; consequently very erroneous were the opinions commonly entertained of him.
>
> Some ("fine fellows") declared him to be a *poor soul*; others pronounced him *stingy*; numbers thought him *very queer*; and many said that he was *good for nothing*.
>
> Still more erroneous was the general decision respecting his knowledge and sentiments; for he very seldom spoke in a way which *proclaimed himself* a wise man. No one could possibly think him deficient in sense, but, excepting by people of great penetration, he was considered only as a man of good plain understanding and common abilities . . .
>
> Attached to no party, and dupe to no sect, . . . his conduct through life . . . was regulated by a sincere wish to do right.[37]

Littleton died in 1812 and his estates passed to his great-nephew, Edward John Walhouse (later Littleton). Teddesley Hall was demolished in 1953.

Cox Macro (1683–1767)

Cox Macro was born in 1683, the son of a prosperous Suffolk tradesman and alderman.[1] He was educated at Bury Grammar School and in 1699 went up to Jesus College, Cambridge, where he remained until January 1702.[2] He then transferred to Christ's apparently for reasons of health, and to benefit from the teaching of two distinguished Doctors of Medicine then resident.[3] From here he moved to Leyden to continue his studies at the University under the famous Professor of Medicine, Hermann Boerhaave.[4] By 1710, however, he had returned to England and proceeded

36 Thomas Nevile, *Imitations of Horace*, 1758, pp. 139–41.

37 [Mary Barker], *A Welsh Story*, 3 vols., 1798, iii. 163–5.

1 Samuel Tymms, 'Little Haugh Hall, Norton', *Proceedings of the Suffolk Institute of Archaeology, Statistics, and Natural History*, Lowestoft, ii (1859). 283; Tymms, 'Cupola House, Bury St Edmund's', *Proceedings of the Suffolk Institute*, iii (1863). 378.

2 *Alum. Cantab.*

3 *Biographical Register of Christ's College 1505–1905 And of the Earlier Foundation, God's House 1448–1505*, compiled by John Peile, 2 vols., Cambridge, 1910–13, ii. 152.

4 *Alum. Cantab.*

LL.B.[5] In 1716 he was ordained deacon and priest, in 1717 took the degree of D.D.,[6] and by 1719, as appears from the dates and addresses on his correspondence, had moved to Little Haugh Hall, his family's country property near Norton in Suffolk.[7] Here he devoted himself to a broad range of studies, and to the collection of "antiquities": coins, medals, paintings, books and manuscripts. His collection of the latter was exceptionally fine, including the Great Register of Bury Abbey during the abbacy of William Curteys; a Ledger Book of Glastonbury Abbey; a cartulary of the religious house at Blackborough in Norfolk; a vellum manuscript of the works of Gower; and the original manuscript of Spenser's 'View of the State of Ireland'. He also obtained a large collection of manuscripts relating to Cambridge University which had been amassed by John Covel or Covill, Master of Christ's from 1688–1722, and a considerable body of charters relating to the immediately surrounding area.[8]

In 1714, before moving to Norton, Cox Macro had married Mary Godfrey, the daughter of Edward Godfrey, Privy Purse to Queen Anne, and about 1717 their first child, a daughter, was born. According to an account book kept by Macro, another child was born after this, but died, and a third and last child was born in 1719 on 24 August.[9] This was a son, whom they named Edward.

The number and variety of entries in the account book during the 1730s and 1740s indicate that the running of the family estate took considerable time and attention. But Cox Macro was also much involved in improving his house, and in commissioning works of art to decorate it.[10] One of his first ideas (c.1734) was to reface the building; the work was completed for "£47.0.0" and the effect celebrated in a specially commissioned painting.[11] Some time later he decided to erect a cupola, enhancing not only the exterior of the house, but the interior, with the dome, painted by Francis Hayman, rising over a fine staircase.[12] These major alterations, plus a great deal of carving and stucco-work, were carried out throughout the 1730s and early 1740s. In addition to the local craftsmen employed on most of the building and decoration, Macro commissioned more important artists like Hayman for particular pieces of work. Amongst these was Pieter Tillemans (1684?–1734), a Belgian painter of some repute. Tillemans was popular in England as a painter of landscapes, country seats, and horses, and since his first visit in 1708 had executed a number of paintings for various patrons, including Lord Byron of Newstead, the Earl of Derby, the Dukes of Devonshire, Kent and Kingston, and the Earl of Radnor.[13] Cox Macro, however, was one of his most faithful patrons, and he was staying with the family when he died in

5 Peile, *Register of Christ's*.
6 *Alum. Cantab.*; Peile.
7 MS BL, Add. 32556, 32557.
8 Tymms, 'Little Haugh Hall', p. 284.
9 Cox Macro, Personal Account Book 1717–53, MS Bodleian Library, Eng. Misc. e. 346. An undated entry records payment for the christening of "Molly", and a later undated entry the payment for christening a "2d child". Edward's date of birth is given, though not his name.
10 A catalogue of the paintings owned by Cox Macro was compiled by his nephew, Edmund Wilson. It forms part of A *Catalogue of the Library etc of Cox Macro, D.D. 1766*, MS BL, Add. 25473.
11 Norman Scarfe, 'Little Haugh Hall, Suffolk', *Country Life*, 5 June 1958, p. 1238.
12 *Ibid.*, p. 1241. See also Robert Raines, 'An Art Collector of Many Parts', *Country Life*, 24 June 1976, pp. 1692–94.
13 Robert Raines, 'Peter Tillemans, Life and Work, with a List of Representative Paintings', *Walpole Society*, xlvii (1978–80). 21–59.

1734.[14] At least five large paintings and a number of his drawings were in their possession at his death, and he had also completed three "Doorpiece[s]" and other decorative work in the house.[15] Almost immediately after his death, Cox Macro commissioned a terracotta bust of Tillemans from Michael Rysbrack, together with another of the sculptor himself. The former was designed to stand in a specially constructed niche at the top of the stairs, with below it, the inscription "Tillemansio suo Rysbrachius".[16]

From the time that he met the Macros Hurd was much interested and involved in the building and artistic work embarked upon at Norton. He produced, for example, a list of alternative verses and epigrams to accompany the busts of Tillemans and Rysbrack, now preserved amongst Cox Macro's papers.[17] His knowledge of art was substantially increased by his contact with the family, and his taste, initially at least, formed under their influence.

The even tenor of the Macros' life was disrupted in the 1750s. First, Edward Macro was involved in a court case in 1750, which Hurd calls an "ugly affair", though two other friends, Sir Edward Littleton and Osmund Beauvoir, make little of it.[18] Then in 1753 Mary Macro died. Her letters, and those of Cox Macro too, suggest that she was an intelligent and entertaining woman, and very much the focus of the family; her death, therefore, was a great loss.[19] From this time, the chief anxiety was again Edward. By 1754 he was managing the family's farmland in Suffolk,[20] but apparently with little success. Between 1755 and 1762 he borrowed over £1,000 from various associates, and other large sums from Sir Edward Littleton, who stood surety for him in his financial dealings. However, despite these loans he got into such severe difficulties that he was unable to extricate himself.[21] The strain on his relationship with his father which this caused ended in his disinheritance, and in 1766 he died, apparently in "rather mysterious circumstances".[22]

Cox Macro survived his son by nearly a year and died on 2 February 1767. The *Ipswich Journal* recorded his death noting that he had been "the Senior Doctor in Divinity of the University of Cambridge; who, during the course of a long life, had indefatigably applied himself to his studies, and acquired a general knowledge of all arts and sciences".[23] He was buried on 9 February in Norton churchyard "in an inclosure between the side of the Vestry and one of the buttresses which support the Church-wall".[24]

14 *Ibid.*, p. 26.
15 *Ibid.*, pp. 26, 38–40.
16 *Ibid.*, p. 42; Scarfe, p. 1240.
17 MS BL, Add. 25103.
18 RH to Littleton, 6 April 1750.
19 The *Macro Letter-book* contains 11 letters written by Mary Macro and, to 1753, three letters from Cox Macro.
20 *Macro Letter-book*, Littleton to Macro, 13 June 1753; RH to Littleton, 2 September 1754.
21 See Biography of Edward Macro, n.10.
22 *Alum. Cantab.*
23 John Nichols, *Literary Anecdotes of the Eighteenth Century; Comprizing Biographical Memoirs of William Bowyer, Printer . . . and Biographical Anecdotes of a Considerable Number of Eminent Writers and Ingenious Artists*, 9 vols., 1812–16, ix. 364.
24 *Ibid.*, p. 365.

Mary Macro (1689–1753)

Mary Macro was born in 1689. Her father was Edward Godfrey, Privy Purse to Queen Anne, but the family came from Risby in Suffolk, close to Bury St Edmunds where the Macro family had been established for some generations.[1] Her marriage to Cox Macro took place in 1714 and their first child, christened Mary, was born about 1717. A second child was born a year afterwards but died almost immediately, and a third child, Edward, was born in 1719.[2] At about this time the family moved to Little Haugh Hall at Norton in Suffolk, which remained Mary Macro's home for the rest of her life, and which she only rarely left. In her letters to Edward, she often mentions visits having been made to Little Haugh Hall by friends and relations, and there are also quite frequently plans afoot for Molly (her daughter) or Edward to "return the compliment".[3] But she herself clearly preferred to entertain rather than be entertained. Her particular pleasure was in having Edward's university friends to stay. These she quickly made friends with, and when they left, her favourites would receive presents (as Hurd did) of cakes and tea, along with letters from Norton.

It is clear from Mary Macro's correspondence with Edward that she was of an indomitable character. She suffered severe and long illnesses without complaint or self-pity, and maintained a steady air of cheerfulness. Her letters make fascinating reading; they are densely detailed and written with an animation that gives a striking impression of her personality. Hurd responded to her warmth and vivacity with delight and evidently tried to match the pace and tone of her letters. In many ways she was an ideal correspondent, sufficiently well read to recognise literary allusions, and interested in contemporary publications: for example, Young's *Night Thoughts* and Whitehead's early poetry.[4] She could also read French and therefore share in Hurd's enthusiasm for French literature as he began to discover it in the 1740s. Their friendship endured till her death on 31 August 1753, when as usual, Hurd had spent some weeks visiting the family at Little Haugh Hall.

Edward Macro (1719–1766)

Edward Macro was the second of Cox and Mary Macro's two surviving children. He was educated in London and was admitted to Emmanuel College, Cambridge, in June 1739.[1] He resided there fairly continuously from the autumn of that year till June 1743, though with lengthy summer vacations; but from then on, having been made a Fellow-commoner in the preceding January, he only occasionally attended during the term.[2] On 14 June 1744 he took his name off the college books.[3] There is a suggestion

1 Miscellaneous genealogical notes, Norfolk RO, Macro family, Box 1, Temp. no. 2.
2 See Biography of Cox Macro, n.9.
3 There are 11 letters written by Mary Macro in the *Macro Letter-book*. Other letters from Cox Macro (three to 1753) give more details of family life.
4 RH to Mary Macro, 26 February 1743; 22 June 1743.

1 *Alum. Cantab.*; *Emmanuel College Register*, COL. 9. 1(A).
2 *Commons Accounts Books*, STE. 15. 8; STE. 15. 9.
3 *Commons Accounts Book*, STE. 15. 9.

in Nichols' *Literary Anecdotes*[4] that at some point after this he proposed to join the army, and Venn in *Alumni Cantabrigienses*, quoting an unidentified authority, states that he did join the army and "was in the expedition to Flanders".[5] There is no other evidence for this and no mention of such a plan in the fairly regular succession of letters either to him, or mentioning him, which covers the years 1744 to 1763. It seems unlikely therefore that his proposal was ever carried out.[6]

Throughout the late 1740s and 1750s Edward Macro lived comfortably and pursued an interest in art which kept him for long periods in London. He was much in demand with his friends both as a lively companion and as a connoisseur of the arts, whose taste was esteemed and advice sought after. When in London he frequented the sale rooms and the studios of such artists as Benjamin Wilson and the sculptor Michael Rysbrack; and socially, depended on his connections with the Godfrey family on his mother's side, and his friendship with Sir Edward Littleton.

In 1753, however, financial and, perhaps, family pressures, obliged Edward to leave London for Suffolk where he took over the management of farmland belonging to his father.[7] This prevented him from moving as freely as he had done in previous years, although he nevertheless contrived to spend enough time in London to engage in the courtship of a Miss Egerton (an affair that came to an acrimonious end in 1756) and to assist Sir Edward Littleton in matters of taste.[8] These ranged from buying paintings and engravings for him at sales, to keeping an eye on the progress of various works of art commissioned by Littleton from London artists, and in particular from Rysbrack.[9] Littleton's letters contain a constant stream of requests, comments and applications for advice. In one letter he objects to many of the things that have been bought on his behalf (particularly a piece by Michelangelo of fruit and flowers, a subject which being in the "Fid-Fad Style of painting" he believed could not satisfactorily be painted by an artist who was distinguished for "ye Rougher Strokes" of his "pencil");[10] in another letter he responds to Macro's reports on the terracotta busts that Rysbrack was working on for him, and is not at all pleased that Macro thinks the Milton and Newton only "pretty good";[11] and in several letters of the period he discusses different recipes for picture varnish, constantly seeking the very best preparation for the large collection of paintings that he was building up.

Macro's attempts to apply himself to farm-management were not successful in financial terms and the 1750s saw him fall further and further into debt. In 1755 and 1756 he borrowed a total of more than £200 from Sir Edward Littleton, but this was insufficient, and in 1757 he was offered, and accepted, another £500.[12] In 1759

4 Nichols, *Lit. Anecs.*, ix. 365.

5 *Alum. Cantab.*

6 The *Macro Letter-book* contains letters addressed to Edward dating from 1748 to 1760; RH's letters continue to refer to him till 1763.

7 *Macro Letter-book*, Littleton to Macro, 13 June 1753.

8 *Ibid.*, Edward Macro to Cox Macro, 19 December 1756; two undated letters from "E" [Miss Egerton] to Edward.

9 *Macro Letter-book*, Littleton to Macro, 7 April 1756, and *passim*.

10 *Ibid.*, Littleton to Macro, 31 March 1754.

11 *Ibid.*, 21 November 1755.

12 Macro's debts to Littleton were documented in the latter's Bank Book, and later (in 1806) transcribed as a separate account, totalling not only the principal, but the interest that would have accrued on it. (Accounts Between Sr. Ed: Littleton Bt. & Edward Macro Esq., Staffs. RO, D260/M/E/129A.)

Littleton acted as surety on a loan of £250 for Macro and again in 1761 and 1762, on loans of £200. Two letters of May and July 1760 show that he tried to call a halt to this borrowing but was unsuccessful. With characteristic generosity he nevertheless continued to stand surety for Macro and at the latter's death found himself responsible for £1,150 worth of bonds, which added to his own loans to Macro, brought the principal owed to him to £1,936.2.0.[13]

Macro's manner of living eventually brought him into open conflict with his father. In 1761 he apparently wrote to Hurd explaining that he and his father had quarrelled, his farms had been taken from him, and, in short, that he had been "turn'd out of doors". He intimated that this was "owing to the intrigues of his Sister".[14] No further evidence to substantiate the implications of disinheritance has been found. Accounts of the family, however, generally suggest that Macro was disinherited at this time. In April 1761 Hurd wrote again to Littleton with the gloomy forecast that if Macro did not seek reconciliation with his father, he could see "nothing but ruin before him".[15]

The last reference to Macro in any existing correspondence is in a letter from Hurd to Littleton dated 21 January 1763.[16] The most recent news of the "Squire" is apparently good: he is in London "well employed" and "necessarily engaged". But Hurd cannot understand the "obstinate indifference" in his father, unless it is that he has received "some excessive ill treatment from his Son". He continues. " I think him in great danger, if he do not submit himself to the old Gentleman, and make a perfect reconciliation with him. But how this is to be done," he adds, "considering his imprudence, and untractable humour, I know not".

Beyond 1763 no further record of Edward Macro's activities appears to have survived. Littleton noted that he died on 4 April 1766, "at his Lodgings in Park Street, Gros[veno]r . Squ[are]", and was buried by Osmund Beauvoir "in the Burial Ground of Mount Street belonging to St Georges Church, Hanover Square".[17]

William Mason (1725–1797)

William Mason was the son of the Rev. William Mason, Vicar of Holy Trinity, Hull, by his first wife, Mary. He was born on 12 February 1725, and baptized on 11 March at his father's church. Mason the elder was said to be "an extraordinary good and diligent pastor, of exemplary life and conversation, charitably disposed and ready to do all human good offices and well affected to His Majesty King George and the present Government in Church and State".[1] The family was well connected and Mason's life was considerably influenced by his relations. Through his great-grandfather's niece he was related to John Hutton of Marske, at whose death he inherited an estate worth about £1,500 p.a., enough to make him financially secure for the

13 *Ibid.*
14 RH to Littleton, 6 March 1761.
15 To Littleton, 12 April 1761.
16 Letter book, Staffs. RO, D1413/1.
17 Accounts, Staffs. RO, D260/M/E/129A.

1 K.J.R. Robson, 'The S.P.C.K. in Action. Some Episodes from the East Riding of Yorkshire', in *The Church Quarterly Review*, clvi (1955). 273.

remainder of his life. Hutton's younger brother was Matthew, Archbishop of York (1747–57), through whom Mason obtained a canonry and prebend at York Minster; his second wife was Elizabeth D'Arcy, a relative of Robert D'Arcy, 4th Earl of Holdernesse, who was to become Mason's principal patron.

Mason's formal education was begun at Hull Grammar School. At home his father instructed and encouraged him in poetry, art and music.[2] On 1 July 1742 he was admitted to St John's College, Cambridge (his father's college), under Henry Wrigley,[3] but was also tutored by William Powell and Thomas Balguy. In 1746 he took his B.A. and on 17 April 1747 published his first work, *Musaeus: a Monody to the Memory of Mr Pope, in Imitation of Milton's Lycidas*.[4] By this time Mason had made the acquaintance of Hurd through their mutual friends at St John's, and during 1747 he made the acquaintance of Thomas Gray. The latter with the backing of William Heberden proposed him as a Fellow of Pembroke Hall in the autumn of this year. Pembroke was unusually hospitable to graduates of other colleges, and unlike St John's did not require fellowship candidates to sit an examination.[5] On Gray and Heberden's recommendation, Mason was elected by the Fellows, but was prevented from taking up his fellowship by the Master, Dr Roger Long, who exercised his power of veto against him for a further eighteen months.[6] He relented early in 1749 and on 2 March Mason was once more elected and on 16 March admitted as a Fellow of the college. In July he took his M.A. and executed his first official poetical commission, an ode for the installation of the Duke of Newcastle as Chancellor of the University, set to music by William Boyce. In the same year he published *Isis. An Elegy. Written in the Year 1748*, an attack on Oxford Jacobitism, which elicited a reply from Thomas Warton, which was acknowledged by Mason as a better poem.

Mason was passionately fond not only of poetry but of music and drama. As an undergraduate he left Cambridge for London whenever he had "five guineas to spare", and each afternoon bought a seat in the pit of one of the theatres, until his money ran out.[7] His next, more ambitious publication, *Elfrida, a Dramatic Poem. Written on the Model of the Ancient Greek Tragedy*, 1752, was influenced by his love for the theatre, and was originally intended for the stage, until Gray persuaded him against the idea.[8] The poem sold well and was reissued almost immediately in a second octavo edition. But soon after this, Mason's career suffered an upheaval caused by the death of his father on 26 August 1753. His fellowship, worth £100 p.a., was insufficient for his needs and had been supplemented by an allowance from the elder Mason which ceased on his death, his estate being made over to Mason's step-mother.[9] Fortunately, Mason had both the option of entering the Church and a patron, Lord Holdernesse,

2 *A Candidate For Praise. William Mason 1725–97 Precentor of York*. Catalogue of an exhibition, compiled by Bernard Barr and John Ingamells, York, 1973, p. 51.

3 Scott-Mayor, *Admissions to St John's*, ii. 106.

4 Philip Gaskell, *The First Editions of William Mason*, Cambridge Bibliographical Society, Monograph No.1, 1951, p. 1.

5 D.A. Winstanley, *Unreformed Cambridge*, pp. 229, 238.

6 *Ibid.*, pp. 229–30.

7 *The Yale Edition of Horace Walpole's Correspondence*, ed. W.S. Lewis, 48 vols., 1937–83, Vol. 28, Mason to Walpole, 3 March 1775.

8 Gray, *Correspondence*, Letter 158. *Elfrida* was, however, produced successfully in 1772, though without Mason's permission.

9 *Ibid.*, Letters 180, 181, 182.

to secure him a living. It seems probable that he spent part of the winter of 1753–54 acting as secretary to Holdernesse, who was a Secretary of State, at his house at Syon Hill.[10] The following year he was ordained deacon on 17, and priest on 24 November 1754, in St Margaret's, Westminster, with Edmund Keene, the Bishop of Chester, officiating. On 27 November, on the presentation of Lord Holdernesse, he was instituted Rector of Aston, West Yorkshire, where he remained for forty-three years. According to William Whitehead, another of Mason's close friends, he was "by much the finest preacher in the whole country, & villages, & towns flock to hear him".[11] In the course of his forty-three years, Mason installed a new paved floor and pews in the church; he worked hard to improve the quality of the church music, obtaining a barrel-organ which could play twenty-four tunes; he built a new rectory; and contributed the larger part of the cost of a new village school.[12]

Not all the year was spent at Aston. Mason retained the post of secretary to Holdernesse for about seven years, which entailed his attendance in London. He had also been appointed his domestic chaplain, and in the summer of 1755 accompanied him to Hanover following the King, who had left for Germany at the end of April.[13] Other preferments also came his way, although the political influence exercised by Holdernesse gradually declined in the 1760s. He was unable to secure any major promotion for Mason, whose whig sympathies probably also hindered him in his career. Nevertheless the latter part of the 1750s and the early 1760s were active years for him. On his decision to go into the Church, Warburton, who knew him through Hurd, had emphasized the necessity of putting aside thoughts of poetry for more serious studies.[14] At the time, Mason had concurred with this view. However, his desire to write was much too strong; as Gray had said of him in 1748, he had "much Fancy, little Judgement, and a good deal of Modesty . . .: he reads little or nothing, writes abundance, & that with a Design to make his Fortune by it".[15] In 1756 he published a collection of Odes and from that year on was working hard at Caractacus, another dramatic poem, eventually published in 1759. On 6 December 1756 he was collated to the canonry and prebend of Holme Episcopi in York Minster, a preferment procured for him by the Archbishop, Matthew Hutton.[16] In the summer of 1757[17] he was appointed chaplain to George II by the interest of the Duke of Devonshire, father of Lord John Cavendish, who had been up at Peterhouse and privately tutored by Mason. Mason was still holding a fellowship at Pembroke. On his institution to Aston, he had been allowed a year's grace before resigning his original fellowship in December 1755. But on 23 March 1756, he was elected Smart Fellow (a bye-fellowship with a small emolument). However, in order to keep this fellowship he was

10 *Ibid.*, Letter 184, n.4; Barr and Ingamells, *Candidate for Praise*, p. 10.

11 William Whitehead to Viscount Nuneham, 1 August 1757, *The Harcourt Papers*, ed. Edward William Harcourt, 14 vols., Oxford, [1880–1905], vii. 214.

12 Barr and Ingamells, pp. 54–5.

13 Gray, *Correspondence*, Letter 195, n.14.

14 *Prelate*, p. 125.

15 Gray, *Correspondence*, Letter 145.

16 *John Le Neve. Fasti Ecclesiae Anglicanae 1541–1857. IV York Diocese*. Compiled by Joyce M. Horn & David M. Smith, 1975, p. 42.

17 Scott-Mayor, *Admissions to St John's* gives the date as 2 July (ii. 531); Barr and Ingamells, p. 55, date the appointment 2 August.

obliged to take the degree of D.D., which he declined to do. He therefore resigned the fellowship on 15 February 1759.[18]

In the 1760s, Mason's first appointment was as chaplain to George III, on 9 September 1761, which entitled him to take part in the Coronation procession on 22 September. A few months later in January 1762, he received even greater preferment, first, to canon residentiary at York, worth, according to Gray, £200 p.a.; and then, in February, to a precentorship "worth as much more", also at York.[19] The canon's stall had been promised to him by Frederick Montagu, a contemporary at Cambridge, and a friend of both Gray and Horace Walpole, the latter of whom Mason had known since 1754. The precentorship (in the gift of the King) had been obtained for him by Lord Holdernesse. It carried with it the prebend of Driffield, which Mason took, ceding his other prebend of Holme. His personal life was substantially altered by his marriage, on 25 September 1765, to Mary Sherman. But their happiness was brief. During the winter of 1765–66, Mrs Mason showed signs of what was later definitely identified as consumption, and on 27 March 1767, she died in Bristol. On the literary front Mason published a slim volume of three *Elegies* in 1762, the first edition on 7 December, and the second on 28 December (both dated 1763).[20] In December 1763, but with a title-page dated 1764, he published a volume of his collected *Poems*, new editions of which appeared periodically throughout the rest of his life.[21]

Mason's political affinities and his lack of a really influential patron were effective barriers to his obtaining a deanery or bishopric. This became increasingly clear in the 1760s and 1770s, and since Mason had been made financially independent by his inheritance of the Hutton estate in 1768, he resigned his chaplaincy to the King in 1772.[22] Whilst still mindful of his obligations at Aston and York, he now devoted increasing time and energy not just to his writing, but to the other interests which dominated his life: gardening, painting, music, and, perhaps to a lesser extent, politics.[23] In gardening he was an admirer of 'Capability' Brown, but his own talent lay particularly in the creation of flower gardens. His own garden at Aston was renowned, and he is credited with designing or helping to design a number of other gardens, amongst them a flower garden at Nuneham (the home of his friend the second Earl Harcourt),[24] and gardens at Thurcaston (for Hurd) and at Papplewick (for Frederick Montagu).[25] This practical interest is reflected in his longest poem, *The English Garden*, modelled on Virgil's *Georgics* and published in four books between 1772 and 1781.

18 Gray, *Correspondence*, Letter 284, n.4.

19 *Ibid.*, Letter 353; *Fasti*, ed. Horn & Smith, p. 11.

20 *Ibid.*, Letter 364, n.6; Gaskell, *First Editions*, pp. 8–9.

21 *Ibid.*, Letter 368, n.3; Gaskell, pp. 9–10.

22 Barr and Ingamells, p. 55.

23 Mason was a prominent member of the Yorkshire Association, critical of the government of Lord North and its conduct in the American War of Independence, and policy in India. In 1783, however, following the younger Pitt's appointment as prime minister, he and his friend Lord Harcourt went over to the King.

24 Mason met George Harcourt (1736–1809), then Viscount Nuneham, in 1755 whilst on the continent with Lord Holdernesse. Nuneham was on a tour with Lord Villiers and their tutor, Mason's friend, William Whitehead. Their subsequent correspondence spans the years 1755 to 1785 and is recorded in *The Harcourt Papers* (see n.11 above).

25 Mason's activities as a gardener are well documented in Mavis Batey's 'William Mason, English Gardener', in *Garden History. The Journal of the Garden History Society*, Vol. I, No.2, February 1973, pp. 11–25.

An interest in both theory and practice is demonstrated also in Mason's abiding enjoyment of the fine arts. Already at Cambridge he was translating Du Fresnoy's *Art of Painting*, which he finally published in 1783, and though his practical ability was poor he produced several sketches of Gray, painted an altarpiece for Lord Harcourt's chapel at Nuneham, a portrait of Whitehead, a *Bard* and a *Holy Family*. He was on friendly terms with Joshua Reynolds, and friends too with William Gilpin.

Other than *The English Garden*, Mason's most important literary work in his later years was his edition of *The Poems of Mr Gray*, published in 1775. This was prefaced by *Memoirs* of the poet, which for the first time introduced the 'life and letters' concept of biography, and influenced the development of the genre for decades to come. Many biographers adopted Mason's original idea, the most significant amongst them, James Boswell, who in his *Life of Johnson*, acknowledged the excellence of Mason's plan. Mason produced a similar volume of *Memoirs* of William Whitehead in 1788, but the majority of his publications in the 1770s and 1780s were poetical, many of them satirical. He also published *A Copious Collection of those Portions of the Psalms of David, Bible, and Liturgy, Which have been set to Music, and sung as Anthems*; a pamphlet on the government of the York Lunatic Asylum; and a sermon on the slave trade, both dated 1788.[26] His last preferment was to the rectory of Langton-upon-Swale in 1777 on the presentation of Lord Holdernesse. Apparently, however, Mason was "only the nominal Rector", accepting the benefice on behalf of the son of his friend, and erstwhile curate, Christopher Alderson, and paying him the stipend until 1793 when he was able to take it over himself.[27]

Mason died at Aston on 5 April 1797 and was buried at his church on 11 April. Hurd noted his death in his *Dates of some Occurrences in my own Life* and added, "He was one of my oldest and most respected friends. How few of this description now remain!" A monument was erected in Westminster Abbey in 1800, and other memorials were placed in Mason's garden at Nuneham and in his church at Aston.[28]

For a detailed biographical study of Mason, see John W. Draper, *William Mason. A Study in Eighteenth-Century Culture*, New York, 1924.

John Potter (1716–?1770)

John Potter was born in Somerset on 15 June 1716.[1] His father, also John Potter, was Vicar of Cloford, but in 1719 resigned the living and was instituted to that of Podimore, which he held with the living of Wheathill (from 1723), till his death in 1739. In 1718 he became prebendary of Barton St David, but resigned the prebend almost immediately and was instituted to that of Whitelackington. In 1726 he resigned the latter and was instituted as prebendary of Whitchurch.[2]

John Potter the younger was the eldest of five children, one of whom died very young, leaving three sons, John, Robert (born in 1721, see post To Potter, 7 August 1739, n.15), and Thomas (born in 1723), and one daughter, Susanna (born in 1726).[3]

26 Gaskell, *First Editions*, pp. 27, 35, 34.
27 Barr and Ingamells, p. 55.
28 *Ibid.*, pp. 48–9, 77.

1 Somerset RO, Cloford Parish Register.
2 Information supplied by County Archivist, Somerset RO.
3 Somerset RO, Cloford Parish Register.

The two older boys were both educated under an Emmanuel man, John Gaylard, though at different schools. Gaylard was Master of Wells Grammar School (which John Potter attended) from 1728 to 1733, and then moved to Sherborne (to which school Robert was sent) to become Headmaster.[4] This possibly accounts for the Potters' subsequent choice of Cambridge and Emmanuel, when they came to read for a degree, rather than their father's Oxford College, Exeter. John Potter was admitted a sizar at Emmanuel on 30 January 1734.[5] He matriculated in the same year, coming into residence in June. Hurd had been admitted in 1733, also as a sizar, but did not come into residence until a year after Potter.[6]

In certain respects the college careers of the two men were very similar. Neither of them came from a wealthy family, and both were therefore admitted to Emmanuel as sizars, and were partly supported by the college. Originally the system in Cambridge allowed free commons to the sizars in exchange for their serving at the Fellows' table. Later they were given an allowance and freed from the obligation of serving at table. In the late 1730s commons bills for sizars in Emmanuel were about 2s.6d. a week, compared to a sum of about 5s. for pensioners.[7] It is not clear whether they still served at table, but they continued to be listed in the same accounts book as the Fellows and Fellow-commoners, a separate book being used for scholars and pensioners.[8] Within three years, however, both John Potter and Hurd had won scholarships which considerably eased their position. Both were chosen Thorpe exhibitioners, Potter on 18 October 1736 (his exhibition to run from the previous Midsummer Quarter), and Hurd, his successor, on 24 November 1738.[9] The Thorpe foundation had been established originally to provide five sums of £15 a year to be paid to five undergraduates "of sober and every way unblameable Life and Conversation, and of ye most hopeful parts and ingenuity, and of ye best proficiency in Learning for their time".[10] Certain obligations were imposed upon the recipients of this benefaction, perhaps the heaviest being that of undergoing an annual examination of their proficiency by at least two of the Fellows. Thorpe had wished that particular regard should be had "in ye first place to ye Holy Scripture, desiring they might be very conversant therein even in their Original Languages, and next to them in ye Articles and Canons of our Church with its Liturgy, and ye best Expositions of any of them; And as many of ye most antient Fathers as their time and abilities may reach, with ye study of ye learned Languages and all other parts of solid and useful Learning."[11] In addition to this, one of the exhibitioners was chosen each year to give a Latin oration at the service of Commemoration of the Founder (Sir Walter Mildmay) and Benefactors, which was also instituted by Thorpe, and which took place in November. For this oration the exhibitioner was paid 10s. John Potter never spoke the oration, although he had to write one (see To Potter, 25 August 1740), but Hurd did give it on 24 November 1740.[12]

In addition to winning Thorpe exhibitions, Potter and Hurd both also won the

4 Biographical note on Robert Potter, Nat. Lib. Wales, MS 12502E; *Alum. Cantab.*; *Lond. Mag.*
5 Emmanuel College, *College Register*, COL. 9. 1(A); *Commons Accounts Book*, STE. 15. 9.
6 *Ibid.*
7 *Commons Accounts Book*, STE. 15. 9.
8 *Commons Accounts Book*, STE. 15. 8.
9 *Thorpe Scholarship Accounts*, SCH. 1. 17.
10 *Statuta Collegii Emman: apud Cantabrigiam*, COL. 18. 4. A copy of 1735.
11 *Ibid.*
12 *Thorpe Accounts*, SCH. 1. 17.

Sudbury Plate, awarded to whoever "at ye time of his taking ye Degree of B. of Arts . . . shall be adjudg'd . . . to be ye most worthy of ye year for his Piety, Learning and Parts".[13] £6 p.a. was laid out for the plate, and appears to have been paid directly in two instalments to the undergraduate concerned.[14] Potter was awarded the plate for the year running from Ladyday 1737 to Ladyday 1738; and Hurd, following him, for the year 1738–39,[15] that is, their last years as undergraduates. Finally, on taking their degree as B.A. the two men were awarded a second scholarship. In Potter's case the award was made on 11 March 1738.[16] However, as he took his name off the college books on 1 September of the same year it is impossible to establish which scholarship he had won; no payments were made to him during the summer, and the record of the award does not specify the particular benefaction.

Having taken his degree, Potter spent very little time in college. B.A. examinations were held in early February,[17] and he stayed on in Emmanuel till the end of March. From April onwards he was away on and off till the second week of June, after which there is no further record of his being in residence. He took out his name on 1 September[18] and on 23 September 1738 was ordained deacon with a title to the curacy of Batcombe, Somerset.[19] On 21 September 1740 he took priest's orders, but was not able to obtain a more profitable living until 1744, when, in May, he was licensed as curate of Pylle (or Pill).[20] His progress continued to be slow; by 1754 he had added another curacy, that of Shepton Mallet,[21] to his other means of subsistence, and in the same year he was instituted Rector of Badgworth, near Axbridge.[22] (According to contemporary reference, he had by now been made an M.A.)[23] At some time following his institution, Potter moved to Axbridge (Hurd's letter of 16 November 1756 is addressed to him there), and then, in 1767, moved once more, to Frome.

Potter had married in 1755 after obtaining the Badgworth living and hence a more substantial income. Hurd's letters of the 1740s mention a woman named "Hetty" with whom Potter evidently had a sometimes turbulent relationship, but there is no record of the outcome of their courtship. His wife to be was Catherine Conway, whom he married on 6 February 1755.[24] Their first child was born in November 1757, and according to the Badgworth parish register four other children were born between 1759 and 1763.[25] Although it seems that Potter and Hurd kept in touch occasionally

13 *Sudbury Foundation*, SCH. 1. 19.
14 *Sudbury Plate*, SCH. 1. 11.
15 *Ibid.*
16 *Commons Accounts Book*, STE. 15. 8; *Order Book*, COL. 14. 2. A few awards were noted in the Emmanuel *Order Book*; the majority of awards are indicated only in the accounts of the separate foundations.
17 *Commons Accounts Book*, STE. 15. 8.
18 *Ibid.*
19 Somerset RO, *Clergy Subscription Book*, D/D/BS no.9.
20 Somerset RO, *Clergy List*, D/D/VC 87. See RH's letter of 25 November 1743 which indicates that Potter was already certain of obtaining the living by the end of this year.
21 Somerset RO, Visitation and Marriage Register (Shepton Mallet).
22 Somerset RO, *Clergy List*, D/D/VC 87.
23 *Ibid.*
24 Information supplied by County Archivist, Somerset RO.
25 Somerset RO, Badgworth Parish Register.

through the 1750s, it is clear from the last letter in the National Library of Wales collection (16 November 1756) that the correspondence had become merely an exchange of particularly important news, and it seems unlikely that even this continued much beyond the 1750s. Potter himself received no further preferments and died late in 1770 or early in 1771.[26] His wife and three of his children survived him.[27]

William Warburton (1698–1779)

The life of William Warburton has been extensively documented in a variety of different sources. The following is therefore a synopsis of the salient facts of his life which may be supplemented by consultation of the works listed at the end.

William Warburton was born on 24 December 1698, the second and only surviving son of George Warburton, attorney and town clerk of Newark, Nottinghamshire, and his wife Elizabeth. He was sent to school in Newark under a Mr Twells, and then moved to Oakham, where he remained until 1714. He then returned to Newark and is said to have studied briefly under the tuition of his cousin, also William Warburton, who had been newly appointed headmaster of the public grammar school there. Warburton's father had died in 1706 leaving his wife with three other children (all daughters) to support. This, combined with the fact that William's father and grandfather had both been attorneys, probably accounts for his being articled as a clerk to John Kirke, an attorney at East Markham, in Nottinghamshire, on 23 April 1714. He served his term of five years with Kirke and in April 1719 returned to Newark. The following four years remain obscure. Warburton may have practised as an attorney, or may have assisted his cousin in his school. He did apparently spend much time studying with his cousin, having discovered a voracious appetite for reading, which he frequently indulged late into the night.

Warburton's appetite for learning coincided with a determination to take orders, for which, according to Hurd,[1] he prepared himself with scrupulous attention. On 22 December 1723 he was ordained deacon by the Archbishop of York, and about the same time published his first work, *Miscellaneous Translations, in Prose and Verse, from Roman Poets, Orators, and Historians*.[2] Warburton's ordination as priest did not take place until 1 March 1727, when he was ordained by the Bishop of London, with a title to the small vicarage of Greaseley in Nottinghamshire. This living was in the gift of Sir Robert Sutton,[3] to whom Warburton had dedicated his *Miscellaneous Translations*, and who was to prove a useful patron in the early years of his career. The year 1727

26 No record of Potter's death has been traced. His signatures in the Badgworth Parish Register (Somerset RO) cease in 1767, and the living was presented to Robert Potter, who was instituted on 15 June 1771. A letter dated 29 January 1771 from Potter's widow, Catherine, indicates that his death had occurred recently, but does not give a specific date. (Nat. Lib. Wales, MS. 12435E.)

27 Letter from Catherine Potter, 29 January 1771, Nat. Lib. Wales, MS 12435E.

1 *A Discourse, By Way of General Preface to the Quarto Edition of Bishop Warburton's Works, Containing some Account of the Life, Writings, and Character of the Author*, 1794, pp. 5–6.

2 The date of this work is variously given as 1723 or 1724. The title-page, however, is dated 1724, although the dedication, to Sir Robert Sutton, is dated 1723.

3 Ecton, *Thesaurus Rerum Ecclesiasticarum*, second edition, ed. Browne Willis, 1754, p. 555.

also saw the publication of *A Critical and Philosophical Enquiry into the Causes of Prodigies and Miracles, as related by Historians* (the manuscript of which Warburton had given to Matthew Concanen) and *The Legal Judicature in Chancery Stated*, a work in which Warburton joined with Samuel Burroughs, a master in Chancery.

In the following year another living in the gift of Sir Robert Sutton fell vacant, and was offered to Warburton. This, the rectory of Burnt, or Brant Broughton, was significantly more valuable than Greaseley, and was said to be worth £560 p.a. Warburton resigned Greaseley and was presented to Brant Broughton in June. His mother and sisters joined him, and the family remained there till 1746. Sutton's patronage also apparently secured Warburton a Cambridge M.A. on 25 April 1728, when George I visited the University, although handsome compliments paid to the King and Cambridge University in Warburton's *A Critical and Philosophical Enquiry* may have had some influence. Having begun to achieve some recognition in the world, Warburton was further rewarded by the presentation to the living of Frisby in Lincolnshire, which was estimated at £250 p.a. The living, in the gift of the King, was offered to him by the Duke of Newcastle, and he held it, without residence, till 1756. Now comfortably established, he was able to turn his full concentration to study and writing.

From 1726 onwards, Warburton had begun to forge links with other writers, some of whom he appears to have become acquainted with in London. Amongst these were Matthew Concanen and Lewis Theobald, with both of whom he corresponded over a period of years. He also established contact and corresponded with William Stukeley, Peter Desmaiseaux and Thomas Birch. His first publication of these years was probably *An Apology for Sir Robert Sutton*, issued anonymously in 1733 in defence of Sutton who, as a director of the 'Charitable Corporation' was involved in allegations of corrupt practice.[4] In 1736 Warburton was contemplating a new edition of Velleius Paterculus, but although a specimen of the projected work was published in the *Bibliotheque Britannique* the advice of Conyers Middleton and Bishop Hare dissuaded him from continuing further with the project. However, 1736 was notable for the publication of *The Alliance between Church and State, or, The Necessity and Equity of an Established Religion and a Test-law demonstrated*, usually considered to be Warburton's most distinguished work. In it, he sets out to prove the necessity of an alliance between the state and the Church, in which the Church relinquishes its independence in exchange for the support and protection of the state, in the course of which he justifies the existence of the established Church and test law. The *Alliance* impressed many of Warburton's contemporaries, among them, Bishop Hare, who recommended Warburton to Queen Caroline. Her death in 1737, however, prevented him from deriving any benefit from the recommendation.

The *Alliance* was intended as a corollary to a work of much greater scope and significance, *The Divine Legation of Moses demonstrated, on the Principles of a Religious Deist, from the Omission of the Doctrine of a Future State of Reward and Punishment in the Jewish Dispensation*. The first part of this ambitious work was published in January 1738 and Warburton worked on it for much of the rest of his life, adding further sections, and altering and extending those already published, in new editions. In it, he put forward what he believed was a new and powerful argument in defence of

4 Warburton never claimed the authorship of this pamphlet, but it is usually attributed to him.

Christianity. His thesis was, briefly, that every society has supposed the existence of a future state of rewards and punishments, and that the belief in such a future state is necessary to the well-being of the society; however, no such provision is suggested in the Mosaic dispensation, which therefore indicates that the law of Moses is unique and of Divine origin. Few works, even in the eighteenth century, provoked as much controversy as the *Divine Legation*. One of the first attacks made on Warburton was by William Webster in his anonymous 'Letter from a Country Clergyman', which insinuated that Warburton shared the views of Conyers Middleton, who was suspected of covert infidelity. Warburton replied to Webster in *A Vindication of the Author of the Divine Legation of Moses*, defending Middleton, but asserting his own orthodoxy. The second part of the *Divine Legation* was published in May 1741 in two volumes. Again, there was much criticism, to which Warburton replied with some savagery in two volumes of *Remarks on Several Occasional Reflections*: the first, issued in 1744, in answer to Conyers Middleton, Richard Pococke, Nicholas Mann, Master of Charterhouse, and Richard Grey; the second, dated 1745, in reply to Henry Stebbing and Arthur Ashley Sykes.

On a less contentious front, the years 1738 to 1741 provided other satisfactions. In 1738 Warburton was acting as chaplain to the Prince of Wales; and in December of the same year he published the first of five letters defending Pope's *Essay on Man* against the accusations of Jean Pierre de Crousaz, Professor of Philosophy and Mathematics at Lausanne. This timely defence led to a correspondence and, in 1740, the invitation to visit Pope at Twickenham, from which point the friendship between the poet and his admirer, and later commentator and editor, never flagged. In November 1741 Warburton received a joint invitation from Pope, who was staying at Prior Park, and his host Ralph Allen, to whom Warburton had not yet been introduced. He accepted, and was evidently found to be as congenial a guest as he had proved himself a friend to Pope. Further invitations were issued leading finally to Warburton's marriage to Gertrude Tucker, a niece and favourite of Ralph Allen. The wedding took place on 5 September 1745 and Warburton moved from Brant Broughton to reside mainly at Prior Park.

Warburton's connection with Pope caused him to direct his energies in a more literary channel than heretofore. He had actively encouraged Pope in the writing of a fourth book of the *Dunciad*, which had been published, with Warburton's notes, in 1742. When Pope died on 30 May 1744, he left Warburton half his library and the properties of all those printed works on which he had already or would in the future, write commentaries, providing only against alterations of the text. Accordingly, soon after his death, Warburton brought out a new edition of the *Dunciad*, and then set about preparing an edition of Shakespeare, incorporating his own and Pope's notes and comments. The project was one for which he was, in some respects, well prepared. From 1726 he had corresponded with Lewis Theobald, contributing textual emendations and remarks which were used in Theobald's edition of Shakespeare. Their collaboration, however, did not last and ended in a bitter estrangement. Warburton subsequently entered into a correspondence with Sir Thomas Hanmer, and appears to have hoped that they might be associated in producing a new edition of Shakespeare. But again a quarrel ensued, and he withdrew his help and friendship. His own edition was published in eight quarto volumes in 1747, and met with what was, to Warburton, an unexpected hostile reception. He was attacked with some ferocity by Zachary Grey, but more damagingly by Thomas Edwards, who ridiculed his editorial methods. Johnson was more lenient, but later critics have generally concurred with Edwards, whose *Supplement to Mr Warburton's Edition of Shakespeare*, re-titled *The Canons of Criticism* in its third edition, proved a popular success.

Warburton's association with Pope also brought him further preferment in his career as a churchman, partly through Ralph Allen and his connections, and partly through William Murray, Lord Mansfield, to whom Pope is said to have introduced him.[5] Through Murray's interest Warburton was chosen as Preacher to Lincoln's Inn, which brought him a small salary, and entailed his presence in London during term time. The appointment was made in April 1746 and on Allen's advice, Warburton took a house in Bedford Row, which he retained until 1757, when he moved to Grosvenor Square, to a house that he kept till his death. Other preferments came his way in the 1750s. Lord Chancellor Hardwicke, the father of Charles Yorke, one of Warburton's oldest friends, presented him to a prebend in Gloucester cathedral in April 1753. In September 1754, he was appointed King's chaplain in ordinary, and was made a D.D. by the Archbishop of Canterbury. Then in 1755 Murray was again instrumental in securing him a prebend at Durham, worth £500 p.a. Warburton resigned his Gloucester prebend, but was allowed to keep that at Durham even after his elevation to the episcopacy. The following year he also resigned his living at Frisby, but this was more than compensated for by his being appointed Dean of Bristol in the autumn of 1757. The deanery he owed to the influence of William Pitt, a friend of Ralph Allen, and the newly elected M.P. for Bath. On 22 December 1759 Warburton's steady progression through the ranks of the church culminated in his nomination as Bishop of Gloucester, a preferment for which, again, Pitt was largely responsible.

The advances that Warburton made in his career during this productive decade did not, however, distract him from his writing. In 1750 he published *Julian, or a Discourse concerning the Earthquake and Fiery Eruption which defeated that Emperor's Attempt to rebuild the Temple at Jerusalem* in answer to Middleton's *Free Inquiry*, part of the debate on the nature and existence of miracles in the early Christian church. At the same time, he had in preparation a new edition of Pope's *Works*, which was published in 1751, in two separate editions, and was re-issued a further seven times in the next nine years. He also produced two volumes of sermons preached at Lincoln's Inn under the title *The Principles of Natural and Revealed Religion*, the first in 1753, the second in 1754, and revised editions of the two parts of the *Divine Legation*. The most important new works published in these years were *A View of Lord Bolingbroke's Philosophy; In Four Letters to a Friend*, 1754–55, and *Remarks on Mr David Hume's Essay on the Natural History of Religion* written in collaboration with Hurd. The decade following Warburton's consecration, in contrast, produced more revisions, but little original work. He expanded an earlier sermon and issued it as *A Rational Account of the Nature and End of the Sacrament of the Lord's Supper* in 1761. His next work was also an elaboration of one of his sermons, but very much extended into a treatise, devoted largely to the refutation of Wesley, Whitefield, and other "enthusiasts". It was published in 1762 as *The Doctrine of Grace; or The Office and Operation of the Holy Spirit vindicated from the Insults of Infidelity and the Abuses of Fanaticism.* Fourth editions of

[5] This is contested by Robert M. Ryley in his study, *William Warburton*, citing a letter from Warburton to Murray dated 1738 as evidence of a previous acquaintance. (Ryley, *William Warburton*, Boston, 1984, pp. 8, 112.) This letter, however, serves a formal business purpose and it is perhaps the case that although Warburton had already met Murray before his friendship with Pope, he had not previously been drawn into his intimate social circle.

the *Alliance* and the *Divine Legation* were put to press, and a last volume of Warburton's Lincoln's Inn sermons was also compiled and released in 1767.

The 1760s marked a decline in Warburton's health. In 1763 he broke his arm, an injury which took a long time to heal and troubled him for months afterwards. In 1764 another blow fell with the death of his old friend Ralph Allen at Prior Park, and in the same year he is complaining of his "usual dizziness".[6] Failing health finally forced him to give up Prior Park in 1769, and remain permanently at his episcopal palace in Gloucester. Here, after a bad fall in 1770, he became increasingly senile, and had his last years saddened by the death of his only child, Ralph (b. 6 April 1756), who died on 18 July 1775 of consumption. Warburton lived a few years longer becoming ever more debilitated, and died in the palace on 7 June 1779. His death was little noticed by the newspapers and journals of the day. But his life and works were handsomely commemorated by Hurd, who edited and published 250 copies of a seven volume quarto edition of the *Works*, added a separately published *Discourse* giving an account of his life, and prepared the edition of letters issued after his own death, *Letters from a Late Eminent Prelate to One of His Friends.*

Printed Biographical Sources

Hurd, *A Discourse, By Way of General Preface to the Quarto Edition of Bishop Warburton's Works*, 1794.

John Selby Watson, *The Life of William Warburton, D.D. Lord Bishop of Gloucester . . . With Remarks on his Works*, 1863.

Nichols, *Lit. Anecs.*, v. 529–658

A.W. Evans, *Warburton and the Warburtonians. A Study in some Eighteenth-Century Controversies*, 1932.

Robert M. Ryley, *William Warburton*, Twaynes's English Authors Series, Florida State University, Boston, 1984.

The Minor Correspondents

Anthony Askew (1722–1772)

Anthony Askew[1] was born in Newcastle, the son of a well-known physician. He was admitted to Emmanuel College, Cambridge, as a pensioner on 11 July 1739, matriculated in 1741, and took his M.B. in 1744. He left the college some weeks later, and in 1745 moved to Leyden in order to continue the study of medicine. His time was, however, much taken up with the study and collection of manuscripts and editions of the classics. Whilst in Leyden he produced and had published a specimen of a new edition of Aeschylus, which he evidently proposed to prepare in full. The specimen, *Novae Editionis Tragoediarum Aeschyli Specimen* was dedicated to Richard Mead, who was to become a life-long friend. After about a year in Leyden, Askew set out on a tour in 1746 visiting Hungary, Athens, Constantinople, Italy and other countries. His motivation was at least in part the wish to acquire such books and manuscripts as

6 *Letters from a Late Eminent Prelate to One of His Friends*, [1808], p. 260.

1 *Emmanuel College Commons Accounts Book*, STE. 15. 8; *Alum. Cantab.*; *D.N.B.*; Nichols, *Lit. Anecs.*, iii. 494–7; William MacMichael, *The Gold-headed Cane*, 1827, ed. George Peachey, 1923, pp. 111–29.

would satisfy his taste for fine editions and the scarce or curious. These acquisitions formed the basis of what was to become a famous library, the *Bibliotheca Askeviana.*

On his return to England, Askew was made a F.R.S. in 1749, and set up practice, at first in Cambridge, about 1750. In the same year he was made M.D. and in 1753 a Fellow of the Royal College of Physicians. During the 1750s he moved his practice to London where he was also appointed Physician to St Bartholomew's and to Christ's Hospitals, and Registrar of the College of Physicians. His collection of books and manuscripts continued to expand, Askew's intention being, it is said, to own a copy of every edition of a Greek author. His house was frequently visited by other scholars and collectors, amongst them Richard Farmer, Sir William Jones, Samuel Parr, and "Demosthenes" Taylor. He died on 27 February 1772; and in 1775 his library of books was dispersed in a sale which lasted twenty days and produed £3,993.0s.6d.

William Bowyer (1699–1773)

William Bowyer[2] was the only son of William Bowyer, the elder, a successful London printer. He was educated privately and in 1716 entered St John's College, Cambridge, as a sizar. He won an exhibition in 1719 but left college without taking his B.A. and joined his father in the family business. His success as a printer led to a series of important official appointments, the first of which was as Printer of the Votes of the House of Commons (1729). At the same time he began to write and during his life published a number of learned pamphlets, essays and prefaces. The earliest of these, *A View of a Book entitled Reliquiae Baxterianae*, appeared in 1727. In the 1750s he took on an assistant, John Nichols, later the author of the nine volume work *Literary Anecdotes of the Eighteenth Century* based on biographical memoirs of Bowyer.

Sir John Danvers (1722?–1796)

Sir John Danvers,[3] born about 1722, was the son of Joseph Danvers of Swithland, Leicestershire. His father was Sheriff of the county from June to December 1721, and in 1722 was elected M.P. for Boroughbridge. He represented the latter and subsequently two other constituencies from that date until 1747, and was created Baronet in July 1746. His son succeeded him on his death in October 1753. Little is known of Sir John. He apparently avoided public life, although acting as Sheriff of Leicestershire from 1755–56. He married Mary Watson of Clapham, Surrey, by whom he had one daughter, who married the Hon. Augustus Richard Butler. On Danvers' death on 21 September 1796, the Baronetcy became extinct.

Robert Hay Drummond (1711–76)

Robert Hay Drummond[4] was the second son of George Hay, Viscount Dupplin, and assumed the name Drummond in 1739. He attended Westminster School and Christ Church, Oxford, where he gained a B.A. in 1731. After making the grand tour with a

2 *D.N.B.*; Scott-Mayor, *Admissions to St John's*, ii. (Part 3). 5, 302–4.

3 G.E. C[okayne], *Complete Baronetage*, 5 vols., Exeter, 1900–6; John Nichols, *The History and Antiquities of the County of Leicester*, 4 vols., 1795–1811; vol. iii, part 2, p. 1048.

4 *D.N.B.*; Robert Drummond, *Sermons on public occasions and a letter on theological study . . . To which are prefixed memoirs of his life, by George Hay Drummond*, A.M. (Edinburgh, 1803).

cousin he was ordained priest with a presentation to the family living of Bothal in Northumberland. He was subsequently appointed a royal chaplain, admitted B.D. and D.D. at Oxford (1745) and in 1748 consecrated Bishop of St Asaph. In 1751 he was translated to Salisbury and a few months later elected as Archbishop of York. In politics Drummond was a whig and an adherent of the Duke of Newcastle. He died at the archiepiscopal palace in 1776.

Thomas Gough (1720–1786)

Thomas Gough[5] was the third son of Walter Gough of Perry Hall, Staffordshire. He was admitted to St John's College, Cambridge, as a pensioner on 26 May 1738, and matriculated the same year. In 1744 he graduated LL.B., and on 20 May was ordained deacon by the bishop of Norwich (in the chapel of Gonville and Caius College, Cambridge), with a licence to the curacy of Little Wratting, Suffolk. He had held the curacy for only four months when he obtained the title to the two livings of Fornham St Genevieve and Risby, both rectories in the county of Suffolk; he was ordained priest on 23 September and instituted on 25 September 1744. Gough remained in Suffolk for the rest of his life and was buried at Risby on 6 January 1786. He was married, but his wife, Alice, predeceased him, dying in September 1765.

Thomas Gray (1716–1771)

Thomas Gray[6] was born on 26 December 1716 in Cornhill, London. He was the fifth and only surviving child of twelve born to Philip Gray and his wife Dorothy. His father was a scrivener and his mother, in partnership with her sister, ran a milliner's shop. Gray was sent to Eton about 1725 where he formed the "quadruple alliance" with Horace Walpole, Richard West and Thomas Ashton. He remained at school there until 1734 when he was admitted to Peterhouse, Cambridge. His parents wished him to study law, and to this end he was also admitted to the Inner Temple in November 1735. Although he was resident in Cambridge for four years, Gray found the prescribed studies in mathematics and philosophy uncongenial. He left, without a degree, in September 1738 and spent some time in London before accepting an invitation from Horace Walpole to accompany him on a tour of France and Italy. The two friends left England on 29 March 1739 and, in the course of two years abroad, visited Paris, Rheims, Lyons, Geneva, Turin, Genoa, Bologna, Florence, Rome and Naples. On their return journey en route for Venice, a quarrel of a serious nature erupted and they parted company. Gray continued on his own to Venice, and arrived back in England in September 1741. A year later, in October 1742, he resumed residence at Peterhouse as a Fellow-commoner, and although determined against taking up law as a profession, he applied himself to the studies requisite to a degree in civil law. In December 1743 he was admitted as LL.B. Meanwhile his father had died (in November 1741) and his mother with her sister had moved to Stoke Poges where they set up house with a third, widowed, sister, Mrs Rogers.

From 1742 to 1756 Gray remained settled at Peterhouse, and addressed himself to the study of the Greek classics and other subjects more suited to his tastes than law or

5 *Alum. Cantab.*; Scott-Mayor, *Admissions to St John's*, ii (Part 3). 90, 493; Nichols, *Lit. Anecs.*, ix. 360, 365, 747.

6 *Alum. Cantab.*; *D.N.B.*; *Correspondence of Thomas Gray*, ed. Paget Toynbee and Leonard Whibley, 3 vols., Oxford, 1935, reprinted with corrections and additions by H.W. Starr, 1971.

mathematics. His inheritance from his father was sufficient for his needs, and not until the late 1760s did he hold any university post. He was never made a Fellow of a college, but was registered on the books, first at Peterhouse and subsequently at Pembroke, as a "Fellow-commoner". He had begun to write poetry in the 1730s, but his earliest publications did not appear until the 1740s. Walpole, to whom Gray had been reconciled in 1745, was an enthusiastic critic and urged him to publish. His first published poem was the *Ode on a Distant Prospect of Eton College*, issued in 1747. A further three poems were published in 1748 in Robert Dodsley's *Collection of Poems*, but Gray's next major publication was the *Elegy written in a Country Church-Yard*. The poem had been started years earlier, but was only completed in June 1750. It was published in February 1751, pre-empting a threatened pirated printing, and went into four editions in two months. Further editions followed, and numerous piracies.

Other important poems were published at intervals, but Gray devoted much of his time to botanical, antiquarian, literary and linguistic studies. In July 1752, or perhaps earlier, he began work on the *Progress of Poesy*, a pindaric ode completed at the end of 1754, and paired with another ode, the *Bard*, which he was writing in 1755. The two poems were the first works to be printed on Walpole's Strawberry Hill Press, and were published by Dodsley in August 1757. They were warmly praised and admired by many, although there were also complaints of their obscurity. In December 1757 Gray was offered the Poet Laureateship, on the death of Colley Cibber, but declined the position as he had declined the offer of the secretaryship to the Earl of Bristol in Lisbon, made to him in 1755.

From 1756 Gray had been in residence at Pembroke College; but in July 1759 he left Cambridge altogether and took lodgings in London, where he continued his studies at the newly opened British Museum. He returned to Cambridge briefly in 1760, and then for longer periods from November 1761. The following year his name was suggested for the Regius Professorship of Modern History, but his nomination was not accepted. The post became vacant again in 1768, and on this occasion he was immediately appointed. Earlier the same year an edition of his *Poems* was published, the last substantial publication in his lifetime. On 30 July 1771 he died.

John Green (1706?–1779)

John Green[7] was born at Beverley, Yorkshire, about 1706, the son of a tax collector. He went to a private school and in June 1724 was admitted to St John's College, Cambridge. He took his B.A. in 1728, and soon after assumed the position of usher at Lichfield school, where Johnson was then a master and Garrick among the pupils. He is said to have remained there for about a year. In 1731 he was elected a Fellow at St John's, proceeded M.A., and was ordained deacon (June) and priest (September). Six months later, in 1732, he was instituted as Vicar of Hinxton, Cambridgeshire, a living in the gift of Jesus College, Cambridge, and tenable with his fellowship at St John's. His career was further promoted during the course of the following decade by his introduction to the Duke of Somerset, who proved a valuable patron and recommended him to the Duke of Newcastle. He became domestic chaplain to Somerset in 1743 and in 1747 was presented to the rectory of Burrough (or Borough) Green, near Newmarket, another living compatible with his fellowship.

7 *Alum. Cantab.*; *D.N.B.*; Scott-Mayor, *Admissions to St John's* ii (part 3). 370–2; D.A. Winstanley, *The University of Cambridge in the Eighteenth Century*, Cambridge, 1922.

At Cambridge, meanwhile, Green had taken his B.D. in 1739 and was made D.D. in 1749. In the same year he was elected Regius Professor of Divinity, in which position of seniority he was able to contest the title to the rectory of Barrow in Suffolk. The living was in the presentation of St John's College, who were obliged to bestow it on their senior member. Green demanded it by his right as senior of the faculty but was challenged by Thomas Rutherforth. The case went to Chancery and Rutherforth was forced to withdraw. Green was instituted in 1750, in which year, on the recommendation of Archbishop Herring, he was also elected Master of Corpus Christi College (Benet). His election coincided with the increasingly acrimonious dispute at Cambridge over the new university disciplinary code. As a head of college, Green supported the new regulations and took an active part in the dispute. On the appointment of a tribunal in 1752 to decide the matter, Green was one of the three heads chosen to represent the university. In college he seems not to have been popular, but he remained as Master until 1764, and in 1757–58 acted as Vice-Chancellor of the university.

Green's involvement in university life did not prevent his further rise in the Church. In 1756 he was collated to a prebend in Lincoln Cathedral and was elected and installed as Dean of Lincoln; in 1761 he was nominated to the bishopric, and vacating his prebend and rectories, was consecrated on 28 December. Ten years later he was granted a prebend of St Paul's Cathedral *in commendam* on the grounds that his bishopric was poorly endowed. He died suddenly at Bath on 25 April 1779.

Although he published little, Green established a considerable literary reputation. He was associated with Philip Yorke, Viscount Royston, as a contributor to the *Athenian Letters*, published in 1741, and was also the author of two letters against the Methodists. He was on friendly terms with Gray and Mason, as well as with Thomas Balguy and Hurd. His acquaintance with both the latter is unlikely, however, to have commenced before 1752, up to which time their mutual opposition over the university regulations would have been a barrier to friendship. Green's elevation to the episcopacy and appointment to Hurd's own diocese, when he was at Thurcaston, does not seem to have strengthened the connection between them.

Frederick Hervey (1730–1803)

Frederick Hervey[8] was the third son of John, Lord Hervey of Ickworth, and grandson of John Hervey, 1st Earl of Bristol. He went to school at Westminster and in 1747 was admitted at Corpus Christi College, Cambridge. In the following year, being originally intended for the bar, he was also admitted at Lincoln's Inn. However, he abandoned the law and after graduating M.A. in 1754, as a nobleman, he was ordained priest on 26 January 1755. Some preferment had already come his way (he had been made a Clerk of the Privy Seal in 1753), but subsequent advancement came slowly despite his solicitations. He became Principal Clerk of the Privy Seal in 1761, and in 1763 was made a Royal Chaplain, but being otherwise unoccupied, he spent a good deal of time on the continent, particularly in Italy. He was a man of considerable culture and taste, and passionately fond of art, collecting many valuable pieces on his travels. He also became much interested in volcanic phenomena after witnessing an eruption of Vesuvius.

8 *Alum. Cantab.*; *D.N.B.*; G.E. C[okayne], *The Complete Peerage, or a History of the House of Lords and all its Members from the Earliest Times, revised and enlarged*, 12 vols., 1910–59.

In 1767 during his brother George's brief tenure as Lord-Lieutenant of Ireland, Hervey received his first substantial appointment, the nomination to the see of Cloyne. He held the bishopric for one year, and in 1768 was translated to the rich see of Derry. As bishop he made many improvements in the diocese affecting not only the clergy but the people in the area. He laid down roads, encouraged the introduction of more effective agricultural methods and supported new building. In 1770 he was presented with the freedom of Londonderry. He also took a prominent part in opposing the Union with Ireland and was one of the Volunteer delegates from county Derry in 1783.

Hervey succeeded to the family title in 1779, becoming the 4th Earl of Bristol. In 1782 he was made a F.R.S. and inherited a further title, the Barony of Howard de Walden. He died at Albano, near Rome, on 8 July 1803. During his life, Hervey aroused a mixture of admiration and contempt in his contemporaries. Lord Charlemont, who knew him well, described him as "vain to excess, inconstant in his friendships . . . fond of intrigue in gallantry as well as in politics, and sticking at nothing to gain his ends in either . . . His ambition and his lust can alone get the better of his avarice".

Lady Frances Littleton (c.1730–1781)

Lady Frances Littleton[9] was born Frances Horton, the daughter of Christopher Horton and his wife of Catton Hall, Derbyshire. She married Sir Edward Littleton in 1752 and resided henceforth at Teddesley. Little is known of her other than that her health was always fragile. She seems not to have made any mark on society but to have been generally well liked. On a material level, however, a highly detailed picture can be reconstructed from Sir Edward's accounts books which document all expenditure (on clothes, jewels, etc.) incurred by him and his wife. Each account is itemised and provides an illuminating insight into the nature and extent of domestic outlay.

The Littletons had no children, and spent their time between Staffordshire, London and spas in various parts of the country, where Lady Littleton took the waters in the hope of improving her health. She died in 1781.

Thomas Warton (1728–1790)

Thomas Warton[10] was born at Basingstoke on 9 January 1728, the son of Thomas Warton the elder (author of *Poems on Several Occasions*, and Professor of Poetry at Oxford), and younger brother of the poet, Joseph Warton. He was tutored by his father and attended Basingstoke school until 1744 when he was admitted at Trinity College, Oxford. Warton began experimenting with verse at a precocious age, and was said to be author of a volume of *Five Pastoral Eclogues* published in 1745. The first publication that can be attributed to him with certainty is the *Pleasures of Melancholy*, issued in 1747, followed in 1749 by his poem, *The Triumph of Isis*, which met with some acclaim. His literary successes did not deflect him from academic studies, however, and he took his B.A. degree in 1747, his M.A. in 1750, and was elected a Fellow in 1751. Warton also, like his father, took orders in 1748, although he did not hold a living until 1771, when he was offered the Oxfordshire rectory of Kiddington.

9 Staffs. RO, Littleton family papers.
10 *Alum. Cantab.*; *D.N.B.*; Nichols, *Lit. Anecs.*, vi. 175–85.

As a Fellow of Trinity, Warton believed that he took his duties seriously, although there are conflicting reports on how much time he devoted to his undergraduates. He did not claim to be a professional man of letters, but continued to produce a regular output of verse (much of it satirical), and some notable prose studies. His earliest important work in this field was the *Observations of the Faerie Queene of Spenser* published in 1754, which established his reputation as a critic and brought him to the attention of Samuel Johnson who became a life-long friend. A second, enlarged edition of the *Observations* was published in 1762. Academic honours followed Warton's literary success with his appointment as Professor of Poetry at Oxford in 1757. The post had a five-year tenure, and was held by Warton for two successive terms. During his professorship he divided his attention between classical studies and the preparations for a history of English poetry. Such a work had been thought of by both Pope and Gray, but never executed. Warton began writing his history in the 1760s and sent his first copy to the press in 1769. Volume One of the *History of English Poetry*, however, was not ready for publication till 1774; the second volume appeared in 1778, and the third in 1781. This last volume brought the history to the end of the Elizabethan age, and Warton managed little more. Part of a fourth volume had been printed when he died in 1790, and was published, undated, some time after; but effectively, the enterprise ended with the Elizabethans.

Although he did not complete further volumes of the history of English poetry, Warton did continue to produce other work. In the late 1770s he published a collection of his poetry which went into three editions between 1777 and 1779. In 1781 and 1782 he had printed a few copies of the *History of Kiddington*, as a specimen of a *History of Oxfordshire*, a project which remained at the conceptual stage. The year 1782 saw the publication of a pamphlet contributing to the Chatterton controversy (Warton believed the poems were fabrications), and *Verses on Sir Joshua Reynolds' Painted Window at New College, Oxford.* His most distinguished work of the 1780s was, however, an edition of Milton's early poems, intended as the first of a series, and considered one of the best critical editions of Milton to have been published. There was no lack of recognition of the merit of these literary and historical works. At Oxford, Warton was made Camden Professor of History in 1785 and in the same year was offered the Laureate on the death of William Whitehead. He held both posts till his death. The esteem with which he was regarded also secured him a place at the Literary Club (in 1782), then boasting Johnson, Burke and Reynolds amongst its members. Warton died suddenly on 20 May 1790 whilst spending the evening in his customary fashion in the common room at Trinity College.

Charles Yorke (1722–1770)

Charles Yorke[11] was born on 30 December 1722, the second son of Philip Yorke, Lord Chancellor and 1st Earl of Hardwicke. He was educated in London and went up to Corpus Christi College, Cambridge, in 1739. However, Yorke, from an early age, had been destined for the bar, and in December 1735 had been admitted a member of the Middle Temple. On 23 October 1742 he transferred to Lincoln's Inn, and on 1 February 1746 was called to the bar. He was elected a bencher on 8 May 1754.

Success came quickly to Yorke and his career seemed almost certain to lead to the

[11] *Alum. Cantab.*; *D.N.B.*; *The House of Commons 1754–1790*, ed. Sir Lewis Namier and John Brooke, 3 vols., 1964.

position of Lord Chancellor, a post held by his great-uncle and, for nearly twenty years, by his father. His abilities were widely recognised and while he was still only in his early twenties he was in correspondence with William Warburton and a little later with Montesquieu, Thomas Birch and Thomas Secker. He was one of the major contributors to the *Athenian Letters*, and in 1745 published *Considerations on the Law of Forfeiture for High Treason*, a defence of a measure instigated by his father, which established his reputation as a constitutionalist. In 1747 his father was able to offer him the sinecure post of Clerk of the Crown in Chancery, worth £1,200 p.a., to be held jointly with his brother. During the same year he was elected M.P. for Reigate, the family seat, which he continued to represent until 1768 when he was returned instead for the University of Cambridge. From 1754 to 1756 he acted as Solicitor-General to the Prince of Wales, and when his father retired, was promoted to Solicitor -General, a position he held from 1756 till the end of 1761. On 14 December that year he resigned, following the fall of Pitt. In January 1762, under the new Administration, he was offered and accepted the office of Attorney-General. Tenure of this office, however, became increasingly difficult, with Newcastle, one of his father's oldest and closest friends, in opposition and anxious to secure the support of the Yorke family. Charles resisted these pressures for some time; he was consequently in office when Wilkes' *North Briton* No.45 was published, and was called upon to give an official opinion on the difficult questions of constitutional law raised by the publication of the pamphlet, and concerning Wilkes' imprisonment. But in November 1763 he bowed to circumstances and resigned.

The ensuing years were also difficult for Yorke. He was uncomfortable in the ranks of Newcastle's Opposition and unhappy out of office. After an interval he made overtures to the Administration, but when offered a place found it impossible to determine either for or against acceptance. Under Rockingham's Administration he was invited to take up the position of Attorney-General again, and with considerable hesitation finally agreed in August 1765. However, the Administration was of brief duration and in the summer of 1766 Pitt was called upon to form a new government. Yorke had anticipated Pitt's return to power and evidently hoped at least to attain his ambition of the Great Seal. He was therefore mortified when the Lord Chancellorship was offered to Charles Pratt, created Lord Camden. On 1 August he resigned as Attorney-General. His further reaction to this disappointment was to retreat from active political life, taking only a limited part in parliamentary debate, and employing himself instead on landscaping the gardens of his villa at Highgate, and devoting more time to his friends, Warburton, Garrick, Hurd and others. The seals came once more within his grasp at the beginning of 1770. Camden was dismissed in January, and Grafton asked Yorke to be his successor. Again Yorke was torn by indecision, advised by some (Lord Chief Justice Wilmot and Lord Mansfield) to accept, and by others (his elder brother, Lord Hardwicke, Rockingham and John Yorke) to refuse. Finally, in an audience with the King on 17 January he deferred to pressure and kissed hands for the Great Seal and a peerage. The following day he was in a state of melancholy, on 19 January he began to vomit blood, and on 20 January 1770 he died.

In addition to his undoubted ability in the legal profession, Yorke was also an able Italian scholar and a man of culture and learning. He had been made a F.R.S. and was a trustee of the Warburton Lecture and of the British Museum. He was the author of three verse essays published in the *Gentleman's Magazine* and the *Annual Register*.

THE CORRESPONDENCE

The correspondence presented in this edition comprises 276 private letters or sections of letters dated from 1739 to 1762. The earliest surviving letter from Hurd to have been traced is addressed to John Potter and is dated 15 April 1739. It was written when Hurd was nineteen and in his fourth year at Emmanuel College, Cambridge, where he had begun to study for an M.A. The correspondence covers the following eighteen years at Emmanuel and six years when Hurd was rector of Thurcaston, in Leicestershire. The year 1762 has been taken as the concluding date for this earlier part of the total correspondence and marks a turning point in Hurd's life. In this year he published his most famous work, *Letters on Chivalry and Romance*, which, in the opinion of many modern critics, makes Hurd a significant figure among the "pre-romantics". After its publication, however, Hurd's interests as he rose in the church became less literary, as does his later correspondence.

There are six distinct groups of letters within the body of Hurd's correspondence to 1762. The first of these is the collection of letters addressed to Potter: 27 have survived, 26 of them covering the years 1739 to 1748 and one dated 1756. A group of 37 letters sent to the Macro family (Cox, Mary and Edward) run almost concurrently with these from 1741 to 1758. The largest section of the correspondence also dates from the early 1740s: these letters are addressed to Sir Edward Littleton. There are 93 written between 1744 and 1762; other letters to Littleton (31 not included in this edition) span the years 1763 to 1801.

Three further series of letters make up the bulk of the remainder of the correspondence. The recipients were William Mason, Thomas Balguy and William Warburton. Of the letters addressed to Mason 21 survive in their entirety, and fragments of 18 more were transcribed by Hurd's nephew, Richard Hurd. The latter is responsible for having destroyed the originals from which these fragments were taken, and 81 other letters from Hurd to Mason covering the period 1747 to 1790.[1] The earliest letter of those that now remain, is dated 7 May 1747. Hurd's letters to Balguy date from 18 August 1749, and comprise a group of 18, the originals of which were recently discovered and sold at auction in 1984. There are also 19 letters addressed to Warburton dating from 25 October 1749. In all three cases further letters covering the 1760s and the early part of the 1770s survive in either published or manuscript form.

The remaining correspondence incorporates an early group of 13 letters written to James Devey between 1741 and 1747, and a number of miscellaneous letters and notes that seem to have survived haphazardly and do not necessarily indicate the existence of more extensive correspondence now lost. These are addressed to: Anthony Askew (1); William Bowyer (2); Sir John Danvers (5); Robert Hay

1 *Hurd-Mason Corr.*, p. xviii.

Drummond (1); Thomas Gough (2); Thomas Gray (4); John Green (1); Frederick Hervey (3); Lady Frances Littleton (1); Thomas Warton (1); and Charles Yorke (9).

The majority of the letters in this edition have never been printed. The text of those previously printed is that of the original manuscript, where it exists. While the correspondence is viewed primarily as a literary correspondence, and the remainder of this section of the Introduction will delineate the more significant characteristics of Hurd as a letter-writer, the annotation is comprehensive, intended to elucidate the social and intellectual milieu in which Hurd moved. A few of the letters, those to Mason, have been annotated before. The annotations of the editors have, however, been checked, expanded, and where mistakes had previously arisen, silently corrected.

The Potter Correspondence

The Potter correspondence, we are told by Hurd, began in 1738. In a letter of 27 April 1740 he says that it is "now two years since I had the happiness of conversing with you in Person". Their correspondence by letter he believes to have been "kept up with more spirit, & vigour, than perhaps betwixt any other of our old Acquaintance". Certainly the letters are not only lengthy, but are the product of a creative energy which had not yet been channelled into other directions. Like many of his contemporaries, Hurd had adopted the concept of letter-writing as conversation. In the same letter he says,

> I could be larger upon this head, but that I have ever look'd upon it as a most ridiculous practice among intimate friends to waste in formal Apologies that time & paper, wch. is much better employ'd in freer, & more material conversation.

But the style is not as easy, nor the letters as varied as we might therefore expect. They do seem, though, to represent the type of discourse that existed between Hurd and Potter as undergraduates. Hurd knew, for instance, that he had no need to entertain with anecdotes, although there are some dramatic vignettes. There was also less room for news and gossip as the memory of Potter's own college days receded. What remained was a common interest in literature, sympathetic tastes, and a desire to experiment in composition and criticism; nowhere else does Hurd allow his fancy such indulgence as he does in his correspondence with Potter. A letter of 2 December 1739 gives some evidence of this, and of Hurd's absorbing interest in the pastoral which characterises these earliest years. He first of all thanks Potter for his description of the rural beauties that surrounded him in Somerset.

> My imagination was fir'd at the lively portraiture, & flew with impatience o'er the flowry lawn, & cloud-invelopt Hill. Not a beauty in the Vale, you mention, escap'd my notice, not a single rill, or flower, murmer'd, or bloom'd without my particular observation. Methought I was plac'd (such is the strange power of fancy!) upon the summit of that mountain, on whose side your house is, or really, or ideally situated. Methought too my friend stood near me, & with an obliging civility pointed out to my view the several charms of ye. country, yt. lay before us . . . As we stood thus, happy in surveying distant beauties, I could not help thinking our situation something like that of Aeneas, & Achates in Virgil, when plac'd upon the Hill, that commanded the walls of rising Carthage. They too were friends; they too gaz'd with pleasure, & amazement upon the objects, yt. surrounded 'em.

Hurd could be unguarded with Potter, having no need to impress or indeed compete with him. The lack of constraint evident in these letters allows him to follow his musings, develop elaborate metaphors, and, as he says himself, to "ramble". He acknowledges this freedom in a letter of 28 August 1740, which he describes as "rambling, & tedious". but recommends as a "model" in terms of length. In the next letter, by contrast, he is more severe on himself, concluding,

> From the whole tenor of this Epistle you'll easily perceive I am in a very idle humour, & have wrote with Ease. This indeed generally passes for a complement, but then it must be such ease, as proceeds from art, not Chance: The latter of wch. has been the chief governess in this Scroll. (14 December 1740)

By March 1741, however, Hurd has rationalised, and can justify, the lack of coherent order in his letters. This letter, he says, writing on 22 March, "will be a series of unconnected observations, on the several subjects that start up in my Imagination, without being at the pains of reducing 'em into any order. This", he continues, anticipating Potter's objections, "you'll be inclin'd to think I do merely to indulge an idle humour, & to shift off all the little labour, yt. attends the observation of method. But what", he asks, "if I should maintain yt. a methodical, and as I wd. term it, a consequential Epistle is much easier to write, than one of an opposite stamp & character?" And that this is the case, he goes on to prove.

The lack of reserve and the assumption of mutual understanding that characterise the early correspondence with Potter did, however, begin to alter. The change seems to have been prompted by Hurd's acquaintance and then friendship with the Macro family, and the changing circumstances brought about by their influence. The letters begin to show signs of this development from April 1742 when Hurd tells Potter that he has been offered the living of Reymerston. The alteration is partly due to the fact that there is simply more to be reported in each letter. On 14 July 1742, for instance, Hurd wrote to Potter to inform him of his ordination which had taken place in London, and added,

> The week was spent agreeably in seeing the curiosities of the Town. Vaux-Hall and Ranelagh, you may be sure, were of this Number. The former of the two places I approve, and admire; the latter I think Ridiculous, and detest.

The clipped sentences and abrupt judgments are quite untypical of the earlier correspondence.

As the letters become more animated, so also they become increasingly distant. In the past Potter had been invited to follow the unfolding of Hurd's thoughts and the vagaries of his imagination. This intimacy gradually disappears and is replaced by accounts of Hurd's actions. Potter evidently perceived this, and in 1743 accused Hurd of wishing to drop the correspondence. In fact it was maintained, but probably on a lesser scale than previously.

The Macro Correspondence

By the autumn of 1742 Hurd was in correspondence with Cox, Mary and Edward Macro, a prominent Suffolk family, with whom Hurd became acquainted on Edward Macro's admission to Emmanuel. His letters make a most intriguing collection, each set differing substantially from the others. The most strikingly individual correspondence is that with Mary Macro, Edward's mother and 31 years older than Hurd. In these letters Hurd exerts himself to entertain and amuse, avoiding the meditative and abstract. The earliest letter to have survived opens in characteristic style. "Madam", writes Hurd, "I have just made my escape from a dish of Tea & a violent fit of laughing, to do myself the pleasure of answering your last kind favour". His next half page is an apostrophe to Mrs. Macro, remonstrating with her at the apology given for the length of her letters.

> Ah! Madam, did you but know the Satisfaction, they always bring along with 'em, were you but sensible of my happiness in receiving, opening, reading, & reviewing ev'ry half Sheet, that bears the date of Norton, & in a particular manner the name of Mrs. Macro, you could not but think it needless, or rather unkind, to make the least apology for what you modestly, but permit me to say unjustly, call the Impertinence of a female Pen.

This is followed by the news that Edward had safely arrived (at Reymerston) the previous Tuesday, but "wet, dagg'd & tir'd past Expression". Hurd, adopting the self-deprecatory stance that is often typical of these letters, "administr'd all the little comforts, my cell wd. afford, and got him well enough by the next afternoon to laugh away a few hours with the Ladies at Mr. Grigson's." However, a more interesting social encounter was yet to come. On Saturday night they were invited to supper with Dr and Mrs Gardiner and went with the "resolution of *shining* before a Lady of Mrs. G.['s] character". But alas, says Hurd, they "were surely never less bright".

> As for my part, she struck me blind & immoveable at once upon our very entrance into the Room. Pray, says She, Mr. H– how does your Father do? – What the duce, thought I, can the woman mean? God forbid she & my Father should have ever been acquainted – In short I look'd silly, & said just nothing. – This gave her time to reflect, & the mistake immediatly appear'd that I was taken for some Billy Hurd the Lord knows where.

Edward fared little better, attempting a witticism that misfired, and both appear to have been rather overcome by their "Supper". Finally, Hurd says,

> apprehending, if we stay'd longer, we might betray ourselves by down right snoring, I mov'd going . . . & accordingly we took leave, and departed. We departed, but with such a blot on our reputation in regard of wit & smartness, as we are afraid will scarcely ever be wip'd off by any future amendments.

Similar descriptions, often of social occasions, are a feature of Hurd's letters to Mary Macro. The characters are generally cast in a more favourable light, but Hurd is frequently tempted, as here, to project himself as a pathetic figure, a "poor puny parson", a "certain thin creature", and, like his "own crack'd fiddle: . . . harsh & untun'd at best". There are memorable accounts of a projected dinner for his parishioners; a meeting with an Emmanuel man, Nathaniel Smalley, and his wife; a difficult and miserable journey from Norton to Cambridge; and a visit from the Cambridge bookseller, Thurlbourne. In dramatising these incidents, Hurd makes more use of direct speech than in any other group of letters, with corresponding immediacy and liveliness of effect.

None of Mary Macro's letters to Hurd has survived, but there are a number still extant, addressed to Edward Macro, preserved in the *Macro Letter-book*. One of these describes the occasion of Mary Macro's first writing to Hurd, and is some indication of the quality of her letters.

> On monday evening last, Mr Hudson arrived here on his dapple-Gray: He set out the next day in the afternoon (for we wou'd not let him go before) for Reymerston with the same directions as Mr Hurd was furnish'd with; and I hope he was as successfull in finding the way. There I'll leave him, and Imagine what Pleasure the two socios had at meeting each other. Mr Hurd did me the Favour, and consequently the Pleasure to write to ME, by the return of the man & nag which had convey'd him to the above mention'd place. And what do you think Ned? Frail, Frail Human Nature that cou'd not withstand temptation! Mr Hurd at the latter end of his entertaining letter said something, which I thought amounted to an expectation of an answer; so I, Presumptive I, wrote an answer back to him, without considering the Inequality of our Pens. (1 July 1742, *Macro Letter-book*.)

Hurd's replies, as well as being intended to entertain, are a flattering reflection of the letters written to him, and an evocation, sometimes playful, sometimes serious, but always fond and admiring, of his image of Mary Macro. This is consistent with his own view of letters, recorded in his Commonplace Book:

> Private letters between friends are supposed to give a faithful picture of the dispositions and sentiments of those who compose them. This is a mistake; the purpose of them is to please (I will suppose in a manly and honourable way) the person to whom they are addressed. They therefore reflect the character, *i.e.* the opinion entertained of the person written to, not of the writer. ('Selections from Bishop Hurd's Commonplace Book', in Kilvert, *Memoirs*, p. 287.)

Nevertheless this act of pleasing involves the projection of different facets of the writer's own character, designed to elicit a certain response. From Mary Macro, Hurd usually wanted sympathy; from Cox Macro he seems to have sought academic and intellectual approval, and he used him to test his own scholarship or the persuasiveness of his arguments.

The correspondence with Cox Macro is very different from that with his wife. Many of the letters read like essays and it is not uncommon for Hurd to begin immediately upon his chosen topic with little or no preamble. (See for instance, 5 March 1743, 1 January 1746.) The earliest letters bear a resemblance in subject matter to those written to Potter. Among them are letters discussing instances of mistaken chronology in the classical poets, the "Progress of a Shepherd's thought in his Invention of the Pipe", and the power of the human imagination. The similarity with the letters to Potter, however, does not extend beyond likeness of content. This is illustrated in a letter of 17 July 1742, in which Hurd introduces the subject of poetical images used to represent the "motions of the Mind under outward and sensible Images", and, in particular, a comparison which he believed had not previously been observed by the poets. In fact the image and its possible application had occurred to him the previous year, and he had announced his discovery to Potter on 18 January 1741. The image is that of a tree covered in dew or rain, sparkling in the sunlight, or shaken by a light breeze. In the letter to Potter, Hurd describes the dewdrops as gems, watery splendours, and quivering globules. In the letter to Macro, the globules disappear and the whole account is more succinct. The application of the image to the character and mental state of a "good-natur'd, passionate man", however, is much extended. The passage is obviously adapted to what Hurd conceived of as Cox Macro's more serious cast of mind.

In subsequent correspondence the emphasis on the classics and poetry gives way to an interest in theology, and in these letters Hurd discusses at some length "the Fall &

Redemption of Man" (5 March 1743), emendations to the Greek New Testament (25 February 1744), and, in three letters, the origin of sacrifices (4 December 1745, 1 January 1746, 28 April 1746). It is significant in the light of this preoccupation with theological problems, that Hurd's first publication should have been a pamphlet concerned with the debate over miracles; and it is tempting to assume that Macro's influence had directed Hurd's intellectual energies into this channel. The tenor of many of Hurd's letters to Macro suggests a tutor-pupil relationship: Hurd defers to him, presents him with elaborately worked hypotheses for comment, and while able to participate in family jokes (the reference to "Sesquipedalian" [10 September 1742], for instance), nevertheless maintains a respectful distance.

The correspondence with Edward Macro which makes up the remainder of the Macro collection is different again from either of the correspondences with his parents. Hurd was in contact with Edward from their college days together in the early 1740s, until at least 1763. Their friendship was strengthened by a mutual connection with Edward Littleton, Hurd as tutor and friend, and Edward as friend and agent, acting for Littleton in his purchase of paintings and engravings in London. But Edward Macro's unsettled life probably prevented a regular correspondence, and no doubt contributed to the disappearance of many letters. The eight that do remain are of a miscellaneous nature. The two earliest (2 October 1741 and 1 January 1742) bear some resemblance to letters to Potter, are varied in content, and contain sections of verse. Writing to Edward Macro, though, seems to prompt Hurd into a more serious philosophising strain. In the first letter, for example, he comments on a dream that Edward had described to him, in which he (Hurd) had apparently figured, "taking a survey of, & despising Ambition". This leads him on to review "life". The few years he has lived in it, he says,

> have been sufficient to shew me the emptiness and vanity of it. They have not, I thank God, been distinguish'd by any extraordinary afflictions, or calamaties beyond the ordinary lot of mankind. Yet ev'n these, small & common as they are, have serv'd to convince me, that happiness is not to be expected here, or, if it be, that it lies in the Shades & private paths of Life.

This thought is expanded at some length, drawing Hurd to the conclusion that if he could choose his manner of life, he would settle for "a tolerable competency in an obscure retreat".

Another three letters date from 1743. The first (22 June 1743) is a brief exchange of news; the second and third, which have survived only as copies, are particularly interesting, dealing with Edward's feelings about his friendship with Hurd, and implicitly with Hurd's own emotions. In the first of these, Hurd replies to the accusation that he has encouraged Edward to write to him while at the same time despising his letters because of their "common" thoughts and "common language". The letter is passionately argued and contains a very unusual declaration of Hurd's feelings.

> You have some knowledge of Mankind; & 'tis usual with such to suspect the obvious & pretended motives to action, & assign others of a deeper policy which tho' sometimes just enough in their application are, I incline to think oftener wrong. Dear Sir, you have known me for some time. I am not forward to engage in friendships, & indeed have but few acquaintances which I can properly call by that name. The consequence of this is, that I am more than commonly sollicitous in supporting & improving those few. I would extract all the happiness from them, that I can, & perhaps for that reason am troublesome, when I mean nothing less.
>
> (19 September 1743)

Reassured by this, Macro evidently replied that he wanted no other friend than Hurd. Hurd is flattered by this, but feels bound to suggest the difficulties that might ensue if, for instance, his "Character should alter! what if some Spots should appear in it which you did not expect!" (31 October 1743). This, like the letter before it, is a long letter and confined almost entirely to the same subject. The three remaining letters date from 1744, 1746 and 1751. The crisis over their friendship had been surmounted and these are mildly interesting letters indicative of Hurd's preoccupations at the time (reading, university matters, publications, etc.).

Taken as a whole, the Macro correspondence makes fascinating reading. It contains some splendid letters, probably the most animated that Hurd wrote, and demonstrates how versatile he could be as a letter-writer. Indirectly, the correspondence provides a fund of information on Hurd's activities (in college, as curate of Reymerston, on vacation), his intellectual development, and his emotional maturity.

The Littleton Correspondence

Hurd's letters to Littleton are more functional than those to Potter or the Macros, and illustrate a different relationship between writer and recipient. They are also much shorter, averaging just over one page in transcription compared to nearly three pages in the case of the Macros, and over three pages to Potter. Hurd was chosen as tutor to Littleton on the advice of William Budworth, schoolmaster to them both, and the connection was to be of mutual benefit. When Littleton came up to Emmanuel in 1744, Hurd was established as a Fellow, had made friends advantageously (most notably with the Macros), and looked set to pursue a successful career both academically and in the Church. He moved in learned and literary circles, and might also be expected to become known as an author himself. Littleton, having inherited a large estate, had wealth and social position. As patron and client each had much to offer the other, and out of this grew a genuine friendship which lasted till Hurd's death in 1808. The nature of their relationship can be deduced from the correspondence.

Hurd's tone as tutor to his pupil is friendly without actually professing great friendship. His letters are full of news, sometimes offer advice, sometimes give support. They were not intended, as "familiar" letters, to amuse, and such an intention might have appeared presumptuous in a social inferior. That is not to say that they totally lack humour. For instance, in a letter of 18 December 1745, Hurd commences with a remark both humorously self-deprecatory and mildly rebuking.

> My Epistolary Preachment, I find, had the same fate, as our Pulpit ones generally have with You young Gentlemen, the fate of being laugh'd at. And therefore not to do a second Violence to your Muscles, I shall continue the Style & Manner of my last, in chatting with you on indifferent Occasions.

But there are no anecdotes or attempts to evoke a shared imaginative experience: in this respect, the letters are totally straightforward and factual. Their interest, within the correspondence as a whole, is twofold. First there is the information they give about Hurd's attitude to Littleton: the mingled sense of deference, in recognition of their different social status, and of confidence and authority, as tutor to pupil, and later as an established friend of acknowledged literary and ecclesiastical standing. Second, there is the mass of information incorporated in the news and opinions that

Hurd records. The earliest letters are dominated by events in Emmanuel and in the university, and by the '45 rebellion. Later letters, while still recording much of note regarding college life, also reveal a shared interest in literature, art, and, to a lesser degree, politics. The literary impetus comes mainly from Hurd, and his letters contain frequent references to books just published or about to be published, with bits of literary gossip, advice on Littleton's collection of books and manuscripts, and details on the progress of his own publications.

The interest in art, on the other hand, was largely sustained by Littleton. Like many eighteenth-century men of means, he was building himself a large new family house which was to be stocked with books, manuscripts, paintings and sculptures. To this end, Macro was a useful friend, with apparently numerous connections in the London art world, and a knowledge of, and taste in art which was much esteemed by his acquaintance. Hurd could only profess a growing interest and the desire to build up a modest collection of his own. But he acted for Littleton by passing on news and information from Macro, and by keeping an eye out for good collections and sales in the Cambridge area. There is an illuminating contrast in the quality of material which he was able to collect as the Fellow of a college (and indeed with generous assistance from Littleton), and the kind of paintings that Littleton selected for his collection. Many of these were paintings of the seventeenth century, by such artists as Cheron, Hals, Hobbema, Rubens, Ruysdael, Trevisani, and Van De Velde. But Littleton also commissioned pictures from contemporary artists. He had a number of portraits done (by Francis Hayman, William Hoare, and Gainsborough), and ordered other paintings from the sea painter Samuel Scott, and Hogarth, though this work may not have been executed. One of his great enthusiasms was for the work of the sculptor, Michael Rysbrack, from whom he ordered more than a dozen busts, including one, now lost, of Hurd himself. The latter, with more limited resources, also collected "heads", but in this case, prints, of which there was a plentiful and fairly cheap supply on the market.

In matters of art and literature, Littleton could consult with and even defer to Hurd; on the question of politics, he appears to have been more reserved, though not uncommunicative, and Hurd expresses general, sometimes rather naive, opinions. By virtue of his wealth and position, Littleton had some political weight in Staffordshire, but his power and influence there were not subjects on which Hurd was qualified to give advice. On one occasion he admits that he and other mutual friends had been amused at the outcome of events in the county (22 February 1754), but he quickly returns to a more serious vein, and, on the whole, confines himself to comments of support and approbation.

In the later years of the period covered in Hurd's early correspondence, the letters are briefer and are a good deal concerned with practical matters. As rector of Thurcaston in Leicestershire (from 1758 when he moved there), Hurd was much closer to Littleton's home and could ride over to see him. His letters are therefore more often restricted to news of friends (particularly Warburton and Macro), details of his plans in coming months, advice on appointments (e.g. the preacher of the assize-sermon; the schoolmaster at Brewood), acknowledgments and best wishes for Sir Edward and Lady Littleton's health.

The Mason Correspondence

Hurd's letters to William Mason are the best known part of his correspondence, and as a group are among the most closely knit. The subject matter (at least as far as can be judged from the selection left to us) is consistently literary, and the letters clearly respond with some precision to those received from Mason. There is a strong sense of mutual affinity and similarity of outlook, expressive of close personal friendship. The correspondence is of considerable importance from a literary point of view, providing valuable documentary evidence of Hurd's reading and the genesis and publication of much of his own and Mason's work. The letters reveal, for instance, that Hurd had begun work on the *Moral and Political Dialogues* in 1756. On 7 August 1756 he wrote to Mason:

> I told You of my Political Dialogue. It runs out into two parts, each of them pretty long, but the subject, at least if I don't spoil it in the handling, not uninteresting. The first of these is quite finishd, I mean thrown completely into form, so that I might have taken your judgment of it.

Mason was also at work on a new literary project, and Hurd adds:

> If You get Caractacus in the same forwardness I promise to repay your criticism, not with the dull civility current amongst authors, but with the free censure of one that takes a greater interest in what You write than in any trash of his own.

The progress made in the writing and revisions of *Moral and Political Dialogues* and *Caractacus* is recorded in Hurd's subsequent correspondence, up to the publication of both works in May 1759. Other letters reveal that Hurd's most famous publication, *Letters on Chivalry and Romance*, was originally intended as a "Dissertation on the *Rise and Genius of Chivalry*", to be appended to the *Dialogues*. (14 August 1758) Again, the development of this idea is recorded in the correspondence, although in this particular instance, all that remain are some fragments of letters, transcribed by Hurd's nephew and inserted into copies of the appropriate volumes of Hurd's works, now at Hartlebury Castle, before he destroyed the letters themselves. In a fragment of 4 May 1759, Hurd says that the *Dialogues*, being printed by William Bowyer, are practically ready ("Three or four Sheets more, I fancy will finish all") and that the "*Dissertations on Chivalry*" have been withdrawn. Then nothing more is heard of this work until 3 May 1761, when he announces insouciantly,

> I have just finish'd a trifle in 12 short Letters, which You & one or two more will perhaps take the trouble of reading, & which no body else will. I may perhaps take the fancy to bring it with me to Prior-Park.

In the intervening two years Hurd's *Dissertations* had been transformed by the introduction of "romance". Some indication of the source of this new interest is given in the letters of 1760 and 1761. A few years earlier in 1755 Hurd had begun to learn Italian at the instigation of Cox Macro, and was already convinced that the Italian poets were "above evry thing which is call'd poetry in the other modern languages, except perhaps in our own, which I am us'd to prefer before all others for the force of colouring and height of Invention". (31 December 1755) On 8 January 1756 he was writing again about Italian poetry, and confesses to Mason,

> You'll think from my saying so much of this subject, that I am quite wild about the

> Italian poetry. You would think so much more if I was to tell You that I have ev'n gone so far myself as to write a sonnet.

His further reading is not documented in the letters that have survived, until, in a letter of 30 November 1760, he explains to Mason that he is in the right frame of mind for poetry, having just come from the "reading of Tasso's *Gierusal*. *Liberata*; in which", he continues,

> it is my odd fortune to dislike ev'rything which Voltaire, & such critics as He, commend, & to admire evrything which they censure. As a Copyist of Virgil & the antients, He is but feeble, & passable at the best. As an original painter of the world of Magic & Enchantments, he is inimitable.

Tasso figures large in *Letters on Chivalry and Romance* but the *Gierusalemme Liberata* may not have been the only influence on Hurd, if the most direct. He was even more enthusiastic about Rousseau's *Nouvelle Héloïse*, which he read in 1761, and, describing the impact the book made upon him, he suggests a view of narrative pattern that colours much of what he wrote on romance in the *Letters*. The *Nouvelle Héloïse*, he states to Mason on 30 March 1761,

> is the most exquisite work of the kind that ever was written. I have read it a second time, & could read it twenty times, with fresh pleasure. The reason is, the author is a man of *virtue*, as well as genius. This *last* indeed is so transcendant in him, that it makes one overlook the most improbable, & worst contrived story that ever was. But, if he had totally wanted Genius, the magic of his *Virtue* is enough to charm evry reader, who is not wholly devoid of it, himself.

In *Letters on Chivalry and Romance* Hurd defends Spenser's *Faerie Queene* on a similar principle. If you judge the poem by classic models, he says, "you are shocked with it's disorder". (p. 62) But it does have a unity. It is true this

> is not the classic Unity, which consists in the representation of one entire action: but it is an Unity of another sort, an unity resulting from the respect which a number of related actions have to one common purpose. In other words, It is an unity of *design*, and not of action. (p. 66–7)

Information about Mason's work is also incorporated in the correspondence. His verse drama *Caractacus* is commented on at some length in letters which convey not only Hurd's view but Warburton's criticisms. Other works mentioned are *Musaeus*, the 'Epistle on Fashion', Mason's *Odes*, *Elfrida*, and the 'Elegy' to Hurd prefixed to *Caractacus*. Reflecting on his friend's poetry often led Hurd on to other literary news, and some interesting comments on contemporary literary opinion. On 30 May 1747, he remarked, for instance,

> This Afternoon I have seen a small Poem of Mr Nevile's (for the fame of Musaeus has kindled up a flame which I thought expiring) call'd an Essay in the Art of writing Tragedy.

But, he adds,

> The Essay-way, You know, has been worn quite thread-bare.

On another occasion (16 June 1756), he writes to console Mason following a disappointing response to the publication of his *Odes*. Public taste, he says, has been so corrupted by a "long run of insipid Romances", that there is now no appreciation of what is "manly or great". "A little easy sing-song, intermixd with what they call *Sentiment*, is the utmost that common readers have any idea of."

Again and again, however, he returns to Mason and his poetry, pressing him to send his latest work and encouraging him to write more. His tone varies from the teasingly reproachful, as in a letter of July 1747:

> Your letter, instead of bringing the long-expected poem on Dress, puts me off with an Excuse, which has so much ceremony in it, that, for friendship's sake, I could wish You had not made it. You bid me neither "scold nor repeat the Request", which, it must be own'd, are two very reasonable Injunctions, considering that You ought certainly to expect both.

to an affectionate scolding:

> You are an impudent bard, that You are, to satirize two Lords at once, & certainly fall under the Statute of *Scandalum Magnatum*, in the proper sense. However it is my weakness to approve all You do. The Epigram is not without it's salt. Tho' what You mean by writing such lawless things, at the time You are solliciting preferment, I cannot imagine. (3 May 1761)

But the underlying affection for Mason remains constant. At Thurcaston, his correspondence with him was even more important to Hurd. "I should not enjoy myself in this *sequesterd bower*, as I do," he wrote on 1 June 1759, "if my heart were not attuned to Your's in every virtuous affection". On 25 June he had still not received a reply to this letter, and so wrote again in disappointment and vexation: "You don't write, and yet You know I am quite alone, and You know too how much I depend on your Letters for the relief of my solitude."

Hurd's feelings for Mason are summed up in a letter of 30 March 1761.

> We are made to comfort each other, or rather we are made to be happy in each other, witht standing in need of any comfort, under such petty disappointments as these. Take my word for it, my dear friend, we are neither of us fated to be rich. For I hold we were born under the same stars, tho' their various influence destined You to be a great poet, & me, to be a poor critic. But, courage, my friend: we will be happy in spite of our starrs, I mean your poetry, & my criticism. Heaven has given us an equivalent for this curse, in the blessing of an equal mind. It has done more. It has given us, what no fortune could have done, the love & friendship of each other. I have said all in saying this.

The Balguy Correspondence

Parallel to his correspondence with Mason is Hurd's correspondence with Thomas Balguy, a contemporary and Fellow of St John's. The latter correspondence, however, bears a markedly different character from that addressed to Mason. The letters, mainly written in the vacation, are full of news and are written with a conscious wittiness, not infrequently spiced with malice. An example of this is the way in which Hurd speaks of Mason when writing to Balguy. On 26 September 1752, for instance, he writes from Cambridge with the current news, in the course of which he remarks that Mason too is in college. And he adds,

> Betwixt ourselves he keeps wretched company. I saw him yesterday speak to Green

> of Cottenham and S. Jennins Esquire. *And* the morning he owned to me was entirely spent in chit-chat with Daniel Wray.

Again on 14 March 1753 he writes of his amiable but apparently unworldly friend:

> Poor Mason is a wretched politician. He has taken it into his head to serve a friend, but has contrived such a way of doing it as, if the world knew it, would disgrace the very name of poetry . . . When will these simple-minded men of Parnassus learn a little prudence?

The greater acidity of Hurd's style, when compared with the letters to Mason, complements a sense of excitement also apparent in this correspondence. Hurd had been appointed a Whitehall Preacher in 1750 and now regularly spent some time in London to give his sermons in the Royal Chapel; in 1752 he was chosen to make the Assize sermon in Norwich Cathedral, which was subsequently published; and, too, he was being invited to join the sophisticated and influential circle at Prior Park. His references to these events are not boastful but he is clearly pleased at his successes and enjoys the sense of belonging in a more worldly environment. On one occasion, he is invited to dine with the Allens in London and meets Henry Fielding, who is described to Balguy as "a poor, emaciated, worn out rake, whose gout and infirmities have got the better ev'n of his buffoonery". (19 March 1751) On another occasion, also in London, he calls on the Bishop of Norwich.

> I am a little of Pope's humour, to love a courtier in disgrace. This, and a little business I had with him, carried me this morning to my Lord Bishop of Norwich. The oily smoothness of this prelate ran over upon me in all manner of civilities, and I am to eat a bit of mutton with him on Sunday. (14 March 1753)

The image projected in these letters is of a distinctly more experienced man of the world than is elsewhere evidenced in the early correspondence. The striking of such an attitude may have been prompted by a sense of competition. Balguy came from a more privileged background than Hurd, and had the advantage of knowing that he would obtain preferment through the patronage of Bishop Hoadly, who had acted as patron to his father before him. He was obviously an able man and active within the university. But at the same time, Hurd's letters also project a mutually gratifying image of one clever young man wittily conversing with another. Balguy's early connections were better than Hurd's, but Hurd was able to introduce Balguy into the Warburton circle, and they were equally accepted into a body of distinguished acquaintance made at, or through, St John's. (William Heberden and William Powell are examples.) It gave Hurd much satisfaction to be able to write from London:

> You lost a great pleasure in not seeing the pictures at Devons. House, which Lord George was so kind to shew me. I mentioned your short stay in town (for I suppos'd it likely he would hear of you) and your indisposition, and your great concern, that you could not wait upon him. He spoke very kindly of you and desired his compliments. (19 March 1751)

Interestingly, whilst being captivated by secular power and authority, Hurd is frequently deprecating in his allusions to the ecclesiastically powerful. His description of the Bishop of Norwich is a case in point, but there are similar comments in a letter of 18 August 1749 and another undated letter written c.1753. Even less worthy of esteem, in the opinion of the two young Fellows, were their college superiors, the Heads of Houses. Both men were much involved in the university dispute over new diciplinary regulations which came to a head in 1750–51 and only petered out in

1753. The association of M.A.s that was formed in opposition to the Heads on this occasion had its strongest representation in Emmanuel, closely followed by St John's. Balguy was a leading member, and Hurd an ardent supporter of the cause, which is another focus of excitement and indignation in the early letters, moving Hurd on one occasion to an unusual vehemence of language. In a letter of 29 March 1751 he delivers a sharp attack on a pamphlet written by Thomas Chapman, the Master of Magdalene, and "an insolent coxcomb". (19 March 1751) This pamphlet, he said, contained "many vile and injurious insinuations, much courtly sycophancy, and not less *head-like* insolence". He believed it should be answered immediately by Balguy, in order to "vindicate the honour of the university, [and] disgrace these reptiles for ever". Balguy evidently demurred, and it was left to Hurd himself to reply to Chapman, as he did in his pamphlet, *The Opinion of an Eminent Lawyer*.

There are nine letters attributable to this period from 1749 to about 1753; but there then follows a silence of six years where all correspondence has disappeared. The letters resume (with no sense of an actual interruption in the sequence) in 1759. By this time Balguy had been made Archdeacon of Winchester, Hurd had become Rector of Thurcaston, and the character of the correspondence had altered. In place of the animated accounts of visits and dinners, or Cambridge controversy, intermixed with gossip and college news, there is more substantial discussion of books or abstract subjects suggested by them (see, for example, 6 September 1759, 2 November 1759, 1 May 1761), and a pervading sense of restraint and responsibility. In the letter of 2 November 1759, Hurd describes his situation to Balguy:

> I must tell You that I lead a life here, which You will think pitiable, & most men, wretched. I am so entirely alone that for weeks together I see no human face, but that of my own Servants, & of my parishioners at Church on Sundays. Yet with all this, one day slides after another so easily & insensibly, that I have no complaints to make of my situation. 'Tis true I should be happier far with You, & others of my friends, but *use*, that great friend to human life, reconciles me to my lot, & keeps me from being positively unhappy. My chief amusement is in my books, & the correspondence of my friends.

There are, indeed, numerous references to Hurd's reading interests in these letters. He writes in some detail of Clarendon's *Life* published in 1759, both in the letter quoted above, and in that which precedes it, of 6 September 1759. In subsequent correspondence he mentions, most notably, Sterne's *Tristram Shandy*, Rousseau's *La Nouvelle Héloïse*, Hume's *History of England*, Macpherson's *Fingal*, Lowth's *Grammar*, and the Italian poets (Tasso, Ariosto, Metastasio). Perhaps as a reflection of Balguy's tastes, though, he deals at length only with Clarendon. *La Nouvelle Héloïse*, which is written about quite copiously in correspondence with Mason, is here defended in a paragraph.

> I require you, upon pain of my displeasure, to retract your opinion of Rousseau. The New Heloise, I do not say as a romance, but as a moral composition, is incomparable. I do not care what you and Mr. Gray in the pride of criticism may pretend to the contrary. I appeal not to your taste, but to your *moral sense*. (1 May 1761)

Again, with an eye to Balguy's interests as well as his own, Hurd remarks, rather unkindly, in a letter of 3 December 1762:

> You are too old, & too much of a Philosopher, to read Ariosto, with enthusiasm. The Italian Poets address themselves to a young Imagination, & You & I are, alass, turn'd of forty . . . But if You love the pathetic, read Metastasio, where You will find the tenderness, not to say, the morality & good sense of Euripides."

Hurd's own publications are also considered in the letters, but since Balguy's comments clearly focused on the factual, rather than the literary, there is little extended discussion of either *Moral and Political Dialogues* or *Letters on Chivalry and Romance* from a literary point of view. (See 6 September 1759, for the main discussion of the *Dialogues.*)

Despite long spells of "retirement" at Thurcaston, Hurd's contact with Warburton ensured him periods of activity: in attendance as chaplain, when Warburton was created Bishop of Gloucester, and as a guest at Prior Park. In the letters to Balguy of 1759 to 1762, it is Warburton who figures predominantly in reports of their mutual acquaintance, and bishops are no longer mocked. Ecclesiastical affairs in general make up a good part of the news contained in these letters. There are interesting remarks on contemporary ecclesiastical preferments (including Hurd's own appointment to the sinecure of Folkton); an account of Warburton's 1761 visitation; and some illuminating references to the problems encountered by Hurd in the "dirty business" of enclosure (26 July 1761). Much of this news was omitted by Kilvert in his editing of the letters to Balguy, and has only now come to light with the discovery of the original letters. At this stage of his career in the Church, Hurd seems to have included more comment on ecclesiastical matters in his letters to Balguy, than to anyone else.

The Warburton Correspondence

Only one set of letters out of all his correspondence was actually selected for publication by Hurd himself. These formed part of his correspondence with William Warburton, and were chosen to accompany letters from the bishop which were to take precedence. The collection (28 letters from Hurd and 227 letters from Warburton) was printed at Kidderminster in 1795, and held for publication under Hurd's instructions until after his death. It was issued as *Letters from a Late Eminent Prelate* in 1808.

It is impossible to say to what extent Hurd edited the correspondence in preparing it for publication, but two factors emerge as influencing the character of the selection. First there is Hurd's veneration of Warburton, whom he treated always with great deference: his letters to him are, in this respect, amongst the least "familiar" of his total correspondence. Second, and related to this, is his clear intention of illuminating Warburton's greatness rather than illustrating equally both sides of the correspondence.

In the period covered by the early correspondence to 1762, only one other letter to Warburton and a fragment have been traced. The letter is a reply of 1756 to an offer of financial assistance and suggestions as to Hurd's future career. Part of it was printed by Kilvert in the *Memoirs*, but no suggestion of the financial transaction is given. In style the letter does not differ substantially from those published in *Letters from a Late Eminent Prelate*, but the contents indicate a dependency on Warburton, that Hurd would not have publicised himself. "Let me own to You", he says,

> that, tho' my little Income, made up of several odd ends, be abundantly sufficient for the wants I have in this place, yet the expences I have been sometimes put to in my attendance on my friends, on some by the calls of duty, and on others, by civility, but especially in the attendance in my unsettled state of health, have so far run me behind hand in my finances as to render this gratuity of your's doubly welcome.
>
> (20 October 1756)

Hurd's devotion to Warburton has often been ridiculed as being foolishly indulged, blinding him to faults and virtues alike. The most extreme manifestation of his uncritical support is his pamphlet, *On the Delicacy of Friendship*, quite unjustly castigating John Jortin for what Hurd supposed to be an attack on part of Warburton's *Divine Legation*. His admiration of Warburton as illustrated in the letters is, in some ways, equally undiscerning, but it is conveyed with such warmth that it is hard to judge Hurd totally unfavourably. And indeed in much of what he says there is some truth. For instance, on 23 March 1755, having learned that Warburton had been appointed to a prebend at Durham, Hurd wrote:

> The Church has been so long and deeply in your debt, that it will seem but common justice if it now pays you with interest.

Although containing a good measure of exaggeration and flattery, this statement is not quite false, for Warburton was, as even his opponents would admit, as energetic a champion of the Church as one might hope to find.

Hurd's estimation of Warburton's talents led him to approve each one of his works as the product of genius. This extended even to his earliest publications, of which Warburton himself was dismissive. In particular, though, Hurd emphasised the importance of the *Divine Legation*. Even the Preface to the first edition of the second volume he felt to be one of Warburton's "master-pieces", (30 December 1756), and in encouraging him to continue writing, he explained his view of the work as a whole.

> I do not expect to see all your plans filled up. For, besides that you have many upon your hands, you will always be forming new ones. But this favourite [the *Divine Legation*], this capital one must be completed. It signifies little that people clamour for it and expect it. You owe it to yourself, to truth, and to posterity. You think it immaterial perhaps that this monument of yourself should be entire. And the *virtuosi*, for any thing I know, might like it the better for its not being so. But who hereafter will be able to throw those lights on *religion* which these preparatory volumes now enable you to throw upon it? And would you envy these lights to the *ages to come*, that are more and more likely to stand in need of them!
>
> (22 January 1757)

Hurd's belief in the value of the *Divine Legation* to posterity proved unfounded, but in his day the work had many admirers as well as detractors, and even now though regarded as a curiosity, it is also demonstrably a monument of learning. Where such enthusiasm and praise abound, it is hard not to be convinced that Hurd's feeling was genuine, if sometimes misguided, and often excessive. And whilst Warburton's critics are summarily dismissed as ignorant "*foolish men*" (2 July 1754), "wretches" (9 January 1757), or "worthless enemies" (22 January 1757), this seems more acceptable than the extended and offensive irony of *On the Delicacy of Friendship*.

The earliest of the letters written to Warburton printed in *Letters from a Late Eminent Prelate* is dated 25 October 1749, and there are seventeen letters printed to 1761, none being included for 1762. In content, they are fairly varied. Four are concerned almost exclusively with Hurd's family, the earliest (dated 2 July 1754) describing his parents and their devotion to their children, and to him in particular; two others written at the time of his father's last illness and death; and a further letter of 27 August 1757 printed in part, expressing his gratitude at Warburton's goodness to his mother, and again dwelling on the exemplary character of his parents. Warburton's replies differ in the extent of their response. He speaks very warmly on the subject of Hurd's parents, but briefly in answer to the account of John Hurd's illness, suggesting that, in this instance, Hurd included these letters not just as an embellishment of Warburton's correspondence, but as a tribute to "the best of parents, and the best of friends". (27 August 1757) Recollections of the past occur in another letter of this period (30 December 1756) in which Hurd describes his first acquaintance with Warburton's works and the effect this produced upon him. This story is urged as part of an argument to retain the original Preface to the second volume of the *Divine Legation*, which Warburton had proposed rewriting.

Several of the letters printed here contain similar passages giving detailed consideration to particular sections of Warburton's work. In themselves they can make dull, sometimes incomprehensible reading. They do, however, illustrate the intense interest Hurd showed in all Warburton's writings, an interest which was not infrequently reciprocated, affecting the revisions each made of their respective works. (See, for example, Warburton's replies of 3 January 1757, 15 January 1757, 24 March 1761.)

As in his other correspondence, the letters following Hurd's removal to Thurcaston contain more, and more sustained references to his reading. Clarendon's *Life*, in particular, is commented on at some length, Hurd taking his cue from the opinion expressed by Warburton in a letter of 14 August 1759. Another book examined in detail is Atterbury's *The Rights, Powers, and Priviledges, of an English Convocation, Stated and Vindicated*, 1700. (October 1760) In reply to Hurd's letter, Warburton wrote:

> I know your drift, and nothing could be more tender. If it was possible that I could love you more than I do, it would be for this letter. From a few words that passed on the subject of convocations, I know you was afraid I might sometime or other publicly declare myself with more warmth than was fitting, in favour of so unpopular a thing as convocations. (*Prelate*, p. 231)

He continues with an explanation of his view of the practice of holding convocations, asserting that from one extreme the Church had fallen into another. Apart from illustrating Warburton's extensive reading and understanding of Church affairs, these two letters indicate a desire on Hurd's side to act occasionally as a restraining influence on Warburton. The latter was flattered and pleased by this friendly interest, although Hurd's attempt at moderation probably had little effect.

La Nouvelle Héloïse is another work described in a letter from Thurcaston, and, to a fellow enthusiast. Warburton agreed entirely in Hurd's admiration of the work, concurred with his views and concluded that Rousseau was "one of those glorious madmen, that Cervantes only saw in Idea". (*Prelate*, p. 241) *Tristram Shandy* is mentioned in the same letter, but with no response from Warburton. Some months later, the recently published poem, *Fingal*, comes under discussion. Warburton had been taken in by the "editor's" statement that the poem had been handed down, as Hurd describes it, "by *oral tradition*, for 1400 years, without a chasm, or so much as a various reading". (*Prelate*, p. 245) Hurd, however, had immediately concluded the work to be a forgery, and his clear exposition of the evidence convinces Warburton in turn.

Although Hurd's letters to Warburton are almost always designed to reflect flatteringly on the latter, they do nonetheless become more relaxed as the years and their friendship progress. The communication between the two men, made up of personal visits, official meetings (as in the visitations), and letters, was very frequent. They came to know each other extremely well and shared many interests. The rather miscellaneous nature of Hurd's letters is, in part, due to this. Those that are included in *Letters from a Late Eminent Prelate*, particularly from the late 1750s onwards, with their remarks on each other's writing, information on family and friends, news of ecclesiastical preferments, comments on recent publications and older works, all rather loosely assembled, form part of a continuing and very dense correspondence. As is the case in his letters to Littleton, Hurd is too conscious of Warburton's superiority to even attempt to be entertaining, but what the letters lose in animation, is made up for by the confidence and warmth of a very close friendship. In his *Dates of Some Occurrences in my own Life*, Hurd recorded, amongst details of publications and preferments, the deaths of his closest friends. Balguy and Mason were described as old friends, in one case "much esteemed", and in the other, "most respected". Warburton was described, fittingly, as his "old and best friend".

List of Letters

No. of Letter	Date	Place	Correspondent	Original Source	Printed Source or Transcript
			1739		
1	15 Apr.	Cambridge	Potter	N.L. Wales	
2	7 Aug.	Hatton-Grange	Potter	N.L. Wales	
3	11 Nov.	Cambridge	Potter	N.L. Wales	
4	2 Dec.	Cambridge	Potter	N.L. Wales	
			1740		
5	13 Jan.	Cambridge	Potter	N.L. Wales	
6	17 Feb.	Cambridge	Potter	N.L. Wales	
7	27 Apr.	Cambridge	Potter	N.L. Wales	
8	[June/July]	[Hatton-Grange]	Potter	N.L. Wales	
9	28 Aug.	[Hatton-Grange]	Potter	N.L. Wales	
10	14 Dec.	Cambridge	Potter	N.L. Wales	
			1741		
11	18 Jan.	Cambridge	Potter	N.L. Wales	
12	23 Jan.	Cambridge	Devey		Memoirs
13	15 Feb.	Cambridge	Potter	N.L. Wales	
14	14 Mar.	Cambridge	Devey		Memoirs
15	22 Mar.	Cambridge	Potter	N.L. Wales	
16	19 Apr.	Cambridge	Potter	N.L. Wales	
17	3 May	Cambridge	Devey		Memoirs
18	27 May	Cambridge	Potter	N.L. Wales	
19	19 Sep.	Hatton-Grange	Potter	N.L. Wales	
20	2 Oct.	Hatton-Grange	E. Macro		Transcript at Norfolk R.O.
			1742		
21	1 Jan.	Brewood	E. Macro	B.L.	
22	15 Apr.	Hatton-Grange	Potter	NL. Wales	
23	1 May	Hatton-Grange	C. Macro	B.L.	
24	14 July	Reymerston	Potter	N.L. Wales	
25	16 July	Reymerston	Devey		Memoirs
26	17 July	Reymerston	C. Macro	B.L.	
27	6 Aug.	Reymerston	T. Gough		Lit. Anecs.
28	25 Aug.	Reymerston	Potter	N.L. Wales	
29	10 Sep.	Norwich	C. Macro	B.L.	
30	[19 Sep.]	[Reymerston]	M. Macro	B.L.	

No. of Letter	Date	Place	Correspondent	Original Source	Printed Source or Transcript
31	24 Sep.	Reymerston	Devey		Memoirs
32	27 Sep.	Reymerston	C. Macro	B.L.	
33	3 Oct.	Reymerston	M. Macro	B.L.	
34	8 Oct.	Reymerston	Potter	N.L. Wales	
35	22 Oct.	Reymerston	M. Macro	B.L.	
36	23 Oct.	Reymerston	C. Macro	B.L.	
37	7 Nov.	Reymerston	C. Macro	B.L.	
38	[Nov.]	[Reymerston]	Devey		Memoirs
			1743		
39	27 Jan.	Cambridge	Potter	N.L. Wales	
40	5 Feb.	Cambridge	M. Macro	B.L.	
41	26 Feb.	Cambridge	M. Macro	B.L.	
42	5 Mar.	Cambridge	C. Macro	B.L.	
43	28 Mar.	Cambridge	Devey		Memoirs
44	22 Apr.	Cambridge	M. Macro	B.L.	
45	9 June	Brewood	T. Gough	Beinecke	Lit. Anecs.
46	22 June	Hatton-Grange	M. Macro	B.L.	
47	22 June	Hatton-Grange	E. Macro	B.L.	
48	11 July	Hatton-Grange	Potter	N.L. Wales	
49	17 [Aug.]	Cambridge	Potter	N.L. Wales	
50	27 Aug.	Cambridge	M. Macro	B.L.	
51	17 Sep.	Cambridge	M. Macro	B.L.	
52	19 Sep.	Cambridge	E. Macro		Transcript at Norfolk R.O.
53	11 Oct.	Cambridge	Potter	N.L. Wales	
54	31 Oct.	[Cambridge]	E. Macro		Transcript at Norfolk R.O.
55	25 Nov.	Cambridge	Potter	N.L. Wales	
56	26 Nov.	Cambridge	C. Macro	B.L.	
57	29 Nov.	Cambridge	Devey		Memoirs
			1744		
58	17 Feb.	Cambridge	Devey		Memoirs
59	25 Feb.	Cambridge	C. Macro	B.L.	
60	16 Mar.	Cambridge	C. Macro	B.L.	
61	23 Aug.	Cambridge	Devey		Memoirs
62	2 Sep.	Cambridge	A. Askew	Bodleian	
63	25 Sep.	Cambridge	E. Macro	B.L.	
64	21 Dec.	Cambridge	E. Littleton	Staffs R.O.	
			1745		
65	25 May	Cambridge	Devey	Memoirs	
66	29 Aug.	Cambridge	M. Macro	B.L.	
67	24 Nov.	Cambridge	E. Littleton	Staffs R.O.	
68	29 Nov.	Cambridge	E. Littleton	Staffs R.O.	
69	4 Dec.	Cambridge	C. Macro	B.L.	
70	18 Dec.	Cambridge	E. Littleton	Staffs R.O.	
71	Dec./Jan.	Brewood	Devey		Memoirs

No. of Letter	Date	Place	Correspondent	Original Source	Printed Source or Transcript
			1746		
72	1 Jan.	Cambridge	C. Macro	B.L.	
73	2 Jan.	Cambridge	E. Macro	B.L.	
74	9 Jan.	Cambridge	E. Littleton	Staffs R.O.	
75	27 Jan.	Cambridge	E. Littleton	Staffs R.O.	
76	14 Mar.	Cambridge	E. Littleton	Staffs R.O.	
77	28 Apr.	Cambridge	C. Macro	B.L.	
78	22 Aug.	Cambridge	M. Macro	B.L.	
			1747		
79	5 Jan.	Cambridge	C. Macro	B.L.	
80	15 Jan.	Cambridge	E. Littleton	Staffs R.O.	
81	17 Mar.	Cambridge	Devey		Memoirs
82	7 May	Cambridge	Mason	Hartlebury	H-M Corr.
83	30 May	Cambridge	Mason	Hartlebury	H-M Corr.
84	July	[Cambridge]	Mason	Hartlebury	H-M Corr.
85	17 Oct.	Hatton-Grange	E. Littleton	Staffs. R.O.	
			1748		
86	15 Feb.	Cambridge	E. Littleton	Staffs. R.O.	
87	20 Feb.	Cambridge	E. Littleton	Staffs. R.O.	
88	20 Apr.	Cambridge	E. Littleton	Staffs. R.O.	
89	7 Oct.	Cambridge	E. Littleton	Staffs. R.O.	
90	14 Oct.	Cambridge	E. Littleton	Staffs. R.O.	
91	27 Oct.	Cambridge	E. Littleton	Staffs. R.O.	
92	15 Nov.	Cambridge	E. Littleton	Staffs. R.O.	
93	26 Dec.	Cambridge	Potter	N.L. Wales	
94	31 Dec.	Cambridge	C. Macro	B.L.	
			1749		
95	23 Feb.	Cambridge	E. Littleton	Staffs. R.O.	
96	2 Mar.	Cambridge	E. Littleton	Staffs. R.O.	
97	21 Mar.	Cambridge	E. Littleton	Staffs. R.O.	
98	4 May	Cambridge	E. Littleton	Staffs. R.O.	
99	8 May	Cambridge	E. Littleton	Staffs. R.O.	
100	26 May	Cambridge	E. Littleton	Staffs. R.O.	
101	5 June	Cambridge	E. Littleton	Staffs. R.O.	
102	7 Aug.	Cambridge	E. Littleton	Staffs. R.O.	
103	18 Aug.	Cambridge	Balguy	Beinecke	Memoirs
104	22 Sep.	Cambridge	E. Littleton	Staffs. R.O.	
105	25 Oct.	Cambridge	Warburton		Prelate
106	28 Dec.	Cambridge	E. Littleton	Staffs. R.O.	
			1750		
107	17 Jan.	Cambridge	E. Littleton	Staffs. R.O.	
108	9 Mar.	Cambridge	E. Littleton	Staffs. R.O.	

No. of Letter	Date	Place	Correspondent	Original Source	Printed Source or Transcript
109	29 Mar.	Cambridge	E. Littleton	Staffs. R.O.	
110	6 Apr.	Cambridge	E. Littleton	Staffs. R.O.	
111	11 June	Cambridge	E. Littleton	Staffs. R.O.	
112	14 June	Cambridge	E. Littleton	Staffs. R.O.	
113	20 Aug.	Brewood	E. Littleton	Staffs. R.O.	
114	4 Sep.	Cambridge	E. Littleton	Staffs. R.O.	
115	1 Oct.	Cambridge	E. Littleton	Staffs. R.O.	
116	21 Dec.	Cambridge	E. Littleton	Staffs. R.O.	
			1751		
117	19 Mar.	Inner Temple	Balguy	Beinecke	Memoirs
118	29 Mar.	Inner Temple	Balguy	Beinecke	
119	26 Apr.	Cambridge	E. Littleton	Staffs. R.O.	
120	21 May	Cambridge	E. Macro	Macro L-book [in private hands]	
			1752		
120A	14 Feb.	Cambridge	Bowyer		Lit. Anecs.
121	18 June	Cambridge	E. Littleton	Staffs. R.O.	
122	1 July	Cambridge	E. Littleton	Staffs. R.O.	
123	28 Aug.	Cambridge	C. Macro	B.L.	
124	26 Sep.	Cambridge	Balguy	Beinecke	Memoirs
125	29 Oct.	London	Mason	Hartlebury	H-M Corr.
126	6 Nov.	Reymerston	E. Littleton	Staffs. R.O.	
127	1 Dec.	Cambridge	E. Littleton	Staffs. R.O.	
			1753		
128	20 Jan.	Cambridge	Mason	Hartlebury	H-M Corr.
129	12 Feb.	Cambridge	E. Littleton	Staffs. R.O.	
130	14 Mar.	Devereux Court [London]	Balguy		Memoirs
131	3 Apr.	Cambridge	E. Littleton	Staffs. R.O.	
132	12 Apr.	Cambridge	E. Littleton	Staffs. R.O.	
133	2 July	Cambridge	Warburton		Prelate
134	26 Aug.	Norton (Suffolk)	E. Littleton	Staffs. R.O.	
135	27 Sep.	Cambridge	Balguy	Beinecke	Memoirs
136	22 Oct.	Cambridge	Mason	Hartlebury	H-M Corr.
137	7 Nov.	Cambridge	E. Littleton	Staffs. R.O.	
138	–	Cambridge	Balguy	Beinecke	
139	–	[Cambridge]	Balguy	Beinecke	Memoirs
140	–	Cambridge	Balguy	Beinecke	Memoirs
			1754		
141	10 Feb.	Cambridge	E. Littleton	Staffs. R.O.	
142	22 Feb.	Cambridge	E. Littleton	Staffs. R.O.	
143	29 Apr.	Cambridge	E. Littleton	Staffs. R.O.	
144	21 May	Cambridge	E. Littleton	Staffs. R.O.	
145	2 July	Cambridge	Warburton		Prelate

No. of Letter	Date	Place	Correspondent	Original Source	Printed Source or Transcript
146	2 Sep.	Cambridge	E. Littleton	Staffs. R.O.	
146A	[mid Nov.]	[Cambridge]	Bowyer		Lit. Anecs.
147	17 Dec.	[Cambridge]	Hervey	Hartlebury [copy letter]	
148	20 Dec.	Cambridge	Hervey	Hartlebury [copy letter]	
149	22 Dec.	Cambridge	Hervey	Hartlebury [copy letter]	
			1755		
150	Feb.	Cambridge	Warburton		Prelate
151	19 Feb.	Cambridge	E. Littleton	Staffs. R.O.	
152	15 Mar.	London	E. Littleton	Staffs. R.O.	
153	23 Mar.	Cambridge	Warburton		Prelate
154	3 June	Cambridge	E. Littleton	Staffs. R.O.	
155	18 June	Cambridge	E. Littleton	Staffs. R.O.	
156	21 July	Prior Park	E. Littleton	Staffs. R.O.	
157	21 Aug.	Shifnal	E. Littleton	Staffs. R.O.	
158	13 Sep.	Shifnal	Warburton		Prelate
159	31 Oct.	Cambridge	Mason		HC(RHn)M.L.R.
160	1 Dec.	Cambridge	E. Littleton	Folger	Memoirs
161	1 Dec.	Cambridge	Warburton		Prelate
162	13 Dec.	Cambridge	E. Littleton	Folger	Memoirs
163	31 Dec.	Cambridge	Mason	Hartlebury	H-M Corr.
			1756		
164	8 Jan.	Cambridge	Mason	Hartlebury	H-M Corr.
165	19 Jan.	Cambridge	Mason		HC(RHn)/M.L.R.
166	3 Apr.	Cambridge	Mason	Hartlebury	H-M Corr.
167	30 Apr.	Cambridge	Mason		HC(RHn)/M.L.R.
168	6 June	Cambridge	E. Littleton	Staffs. R.O.	
169	16 June	Cambridge	Mason	Hartlebury	H-M Corr.
170	19 July	Brighthelmston	E. Littleton	Staffs. R.O.	
171	7 Aug.	Brighthelmston	Mason	Hartlebury	H-M Corr.
172	20 Oct.	Cambridge	E. Littleton	Folger	Memoirs
173	20 Oct.	Cambridge	Warburton	B.L.	Memoirs
174	16 Nov.	Cambridge	Potter	N.L. Wales	
175	30 Dec.	Cambridge	Warburton		Prelate
			1757		
176	7 Jan.	Cambridge	Gray	Hartlebury	H-M Corr./Gray Corr.
177	9 Jan.	Cambridge	Warburton		Prelate
178	22 Jan.	Cambridge	Warburton		Prelate
179	[Mar./Apr.]	Cambridge	Gray	Hartlebury	H-M Corr./Gray Corr.
180	15 May	Cambridge	Mason		HC(RHn)/M.L.R.
181	29 May	Cambridge	E. Littleton	Staffs. R.O.	
182	16 June	Cambridge	Mason		HC(RHn)/M.L.R.
183	3 July	Cambridge	E. Littleton	Staffs. R.O.	

No. of Letter	Date	Place	Correspondent	Original Source	Printed Source or Transcript
184	12 July	Cambridge	E. Littleton	Staffs. R.O.	
185	16 Aug.	Cambridge	Gray	Hartlebury	H-M Corr./Gray Corr.
186	17 Aug.	Cambridge	Mason		HC(RHn)/M.L.R.
187	27 Aug.	Cambridge	Warburton		Prelate
188	28 Aug.	Cambridge	Gray	Hartlebury	H-M Corr./Gray Corr.
189	20 Oct.	Cambridge	Yorke	B.L.	
190	21 Oct.	Cambridge	E. Littleton	Staffs. R.O.	
191	27 Oct.	Cambridge	C. Macro	B.L.	
192	6 Nov.	Cambridge	Yorke	B.L.	
193	30 Nov.	Prior Park	Mason	Hartlebury	H-M Corr.
194	21 Dec.	Prior Park	Mason	Hartlebury	H-M Corr.
195	27 Dec.	Prior Park	E. Littleton	Staffs. R.O.	
			1758		
196	26 Jan.	Prior Park	Mason		HC(RHn)/M.L.R.
197	4 Feb.	Prior Park	E. Littleton	Staffs. R.O.	
198	10 July	Thurcaston	Mason		HC(RHn)/M.L.R.
199	28 July	Thurcaston	E. Littleton	Staffs. R.O.	
200	13 Aug.	Thurcaston	C. Macro	B.L.	
201	14 Aug.	Thurcaston	Mason		HC(RHn)/M.L.R.
202	20 Aug.	Thurcaston	Danvers	Leics. R.O. [copy letter]	
203	27 Aug.	Thurcaston	Danvers	Leics. R.O. [copy letter]	
204	3 Sep.	Thurcaston	E. Littleton	Staffs. R.O.	
205	17 Sep.	Thurcaston	Danvers	Leics. R.O. [copy letter]	
206	23 Sep.	Thurcaston	Danvers	Leics. R.O. [copy letter]	
207	2 Oct.	Thurcaston	Danvers	Leics. R.O. [copy letter]	
			1759		
208	3 Feb.	London	E. Littleton	Staffs. R.O.	
209	14 Mar.	Leicester	Mason		HC(RHn)/M.L.R.
210	9 Apr.	Leicester	E. Littleton	Staffs. R.O.	
211	17 Apr.	[Thurcaston/ Leicester]	E. Littleton	Staffs. R.O.	
212	4 May	Thurcaston	Mason		HC(RHn)/M.L.R.
213	26 May	Thurcaston	Mason		HC(RHn)
214	1 June	Thurcaston	Mason	Hartlebury	H-M Corr.
215	25 June	Thurcaston	Mason	Hartlebury	H-M Corr.
216	5 July	Thurcaston	E. Littleton	Staffs. R.O.	
217	29 July	Thurcaston	Mason		HC(RHn)/M.L.R.
218	8 Aug.	Thurcaston	E. Littleton	Staffs. R.O.	
219	8 Aug.	Thurcaston	F. Littleton	Staffs. R.O.	
220	26 Aug.	Thurcaston	Mason		HC(RHn)/M.L.R.
221	26 Aug.	Thurcaston	Warburton		Prelate
222	30 Aug.	Thurcaston	E. Littleton	Staffs. R.O.	

No. of Letter	Date	Place	Correspondent	Original Source	Printed Source or Transcript
223	6 Sep.	Thurcaston	Balguy	Beinecke	Memoirs
224	28 Sep.	Thurcaston	Mason		HC(RHn)/M.L.R.
225	2 Nov.	Thurcaston	Balguy	Beinecke	Memoirs
226	6 Nov.	Thurcaston	Mason		HC(RHn)/M.L.R.
227	13 Dec.	Prior Park	Yorke	B.L.	
228	17 Dec.	Prior Park	Yorke	B.L.	
			1760		
229	8 Feb.	Thurcaston	Balguy		Memoirs
230	17 Feb.	Thurcaston	E. Littleton	Staffs. R.O.	
231	27 Feb.	Thurcaston	Mason		HC(RHn)/M.L.R.
232	4 Mar.	Thurcaston	Warburton		Prelate
233	11 Apr.	Thurcaston	Mason		HC(RHn)/M.L.R.
234	14 June	Thurcaston	E. Littleton	Staffs. R.O.	
235	22 June	Thurcaston	Warburton		Prelate
236	27 Sep.	Prior Park	Mason		HC(RHn)/M.L.R.
237	Oct.	[Thurcaston]	Warburton		Prelate
238	29 Oct.	Thurcaston	E. Littleton	Staffs. R.O.	
239	30 Nov.	Thurcaston	Mason	Hartlebury	H-M Corr.
			1761		
240	1 Mar.	Thurcaston	Yorke	B.L.	
241	6 Mar.	Thurcaston	E. Littleton	Staffs. R.O.	
242	18 Mar.	Thurcaston	Warburton		Prelate
243	30 Mar.	Thurcaston	Mason	Hartlebury	H-M Corr.
244	8 Apr.	Thurcaston	Yorke	B.L.	
245	12 Apr.	Thurcaston	E. Littleton	Staffs. R.O.	
246	1 May	Thurcaston	Balguy		Memoirs
247	3 May	Thurcaston	Mason	Hartlebury	H-M Corr.
248	26 July	Gloucester	Balguy	Beinecke	Memoirs
249	30 Aug.	Birmingham	E. Littleton	Staffs. R.O.	
250	28 Oct.	Thurcaston	Mason	Hartlebury	H-M Corr.
251	22 Nov.	Thurcaston	E. Littleton	Folger	
252	27 Nov.	Thurcaston	Mason	Hartlebury	H-M Corr.
253	14 Dec.	Thurcaston	E. Littleton	Staffs. R.O.	
254	23 Dec.	Thurcaston	E. Littleton	Staffs. R.O.	
255	25 Dec.	Thurcaston	Warburton		Prelate
			1762		
256	1 Jan.	Thurcaston	E. Littleton	Staffs. R.O.	
257	29 Jan.	Thurcaston	Balguy	Beinecke	Memoirs
258	31 Jan.	Thurcaston	Green	Hartlebury [copy letter]	
259	28 Feb.	Thurcaston	E. Littleton	Staffs. R.O.	
260	12 Mar.	Thurcaston	E. Littleton	Staffs. R.O.	
261	24 Apr.	Thurcaston	E. Littleton	Staffs. R.O.	
262	26 Apr.	Thurcaston	Balguy	Beinecke	Memoirs
263	20 May	Thurcaston	Yorke	B.L.	

No. of Letter	Date	Place	Correspondent	Original Source	Printed Source or Transcript
264	5 June	Thurcaston	E. Littleton	Staffs. R.O.	
265	1 July	Thurcaston	Balguy	Beinecke	Memoirs
266	30 Aug.	Weymouth	E. Littleton	Staffs. R.O.	
267	23 Sep.	Prior Park	E. Littleton	Folger	
268	25 Sep.	Prior Park	Yorke	B.L.	
269	14 Oct.	Thurcaston	Warton	B.L.	
270	26 Nov.	Thurcaston	E. Littleton	Folger	
270A	29 Nov.	Thurcaston	Drummond	Borthwick Institute	
271	3 Dec.	[Thurcaston]	Balguy	Beinecke	Memoirs
272	10 Dec.	Thurcaston	Warburton	B.L.	Illusts.
273	10 Dec.	Thurcaston	Yorke	B.L.	

THE TEXT

The manuscripts of the letters

The letters to John Potter are in the National Library of Wales (12432E); they have never been published either wholly or in part. The letters to Cox, Mary and Edward Macro form part of the second volume of Macro correspondence in the British Library (Add. MSS 32557) and are also unpublished. Three letters to Edward Macro survive only as copies in the Norfolk County Record Office, and one letter is included in the *Macro Letter-book*. The majority of the letters to Sir Edward Littleton are preserved at the Staffordshire County Record Office (D1413/1); six other letters are in the Folger Shakespeare Library (w.a.57). Of the latter, three were transcribed or partly transcribed by Francis Kilvert and printed in his *Memoirs* of Richard Hurd.

The letters to William Mason are preserved at Hartlebury Castle, including those fragments transcribed by Hurd's nephew onto separate sheets of paper and inserted into volumes in the library. The complete letters have been published in Pearce and Whibley's edition of 1932 (*The Correspondence of Richard Hurd & William Mason*), and the fragments by James Nankivell in the *Modern Language Review* ('Extracts from the Destroyed Letters of Richard Hurd to William Mason'). For this edition the originals have been re-transcribed and more extensively annotated. Hurd's letters to Balguy had been consulted by Francis Kilvert for his *Memoirs* and were then apparently lost. They were re-discovered in the early 1980s and now form part of the collection of the Beinecke Rare Book and Manuscript Library at Yale University. Permission was given to consult the photostat copies retained by the British Library. The majority of these letters were printed by Kilvert, but with many un-noted excisions and without annotation. The full text is presented here for the first time. The correspondence with Warburton was edited by Hurd and first published in 1808. The originals of the few letters of his own that were included have since disappeared. The text therefore comes from the (unannotated) published edition of 1808.

Many of the miscellaneous letters to minor correspondents have been preserved either in the original or as copies at Hartlebury Castle. These include the letters to Thomas Gray, John Green, Frederick Hervey, Thomas Warton and Charles Yorke. For some letters both the original and the copy have survived, as in those addressed to Thomas Warton and Charles Yorke, where the originals have been preserved at the British Library. In these cases the text is that of the letter sent, and a note indicates the existence of a copy elsewhere. The letter to Anthony Askew is part of the Bodleian Library archive; the letters to Sir John Danvers are preserved at the Leicestershire County Record Office; the letter to Archbishop Drummond is at the Borthwick Institute; one letter to Gough is in the Beinecke; and the letter to Lady Frances Littleton is included in the correspondence to her husband, Sir Edward. Of these, only the letters to Gray and to Gough have been published.

The Macro Letter-book

The *Macro Letter-book* has been more extensively used than any other manuscript source of documentation. It is a bound collection of 130 letters written to Edward Macro from the 1730s to 1760. Many of the letters are from Sir Edward Littleton and are largely devoted to the discussion of his art collection and the building of Teddesley Hall. Other letters are from the Macro family (both immediate and more distant relatives) and friends in Cambridge, London and elsewhere. The letters provide an enormous quantity of information on matters touched upon by Hurd in his own letters from the time of his appointment as curate of Reymerston, throughout the 1740s and 1750s. The *Letter-book* is therefore an invaluable source of information, providing factual information and illuminating insights into the quality of life in the mid eighteenth century. I am grateful to the owners for their permission to consult the *Letter-book* and for the encouragement they have given me.

List of printed sources

Correspondence of Thomas Gray, ed. Paget Toynbee and Leonard Whibley, 3 vols., Oxford, 1935, reprinted with Corrections and Additions by H.W. Starr, 1971.

The Correspondence of Richard Hurd & William Mason, and Letters of Richard Hurd to Thomas Gray, ed. E.H. Pearce and L. Whibley, Cambridge, 1932.

Francis Kilvert, *Memoirs of the Life and Writings of the Right Rev. Richard Hurd, D.D., Lord Bishop of Worcester; With a Selection from his Correspondence and other Unpublished Papers*, 1860.

James Nankivell, 'Extracts from the Destroyed Letters of Richard Hurd to William Mason', *Modern Language Review*, xl. (1950). 153–63.

John Nichols, *Literary Anecdotes of the Eighteenth Century; comprizing Biographical Memoirs of William Bowyer, Printer . . . and Biographical Anecdotes of a Considerable Number of Eminent Writers and Ingenious Artists*, 9 vols., 1812–16.

John Nichols, *Illustrations of the Literary History of the Eighteenth Century*, 8 vols., 1817–58.

[William Warburton and Richard Hurd], *Letters from a Late Eminent Prelate to One of His Friends*, Kidderminster, [1808].

EDITORIAL PRINCIPLES

Spelling. The exact spelling of the original is retained. When a word appears to have been mis-spelled through inadvertence, it is corrected, and the original reading is given in a footnote. Diphthongs are expanded.

Capitalisation. All capitals are retained, even when the editor may consider them indiscriminately used. Where it is impossible to determine whether a letter in the MS is upper or lower case, a choice has been made on the basis of the author's usual practice.

Superior letters. All superior letters are lowered.

Slips of the pen. See spelling (above). Omitted words are supplied in square brackets.

Mutilated text. The reconstructed text is given wherever possible in square brackets.

Interlineations and marginalia. Interlineations and marginalia are inserted into the text without comment, unless there is a question about the proper point at which they should be inserted, or some special reason to discriminate between the text and the insertion.

Deletions. Deletions are incorporated in the text, within angle brackets wherever possible. If it is not possible to include the deletion without obscuring the text it is reported in the footnotes.

Punctuation. The original punctuation is retained. Square brackets are used for any marks supplied where there had been no punctuation.

Brackets. Square brackets are reserved for editorial use; angle brackets indicate authorial emendation.

Italics. Underlinings which appear to the editor to be used for purposes of emphasis are retained; underlinings which appear to be meaningless flourishes are ignored.

Postmarks. The heading "Postmarked" always appears at the beginning of a letter, even when the postmark is missing; it does not appear when the letter in question has been enclosed with another, or has been conveyed by some other means than the usual postal services.

THE LETTERS

1 To JOHN POTTER 15 APRIL 1739

Text: MS NLW 12432E; unpublished.
Addressed: To/the Revd. Mr. Potter at Dr. Burnett's/at Doddington near Marshfield/in Gloucestershire./By London[1]
Postmarked: CAMBRIDGE 16 AP

Camb: April 15th. 1739.

Dear Sir

I had the favour of your's,[2] when I was deeply engag'd in Homer & Burgesdicius,[3] otherwise should have answer'd it sooner. I hope you don't think, I preferr'd the old musty Greek, or the trifling Logician to a correspondence with a valuable friend: no; 'twas necessity, not choice, yt. restrain'd my Pen, & prevented my writing. But being now free'd from Business your friend is at leisure to send you as much Nonsense as he can crowd into an Epistle.

The perusal of your Letter has been very agreeable to me, nor did your verses afford the least pleasure: if they were, as you assert, the product of your horses trotting, I can't but envy you so musical an animal, & must confess his pace is the most regular, & harmonious, I ever remember to have met with.

Having no news to send you, I shall fill up the remainder of my Letter with a parcel of verses, wch. my hasty pen threw together the other day, without much order, or accuracy. I can plead nothing in their behalf, only that they were the amusement of an idle hour, or two, & if they prove of the same service to you, it is as much as I expect from them. They run thus.

Zelinda.

O'er the transparent Stream Zelinda stood;
And view'd her beauties in the chrystal flood;
With ev'ry grace the blooming virgin glow'd,
Her ev'ry grace the faithfull mirrour shew'd:
The snowy whiteness of her heaving breast
Full in the watry Image stood confesst;
While her fair Tresses round her head display'd
Unnumber'd beauties, & a pleasing shade.

1 Thomas Burnett, D.D. (c.1671–1750), rector of Dodington, Gloucestershire, 1738–50. (*Alum. Cantab.*) His connection with Potter is not known.

2 The correspondence with Potter probably began in the summer of 1738. He actually removed his name from the college books on 1 September but had been almost continually absent since April. (Emmanuel College, *Commons Accounts Book*, STE. 15. 8.)

3 Francis Burgersdijk or Burgersdicius (1590–1629) had been Professor of Philosophy at Saumur, and afterwards, of Logic at Leyden. In 1626 he published *Institutionum Logicarum Libri duo, . . . Ex Aristotelis, Keckermanni, aliorumq. praecipuorum Logicorum praeceptis recensitis, nova methodo ac modo formati, atque editi*. This was widely reprinted and an edition "Ad juventutem Cantabrigiensem" was published in Cambridge in 1637. Although Burgersdijk was evidently still a prescribed text in Emmanuel, at least, the study of logic was being largely superseded by that of mathematics. ([Daniel Waterland], *Advice to a Young Student. With a Method of Study for the Four First Years*, 1730, pp.18–20; John Gascoigne, 'Mathematics and Meritocracy: The Emergence of the Cambridge Mathematical Tripos', in *Social Studies of Science*, xiv (1984), 570–2.)

As thus the maid survey'd each blooming grace,
Fresh rising Sorrow veil'd her lovely face;
As when the Sun clad in a vernal Show'r
Darts milder glories, & a softer pow'r.
Silent she stood, with thoughtful grief oppresst,
A secret woe her downcast Eyes confesst,
And thick with sorrows beat her throbbing breast.
Then pointing to the smiling flow'rs, yt. grew
Around the stream in blooms of brightest Hue,
In sighs, she cry'd, Alass! unhappy maid!
How soon shall thine, like those fair beauties fade?
How soon these Roses leave thy youthfull face,
Now gently blushing in the watry glass?
These Eyes, where Damon's flatt'ring tongue has say'd,
The graces dwelt, & smiling Cupids play'd,
How soon alass! shall cruel rage disarm,
And all their little honours cease to charm?
This forehead too, where some small beauties lye,
(Pass but a few, unheeded Summers bye)
Stript of each charm, in wrinkles shall make known,
How vain those charms, those beauties, not it's own.
As thus the maid in softest Sorrow sings
The sure decay, yt. Age on beauty brings,
Down her fair cheeks a pearly current flows
Like glitt'ring dew-drops from the op'ning Rose.
Damon, who all the while securely stood
Within the covert of a neighb'ring wood,
Attentive hear'd the weeping nymph complain,
And thus address'd his fair in softest Strain.
Weep not, dear maid, restrain those flowing tears,
Let not Zelinda dread approaching years!
Those short'-liv'd charms, yt. like a tender flow'r,
Live thro' a day, & blossom but an hour;
To some kind swain thou lovely fair resign,
(And may that lot, propitious Gods, be mine!)
Who shall repay those charms, & bloom of youth
With sure returns of constancy & truth.
Beauties, like these, nor dread th' assault of Age,
Nor fear to cope with adverse fortune's rage.
But still from time a nobler grace receive,
Than youth imparts, or beauty knows to give.

I am, Sir, your sincere friend, & Servt.

R. Hurd.

P.S.

One piece of bad news I had almost forgot; Poo[r M]r. Sanderson[4] is ill of a

4 Nicholas Saunderson (1682–1739), Lucasian Professor of Mathematics at Cambridge. He was particularly distinguished for his ability as a teacher, most notable in his explication of the works of Newton. He was also regarded as a good mathematician in his own right, despite the loss of his sight in infancy. He died on 19 April. ('The Life and Character of the Author', [by John Saunderson], prefixed to Saunderson's *The Elements of Algebra, in Ten Books*, Cambridge, 2

mortification; all the Physicians have giv'n him over. Sad news for Cambridge.

I shall go into the country next week, where I shall expect a letter from you soon.[5]

2 To JOHN POTTER 7 AUGUST 1739

Text: MS NLW 12432E; unpublished.
Addressed: To/the Revd. Mr. Potter at Batcombe/near Brewton in/ Somersetshire/By London[1]
Postmarked: 10 AV

August 7th. 1739.

Dear Sir

What Virgil says of Liberty may without any Strain in the application be said of your letter –

> Sera, tamen respexit inertem
> Respexit tamen, et longo post tempore venit.[2]

You'll pardon the pedantry of this quotation, because I know no other words so proper to express your negligence of a friend, who waited <. . .> with impatience to hear from you. But there is a further reason for my quoting this passage; the word inertem happily enough expresses that life of indolence & ease, I here enjoy in the country. The mention of this last particular insensibly leads me to send you some acct. of the manner in wch. I spend those many solitary hours yt. fall to my share in this distant region. But before I enter upon that subject I must beg leave to premise, yt. I have chang'd my place of residence from Penford to Hatton-Grange near Shiffnall in Shropshire.[3] I was going to <paint> enumerate the beauties of this new seat, & say how much it excells my old one; I was preparing to tell, what streams murmur, what Birds warble, & what Landskips smile around me; I[a] had almost begun to describe, what a lovely appeara[nce] the corn-fields make, & what sweet variety of hill, & Dale this happy Spot affords. Incautious! to attempt a description of such prospects, as would require the utmost art of the inimitable Virgil! Imprudent, to think of expressing in rough, untuneful phrase those lulling murmers, & warbling notes, wch. even Handel would imitate in vain! Fool! not to know, yt. the Stars disdain to submitt to number, & yt. the charms of this sweet retirement are more numerous than the Stars! But where have I wander'd? I propos'd to send you some acct. of my life, & the manner in wch. I spend it. Scilicet – ea cura quietum te vexat![4] Nevertheless I shall

vols., 1740; Christopher Wordsworth, *Scholae Academicae: Some Account of the Studies at the English Universities in the Eighteenth Century*, Cambridge, 1877, pp. 66–70.)

5 RH left Emmanuel on 23 April. He returned briefly in May, but was then away again until 11 October. (*Residence Book*, TUT. 11.1.)

1 John Potter was curate at Batcombe, having been admitted to deacon's orders on 23 September 1738. (Somerset RO, *Clergy Subscription Book*, D/D/BS no. 9.)

2 Virgil, *Eclogues*, i. 27, 29.

3 RH's parents lived at Pendeford, Staffordshire; his brother at Hatton Grange, Shropshire.

4 Perhaps an allusion to *Aeneid*, iv. 379.
"scilicet is superis labor est, ea cura quietos
sollicitat".

a MS: "I I had".

for once be so impertinent as to tell you, yt. my life passes away here as agreeably, as can be expected in a place, where fate deprives me of the society of those friends, for whom I have the greatest value. Yes! the time has been – But the thought is tormenting: I'll dwell upon it no longer. I'll endeavour, if possible, to blot it out of my memory, & be, as tho' it had never been. What have I said? no: rather let me feed upon the pleasing remembrance of that fortunate season, & in the midst of ye. troubles of life comfort myself yt. I once was happy. But I am wandering again (excuse my roving thoughts!) & had almost forgot the chief design, & purpose of my letter; wch. was to tell you yt. my life here is spent betwixt Books, & musick. The former of wch. are my business, the other my diversion.[5] Among the many antient Gentlemen, who share my more serious Hours, there is none I visit more frequently than Virgil. His conversation is so engaging, his treat so elegant, & the whole man so perfectly <elegant> polite, yt. I am sure you cannot blame my choice. Sometimes you might find me seated with him upon the banks of the Mincius[6] & listning with the deepest Attention to the musick of an oaten reed, wch. he blows so harmoniously, yt. I never heard anything sweeter. As I wander with the good old Gentleman thro' his estate, I can't help taking notice of the number of his flocks, & the wonderful beauty of his prospects. In short, the whole country is inexpressibly charming, & can, I am sure, be nothing inferior to those fortunate Islands, wch. Mr. Horace makes so much noise about.[7] Sometimes he takes a pipe of a different make from the former, & plays a tune of the didactick kind, (thus he calls it, tho' I don't remember to have met with the term in musick before)[8] but in so charming a manner, yt. all the concerti's, sonatas, &c. of Corelli,[9] tho' play'd in the utmost perfection, are in comparison of it nauseous to the Ear. It is impossible to tell you, what unaffected graces, easy swellings, & natural shakes are every where with the utmost beauty scatter'd thro' his compositions of this sort. In a word, one day being more than ordinarily transported with so divine a piece of musick, I cry'd out in rapture, that it was impossible for anything to exceed it. Upon wch. the old gentleman smil'd at my ignorance, & being willing to convince me of my error, took up a trumpet, that lay near him, & fill'd it with such inimitable delicacy & sweetness, as well as shrillness, & majesty of tone, yt. it is not easy to conceive, how much it mov'd me.[10] Never before that time was I so affected with sounds; ev'ry note seem'd to breathe war & fury, & transported me into the midst of heroes, wounds, & deaths. The middle part of the tune, indeed especially the end of the first third part, was compos'd in something a softer strain; the notes were sometimes soft, sweet, & lulling, & excited images of love; then again they were short, quick, & interrupted, & rais'd ideas of passion, & disturbance of mind. At last, the strain was so sorrowful, & affecting, yt. it brought scenes of death to my view, & made me almost weep for imaginary afflictions. Thus in the various parts of this wonderful piece of musick, he by turns rais'd in me different passions, & emotions of soul. So that he seem'd to play upon me, as well as his trumpet. But in general, his notes

5 RH was beginning to read for his M.A. He may also have known that he was likely to be appointed a Sub-lecturer the following October and have been preparing for that. (*Emmanuel College Order Book*, COL. 14. 2, 1 October 1739.)

6 Mincius, now Mincio, a river of Venetia, flowing from the lake Benacus, and falling into the Po. Virgil was born on its banks. (See *Eclogues*, vii. 13; *Georgics*, iii. 15; *Aeneid*, x. 206.)

7 Horace, *Epodes*, xvi. 39–66. Horace describes the mythological "Islands of the Blest".

8 This expression has not been traced.

9 Arcangelo Corelli (1653–1713), the great violin player and composer.

10 RH refers to his reading of the *Aeneid*.

inspir'd me with martial courage; & hurry'd me into so many dangers, & military hazards, yt. at last methought I could have fac'd the Spaniards, & march'd with intrepidity among swords, & canons.

After this particular acct. of Virgil's musick, would you not be surpriz'd to hear, yt. I often chuse to exchange his harmony for a squealing tune upon my own fiddle? Would you think it possible, I should leave such caelestial sounds, "stridenti miserum stipulâ dispergere carmen"?[11] Yet such is the unaccountable love of variety! such the strange turn of man, yt. he often prefers the worse to the better! Hitherto I have talk'd of nothing but musick, it remains now to inform you, yt. I sometimes walk into those pleasant fields, mention'd above, & enjoy the beauties of nature; & sometimes entertain myself with the conversation of a friend, or the Parson of the Parish.[12] Thus, Sir, you see, I would willingly talk myself into a good opinion of yt. sort of life, wch. fate has allotted me. And tho' perhaps you cannot agree with me in commending such a life, as is here describ'd, you will at least joyn with me in this, (viz:) yt. it is prudence in me to commend it.

It would be a pleasure to converse with you much longer, would the limits of my paper permit, & were I not afraid of having tir'd you with the incoherent nonsense I have already scribbl'd. I shall therefore only lengthen my letter with one other line, wch. tells you, yt. I am, Dear Sir, your's sincerely, &c.

Richd. Hurd.

P.S.

I am sorry, after my late promise, to trouble you again, but I have a favour of consequence to ask of you, that I did not think of before. I must speak the next 5th. of Novr. Speech at Emman:,[13] & should be particularly oblig'd to you, if you would lend me yours for yt. purpose. I remember you had one, but never spoke it. If you can oblige me in this particular, please to let me know, as soon as possible. If you can, I could be glad, if you would send it to Sam: Stavely by the beginning of October, at wch. time I shall return to college.[14] I need not repeat my request; I dare say, you will do me this favour, if you can.

My Service to your Brother.[15 b]

11 Virgil, *Eclogues*, iii. 27. (. . . disperdere . . .)

12 Probably James Devey, who was rector of Beckbury and Kemberton, villages about two miles either side of Hatton Grange.

13 A special service and dinner took place in Emmanuel on 5 November commemorating the discovery and forestalling of the Gunpowder Plot. It is not known at what point the "speech" was given.

14 Samuel Staveley (c.1720–62) was a contemporary of RH's at Emmanuel and came from Dorset. The arrangement for him to bring Potter's speech to Cambridge was probably to save the cost of postage.

15 Robert Potter (1721–1804) had been admitted to Emmanuel on 19 July 1737, and came into residence in February 1738. He was made B.A. in February 1741 and returned to Somerset where he took orders a year later. In 1743 he replaced RH as curate of Reymerston, Norfolk (see *post* To Potter, 27 January 1743). He subsequently received further preferment in Norfolk, becoming a canon of Norwich in 1788. Potter published numerous poetical works and was the translator of Aeschylus, Euripides and Sophocles. (*Commons Accounts Book*, STE. 15. 9; *Alum. Cantab*; *D.N.B.*)

b "[?] Turcius Tourament" added at the foot of the letter in another hand.

3 To JOHN POTTER 11 NOVEMBER 1739

Text: MS NLW12432E; unpublished.
Addressed: To/the Revd. Mr. Potter at/Batcombe near Brewton/in Somersetshire/By London.
Postmarked: CAMBRIDGE 12 NO

Camb: Novr. 11th. 1739.

Dear Sir

I am now sate down to answer your two Letters. And as to ye. first, I cannot but observe yt. yr. passion for the happy Lady,[1] you mention'd, is perfectly honourable, & altogether worthy a Gentleman, & a Clergyman. There is certainly something in love of a very refin'd, & delicate nature, when founded upon virtue, & good sense, & under the guidance of reason. And I can't but rejoyce to find your's of yt. kind; a remarkable instance of wch. you have given in being so exact in a point, in wch. it had been excusable to have offended. As warm a lover with a less share of good sense would hardly have prevail'd upon himself to neglect the completion of his happiness, for the distant, possible difficulties, yt. might arise in the remainder of his life. But you have judg'd better, & giv'n the Lady at once a convincing proof of your affection & prudence. Pecuniam in loco negligere, maximum interdum est lucrum, says Master Terence,[2] & to neglect happiness in it's proper place is sometimes the best way of encreasing it. The case before us is, I think, one of yt. nature, & I don't in the least doubt but Providence will hereafter make up your loss with ample Interest. And that she may do this by bestowing upon you as large a living, as you can desire, in a short time is the sincere wish of one, who at present lies under the disgrace of a suspected friend. By the conclusion of this last sentence you'll easily <see> perceive I am passing from your former, to your late letter. And of wch. give me leave to say, yt. it is ye. only disagreeable one, I ever receiv'd from Mr. Potter. To suspect my friendship, & sincerity, to accuse me of coolness & indifference, & to represent me either as forgetfull, or designedly negligent of a friend, for whom I have often profess'd great esteem, & respect, these, Sir, are particulars that bear so hard upon my reputation, yt. I could not peruse your letter with that pleasure, & satisfaction, I was wont to do. It would be easy to enlarge upon this subject but as it is in itself very disagreeable I shall leave it; after having first observ'd to you, yt. you have prevented me in making any Apologies for my long Silence, by mentioning the fifth of November.[3] Nor will you be surpriz'd at it's engrossing the greatest part of my Time, if you consider the niceness of Em̃anuelian[a] Ears, & the slow Invention of their Orator. But of this enough; proceed we now to answer the remaining part of your letter. And here, if it had not the appearance of flattery, I should immediatly say, you might have spar'd yourself the trouble of proving to me, yt. the Country had not yet vitiated your taste of polite learning. The Style & manner in wch your letters are wrote, abundantly convince me, yt. the Revd. Mr.

1 It is not known to whom this refers, though later RH calls her "Hetty". (See *post* To Potter, 15 April 1742.) The relationship continued for some years, but probably did not end in marriage. (See Biography.)

2 *Adelphoe*, l. 216.

3 RH had to give a speech at an Emmanuel dinner on 5 November. (See preceding letter.)

a MS: "Em̃anueian".

Potter of Batcombe is not chang'd from Ds. Potter[4] of Em̃anuel, & yt. Pope, Prior, & Addison are not less your Favourites in Somersetshire, than formerly they were in the Seat of the Muses. The Pierian Spring has too delicate a flavour, ever to be exchang'd by any thinking man for a more ignoble liquor; & tho' his health, or some other extraordinary cause may oblige him to draw from a common, or insipid stream, yet his taste can never so far degenerate as to forget the delightful relish of the one, & prefer a less pure draught of the other. This, Sir, is the case of all those, who have ever tasted that sacred Spring; but you who have drunk largely of it, & whose Brain has been sober'd by copious draughts, can never forget the richness of it's flavour, or drink with pleasure of any other Stream.[5] If you will excuse the coarseness of the Comparison, I would venture to say, yt. the Mental Taste, I have hitherto been speaking of, is not very unlike the[b] corporeal Taste of those good Wives, who by degrees contract so great a love for Gin, yt. it is not in their power to lay it aside, & betake themselves to any other liquor. I have indeed beg'd pardon for the meaness of my Allusion; but upon a review it is so nauseous upon so delicate a Subject as that of Taste, yt. I am very sensible, if it meets with pardon, it deserves none. I have run directly counter to the practice of all polite writers, & instead of discovering a fineness of taste in my manner of talking upon that subject, have only convinc'd you, yt. I want that Taste I commend, & am entirely ignorant of the Elegancies of a genteel Style. We are told of Longinus, yt.

"His own Example strengthens all his Law"
And yt. "He is himself the great Sublime he draws."[6]

But it may be said as truly to my honour, yt. my own Example weakens my observations, & yt. I am just the reverse of that polite Taste I would describe. From what has been said it appears a dubious case, whether I am a proper judge of a fine taste, or no, or rather it evidently appears, I am not. The consequence of wch. is, yt. I pay no great complement to your letters, when I affirm them to be written in an elegant taste. But whatever may be determin'd of that point, this I can affirm, yt. they are always particularly agreeable to me, and always discover that taste wch. I have ever look'd upon to be a fine one. And therefore give me leave to say further, yt. you cannot oblige me more, than by writing very frequently; and (if I thought <it could> my letters could be as agreeable to you), I would faithfully promise, they should be as frequently answer'd by, Sir, your unjustly suspected Friend, & Humble Servt.

R. Hurd.

P.S.

I need say nothing of your Brother, because he writes by this post.

4 Dominus. Style used to denote scholars and B.A.s.

5 Pope, *An Essay on Criticism*, ll. 215–18.

A *little Learning* is a dang'rous Thing:
Drink deep, or taste not the *Pierian* Spring:
There *shallow Draughts* intoxicate the Brain,
And drinking *largely* sobers us again.

6 Pope, *ibid.* ll. 679–80.

Whose *own Example* strengthens all his Laws,
And *Is himself* that great *Sublime* he draws.

b MS: "at" deleted; "e" substituted.

4 To JOHN POTTER 2 DECEMBER 1739

Text: MS NLW12432E; unpublished.
Addressed: To/the Revd. Mr. Potter at Batcombe/near Brewton/in/ Somersetshire/By London.
Postmarked: CAMBRIDGE 3 DE

Camb: Em̃an: Decr. 2d. 1739.

Dear Sir

The lovely draught you give me of your <happy> sweet Country<s>, & the happiness of your retirement, awake in my mind all those agreeable rural Images, that had for some time slept there, conceal'd & unattended to. My imagination was fir'd at the lively portraiture, & flew with impatience o'er the flowry lawn, & cloud-invelopt Hill. Not a beauty in the Vale, you mention, escap'd my notice, not a single rill, <&> or flower, murmer'd, or bloom'd without my particular observation. Methought I was plac'd (such is the strange power of fancy!) upon the summit of that mountain, on whose side your house is, or really, or ideally situated. Methought too my friend stood near me, & with an obliging civility pointed out to my view the several charms of <of> ye. country, yt. lay before us. Every thing around us shone with unusual Splendor, & yet methought every thing receiv'd an additional beauty from the manner, in wch. your enlivening fancy represented them. The verdure of the landskip seem'd heighten'd by your remarks upon it, & the colours of the flowery plain borrow'd a more agreable lustre from the light, in wch. your imagination plac'd 'em. As we stood thus, happy in surveying distant beauties, I could not help thinking our situation <not much un> something like that of Aeneas, & Achates in Virgil, when plac'd upon the Hill, that commanded the walls of rising Carthage.[1] They too were friends; they too gaz'd with pleasure, & amazement upon the objects, yt. surrounded 'em. But here indeed lies some difference; they survey'd the imperfect works of art, we the finish'd works of Nature. They saw with wonder lofty temples arise, & shining palaces hang in air unfinish'd; we beheld the humble cottage of the vale, & a Parish-Church, or two built in the simplicity of better ages. In short, their prospect was possibly more noble, ours more beautiful. If you'll give me leave to mention another difference betwixt the circumstances of their situation, & ours, it should be this. That, whereas Aeneas saw the palace, & city of the amorous Queen, whose easy faith he beguil'd; my friend beheld with rapture the more humble habitation of the virtuous Lady, who is bless'd with <the> his return of as warm & virtuous a love. But to return from this digression. From the imaginary entertainment,[a] your letter afforded me, <you will> & the pleasure, with wch. I enlarge upon it, you will readily perceive how enamour'd I am with the Rural Scene. And indeed there is something in that kind of life so wonderfully entertaining to the imagination, & so agreeable to the turn of mind, I experience in myself, yt. were it not for the sake of better company, than is generally to be met with there, nothing but necessity could prevail upon me to leave it.

"Rura mihi, et rigui placeant in vallibus amnes,
Flumina amem, sylvasque inglorius"![2]

1 Virgil, *Aeneid*, i. 418–49.
2 Virgil, *Georgics*, ii. 485–6.

a MS: "entertaiment".

From this quotation, & the romantick air, that runs thro' this whole letter, you'll be apt to look upon me in the light, you would a young [P]oet, whose Fancy loves to indulge itself in rural Images, & wantonly roves thro' all the gayeties of the Spring. Or else you'll regard me as a youthful lover, whose head is fill'd with shady walks, & smiling plains; who loves to wander in the gloomy grove, & languish it in painted meadows, <&> or on the banks of purling streams. And this weakness you'll be more inclin'd to wonder at in one, whose thoughts have been long <since> diverted from such objects, & confin'd to those of a quite different nature. 'Tis not the murmer of the fountain, or the colour of the rose, yt. has engag'd my meditation of late years; but the reason, why sound was communicated from the one, & why reflected light blush'd in the other. Reasoning, & Philosophy (those known enemies to the excursions, & rovings of fancy) have been so much my employment of late, yt. I must add, you may justly wonder to find this weakness (for so I fear you'll call it) still remaining with me. But how will that wonder be encreas'd, when you hear yt. I am actually fool enough to turn Poet, & yt. I have indulg'd myself in writing upon the most copious, & fanciful subject in nature, viz: a country life? But such <is> was the influence of rural beauties, & the charms of my late habitation in Shropshire,[3] yt. I could not help throwing out upon paper some wild, & hasty conceptions, wch. offer'd themselves upon that delightful, but puerile subject. A Specimen of this I intend to give you in my next, & if that [h]as the good fortune not to displease you, may possibly in some future letter give it you all. I shall only add in this place, 1st. yt. I wrote in blank verse, being unwilling to fetter myself in Rhyme. I do not mention this with a design to intimate the excellency of it, but only to apologize for the want of Rhyme, wch. in a poem of this kind you may possibly expect.[4] If you should, all I can say, is, yt. the difficulty of the thing deterr'd me from such an undertaking. 2dly. I must desire you to look upon it, not as a descripti[on] of any particular country, but of the pleasures of the country in general. For tho' it was at first design'd to celebrate the charms of my rural Villa in Shropshire, yet as I proceeded in the work, I chose to admitt several particulars, yt. are of a more general nature, & not such as relate<d> only to the above-mention'd situation. Those passages, wch. are of a relative kind, will be easily distinguish'd from the rest; but to prevent all confusion, they shall be marked thus. ". . . This is all, yt. I think necessary to be mention'd by way of preface, I shall therefore in my next proceed to the poem itself without any further ceremony.

There is a great deal of news stirring in College now,[5] wch. I must for want of room leave to your Brother to give you an acct. of; wch. he will not fail to do, as soon as he

3 RH had been staying with his brother at Hatton Grange over the summer.

4 The influence of Dryden and Pope and the predominance of the rhyming couplet had, for a time, displaced blank verse as a generally used medium for poetry.

5 There were a number of elections taking place at this time: two were of Fellows (29 November and 4 December) and one was of an undergraduate to a scholarship (29 November). (*Emmanuel College Order Book*, COL. 14. 2.) The following perhaps significant entry also appears in the Order Book: "Nov. 23. 1739. Agreed that any Person, who shall discover any Woman of ill fame conceal'd in any Chamber in ye College wth. ye knowledge of ye Person in whose Chamber She is, shall be intituled to 5 Guineas Reward to be paid by the Master upon such Conviction as shall be satisfactory to the Master & Fellows or ye major Part of them."

receives a letter from you. You may possibly think it a little unkind to leave you in suspense thus, but you see it cannot be avoided. I am, Dear Sir, your Faithful friend, & Servt.

R. Hurd.

P.S.

Your Brother desires his love to you.
I have not hear'd from Hudson this age.[6]

5 To JOHN POTTER 13 JANUARY 1740

Text: MS NLW12432E; unpublished.
Addressed: To/the Revd. Mr. Potter at Batcombe/near Brewton in Somersetshire/By London
Postmarked: CAMBRIDGE 14 IA

Camb: Jan: 13th. 1739

Dear Sir

After what I have said in my last, I shall immediatly proceed to the case in hand without any further ceremony. Only, just give me leave to tell you, yt. I should have done it sooner, had not illness prevented me.

A VIEW[a]
of the beauties of the Country, particularly those of Hatton-Grange,
in Shropshire.

"Rura mihi, et rigui placeant in vallibus amnes.
Flumina amem, sylvasque inglorius" ! – Virg.
"Fortunatus et ille, Deos qui novit agrestes,
Panaque Sylvanumque patrem, Nymphasque sorores." Idem.[1]

Soon as the Morn her purple Couch forsakes
Fresh-rising, beauteous, & with orient pearl,
And blushing roses strows the Eastern sky,
Wakeful I start from Slumber's sweet repose,
And willing quit the downy bed to breathe
A Among the pleasant Villages & farms,
And taste the fragrance of the Morning Air.
Yet not alone, two Nymphs of fairest grace,
And sweetest aspect on my steps await,
Self-pleasing Chearfulness, with smiling face,
And rosy Health, with youthful Beauty crown'd.
Attended thus, I bend my early way,
Where Chance conducts, or fairest prospect charms;

A Milton.[2]

6 Robert Hudson (?1720–85), an exact contemporary of RH's at Emmanuel. He had taken his B.A. in 1738, was ordained deacon in March 1739, and was now living at Wherstead in Suffolk. (*Alum. Cantab.*)

1 Virgil, *Georgics*, ii. 485–6, 493–4. (. . . agrestis,) (. . . Silvanumque senem . . .)
2 *Paradise Lost*, ix. 448.

a Written in very large lower case letters.

Delights around sollicit ev'ry sense,
Each sense awaken'd with the fresh delight
Sweet recreation tastes, & rapture high.
  Aloft in Air the Lark with early Song,
And sweetest Mattin greets the op'ning day;
Not half so sweet the labour'd Strain, yt. lulls
To downy Sleep some Asiatick prince,
Or Eastern Monarch, whose nice ears disus'd
To the rude Musick of a manly voice,
Drink in with ecstacy the softer notes,
That flow soft-trilling from an Eunuch's tongue.
Not half so sweet Italian Airs, or thine
O! Farinelli,[3] on whose tuneful Strain
The British Theatre with rapture hung,
Nor wonder'd to behold the Temple left
For the soft Musick of a foreign Song.
  Yet not the Air alone with joyous notes
Resounds harmonious, ev'ry peopl'd bush
Breaks forth in singing, & with social song
Joyns the full concert, yt. the Country rings
With joy, & gladness spreads o'er all the plain.
A   Charm'd with the artless musick of the grove
I walk attentive o'er the flow'ry lawn;
Yet not unmindful of the various charms
That with soft lure attract the wand'ring eye.
B   "Far to the west a Mountain rears it's head
"Stately & <vast> huge, as the vast Appennine,
"Or tow'ring Alps; the Trav'ler with surprize
"Sees dusky Clouds & floating vapours rest
"In midway hov'ring, all the top sublime
"Obscur'd, & scarce in brightest sunshine view'd.
C "Two other Mountains on the left ascend
"More distant, but of size less eminent,
"As blueish clouds they seem, whose azure sides
"With circling border part th'expanse of Heav'n,
"And Earth's wide surface. O'er th'extended plain
"Lie groves, vales, meadows, forests interpos'd,
"In verdant Mantle dresst; & smiling <flow'rs> fields,
"Whose wavy surface nods with future Harvests;
"The fertile Valleys stand so thick with corn

A Leg. Pleas'd.
B the Wrekin.[4]
C The Clay-Hills in Shropshire.

3 Carlo Broschi Farinelli, the most famous castrato singer of his day. He was born in 1705, and made his first visit to England in 1734. The following anecdote has been recorded as an indication of his popularity: "The excessive fondness which the nobility discovered for this person . . . indicated little less than infatuation; their bounty was prodigality, and their applause adoration. 'One God, one Farinelli!' will be long remembered of a lady of distinction, who, being charmed with a particular passage in one of his songs, uttered aloud from the boxes that impious exclamation". (Stephen Jones, *A New Biographical Dictionary*, Second Edition, Corrected: With considerable Additions and Improvements, 1796.)

4 The Wrekin is a high hill with a fort, near Shrewsbury.

"They laugh, & sing.[5] A prospect fair & large!
"Such not the curious Eye from far surveys
"From Caucasus's amazing height, or thine,
"O! Gogmagog,[6] tho' Athens grace the Scene
"Magnificent, & Royal temples strike
"The wondring Eye. O! for the sacred Muse
"That fir'd whilere the Mantuan Shepherd's breast,
"To sing in lovely phrase, & aptest v[er]se[b]
"Th'unnumber'd flocks, yt. o'er the mo[u]ntains rove
"Whit'ning the cover'd plain; & lowing [h]erds
"That might in comely form, & stature vye,
"Io, with thee, tho' once a lovely fac[e],
"And by a God for am'rous purpose chang'd.
"Not fam'd Arcadia's vales did erst ab[ou]nd
"With flocks more num'rous, or with he[rd]s more fair.
Next would I paint the beauties of [t]he plain,
Blossoms & flow'rs of various colour m[i]xt
In elegant confusion. Such their h[ue],
The happiest pencil would in vain attem[p]t;
In Raphael's draught such colours neve[r] shone,
Ne'er grew such flowers in his faires[t] piece.
Their fragrance such, fresh odours [fi]ll the Skies,
Breathing perfume, sweet as the spic[y] Gale
Of Arab's coast, an incense fit for Heav'n!
But ah! my Muse in vain the lovely theme
Fearless pursues; so sweet a Scene disdains
The poor description of my humble thought,
And only is in Milton's verse express'd,
Where Paradise is open'd to our view,
Profuse of bliss, a wilderness of sweets.
Tantum.

The Marks you see prefix'd to each line in the Paragraph, beginning with "Far to the &c. denote, yt. the particulars contain'd therein are peculiar to Hatton, or at least remarkably famous there. And the same must be understood, wherever they appear. Tho', if I mistake not, something like this was observ'd in my last. I could not send you the whole in one letter on acct. of it's length. Besides I have often observ'd, yt. upon <one of> our exceeding days I have been able to manage two halfs, when a whole Mince-pye would have surfeited me.[7] Something like this will, I presume, hold good also with respect to the Mental taste & appetite. And I am in great hopes yt. this tedious string of verses will meet with a tolerable easy digestion, when 'tis thus divided into two Messes, tho' I have good reason to believe it must have been loath'd in one. If this allusion to Mince-pyes does not please you, consider 'tis Xstmas time, & on yt. acct. at least excuse it. To conclude, I have here sent you a specimen of the Poem, I

5 *Psalms*, lxv. 13.

6 The higher of two hills about three miles south east of Cambridge.

7 Exceeding days were days on which extra dishes were allowed at dinner in college. There were nine such occasions each year at Emmanuel: New Year's Day, Twelfth Night, Candlemas Day, Easter Sunday, Whitsunday, 29 May, 1 November (the College Michaelmas feast), 5 November and Christmas Day.

b MS badly creased obscuring parts of words down to "spic[y] Gale".

promis'd you; if you don't dislike this, the remainder shall be sent [y]ou in my next. There are indeed in[c] this part many particulars, yt. might be much mended, would [b]usiness, & health at present give me leave to set about [. . .][d] very many, yt. must give offe[nc]e to an unprejudic'd reader. However <with all it's> [. . .] sent it you with all it's faults [. . .] to your known candour, & humanity.

I am, Sr., your's most sincerely

R. Hurd.

6 To JOHN POTTER 17 FEBRUARY 1740

Text: MS NLW 12432E; unpublished.
Addressed: To/the Revd. Mr. Potter at Batcombe/near Brewton in/ Somersetshire/By London

Camb. Feb. 17th. 1739–40.

Dear Sir

I am extremely oblig'd to you for your Poem upon shooting. The pleasure, the perusal of it gave me, was much greater than I could have expected from a Poem upon an art, of wch. I am neither skill'd, nor studious. But 'tis not the subject, but the manner of treating it, wch. recommends a Performance in Poetry. And when the subject has nothing in itself fit to strike the Fancy in a very extraordinary manner, the most delicate touches of the master's hand are requisite to make it please. To say more upon this Subject, would ill become that familiarity, wch. is betwixt us. I shall therefore only add, yt. I think myself very happy in setting your pen on work; & shall be the less sollicitous about the many faults, wch. I have good reason to think you'll find in my mean performance, since it has been the means of procuring a very beautiful one from yourself. This I must confess was one view I had in entering upon such a design; & I hope as you have begun, you will proceed to oblige me in yt. way pretty frequently. I shall not prolong my preface with tedious Apologies for the remainder of the Poem, I promis'd you, but give it you as it is, without form, or ceremony.

Continu'd.

O! more than fortunate the Village-Swain
That wanders o'er these happy plains, to cull
The choicest blooms, or count his straggling sheep.
How sweet his Slumbers in the cooling shade
At noontide's sultry hour! Him, nor the mad,
Discordant din of hellish war alarms;
Nor from the mossy couch the hideous Snake
With dreadful hiss awakes.[1] Not so the Swain
In Latian Realms, & sad Calabria's woods
Sleeps undisturb'd, & safe enjoys the grove.
Oft to some shady bank, where flow'rs invite,

c MS: "on" changed to "in".
d The rest of the letter is very torn and creased.

1 From here to "Cruel to execute." RH is paraphrasing Virgil, *Georgics*, iii. 425–39.

Or his lost Lambkin crops the tender food,
Repairs the Swain; the shady Bank admires,
The fragrant Sweets, & sleep-inviting gloom:
Nor long admires, e'er to the flowry bed
His weary limbs th'incautious Shepherd trusts.
There lost in sleep, & easy dreams awhile
Secure he lies: perhaps in fancy'd form
His Amaryllis rises to his view,
And to his am'rous tale with kinder look,
Or lessen'd fury listens.[a] When anon
Scorch'd with the Summer's heat, & mad with thirst
Darts forth a Serpent, many a sinuous maze
Of burnish'd gold convolving; on he drags
His speckl'd train, & now with breast erect
And crest sublime, shoots forth his forky tongue,
(Tremendous, as the triple Bolt of Jove)
And rolls around his fiery eyes, yt. cast
A dreadful Glare, to thee, unhappy Swain,
Threatning destruction<s> nor his threats delays
Cruel to execute. The wounded Swain
With shudd'ring horror pale, & eyes aghast
Starts from the fatal Couch; alass! too late,
The baleful Pest spreads o'er th'infected veins,
And Death in poison stops the vital tide.
  But where in verse digressive roves the muse
Advent'rous? to the flowry seats return,
There paint the beauties of the verdant lawn
Glist'ring with dewy pearls. Soon as the Sun
Fresh-rising glitters o'er the eastern wave,
And gilds the Wrekin, cloud-aspiring Hill;
Ten thousand Spangles deck the shining plain,
And hang resplendent from the dewy Thorn.
Not brighter Stones in India's Mountains glow,
The Nurse of Gems! Nor in Lucinda's Hair
At Ball magnificent, or splendid court
Trembles the Emerald green, or Di'mond bright
With blaze more sparkling, or a fiercer ray.
O! cheap magnificence of nature's works!
Not all the costly pride of Eastern Kings,
Or thine, o! Solomon, could e'er devise
(Tho' her exhausted mines sad India mourn'd,
And Ophir's mountains open'd all their stores)[2]
A pavement in more gorgeous splendor dresst,
Than that on wch., (sad impotence of pride!)
Crawls the slow Worm, & much detested Snake.
  "The silver beauties of the mazy brook,
"That gently winds thro' fair Hattonia's meads,[3]

2 An unidentified territory, famed in the *Old Testament* for its fine gold, possibly in S.E. Arabia. (See I Kings 9. 26–8.)

3 The land around Hatton Grange where RH's brother John lived.

a MS: "listnens".

"It's wondrous Source, & fertilizing Stream
"I next prepare to sing. O! all ye powrs,
"Who haunt the Stream, unlock your watry <. . .> Stores,
"And thro' your inmost cells, recesses sweet!
"Conduct a Muse, yt. with advent'rous wing<s>
"Attempts to soar, & in fit numbers tell
"Your sacred Haunts, by other Bards unsung.
"Far on the Utmost Limit of the plain
"Descends a path, by human footstep scarce
"Distinguish'd: Such the horror of the place,
"The vulgar[A] led by superstitious[b] fear,
"And coward Ignorance, have feign'd the way
"To shades of Erebus & gate of Hell.
"Idle suspicion! to far other shades
"Descends the happy Passage. On each side
"The parted Vale retreats, & forms between
"A Bottom large, & fair, capacious Bed
"Of waters! Here the liquid Mirror stands
"Fixt as the stable plain, inspiring thought
"And Meditation, to the busy Soul
"Grateful retirement! O'er the lake profound
"Impending Oaks their aged Arms extend
"Looking Tranquillity. And antient rocks
"With creeping Moss, & mantling Ivy hung
"Shoot forth their craggy tops, as they would meet,
"Threat'ning sad ruin. Hence with silent course
"Steals a slow Stream, but soon with headlong fall
"Down rugged Rocks rolls rapid. Till anon
"Lost in the distant plain with gentler course
"O'er golden Sands the happy waters flow
"In various folds, & turns of artful round
"Sweet-winding thro' the mead; as loth to quit
"The much-lov'd plain, & visit other seats.
"So smooth it's gentle course, as if to rest
"And quiet sleep retir'd; save what small sound
"And murmur soft, as hum of distant Bees,
"Or Zephyr's lowest whisper, from the Stream
"Is hear'd, soft-bubbling o'er the pebbl'd way.
"To troubl'd minds sweet Harmony! So clear
"It's amber <Stream> wave, the smallest sand appears
"In clearest Light reveal'd. The musing Swain
"Spies rustling Oziers tremble in the flood,
"And Birds among the waving boughs unfurl
"Their painted plumes, & flutter in the <. . .> wave.
"The flow'rs, yt. on it's smiling border grow,
"In the fair brook a milder lustre shed
"And bloom more lovely in the colour'd Stream.
"Not yt. the Current smooth alone delights

A The path, here mention'd, leads to a pool call'd by the common people thereabouts, "Hell-Pool".

b MS: "supersitious".

"Or wave translucent; higher honours far
"Wait the rich Stream, along the smiling vale
"Shedding sweet Influence. On either Bank
"Herb, flower, plant in gay confusion mixt
"Spring lovely, & with particolour'd robe
"Bedeck the plain. Less pleasing to the sight
"The fulgent Vest by mimick art inwove
"With gilded flow'rs, & many a bloomy Spray,
"On day of nuptials, or high festival
"Worn[c] by illustrious maids: the Eye from far
"Haply descrys not, but the painted flow'rs
"On near approach sees lifeless, & with nature
"Perceives how impotent the strife of Art.
"With such superior Beauty smiles the mead
"Profuse of living sweets. The tender herb
"Rises luxuriant, to the grazing ox
"Grateful repast! nor wants he large recruit:
"How much is cropp'd in length of Summer's day,[A]
"In one short night the fatning streams restore.
O! had the Mantuan Swain (of Mortal Bards
Discreetest, wisest, virtuousest, best)
Had he his Flocks along thy fertile banks
Tended, or tun'd his past'ral[d] reed, thy Stream
Had not in vale obscure now dragg'd along
It's humid train ignobly, had not stray'd
A nameless Rivulet, unknown to fame.
Thyself, a Mincius, then hadst proudly flow'd,
And run for ever in immortal Song.
But now to night, & long oblivion doom'd
In silence rolls thy lovely stream along.
Nor more avails my Muse with mimick voice
Hoarse-screaming, than the tuneful Swans among
On fam'd Cayster's stream the babbling Goose.[5]
For me sufficient, yt. in humble strains
First on thy Banks I tun'd the slender reed,
And in the silent shade inglorious sung
A painted Meadow, & a purling Stream.

[A] Virgil's Georg. B.2. L.201.[4]

You see now by the tedious length of this Scroll, yt. the politick reason mention'd in my last was not the only, (tho' the chief) cause of my dividing it into two parcels. It was the diversion of a few leisure hours in the finest Season of ye. year, & in one of the

[4] *Georgics*, ii. 201–2.
"et quantum longis carpent armenta diebus
exigua tantum gelidus ros nocte reponet".

[5] Probably an allusion to Virgil, *Eclogues*, ix. 32–6, where Lycidas compares himself, as a poet, to a goose among melodious swans. The Cayster was the name of a river in Asia which, according to the poets, was much frequented by swans.

[c] MS: ? "e" deleted; "n" substituted.

[d] MS: "past'rral".

finest Countries, I ever yet saw. If it affords you but half the entertainment, & amusement it did me in composing it, I shall think myself very happy by thus contributing to your diversion. When I say the composing[e] it gave me much pleasure, mistake not that for an Encomium upon my own Work. This I am so far from designing, yt. I am very sensible, both the subject & manner of treating it will seem very trite, & mean in the eyes of a much worse Critick, than he, into whose hands I am going to deliver 'em. But there is something so exquisitely pleasant in the nature of the Ideas, of wch. this Poem consists, that, however[f] coarsely handl'd, they must please <. . .> at least their own Parent. To detain you no longer, they must speak for themselves. I can only say in their behalf that they were intended for your amusement, & <written> yt. they are ye. product of a Muse, <yt> who is, together with her <. . .> Master, your most sincere Friend & Servt. <. . .>

Parnassia.

P.S.

Your Brother desires Service &c.

Sam: Stavely (whom I trouble with the Carriage of this,) will I believe bring your Plate along with him.[6]

7 To JOHN POTTER — 27 APRIL 1740

Text: MS NLW 12432E; unpublished.
Addressed: To/the Revd. Mr. Potter at Batcombe/near Brewton/in Somersetshire./By London
Postmarked: CAMBRIDGE 28 AP

Camb: April 27th. 1740.

Dear Sir

Your friendly, genteel Letter deserv'd a much speedier Answer, than it has had the fortune to meet with. To excuse myself in this matter, I shall only say, that Business, & a slight Illness or two have so necessarily engag'd my time since the receipt of yours, that it was not in my power to do it sooner. I could be larger upon this head, but that I have ever look'd upon it as a most ridiculous practice among intimate friends to waste in formal Apologies that time & paper, wch. is much better employ'd in freer, & more material conversation. Only give me leave to say further, yt. nothing, but necessity, can at any time make me defer writing to one of my oldest, faithfullest, politest, & most ingenious Friends. This & a great deal more I ought in justice to say, did I intend to imitate that Style of compliment, & ceremony, in wch. your last address'd me. But as you cannot but be sure of my good opinion, & esteem, so I think it unnecessary to tell you so. As to the favourable reception, my Poetical Trifle met with at Batcombe, I look upon it as a singular instance of your respect for me, & for anything I compose;

6 This was probably the Sudbury Plate awarded each year at Emmanuel to the "best commencing Bachelor". Potter was awarded the Plate after the results of the B.A. examinations in February 1738. He had been placed in the second class of honour, the "senior optime". (*College Register*, COL. 9. 1. (A).)

e MS: "ition of" deleted; "ing" substituted.

f MS: "howevever".

but cannot from thence draw many conclusions in favour of your Judgment: But on the contrary, should be apt to suspect the weakness & depravity of it, had I not been convinc'd by numberless other Instances, that your judgment is at least equal to your sin[cer]ity, & respect for me; & did I not know to what cause the present seeming weakness of it is to be ascrib'd. 'Tis enough for me, if it serv'd to amuse a few vacant moments, when entertainments of a higher kind began to weary your spirits, or indisposition should render such reliefs in a manner necessary. Thus a foolish, & stupid Pamphlet shall sometimes please, when a more sensible & ingenious author lies unopen'd; & ev'n a silly & insignificant conversation is sometimes agreeable, when we should have crept on slowly, & painfully thro' a Page of the admir'd Locke, or Newton. This then is the main end & use I would propose in my letters, especially Poetical ones, & if they attain that, I am satisfy'd. And here I cannot but congratulate myself, (tho' I know not whether I have not done so upon a former occasion) in having set to work by my little Poetical performances a much better Muse than my own. I consider myself in this case as a <little> small, & in itself inconsiderable weight, or Spring, in a Clock, or other such Mechanical Engine, wch. yet by it's own little pow'r knows to communicate motion to some great & nobler part, & put the whole machine into a beautiful & regular motion. This reflection I am led into from the very ingenious Character, you sent me in your last, wch. from the name of the person characteris'd, I shall term AVARO.[a] 'Tis in itself an uncommon as well as humorous Character, & wrote in a Style proportionably[b] comical & entertaining. There is much ease & spirit in the expression, & 'tis a good deal in the taste of Swift, or the most free, & humorous parts of Prior. I could say a good deal of the unexpected turn not only of Avaro's life, but of your Poem towards the close, & of the remark you make upon it in the last line (wch. gives the whole all the air & spirit of a good Epigram, & leaves us quite satisfy'd, & compleatly entertain'd) but that I am afraid of offending by too minute an admiration of particulars. Thus far with regard to you & myself; what if we now make room for a third Person? 'Tis Gould:[1] Of whom I can only say, what you have, that he has not wrote to me a long time. I cannot imagine the reason of it, not being sensible of having offer'd the least affront, <. . .> or of having treated him with any the least disrespect. And here I cannot but take an opportunity of observing how distant friendships grow every day less glowing & intense, & (as I would perhaps say, were I writing in verse) <insensibly> like the northern lights insensibly decay, till after a few struggles, & forc'd, interrupted flashes, they at last die away into obscurity, & confusion. This reflection would give me great uneasiness, was I not sensible, that I am now addressing myself to one of those friends, whose heat (to carry on the allusion from the element of fire) is not like that of the northern Aurora transient, & fading, but like that of the Sun vigorous, & lasting. And that, tho' business, & such like necessary occurrences may sometimes seem for a while to obscure it's splendor, & damp<s> it's heat, (as that luminous Body is, you know, sometimes intercepted from our sight by clouds, or such like intervening bodies) it

1 William Gould was an exact contemporary of John Potter at Emmanuel. He had graduated B.A. in 1738, and was ordained deacon in the same year. In 1741 he was made an M.A. and two years after was ordained priest to become vicar of Hoxne in Suffolk. (See *post* To Potter, 11 October 1743.) He held this living until his death in 1772. (*Alum. Cantab.*) For further description of him, see *post* To Potter, 15 February 1741.

a Written in very large lower case letters.
b MS: "proportiably".

will nevertheless at last shine forth in all it's warmth, & beauty, & instead of being weaken'd draw strength, & splendor from such interruptions. I know from the nature & circumstances of this long, tedious allusion (for such all long Allusions must be) that I can only be look'd upon as the Earth, or some other revolving Planet, whose heat as well as light must therefore want much of your's. But here it may however be consider'd, that the little heat <&> or light, wch. the Earth enjoys, is not less durable, & constant, than that of the Sun, & yt. it is capable of being still greater by a nearer or more intense application of that noble Luminary. Of all that has here been said the Sum is this. I shall always endeavour to make out in sincerity & constancy what I want in perfections of any other kind; And that frequent conversation with you will be a means of <giving> supplying me with that light, & heat, wch. I want. But to drop the Allusion (for tis high time) & proceed: I cannot but remark further in this place, that the correspondence wch. is betwixt us, has been kept up with more spirit, & vigour, than perhaps betwixt any other of our old Acquaintance. And tho' 'tis now two years since I had the happiness of conversing with you in Person, yet I cannot find that our respect & esteem for each other is at all lessen'd, or abated. Whether this may not proceed from a similitude of taste & manners, or <from any> some other cause of the like nature, I shall not here enquire, but methinks this is no bad omen of <our> the constancy of our future friendship; but rather seems to promise that an Acquaintance hitherto carried on with so much vigour, & success is calculated for a longer time, than University friendships generally last. That this may be the case of our's (if agreeable to you) is the hearty wish of your sincere, & Affectionate Friend

R. Hurd.

P.S.

Having now spent 7 or 8 Months in Cambridge I begin to think of changing the Scene & <repairing> retiring into Shropshire, where I shall expect your next.[2] Direct [to] me as usual, & let me hear from you in a fortnight, or 3 Week's time at mo[st,] for then I hope to be in the Country at Hatton-Grange. Till then I scarcely know where I shall be myself, much less can I direct you where to find me.

Your Brother is well, & at your Service. When Rob Hudson was here we talk'd much of our friends, & particularly you, & drank your Health, whenever we met over a glass of wine, or a Bowl of Punch.

Your's once more

R. H.

Endorsed by Potter: "Ans: June: 2d".

2 RH had been in residence since the beginning of October 1739. He left college in the second week of May. (*Commons Accounts Book*, STE. 15. 8.)

8 To JOHN POTTER [JUNE/JULY 1740][1]

Text: MS NLW 12432E; unpublished.
Addressed: To/the Revd. Mr. Potter at Batcombe/near Brewton in/ Somersetshire/By London
Postmarked: [SHIFNALL]

Beginning.

Strange! how the Love of Poetry can spread
And propogate it's Rage from Head to Head!
Soon as I saw thy brilliant Humour shine,
Live thro' each Page, & sparkle in each Line,
My eager Soul soon knew to catch the flame,
The same my passion, were my pow'r the same.
But with vain toil the lab'ring Muse essays
With easy wit to grace her sprightly Lays;
In vain from thee would learn the pleasing Art
To charm the fancy, & improve the Heart;
To paint the wretch, who dying never dy'd,
And him, who bore a crooked Soul & Side.
Yet to the last why so severe? Thy wit,
His body spar'd, his mind had blameless hit.
The follies of the mind ourselves create,
Just then the Recompence of Scorn <of> or hate.
The Body's[a] Marks far other Treatment claim,
Faultless ourselves, from Heavn's high hand they came.
This fault alone your last fair Poem knows,
And this one fault an honest Critick shews.
In all things else sense, humour, wit prevail,
And ev'ry grace adorns the easy tale.
  Go! (since to *sport*[b] thy merry Muse inclines,
And with Hibernian Swift to *hit*[c] the times)
Beat ev'ry thicket, start the fluttring game,
At Folly's mark the[d] certain Arrow aim! –
– See! to the mark thy certain Arrow flies,
At ev'ry shot some fav'rite folly dies! –
To thee this Counsel. – To myself belong
Some humbler Subject, & some softer Song.

1 This letter can be dated to the summer of 1740 partly on the basis of the handwriting, and partly on the following internal evidence. In the first paragraph of his verse RH criticises Potter for his satire on bodily ugliness; in the following letter he compliments him on his equable acceptance of criticism, and continues a discussion on whether "deformed" souls are more likely to be found in deformed bodies than in sound ones. Secondly, RH suggests that Potter might write a poem on the "change of manners in the countryside"; again, in the next letter there is a reference back to this in the postscript.

a MS: "Body's" written over "Bodies".
b Written in large lower case letters.
c Written in large lower case letters.
d MS: "the" written over "thy".

My artless Muse knows not to sneer the Age,
And fears to combat with Satyric rage.
*Come then, ye gentle, inoffensive Themes,
Ye whisp'ring Zephyrs, & ye purling Streams!
With softest sounds smooth ev'ry liquid line!
And all ye Graces, in my numbers shine!
O! <as> while along the flowry path I stray,
May no rude Censure interrupt my way!
Still let the Muse in soft description rove,
Deck out the painted Lawn, or [verd]ant Grove,
[?Streak] the gay Tulip, pai[nt the] blushing Rose,
[?And] all the Sweets of op['ning Sp]ring disclose!
This soft employment suits my [? am]'rous frame,
And innocent of censure, who can blame?
Yet should some Squire swoln out with Beef & Beer,
Possess'd of full – six hundred pounds a year,
Who ne'er to Church for very spite repairs,
And hates his Parson, as he hates his pray'rs;
Who knows no letters, & to know none cares;
Herds all the day with wiser Brutes, his Dogs,
And snores all night supinely, as his hogs;
Dreams not, or if he dreams, like Jowler, views
A hare, starts eager, opens, & pursues;
Laughs loud, jests coarsely, if he jests at all,
And lives the booby Lord of some old Hall –
Should such a monster chance to come abroad,
(Avert the Omen, Heav'ns!) & cross my Road,
At him one thirsty Shaft should freely fly
Flung with full force, & sing along the Sky.
And o! if ever I deserv'd thy care,
Now, now Apollo grant the pious pray'r!
Drive the sure weapon with relentless hate
Full in his bloted Paunch, or brainless pate,
Down sink the Brute unwieldy on the Ground! –
– Hark! the fields tremble, & the woods resound.
Yes, this one Brute of all, the Country gives,
This, sacred to my hate & fury lives.
Safe all ye rest! – Pass unmolested by!
No Past'ral Scribe so innocent, as I.
Yet could I sing like you, or knew to bite,
There still is Room for Poetry & wit.
The rural Scene, in these unhappy Days,
How chang'd from that, wch. charms in Virgil's Lays!
Then love, & Innocence to shades retir'd;
Each modest Nymph her honest Swain admir'd,
And each Swain lov'd, by modest beauty fir'd.
The peaceful Slumber, stranger to the Great,
Shed all her blessings on the calm retreat;
Not in sear'd Fancy's guilty Visions thrown
O'er the proud Palace or the gilded Throne,
But soft, & pure with healing Wing o'erspread
The straw-clad Cottage in the silent Shade.
Man then had Peace: the Soul, serenely gay,

Knew not a thought, that fear'd the face of Day;
But each, unconscious of the die of Art,
Thro' honest Sounds ran spotless <of> fm. the Heart.
Not so with us; (whom may we now believe?)
[The] Swain can flatter, & the Nymph deceive,
[Scan]dal & fraud well-pleas'd to shades resort,
[And] haunt alike the Cottage & the Court.
[For] baser Pelf each Sterling Vertue's sold,
And the rude Age forgets to flow in Gold.
  Not but the Country boasts some blessings still,
The peaceful Grotto & the purling Rill;
The spreading Oak still casts a grateful Shade;
The Breeze still whispers & still smiles the Mead.
Nature, unchang'd, retains the Art to please,
With her still dwells Health, Liberty, & Ease.
  O! to the rural Scene then let me fly,
Seize the glad hour, & feel the guiltless Joy!
Quit, for the peaceful pleasures of the plain,
Fame's flatt'ring Breath, & fortune's gilded Train;
In life's low Vale, far from the pride of Pow'r,
Easy & free enjoy the coming Hour,
Nor anxious ask, of Nature's charms possesst,
What Monarch rules, or Minister's caresst!
  Not that the lazy years should useless die,
Or in rude, rustick Sports unheeded fly,
While Virgil's Italy so fair appears,
Fresh in full Bloom, thro' such a length of years,
Or thine, accomplish'd Addison, remains,
Thy Classick Mountains, & Poetick Plains;[2]
And Windsor Groves (such Pope's enchanting Tongue) }
Like those "of Eden, vanish'd now so long, }
Live in Description, & look green in Song."[3] }
  With joys, like these, be all my moments blesst,
  And thou, great George, or Walpole, take ye. rest!

Thus far, dear Sir, I have hobbl'd on in Rhyme; & considering the difficulty of the roads, & the badness of my Hackney, methinks I am got a good way of my Journey. 'Tis therefore the more disagreeable to be oblig'd to walk the rest of it; & yet such is my misfortune, yt. if I would see the end of it, I must ev'n do so. In short, Sir, to speak plain English, I am quite us'd with rhyming, & must therefore descend to Prose. Besides upon a review of this poetical Epistle, (or what else you may please to call it) I find I have been acting the part of those, who are humourously enough said to talk a great deal, & say nothing. In order therefore to explain myself, I must come to plainer language. What I would say then, is this: Both the Style, & manner, you have us'd in those little poetical performances I have been favour'd with, shew you well qualify'd for sneering the follies, & inconsistencies of mankind. I would therefore advise you to

2 *A Letter from Italy, To the Right Honourable Charles, Lord Halifax. By Mr. Joseph Addison. 1701. Together with the Mourning Muse of Alexis . . . By Mr. Congreve.* 1695, 1709, ll. 11–12.
"Poetick Fields encompass me around,
And still I seem to tread on Classick Ground".

3 *Windsor-Forest*, 1713, ll. 7–8.

proceed in that kind of writing; it will prove an elegant, & useful employment to yourself, & to me (for you cannot oblige me more than by giving me a sight of what[ever] you do in this, or any other kind of composition) a most agre[able] Amusement. I have in the latter part of these Verses hi[nted] a subject to you, wch., I can't but think, would please, if d[ressed] up in your language. The change of manners in the country[side,] or if that be too grave a theme, their little oddnesses (pardon [the] word!) & rusticities &c, would furnish out a very humourous [&] diverting draught in Poetry, & seem admirably fitted for the burlesque way of writing. As to myself (for you importune me I find, to do something in the same way) I am very serious in what I say above. I am by no means qualify'd for that kind of Poetry; it requires a peculiar taste & happiness of Expression, wch. I am very sensible I am not possess'd of. If I pretend to do anything in Poetry, it must be upon more low & trifling Subjects, such as I have sometimes troubl'd you with. (For yt. I think such subjects trifling is evident from the very turn & run of those verses a[bove,] wherein I make mention of them; See this mark * above.) But even there I am [?conscious] how unable I am to compose anything, that can deserve those kind Eulogiums, you have formerly pass'd upon some of my performances of that kind. What I have further to say is only to beg pardon for the freedom I have taken in censuring the last copy of Verses, you oblig'd me with. Indeed, if I was not as well assur'd of your good nature, & good Sense, as a Man, as I am of your qualifications, as a Scholar, it might seem a pretty bold step in me to pass so free a censure. But as nothing is more the aversion of a wise man, than flattery in a friend, so nothing is more agreable to him than an honest, & undissembl'd freedom, wch. prompts him at all times to speak his mind, & to blame, or commend with openess, & sincerity. In short, I am so little apprehensive of your resenting the freedom, I have taken, yt. I am pretty sure nothing could recommend me more to your esteem. And I can have no other view in dwelling thus long upon such a subject, than to excite you to follow my example. I now put into your hands a Scroll in wch. if you'll be as free with me, as I have been with you, I doubt not <but you'll> but you'll find a multitude of faults, instead of one. Use then that freedom, & be assur'd, Sir, the more faults you find in it, the more I shall be pleas'd, & the more I shall be oblig'd to you. For by this means I shall grow wiser, & ev'ry fault, you take notice of, will bring instruction along with it. Which is what I value much more than the kind Eulogiums of an obliging Friend, even <. . .> if they were just; certainly then more than any praises you can bestow upon my compositions, wch., I am afraid, rather call for your censure.

I am, Dear Sir, your most sincere Friend, & Servt.

R. Hurd.

P.S.

Pray write to me as soon as possible. – My Service to your Brother.

N.B.

I had wrote sooner, but have been constantly engag'd in Company for this fortnight or three Weeks.

9 To JOHN POTTER 28 AUGUST 1740

Text: MS NLW 12432E; unpublished.
Addressed: To/the Revd. Mr. Potter at Batcombe/near Brewton in/ Somersetshire/By London.
Postmarked: SHIFNALL 1 SE

Hatton-Grange August 28th. 1740

Dear Sir

Call me deceitful, flatterer, what you will, I must tell you, yt. your late letter has giv'n me a very high, & in one respect a new Idea of your worth, & accomplishments. I have indeed, ever since I had the happiness of being acquainted with Mr. Potter, always observ'd something in him, wch. I could not but like, & esteem. But your late behaviour has rais'd yt. esteem to a pitch, I think, it never reach'd before. To have a fine taste for learning, & to excel in the Sciences, are, it must be own'd, very valuable qualifications, & such as deserve our approbation, & regard; but in the present Age those qualifications are not extremely uncommon. But to receive admonition from a friend,[1] to renounce our own Opinions for his, & in consequence of that acknowledge our own mistakes, & weaknesses, & to do all this with Temper, Candour, & Politeness, this, Sir, is such an instance of ingenuity, humility, & good sense, as is very rarely to be met with in Men of Letters. The "monitoribus asper"[2] wch. Horace takes into his Character of a young Man, is applicable in a particular manner to Men of learnng, especially the younger sort of them. They are always impatient of Contradiction, & always affronted at the freedom of an honest friend, that pretends to charge 'em with an Error, however insignificant, & trifling. But hold: I correct myself, I should not have said always: there is One, I find, (e tot millibus unus) who knows better, & is convinc'd yt. the honest freedom, I mention'd above, is the greatest advantage of friendship. This I the more wonder at in the present case, as you had a very fair opportunity of defending yourself; (for, while Men have anything to urge in their own behalf, they are seldom us'd to admit the objections of another.) Indeed the reasoning,[a] you just hint at, <for your former> wch occasion'd your mistake, has in it something so subtle, if not solid, yt. I think myself oblig'd to give it a particular Consideration. I shall begin with an observation in your favour; it has been suppos'd by Physiognomists, (& a late admir'd writer seems to be almost of the same opinion)[3] yt. different sorts of Souls require different sorts of bodies, & consequently according to their principles the most deform'd bodies are joyn'd to the most deform'd Souls. This at first sight seems to declare greatly in your favour, & authorize your Hypothesis, that Nature is careless in forming those bodies, wch. are design'd for crooked Souls, & therefore intends, they should both be despis'd. But, as I have no great Opinion of Physiognomy, & as in fact the case is often otherwise, & we often see fine Souls united to the most disagreeable bodies, I shall not <lay> much <stress upon> regard such reasonings. To come therefore to the point in hand; if, according to your Hypothesis, Nature foresaw the defects, & imperfections of the Souls of some men, & for that reason gave them deform'd bodies, I would beg leave to ask, why she was not

1 RH had criticised Potter for satirising bodily ugliness. (See preceding letter, n. 1).
2 *Ars Poetica*, l. 163.
3 Unidentified.

a MS: "reason" changed to "reasoning".

more impartial in her distributions, & why all Souls of yt. kind had not such bodies allotted them? If she design'd Deformity, as a just Object of Ridicule, 'tis plain the deform'd Man with a defective Soul must be much more ridiculous, & therefore miserable, than the well-shap'd Man with a Soul equally defective; tho' the former contributes no more to make himself defective than the latter. Nor can it be reply'd with reason, yt. there is the same inequality in the dispensations of Providence, & that therefore it is no more unreasonable for one of equal, mental, defects with another, to have greater corporeal ones, than for a man, equally vicious with another, to have more wealth, pow'r, or good fortune; this, Sir, I think, cannot be reply'd, since in the latter <course> case we have recourse to a future State in order to solve the inequality, wch., I presume, we shall hardly be allow'd to do in the former. For it seems pretty odd to say, that a reward will be giv'n hereafter to Deformity, or that a Man will be happy in the next life for being ugly in this. I would therefore suppose that Deformity of body is neither any just Object of Ridicule, nor was so intended by Nature, but that all who are equally perfect in their better part, ought to be equally valu'd, however they may differ in externals; & on the contrary, that all who are equally imperfect, are for the same reason equally despicable. I must own indeed, according to our present corrupt, & prejudic'd estimation of things, we are inclin'd to think beauty a very valuable gift; & indeed there is some Advantage in being Master of a well-turn'd Person with regard to our intercourse with Mankind. But then to ballance this, there is, as I may so speak, an Advantage in being ugly, wch. does not always happen to the handsome. For, I believe, it is an observation, that will generally hold, that bodily imperfections are attended with some perfections of an extraordinary nature, & yt. the latter sufficiently compensate for the former; & that beauty on the other hand receives some abatement of it's excellency from it's concomitant imperfections. I shall explain myself by giving some examples of both sorts: Ist. then a deformity or deficiency in one part of the body is generally attended with some extraordinary perfection in another, thus the late Dr. Sanderson, who was blind, & therefore so far deform'd, had his senses (not to insist upon his memory & reason) wonderfully acute.[4] 2dly. if the deformity is general, &, to borrow your expression, wanders over all the limbs, that imperfection is compensated by the greater perfection of the Soul. As an Instance of this I shall not produce Aesop, or any of the antient, deform'd, worthies, but shall confine myself, as in the former case, to our own times; such kind of examples being more convincing, than those of foreign extraction (excuse the harshness of the Metaphor) & an antient Date. Suppose then I should mention Mr. Pope, could you refuse to admit him as a wonderful instance of a fine Soul in a foul Body? Or again, should I put you in mind of Mr. Johnson, than whom I don't know a man more deform'd, must not you allow, that there is something in his Satire, call'd London, wch. bespeaks a Soul, that makes ample amends for the deformity of his body?[5] These, Sir, are very remarkable instances, but the observation will hold, tho perhaps in a less degree, in all other forms of ugliness; & I doubt not in the

4 Saunderson's sense of hearing was said to be so acute that "he could readily distinguish to the fifth Part of a Note"; and among other anecdotes told to illustrate his highly developed sense of touch, was the account of how he was once able to distinguish "in a Set of *Roman* Medals, the genuine from the false, though they had been counterfeited with such Exactness as to deceive a *Connoisseur*, who had judged by the Eye". ('The Life' of Nicholas Saunderson, prefixed to his *Elements of Algebra*, 1740.)

5 *London: a Poem, in Imitation of the Third Satire of Juvenal*, 1738.

least, but that Oldershaw himself, had he follow'd the bent of his genius, & had not been wanting to himself, had some latent qualifications, that might have made him famous in some method of life, or other.[6] I promis'd to give you, besides these examples of *Advantagious* Ugliness, some others of disadvantagious Beauty. But here I shall not instance in particulars, but refer you to the whole race of Beaus, & Belles in Great Britain for a proof of it; & I doubt not but you will find, in almost evry individual of that pretty Species, imperfections enough to lessen the merit of their charms, & that throw a kind of Shade o'er their dazzling beauties. Upon the whole therefore Nature seems to me to have taken care that the deform'd, even in our present, & corrupt judgment of things, should not be the objects of Ridicule; but then if we could but conquer our prejudices, & think justly, I am of Opinion, we should not look upon any kind of form, as ridiculous in itself; &, if you'll excuse a wild conjecture, we should perhaps in this imitate superior Beings, who, I would suppose, make no difference between the ugly, & the handsome, but look with the same complacency, (setting aside the different perfections of their minds) upon Thersites, & Achilles.

Having mention'd Thersites, it seems necessary to say something of Homer's description of him, since the practice & Authority of so great a Man may possibly be alledg'd in favour of that kind of writing.[7] 'Tis, if I remember right, very severe; so severe, yt. Mr. Addison is of opinion, yt. he design'd yt. spiteful picture for some of his Cotemporaries, that had perhaps affronted him.[8] But if so, I think, it makes but little for the Honour of the Prince of Poets (as some presume to call him) to revenge himself so mean a way, & be eloquent upon a Subject, on wch. the Hags of Drury Lane,[9] or the Ladies of the British Fishery would probably harangue with greater fluency, & Sharpness. But to overturn the Authority of this mighty Monarch of Parnassus, let us cast our Eyes upon one of his Brethren, who indeed is less haughty, & presuming, but stands full as high upon the Hill of Fame. You'll know by this introduction, yt. I mean the Humane, the wise, the inimitable Virgil; let us then examine into his Conduct upon a similar Occasion. Drances in the IIth. Aeneid is without doubt

6 Probably Francis Oldershaw, an undergraduate at Emmanuel, contemporary with RH and John Potter, but some years older than either. He had died in college in April. It is not known to what "deformity" or ugliness RH refers.

7 *Iliad*, ii. 211–22.

8 Addison suggests this in A *Discourse on Ancient and Modern Learning*, 1739, p. 3. "I don't question but *Homer*, who in the Diversity of his Characters has far excell'd all other Heroic Poets, had an Eye on some real Persons who were then living, in most of 'em. The Description of *Thersites* is so spiteful and particular, that I can't but think it one of his own, or his Country's Enemies in disguise."

9 Drury Lane had a bad reputation throughout the eighteenth century. A description of the area is given in an appeal made by the shopkeepers and traders of Covent Garden to the Westminster Sessions in 1730. They wrote that: "several persons of most notorious characters and infamously wicked lives and conversations have of late years taken up . . . their residence in the said parish. And that there are several streets and little courts, as Russell Street, Drury Lane, Crown Court and King's Court, and divers places within the said parish, and more particularly in the neighbourhood of Drury Lane, infested with such vile people; that there are frequent outcries in the night, fighting, robberies and all sorts of debauching committed by them all night long, to the great inquietude of his Majesty's good subjects . . ." (Middlesex County Records. Calendar of Sessions Books and Orders of Court, January 1729–30 to May 1732, ff. 105–6 (typescript of MS in BL); quoted in M. Dorothy George, *London Life in the Eighteenth Century*, 1966, pp. 92–3.)

intended as a despicable Character, perhaps the thought was originally taken from Homer; but how does he manage it? Not with taunts, & invectives upon his person, but his pride, insolence, & Cowardice; not a word of bodily deformities, wch. Virgil well knew were no proper Object of Ridicule, but a great deal about the Ventosâ linguâ, pedibusque fugacibus.[10] This one passage abundantly convinces me, yt. Virgil thought it wrong to object those defects ev'n to the most ridiculous Character, wch. it was not in his power to help, & with submission to all the Admirers of Homer, I would sooner rely upon the Judgment of the Roman, than the Practice of the Graecian Poet. Indeed there is something so ill-natur'd, & inhuman in this practice, yt. if no other reasons could be brought against it, I should think that alone sufficient to bring it into disrepute. For this reason I have been often greatly offended at a passage in Xenophon's History of Cyrus the Great, where he introduces his Hero, whom he proposes as a Pattern of Perfection, ridiculing an unhappy Stranger, that sat at table with him, on acct. of his deformity.[11] This is the more remarkable too, because his Hero is said to be φιλαν 'Θρωπότατος, & the Historian himself passes for a writer of Delicacy, & Politeness, nay, what is more, for a Man of Humanity, & sweetness of Temper. Besides this, the youth, he ridicul'd, was a Stranger, as was hinted above, & Cyrus was not then a Child, but a perfect Man, τελειὸς ἀνὴρ, as the Persians term those of an advanc'd age, & at the head of an Army in Media. I shall not enlarge upon particulars, but refer you to the passage itself, wch. you'll find about the middle of the second book of his Cyropaedia. All the inference I shall make from these Examples is, yt. 'tis no wonder, you should give into a practice, yt. is countenanc'd by two of the greatest Wits in Greece, & thought not unworthy the greatest Hero, yt. ever liv'd.

As I design'd this for a kind of Dissertation upon, or rather Apology for Ugliness, I have <hitherto> treated it in something a close, & serious way. I shall now, to alleviate the severity of my letter, (wch. has hitherto been more grave, than perhaps it should be), conclude this Topick with a humourous Story, I have somewhere hear'd, tho' I cannot now recollect where.

A Gentleman, (whom for Distinction's sake I shall call Cynthio,) <having> who had the Misfortune to have a pair of none of the handsomest legs, was one day in Company with several other Gentlemen, & one Lady, whose name, if you please, shall be Delicatessa. His Situation in the Company happen'd to be such, that his worst leg, (for there was a difference betwixt 'em) lay conceal'd under the Table, whereas the other did not fear to expose itself to all the Company. Delicatessa, upon a Rest in Conversation, chancing to fix her Eyes upon it, was so delighted with the novelty, & oddness, of the Object, that she could not help breaking out into a pretty loud laugh upon the Occasion. And being ask'd, what it was, diverted her so highly, She protested with half a laugh, she had never seen so delicate a Leg in her life, as Mr. Cynthio's. The Gentleman, not at all confounded at the unexpected freedom of her Ridicule, told her, yt. notwithstanding the queer Shape of the leg, that had had the unhappiness to offend her, he durst venture a small Wager with her, there was one of a much queerer in the Company. Delicatessa being a good deal surpriz'd at his proposal, & fearing the Company should suspect the <stateliness> shape & beauty of her own Supporters, & being besides, tis thought, a little conscious of some small defects in

10 *Aeneid*, xi. 390 (ventosa in lingua . . .). The speech made against Drances, to which RH refers, runs from l. 376–444.

11 *Cyropaedia*, II. ii. 28–31.

point of Symmetry, & Proportion (perhaps <She had> there was something of the *Elephant* in the make of 'em) answer'd with a good deal of smartness, & confusion, that she could not tell what he meant by talking at that rate, but yt. for her <her> part she was sure she had no such a leg as that. Excuse me, Madam, says Cynthio, I could not presume to mean so; but here's a leg under the Table, wch., I believe, has escap'd your Observation, yt. I would not fear to say, quite exceeds it. Upon wch. he immediatly produces the other leg, wch. was indeed turn'd, & twisted in <a superior greater> very great perfection. At the sight of wch. Delicatessa's resentment soften'd into a Smile, the whole Company fell a laughing, & Cynthio himself with a great deal of good Humour, joyn'd the Chorus.

Whatever you may think of the freedom of Delicatessa, I dare say, you'll be pleas'd with the behaviour of Cynthio, who dar'd to be ugly in so nice a juncture, & as it were boast of his deformities, tho' <a Lady was> in the presence of a Lady.

After this rambling, & tedious letter, I have but just room enough to thank you for your ingenious version of the pretty Story in the Spectator; Of wch. I will say no more, than that it pleases me very much, since, was I to say anything more, I might run the hazard of being suspected for a flatterer.

Before I conclude I have one favour to beg of you. You know, last year I importun'd you for the 5th. of Nov.'s Speech thro' a mistake. I am now going to beg the favour of you to lend me your Thorp's, it being my turn to be *Orator* this year upon that Occasion.[12] If you think your Brother will have occasion for it, I will promise you not to turn Plagiary, only it will be of service to me to have a view of it, since I am at present quite unacquainted with the Subject, & usual manner of treating it. If the expence is not much, I would desire you to send it me in a packet, but if the carriage will rise high, you may send it by your Brother to Cambridge, when he goes thither.

I have only to say further, that I would beg of you to write to me soon; & give me leave to recommend this letter to you as a model for the length of yours; for I always estimate your letters by the quantity of Paper they take up.

I am, dear Sir, your's most sincerely, & heartily

R. Hurd.

P.S.

My Service to your Brother.

I wait impatiently for your Rural Portrait.[13]

Endorsed by R.H.: "NB. A Single Sheet."
In Potter's hand: "Pd: 7ber; 7th".

12 For RH's request for the 5 November speech, see *ante* To Potter, 7 August 1739. The Thorpe oration was a speech in Latin, which had to be given each year by one of the five Thorpe scholars on 24 November, the day of the Commemoration of Emmanuel's Founder and Benefactors. ('Thorpe Exhibitions' in *Statuta Collegii Emman: apud Cantabrigiam*, COL. 18. 4.) The Thorpe Scholarship accounts record a payment of 10s. to "Ds Hurd for his Speech". (SCH. 1. 17.) John Potter, though a Thorpe scholar, did not give a speech the previous year; payment was made to "Ds. Bunbury". (*Ibid.*)

13 See RH's request in the preceding letter.

10 To JOHN POTTER 14 DECEMBER 1740

Text: MS NLW 12432E; unpublished.
Addressed: To/the Revd. Mr. Potter at Batcombe/near Brewton/in/ Somersetshire./By London.
Postmarked: CAMBRIDGE 15 DE

Camb: Decr. 14th. 1740.

Dear Sir

I am at last at leisure to answer your very obliging Letter, and shall begin with thanking you for the Speech, you sent me by yr. Brother.[1] It was indeed, as you foretold, of no great Service to me, & therefore I cannot easily admit your Excuse for not sending your own. "But it was incorrect, it seems, & therefore you would not let me see it". Surely my friend has no great opinion of my Candour & sincerity to make such an Apology. Incorrectnesses I could have pardon'd, nay perhaps should have admir'd. For there is something beautiful in the negligent, careless strokes of a Master hand.

As to your Brother's Affair, twas a great plea[su]re to me to find it so soon, & so happily compos'd.[2] <Your Brother,> I suppose, He has wrote you an acct. of Particulars, & therefore you'll not expect me to enlarge upon it. Only this I must add by way of reply to your request, yt. had there been any occasion for my advice in the Affair, he should not have wanted it.

Sometime ago he favour'd me with the sight of a small paper of verses, written upon Dr. Bowden, that shew'd a truer spirit, & a more masterly turn of Expression, yn. I had before observ'd in his Compositions.[3] Upon a perusal of them, I gave him the commendation, he deserv'd, & encourag'd him to employ his more vacant hours in amusements of that kind. In doing which I had this double view; Ist. by putting him upon composition to improve his taste in polite learning; & in the next place, to draw him off by that means from some little indiscretions to wch. the fire & vivacity of his youth & temper are in his more disengag'd moments apt to subject him. For the same reason I have sometimes recommended to him books of polite Amusement, yt. were new to him, & have endeavour'd to mix 'em so with his other Studies, as to give no interruption to them. If you think me right in this, I shall receive some pleasure, as I have contributed something to his instruction & interest, and as it may serve to shew my respect for you both.

The Amatorial Differences, you mention'd, surpriz'd me a good deal, & are a fresh instance of the hypocrisy, & falseness, of that Sex, we call fair.[4] I faithfully believe an Elegant, but idle Writer of the Augustan Age, when he tells us from his own Experience,

1 See preceding letter.

2 It is not known to what "Affair" RH is referring.

3 Samuel Bowden, (fl. 1732–61) a physician at Frome, Somerset. He was the author of two volumes of *Poetical Essays*, published in 1733 and 1735. A manuscript copy of Robert Potter's verse on Bowden was still in existence in 1936. It had been preserved in a collection of papers originally belonging to Cox Macro, to whom, perhaps, Potter had presented it as a curiosity (it was one of his very earliest works). It cannot now be traced. (*Historical Manuscripts Commission*, Twelfth Report, Appendix, Part IX, p. 160.)

4 This was the beginning of the difficulties Potter was to experience in his relationship with "Hetty". They were to continue for some time.

Difficile est subitò longum deponere amorem.

Catullus.[5]

But at the same time I don't doubt but my friend will remember, that to conquer such difficulties is the business, & province of noble & exalted Spirits. The Occasion must necessarily suggest to you the first Scene of Terence's Eunuch,[6] & perhaps some other passages of the <like> like Nature in Heathen Literature. And indeed such helps may be of no inconsiderable Service to a delicate, & refin'd Imagination. But besides these, I doubt not but Mr. Potter will draw such assistances from Religion (for the importance of the Occasion will, I think, justify so serious a thought) and Philosophy, as will enable him to bear up against all the Attacks of love, & Beauty, of faithlessness & Woman. Methinks I see you after a certain intermediate Space, post aliquod spatium requiemque furoris,[7] look back with transport upon the dangers, & difficulties, you've <escap'd> past. 'Twill be something like a review of the many hazards, & fortunate escapes, wch. an old traveller entertains himself with, upon retiring to a calm retreat, far from the uncertain & delusive Deep, that had once tempted him to leave the Shore, & had been the Scene of his former disquietudes, & misfortunes. It were easy to carry on this Allusion much further, had not Horace already done it with infinitely greater beauty in one of his Odes.[8] All yt. I shall add is an hearty wish, yt. you may happily escape the present Shipwreck; & may soon be in a condition to testify your happiness, not by suspending, but sending a votive Table to your well-Wisher. In short, you must give me leave once more to press you to undertake your promis'd work. And this I am the more inclin'd to do at present, as it will serve for an agreeable amusement in your present troubles, &, I hope, call off[a] your thoughts from yt. Object, that had hitherto engross'd but too many of them.

What you mention about coming to Camb: next Summer gives me great pleasure, & I will, if possible, contrive to meet you there. Hudson has not wrote to me since April; & Gõld has been silent a long time. Whether I am to be favour'd with a continuance of their correspondence, is a secret, wch. my undiscerning[b] Eyes cannot at present pry into. But however that be, it will be some comfort to me, yt. I have not yet lost the regard, & correspondence of my good friend of Somerset.

From the whole tenor of this Epistle you'll easily perceive I am in a very idle humour, & have wrote with Ease. This indeed generally passes for a complement, but then it must be such ease, as proceeds from art, not Chance: The latter of wch. has been the chief governess in this Scroll. Notwithstanding wch. believe me to be (what I am not the less on acct. of my present disposition) your most Sincere Friend, & Servt.

R. Hurd.

P.S.

Your B: is yours: write very soon.

[5] Catullus, lxxvi. 13. (. . . longum subito . . .)

[6] Terence's *Eunuch* opens with Phaedria, a young gentleman, deliberating on whether or not to go to Thais, his mistress; because although she had asked to see him that morning, the previous night when he had gone to see her, he had been refused admittance to the house.

[7] Perhaps an allusion to Virgil, *Aeneid*, iv. 433.

"tempus inane peto, requiem spatiumque furori".

[8] Probably a reference to Horace, *Odes*, II. vi.

[a] MS: "call of".

[b] MS: "prophetick" deleted; "discerning" substituted.

11 To JOHN POTTER 18 JANUARY 1741

Text: MS NLW 12432E; unpublished.
Addressed: To/the Revd. Mr. Potter at Batcombe/near Brewton in/ Somersetshire./By London.
Postmarked: CAMBRIDGE 19 IA

Camb: Jan. 18th. 1740.

Dear Sir!

Your last very obliging letter was the more agreeable, as it contain'd <some> some news relating to yourself, wch. I was not displeas'd to hear. You'll be surpriz'd to find, I mean yt. part that describes your passionate, & resentful disposition; & wch. instead of perfection argues only weakness in my Friend. No Beauty could be more happy in spying a blemish, or irregular feature in a Rival, nor Poet in meeting with a low thought, or slovenly expression in the sonnets of a rhyming Antagonist, than he, who has so often call'd himself your most sincere friend, was in finding so great a foible, as pride, amid your many excellencies & perfections. Go on, & cherish this weakness; 'tis honourable, 'tis glorious, 'tis lovely. 'Tis a weakness of yt. peculiar sort, as ends in manliness, & strength, and is necessarily productive of satisfaction & ease. Hitherto you'll think me very paradoxical: 'tis fit I should explain myself. Your pride, & resentment with regard to that lady, with whose perfidious name I shall not trouble you, are weaknesses, I was pleas'd to hear you own yourself guilty of. The pleasure was perhaps equal, but far unlike in it's cause, to that of a jealous Beauty, or Poet in the cases, mention'd above. 'Tis ambition, & vanity, yt. actuate them; 'tis friendship, & benevolence, that occasion a satisfaction, & pleasure in me. Not that I deny myself to have some regard to my own interest, and advantage: For thus I reason; <with my self.> "If this foolish girl can once be driven out of his head & heart, he will have more <plea> leisure to converse with his friends. His letters will be then more frequent, & the efforts of his geni<o>us more strong & vigourous. Future Rusticks will not lie so long upon his hands, & "give th<e>' expecting reader cause to curse
So long delay."
So yt. you see I am concern'd in this affair, as well as you.

What you say of the uneasiness & commotion, rais'd in the Soul by the eager contest of such opposite passions, as anger, love, & resentment, puts me in mind of that fine distress, in wch. we find Aeneas in the beginning of the 8th. Aeneid.[1] The comparison the Poet makes use of in order to illustrate this, is so remarkably beautiful, yt. I need not make any apology for transcribing it.

"Sicut aquae tremulum labris ubi lumen ahenis
Sole repercussum, aut radiantis imagine lunae,
Omnia pervolitat late loca, jamque sub auras
Erigitur, summique ferit laquearia tecti."[A]

You see I have made no scruple to compare you in this respect to one of the most amiable Heroes of Antiquity: (at least if we view him in the light, in wch. Virgil, the best of Painters has plac'd him) I wish I could as easily compleat the remaining part of

A If you wd. see this, or any other passage <well of> in Virgil, well translated, read Mr. Pitt.[2]

1 *Aeneid*, viii. 22–5.
2 Christopher Pitt (1699–1748) had published *The Aeneid of Virgil* translated into English, in two

the likeness, & draw <so fine> a picture of your distress in so fine a Simile. But this is presumption, even if it go no further than a wish. However, while I am writing this, an image occurs to me, wch. <if taken by> in the hands of a Master, <. . .> would be susceptible of all the grace & beauty, his art could bestow upon it. I need not observe to you, how few corporeal images there are, yt. with sufficient life, & beauty represent the various motions, & shiftings of the mind of man. That of Virgil, wch. I have just mention'd, is the most known, & perhaps the most lovely of any in the whole compass of Poetry. The image, I am going to present you with, is consider'd in itself extreamly agreeable, & I believe, quite new. At least I never yet saw it work'd into a comparison. In this respect therefore, it has the advantage ev'n of Virgil's, wch. has been imitated by a variety of hands. And whether it ben't as beautiful, as his, you will judge for yourself, when you've hear'd it.

Have you not seen <after> in a dewy morning, or after a gentle show'r, a tree full of leaves, & dew-drops hanging from each of 'em? & have you not <seen,> upon the rising of the Sun, or <the> it's breaking out from behind a cloud, seen every dew-drop converted into a gem, & the whole tree in one continu'd, lovely glow? And is there a finer image of the calm, bright sunshine of the mind than this? Suppose then a small wind should rise, & put into motion these watry splendors; can you conceive a more lively image of the violent tossings & perturbations of the mind, than what wd. arise from the quick dazling, & dancing of the rays of light, yt. stream from those quiv'ring globules? Sure there cannot be a more charming picture than this in all the wide regions of nature. At least that this is my opinion of the matter, you'll in some measure infer from my endeavouring to express it in numbers. Which, after having mention'd Virgil's, nothing but the wonderful beauty of the Image itself could excite me to do. It is drawn up in the form of a Simile, and has this additional disadvantage to it's other defects, yt. it waits upon you without any ceremony of introduction. 'Tis a little like the freedom of those impertinent visitors, that break in upon <you> us, without giving the least notice. However, to leave my candid friend to pardon it's faults, & make the application himself, it runs thus:

So, when the Sun, fresh-rising from the main,
Impearls the grass, & sparkles o'er the plain,
Stands a fair tree, all lovely to behold,
Hung round with Spangles, & bedrop'd with gold;
Steddy & soft the pendant glories beam,
Shine in fixt light, & shed a gentle gleam:
But, if a gale with softest motion heaves
In the still Boughs, & stirrs among the leaves,
The quiv'ring Branches cast a trembling light,
And a quick [lu]stre darts upon the Sight;
This way & yt. the flitting splendors fly,
Dance o'er the plain, & glitter to the Sky.

Odd enough the order & Succession of our Ideas! I began with expressing my satisfaction in hearing of your Aversion to the delusive fair, & congratulating you upon the prospect of your delivery from the worst sort of Slavery, & Subjection. And now I am insensibly got upon beautiful Images, the charms of nature, & Poetry. Tho'

volumes, in April 1740. (*Lond. Mag.*) He did not publish any other translations of Virgil's poetry.

upon second thoughts 'tis no wonder yt. Poetry should grow out of liberty, & yt. a freedom from Tyranny should naturally inspire pleasing thoughts, and agreeable meditations. You see I would fain entice you to throw off[a] the yoke of Slavery to <. . .> an unconstant woman, and at the same time do what I can to make you think I have been entertaining you in a very agreeable manner. But however I may have fail'd in the last, I would hope I have not been altogether unsuccessful in the former. Mr. Potter is, if I know him right, too prudent a man, to give way to a weakness, yt. would make greatly against his own interest, & happiness; and too respectful a friend to do anything, that would give uneasiness, & concern to his most sincere, and affectionate Friend & Servt.

R. Hurd.

P.S.

Your Brother is very well, & desires Service.

He has an Act upon his hands.[3] Write soon.

Endorsed by R.H.: "N.B. A Single Sheet".

12 To JAMES DEVEY 23 JANUARY 1741

Text: *Memoirs*, 6.

Emmanuel College, Cambridge, Jan. 23d, 1740.

Rev. Sir,

. . . As I write from a famous seat of learning, you will probably expect some news relating to the republic of letters. I shall therefore tell you that yesterday was published an answer to the third volume of The Moral Philosopher, by a gentleman of St. John's. 'Tis wrote a good deal in the taste and spirit of Bentley's Phileleutherus Lipsiensis, and is expected to be a good thing.[1] Dr. Delany's Life of David is a

3 "Keeping an Act" was a form of examination in Oxford and Cambridge, which continued until the nineteenth century. In Cambridge, the undergraduate being examined for the degree of B.A. had to present three theses in Latin and defend each against the arguments and objections of three opponents. Most undergraduates were expected to take part in these disputations several times, both as "Respondents" and as "Opponents". According to Christopher Wordsworth, the Moderators, i.e. the examiners, sent notice "on the second and subsequent Mondays in Lent Term to five students to 'keep their act' on the five first days beginning with that-day-fortnight". (Wordsworth, *Scholae Academicae*, p. 34.)

a MS: "of".

1 This was *The Ancient History of the Hebrews Vindicated: Or, Remarks on Part of the Third Volume of the Moral Philosopher*, By Theophanes Cantabrigiensis, Cambridge, 1741. It was a reply to Thomas Morgan, a Free-thinker, who had put forward the proposition, "Superstition and Tyranny inconsistent with Theocracy", in the third volume of his *Moral Philosopher*, published in 1740. Theophanes Cantabrigiensis was Samuel Squire (1713–66), then a Fellow of St John's, and later Bishop of St David's. Phileleutherus Lipsiensis was a pseudonym for Richard Bentley. Under it, amongst other things, he wrote *Remarks upon a Late Discourse of Free-Thinking*, 1713.

charming performance;[2] if you have not seen it, I am sure it will please you . . . I am, Sir, with service to Mrs. Devey and your son,[3] your most humble servant,

Richard Hurd.

13 To JOHN POTTER 15 FEBRUARY 1741

Text: MS NLW 12432E; unpublished.
Addressed: To/the Revd. Mr. Potter at Batcombe/near Brewton in/ Somersetshire./By London.
Postmarked: CAMBRIDGE 16 FE

Camb. Feb. 15th. 1740–41.

Dear Sir!

After sitting up pretty late last night, I find myself much indispos'd for Study this morning, & know not how to pass the intermediate hours betwixt this & Dinner more agreeably, than in writing to my Friend of Batcombe. And this I am the more inclin'd to do, as I have got a little news to tell you. On friday night last I went according to my weekly Custom to hear a concert of Musick at the Tons.[1] The Room was made very comfortable by a couple of good fires, & a considerable number of Candles. After a little chat among the Auditors, & a few preparatory flourishes among the performers, we were most elegantly entertain'd with a very fine Sonata. Whether Corelli's, Vivaldi's, or Geminiani's[2] is not very material to determine: 'tis enough yt. the musick was good, & we pleas'd. In the mean time two or three of us retir'd to a freer, & more disengag'd part of the Room, in order to listen with less interruption, & to make such remarks upon our entertainment, as persons of some whim, & little judgment usually throw out on those Occasions. 'Tis possible I might be blaming a very fine Adagio, or commending a wretched Allegro, or ill-plac'd Piano, when lo! a venerable form advanc'd! His Stature was of such a kind, as plainly spoke him to be none of the Descendants of Gog, & Magog. Should I allow him a yard & half, I should probably

2 Patrick Delany, *An Historical Account of the Life and Reign of David King of Israel*, 1740. Only the first volume of Delany's *Life of David* was published in 1740. (See RH's further comments on this part in To Devey, 14 March 1741.) The second and third volumes were advertised for sale in July 1742. (*Lond. Mag.*) These were even more enthusiastically spoken of by RH. (See *post* To Potter, 25 August 1742 and 8 October 1742.)

3 James Devey (c.1725–1809). Devey was admitted to Emmanuel in March 1741 and matriculated in 1742. In 1747 he was elected Fellow, and in 1766 he took over the college living of Stanground in Huntingdonshire, where he remained until his death. (*Alum. Cantab.*). Although he and RH came to know each other fairly well at Emmanuel, there seems not to have been any particular friendship between them.

1 The Tuns was one of four taverns licensed by the university, the others being the Rose, the Mitre, and the Hoop. (Edmund Carter, *The History of the County of Cambridge, From the earliest Account to the present Time*, Cambridge, 1753, p. 15.)

2 Francesco Geminiani (1687–1762) was an Italian violinist and composer. He was one of the foremost representatives of the school of Corelli, and had a great reputation as a virtuoso in England. He first came to London in 1714 and had lived there for some years. In the 1730s he had been in Dublin, but he returned to England in 1740, after George II had granted him a licence to print and publish his compositions for the next fourteen years. (*Grove's Dictionary of Music and Musicians*, ed. Eric Blom, 1966.)

seem too liberal in my Allotment. His countenance was one of the most grave, & manful I had seen, & by the length of Beard, yt. overshadow'd the greatest part of it, it had been easy to have mistaken him for Socrates, or some of the old Bearded Worthies. What still added to the gravity of his look, & deportment was the Clerk-colour'd Coat, he appear'd in. By all wch., & some other Symptons, wch. I forbear to enumerate, I soon knew him to be the little, grave Gentleman, known formerly by the name of Will: Gould. – I arose: we met: we complemented: we sat down: we chatted a good part of the Ev'ning. I invited him, & Sir Richd. Jenoure,[3] (who is now at Peter-house, & on whose Acct., I believe, he came down) to spend the following Ev'ning with me at Emmanuel. Accordingly they came, & we were tolerably merry. He talks of staying but a week with us, but I fancy he will at last resolve to stay here till the Commencement. For he has, it seems, no Cure upon his hands, & has some thoughts of going into Priest-Orders on Trinity Sunday next at Bugden.[4]

Thus much for news, wch. I have sent you, without his knowledge. Now, Sir, give me leave to answer your letter. The condition, you are in at present, seems distressful enough, I wish it lay in my power to relieve you. If I might give my Advice in the case, I would by all means put you upon bringing the matter to a conclusion with all possible Expedition. Make known your intentions to her immediatly; if she accepts the offer, 'tis well; if not, strive, nay force yourself to hate her mortally. The uncertain, & wav'ring state, you are now plac'd in, cannot but be very injurious to your peace, & interest. And either of them, particularly the first, is of too great value to be sacrific'd to the capricious Smiles of the most accomplish'd Fair <of> in Christendom.

As to your wishing, yt. you had push'd your interest in College, if yt. would have contributed to your greater happiness, I am very ready to joyn my wishes to yours. But that is what I greatly suspect: shake but that love off, & I think you have it in your power to be more happy in the Country, yn. you could be here. At least yt. these are my sentiments, you'll easily conclude, when I tell you, yt. I intend to leave College myself, as soon as ever 'tis convenient for me. The reasons, yt. have inclin'd me to make this resolution, I have neither room nor inclination to mention here. Perhaps some future letter may be charg'd with contents of that Nature. In the mean time I proceed to answer the Queries, mention'd in your Postscript.

What you may have hear'd of Mr. Pitt, does not, I dare say, exceed his merit. His Translation is, at least as far as I am able to judge of Poetical Translation, extremely spirited, delicate, & just. Scarce Pope himself equals him in the harmony and beauty of his versification. And those, who blame him for want of Spirit, & fire, have not, I believe, duly consider'd the closeness, & peculiar Spirit of the Original, wch. he

3 Richard Day Jenoure (1718–44) was a Fellow-commoner at Peterhouse, but had just been admitted at Lincoln's Inn (19 January). He had become fifth Baronet of Much Dunmow in Essex in 1739. (*Alum. Cantab.*) For Gould see *ante* To Potter, 27 April 1740, n. 1.

4 The Commencement was the first Tuesday in July and was the day on which degrees were conferred. (Edmund Carter, *The History of the University of Cambridge, From its Original, To the Year 1753*, 1753, p. 6.) Gould was in Cambridge to receive his M.A. and had his name put back on the college books from 1 July to 21 October. (*Commons Accounts Book*, STE. 15. 9.) He was not ordained until 1743. (*Alum. Cantab.*) Buckden (here Bugden) was the official residence of the Bishop of Lincoln; ordinations were frequently held there (or in churches in London) rather than in Lincoln cathedral. (Norman Sykes, *Church and State in England in the XVIIIth Century*, Cambridge, 1934, p. 97.)

translates.[5] I said peculiar Spirit, for yt. Virgil has[a] a great deal of Spirit in his works, nay as much Spirit, as a Poet ought to have, is what I must maintain against the assertions of any the greatest Criticks. But then yt. the Spirit, wch. appears in his works, is not of the same kind with yt. we meet with in Homer, is what I am always ready to own. And I can't help thinking, it is much for his honour, yt. it is not. Now they, who have form'd their taste of a poetical Spirit entirely upon Homer, will probably censure Mr. Pitt's Translation for being spiritless; but then it must be observ'd, yt. the same gentlemen would in all probability make the same Objection to Virgil himself. And if so, I believe you will agree with me, that their judgment is not much to be regarded. But to reply to your particular questions:

The Aeneid, wch. is all, I believe, Mr. Pitt intended to translate, is completed. It came out in 4to., & sold for about 20 Shill: 2. Vols. – But we expect very soon a new Edition of it in 12o.[6] – You will therefore, I imagine, chuse to wait till this Edition. In the mean time, yt. Mr. Pitt may administer some pleasure to you, let me recommend his Translation of Vida's Art of Poetry to you. If you have not seen it, I know, it must please you: 'tis a very thin Duodecimo, & will cost you 2, or 3 Shillings.[7]

Mr. Whiteheads Poem,[8] wch. 'tis probable you have seen before this, has had the good fortune to meet with a great many Criticks, that think it much too good a Poem to pass uncensur'd. May all his future performances displease 'em as much, and then, I am sure, they will please every body else. The following Passage,

('Tis powerful Reason holds the straighten'd Rein
While flutt'ring fancy to the distant Plain,
Sends a long look, & spreads her wings in vain)

has been objected to, because the Metaphor in the 1st. line was not continu'd thro' the other two. In answer to this objection I shall insert an alteration of the passage, <in order> wch. was made by a humorous fellow, in order to ridicule the trifling Objector. The metaphor not carried on? says he – no more it is, faith; how much better had it been thus!

5 In his life of Pitt, Johnson describes his translation of the *Aeneid* as one of the "two best translations that perhaps were ever produced by one nation of the same author". (The other translation was Dryden's.) However, he continued, if the translations were compared, "perhaps the result would be, that Dryden leads the reader forward by his general vigour and sprightliness, and Pitt often stops him to contemplate the excellence of a single couplet; that Dryden's faults are forgotten in the hurry of delight, and that Pitt's beauties are neglected in the languor of a cold and listless perusal; that Pitt pleases the criticks and Dryden the people; that Pitt is quoted, and Dryden read." (Johnson, *Prefaces, Biographical and Critical, to the Works of the English Poets*, 1779–81, viii. 5–7.)

6 This was published in 1743. The quarto volumes had come out in 1740, price one guinea. (*Lond. Mag.*)

7 Pitt's translation of Marcus H. Vida's *Art of Poetry* was published in duodecimo in 1725, price 2s. Johnson says of this translation, that it was distinguished both for its "general elegance", and for the way that Pitt had skilfully adapted "his numbers to the images expressed; a beauty which Vida has with great ardour enforced and exemplified." (*Prefaces*, viii. 3.)

8 William Whitehead, *The Danger of Writing Verse: An Epistle*, 1741.

a MS: "has" written over "had".

Tis pow'rful Reason holds the straighten'd Rein,
While PRANCING[b] Fancy to the distant plain,
Sends a long look, and COCKS HER TAIL[c] in vain. } Judicet lector.

I am, Dear Sir, your sincere Friend, & Servt.

R. Hurd.

P.S.

You know what I expect by answering your last so soon.
Your Brother desires Service &c.

Endorsed by RH: "N.B. A Single Sheet."

14 To JAMES DEVEY 14 MARCH 1741

Text: *Memoirs*, 6.

Cambridge, March 14, 1740–1.

. . . With regard to systems of logic, which you inquire after, it will perhaps surprise you to hear that we can hardly be said to use any at all. The study of logic is almost entirely laid aside in this university, and that of the mathematics taken up in its room.[1] It is looked upon as a maxim here, that a justness and accuracy in thinking and reasoning are better learned by a habit than by rules; and it is an observation founded upon long experience, that no men argue more closely and acutely than they who are well versed in mathematic learning, even though they are ignorant of the rules delivered by the great masters in that other science. Indeed, as our disputations in the schools are always carried on in syllogism, a small part of that study is still requisite;[2] but, as this is very easily learned from any system, we are not very curious in the choice of one. However, those that are generally made use of on this occasion are Le Clerc's and Dr. Watts's[3] . . .

I thank you, Sir, for your judicious remarks on the Life of David, and can't but admire the complaisant and genteel turn you give to my bad taste and wrong judgment of that author.[4] For both these I am justly chargeable with, if there are those superfine triflings and laboured overflowings of the sublime you speak of. Your sentiments, indeed, have great weight with me, and it must carry in it the appearance of much pertness and presumption to think of disputing the justness of them. However,

b Written in very large lower case letters.

c Written in very large lower case letters.

1 Mathematics was particularly strong in Cambridge at this time, due primarily to the influence of Newton, who had been a Fellow of Trinity. The spread and continuance of his influence, though, is said to have owed much to the excellent teaching of Nicholas Saunderson, Richard Laughton, a Fellow of Clare from 1686–1710, and William Whiston, also a Fellow of Clare from 1691, and Lucasian Professor from 1702–10. (See *ante* To Potter, 15 April 1739, nn. 3 and 4.)

2 RH refers to the keeping of Acts in the Senate House. (See *ante* To Potter, 18 January 1741, n. 3; and Wordsworth, *Scholae Academicae*, pp. 22–43.)

3 John Le Clerc, *Logica: sive, Ars Ratiocinandi*, 1692. Isaac Watts, *Logick: Or, The Right Use of Reason in the Enquiry after Truth*, 1725. These were standard textbooks in the first half of the eighteenth century.

4 RH had recommended Patrick Delany's *Life of David* in a previous letter. (See *ante* To Devey, 23 January 1741.)

with your leave, Sir, I will just mention one or two particulars that may serve, perhaps, if not to overcome your opinion, at least in some measure to excuse my own. I would flatter myself, then, that the reason of my differing from you in this case, is the viewing it in a light which perhaps did not immediately present itself to you. This I ascribe, not to my own penetration, but to the hints of others of much more learning and experience: 'tis in short this: 'tis probable you might expect to find it wrote according to the strict laws of history, and therefore containing only a plain narrative of the life and actions of David, collected from sacred writ. This expectation would be in some sort confirmed by the title-page, which, as I remember, calls it the History of the Life of David.[5] Considering it, therefore, in this light, it might very well seem affected and unnatural to insert so many disquisitions and conjectures, and to run out into digressions of almost a poetical nature.[6] But, if we look upon it (as I believe it was intended) as an essay or dissertation upon the life and actions of that hero, the particulars you blame are so far from being faults, that I dare say you'll think them beauties. This way of considering that performance will account not only for the manner but the style also in which 'tis wrote. In the character of an exact history the language is, perhaps, too florid, and savours too much of the sublime; but in that of an essay, 'tis, I conceive, otherwise; the diction must be spirited, and raised above the common pitch, to entertain and please.

You see, Sir, how impertinent we young lads are, and what trouble we give both ourselves and others, rather than own (what would perhaps better become us) that we are mistaken. But, notwithstanding this common failing of young men, if Mr. Devey, upon viewing the Life of David in this light, should still continue in his opinion, I shall be so far from standing out any longer against him, that I shall immediately embrace his sentiments, and endeavour to correct the error of my own judgment by submitting to a much better . . .

15 To JOHN POTTER — 22 MARCH 1741

Text: MS NLW 12432E; unpublished.
Addressed: To/the Revd. Mr. Potter at Batcombe/near Brewton in/ Somersetshire./By London
Postmarked: CAMBRIDGE 23 MR

Camb: March 22d, 1740–1.

Dear Sr,

'Tis now exactly ten o' clock, & the two intermediate hours betwixt this & twelve I shall devote to your Service. This is all the preface I shall use to introduce the following letter, wch., as far as I am able to foresee at so great a distance, will be a series of unconnected observations, on the several subjects that start up in my Imagination, without being at the pains of reducing 'em into any order. This you'll be inclin'd to think I do merely to indulge an idle humour, & to shift off all the little labour, yt. attends the observation of method. But what if I should maintain yt. a methodical, and as I wd. term it, a consequential Epistle is much easier to write, than

5 The title-page of the *Life of David* runs as follows: *An Historical Account of the Life and Reign of David King of Israel: Interspersed with Various Conjectures, Digressions, and Disquisitions.*

6 For such a digression, see *post* To Potter, 25 August 1742, n. 4.

one of an opposite stamp & character? Could you think me serious?, or wd. you not rather imagine I design'd to trifle with you, or at least to shew myself very singular & affected? And yet I must repeat it; a piece compos'd according to the nice Rules of order is the product of much less labour, than the irregular, &, as I may so speak, desultory Composition. You'll be apt to joyn with me in this, if you reflect yt. the Ideas of men easily & naturally run in a pretty regular Succession, & yt. therefore it can not be very difficult to throw them into an exact train, & series of words. To this I might add, yt. the dullest Heads are commonly the most methodical, & observant of order. Was I to give a reason of this, it should be, yt. they find yt. way of writing to be far the easiest. After a vain effort or two experience convinces 'em, how unable they are to fling out into a variety of new, or daring thoughts, & [they] therefore very wisely confine themselves to one strait, & beaten track. Thus it wd. require more force to guide the Earth in irregular wandrings thro' the caelestial Space, than is necessary to preserve it's motion, & keep up it's progressive state in it's own plain, & simple Path. A Body once in motion is by a small addition of force easily carried on in the same successive line; but calls for the application of an immense power to turn it here, or there at pleasure, & direct it's course thro' numberless by-ways, & unfrequented tracks. In short, (to descend from the figurative style) 'tis easy to follow the copy, set us in our own minds, & to write in order, since we generally think so; but a composition in the other way, as 'tis rather unnatural, will be difficult, & tho' judgment will perhaps have less to do, Invention will have much more. You see, Sr., what pains I take to clear myself from any imputation of Idleness, & to let you know what labour it costs me to write ill. Tho' after all, I believe, I must be oblig'd to recant, and drop the cause, I have hitherto been defending, since, notwithstanding what has been said, Mr. Potter, I am sure, can never persuade himself, yt. the author of this Scroll <took> had any trouble in writing it. – But for a Specimen or two of the unconnected manner! –

Your Brother tells me, he promis'd you, I should say something of our English Cicero.[1] He did not think, I suppose, how difficult a thing it wd. be to discharge a promise of that nature. Should I lay before you the remarks, our News papers have been stuff'd with lately? That wd. be trumpery: besides you must have seen 'em. Would you know the opinions of our Dons in Criticism? Alass! I fear, they are prompted either by Envy or Prejudice. Or wd. you have me deliver my own thoughts upon the matter? That must be conceit, & arrogance. Thus, you see, whatever way I turn myself, I am straiten'd with almost insuperable difficulties. As something however must be said upon the occasion, rather than teaze you with the trash of Party-Zealots, or expose the characters of others, I shall run the hazard of blotting my own reputation, & am resolv'd to bear the title of arrogant, & conceited, or what other name you shall think I deserve. And here, if I had not disclaim'd all method, I would for my greater ease, divide, what I have to offer upon this work, into two heads; the first of wch. may comprehend the matter, the latter the manner of it.

As to the matter, you must necessarily imagine it to be extreamly entertaining. The whole History comprizes all the most curious & interesting events, that fell out in the

1 Conyers Middleton (1683–1750). He had just published *The History of the Life of Marcus Tullius Cicero*, which was long regarded as a model of style. Middleton had held the post of Librarian at Cambridge University since 1721 and had a house in the city described by Thomas Gray as "the only easy Place one could find to converse in at Cambridge". (*Alum. Cantab.*; *Correspondence of Thomas Gray*, ed. Paget Toynbee and Leonard Whibley, 3 vols., Oxford, 1935, reprinted with Corrections and Additions by H.W. Starr, 1971, Letter 154.)

Roman State during the life of Cicero. The conspiracy of Catiline, the actions & tragical Death of Caesar, the proceedings of the triumvirate, & wars of Pompey make some part of this Work. In all this time great was the struggle between liberty & Tyranny; Rome was never fill'd with nobler & more exalted Spirits, than in this critical Period, nor do we anywhere meet with such a complication of intrigues, & interests carrying on, or so many memorable actions atchiev'd, as in those 60 years, yt. preceded the unhappy Death of Cicero.

The manner of it is this: The Dr. has divided his work into 12 Sections, all wch. conclude naturally with some remarkable change or pause in the life & actions of his Hero. The last Section is entirely taken up in giving us an acct. of his character & writings; both wch. he performs with ye. utmost accuracy & beauty. The Style is inimitably pure & delicate; there is a spirit of liberty breathes in ev'ry expression, equal to that, wch. inspir'd the great Orator, whose life he writes. 'Tis flowing, sprightly, strong, & full; he every where discovers a most happy Genius, & a finish'd taste of politeness. In short, 'tis, as far as I am able to judge, a most charming performance. Several indeed have objected to his translations, but I believe without much reason. I took only a cursory view of the History, & therefore did not stay to compare the translations with the Original; but suppose 'em to be very just from the Author's being so well acquainted with the writings of Tully. It must indeed have been very difficult to translate some of the most florid and elaborate parts of the Roman Orator's compositions, & perhaps our language cannot always reach the strength & beauty of the Original. But, I believe, you'll find in Middletons translations all that can reasonably be expected from the English Language in the hands of the greatest Master of it. These you'll think great words; but if, after reading the work, you don't look upon Dr. Middleton as the greatest Master of Style, you ever read, or met with, I am much mistaken.

But the Bell rings for Dinner, & I must haste to subscribe myself your sincere Friend & Servt.

R. Hurd.

P.S.

Now Dinner is over, I'll fill up my paper with a postscript. Your Brother is very well, but busy in studying for his Degree.[2] He desir'd, I'd make his complements to you. We have a polite Scheme in our heads, of wch. more in my next.

Your last makes me envy & pity you, two strange passions, you'll say, to meet at ye. same time. For Heavn's sake contrive some means to make your love, & therefore your life, easy to you. If I had room, I could say more on that Subject.

Let me count over, what you call, your copper-coin very soon. A single Simile is as much as you must expect from me in half a year. Vale!

Endorsed by RH: "NB: A single Sheet".
In Potter's hand: "Pd: MR 28."

2 Robert Potter took his degree later on in the year, in the Easter Term. This was a bye-term, the more usual time for taking degree examinations being in February, during the Lent Term. Potter's deviation from the general practice cannot be explained. (*Emmanuel College Register*, COL. 9. 1. (A); Carter, *History of the University of Cambridge*, 1753, pp. 6, 10.)

16 To JOHN POTTER 19 APRIL 1741

Text: MS NLW 12432E; unpublished.
Addressed: To/the Revd. Mr. Potter at Batcombe/near Brewton in/ Somersetshire/By London.
Postmarked: CAMBRIDGE 20 AP

Camb. April 19th. 1741.

Dear Sr,

Your last very handsome & obliging letter gave me that pleasure, I always receive from the correspondence of a sincere & ingenious Friend. As the contents of it were elegant, I was entertain'd; as they were friendly, I was delighted. For both I am oblig'd to you. Only one part has thrown me into a Dilemma, yt. I hardly know how to get over. Your manner of expression in some places carries in it so great an Air of complement, yt. it must infer no small degree of vanity to believe you; & yet there is something so truly cordial, & affectionate runs thro' the whole; yt. I cannot disbelieve you. The most prudent way perhaps is to moderate the affair a little: I hope, I believe, I know you respect me; that respect might carry you too far in your profession of it, & heighten your colouring too much. However it be, I am determin'd rather to be thought vain, than suspicious; the one <implies> indeed implies a weakness, but such a one as is pardonable; whereas the other has something criminal in it's nature, & betrays a darkness of Soul, I should be sorry to be charg'd with.

Should I enlarge upon the ease, & beauty of your Poetry at this time, it would look too much like an exchange of complement, & a mere return of words. I cannot however omitt saying, the<y> lines pleas'd me; & if there be any fault in them, 'tis that they are too much in the taste, & manner of Prior's. A little paradoxical this, you'll think, yt. to be very like one of the best of Poets, is to be faulty! But 'tis easily explain'd: our taste for poetry in this age is founded entirely upon the practice, & manner of Mr. Pope, & as Prior happens to differ from him in the turn, & run of his versification, he is not look'd upon as an exact model. This indeed seems to be his only fault; he is rather loose & careless in his numbers, & often so, as to take off from the delicacy & beauty of a Sentiment. I ascribe not this to negligence, or the want of a discerning Ear; Mr. Prior is well known to have excell'd in the later, &, I believe, he us'd much care. 'Twas perhaps rather owing to too great an affectation of ease in writing, wch., tho' justly admir'd in this poet, & indeed the greatest perfection in works of Genius, should never be aim'd at, & observ'd at the expence of Strength, harmony, & beauty. But I ask pardon <both> for the freedom I have taken both with your (justly) favourite Poet, & with you. Sincerity is one of the first qualifications you require in yr. Ideal friend, & if I could be vain enough to think any part of so amiable a character belong'd to me, 'tis that. The other eminent virtues, requir'd[a] in your piece, I presume not to lay any claim to, but this I arrogate to myself with so much confidence, yt. I shall venture to assert in the following couplet,

> "My tongue impartial never will commend
> The slightest Errors ev'n in a Friend."[1]

[1] This couplet appears to be of RH's own composition.

[a] MS: "site" deleted; "r'd" substituted.

It gives me some pain to observe, yt. the word Pen wd. suit this place, much better than Tongue. A length of days has pass'd, since it was in my power to use ys. member in your Service. Too many mountains rise between us to suffer any sounds to reach your ears, from this quarter, except what are made visible upon paper. And this way (thank Heav'n) we can converse. Nor Seas, nor deserts can prevent this kind of Intercourse; but our thoughts, fleeting & transient, as they are, become permanent & lasting, & take a secure flight to whatever part of the Globe, it may please their master to send them. 'Tis for this reason, yt. the absence of friends becomes tolerable, & 'tis from this expedient, if anything should hinder our meeting at Cambridge this year, that I promise myself some comfort. Believe me, Sr., to see you here wd. be the greatest pleasure, & if it can be done with any sort of convenience, you may be sure, I shall endeavour to do it. But Cambridge is not at present so agreeable to me, as once it was, & whether other reasons may not conspire to hurry me away before the commencement, is what I cannot now promise.[2] In the mean time be assur'd of my affection for you, & doubt not of my sincere endeavours to see you, & to serve you.

Your Brother the other day recd. a very handsome letter from the Author of the late English Aeneid. It was occasion'd by a complement <your Brother> he made him upon his Translation; a pretty Poem, but not quite so correct, as 'tis wish'd it had been.[3] I had seen it some time before, but as yr. Brother never gave me the least hint of his design, I did not pass so severe a judgment upon it, as otherwise I should have done. However Mr. Pitt seems to like it very much: the complement he has recd. upon this occasion, & indeed the whole letter, do him more honour, than 'tis proper any other person should mention to him.

I am glad to find, you have read Dr. Delany's life of David; I am certain it pleas'd you. There is an uncommon Spirit runs thro' the whole performance, & something so ingenious in the digressions, disquisitions, &c that, I think, I never met with anything more entertaining. In his remarks on the 18th. Psalm, the Dr. observes (if I remember right, for I have not the book by me) that the word Temple is us'd by the inspir'd Author to signify the Heavens with great beauty in the follow[ing Pas]sage.[4] "In my distress I called upon the Lord, & cried unto my God: [He] hear'd my voice out of his Temple &c." Ps.18. v.6.

I was pleas'd the other day to find it us'd exactly in the same [sense] by the Sublime Lucretius:

> . . . jam nemo, fessus satiate videndi,
> Suspicere in caeli dignatur lucida *Templa.*
>
> L.2. v.1037.[5]

It occurs also in a passage of the first Book, where the Epithet Tonitralia, to wch. it is

[2] The Commencement fell on 7 July in 1741. RH left college on 4 June. (*Residence Book*, TUT. 11.1.)

[3] Robert Potter's poem complimenting Christopher Pitt (translator of the *Aeneid*) was still extant in 1936, and with his verses on Samuel Bowden was sold in that year. (See *ante* To Potter, 14 December 1740, n.3.) Their present whereabouts have not been discovered.

[4] Delany had actually asked, (i. 88): "Can there be a nobler idea, than to consider the heavens as the temple of GOD!"

[5] Lucretius, *De rerum natura*, ii. 1037–8; i. 1098. The line numbers given by RH agree with eighteenth century editions of Lucretius; Loeb edition line numbers are ii. 1038–9 and i. 1105. (See also following quotation.)

joyn'd, wd. not improperly mark the Idea, we have of that Temple, when "the Lord thunders in it, & the High[est] gives his voice." Ibid: v:13.

"Neve ruant caeli Tonitralia Templa supernè."
L.1. v.1098.

I don't recollect, that this form of Expression is ever us'd by Virgil.[6]

An excellent paragraph in yr. last letter to yr. Brother has prevented my saying anything upon the Subject of yr. Love. Keep to your resolution, & all's well.

You see I did a politic thing in my last to explode method, since I should [have fou]nd it a very difficult task to have connected so many different Scraps, as this letter consists of, in any tolerable form & order. It has been of vast Service to me thro' the whole, & gives me an opportunity ev'n at the last of letting you know, without any form, yt. the polite Scheme, I hinted to you, was learning French. And to shew you I have made some progress in the language, give me leave to subscribe myself, but with the sincerity of an Englishman, Vôtre trés humble Serviteur

R. Hurd.

P.S.

Yr. Bro: is all but Bachelor, & at yr. service.[7]

Endorsed by RH: "A Single Sheet".

17 To JAMES DEVEY 3 MAY 1741

Text: *Memoirs*, 8.

Cambridge, May 3d, 1741.

Rev. Sir,

You see what it is to engage in a correspondence with boys. We are a most impertinent set of people, and never know when to give over talking. Methinks the epithet *garrula*, which from the age of Nestor to the present times has been constantly given to *Senectus*, would suit full as well with *Juventus*. There is, indeed, this difference between the two cases, that talkativeness in old men is ever seasoned with experience and good sense, whereas the tattle of the young is light and trivial, and has seldom any solidity to compensate for its exuberance. For this reason it was perhaps not so ridiculous in the old sage, as some are apt to imagine, to enjoin a profound silence to his pupils for a certain term of years.[1] His design, without doubt, was to instruct them in their duty, and prevent them from talking at all till they had learnt to talk well. And, indeed, this conduct is so reasonable, that I believe I should immediately give

6 This reference to Virgil is prompted by the comparison that Delany had made between Virgil's description of Jupiter's anger, and David's description of God's wrath. The difference between the two is that Jupiter uses the elements as an expression of his fury, whereas when God becomes angry, the universe reacts independently and in fear, trembling and giving way before Him. (*Life of David*, i. 90–1.)

7 Robert Potter apparently left Emmanuel at the end of April. (*Commons Accounts Book*, STE. 15. 8.) The actual date of his taking his degree is not known.

1 Pythagoras (the Sage of Samos) required the most talkative of his pupils to remain silent in his presence for five years. Those who were more reserved were allowed to speak after a probation of two years. (*Lemprière's Classical Dictionary of Proper Names mentioned in Ancient Authors Writ Large*, 1788, Third Edition (revised and rewritten), 1984.)

into it, but that I have now an opportunity of conversing with one whose candour would incline him to pardon anything his judgment should dislike. Of that I have had a remarkable instance in the case of Delany's Life of David; of which I shall only add further, that it has given me great occasion to admire not only the judgment but politeness of Mr. Devey.

I know not whether the following remark be worth mentioning to you, but the name of David naturally brings it to my mind.[2] The word "temple" is used by that inspired poet to signify the heavens in the following passage, "In my distress I called upon the Lord, and cried unto my God: He heard me out of his temple," Ps. xviii. 6. Dr. Delany, if I remember right, adds that this form of expression is very beautiful. I was pleased the other day to find this term used exactly in the same sense by the sublime Lucretius:

> – jam nemo, fessus satiate videndi,
> Suspicere in coeli dignatur lucida templa.
>
> L. ii. v. 1037.

It occurs also in a passage of the first Book, where the epithet "tonitralia," which is joined to it, would not improperly mark the idea we have of that temple when the Lord thunders in it, and the Highest gives his voice. Ibid. ver. 13.

> Neve ruant coeli tonitralia templa superne
>
> L. i. 1098.

Think not, Sir, I mention this as though I thought the poetry of David could receive any additional glory or merit from any resemblance it may be found to bear to the flights of Pagan writers. That I know is impossible; but must own it gives me some pleasure to meet with passages in heathen learning that are parallel to those in sacred writ, since it is by such kind of proof only that many classical pretenders to criticism will suffer themselves to be convinced of the beauty of those sublimest of compositions . . .

18 To JOHN POTTER 27 MAY 1741

Text: MS NLW 12432E; unpublished.
Addressed: To/the Revd. Mr. Potter at/ Batcombe near Brewton/in Somersetshire.

Camb. May 27th. 1741.

Dear Sr,

I mention'd to your Brother my design of writing to you, & yt. an ordinary sheet wd. scarcely contain what I propos'd to say; upon wch. he complimented me with one of a more unusual Size, & in wch. I might have room to throw out myself at full length. The offer was too agreable not to be accepted, & you see what a frightful length of Paper you are to travel over, before you can hope to arrive at your Journey's End. However as the following Scroll will consist of very different Subjects, you'll stand a fair chance of meeting here & there with some commodious resting-places, wch. may serve in the capacity of Inns to lessen your fatigue, & render your whole

[2] The following is an almost exact transcript of the note on the word "temple" in the preceding letter to Potter.

course the more supportable. One has sometimes odd thoughts, or you wd. not know <what> how to acct. for a whimsical Simile, yt. forces itself upon me on this Occasion. The several little pauses, & interruptions, wch. you'll find scatter'd up and down this Epistle, make me think, the case of <the> it's reader <of<this letter> it>[a] is not very unlike that of a Traveller crossing the Aegean Sea. Numberless Islands lie straggling here & there <in that Sea,> without order or regularity, wch. the Mariner by *putting in at* (I think yts. the Sea-Term) furnishes himself with conveniences for his voyage, & thinks he finds the way shorten'd, in proportion to the number of Isles, that lie before him. To explain what I mean, conceive yourself in the beginning of this Sheet just loosing (E:G:) from Carystus in Euboea, & bound to Caria in Asia; & when you've done this, the following Pause may serve to represent to you Andros, or some other neighb'ring Island, where you may rest a little & refresh yourself. – Tell me in yr. next if you don't think this Simile perfectly new.

If you have by this time <sufficiently> got over your last fatigue, let us set Sail again. I entirely agree with you in regard to what you say of Method in writing. Nor was I ever of a different Opinion, the few thoughts, or rather expressions, yt. escap'd me in the letter, you mention, were not serious. 'Tis however a pleasure to me to have giv'n an occasion, by a ludicrous turn, to those handsome remarks, you have made on yt. Subject. All I shall add upon yr. love, is, yt. I wish it successful soon, or never. It grieves me to think it should prey upon that time, wch. wd. otherwise be employ'd to the best purposes, & on the noblest Subjects.

But now comes a Theme, yt. concerns me nearly. Whether Cambridge should be left before the Commencement, or no; that's the question. What can I reply to it? Should the answer be in the affirmative, how must I stand out against the reproches of a sincere, & seemingly injur'd friend? Or rather how can I [be]ar up against the reproches of my, more injur'd, Self? Would not ev'n friendly zeal condemn me as insincere, as disrespectful, as treacherous? Or cd. I, who know the honesty of my own thoughts, excuse myself for letting slip so favourable an opportunity of seeing the best of Friends? – These are the reasons, & weighty ones they are against the Affirmative Side. But let us, if you please, weigh those for it. Your Brother can tell you, (for he knows) how uneasy my situation is at present in this Society. This uneasiness springs not from the discipline of our Governours,[1] for this gives me little trouble; no, not from the treatment, I met with the other day at the hands of Dr. R–.[2] Your Brother tells me he has giv'n you an acct. of that affair, and, I doubt not, with his usual Archness. But in truth, I acquit him of all Blame, & have a very great & sincere regard for him. Were they all like him – but I cannot stay to be particular, I refer you to Sr. Robert.[3] But besides this there is another reason, wch., could I get over, the rest might perhaps be dispens'd with. The case is this: the Qr. ends next week, & was I to

1 The Master, William Richardson, and Henry Hubbard, one of the Fellows, were both known as "Disciplinarians". (John Nichols, *Literary Anecdotes of the Eighteenth Century; comprizing Biographical Memoirs of William Bowyer . . . and Biographical Anecdotes of a considerable number of eminent writers and ingenious artists*, 9 vols., 1812–16, viii. 420.) Richardson was Master from 1736 to 1775; Hubbard was a Fellow from 1732 to 1778.

2 Possibly William Richardson; but no evidence has been found to explain RH's "uneasiness" in college at this time.

3 Robert Potter.

a RH altered this sentence twice from "the case of the reader of this letter" to "the case of the reader of it" to "the case of it's reader".

stay a month longer, the expence wd. be nearly the same (such is the villany of this place) as if I staid the whole Quarter. From hence arises a plea for my leaving Cambridge, that will, I dare say, in a great measure excuse me with you. I am indeed sorry, yt. our meeting should be prevented on a pecuniary Acct., but ye. readiness & even chearfulness, with wch. my Father has contributed to a pretty expensive Education makes me very cautious of admitting any considerable expence, yt. may be avoided. To dwell longer on this topick, & run out into vehement professions of the sincerity of my friendship, wd. be to betray some consciousness of it's being insincere. I shall therefore leave it to your good sense, good nature, & knowledge of me to plead in my behalf, & doubt not from such Advocates to receive a favourable Sentence, when you, the Judge, come to give it.

See! the strange disposition[b] of things! – Those friends, yt. are valu'd in a less degree, I can often converse with; those yt. stand in a higher rank, like other rarities, are seldom met with. Last week came hither for Priest's Orders, & staid a week, our old, & honest, (but upon the whole not quite so valuable, as some I could name) friend Bob Hudson. I was pleas'd, you may imagine, to have his company, & talk over some of our old affairs; but there was still something wanting to render the pleasure so compleat, as the converse of some others might have done. Nevile[4] & I rode with him yesterday to New-market in his way home, where having fed upon Beef Stakes, & mutton chops (wch. by the by were the best I ever eat) we did not forget to drink the Curate of Batcombe, & our London Friend.[5] Oh! have you hear'd, pray, of his being ill of the small Pox? Sr. Richard Jenoure is now at London, & I wait for his return impatiently to know how he does. Perhaps I may see him, before this goes; (for yr. Bro: is to be my Post) if so, I'll tell you more of it.

Last friday night we had a concert of Musick at Trinity College Hall, for the benefit of Signor Caporalli,[6] the famous Bass-Violist: Signor Pasqualli,[7] our constant master in Cambridge, play'd the first Fiddle. They are both incomparable in their respective ways, and upon this occasion exerted their whole Art. You know how fond I am of Musick, & need not be told therefore what pleasure I receiv'd that Ev'ning. Hudson & yr. Brother went with me, & you'll hardly imagine we forgot to wish for a certain other gentleman, in order to make our happiness compleat.

May 29th.} After an interval of two days, I am again at leisure to write. The rains, that fell this afternoon, & the lovely harmony of St. Mary's Bells,[8] yt. are now ringing, conspire to raise my Spirits, if they needed such assistance, & throw me into that kind

4 John Nevile (c.1720–58) was also at Emmanuel. He matriculated in 1737, became B.A. in 1740, M.A. in 1743, and was made a Fellow at the same time as RH in December 1742. (*Emmanuel College Order Book*, COL. 14. 2.)

5 William Gould.

6 Andrea Caporale (?–c.1756) was an Italian violoncellist and composer. He had arrived in England in 1734 and excited a great deal of attention. Since then he had become famous as a performer, but rather for the tone and expression of his playing than for his execution. (*Grove's Dictionary of Music and Musicians*, ed. Eric Blom, 1966.)

7 Presumably Niccolo Pasquali (?–1757) an Italian violinist and composer, who lived mainly in Edinburgh. He wrote music for a variety of instruments including two sets of sonatas, one for violin and bass, and one for two violins, viola and continuo. (*Ibid.*)

8 Great St Mary's is the university church. According to Edmund Carter it had "a ring of ten excellent bells, with a clock and quarters, and . . . a set of chimes". "St. Mary's the Less" had "but one bell". (Carter, *History of the County of Cambridge*, 1753, pp. 35, 36.)

b MS: "dispostion".

of temper, that suits best with an Epistolizer. But to say the truth: this is what I seldom want, when writing to Mr. Potter. The moment I sit down with yt. design, a thousand agreeable Ideas croud in upon me, & such a complacency spreads itself over my mind, yt. the chief difficulty I find is to know when to leave off.

A part of your last turns upon a refin'd Subject; you observe the folly of setting a greater value upon things, than they deserve. The application of that remark seems chiefly to respect Love, and such as have the misfortune to be unhappy in it. With your leave [I'll] widen the thought a little, & extend it to some other particulars of a different nature. 'Tis this extravagant estimation of things, yt. to me appears the most considerable source of our dissatisfactions, & unhappiness in life. There's scarce a man, that does not propose to himself some certain method of life, wch. he doubts not will render him happy. That method is attain'd: the man is unhappy. Is it not, yt. he expected more from it, yn. it was capable of bestowing? Let <but> a Middleton, or a Pitt publish a History, or a Poem: the world's alarm'd: from such works what pleasure is not expected? – The works are read: the readers feel no extraordinary pleasure, perhaps are dissatisfy'd. Were I call'd upon to solve this appearance, (wch. daily observation presents us with) it should not be, as is usually <the case> done, by charging the performances themselves with numerous faults & imperfections, but ourselves with unreasonable expectations. The case is still the same in other Instances: thus we are apt upon hearing of a <great> famous General, or fine prospect, to form greater Ideas of the valour & capacity of the one, & the extent & beauty of the other, than are to be found existing together in nature. The mind immedia[tly] takes the hint, forms to itself notions of a wild and extravagant kind, & outruns the reality of things. 'Tis no wonder therefore, if upon an intimate view of them, we find ourselves disappointed, & abate something of yt. admiration, wch. before transported us. The Hero indeed may be as extraordinary as the condition of human Nature will permit; & the prospect as agreeable, as rivers, woods, & plains can make it; but if in our Ideas of them the one rises into a God, & the other brightens into a Paradise, we need not be surpriz'd, if a more exact Enquiry convinces us of our Error, & the God after all should dwindle into a mere Man, & the Paradise fade away into a plain, & natural Landskape. 'Twere easy to extend this thought further: but 'tis time to give over, &, in the language of the first part of this letter, land you on the first safe Shore; from whence, like a weary mariner, you may view the length of Sea<s> you've cross'd, &, tho' sick of winds & waves, receive the no small pleasure of reflecting upon the toils & difficulties, you've securely pass'd.

I am, dear Sr., your's most sincerely

R. Hurd.

P.S.

The two following lines contain something remarkable: I shall leave it to yourself to apply 'em, as you think fit.

> "Tu, quamcunque Deus tibi fortunaverit HORAM,
> Gratâ SUME manu, nec DULCIA differ in ANNUM."[9] [c]

Write to me very soon, & direct to me at Hatton-Grange in Shropshire, as usual.

[9] Horace, *Epistles*, I. xi. 22–3.

[c] Words in capitals written by RH in very large lower case letters.

19 To JOHN POTTER **19 SEPTEMBER 1741**

Text: MS NLW 12432E; unpublished.
Addressed: To/the Revd. Mr. Potter at Batcombe/near Brewton/in Somersetshire./By London.
Postmarked: SHIFNALL 2[?] SE

Hatton-Grange Septr. 19th. 1741.

Dear Sir,

'Tis very common to hear persons, upon being ask'd to sing, profess they have no voice, when the very tone & accent, in wch. that profession is made, discover<s> they have: 'tis very common to hear persons, upon being ask'd to dance, profess, they cannot, when they do[a] not ev'n move, without shewing they can. Mr. Potter, I find, has, contrary to his usual custom, giv'n into this trite phraseology, and asserted, he knows nothing of Pastoral, at the same time that he has shewn he is well acquainted with it. Believe me, Sir, I had never appli'd to you on that occasion, if I had not previously known your taste & genius, & which way the bent of your Soul lay. Your late poem has convinc'd me, I was not out in my conjecture; & tho' there is not perhaps that correctness in ev'ry part, that you are capable of giving it, yet permit me to say, there is an air of simplicity and nature breathes thro' the whole, that is extremly pastoral. I shall not detain you with further complements, but own myself sincerely oblig'd to you for the Favour. – And now give me leave (for I may with some reason) to renew my request. That you may be induc'd to grant it the more readily, I shall lay before you the reasons, that put me upon making it. Tho' this secret, notwithstanding it be void of anything sacred, & mysterious, must, like the antient rites of Religion, be introduc'd with a Faveto linguae. – But I need say no more.

The case then is this: I am now engag'd in drawing up a treatise on Pastoral Poetry. The thought took me some years ago, & something was ev'n then attempted; but I soon found my strength unequal to the task, and laid it aside. My natural fondness for this subject insensibly drew me over, I know not how, to the same attempt in the beginning of the last Spring. A part was soon work'd off, in a manner, I thought, more successful than before, & with greater ease to myself. This you may imagine was enough to flatter the vanity of a young man; and I began to hope, I was not so ill-qualify'd to attack the whole, as I had found myself before. However I had still many doubts hanging about me, and durst not absolutely resolve to proceed. The wonderful delicacy of the Subject, the elegant manner in which it would require to be handl'd, the great names I found myself oblig'd to dissent from in such a performance, the reading necessary to discharge it in a masterly manner, &, to mention no more, the time, I perceiv'd, a work of this nature wd. take up, these were the difficulties that offer'd themselves to me in a frightful train, whenever I turn'd my thoughts that way. These were the Rocks & shelves, these the gulphs & Hurricanes, that kept me on the Shore, and prevented my setting sail. However time, & frequent reflection began at last to familiarize the thing to me, & I pursu'd my plan. But, as I went along, the distrust I had of my own capacity, & abilities for so nice an undertaking, by turns interrupted the design & stop'd my Pen. But not to trouble you with more circumstances, a favourable opportunity at last offer'd of desiring the judgment of a friend,

[a] MS: "can" deleted; "do" substituted.

whose Sincerity I could not doubt, & whose taste is indisputable.[1] The partiality & indulgence of his approbation encourag'd me once more to proceed; & tho' it did not free me from all suspicion, & fearful apprehension (for he is of that kind of men, the world calls polite) yet it had this good effect, yt. I have wrote since with less concern, & interruption. Thus, Sir, you see by what degrees I have been led into a rashness, almost equal to Phaeton's. That daring Spirit had an ambition to enlighten the world, and for a day hold out the Sun to mankind. Your friend has folly enough to undertake an illustration of Virgil, and attempt to display the Beams of that Sun of the Poets. <. . .> His fate you know; your friend perhaps is to have no better a destiny. And if so, 'twill be but a poor consolation to have it said of him, "magnis tamen excidit ausis".[2] To prevent this, the assistance of my more ingenious friends will be necessary. I shall thank your Brother for his in a particular letter. But he mistook my design; I want not any distinction of pastoral into it's several species, that being a kind of criticism, wch., tho' very good in it's way, I cannot for some reasons give into. What wd. come up to my purpose better is an explication of some passages, or an illustration of the more retir'd beauties, in Virgil's Eclogues, or Theocritus. If you are at leisure, it wd. be extremely obliging in you to read over some parts of those works with that view. Ev'ry Reader has some peculiar remarks to make upon an Author <that escape another;>; & I can trust your judgment for selecting such as wd. be useful to me. But if this employment be dry, or disagreeable, give me leave to mention another way in wch. your Assistance wd. be serviceable. If you make any remarks, or have already any by you, upon rural Images, & the Scenary of a pastoral Life, a communication of them wd. much oblige me. I know the Subject to be what you like, & I know your fancy would suggest a variety of observations upon it.

In short, the plan & nature of my design lead me to speak of ev'ry thing, that regards the Country life, & the manners of it; I mean, yt. country life, & those manners, that we conceive to have been in antient times, in what the Poets call the Golden Age. As to modern[b] Pastoral, I shall not much concern myself with it, it being, as Mr. Pope says of Ogylby's Translations, generally speaking, too mean for Criticism.[3] [c]

I am sensible of one great Objection, that will be made against my whole plan, & the very nature of this work. To admire pastoral Images is thought the effect of a boyish Fancy, and expressive of a certain puerility in the turn of the Admirer. The attention of a Scholar, or indeed of a Man is suppos'd to be employ'd upon Subjects of a higher, & more useful concern; pastoral, & it's attendant Trumpery, is fit only for Schoolboys, & young Poets. They indeed may be delighted with a chrystal Rill, or flow'ry meadow, the circling vale, or swelling Ascent, but Men should have other thoughts, Men should contemplate other Objects. Yes – I allow it, – a Bottle, or whore, a gaming-table, or, if they happen to be more unfashionable, a pack of Hounds. [Go wiser then, &] then, run thro' all the follies, & vices of the age, ruin <your> health, fortunes, peace, Souls, and all, then put on a superior smile, & laugh at empty fools, that are queer enough to love a prospect. – Forgive me, Sir, I have been betray'd

1 Unidentified. Perhaps Edward Macro. (See Biography.)

2 Ovid, *Metamorphoses*, ii. 328. This was part of Phaeton's epitaph.

3 Pope, *The Iliad of Homer. Translated*, 6 vols., 1715-20, Preface, [p.xxxii]: "His [Hobbes'] Poetry, as well as *Ogilby's*, is too mean for Criticism".

b MS: "moden".

c Note by Potter: "NB: Such must be a Satyr".

here into a fit of declaiming, contrary to my design. I thought only to have told you, that notwithstanding the sneers of worldlings, and pretty Fellows, I must own my love of Pastoral, & that I think I can defend my taste, however awkward & unfashionable it may be, by the severest reasoning. This I shall not fail to do, as convenient parts of the work may give a proper occasion. – I need not question your doing me the justice to think, I don't me[an] by a love of pastoral, (wch. I wd. recommend) an affected admiration of s[t]rea[ms] and groves, or an unmea[n]ing rapture upon reading a flow'ry description. The regard for pastoral, I speak of, is founded in nature, & reason; is productive of many good ends, and therefore is, as it also has been, worthy the greatest & most refin'd minds. But I need not preach this to you: nor need I vindicate a taste for pastoral to the Author of George & Ned.

You see to what a length I have spun out my letter; another word or two however, before I conclude. The contents of this will afford you a good reason, should I chance to be less punctual, or shorter in my letters for [s]ome time. Tho' nothing but necessity shall force me to be either. But admitting the Supposition, I must charge you not to imitate me. Let me hear frequently from you, and, if I don't write soon, stay not for an Answer. This will be doubly obliging, as it will be giving me more pleasure with less trouble. For really writing is become a trouble, since I have had so much of it; what vacant time I steal from business of that kind at present I am glad to employ upon my fiddle, or Company. But tho' this be my case now: yet neither musick, company, nor Business, shall make me one jot less, dear Sir, your sincere Friend & Servt.

R. Hurd.

P.S.

My service to yr. Brother; he may expect to hear from me soon.

Endorsed by RH: "NB. A single sheet."

20 To EDWARD MACRO 2 OCTOBER 1741

Text: MS NORFOLK RO; copy in a later hand; unpublished.

Hatton Grange Oct. 2. 1741.

Dear Sir,

I thank you for your Dream. If that be your way of thinking in Sleep, 'tis pity, methinks, you should ever be awake. From a review of it, I can't but observe how well you seem to understand the Person, to whom 'tis address'd. You introduce me taking a survey of, & despising Ambition, and this I'll venture to say, was no random guess, no flying compliment. Yes Sir, I do most sincerely despise, what the world calls Greatness; nor have I the least, lurking fondness in my heart for the pomp of Life. This, I know, will seem a rant from the mouth of a young Man; it will be said, that one of my Age, ignorant as yet of the turns of fortune; and but slenderly acquainted with the world, cannot have seen enough of life, to be sincere in such professions. It will rather seem affectation in me, and a forwardness to talk in the air, & manner of a Philosopher; or lastly it may be looked upon as a pretended dislike, & contempt of a manner of life, which 'tis probable I shall never be troubled with. I think, I could depend upon your knowledge of me for an answer to these objections; but as I have paper enough before me, give me leave to send you my own thoughts on this subject.

With regard to life, my friend, the few years I have liv'd in it, have been sufficient to shew me the emptiness and vanity of it. They have not, I thank God, been distinguish'd by any extraordinary afflictions, or calamaties beyond the ordinary lot of mankind. Yet ev'n these, small & common as they are, have serv'd to convince me, that happiness is not to be expected here, or, if it be, that it lies in the Shades & private paths of Life. My Eyes have been open to the lives, & actions of the modern great; & my mind has attentively consider'd those of the most illustrious dead. The result of this enquiry has been, yt. their days were wretched in proportion to their greatness; that the hurry & tumult of their elevated state were inconsistent with their happiness, and that many a Cloud had obscur'd the lustre of their lives, which humbler mortals knew nothing of. An illustration of this that very Welkin, you have seen, will afford me. Tis common, to see that aspiring mountain, lab'ring beneath the weight of dusky vapours, & wrapp'd in Clouds, at the same time, that the neighbouring vallies enjoy a serene & lovely day. The Sun, regardless of its proud Summit, pours all its brightness on the humble plain, & disdains not to gild the cottage with those rays, that had been refused to the Welkin's loftier Rocks. Tis thus, I suspect, with regard to greatness; many a blessing escapes it, that is only to be found in privacy & retirement. This I am the more confirm'd in, when I recollect the many testimonies of the fall'n Great. Then they own the happiness of an humbler station, condemn their fond ambitious views, & find at last that real bliss, that home felt ease in Solitude, which they had in vain sought for in courts & crowds. When I indulge reflections of this kind, and consider further the fitness of solitude for ev'ry more serious, & worthy employment, 'tis with some difficulty that I refrain from breaking out into that poetical Rapture:

> Bear me, some God! o! quickly bear me hence,
> To wholesome solitude, the nurse of Sense;
> Where Contemplation prunes her ruffl'd wings,
> And the free Soul looks down to pity Kings.
>
> Pope.[1]

In short, whatever kind of life falls to my share, I shall think it my duty to be as easy under it, & to discharge it as well, as I can. But could I choose my manner of Life, believe me, Sir, (I speak with the utmost sincerity) a tolerable competency in an obscure retreat is all I desire. A few honest & well natur'd Friends would there afford a real Satisfaction, & together with a few books, & a little business (unless perhaps I were to mention an agreable Wife) are all the blessings, your friend could wish. But you'll think me grown melancholy, If I go on at this rate, & will begin to think, you've met with no very agreable correspondent. 'Tis time therefore to change my note; & 'till fortune favors me with the life[a] I pant after, let me talk like other folks, & assume the air of one, who is not yet removed out of the world.

As a proof of my not being quite so wise, as I would seem to make myself above, I shall fill up the remainder of this letter with a string of Rhymes, I was fool enough the other day to spin out. The beauty of the subject must attone with you for the faults of the piece. If they serve to entertain you a little, I have my end; if not, you'll at least excuse 'em. NB. Tibullus accompanying his friend Messalla on an expedition, was taken ill in the island of Corcyra. The following lines are a Translation of some part of the Elegy, he compos'd on that occasion.

1 *The Fourth Satire of Dr. John Donne*, 11. 184–7.

a MS: "wife" changed to "life".

A Translation of part of E.1.3. B.1. of Tibullus.[2]

Hail! happy world! hail Saturn's gentle reign!
ee'r Earth was cross'd or journey'd o'er the main;
or Pine had brav'd the Surge of rolling Seas,
Or loos'd its swelling canvass to the breese.
No costly wares, or freight of glittering ore
Heap'd the rich vessel from a Foreign Shore.
The bounding steed no galling fetters broke,
Free graz'd the Ox, unconscious of the Yoke.
No cot was door'd, nor useless Stone was seen
To fix the limits of the common Green.
From dropping Oaks were brush'd mellifluous Dews,
And milk flow'd copious from unguarded Ewes.
No wrath was there, no dreadfull war to wage,
No faithless friend to fear, or foe engage;
Nor artists yet had learn'd the cruel Skill
With murd'rous pow'r to arm the sharpen'd Steel.
But under Jove are Seas & wounds & wars,
And various Death in frightful forms appears.
Spare mighty Sire! the vengeance[b] of thy hand
No Gods blasphem'd, no perjuries demand.
But if (alass!) the fatal hour be come;
May this sad couplet mark the figur'd Tomb!
Here lies Tibullus: over land & Sea
Messalla following, snatch'd by fate away.
But me obedient to the voice of love
Venus shall lead to the Elyzian Grove
The tunefull Song here glads the happy hours,
Here the dance echoes thro' the blissfull bow'rs.
The Birds around with warbl'd raptures strain
Their little throats & flutter oer the plain.
The fragrant fields spontaneous sweets disclose,
Here Casia springs, there blows the blushing rose.
While gentle Youths the tender Virgins lead
In mirthfull frolick to the flow'ry mead.
Love smiles around, pleas'd with their amrous play,
And sees soft battles crown each happy Day.

I am dear Sir, your's sincerely

R. Hurd

P.S.

My Service to Mr. Cox,[3] – let me hear from you soon.

2 Tibullus I. iii. 35–64.

3 Hadley Cox was a relation of Edward Macro and had come up to Corpus Christi, Cambridge, in 1739. His college elected him a Fellow in 1746, but he remained there only till 1751, when he obtained a living in Essex. He finally became Archdeacon of Bedford in 1771, and died in 1782. (*Alum. Cantab.*; *Macro Letter-book.*)

b MS: "vengeange" changed to "vengeance".

21 To EDWARD MACRO 1 JANUARY 1742

Text: MS BL Add. 32557, ff. 29–30; unpublished.
Addressed: To/Mr. Edward Macro at the Revd. Dr./Macro's in Norton near St. Edmunds Bury/Suffolk.[1]/By Lond[on]
Postmarked: WOLVERHAMPTON 4 IA

Brewood Jan: 1st. 1741–2

Dear Sir,

Your last found me in the middle of a Sermon; and as that kind of business does not love Interruption, you'll forgive my deferring to answer it, till I had in some sort brought it to a conclusion. I thank you, Sir, for that regard, I might almost say, zeal, you shew for my Interest: it discovers a Sincerity and warmth of friendship, <for me,> and therefore lays me under the most agreable Obligation. As to the Curacy, you mention, I am not in a capacity to take it at present; I am not, nor can be in orders till Lent, and the Gentleman, I suppose, cannot wait till then. Thirty five pds. a year is indeed but a small thing; however, as I have a desire to settle in that part of the world, if that difficulty could be got over, I should incline to accept it.[2] I do not conceive, of what use the house, you speak of, can be <. . .> to me, since my income would hardly enable me to set up for an Housekeeper. I should like too to know the distance of the place from Bury, and whether the Rector resides at it. If Mr. Lyne writes, I shall take care to send letters of thanks both to him and Mr. Elliot:[3] till then I dare say you'll think it more prudent in me to omit them. An obligation I am as ready to acknowledge as any man, but am afraid, that to be forward in this case would have too much the Air of Sollicitation, and Assiduity; things of wch. you know I am not very fond. In the mean time 'tis a very sensible pleasure to me to find Mr. Elliot interesting himself in my behalf; as the worthiness of his character had always attracted my esteem, and as the many valuable qualities, he possesses, makes it an honour to be regarded by him. To say the truth, he is almost the only Man of fortune, whose acquaintance I have ever had the honor of, to whom I could have been pleas'd to have recommended myself. – The favour of Mr. Lyne you may imagine I take kindly, as it comes from one, whose kindness I had no reason to expect. But as I consider Mr. Macro, as the primum

1 The Macro family lived at Little Haugh Hall at Norton in Suffolk.

2 Edward Macro was trying to secure a curacy for RH through the influence of his friends and his father, both to help him in his career, and to secure his presence near to the Macros' own home. (*Macro Letter-book.*) The value of the curacy was above average for the first half of the eighteenth century (see the figures for the rich diocese of Durham and for St Asaph in J.C. Shuler, 'The pastoral and ecclesiastical administration of the diocese of Durham 1721–1771; with particular reference to the archdeaconry of Northumberland', Ph.D. dissertation, University of Durham, 1975, p. 101; and J.L. Salter, 'Isaac Maddox and the dioceses of St. Asaph and Worcester', M.A. dissertation, University of Birmingham, 1962, p. 58.) But it was only about £10 more than RH received in scholarship money at Emmanuel. He did not take it in the end, and a more profitable cure was found a month or so later. (See *post* To Potter, 15 April 1742.)

3 Matthew Lyne (of Northamptonshire) was a Fellow at Emmanuel; James Elliot (of London) was a Fellow-commoner. What influence they had in this affair has not been discovered.

mobile, or the Spring, that has set ev'n these in action, 'tis to him I can't but think myself more particularly oblig'd. – I need not apologize for leaving a Subject with some abruptness, wch., if continu'd, would displease you. Let me therefore chuse a less offensive <Subject> Topick. Mr. Cox, I remember, mention'd an Emendation Dr. Macro had made in I Ep. Cor: c. 14. v. 6, where, instead of ἐὰν [. . .] would read ἐὰν μεν, or ἐὰν δὴ, or something like it. The alteration [. . .] let great light in upon a passage, as it now stands, sufficiently obscure. But he seem'd at the same time to doubt, if ἐὰν was ever us'd in that sense in good Greek. I happen'd the other day to meet with it us'd in the new Testament exactly in the same manner, in wch. the Dr. would use it there. 'Tis in the 13. c. of the Acts of Ap: and the 41st. verse, where ἐὰν is to be constru'd etiamsi, and has the same force, as κἄν. The remark, I am afraid, will be but of little Service: however I could not help just taking notice of it.

What luck had I to mention the Muses in my last? Or if I must mention them, why was it done in the sneering and disrespectful form of, si Musis placet? The jades have been even with me for't: they have plagu'd[a] me with rhyme, & it's attendant, Head-ach, pretty heartily since that time; and as if versifying of any kind were not punishment enough, they have put me upon the most painful and laborious part of it. To speak plain English, in the <late> frost, that happen'd about a fortnight ago, and wch. hung the hedges with a Snowy kind of Substance, in forms the most lovely I remember to have seen, the thought struck me, that a description of it would be no disagreable amusement at a time, when I found myself confin'd to the House. But a second thought convinc'd me of the rashness of my design, by putting me in mind of the fine description of winter in Virgil's Georgicks,[4] and that after him an attempt of that kind must be most impertinent. However not being willing to be entirely balk'd of my aim, I resolv'd to attempt a translation of that famous Episode, and apply in some sort the Scythian-winterpiece to our own condition in Staffordshire. The inimitable beauty of the Original, when I came to look into it, somewhat discourag'd me; however I went thro' it, and shall here send you a copy for your amusement. 'Tis usual with tenants to make little presents at this Season to their Landlords; a goose, or Turky is carry'd with great form to the Squire, and tho' he wants them not, & has much better of his own, yet he never fails to accept them, and, if he happens to be, what they call, a well-spoken man, with expressions of great civility and respect. Permit me, Sir, to imitate this laudable custom, and 'tho' there is no want of amusements at Norton, please to accept this, as my Xstmas Offering. A friend, I think, has a greater right to them, than a Landlord; and as this is the only one in my power to make, let not the meaness of it be any Objection. Upon comparing it with the Original you'll perceive I have taken some liberty in two or three places, but it is in such, as I must confess to you I was not able to turn more literally with any tolerable grace.[5] The line, that describes Icicles hanging at the beards of the Scythians, is extremely beautiful in the Latin;[6] but I could not cloath the Image in any English words, that did not evidently turn it into burlesque. Dr. Trap, I remember, says there is

4 Virgil, *Georgics*, iii. 349–83.

5 RH refers to his translation of ll. 355–6 and ll. 377–82 (l. 8 and ll. 29–36 in his own verse). The Latin contains specific details such as the names of trees or plants, and numbers.

6 *Georgics*, iii. 366.

a MS: "plaug'd".

fire in this description of Virgil,[7] but I wish my copy be not too cold and [. . .] have any degree of heat in it. All I shall say further upon it [. . .] this weather lasts, my complement will not be ill-tim'd; since Nature will afford you a pretty exact Image of that, wch. is the Subject of it.

The Scythian W[inter]-piece from Virgil's Georg: L. 3. 1. 349.

Not so, where spreads Mae[oti]s, and the land,
Where turbid Ister whirls his waves of Sand;
Where to the Pole, returning from the Sun,
East-pointing Rhodope is seen to run.
There in eternal Folds the flocks remain;
Unleaf'd the Trees: no verdure on the plain.
Wide the vaste waste in snowy mountains lies,
And frozen Pyramids assault the Skies.
The pow'r of cold for ever rages there,
And wintry winds blow bleakness all the year.
The pale, dank Shades yield not to Phoebus' Ray,
Nor when he's mounted to the noon of Day,
Nor when in western Seas he wheels away.
A sudden crust retards the current tide,
The Icy waters stiff'ning, as they glide.
And wheels now press the Surface of the Main;
Where Ships once floated, rolls the Iron wain.
Brass bursts: their garments freeze: the fluent tide
Of wine's free Juice with Axes they divide.
The depth of Lakes one solid Substance lies;
Ev'n Breath's warm Vapour catches, as it flies.
  Mean time from Heav'n descends the flaky Store;
Perish the Beasts: with Snow stands cover'd o'er
In all his Bulk the Ox: In droves the Deer
Nums the new weight, and scarce their Horns appear.
Them, nor pursuing Dogs, nor Toils beset,
Nor purple plumes scare trembling to the Net;
But vainly lab'ring 'gainst a mountain's weight
With spears they wound them in a closer fight,
Loudly lamenting stab the easy Prey,
And bear their prize with joyful Shouts away.
Jovial and safe in caves, and shelt'ring cells
Deep in the Earth the hardy Offspring dwells.
There Forests falln, and from the mountains roll'd
Warm all their caverns, and forbid the cold.
There the glad Tribes indulge in feast and play,
While the long night steals unperceiv'd away.
The viny Draught, their envious Clime denies,
Less generous Liquor from the Brake supplies.
  Such the rude Race of men, who fix their Seat,

7 See the Introduction to Book III of the *Georgics* in *The Works of Virgil: Translated into English Blank Verse. With Large Explanatory Notes, and Critical Observations. By Joseph Trapp*, 1731. Trapp lists the distinguishing characteristics of Book III, the second of which, he says, is the "wonderful Fire and Elegancy of [Virgil's] *digressive Descriptions*". Amongst these he includes the "*Scythian Winter-piece*. For there is *Fire* in *That* too". See also the Preface to Joseph Trapp, *The Aeneis of Virgil, Translated into Blank Verse*, 1718.

Where fierce Riphaean winds for ever beat,
Of their warm furrs who strip the tawny Bear
And round their lusty limbs the shaggy cov'ring wear.

After this tedious letter, I shall not detain you long. 'Twould however be unpardonable in me to omit the complements of the Season, and my Service to Mr. Cox. The usual mirth and good-humour of this part of the year will furnish you with abundant matter to write upon. I shall therefore expect, you'll keep me in countenance, by sending me an answer very soon, that shall bear some proportion to the length of this. I am, dear Sir, your most oblig'd Friend & Servt.

R. Hurd.

22 To JOHN POTTER 15 APRIL 1742

Text: MS NLW 12432E; unpublished.
Addressed: To/the Revd. Mr. Potter at Batcombe/near Brewton in/ Somersetshire./By London.
Postmarked: 19 AP

Dear Sir,

Your last opens with such tenderness of Sentiment and Expression, that I could not help concluding at first, you had forgot yourself, and directed a letter to me, that was intended only for Hetty. Indeed the profession you make of your regard for me, and my letters, is so much above anything, either I, or they, can pretend to, that I could not well give it any other turn. At least I am to resolve it into that habitual complaisance, wch. grows upon a man in Love, and by degrees wears him, like the Air and converse of a Court, into a degree of Politeness, unknown to the rest of the world. In one point however I am willing to think my comparison fails; for tho' I have charg'd you with a Courtier's politeness, yet you have not, I am sure, his Insincerity; and that is an Idea, wch. the word Courtier has been usually made to convey. In short, I believe you to be, tho' a Lover, that is half a Courtier, a very honest man; and that your letter, however extravagant in point of language, at least means this, that you have a real respect for me. I would willingly shew you the same in my turn, and by some act or other convince you, if it should seem necessary, of a mutual, and, I hope, equal respect from me. This I am now about to attempt by writing you, what I have not done to any one a long time, a whole Sheet. The Subject may indeed chance to want an Apology, for it is of myself. Yet the making one would have in it an air of greater distance, and form than ought to be observ'd between Friends. Take then the following Impertinence, and treat it as you please.

About a Month ago I receiv'd a very obliging Offer, from a friend at Cambridge[1] (whom, I believe, you don't know, and therefore I need not mention) of a little Living

1 Edward Macro. The offer was of the rectory of Reymerston. The right of presentation to this living belonged to Francis Longe (1726–76), the cousin of Edward Macro, on his mother's side. Longe's father had died in 1735, and since then he had been living under the guardianship of Edward's father, Cox Macro. When the living of Reymerston became vacant in February 1742, the Macro family had recommended RH as successor to the previous incumbent. However, it was Cox Macro's particular influence over Longe that decided him in RH's favour. (*Macro Letter-book.*)

in Norfolk, about 70, or 80 pds. a year, and a neat house upon it. As my Inclination leads me to settle somewhere in that part of the Kingdom, and as the Thing itself was not of a contemptible value, you'll imagine I was not backward to accept it. Some small difficulty however arising about it, my Friend advis'd me by the next Post to appear upon the Spot, and settle matters myself.[2] Immediatly upon this I went for Cambridge, and got there last Sunday Fortnight. From thence I rode to my Friend's Father, whose Interest it was, that procur'd me this living, and who was the chief Manager in the affair. Upon consulting him the great Difficulty, I found, was my not being in Orders, and under Age.[3] This made it necessary <for me> to choose a Person to hold it for me; but who that Person, was the Task. Considering however that Hudson was very near, within about 16 miles, and that "Honest" was the Epithet we us'd to give him, I resolv'd to ask the Favour of him. With this design the next Day brought me to Ipswich, or rather Wherestead. I was riding by the house, and was just going to enquire where he liv'd, when Bob came running out, broad awake, you may be sure, and marvelling much to see me there. His Eyes indeed, as well as his words, witness'd his Surprize; but glad he was to see me, and, my horse committed to the care of a Servt., in we went. Osculation, and a Commerce of hands, you'll imagine, pass'd between us. This over, down we sat, and began to chatter. But not to tire you with a Detail of particulars, after Dinner, and over a glass of wine, I told him the design of my coming, and, in short, beg'd him to hold a Living for me. After a few questions about Residence &c he told me, he would; and it was presently agreed, that he should enter upon it by Trinity Sunday, (for it wd. not lapse till after)[4] and that I should be Curate. In order to this <I am> I intend at that time, for I am yet a lay-man, to take Orders. The remaining part of the Evening we spent very chearfully, and among our friends and acquaintance did not forget those in Somersetshire. The next morning I took leave, and return'd to my new Friend, or rather Patron, with whom I pass'd two or three Days most agreeably. He was, I found, a very polite, and learned man, well vers'd in most Sciences, but particularly curious in Manuscripts, Medals, and painting. He has an ex[ce]llent collection in each of these ways, and very obliging in giving me a

2 RH's itinerary was as follows. He arrived at Cambridge on 28 March. From there he travelled to Norton in Suffolk, where he stayed one night with the Macros. He rode on the next day to Wherestead near Ipswich, and stayed another night there. On returning to Norton after this, he paused for two or three days, before going back to Cambridge on 3 April (Saturday). He left Cambridge on Monday, 5 April and arrived in Shropshire on 8 April.

3 It was not possible to be ordained a priest before the age of twenty-four. The official age for ordination as a deacon was twenty-three, but a man could be ordained earlier than this if he was vouched for as sufficiently learned and of good morals. (Canon XXXIV (1603), see Edward Cardwell, *Synodalia. A Collection of Articles of Religion, Canons etc. for the year 1547 to the Year 1717*, 2 vols., Oxford, 1842, i. 245–329.) RH was ordained deacon in 1742, and priest in 1744. Meanwhile, the arrangement that was proposed in order to secure Reymerston, was for RH to find someone who would accept the living as rector, and appoint him as curate. When he became of age to take priest's orders, the living was to be handed over to him entirely. (*Macro Letter-book*.)

4 Thomas Dalton, the previous incumbent, had died in February. (Norfolk RO, St. Giles, Norwich Parish Register.) Francis Longe as a lay patron had six months from this date in which to appoint a new rector. (Richard Burn, *Ecclesiastical Law*, 2 vols., 1763, i. 104, 629.) Hudson was instituted to Reymerston on 30 June (just over two weeks after Trinity Sunday which fell on 13 June) and a mandate for his induction was issued on the same day. (Norfolk RO, Archdeaconry induction register.)

Sight of 'em.[5] From his conversation I with pleasure observ'd an extreme candour, in his judgment both of men, and books. He seems a most generous friend; particularly his civilities to me were beyond anything, I ever met with. On Saturday I return'd to Cambridge, din'd on Sunday with the Master of Emm:,[6] and was the other part of the Day with my Friends. On Monday I set out for Shropshire, met with bad weather by the way, but reach'd Hatton by the Thursday following, wch., to be exact in the chronology of my Expedition, was April 8th. 1742. As I rode thro' the open fields in Northamptonshire, I could not but observe with pity the sad State of modern Shepherds: ah! how unlike the golden dreams I had form'd to myself in considering the Antient. Instead of a lovely Antrum, so much talk'd of in Virgil, a thin, leafless Thorn was all the Shelter; and so far from piping it, like their old Brethren, were they, that not a single note was hear'd throughout the doleful Region. Their condition seem'd to me the more miserable, from <seeing them> their being expos'd at that time to some heavy Show'rs; and from thence instead of regarding them, as I had us'd to do, as the favourites, I now began to look upon 'em as Objects of the peculiar wrath, of Heav'n. But to amuse myself in that disagreeable Situation, I attempted to throw a few thoughts of this kind, wch. the melancholly Scene <before> suggested, into Rhyme, and as Pack Horses may be suppos'd[a] to do with their Bells, divert myself on the road with a little Gingling. What a kind of Sound they may make in your Ears I know not; 'tis a comfort however, that if you do not like, you may refuse to hear, 'em. To be read, or thrown by therefore, just as you please, I have wrote you a Copy of them. I call it, for I know not what other name to give it, a Soliloquy.

A Soliloquy.

Lovely these Flocks, as Mantua's plains could share;
As white their fleeces, and their forms as fair.
Their tender young see! sportful all the day
Frisk in the vale, or on the mountain play!
Intent their dams, so years advise, on gain
Assiduous crop the verdure of the Plain!
Nor less that verdure, or the plenty less
Than yield the vales, that Mincio's waters bless.
Yet wherefore stir no raptures at the Sight?
Why, nor those Meadows, nor those flocks, delight?
Ah! wherefore no involuntary Sigh

[5] Cox Macro's collection of manuscripts was very splendid and included a great variety of material, ranging from autograph letters to collections of charters and other manuscripts from religious houses. He also possessed a vellum manuscript of the works of Gower, and the original manuscript of Spenser's *A View of the Present State of Ireland*. His collection of medals was less spectacular, but also extensive. The paintings he collected were mainly by, or attributed to, Northern European artists, and again, they form a very impressive group. Among the artists represented were Bol, Dou, Droochsloot, Holbein, Hondecoeter, Lely, Rembrandt, Rubens, Ruisdael, Streeter, and Trevisani. He also owned works by his contemporaries Pieter Tillemans, Thomas Ross, Francis Hayman, and Christian Frederick Zincke. For further information on these collections see *Proceedings of the Suffolk Institute of Archaeology*, 1858, ii. 284–7; and Robert Raines, 'An Art Collector of Many Parts', in *Country Life*, 24 June 1976.

[6] William Richardson.

[a] MS: "suppo'd".

To live with Shepherds, and with Shepherds die?
Too plain the case: the meads, and flocks, remain:
But Mantuan Shepherds now we seek in vain.
In the slight shelter of a dropping Thorn,
The Citizen's, and ev'n the Farmer's, Scorn;
Stupid, not simple; gross, not unrefin'd;
Meanest at once, in manners, and in mind:
With rags scarce [cove]r'd, and with Hunger pale,
Lo! shiv'ring stands the Tit'rus[b] of the Dale!
Rude to the Pipe, his Lip alone essays
An uncouth whistle on rare Holydays.
Nor knows his Breast to own the gen'rous Flame,
Untaught the woods an Amaryllis' name.
Above Loves feign'd he sets a real fire,
Or for a Dinner only feels Desire.
Inelegant of Taste, to him the same,
The standing Puddle, and the running Stream;
The same, the marshy flat, o! void of Skill,
And the fair rising of the flow'ry Hill.
– Alass! what wonder? Plenty is no more;
And with it ev'ry rural charm is o'er.
  This pitying verse, lamented Swains, receive;
'Tis all the passing Bard, and Friend can give.
Tho' hapless now, without, or grace, or praise,
Say, there was one, who wish'd you better Days.

Now I am got upon Poetry, pray have you seen the new Dunciad?[7] It is believ'd to be, and certainly is, Mr. Pope's. No one, that I know of, but himself could finish a piece with such exactness. Yet there are some reasons, might tempt one to think otherwise. Pray give me your Opinion in your next. If you have not seen it, it will entertain you; for tho' some other studies may not, yet Poetry is, I think, allow'd to consist with Love. Haec bene conveniunt, et in una sede morantur.[8] (To a Scholar and a Friend I never apologize for a Scrap of Latin.[c]) Tho' I must own I could wish the latter were expell'd it's Seat; I should then hope for more of the former from you. I should then too hope, you'd be at leisure to give me now and then a thought upon my fav'rite Subject, Pastoral. For, tho' I do nothing this way at present, I don't forget it. I have lately appli'd to a Gentleman, that is going to make the Tour of Italy, to inform me in some things relating to Mantua, particularly what is the present face of the Country, and whether it answers in any degree to the description, Virgil has left of it.[9] But this, with ev'rything that concerns this whimsical Design, I beg may be a Secret. Will your Brother do anything tow'rds it? Tell him I wish to see his thoughts. He might in the compass of a few letters write me many valuable hints. Let me hear from

7 *The New Dunciad: As it Was Found in the Year 1741*, 1742. This was the fourth book of the *Dunciad*. The first three books had been published in 1728, and the complete work appeared in 1743.
8 Ovid, *Metamorphoses*, ii. 846. (non bene . . . nec . . . maiestas et amor.)
9 See Virgil, *Eclogues*, i, etc; *Georgics*, iii. 12; *Aeneid*, x. 180.

b MS: "Titi'rus".
c MS: "a Scrap of a Latin."

both of you very soon; 'twill be a pleasure <to me> to be detain'd by each of you, as long as I have detain'd you. I am, dear Sir, your most faithful Friend and Servt.

R. Hurd.

Hatton-Grange: April 15th. 1742.

Endorsed by RH: "NB. A single Sheet."

23 To COX MACRO 1 MAY 1742

Text: MS BL Add. 32557, ff. 31–2; unpublished.
Addressed: To/the Revd. Dr Macro.

Hatton-Grange May 1st. 1742.

Revd. Sir,

I had the favour of your very obliging letter; and am particularly sensible of the Honor you do me in employing me in the Search of Antiquities. I wish indeed there is not a Scarcity of them in our part of the World: but if I hear of any (and they shan't escape me for want of Enquiry) you may be assur'd I shall spare no pains to come at 'em. The letters of Bp. Bedell I got transcrib'd, but beg'd the older Copy for you, because I guess'd it would be something more agreable.[1] This, Sir, together with an English Presentation, in a form, that has been accepted by our, and will therefore, I believe, be refus'd by no other, Bishop, I have hereby sent you. The later you'll be so kind as [to] send to Mr. Hudson time enough for him to give me a Title for Trinity Sunday.[2]

I am so proud of my new name of Antiquary, wch. I find you complaisantly indulge me in the boast of, that I am unwilling methinks to talk entirely out of this Character. Give me leave therefore, for a want of a more proper Subject, to trouble you with a Remark or two on a point in Antiquity, which an Accident in Reading the other day insensibly occasion'd. I wish you won't complain of my detaining you too long upon it; but the Affinity, it bears to your fav'rite Science will, I hope, in some sort excuse for me.

The Criticks, you know, have judg'd it a considerable Objection to the Aeneid, that Chronology is neglected in order to give Occasion to the Episode of Dido in the fourth B: of that Poem.[3] In answer to this it has been justly urg'd, that great allow-

1 William Bedell (1571–1642), Bishop of Kilmore and Ardagh. Bedell had resided at Emmanuel for a number of years as a scholar and Fellow, and at Bury St Edmunds as Vicar of St Mary's, before becoming Provost of Trinity College, Dublin, and finally Bishop. He was the author, with James Wadesworth, of *The Copies of Certaine Letters which have passed betweene Spaine and England in Matter of Religion*. The letters to which RH refers (presumably manuscript) have not been identified.

2 A presentation was a formal letter from the patron of a living to the bishop of the diocese, offering a candidate for institution to the benefice in his gift. At the beginning of the century presentations were drawn up in Latin (see William Watson, *The Clergy-Man's Law: or, The Complete Incumbent*, 1701, pp. 104–5); by the 1760s the standard letter was in English (Burn, *Ecclesiastical Law*, i. 105–6). In this case, the patron was Francis Longe, and the candidate was Robert Hudson. Hudson had agreed to accept the rectory of Reymerston until RH came of age to take priest's orders, when he was to relinquish it in the latter's favour. He was instituted on 30 June, and RH was ordained deacon with a title to the curacy of Reymerston from Hudson, on 13 June (Trinity Sunday).

3 Joseph Trapp summarised the lengthy controversy over Virgil's "famous *Anachronism* in making *Dido* to be contemporary with *Aeneis*" in the 'Remarks' on Book IV of his translation of the

ances ought to be made in cases of so remote Antiquity, especially where there is not direct proof on the other Side; wch. is confessedly the case with regard to the Story of Dido. Now what I would enquire is, whether some other Poets, that have hitherto escap'd censure on this acct., are not, if one should look nearly into them, more deserving of it. Before I bring an instance of this, it is requisite to shew, that the Amour of Theseus and Ariadne, so famous in antient Story, was later than that of Jason and Medea. And this the two or three following incontested points in History will put beyond all possible Doubt.

1. Medea was marry'd to Jason, before she fled to Aegeus.
2. Medea was marry'd to Aegeus, the Father of Theseus, before Theseus was known to be his Son. For upon his Arrival at Athens, he found that Sorceress advanc'd to his Father's Bed, on acct. of the promises she had made of procuring him a Son by means of her Incantations. Plutarch's words are, φαρμάκοις ὑποεχομένῆς † ἀτεκνίας ἀπαλλάζειν 'Αιγέα &c Vit: Thes. sub. Init: –[4]
3. A considerable time pass'd after this, before the Expedition into Crete, and consequently before Theseus' Amour with Ariadne. Plut: ibid: –[5]

The conclusion from hence is, that the Affair of Jason and Medea, falling out before her marriage with Aegeus, *therefore*[a] before the return of Theseus to Athens, and therefore longer still before his Expedition into Crete, did and must necessarily happen before that of Theseus and Ariadne. Now should a writer, tho' with all the allow'd licence of a Poet, contrary to so great a Degree of Evidence, reverse the Chronology of these two Stories, and for the sake of Ornament run into so glaring an Anachronism, I think, Sir, 'twould puzzle ev'n your Candour to find an Excuse for him. Yet this has been the very conduct of no less a Poet than Apollonius Rhodius; who in the 3d. B. of his Argonaut: introduces Jason urging the case of Ariadne as a precedent for Medea.[6] The Passage is thus translated by a tolerable Hand:[7]

"Fair Ariadne, sprung from Minos' Bed,
Sav'd the brave Theseus and wth. Theseus fled,
Forsook her Father and her Native Plain,
And stem'd the tumult of the Surging main.
Yet the Stern Sire relented and forgave
The maid, whose only crime it was to save;
Evn the just Gods forgave; and now on high
A Star she shines, and beautifies the Sky.
What blessings then &c"

The Poet, it seems, has made a Star of Ariadne in this Description, and has not scrupl'd allotting her a very conspicuous Place in the Heav'ns, at a time when 'tis probable she made no extraordinary figure upon Earth. All that seems possible to be

Aeneid, 1718. The anachronism had been discussed by Scaliger (1540–1609), a number of French critics in the seventeenth century, and more recently by Dryden in the 'Dedication' of his own translation of the *Aeneid*, 1697.

4 Plutarch, *Life of Theseus*, xii. 2.

5 *Ibid.*, xix–xx.

6 Apollonius Rhodius, *Argonautica*, iii. 997–1005.

7 Presumably, that is, by RH himself. The first English translation of Apollonius Rhodius did not appear until 1771.

a Written in large lower case letters.

urg'd in his favour is, that 'tis only an Allusion, and not carry'd on to any considerable Length. I should be sorry if this Objection should prove yet stronger agst. an admir'd writer of the Augustan Age. And yet Catullus in his Nuptials of Peleus and Thetis, wch. I need not say is one of the most delicate pieces, ev'n that Age of wonders produc'd, mentions the Genial Bed as adorn'd with the Story of Ariadne and Theseus, and what is more, alludes to it as an antient Tale.

"Haec vestis *priscis* hominum variata figuris
Heroum mirâ virtutes indicat arte."[8]

Tho' this very Author tells us in the beginning of the Poem, that the first opening of this Amour was in the time of the Argonautick Expedition: For Peleus fell in love with Thetis, as he pass'd the Sea to Thrace. When they were marry'd indeed is not express'd; but, I believe, you'll agree with me that it must have been a tedious, an Antediluvian Courtship, if it lasted till Peleus (who began his addresses during the Argonautic Expedition, and therefore long before Theseus' affair was talk'd of) could reflect upon it as an antient Tale.

I am pleas'd to observe that however he may have fail'd in the Acct. of Dido, Virgil has been much more happy in the Use of this Story. He alludes to it in the beginning of the sixth Aeneid, where it serves to grace the Portals of his Cumaean Temple.[9]

"Hic labor ille Domûs et inextricabilis Error.
Magnum Reginae sed enim miseratus amorem
Daedalus, ipse dolos tecti Ambagesque resolvit
Caeca regens filo vestigia." –

You see, Sir, how far an accidental thought has led me! so far, that, I am afraid, I ought to make a fresh Apology for having pursu'd it; at least for giving you the trouble of pursuing it too. Indeed, now I come to consider what I've wrote, and to whom, I am almost asham'd of it. It looks like no great Complement to lead a D.D. thro' so much Classick Trumpery, merely to date the Aeras of two noted Amours, or, in other words, of two noted Whoredoms. All I can say for myself is, that some illustrious names have been tack'd to as low Subjects, and that, if you put me on defending myself, I could mention some great Criticks that have wasted more time on full as scandalous loves as these. Tho' after all my chief dependance is on that indulgent regard, you are ever ready to shew to the innocent Trifles of young men; and as such, I dare promise myself some share of it ev'n to this of, Revd. Sir, your most oblig'd and most humble Servt.

R. Hurd.

You'll please to make my Complements to Mrs. Macro.

8 Catullus, lxiv. 50–1.
9 *Aeneid*, vi. 27–30.

24 To JOHN POTTER 14 JULY 1742

Text: MS NLW 12432E; unpublished.
Addressed: To/the Revd. Mr. Potter/at Batcombe near Brewton/ Somersetshire./By London.
Postmarked: 19 IY

Reymerston July 14th. 1742.
Direct to me at Reymerston to be left at
the Ship in St. Peter's Norwich by London.[1]

Dear Sir,

I have somewhere misplac'd your letter, (for I take too much care of anything of yours to lose it) and in the hurry I've been lately in forgot the purport of it. You'll please to accept this as an Apology for my passing on, without taking any further notice of it, to a less agreeable Subject, but one you'll probably expect to hear something of, myself. If you've hear'd it from no other Quarter then, this will inform you, that I was ordain'd in St. Pauls by the Bishop of Bristol. As Norwich did not ordain, he gave letters Demissary.[2] The week was spent agreeably in seeing the curiosities of the Town. Vaux-Hall and Ranelagh,[3] you may be sure, were of this Number. The former of the two places I approve, and admire; the latter I think Ridiculous, and detest. Hudson, Gould, and Macro, whom your Bro: knows, were the chief of my company. We often, very often, drank your Health, and wish'd for you<r Company> with us. Mr. Macro was so kind to go with me from Camb: merely to bear me company.

1 The post to and from Shipdham (and from there to Reymerston) was collected at the Ship each week.

2 RH was ordained deacon on 13 June 1742. Joseph Butler (1692–1752), the Bishop of Bristol, was also Dean of St Paul's. The Bishop of Norwich was Thomas Gooch (1674–1754). The granting of letters dimissory, authorising the bearer as a candidate for ordination by another bishop, was standard practice in the eighteenth century. (Burn, *Ecclesiastical Law*, ii. 112–13.)

3 Vauxhall was renowned for its beautiful gardens and musical performances. The property had originally been privately owned, but according to Sir John Hawkins, quoted in the *Ambulator: or, A Pocket Companion in a Tour Round London*, Fourth Edition, 1792, it was bought by Jonathon Tyers about 1730, and developed as a place of public entertainment. The gardens were already "planted with a great number of stately trees, and laid out in shady walks", but Tyers converted the house into a "tavern, or place of entertainment", which was "much frequented by the votaries of pleasure". Tyers had opened the gardens with a "Ridotto al Fresco" which proved so successful that he was encouraged to make the gardens a place of musical entertainment on every evening during the summer season. "To this end he was at great expence in decorating the gardens with paintings; he engaged a band of excellent musicians; he issued silver tickets for admission at a guinea each; and, receiving great encouragement, he set up an organ, in the orchestra, and, in a conspicuous part of the garden, erected a fine statue of Mr. Handel." (pp. 239–40.) Ranelagh was a more fashionable place of resort than Vauxhall. It was situated in Chelsea and was particularly famous for its enormous "rotundo", a building somewhat resembling the Pantheon at Rome, which had been built in 1740. In order that it should be "particularly devoted to the entertainment of the best company," Ranelagh was "always opened about the beginning of April, which is before the families of distinction quit London to reside in the country, and it is closed in the month of July". (*The Ambulator; or, the Stranger's Companion in a Tour Round London*, 1774, p. 138.)

Hudson has been over at Norwich for Instit: and Induct: since I came to Reymerston, and staid a week with me.[4] Last week I was at Cambridge to change my Gown. The day after I came there, Smalley accepted a College Living, and the ruling part of the Society, I mean the Master, Mr. Hubbard, and Lyne, did me the honor to signify their Desire of choosing me into his Fellowship.[5] I shall think of it, but believe 'twill be for my Interest to decline it. I am at present happy in the acquaintance and correspondence of a Man, whom but to know, is to esteem.[6] He is the most general Scholar, I have convers'd with; and has by a near and intimate knowledge of mankind, and an Acquaintance [wi]th the whole circle of Sciences, open'd his mind into the widest and most extensive Charity. I use this term perhaps a little particularly: but I mean by it such a candour in judging both of men and Books, as is seldom met with, and is the Effect only of an enlarg'd Education. And I need not tell you, what pleasure one may receive, and what advantage must necessarily arise from the converse of one, whose mind is narrow'd by no prejudices, and who must therefore think beyond the confin'd capacity of the mob of Gentlemen and Scholars. The Gentleman I have been describing is the Person I am oblig'd to for this living, and whom you've hear'd me speak of before. The mention of this may probably suggest a Suspicion, yt. however free from Prejudice he may be himself, his Panegyrist is not likely to be so. As it wd. be difficult for me entirely to refute this, I shall content myself with dropping the Subject, after having told you that he has lately made an Addition to the Obligations, I am already under to him, by getting me a Curacy, within ½ a Mile of Reymerston, wch. I can hold with the Living, and of so easy a Duty, as that both of them give me the Trouble but of one Church.[7]

I am sorry I have nothing better to entertain you with, than an acct. of myself. [In yr.] next, wch. I beg may be by the return of the Post[,] suggest a better Subject. That I may in the mean time trouble you no further, I'll conclude with observing to you, what however I would hope is no news, that there is not any one more sincerely your's, than your Friend and Servt.

R. Hurd.

P.S.

My Service to your Brother: tell him I expect a Scene or two by the Post, you make

4 He was instituted to Reymerston on 30 June, and a mandate for his induction was issued the same day. (See *ante* To Potter, 15 April 1742, n. 4.)

5 Commencement Day in 1742 fell on 6 July. RH had to be present to have the degree of M.A. officially conferred upon him. (It is this that involved a change of gown.) The following day Nathaniel Smalley (c.1708–77), a Fellow of Emmanuel and RH's old tutor, was nominated to the college living of Preston in Suffolk. (*Order Book*, COL. 14. 2.) The college wished to elect RH in his place, and the subject was broached by the Master, Henry Hubbard, and Matthew Lyne. The latter were among the more senior of the Fellows; they held the college tutorships and were therefore an important force in the society. The post of tutor was the only office that could be held indefinitely; all other offices were rotated annually.

6 Cox Macro.

7 This was the curacy of Garveston. It is not known through what connections Macro was able to secure the position for RH.

use of;[8] and yt. I will not fail to answer his last letter, tho' I have not hitherto had time to do it. He will also take some Notice of Butt's affair.[9]

N:B:

I have sent an answer to his last by ys. post.

25 To JAMES DEVEY 16 JULY 1742

Text: *Memoirs*, 10.

Reymerston, July 16, 1742.

Rev. Sir,

The hurry I have been in ever since I left Hatton will be an excuse to you for my not writing sooner.[1] It will be needless to tell you, since you have heard it I suppose from Hatton, that I was ordained at London, that Dr. Macro has procured me a curacy which I can hold with Reymerston, and that all difficulties are over with regard to this affair. I have very convenient lodgings, have met with very civil people, and, in short, am likely to live very comfortably.[2] The only thing I want is such a friend as I left behind me at Beckbury.[3] To say the truth, there is a wondrous scarcity of reputable clergymen in this country; sober are rare, but learned I have not heard of one near me. But this to my friend.

I was at Cambridge last week to change my gown. The day after the Commencement Mr. Smalley accepted of a college living, and the principal persons in the Society were so kind to signify to me their desire of choosing me into his Fellowship. I shall consider of it, but believe it will not be for my interest to appear as a candidate . . .

If you are curious to know particulars with regard to Reymerston, &c. a letter or two which I sent to my father will inform you . . .

8 There are no published plays in English by Robert Potter. Possibly, therefore, he was already engaged in the translation of Greek tragedy, for which he was to become well known. (This may account for RH's own attempts at translating Lucretius: see *post* To Macro, 27 September 1742, and To Potter, 8 October 1742.) The possibility that he was translating Greek drama is supported by the request in To Potter, 8 October 1742, for Robert Potter's tragedy "together with ye. Comment".

9 Edward Butt was an undergraduate at Emmanuel and a contemporary of Robert Potter's. (*Alum. Cantab.*) No records suggest the nature of the "affair" to which RH refers.

1 RH had probably left Hatton at the end of May or at the very beginning of June. For further details of his activities since then, see preceding letter.

2 RH was not living in the parsonage, but in the house that had formerly been the Longe family seat. By this time he may already have met the Grigsons with whom he was on terms of some familiarity by September. (See *post* To Macro, [19 September 1742].) He may also have encountered the Bullocks who were another local family of some standing. (A *Copy of the Poll for the Knights of the Shire for the County of Norfolk; taken at Norwich, May 22nd, 1734*, Norwich, 1734.) They were connected by marriage to Edward Sharpin, who with his wife Mary (née Bullock) moved into the same house as RH at the end of September or beginning of October. (See *post* To Macro, 3 October 1742 and To Potter, 8 October 1742.)

3 Devey was rector of Beckbury, Shropshire.

26 To COX MACRO 17 JULY 1742

Text: MS BL Add. 32557, ff. 33–4; unpublished.
Addressed: To/the Revd. Dr. Macro at Norton/ near Bury St. Edmunds:/Suffolk./By the Bury-Coach from Attleborough.
Postmarked: postmark missing.

Reymerston July 17th. 1742.

Revd. Sr.,

You have doubtless with great pleasure observ'd those passages in the Poets, that represent the motions of the Mind under outward and sensible Images. Mr. Pope has observ'd one in Homer of a singular Beauty:[1] 'tis where he compares a Doubt and sudden Resolution in Nestor to the waves of the Sea, wch. in a calm continue in a ballancing motion, till a rising wind determines 'em to move one way. He observes, that ys. Allusion is the more to be admir'd, because 'tis very difficult to find sensible Images to represent the motions of the mind, and adds, that such comparisons are but rarely met wth. in the best of Poets. He gives us however one Instance from Virgil, where he compares his Hero's mind agitated wth. a great variety and quick Succession of Thoughts to a dancing light, reflected from a vessel of water in motion. The meaning of all this Preamble is to make way for a most ambitious attempt of my own. Not to keep you in Suspense, will you pardon the vanity of offering you a comparison of this Sort myself? If it chance to be new, as I confess it is to me, and be but just in the Application, I have forc'd, you see, a compliment ev'n from Mr. Pope: so you'd best take care how you find fault. The Image I have wrought up into a comparison is this:[2] You must have observ'd in a still dewy morning, or after a Show'r, when the Sun breaks out, the Trees, and Bushes hung round with little drops of water, wch., from the Reflection of the Sun's Rays, shine out in great Beauty. So long as the calm lasts, this Splendor, as it were, sleeps, and is without motion presenting to the Eye one of the softest, stillest, loveliest Scenes in Nature. But if the least Breath of wind shakes the leaves, the little gems, that are at the Extremities of them, seem at once in the utmost flame and agitation; exhibiting on the other hand a Scene of the greatest hurry and confusion. Now this, Sr, I have thought an Image, proper to illustrate the character of what the world calls a good-natur'd, passionate man. Take him in good temper, and no dew-drop'd Tree with all it's gentle splendors looks so placid and lovely. But let the least and most trivial affront, like the softest Breath of air, come upon him, and he's instantly in a state of convulsion: his busy thoughts, like those active rays of Light, shoot and glance a thousand ways, and are in immediate tumult and Disorder. Nor does the Allusion stop here: his fury, great as it is, is soon over: and, let but the gale cease, the dew-drops rest as before. This, Sr, is the whole of my comparison; and could I flatter myself the Execution of it were in any degree answerable to the Beauty of the Image, or it's justness, as an Allusion, I durst almost assure myself, it wouldn't displease you.

The good-natur'd, passionate Man:
A character.

Of mind compos'd, and countenance serene,

1 Pope's translation of the *Iliad*, xiv. 21–30, and note. RH's account is very close to being a transcription of sections of Pope's note.

2 See *ante* To Potter, 18 January 1741 for the first use of this image.

Without all Peace, all Harmony within,
See gentle Flammeo smile! so mild, you'd swear
No ruder passion knew to harbour there;
Bless'd in himself, and cordial to his Friend,
Willing t'oblige, and eager to defend;
Asks He a Sum or favour? In the play
Not Micio's self more fondly kind, than He.
  Yet should this friend in jest familiar chance
To hint a fault, or at a foible glance,
Some innocent neglect but friendly note,
The *traytor* Stocking, or the *wounded* Coat;
Quick o'er his look the wrathful colour flies,
And instant fury lightens in his Eyes;
This way and that his shifting Soul he turns,
Burns, hates, reviles, detests – relents, and mourns.
  So, when the Sun, fresh-rising from the main,
  Impearls the grass and sparkles o'er the plain,
  Stands a fair Tree, all lovely to behold,
  Hung round with Spangles, and bedrop'd wth. gold;
  Steady and soft the pendant glories beam,
  Shine in fix'd light, and shoot a gentle gleam:
  But if a Gale with softest motion heaves
  In the rich Boughs and stirs among the leaves,
  The quiv'ring Branches cast a trembling light
  And dancing Splendors dart upon the Sight,
  This way and that the flitting Lustre flies –
  Lo! the gale ceases, and the Tumult dies!

I'll not trouble you with an acct. of my late good fortune in getting rid of Mrs. Bullock; your Son's letter, wch. should have been a Post or two before this, but that I had no convenience of sending it, will inform you of the whole affair.[3] I am going wth all haste to transcribe Smalldridge's Letters.[4] That the Originals are likely to be, tho' a trifling, yet a no unacceptable present to you, is a thought that gives infinite Satisfaction to your most oblig'd and most Obedt. Servt

R. Hurd.

P.S.

I need not say how great a pleasure 'twill be to me to hear from Dr. Macro.

3 Mrs Bullock had possibly been temporarily lodged in the house that RH lived in, once the seat of the Longe family. By November, however, she was living in the old parsonage, and RH had new lodgers in his own house: Mrs. Bullock's daughter and son in law, Mary and Edward Sharpin. (See *post* To Potter, 8 October 1742, and To Devey, [November] 1742.) The letter to Edward Macro has not been traced.

4 George Smalridge (1663–1719), Bishop of Bristol, had been a highly popular preacher and much esteemed scholar. RH had obtained a number of his letters through Thomas Gough of St John's College, Cambridge, whose family had been well known to Smalridge, and whose father had been tutored by him at Christ Church, Oxford. (See *post* To Gough, 6 August 1742.) A number of these letters are printed in John Nichols' *Illustrations of the Literary History of the Eighteenth Century*, 8 vols., 1817–58, iii. 241–83. A note on p. 241 explains that about half of the letters were originals and the others transcripts in the "hand-writing of the late venerable Bishop of Worcester when a very young man".

27 To THOMAS GOUGH 6 AUGUST 1742

Text: *Lit. Anecs.*, ix. 360–1.

Aug. 6, 1742.

Dear Sir,[1]

I am much obliged to you for the favour of Dr. Smalridge's Letters.[2] I have transcribed a good number of them for you, but not all; many of them were, I found, upon indifferent subjects, and such as I guessed you would not be very curious to keep copies of. However, if you should like to have any more of them, and particularly if you think of any which are valuable to you, and which I have not wrote out, I shall be extremely ready, upon notice of it, to send you transcripts of them. As there was some hazard in a packet finding you at St. John's, if I had sent it, I have wrote this to assure myself if you are there or not. You will please to favour me with an answer immediately, and I will contrive some method of sending them with all the safety I can. If it lies in your way to do me any more favours of this sort, be assured nothing can more oblige me. I remember you mentioned some letters of Addison and Gay, &c. in the hands of your brother;[3] if you could prevail upon him to part with a few of the originals, I should be punctual in returning copies, and think myself under a very particular obligation of being, dear Sir, Your affectionate friend and very humble servant,

R. Hurd.

Direct to me at Reymarston, to be left at the Ship, in St. Peter's, Norwich.

28 To JOHN POTTER 25 AUGUST 1742

Text: MS NLW 12432E; unpublished.
Addressed: To/the reverend Mr. Potter/ at Batcombe near Brewton/ Somersetshire./By London.
Postmarked: 31 AV

Reymerston Augst. 25th. 1742.

Dear Sir,

You are but too kind to me: the Terms, in wch. you choose to express your satisfaction on acct. of my late good fortune,[1] are such as flow from an extreme Benevolence of Soul and could only proceed from yt truly generous and affectionate turn of mind, wch. at the same time that it endears the Friend, makes the Man more valuable. But I am got upon a nice Subject: I'll exchange it to congratulate you upon your [probable] &, I hope, near chance for preferment.[2] Of 20 good livings may my Friends be the best: ev'ry body, but himself, will I am sure think he deserves [it]. From

[1] Thomas Gough (1720–86) of Perry Hall, Staffordshire, was an undergraduate at St John's, Cambridge. RH may have met him through Edward Macro who had a number of friends at the college. (*Alum Cantab.*; *Macro Letter-book.*)

[2] See *ante* To Macro, 17 July 1742, n. 4.

[3] Probably Walter who had inherited Perry Hall in 1730 on the death of his father. Nothing further is known of the Addison and Gay letters although RH himself acquired a letter by Addison at some time, which is now at Hartlebury Castle.

[1] RH's obtaining the curacies of Reymerston and Garveston.

[2] Potter was not successful in seeking preferment on this occasion.

some hints in yr last I conclude you are agst. my re[turning] to College; to say the truth all my Friends are, & [I shall] pay so much deference to their judgmen[t as] to be determin'd by them. It's being offer'd me by that part of the Society, by wch. it is an honor to be oblig'd, was the only thing yt. made me hesitate about it.

I am just return'd from spending a fortnight with Dr. Macro: my time pass'd there in all the Satisfaction, that arises from a due mixture of polite & learned conversation. The Dr. did me the honor to admit me to a sight of his own Manuscripts; amongst other things I read a Paraphrase of his upon the Revelations, connected all along with, & explan'd from, History. The execution of the whole has giv'n me such an Idea of his Taste & Learning, as, I think, exceeds what I had entertain'd of him before. That mysterious Book, as it has hitherto been call'd, is so clear from his Elucidation, that nothing in the whole Scriptures is more intelligible. I press'd him, as far as decency wd. permit, to publish it; but he seems resolv'd agst. being an Author. I know not his reason, but imagine it must arise from his fondness for Manuscripts, wch. may probably represent his works to him as more valuable in his own hand, than in Print.

I am not at all surpriz'd at your admiring Dr. Middleton's Cicero; Cicero himself could not have wrote it with greater Elegance.[3]

The Life of David I have got, & read part of it: I will not prevert yr. better judgment on this performance, (wch. I beg you'll favour me with very particularly in yr. next;) [o]nly let me desire you to read over the 139, & 140 Vol. 2. pages, & tell me if you ever saw anything more deliciously beautiful![4]

What I am going to ask of you is a very great favor, but I don't on that acct. despair of obtaining it. To explane myself at once, I am at a terrible loss for Sermons: I have hitherto made all I have us'd, but begin now to be tir'd of it. I'll [?tell] you my reason. In writing for a country congregation, [?you] are confin'd to such Subjects, and to such manners of treating 'em, as are trite and old. Now I can't but think it a ridiculous misapplication of time & pains to busy oneself in writing for some years, what at last has been wrote many times before. The same time employ'd in reading & writing of another kind might enable one to strike out something new, and, if there should be occasion, of some Importance. I own indeed if by writing oneself the people were better instructed, we ought to submit to the drudgery, however disagreable. But ys. is by no means the case; good plain Sermons, rather in the old way, have a greater Influence, than any others; at least, if enforc'd by a proper Delivery, must be as good. What I am therefore to beg of you after this preamble is to lend, or give me such a

3 The *Life of Cicero*, published in 1741 by Conyers Middleton. RH had written about it with considerable enthusiasm in March of that year. (See *ante* To Potter, 22 March 1741.)

4 The second and third volumes of Patrick Delany's *Life of David* were published in July 1742. (The first volume had been published in 1740.) The pages that RH mentions contain a discussion and description of what Delany takes to be the Jewish custom of erecting tents on the flat roofs of their houses, in memory of the years of exile and wandering. They were also accustomed, he says, to put up "bowers of evergreens of various kinds, on the tops of their houses, at the beginning of the feast, and to dwell in them to the end of it. They also erected bowers in ranges throughout the larger streets of the city . . . Now, to me, a city regularly built, the palace in the centre, crowned with bowers, and all the streets shooting out regularly from it, adorned in the same manner, the city in the centre of many fruitful hills encompassing it like an amphitheatre, and these also covered with tents and bowers, must form one of the most beautiful landskips the human imagination can conceive; especially by night, when an infinite number of lights, glimmering through the branches, exhibited, as it were, so many moons breaking from behind a cloud." (pp. 139–40.)

number of Sermons, as you can conveniently share: the latter wd. indeed be more agreable, but if that be too unreasonable, the former wd. much oblige me. The Numbers you & your Bro: have will make it easy for you to part wth. some,[5] and I will promise you on the word of a Friend, (for I know nothing more solemn) to preach 'em no where but at my two Parishes, Reymerston, & Gaverston. If you cannot absolutely give 'em me, I'll be at the trouble of taking copies, & will take care to return the Originals. Pray communicate this request to yr. Brother, & if betwixt you I can be furnish'd with a parcel, be assur'd nothing in your power could more oblige me. They might be sent very safe, with the same directions only, that you write upon my letters; only take care to nail & cord 'em up well in a little Box! I don't desire any of yr. best Sermons; plain useful Discourses are all that I want. But I'll press you no farther; I know you'll oblig[e me] if you can: Only let me know as soon as possible.

[I] had almost forgot to tell you that my Rector was [at] Norton with us some part of the Time:[6] the Curate & He lay together, and had by yt. means an opportunity of talking over with much pleasure some of our old affairs at Emm: – The morning after he came, he was almost frighted out of his wits by a Larum, wch. went off about 7 o'clock, and awoke him out of the sweetest Slumber, he had known yt. night. Miss Macro & I laid the Scheme, & had, you may be sure, good laughing on the occasion. By the assistance of a little light, yt. play'd thro' the curtains, I could perceive his Eyes, wch. you know were never of the Smallest, at least ½ an Inch larger in the Diameter, than usual. But I am dwindling into a sort of tattle, but ill worth sending 190 miles. Excuse the impertinence, & believe me, Sr., your's most affectionately

R.H:

29 To COX MACRO — 10 SEPTEMBER 1742

Text: MS BL Add. 32557, ff. 39–40; unpublished.
Addressed: To/the Revd. Dr. Macro at Norton/ to be left at Mr. Haywood's/in the Cook-Row/Bury St. Edmunds.
Postmarked: NORWICH

The Popping Jay Norwich:

Revd. Sir,

As the conveyance of letters is more convenient from this place than Reymerston, I shall not stay till I reach thither, before I give you an acct. of my Interview with Mrs. Longe.[1] This morning (viz: Friday Septr. 10th. 1742) about 9 o'clock I set out from Reymerston to Shixworth, and got there about one. I committed my Horse to the care

[5] The borrowing of sermons or use of available published discourses was common practice in the eighteenth century and recommended by such authorities as Bishop George Bull and Samuel Johnson. (James Downey, *The Eighteenth Century Pulpit. A Study of the Sermons of Butler, Berkeley, Secker, Sterne, Whitefield and Wesley*, Oxford, 1969, pp. 6–7.) John and Robert Potter probably used sermons collected by their father who had died in 1739.

[6] RH's rector, Robert Hudson, was still living at Wherestead, near Ipswich.

[1] Elizabeth Longe (née Godfrey) was the sister of Mary Macro and mother of Francis Longe, patron of Reymerston. Correspondence in the *Macro Letter-book* shows that she had been opposed to the appointment of RH as curate of Reymerston and that she deeply resented the influence the Macros had over her son.

of a Servt. & went to the Kitchin-Door. [After] a pulsation or two comes a person to the door: I en[quir]'d first if Mrs. Longe was at home; the answer was, yes; next, if Mr. Longe was, it was reply'd, no: he was gone a gunning, but would return by Dinner. I then desir'd to be admitted to speak wth. Mrs. L– upon wch. a female Servt., whom by the busy pertness of her look, & the sleekness of her hide (for these I think are the marks by wch. we usually distinguish your fav'rite domestic Animals) I guess'd to be Mrs. Margett, told me her Mistress was a good deal engag'd with company, and she believ'd she was not at leisure. I said 'twas no matter, for as I propos'd to see Mr. Longe, I could stay, & therefore she needed not to trouble Mrs. Longe upon the Occasion. I was all this time in the Kitchin; she offer'd to shew me to no Room, nor, I think, ask'd me to sit down. I therefore walk'd about a pretty while; at length crys the same female creature (whom you must know upon the supposition of her being Mrs. Margett I call'd Madam) if you please to tell me your name, I'll carry it up to my Mistress, perhaps she may be at leisure, tho' I don't know – Well – reply'd I, just as you will; my name is H: – & I come from R. – On the mention of the place & name I observ'd a look to spread upon her visage, betwixt a Smirk, and that sort of aspect that goes by the name of Simple – but away she went. – After a space comes a man Servt. and desir'd my name agn.; wch. being told him, he retir'd, but soon return'd with a desire from his Mistress, that I wd. walk up stairs. Up stairs I went, and into a little room on the right hand the passage, not far from the Stairs. As soon as I had well seated myself in [an] Arm-chair by the window, and began to look round me, in sails Madam. Reverent I rose & did Obeysance: she look'd torvous, & waited the opening of your Servant's mouth. Accordingly I open'd my Mouth & said, "that I had done myself the pleasure to wait upon her, & Mr. L– – I had not finish'd my speech, before she interrupted me by saying, She did not know me: I answer'd, my Name is H: I come from Reymerston. – I don't know any such person, reply'd she to this. – Madam, I have receiv'd a very considerable favour from your Family, & therefore I could not but think it my duty to wait upon you to acknowledge it, was my Answer. Upon ys. she colour'd & paus'd. – After a silence of about ½ a minute, she ask'd me to sit down & call'd a Servt. to fetch a glass of wine. In the interim I beg'd to know, if Mr. L. was at home, & how he did; she said, he was well, but not at home, and yt. he was not expected till Night – she added that some company was come in to see him, but wd. be disappointed. I said, I was sorry I was so unfortunate not to find him at home. We sate mute for some time; she look'd very grave, if she was not a Lady, I should say, Sour. When the wine came, I took it, and drank my Humble Service to her, & Health to Mr. L. – After this I sate about 5 minutes. – She said nothing: I then rose, & made my compliments & beg'd she would please to give my H: Service to Mr. L. – She answer'd, [s]he wd. let him know, such a person had been there. I bow'd, & departed. To the stable I went, got my Horse, gave the Servt. a Shillg. & came hither, where I have devour'd, (for I was very hungry), a Beef-Stake, & a couple of tarts.

Since dinner I have been to wait upon the Chancellor;[2] [a] he treated me with great

[2] Dr Robert Nash (1691–1752). As Chancellor of Norwich he was the representative of the bishop in matters of jurisdiction and administration from 1731 till his death. (Hamon Le Strange, *Norfolk Official Lists, From the Earliest Period to the Present Day, compiled from Original Sources*, Norwich, 1890, p. 68.)

[a] MS: "Chanchellor".

civility; we sate & chatted over a Bottle of wine a pretty while. On my saying that I intended waiting on Mr. Baker[3] he insisted upon sending for him; but he was not at home. The Chancellor enquir'd after your Health, and says he will certainly do himself the pleasure to wait upon you, before Summer is over. –

As to the affair of Mrs. Longe; it gives me no uneasiness, only as I am concern'd to reflect yt. I should be the unhappy cause of such a breach between your two families. I am, Sr[.,] your most oblig'd & most Obedt. Servt.

R. H:

I beg my H: S. to Mrs. Macro, Miss Macro & my good friend, your Son.

The hopes of a Sesquipedalian, as you are pleas'd to call it, from Mrs. Macro, give me great pleasure. Please to excuse Tavern-writing.

Endorsed by Cox Macro: "Answer'd".

30 To MARY MACRO [19 SEPTEMBER 1742]

Text: MS BL Add. 32557, ff. 35–6; unpublished.
Addressed: To/Mrs Macro.

Sunday Ev'ning:

Madam,

I have just made my escape from a dish of Tea & a violent fit of laughing, to do myself the pleasure of answering your last kind favour. It reach'd me not before I had often wish'd for it, and was therefore heartily welcome. Only one thing I must own my dislike of, and 'tis I am sure the only thing I ever shall dislike in Mrs. Macro's letters. What I mean is the Apology you make for the length of 'em. Ah! Madam, did you but know the Satisfaction, they always bring along with 'em, were you but sensible of my happiness in receiving, opening, reading, & reviewing ev'ry half Sheet, that bears the date of Norton, & in a particular manner the name of Mrs. Macro, you could not but think it needless, or rather unkind, to make the least apology for what you modestly, but permit me to say unjustly, call the Impertinence of a female Pen. Were ev'ry female Pen like that, by wch. I have been lately favor'd, I should make no Scruple to abridge the Number of my Male Correspondents, & endeavour to supply their places with Petticoats. But to say the least, (for I find by your critical remarks on my last you won't permit me always to write up to the Truth) 'tis unnecessary to excuse your pursuing me, as you elegantly express yourself, to the recesses of my closet, since that very pursuit affords me the greatest pleasure I receive in there. But to have done with prefacing, (wch. I should not indeed have dwelt upon so long but to remove a principal obstacle to my Entertainment,) just as you gave me to hope, my good friend[1] came on Tuesday, but wet, dagg'd & tir'd past Expression. I adminstr'd all the little comforts, my cell wd. afford, and got him well enough by the next afternoon to laugh away a few hours with the Ladies at Mr. Grigson's.[2] Thursday pass'd in that agreable

[3] John Baker, with his brother William, was registrar of the Norwich diocese, and Rector of Garveston, of which parish RH was curate. (*Norfolk Official Lists*, p. 77.)

[1] Edward Macro.

[2] The Grigsons were a Norfolk family with property near Garveston. (See Walter Rye, *Norfolk Families*, Norwich, 1911–13, p. 270.)

sort of conversation, wch. friends are never at a loss for; & friday we set out for Sr. Andrew Fountain's & Houghton.[3] What entertainmt. we met with there you'll better inform yourself from my Friend's mouth, wch. will open itself, I dare say, in large praises of the beauty of the one & Grandeur of the other. What I chuse to insist upon (because perhaps he wont) is our Ev'ning's conversation with Dr. Gardiner & his Lady. The term "conversation" indeed you may probably see cause in a little time to think improper, but as a better does not occur, you must e'en take it. Well: by means of Mr. Gardiner, the Dr.s Son, & a little known to Mr. Macro, we were invited to Supper on Saturday night.[4] (The day we had spent in rambling about Sr. Andrew's & Ld. Orford's.) We went be sure with a resolution of *shining* before a Lady of Mrs. G.['s][a] character; but alass! how vain are human purposes & resolutions! for, whether it were owing to the superior lustre of Madam, the unlucky influence of our Stars, or the preordain'd decrees of <. . .> an overruling Destiny, my friend & yr. humble Servt. were surely never less bright. As for my part, she struck me blind & immoveable at once upon our very entrance into the Room. Pray, says She, Mr. H– how does your Father do? – What the duce, thought I, can the woman mean? God forbid[b] she & my Father should have ever been acquainted – In short I <. . .> look'd silly, & said just nothing. – This gave her time to reflect, & the mistake immediatly appear'd that I was taken for some Billy Hurd the Lord knows where. After ys. I was troubl'd with no more Interrogatories, & had nothing to do but to hear Madam's stories about my Ld. Walpole, & fifty fine things, that I can't remember, till at length lull'd & overpowr'd by the enchanting softness, I suppose, of her voice, compos'd I was going comfortably to sleep, had not a certain Accident, wch. you are now to be inform'd of, come to my

3 Narford, the seat of Sir Andrew Fountaine, was built about 1700. The house is described in the *Norfolk Tour* as "a good one, but not the object of view so much as the curiosities it contains". These included a "cabinet of earthen ware, done after the designs of Raphael"; "antique urns, vases, sphinxes, &c."; and collections of bronzes, prints, and paintings. ([R. Beatniffe], *The Norfolk Tour: or, Traveller's Pocket Companion*, [1772], pp. 52–3.) Houghton, the seat of Robert Walpole, Earl of Orford, is also described in the *Norfolk Tour*: "The whole extent of the building, including the colonade and wings, which contain the offices, is 450 feet; the main body of the house extends 166. The whole building is of stone, and crowned with an entablature of the Ionic order, on which is a balustrade. At each corner of the house is a cupola surmounted with a lanthorn." This "stately" structure was begun in 1722 and completed in 1735. (p. 21.)

4 Macro's acquaintance was Richard Gardiner (1723–81), who had been admitted at St Catherine's, Cambridge, in January 1742. (*Alum. Cantab.*) His father was John Gardiner, a protégé of the Walpoles; he held the positions of domestic chaplain at Houghton, and personal chaplain to Lord Walpole, and was also Rector of Great Massingham, Norfolk. He is described in a letter quoted by R.W. Ketton-Cremer, as "a very pretty man", and his wife as "a very pretty woman". (*Norfolk Portraits*, 1944, p. 110.) Little else is known about Mrs. Gardiner, other than what may be inferred from her son's belief that his real father was the second Earl of Orford. This belief is commented on by Orford's brother, Horace, in a letter to Sir Horace Mann. The "young Gardiner", he wrote, "has pushed his fortune *en vrai batard*, without being so, for it never was pretended that he was my brother's; he protests he is not – but the youth has profited of his mother's gallantries". (*The Yale Edition of Horace Walpole's Correspondence*, ed. W.S. Lewis, 48 vols., 1937–83, Vol. 18, Walpole to Mann, 19 October 1744.)

a MS: "Mrs. G.– character".

b MS: "fobid".

Assistance. My friend, who believe me was much the brighter of the two, had just life enough, tho' partly in my condition, to keep talking. A <smart> complement or two that rebounded with some smartness from the Pidgeons & Apple-pye at Supper promis'd much Success in the remainder of the Ev'ning, & put him I guess, if one knew the truth of the matter, on that bold Attempt, that prov'd so fatal. A picture was mention'd in wch. Harry 8th. was drawn among some ladies[5] – the Dr.s remark was yt. those were creatures his Majesty had considerable dealings with, <. . .>– Oh! I abominate that fellow, adds Madam with a certain pertness & vivacity, wch. you'll better imagine than I can express – the wretch made no conscience of doing any thing. – My friend, who you may be sure was upon the catch for ev'ry opportunity of saying a good thing, snatch'd this to observe to her with some archness, that She hardly suppos'd then the Res – the *Revolution* was owing to any Sting of his conscience.[6] Poor stupid I, who was just *gone* on the other side the table, was so far recover'd by ys. means as to open an Eye, and witness my approbation by a half smile, that unavoidably <crept> gain'd on my countenance. They, that were awake, laugh'd, but whether at the wit, or the mistake, is yet a secret. Warn'd by ys. danger I kept my mouth rather more guarded, than before; for in ye.[c] twilight of reason that broke in upon me in that Interval, I was bright enough to see that if my friend, who had both eyes open, was so much in the dark, I who had neither open to any purpose, should be much more so. Soon after this I made a shift to command attention enough to observe the progress of the conversation, when upon observing considerable pauses in the Revolutionist's discourse, upon hearing him preface some of his remarks with hesitations, & particularly upon taking notice of his beginning some of his Sentences at the wrong End, I concluded he was full as far gone as myself, and apprehending, if we stay'd longer, we might betray ourselves by down right snoring, I mov'd going to him, & accordingly we took leave, and departed. We departed, but with such a blot on our reputation in regard of wit & smartness, as we are afraid will scarcely ever be wip'd off by any future amendments. As Madm. is mightily giv'n to hate things & folks, we are alarm'd at the thoughts of being detested as a couple of insipid creatures. Pray, Madam, administer some relief to me in ys. distress; & endeavour, if you can, to account for this Night's behaviour in such a manner, as may make me think better of myself, than I am now <. . .> able to do, tho' 'tis with a certain vanity I always write myself, Madam, your most Obedt. Humble Servt.

R. Hurd.

I beg my H: Service to Miss Macro.

P.S.

I am pleas'd to hear of your design in regard to the House; 'twill make an excellent Addition to it.[7]

5 This was possibly a picture painted by Holbein and Janet. It was at one time thought to be of Henry VIII with Ann Boleyn and other ladies; but this theory has now been discredited. (Information from the National Portrait Gallery.)

6 The word Macro was looking for was "Reformation".

7 The Macros did a great deal of work on their house in the 1730s and 1740s. What their precise plans were at this point has not been discovered; but see *post* To Mary Macro, 22 June 1743, n. 7 for an account of work done between 1743 and 1745.

c MS: "ye" written over "yt".

I know the character of the Lady, you mention, Mr. Sm–['s][d] quondam Mistress – She's a clergyman's daughter of little or no fortune in Yorkshire – her name Miss Tomlin.[8]

Endorsed by Mary Macro: "answer'd ye 23 of Sept 1742".

31 To JAMES DEVEY 24 SEPTEMBER 1742

Text: *Memoirs*, 11.

Reymerston, Sept. 24, 1742.

. . . July 28, and this September 24! A long time, I own, for so kind a letter from so kind a friend as Mr. Devey to remain unanswered; but I dare promise myself your pardon. I will not waste any of my paper in apologies, only in general give me leave to tell you that sermonizing has been the main cause. Your advice from Dr. Moor weighs much with me, but not more than it had in Mr. Devey's own words and name.[1] Dr. Macro has been informed by Mr. Smalley (who accidentally called upon him one day) of the favour the college designed me.[2] He seemed pleased at the information, but dissuaded my return to college, and added I might be sure in a little time of a second living. The Doctor never mentioned the thing to me, which convinces me that he would be better pleased if I declined the offer, and I know myself under too many obligations to him to act contrary to his pleasure. I shall, therefore, in a few days write to Mr. Smalley to cut out my name, and have resolved with myself, instead of reposing in the shade of a college, to trust my fortune to the world. I confess myself on this occasion something in the state of Adam on his leaving Paradise. I cannot help reflecting, with some regret, on the place I am going entirely to forsake, and am every now and then turning a wishful eye back on those pleasant scenes from which I am about to banish myself for ever. The happy difference is, that I banish myself, and he was banished; in this, indeed, there is some comfort, otherwise the prospect of encountering an ill-natured world is none of the pleasantest. But I must change my theme, or I find I shall grow grave upon you.

The people of Reymerston, whose character you inquire after, are said to be very honest, but very obstinate. I guess the remark is just, from what I've already seen of them . . . I had almost forgot to tell you that there is a very rich, and consequently a very powerful, man in the town, with whom I am in huge favour. By means of Dr. Macro I have been introduced to the acquaintance of the Chancellor of Norwich. He is a very worthy, good-natured man; I have paid him a couple of visits, and have been treated by him with great civility.[3] My good friend Mr. Macro spent the last week with me at Reymerston; only for a couple of days we made an excursion to Sir Andrew

8 RH refers to Elizabeth Tomlin and Nathaniel Smalley. Smalley had relinquished his fellowship at Emmanuel in July to take up a college living at Preston in Suffolk. (See *ante* To Potter, 14 July 1742, n. 5.) He and Miss Tomlin were married there on 24 November 1742. (Suffolk RO, Preston Parish Register.)

d MS: "Mr. Sm– quondam".

1 This reference cannot be explained.

2 The Fellows of Emmanuel still wished to elect RH to the fellowship vacated by Nathaniel Smalley. (See *ante* To Potter, 14 July 1742, n. 5.)

3 Robert Nash. (See *ante* To Macro, 10 September 1742, for one of RH's visits.)

Fountaine's and Houghton. To describe the curiosities of these two places would require a volume. ('Tis most unfortunate that the masters of both of them should be rascals.)[4] One, however, I must tell you of, – I saw my Lord Orford.

As I have tired myself a good deal to-day with writing a sermon, you'll excuse my talking to you thus by bits and scraps. I wish you'd give my duty to my father and mother, and say I wish to hear from them; please too to add my respects to my brothers.[5] Dr. Delany's Life of David is completed in three volumes; if you read it, as I dare say you will, I should thank you for your opinion of it in as full a manner as a letter will permit. Pray let me hear from you very soon: the correspondence of such friends as you, is one of the greatest pleasures I know; at least in my present situation, in which, conversation, I mean such as one would like, is so hard to be come at. I shall consult my own happiness too much to let any letter of yours lie unanswered so long for the future.

Poor Mr. Budworth![6]. . .

32 To COX MACRO 27 SEPTEMBER 1742

Text: MS BL Add. 32557, ff. 37–8; unpublished.
Addressed: To/the reverend Dr. Macro at Norton/to [be] left at Mr. Haywood's in the/Cook-Row/ Bury St. Edmunds.
Postmarked: postmark missing.

Revd. Sir,

What you censure in me as a tenacity of obliging, you'll soon see cause to regard in another light. The first slight view of the following Sheet will convince you, that 'twas rather a piece of prudence in keeping from your too skilfull Eye, as long as I could, a Trifle that by no means deserves to come before it. I confess indeed 'twas what I mention'd myself first upon seeing a small piece of your's on the same Subject; but if I am not hereafter oblig'd to condemn my rashness in doing so, it must be wholly

4 The "master" of Houghton was Robert Walpole (1676–1745), Earl of Orford. RH echoes opposition whig condemnation and the opinion expressed by many contemporary writers. Pope, Gay and Swift all attacked Walpole and many other authors revealed an equivocal attitude to the "Great Man". (See J.A. Downie, 'Walpole, "the Poet's Foe"', in *Britain in the Age of Walpole*, ed. Jeremy Black, 1984, pp. 171–88.)
Andrew Fountaine (1676–1753) of Narford had also incurred Pope's displeasure and had been attacked as the crafty antiquary Annius in the *Dunciad*, who:
"False as his Gems, and cancer'd as his Coins,
Came, cramm'd with capon, from where Pollio dines." (*Dunciad*, iv. 363–4.)

5 John and Thomas Hurd.

6 William Budworth (?1699–1745) had been RH's schoolmaster at Rugeley School, Staffordshire and subsequently at the Free School in Brewood. Following his election as Head Master of Brewood School he had been appointed Vicar of Brewood and was also presented to the donative chapel of Shareshill by Sir Edward Littleton, uncle to RH's correspondent of the same name. (*Notes and Collections relating to Brewood, Staffordshire*, Wolverhampton, 1858, pp. 105–7; James Hicks Smith, *Brewood: a Résumé Historical and Topographical*, Second Edition, Revised and Enlarged, Wolverhampton, 1874, p. 79.)

owing to that Candour, wch. tempers all your Judgments, & of wch. you give a very singular proof in observing only in that poem, wch. the Author himself would not scruple to own very incorrect, "some small Inaccuracies". But I have no paper to waste in Apologies, however necessary. What you are to expect in ys. short Essay is the Progress of a Shepherd's thought in his Invention of the Pipe: the beginning is a little abrupt, but what goes before is not necessary.

The tending of flocks, watering of herds, & other little Affairs of that kind, may be suppos'd the first & most natural Employments of Shepherds. But such Employments fill not all the vacancies & intervals of life. Frequent must be the returns of leisure to this people, & many the hours unoccupy'd in such cases. The flock may be led to pasture, or water'd at a Spring; but when this is done, the free Shepherd may retire to a green Bank, or friendly Shade, & has little more to do than sometimes to cast a watchful glance that way, & prevent their wand'ring. What amusement should he then invent, or what exercise call in to his relief at this Season? The Tree, that affords him Shade, will indeed afford him pleasure, & entertain him with a quire of natural Music from it's Branches. The tinkling of a neighbouring Spring may sometimes draw him to it's bank, where he must be pleas'd to eye at once the running Stream & listen to it's murmurs. The lowing of herds, & sight of rural Objects may, I think, be reckon'd amongst the other delights of his earliest State. Not to mention the cheap, but sweet regalements of Shepherds on the bank of a Rivulet, on the flow'ry turf, in the Shade.

> . . . prostrati in gramine molli
> Propter aquae rivum, sub ramis arboris altae,
> Non magnis opibus jucundè corpora curant:
> Praesertim cum tempestas arridet, et anni
> Tempora conspergunt viridantes floribus herbas.
>
> Luc. L.2. 1.24.[1]
>
> All on a fountain's brink securely laid
> On Earth's soft lap, & in the cooling Shade,
> Their pleasure purchas'd at an easy price,
> O'er cheap repasts the jocund Swains rejoyce:
> Then most, when laughs the year, & vernal Show'rs
> The springing greens have sprinkl'd o'er with flow'rs.

But these are pleasures of too still & equable a Nature to satisfy the busy Soul of Man. Something of Labour must be contriv'd ev'n for his diversion, & a more active Scene of life be disclos'd. The Bird, the Stream, the lowing herd, & flowry Landskape, may have each it's several charm, & by turns contribute to his Entertainment. But his Attention must not be employ'd on them only: himself sure must do something. What then more obvious than Music? The natural love of Harmony he perceives in himself, strongly inclines him that way; & nothing, he soon finds, can better suit the condition of his State. This of itself will most agreably fill up all the Intervals of his leisure, & what is peculiar to it, will not interrupt his pastoral concerns. 'Tis pleasant to consider the workings of a Shepherd's brain on this occasion. At first 'tis probable his Music would consist only in a rude Imitation of the notes of birds, or his natural love of Mimicry would perhaps lead him to copy in his own voice some other accidental Sounds, that pleas'd him. Wrapp'd up in such thoughts, & attentive to ev'ry Sound,

1 In eighteenth century and modern editions of Lucretius the line numbering is 29–33.

he hears, the watering of his herds, or, it may be, mere chance, carries him to the next River. The whistling of the hollow reeds, that grow upon it's banks, & play in the wind, gives a lucky hint, which he fails not instantly to improve. The hollows of those reeds, when fill'd with wind, yield a musical tone; what if he breath'd within 'em? The Experiment is made, and as the reed happens to differ in size, the note, he finds, is different; & a variety of notes, what is it but Music? In short the reeds are joyn'd; and the Pipe form'd. The groves are taught immediatly to repeat it's Strain, & ev'ry Eccho rings with the new Harmony. The Shepherds from the neighb'ring dales flock around him, wonder at the strange Machine, & applaud the happy discovery. The instrument improves; & as added graces bring it to a just perfection, future Shepherds look upon <it> so beautiful an Art with more than common Admiration, & in fullness of gratitude agree in paying divine honors to the Inventor. This was indeed the extravagance of applause, but we shall incline perhaps to treat it with less Severity, when we call to mind the many lovely Strains, with which ourselves have been delighted by it. The poetical Admirer of the pastoral pipe will be pleas'd to find this account of the origin & invention of it in the language & numbers of Lucretius.

. . . liquidas avium voces imitarier ore
Ante fuit multò, quàm laevia carmina cantu
Concelebrare homines possent, auresque juvare.
Et Zephyri cava per calamorum sibila primum
Agrestes docuere cavas inflare cicutas.
Inde minutatim dulces didicere querelas,
Tibia quas fundit digitis pulsata canentum
Avia per nemora, ac sylvas saltusque reperta,
Per loca pastorum deserta, atque otia dia.

Lib. 5. l.1378.[2]

Long e'er the labour'd line was set to Song,
Or man's charm'd ear with warbl'd numbers rung,
The liquid accent of the Linnet's note
Was taught to tremble in his mimic throat.
And zephyrs whisp'ring thro' the hollow canes
To tune the reed first taught observing Swains.
Thence by [degre]es their Sorrows learn'd to flow
Thro' practis'd pipes in a melodious woe;
Hear'd frequent now along the groves & glades,
The Shepherd's lonely haunts, & sacred Shades.

Thus, Sir, you have your request, & my promise. In return (if I could imagine myself intitl'd for such a thing to claim a return) I could wish you'd favour me with your thoughts on that very remarkable passage in I Cor. II. 10. where 'tis said "the Woman ought to have power over her head because of the Angels". I own 'tis a pretty bold transition this from Lucretius to St. Paul, but I was not willing to omit the first opportunity of making this request to you. You see I have not play'd you a country Tune for nothing; I use it as a means of getting from your hand a more masterly Stroke upon the Lyre; something of a <more> sublime & heav'nly harmony, that will not only tickle the Ear, but sink into the mind, and, like ye Strains of Orpheus, & the old

2 RH's line numbering agrees with eighteenth century editions of Lucretius, but in modern editions this passage begins on l. 1379.

ἀοιὸι, those Interpreters of the Gods, as they were call'd, convey Instruction together with Entertainment.[3]

The letters your Son mention'd of Mr. Potter are chiefly queries about some passages in the Classics, wch. therefore without their answers signify nothing; nor is it certain they would signify much with 'em. However if I had kept any of my Answers, you might have commanded 'em.[4]

I hope I shall always retain too lively a Sense of Dr. Macro's favours to be ignorant how much I am, & ought to be his Oblig'd, Humble Servt.

R. Hurd.

27 Sept: 1742. Reymerston.

I beg my complements to your very agreable family: Mrs. Macro may be sure I have too great a regard to my own happiness not to answer her last favour as soon as possible.

The L. of David shall immediatly follow your next.

33 To MARY MACRO 3 OCTOBER 1742

Text: MS BL Add. 32557, ff. 41–2; unpublished.
Addressed: To/Mrs. Macro at Norton to be left/ at Mr. Haywood's in the Cook-row/in Bury St. Edmunds./Suffolk.
Postmarked: postmark missing.

Sunday Night Reymerston.

Madam,

An ugly, vexatious business of a Sermon deny'd me the pleasure of answering your last favour sooner. I have been sacrificing it to day to the people of Reymerston, (or rather to the winds, for they, I believe, had the greatest Share of it.) & now I am retir'd to my peaceful solitary cell, there to indulge a happy hour in writing to Mrs. Macro. To begin with some appearance of Order I thank you, Madam, for your last two Sides, & am only sorry that paper is so scarce at Norton as not to afford you three. Neither Horace nor the Doctor shall intimidate me, so long as the threaten'd verbosity comes from such a Correspondent. The Dr. calls it impetuous, & would thereby intimate it's Allusion to a torrent, but with submission he had been more exact, & kept nearer to the truth, had he compar'd it, as Homer does Ulysse's Eloquence, to the soft fleeces of descending Snows. For like them, were I addressing any but yourself, I should not scruple to say,

> Your copious Accents fall with easy art,
> Melting they fall, & sink into the heart.[1]

[3] αοιδος, singer, minstrel, bard. No direct source for RH's statement has been traced.

[4] This was correspondence with Robert Potter, not John Potter. It does not appear to have survived.

[1] Pope, *Iliad*, iii. 283–6.

> "But, when he speaks, what Elocution flows!
> Soft as the Fleeces of descending Snows
> The copious Accents fall, with easy Art;
> Melting they fall, and sink into the Heart!"

If anything in such a couplet could be objected to, it would be the term *copious*; for as yet I have not been so happy to find that epithet applicable to you.

But, Madam, how could you be so cruel as not to administer a little comfort to one on so sad an occasion as that of the Gardinerian Affair. You are so good [as] to take[a] some friendly notice of the Shixworthian, wch. yet I never regarded; but here, when consolation had been so kind, you quite desert me.[2] Tho' upon second thoughts (for I've learn'd from the Dr. that ev'ry thing has two handles) I believe you did right. You could not well reconcile me to myself without some sort of praise, or Encomium, & I know my weakness too well to think I could stand your praises without Vanity. My modesty indeed you're pleas'd to say would secure me there; & 'tis true I believe it would, were the praises to come from some <. . .> mouths I could mention, as for instance were Mrs. Gardiner's inclin'd, as I am inclin'd to think <. . .> it is not, to heap 'em upon me – but then, Madam, when – but hold I am got into a Sentence that I am sensible I cannot finish without offending, & rather than do that, I'll e'en leave it abruptly, & begin a second.

My new Neighbours Dr. Sharpin & his Lady are come. This afternoon a civil Invitation carry'd me to drink Tea there.[3] I find him a good genteel sensible Man: as he had no company the conversation soon turned on literary Subjects. I encourag'd it's tendency yt. way, & had the Satisfaction of reading a considerable Scholar in him. On my leaving him betwixt Six & Seven (wch. I did to give myself the greater pleasure of writing this) he ask'd me to stay Supper, & on my refusal, attended, as you'll imagine, with an Excuse, added that he was in hopes of seeing me often, & that we should be good Neighbours. My answer to this you'll guess, & therefore I shall not encumber my paper with it. In short his whole behaviour had so much of the Gentleman in it, & his conversation of the man of Sense, that I rejoyce extremely at his arrival, & promise myself, what I did not expect to find, good company in Reymerston. As I know your goodness leads you to rejoyce with your friends on ev'ry instance of their good fortune, I could not help mentioning this to you.

Mrs. Sharpin is really a well-behav'd woman.

Pray my Service to your *Majestic*[b] Son. The grandeur of his Person has charm'd all the Eyes of Reymerston.[4] One of my neighbours says he's a mighty well-look'd Gentleman, a second calls him a brave young man, & a third, Mary Cocker the Blacksmith's Wife, is of opinion that he has the very presence of a Prince. You'll guess after this how their poor puny parson goes down with 'em. In short I am so alarm'd on this

2 For the "Gardinerian Affair" see *ante* To Macro, [19 September 1742]; for the "Shixworthian" affair see *ante* To Macro, 10 September 1742. Spixworth, the name of the village in which the Longe family lived, is repeatedly mis-spelt by RH.

3 Edward Sharpin had matriculated at Caius College, Cambridge, in 1731. He received the degree of M.B. in 1736 and subsequently practised physic at East Dereham and afterwards at Bury St Edmunds. He had married Mary Bullock of Sturston Hall, Norfolk, in October 1741. (*Alum. Cantab.*; see also Norfolk RO, Deed of 1745 relating to the disposition of William Bullock's personal estate on his death, NRS 24379.) Although RH refers to the Sharpins as "Neighbours", they were by this time living in the same house as he was. See *post* To Potter, 8 October 1742, where this Sunday's tea-drinking is again referred to.

4 Edward Macro had come to visit RH at Reymerston on 14 September for a few days. (See *ante* To Macro, [19 September 1742], for an account of their activities.)

a MS: "good to take".

b Written in large lower case letters.

occasion, & am in such a dread lest the admir'd MAJESTICALITY[c] of his Appearance should alienate the good folks' affections from their lawful Pastor, that I could almost wish his last year's consumption had thinn'd him a little more, & sunk his personableness into a narrower dimension. Pray tell him I think myself oblig'd for the good of the public to admonish him, <for the future> either to make his appearance for the future like other folks, or not to appear at all at Reymerston.

Well! 'tis growing late, & yet I don't perceive myself at all drowsy. How you may be indeed by this time I will not take upon me to say; but if you have any Inclination for a nap, there's no likelihood of your taking it yet quietly. Like Mrs. G–'s,[5] my Larum is[d] still upon the run, tho' ev'ry soul chance to be fast asleep round me. In this indeed she has the Advantage: I have no right honourable to ennoble a Sentence with, no high-sounding Ses[quipedali]an Titles to swell my Style <with>, & thunder in the Ears[e] of my Auditors. That, if anything, might bid fair to keep folks awake; but as for my uniform, humble prate, how is it possible that should have any wakeful Effect, or keep a single Eye from closing? But hold, you'll say, what! always upon Mrs. G–r? Why no truly, I'll e'en leave that to my L–d – & since you must by this time be weary of the Subject, I'll promise for your ease not to mention it any more.

You say, you mention'd ev'ry particular of the Shixworth Treatment to Mr. Longe. I wish he would not take it ill from me that I should send you so particular an Account of it. I did not indeed intend it should go any farther. I regarded it not myself, & imagining you would know that, design'd it rather for your Amusement. The account indeed was punctually, literally true; but would it not appear to him like carrying tales, & complaining idly? However I am sensible your Intention was, as in ev'rything else, extremely kind; & after all you would judge much better, than I can, whether it would give Offence. What I am concern'd for is to preserve such a decorum in my behaviour tow'rds Mr. Longe & his family, as not to incur their just censure or Exception, since that would be to bare a more valu'd friend's Side & make their passes at him more easy & successful. In short 'tis, as you observe, thro' me the malheureux Guardian is to be wounded, & if a passage be once made thro' my spare ribs, the Dr. has not long to survive me.[6] 'Tis on this account I have ventur'd to propose the foregoing Scruple; & if it seems to express any sort of dissatisfaction about what two of my best friends have meant in my favour, they will please to consider it, as it really is, as a sincere & unfeign'd proof of my being their Oblig'd, Humble Servt.

R: Hurd.

3 Octr. 1742. Reymerston.

I beg my Service to Dr. Macro and Miss. I hope I need not say how agreable a letter wd. be on yr. first leisure.

Endorsed by Mary Macro: "answer'd ye 14 of Oct 1742".

5 Mrs. Gardiner.

6 The "malheureux Guardian", Cox Macro, and the rest of his family were on good terms with Francis Longe, Macro's nephew and ward, but Elizabeth Longe had still not forgiven them for their successful application to her son over the Reymerston living. The Macros, however, do not seem to have made any effort to be conciliatory. (*Macro Letter-book.*)

c Written in very large lower case letters.

d MS: "Larum's" changed to "Larum is".

e MS: "Ear's".

34 To JOHN POTTER 8 OCTOBER 1742

Text: MS NLW 12432E; unpublished.
Addressed: To/the reverend Mr. Potter/at Batcombe near Brewton/ Somersetshire./By London.
Postmarked: 13 OC

Reymerston Octr. 8. 1742.

Dear Sir,

I thank you for your last; but not for saving me half the Postage. Pray let no pecuniary Considerations on my part be for the future the cause of an Abridgment. Besides I am at a loss to know, what you have sav'd me by it; as tho' three sides were not better worth 8 pence, than one a groat.[1] But, Sir, for the favor of your Sermons, & the much greater of transcribing 'em I am more oblig'd to you than the limits of ys. paper would permit me to express.[2] So tedious a Task no one wd. undertake for me but from a principle of greater friendship & kindness, than I am [sen]sible I deserve! Tis a trouble indeed nothing should suffer me to [gi]ve you, but the last Necessity. When your Parcel is ready, the best way, I think, will be to send it in a Box, wch. you may have made larger, than is strictly necessary, & fill it wth. paper or Straw. My reason for advising this is, that a larger Box will come with greater Safety. A Direction upon it, the same as on my letters, will, I doubt not, bring it without any hazard to Reymerston. 'Tis strange what you tell me of the choice of your female Neighbour; but the word Love is sufficient to account for it. May I hope your Amour is some way or other drawing near a conclusion!

There has been a considerable Addition made to our Neighbourhood here, since my last. A young Physician & his Lady are come to live in the very house with me![3] Tis a pretty large house, formerly my Patron's family Seat; & as there is more room than the Tenant wants, he has set a considerable part to this Gentleman. I drank Tea there on Sunday last: he is a good genteel, well-bred man, & as far as I could learn from 3 or 4 hours Conversation, a Scholar. You'll guess from hence the grounds I have to hope for an agreable Neighbour in him. His Lady is a well-behav'd woman.

Well! I have read David's life: too hastily I begin to think, for I now envy ev'ry one that has not.[4] There is an oddness in some parts would make one laugh; but I love his Spirit, & admire his Ingenuity extremely. I am this next week to send the two last vols. to Dr. Macro, whose opinion of the whole work I intend to sollicit, & am willing to hope I shall obtain. Such Remarks as you make in reading him would also give me great pleasure. As soon as your most welcome present will set me at liberty, I design myself the pleasure of looking a little into Italian. The Dr. accommodates me with Books, & has promis'd me such Instructions as are necessary. He'll be an extremely proper Person, as he's well vers'd in the language, & receiv'd his Rules from one of the best Masters.[5]

1 At this time the cost of sending letters was met by the person who received them. A groat was equal to 4d. It was a silver coin issued between 1351 and 1662.

2 RH had asked for some of the Potters' sermons in August. (See *ante* To Potter, 25 August 1742.)

3 Edward Sharpin and his wife Mary. (See *ante* To Macro, 3 October 1742.)

4 Delany, *Life of David*. (See *ante* To Potter, 25 August 1742.)

5 This was Ferdinando Altieri, the author of a popular Italian-English, English-Italian dictionary, and of an English and an Italian grammar. (See *post* To Devey, 17 February 1744.) According to the title-pages of the grammars, published in 1736, Altieri was a professor of Italian in London.

My Style, I find, has run hitherto pretty much in the first Person: 'tis no very agreable figure, but will you permit me to use it in one case more? I am now reading with all the Attention, I am master of, a little 18 penny Pamphlet, that came into my hands a few days since.[6] If it's doctrine be true, it reverses all the Notions I have hitherto form'd of one of the most important Subjects in life. 'Tis wrote in such a closeness of Style, with such a force of reasoning, & such a delicacy of <. . .> language & conception, as evidently shew it to be the work of no common[a] Author. Who it is I cannot so much as guess. – When you are at leisure, you shall know more of the Subject & the Book I mean. By yt. time perhaps I may be convinc'd on one side or other: at present I am very uncertain.

Your Brother has done me a favour in writing upon the Eclogues, wch. I take very kindly.[7] I doubt not but he has struck out many things, that will be very useful. In the mean time if what I flatter myself is no unsatisfactory Answer to his Queries from Theocritus will be thought any little Return, you may assure him he shall not long expect it. Pray look over the little piece from Lucretius in my last to your Brother: do me the favor to point out what you take to be, i:e what really are, it's faults. Be as rigid as you can; lay aside, if you are able for one moment, the gentleman & the friend, & tho you cannot the haughtiness, yet for once assume the Severity of Bently.[8] The following is another small business, wch. waits upon you for ye same treatmt.

— prostrati in gramine molli
Propter aquae Rivum, sub ramis arboris altae,
Non magnis opibus jucundè corpora curant:
Praesertìm cum tempestas arridet, et anni
Tempora conspergunt viridantes floribus herbas.

Luc. L.2 1.24.[9]

6 Probably *Christianity Not Founded on Argument; and the True Principle of Gospel-Evidence Assigned: In a Letter to a young Gentleman at Oxford*, 1741. The pamphlet had been published anonymously in April 1742 (advertised at "price 1s. 6d.") but was known to be by Henry Dodwell, the Younger. It was a contribution to the deist controversy addressing the central question of whether a belief in revealed religion was reasonable or not, and was professedly written in defence of Christianity. Dodwell's proposition is that Christianity was not founded on any arguments of truth or reason but on faith; yet the tendency of his work was interpreted by some as debasing faith to a weak credulity, and his arguments if taken to a logical conclusion as making nonsense of orthodox Christian belief. Nevertheless, the persuasiveness of the pamphlet has latterly inclined some critics to assert the sincerity of his intentions. (James C. Livingston, 'Henry Dodwell's *Christianity Not Founded on Argument* 1742– Revisited', in *Journal of Theological Studies*, N.S., xxiii, Pt. 2, October 1971, pp. 466–78.)

7 RH had tried to persuade the Potters to give him their comments on Virgil's *Eclogues* and the *Bucolics* of Theocritus in the autumn of the previous year. John Potter seems to have been reluctant to do so, but Robert was keen to assist. (See *ante* To Potter, 19 September 1741.) He had already written something for RH by September but had misunderstood what was required. This confusion had now been cleared up.

8 Richard Bentley (1662–1742). Bentley was known for his "hard-mouthed severity" as a critic; though this was apparently tempered by warmth and sincerity in his character as a friend. (Stephen Jones, *A New Biographical Dictionary*, 1796.) As he had been the Master of Trinity, he was of course well known to Cambridge men.

9 The line numbering of this quotation from Lucretius should be 29–33. See *ante* To Macro, 27 September 1742, for an earlier version of RH's translation of this passage.

a MS: "commmon".

All on a river's bank securely laid
On Earth's soft lap, & in the cooling Shade,
Their pleasures purchas'd at an easy price,
O'er cheap repasts the jocund Swains rejoyce.
Then most, when smiles the year: & vernal Show'rs
The rising greens have sprinkl'd o'er with flow'rs.

There is in particular one word wch. I much suspect: however, I'll not mention it: if it escapes your critique, I shall be satisfy'd.

Pray tell your Brother I shall expect his Tragedy together with ye. Comment.[10]

I wish you could be here to laugh at Boby to his face.[11] He comes the beginning of the next Month to treat his Parishioners & receive his Tythes. I expect he'll stay with me the best part of a fortnight. If to be often remember'd in yt. time were a benefit, or but a complement, I should venture to say you'll have many an Obligation to the large-ey'd Rector, as also to a certain inferior Ecclesiastic on ys. side the country, who, tho' he honours himself with the name of your friend, can yet do you the credit of calling himself by no higher a name than that of the

Curate of Reymerston.

35 To MARY MACRO 22 OCTOBER 1742

Text: MS BL Add. 32557, ff. 43–4; unpublished.
Addressed: To/Mrs. Macro at Norton to be left/ at Mr. Haywood's in the Cook-row,/Bury St. Edmunds,/Suffolk.
Postmarked: postmark missing.

22 Octr. 1742 in the afternoon just before Sun-set. Reymerston.

Madam,

A thousand thanks for your last favour from Norton. I make no scruple to say it is the most agreable of the kind I have yet been honour'd with. 'Tis generally a good rule to judge by other measures than the Length of a performance, but that alone is sufficient to determine the degrees of merit in yours. To speak a plain truth the longer your letters are, the honor I receive is not only greater but the pleasure too; & that I may sollicit another Triplicate with a better grace, I am now meditating one for you.[1] Tho' what my Brain can furnish on the Occasion, Heav'n knows. I am at present in a dull mood, & am therefore in a hopeful way of proving a dull correspondent. You'll ask me then why I chuse this hour to trouble you <with>. – I'll tell you, Madam, with great frankness: 'tis for that very reason, because I am dull. My fiddle, my Books, & all my amusements desert me just at this time: I find myself in a way to relish none of 'em, & were I to run round the whole circle of my pleasures have the mortification to see I should <. . .> still be dissatisfy'd. One only remains, that can be any resource to me; & 'tis happily such as cannot fail. In short I find myself under the necessity of taking a trip to Norton; (a poor complement truly! wch. I make for my own Relief.) & talking myself into better Spirits by a little conversation with you. Perhaps indeed, as

10 Possibly a translation of a Greek tragedy which Robert Potter had been working on since the summer. (See *ante* To Potter, 14 July 1742, n. 8.)

11 Robert Hudson.

1 RH's letter is written on one large sheet of paper folded in half, and consists of three pages.

I am forc'd to talk to you at the distance of twenty miles, a few of my first Sentences may set out heavily, but I doubt not to find myself considerably enliven'd, before I have done. Nor wonder, Madam, that I begin with so melancholly a preface: I as seldom want Spirits, as most folks; but Nature itself wants 'em now. Lo! yon solitary row of drooping Trees: stript of their green honours they look an uncomfortable bleakness <to>, while the Eye <,which> discovers thro' the intervals of their naked branches as many portions of a hazy Sky. But then how worse than naked look yon wither'd <boughs> Oaks! they shew indeed a variety of colours, but 'tis such as puts one in mind of Otways patch'd Witch & her variety of wretchedness.[2] A pallid, sickly yellowness liveries o'er ev'ry leaf, unless where it is interspers'd with a shade of deeper brown, or dies a way in a gradual, fainting green. The sickliness of the Scene receives an Addition too from the languid rays of an almost setting Sun. See, how they feebly fall on those Oaks, & spred a melancholly glimmer, worse & more dispiriting than Night itself. And then what Silence! not a breath of Air stirs, but the fluid, fleeting Spirit seems almost to have lost it's properties, & grown consistent. Nature is, if you'll pardon the Expression, in a very lethargy: she's motionless & dead; her beauty & vigor are no more, or as I might express myself <more delicately> to a Lady more delicately, like a Belle in a Swoon, her Spirit is flown off with her colour. Ah! how unlike the loveliness of another Season! that much-lov'd, lively, laughing Season, when all is sprightliness, & gayety! But turn from the too fair Scene, my fond Attention, nor dwell unprofitably on the springing verdure, breathing gale, or flow'ry landskape. What pleasure to paint <the> grassy walks, leafy Rows, sheltring Shades, & to compleat all, walking, witty, laughing, pretty, charming, lovely Ladies! in one word, what mighty Satisfaction to survey in fancy's prospective the various charms of Norton in July, when remove but the delusive Instrument & the tortur'd Eye sees Reymerston in the arms of October! Yet see the influence of the lov'd Idea: from the dullness of a drooping Solitaire it has rais'd me into chearfulness & Spirits. On a review of some of the last lines it betray'd me, I find, into the mimicry of a Poet's Strain. Rash, idle Ape! sure I was thinking of Pindar's Address to his Lyre,[3] when I was calling so loudly, & so lamentably on my "fond Attention". However my point is gain'd: the turning from my own sad Scene to you, tho' it carry'd me into some impertinence, carry'd me at the same time into a briskness of Spirit: & for the sake of the latter, the former, (for I know you'll pardon it), is not much regretted. What machines we are, to be skrew'd up & let down again by <. . .> mere Imagination! or rather, now I have mention'd Screws, methinks I am mainly like my own crack'd fiddle: the tone is harsh & untun'd at best, but in a misty dull Air intolerable; the only time when the Ear can listen to it with safety, is in a chearful day when the Sun breaks out, dispels the gloom, & by altering the Disposition of the Air renders to my Strings their due size, & tension. 'Tis thus pretty nearly with me: the Season was to me that gloomy day, it's influence had made me unfit to entertain myself or others: ev'ry thing

2 The "widow'd Witch" appears in Thomas Otway's *The Poet's Complaint of his Muse*, 1680. She lived in an "ill-pil'd" cottage,

"Down in an obscure Vale,
'Midst Fogs and Fens, whence Mists and Vapours rise,
Where never Sun was seen by eyes,
Under a desart Wood,
Which no man own'd, . . ." (Stanza 9)

3 *Pythian Odes*, i. 1–14.

in me was jarring, discordant, & unharmonious, & I was in no humour to be touch'd or play'd upon to my satisfaction by anything; when lo! a luminary of a Sun-like pow'r rose upon me from Norton, clear'd up the surrounding gloom, & left me this moment in as tuneable & melodious a disposition, as the poor squeaking <. . .> Instrument is capable of. Well, Madam, for this as well as other your favours I thank you. Wou'd it were any return for 'em <. . .> to fill the remaining Side with the production of such Spirits, as you have giv'n me! But however that be I must go on, & am determin'd now my hand's in to push things to an Extremity.

To give you a little domestic news, I have ys. day order'd, with the Advice of my Landlady, Mrs. Blanchflower, a dinner for my Rector's Parishioners on the 3d. of November.[4] A swinging piece of Beef, a couple of Geese & plenty of Puddings are to be the fillings for some twenty or thirty hungry, hearty Stomachs. The Ale has been long brew'd, & is just in a condition to run. There will be a delicious Afternoon when the Rector of Reymerston with his Curate, to be sure, on his right hand, and a goodly Row of Rustics on his left shall repose under a canopy of Tobacco Smoke, & batten & swill in tubs of rich, fat ale. Then for conversation, none of your fashionable trumpery; what have we to do with the Queen of Hungary, & what is't to us whether his Majesty goes to Flanders or not? As if we car'd what became of Maillebois, or Prince Charles, or whether folks beyond Sea had any Ale & Tobacco.[5] No: none o' your foreign Subjects, I beseech you: a little good home talk about matters in our own town: a *sort* of observations about the weather & seed time, worthy a natural Philosopher; & not a few remarks on the price of corn & Cattle. See the simple, natural converse of my happy Neighbours! O! for the voice of a Poet to sing Saturn's reign & the return of the golden Age! – But I must check my transports; I have room only to say two or three necessary things before I conclude.

I am glad the Dr. made that Apology for my mention of the Spixworth Trans: to Mr. Longe: it has quite remov'd all my Scruples, & made me, as you kindly meant it should, easy.[6]

I am vastly happy in the prospect of Dr. Macro's next: I have found him Subjects, for I perceive he is not so obliging to find 'em himself, for, I hope, a long letter.[7]

4 Robert Hudson was coming to Reymerston to receive the tithes and to "treat his Parishioners". (See *ante* To Potter, 8 October 1742.)

5 The news from Europe in the autumn of 1742 was chiefly of the War of the Austrian Succession. Maria Theresa, Queen of Bohemia and Hungary, and daughter of the last Hapsburg Emperor, Charles VI, had been struggling against repeated attempts by other European countries to invade her territories, since the death of her father in October 1740. RH's reference to Maillebois and Prince Charles probably relates to an attempt made by Marshal Maillebois to reach Prague and relieve the French troops who had taken and were holding the city. His advance, however, had been blocked by Prince Charles of Lorraine, and on 10 October he decided to retire into Bavaria to take up winter quarters. Also during this period, there had been frequent reports in the newspapers about George II's proposed journey to Flanders. This had been repeatedly postponed, though, until in the end it was put off to the following year. (*Norwich Gazette*, September–October 1742.)

6 The Spixworth incident (see *ante* To Macro, 10 September 1742) had been mentioned to Francis Longe as a result of RH's letter to Cox Macro describing his interview with Elizabeth Longe. RH had not wished that Longe should be told, and had felt uneasy about the matter ever since. (See *ante* To Macro, 3 October 1742.)

7 One suggestion that RH had made was that Cox Macro should send him his comments on a "remarkable passage" in 1 Corinthians, chap. ii. (See *ante* To Macro, 27 September 1742.)

Your Son's Rowland was answer'd this week with a very hasty Scroll:[8] what Effect it will have upon him I don't know; if it does not operate sufficiently upon his Idleness, please to forward it with a remembrance or two that so in some reasonable time I may have the rare felicity of a letter from him. I am, Madam, with my best complements to your good & agreable family, your most obedient, Humble Servt.

R. Hurd.

Endorsed by Mary Macro: "answer'd the 1 of Novr: 1742."

36 To COX MACRO 23 OCTOBER 1742

Text: MS BL Add. 32557, ff. 45–6; unpublished.
Addressed: To/the reverend Dr. Macro at Norton/to be left at Mr. Haywood's in/the Cook-row/Bury St. Edmunds/ Suffolk.
Postmarked: postmark missing.

reverend Sir,

'Tis wonderful, I am just now thinking, the power of the Human Imagination. Numberless instances might illustrate this Remark, but I mean at present to confine myself to it's effects in times of danger & distress. At such a Season the generality of men are transported out of themselves, & led to apprehend consequences much worse than they really are. 'Tis sure to set things in the most frightful Situation, & is studious to magnify ev'ry probable difficulty to the utmost. The force of it is seen only in cases of actual & allow'd distress, but in the more indifferent circumstances & events in Life. Whatever little tryal of a domestic Nature is to be sustain'd, or whatever common Business our Duty may oblige us to undertake, so long as it lies at a distance, the Fancy is always prompting some possible difficulty, & terrifying itself with phantoms of it's own Creation. In so much that I am well satisfy'd, the trouble we undergo in the tryal or business itself is seldom half so great as what this distant prospect of it gives us. I believe it may be just to compare the mind under these circumstances to the Eye, which thro' a misty Air, a no unapt Emblem of Distress, is wont to enlarge it's Objects vastly & convert the least plant or tree into a very considerable Substance. It should be the endeavour & work of Reason to correct the Suggestions of fancy in the one case, as it does those of Sense in the other; <to reduce> to reduce the difficulty as well as Object to it's proper size, & institute an exact conformity between Opinion & Truth. The evils of life are confessedly so many & grievous as make it intolerable to sweat under the weight of these imaginary pressures. A wise man will disengage himself from as many of 'em as he can, & be particularly careful of adding to the number of his woes by a voluntary delusion. Tho' after all his care the disease, I fear, lies too deep, & is too effectually wrought into our very frame, to be entirely eradicated. It is perhaps a natural & necessary fear, kindly implanted in the Soul, in order to suggest caution & foresight, & put us upon

8 To give a Roland for an Oliver is to give as good as you get. This expression was first used in the seventeenth century and died out in the nineteenth century. (*O.E.D.*)

providing agst. approaching Ills with the greater earnestness & attention. To explain myself by an obvious comparison, we live, as it were, in a vast Desert, where Beasts of prey are ev'ry where lying in wait for us. The Bush, or Thicket has frequently, we know, been <the fatal> a cover to the famish'd Tyger or <a> foaming Boar; & what tho' it's rustling arise from some slighter cause, a flying Lizard, or a Breath of Air, yet to start at the Signal may be no vain terror, as it may often serve to secure us from a real Danger. 'Tis thus perhaps in life: the greater calamities sometimes break forth without preparing us by any extraordinary notice for their reception, & would therefore commonly find us an easy prey, were it not for this Alarm of fancy, wch. quickens the Apprehension to fear many times what we never feel. All I would propose then upon the whole is to regulate & restrain it: to listen to it as a kind & provident Monitor, but by no means <to> allow it to usurp a Tyranny, & exact the homage of a Slave. In a word it will be prudent to use it as a Gale that may serve to drive us along the Stream of life with greater safety, but not to give it the rein so much as to suffer ourselves to be overset by it. You have been wond'ring, Sir, I doubt not, for some time what might be the cause of this formal dissertation. You may have agreed with me possibly in the truth of my remarks, but are still surpriz'd at the abrupt manner in wch. they are introduc'd. You'll perhaps cease to be so, when I now tell you, that the following passage in Xenophon's Expedition of Cyrus has of late been the Subject of my Attention.[1] In the account that Historian has left us of the return of the Greeks, he mentions a People, call'd Taochoi, not very far from the Euxine, thro' whose <country> territories they were obligd to pass. The rude Inhabitants, unskill'd in the arts of war, & therefore frighted at the sight of such an Army came out with their wives & children in order to prevent their marching thro' & ravaging their country. To this end they posted themselves on a Rock, over wch. by a very narrow pass their road lay; & annoy'd 'em for some time with Stones & fragments of the Rock, wch. they roll'd down upon them. But the artifice & hardiness of the Greeks conquering all difficulties, & some of them finding means to escape to a place, from whence they might easily come upon & dislodge 'em, the poor, unhappy Defendants were in such consternation, & terrify'd themselves so extremely with apprehensions of cruelty, & outrage from the victorious Enemy, that numbers of them, both men & women, threw their children & themselves from the Precipice, & were dash'd to pieces. A melancholly proof this of the pow'r of frighted fancy, that it should ev'n push to the Extreme of chusing the most shocking Death rather than expect a future imagin'd misery! 'Tis going beyond my Subject to make the following remark, but the pleasure of commending a kind & benevolent deed engages[a] me to do it. In the midst of this Scene of death & terror, which the elegant & generous Author most justly styles δεινὸν θέαμα, one Aeneas of Stymphalus, an Officer in the Greek Army, seeing a beautiful youth about to throw himself headlong,[2] was so touch'd with the Sight, as to catch hold of him, & endeavour to prevent his destruction. But the frighted youth, springing forward with <the> great violence, & perhaps quicken'd in the Effort thro' an Apprehension of torture from the hand, that was only stretch'd out to save him, rush'd furiously down the rock, & drew the compassionate Greek along with him.

1 Xenophon, *Anabasis*, IV. vii. 13–14.

2 The usual description of the fleeing man is of a person "wearing a fine robe". (See Loeb edition; see also Edward Spelman, *The Expedition of Cyrus, Translated from Xenophon*, 1742.)

a MS: "engages" written over "engag'd".

What the Character of this Aeneas might be as a Soldier I know not, for he's no where else mention'd in the History, but this single act of generosity, exercis'd from a truly humane & compassionate feeling for the distress of others, has rais'd him (at least in my unwarlike notions) to such a pitch of Heroic fame as equals, if not exceeds that of the most renown'd Adventurers in the Expedition. He fell indeed in the generous Attempt: but ev'ry Breast, that feels for the virtues of Humanity, will heave on the mention of so glorious a deed, & confess in ringing throbs the honor, that is due to a name of so amiable a memory.

Thus, Sir, I have presum'd to refresh your memory with a piece of no incurious, or inelegant History. The pleasure of a Soul, like yours, sensible to the workings of compassion, will receive ev'n from this rude account of it, must plead my Excuse for the length or impertinence of the Reflexions, into wch. it betray'd me. That I may not add to them still further, for I find it difficult to leave a Subject so agreable, I shall haste to an immediate conclusion by writing myself, reverend Sir, your most sincerely oblig'd Humble Servt.

R. Hurd.

23 Octr. 1742. Reymerston.

P.S.

I return you many thanks for the French-Books: they came very safe, and are very welcome: I was only concern'd to find no Mss among 'em. Don't deny me the pleasure of your remarks on David &c as soon as possible: I am impatient to receive 'em.

37 To COX MACRO 7 NOVEMBER 1742

Text: MS BL Add. 32557, ff. 47–8; unpublished.
Addressed: [To]/the reverend Dr. Macro/at Norton to be left at/Mr. Haywood's in the/Cook-Row/Bury St. Edmunds.
Postmarked: postmark missing.

reverend Sir,

You are not singular in regarding *Xstianity not founded on Argument* as a Sneer at Revelation. To me it seem'd rather an Enthusiastic piece, & I was half confirm'd in the opinion from having hear'd some well-meaning men push the Argument almost as far. But I am sensible how much your Judgment ought to weigh with me. The masterly manner, in which it is wrote, has alarm'd, I find, a good many readers; & this I must own, if the Author be an Enemy to Revelation, he appears to me an abler Champion, than I had hop'd the bad cause cou'd afford.[1]

I thank you, good Sir, a thousand times for recommending Pamela to me.[2] I had some how conceiv'd such an unaccountable prejudice agst. it, that nothing less than your good Opinion could have induc'd me to read it. But what a treasure of Beauties

1 See *ante* To Potter, 8 October 1742, n.6.

2 *Pamela: Or, Virtue Rewarded. In a Series of Familiar Letters from a Beautiful Young Damsel, to Her Parents*, 4 vols., 1740–41. Samuel Richardson had published the first two volumes of *Pamela* in November 1740. The third and fourth volumes were published in December 1741. (William Merritt Sale, Jr., *Samuel Richardson. A Bibliographical Record of his Literary Career*, New Haven, 1936, p. 13.)

had I then lost! to say the least of a work, of wch. the most one can say is too little, I never saw Nature in such perfection before. I make no scruple to say there never were any characters more justly drawn, with greater propriety and exactness, or of a more glowing likeness to the life. The whole is literally a speaking Picture, & by reason of the several distressful Incidents, that are work'd up in it, as moving a one as ever did credit to any pencil. As a draught of Nature then I must read, love, & admire it, & stand amaz'd that any Reader of Taste should hazard his reputation so much as to own a dislike of it. But in it's moral capacity I am not so positive. On the other hand I incline to suspect more danger from it to the generality of young readers, than Advantage. Mr. B's character is a little too engaging to make a Debauchee sufficiently distasteful to the youth of his quality & fortune; & the very nature, that strikes so much <of> in Pamela's narrative of her own distresses is, I fear, still more dangerous to most female fancies. 'Tis hazardous, nay I'll go further, 'tis hurtful to paint Nature in such cases too faithfully. The two lively representation warms & inflames – the passions kindle at the view, & want more than the fair complainant's ejaculations, & reflections to cool them again. This, Sir, I cannot but fear will be the probable consequence of some part of Pamela's charming Journal to the unconfirm'd virtuous of both Sexes. I mention it not as an Objection to the work, (for I am satisfy'd 'tis the very perfection of it) but as a hindrance to it's moral Design. 'Twill be a pleasure to find myself mistaken, & too apprehensive in this point, for 'tis with reluctance I observe anything in the lovely piece, that may keep it from being generally read.

I am pleas'd to hear K. David proves so good Company. Your report of him is expected with that Impatience, which your known Judgment in regard both of men & books but naturally excites. The pleasure this last work has giv'n me makes me think it no more than a reasonable compliment to the excellent Author to purchase his other works. So that I hope soon to do myself the pleasure of obliging you with a Sight of his *Rev. examind with candour.*[3] If I can bring it with me to Norton, (for you've hear'd the design I have upon you,) it will make my Expedition still more agreable.[4]

Pray favour me with a Letter very soon; & please always to do me the justice to think me, with a sincere gratitude & Esteem, Sir, your Oblig'd, Humble S:

R. Hurd.

Reymerston: 7 Novr. 1742.

Mrs. & Miss Macro may be assur'd I am always at their Service.

38 To JAMES DEVEY [NOVEMBER] 1742

Text: *Memoirs*, 13.

. . . In respect of the tithes of Reymerston, which you are pleased to mention, I apprehend, not only that they cannot *now*, but that they cannot *ever*, by me be materially altered. The temper of the people is so resolutely obstinate, that upon any such attempt I am certain they would leave the church; of which, though in the

3 [Patrick Delany], *Revelation Examin'd with Candour. Or, a Fair Enquiry into the Sense and Use of the Several Revelations Expresly Declared, or Sufficiently Implied, to be Given to Mankind from the Creation, as They Are Found in the Bible*, 2 vols., 1732. A third volume was published in 1763.

4 RH visited the Macros later in November. He stayed only a short while, leaving on 27 November for Cambridge. (*Macro Letter-book.*)

assertion of my just rights, I should think myself unhappy in being the occasion. The rent-day is over; and the income is (though not, indeed, this year on account of some deductions) a good eighty pounds. I am sensible, as you suggest to me, that it is worth much more; but am assured it will never be in that power of that address you are so polite to compliment me upon, to advance it. And as to gathering,[1] it is what I must never think of: for the inclosures are so small, so perplexed, and lie in such a manner, that the trouble of doing it would be infinite. Though in this case I am prudent enough to keep my thoughts to myself. They would otherwise be apt to take advantages. But I will trouble you no more on this head . . . As to Mr. Fitzer's books,[2] I could like very well to purchase a part of them; but at present cannot afford it. My late expenses in journeys, orders, degree, repairs, and some little conveniences in my rooms, have rose so high, that such a thing would be inconvenient. I am obliged to you, however, for mentioning it.

Dr. Macro continues his favour to me in every way in which it can be expressed. I am welcome at all times to his study, and a noble one it is; and, what is still more valuable, to his advice and instructions in any branch of learning, either by conversation or letter. He is a very learned and amiable man, the most complete scholar and gentleman united that almost ever I saw. If I seem a little extravagant on the subject, you must excuse me, for his treatment of your unworthy friend is so obliging, that, whenever I mention his name, I am hurried by a sense of gratitude into encomiums. Though, really, in what I've said of him, 'tis, if I know myself, the result, not of prejudice, but of my best judgment.

Since my last to you I am become very happy in a new neighbourhood.[3] A very sensible and polite gentleman, a physician, has taken part of the house I live in for himself and family, which consists at present of an agreeable lady, his wife, and as agreeable a young lady, his wife's sister.[4] We are vastly sociable: yesterday they drank tea with me, together with two more ladies and a strange gentleman. The lady that has taken my parsonage, and who was one of them, is the physician's wife's mother.[5] These two families, together with my rich neighbour's, in which are also two ladies, his sister and niece, make Reymerston quite a polite place. We have, and are soon to have, no less than a brace of chariots and a chaise at our church on Sundays. Could you have thought all this of my little village in the woodlands of Norfolk? I shall be impatient for your next, as I expect in it your judgment of King David. However, don't let me wait if you have not yet got it.

My humble service to good Mrs. Devey. Please to tell her I have just read Pamela, and am glad, for the credit of my judgment, that I agree with her in admiring it. Some people have thought it odd in me, but I really like Pamela in low life better than in high. I have not room now, or think I could give excellent reasons for my opinion. If I was as near you as I have been, what pleasure could I take in talking over this and a thousand other subjects with Mrs. Devey and your good self. Alas! all I can now say is that I am hers and your most faithful servant,

R. Hurd.

1 By "gathering" RH refers to the practice of collecting tithes in person.

2 No further information on this sale of books has been found.

3 See *ante* To Macro, 3 October 1742, and To Potter, 8 October 1742.

4 See *ante* To Macro, 3 October 1742, n. 3.

5 See *ante* To Macro, 17 July 1742, n. 3.

39 To JOHN POTTER 27 JANUARY 1743

Text: MS NLW 12432E; unpublished.
Addressed: To/the reverend Mr. Potter/at Bacomb[e] near Brewto[n]/ Somersetshire./by London.
Postmarked: CAMBRIDGE 28 IA

Dear Sir,

I thank you for the Sermons & Alphabet. I am glad you had not the trouble of transcribing, for as I have now time to learn the characters, they will do full as well.[1]

Your last was just what I expected, & shews me how well you can still rally a College life. All I have to say for myself is, that it at present favours some designs, which I am willing to pursue, & is otherwise agreable in a good measure to my Inclination & Taste.[2]

The suddeness of the change after a seeming Resolution to the contrary was what, I can readily imagine, most surpriz'd you.[3] But I had apprehended thro' mistake that Dr. Macro was agst. it; whereas upon my mentioning the affair to him he entirely advis'd it. To lay the whole proceeding on this occasion before you in as short a compass as I can, Smalley marry'd: the College wrote to me: Dr. Macro advis'd: I went to College; learn'd Hebrew in four days,[4] & was chose Fellow.

'Twas a real pleasure to me yt. by this means a way was open'd for a little thing for your Brother;[5] especially as that, I knew, would further introduce him to the Acquaintance of Dr. Macro. There are some few difficulties, or more properly Impositions, which I am sorry to find he must submit to in regard of his board. But notwithstanding these the thing, I hope, will turn out tolerably to his Satisfaction. I had a letter from him yesterday, in wch. he seems to be in spirits, & not displeas'd with his Neighbours.

Our visit to Norton I guess you must have hear'd of: the Dr. has a very favorable opinion of your Brother & will be always glad to see him.

The talk of the University at present is about the late Election of a Provost at King's. Dr. George is the man chose by the Society, but the Bishop of Lincoln, who is Visitor of the College disputes the validity of their proceedings on account of there[a]

1 Potter had agreed to send RH some of his own collection of sermons for use at Reymerston. (See *ante* To Potter, 25 August 1742, and 8 October 1742.) The reference to the "Alphabet" suggests that the sermons, possibly written by Potter's father, were in shorthand.

2 RH refers to his renewed residence in Emmanuel as a Fellow. (See n. 3 below) He had moved back into college by 18 January after an absence of twelve months. (*Residence Book*, TUT. 11. 1.; *Commons Accounts Book*, STE. 15. 8.)

3 The following paragraph explains RH's sudden decision to accept the offer of a fellowship at Emmanuel. According to the College *Order Book* (COL. 14. 2.) Smalley's fellowship had become vacant on 9 November 1742. By statute it had to be filled within four weeks. (*Emmanuel Register*, COL. 9. 1(B).) RH was elected on 7 December. (*Order Book*.)

4 According to the 1735 copy of the Emmanuel College Statutes, proficiency in three languages, Greek, Latin and Hebrew, was required of any candidate for a fellowship. (*Statuta Collegii Emman*:, COL. 18. 4., Statuta XVII, p. 18.)

5 Robert Potter succeeded RH as curate of Reymerston. (See *post* To Potter, 16 November 1756.)

a MS: "there" written over "their".

being improper Officers employ'd in them. All that can be yet concluded about the issue of this Dispute, is that the Lawyers are likely to get handsomly by it.[6]

The controversy betwixt Middleton & our Public Orator grows very warm.[7] The Orator is a good deal gall'd with Middleton's Sneers, & is sending in all haste to the press a voluminous Answer. His friends are under pretty great Apprehensions of the ill Success of this attempt on the *Epistles* of the Old, & the *History* of the Modern, Cicero. It was indeed pretty daring in our new-made Orator to attack the most acute controvertist of the Age, especially on a Subject, wch., if any man, the Author of the L. of Cicero ought to understand. But it seems a little fatal to the Orators to fall under the correction of Middleton; & if this comes off no better than the last, I would advise the next, should Middleton be then alive, to learn from their Example.[8]

Pray give me your thoughts of Dr. Young's melancho[lly] Muse, when you <. . .> write next.[9] I should wish you to be particular because the Critics, I find, are very much divided.

In answer to your next, wch. I beg may be very quick, I shall say a great deal. At this time you must excuse me, if a number of letters, wch. thro' a late neglect of all my friends, pours in upon me, obliges me sooner, than I could wish, to write myself, dear Sir, your most faithful Friend & S:

R. Hurd.

Cambridge: 27. Jan. 1742–3.

6 William George, the Headmaster of Eton, had been elected Provost of King's on Tuesday, 18 January 1743 after a long drawn out contest. (See Charles H. Cooper, *Annals of Cambridge*, 5 vols., Cambridge, 1842–1908; Nichols, *Illusts*., i. 95, 623; and Nichols, *Lit. Anecs*., ii. 193.) No other reference to the intervention of the Bishop of Lincoln (Richard Reynolds) can be found. However, according to *Registrum Regale*, Eton, 1847, William George was not officially recognised as Provost until 30 January 1743.

7 James Tunstall (1708–62) was the Public Orator of Cambridge University from 1741–46. In 1741 he had published an attack on Conyers Middleton's *Life of Cicero*, questioning the authenticity of the letters said to have been written by Cicero to Brutus, of which Middleton had made considerable use in his book. Middleton replied to this in a dissertation prefixed to an English and Latin edition of the correspondence concerned. His allusions to Tunstall are patronising, and even insulting. Tunstall's reaction to this was published in 1744, and entitled *Observations on the Present Collection of Epistles between Cicero and* M. *Brutus, Representing Several Evident Marks of Forgery in Those Epistles*. The controversy does not appear to have been continued after this.

8 The office of Public Orator had previously been held by Philip Williams (1695–1749) who had attacked Middleton on religious grounds. Between 1730 and 1733 Middleton had been involved in a controversy with Daniel Waterland, about the nature of religion and the historical accuracy of the Bible; this had revealed a sceptical tendency in his religious beliefs, which Williams noticed and exposed. In an anonymous pamphlet published in 1733, he proposed that Middleton's books should be burned, and he himself banished from the university (he was University Librarian), unless he recanted. Middleton answered him in another pamphlet published the same year, and then the dispute died down. He did not, however, publish anything more on a theological subject for some time to come.

9 Edward Young (1683–1765) had published three 'Nights' of *The Complaint: Or, Night-Thoughts on Life, Death, & Immortality* by the end of January.

40 To MARY MACRO 5 FEBRUARY 1743

Text: MS BL Add. 32557, ff. 49–50; unpublished.
Addressed: cover missing.

Camb. 5. Feb. 1742–3.

Madam,

The unsettl'd way, I have been in since my coming hither, must be my Excuse for not answering your last sooner & for omitting to thank you for the care, you was so good to take of my Bundle.[1] I am now sate down to discharge yt. debt, & dare take upon me to promise, that you'll seldom find me backward in such payments.

Mr. Macro & his Chum live very comfortably together; & the more so for the late very valuable Accession of Tea & Cake.[2] They are both excellent in their kinds, but I am prejudic'd more strongly in favor of the later, as coming directly from such hands! – <. . .> We have lately been pretty much pester'd with rats, especially your vigilant Son is frequently alarm'd by 'em; tho' 'tis pleasant enough to hear him beat the floor, & fling his Shoes about to silence the noisy Animals, when, God knows, a certain thin creature, that lies by his Side, & says not a single word, does all the Mischief. Mr. Nevile goes to London next week, & lends me his rooms in his absence,[3] so that my friend has some prospect of being soon shut of his Vermin; tho' 'tis great odds if he be not shut of his cake first.

Methinks I am a little curious to know how the Trojan war goes on; whether Achilles or Hector be your fav'rite, & if Paris be not what may be call'd a very pretty Fellow.[4] I am impatient to hear your Sentiments of Andromache, & could wish to be inform'd what Idea you entertain of the admir'd Helen. Tho' let Homer say what he will I doubt not but I could easily find nearer home as faithful & as good a wife as the wife of Hector, & a Lady of equal charms, tho' of greater Modesty, than the Spartan Beauty.[5] This mention of fine ladies puts me in mind of one whom I must give you some account of: For you must know Mrs. Smalley has been here, the elegant, reading, philosophic Mrs. Smalley.[6] She & her Lord came into the red Lyon about 7 o'clock the very night before Mr. Macro return'd to Cambridge. Immediatly a messenger was dispatch'd for his old Pupil. Away went I upon the Summons, & upon entring the room had my Eyes bless'd with the sight of a delicate fine Lady, whom I soon knew to be, & accordingly saluted as, the wife of Mr. Smalley; not indeed without being puzzl'd a little in the execution, on account of numberless patches that overspread her face, & made it some difficulty for me to fix where, to my apprehension at least, there was not a Pimple. Well, ceremonies being adjusted, down we sate, my attention

1 This may refer to arrangements made for transferring RH's possessions from Reymerston to Cambridge.

2 The location of the accommodation shared by RH and Macro in Emmanuel is not known. Mary Macro sent frequent presents of tea, cakes and hams to her son and his friends while they were up at Cambridge. (*Macro Letter-book.*)

3 John Nevile had been elected a Fellow of Emmanuel on the same day as RH (7 December 1742) following an examination of the "State of ye College" which found that the "College-Debt" had been "considerably diminished". (*Order Book*, COL. 14. 2.) He had not left college before his election and there was therefore no difficulty over his rooms. RH's rooms had evidently not yet been allocated.

4 Mary Macro was probably reading Pope's translation of the *Iliad*.

5 Mary Macro and her daughter.

6 Elizabeth Smalley (née Tomlin). See *ante* To Macro, [19 September 1742], n. 8.

seemingly being turn'd to the prate of Mr. Smalley, while my narrowest Observation & regard were cast upon the Lady. As she is one of the philosophic tribe, & as such conceives her words to be of great value, She speaks but little, so that I was forc'd to wait some time before anything more considerable than a yes or no was permitted to fall from her. At length the conversation turn'd upon Mr. Smalley's living, & Madam, quoth I, you are happy, I hope, in a good Neighbourhood at Preston[7] – I can't tell indeed, reply'd she, what the Gentlemen may be, but their wives, I am told, are strange creatures, unsociable creatures that pay a visit once a year – o! hideous, cry'd I, taking the manner of my fair Dialogist at once, such creatures are unsociable indeed; why they deserve not the name of Neighbours. But, Madam, continu'd I, the place is agreable? – Why, tolerable, I think, Sir – we have Trees, & Water, but Mr. Smalley talks of robbing me of my Shade. You must know, interpos'd my queer Tutor, my dear & I cannot quite agree about an Elm-Walk, that is near the House. I say it spoils a quick-Hedge it stands in, & therefore must come down – she urges the beauty of the thing & therefore is against it – to end the dispute, Mr. Hurd, you must come over & give us your Opinion – this Gentleman, my dear, adds he with his prosing face, has a good taste & is – he was going on when, "no, Mr. Smalley, interrupted I, there can be no room, I am sure, for any taste, much less mine, after Mrs. Smalley's." The compliment, tho' coarse enough, had it's effect, it drew her into a more familiar Air, and, "yes, Sir, do come over", said she, "& *rescue the poor Trees*." Besides the softness of the Expression it was deliver'd with that theatrical tone of voice, that sleepy languish of the Eye, & that contortion of the <. . .> hand, that at once surpriz'd me & let me into her true character. We had a good deal of talk after this, but I shall trouble you with no more, as you'll apprehend from this little, as well as from the whole, that the character of Mrs. Smalley is that which a plain man would hardly chuse in a wife, & which must be very insipid to a country Parson, not read in Romance<s>. I shall only add, that Mrs. Smalley is going to publish a correspondence betwixt herself & Mrs. Masters of Norwich. Smalley adds, that he will have it call'd a correspondence between a young Lady & a certain Ecclesiastic, for that some of his own letters come into the course of it, & that some good Judges, to whom the work has been shewn, insist on their being publish'd.[8] I shall now, Madam, leave you to ruminate on the Lady of Preston, & entreat your attention to me no longer, than while I write myself, Madam, your most Obedt. Humble Servt.

R. H:

I beg my H: Service to Miss Macro. – Dr. Macro may be sure I shall with pleasure obey his commands in regard of the Books he has mention'd.

7 Nathaniel Smalley had been nominated to the college living of Preston, near Lavenham in Suffolk on 7 July 1742. (*Order Book*, COL. 14. 2; see also *ante* To Potter, 14 July 1742, n. 5.)

8 No evidence of the publication of this correspondence has been found. Mrs Masters has not been identified.

41 To MARY MACRO **26 FEBRUARY 1743**

Text: MS BL Add. 32557, ff. 51–2; unpublished.
Addressed: To/Mrs. Macro at Norton/to be left at Mr. Haywood's/ in the Cook -row/Bury St. Edmunds/Suffolk.
Postmarked: postmark missing.

Camb. 26 Feb. 1742/3.

Madam,

Not to make the swiftest return of Thanks for such a letter & such a present, were an Omission, which, however you might pardon, I never could. It gives me great pleasure, but no Surprise, that you are fond of Dr. Young. His numbers, as you elegantly observe, swell with such a grief, as must extort a Sigh from the humane, & I doubt not but that when the throb rose in your own generous breast, a certain Lady by your side, who to pay her the greatest compliment I can, inherits all her Mother's virtues, felt the same benevolent call to grief & pity. I am much oblig'd, Madam, by that goodness & condescension with which you are pleas'd to give me your opinion of the whole. Your Decision is, as I expected it would be, too just to leave me any room to dissent from it. 'Tis I take upon me to say with great judgment you pronounce many pats in the second & third Poem very beautiful; which I the rather observe as there are but few I meet with who do not by an undistinguishing sort of Criticism condemn 'em in the gross. The part of conscience in the second piece is, I think, inimitable,[1] which I mention not as if I could believe it escap'd your notice (for that I guess is one of your *peculiar Beauties*) but to give you the pleasure of a second perusal. As to what You say of *our being led in the first by a soothing Sorrow to an ample field of just reflexion*, [it] is[a] most exquisitely, as well as elegantly, true, & marks out the sovereign charm & perfection of the whole. If it did not look like arrogance in me to add anything to reflections like yours, I should further say, that the Soliloquy-form, in which it is wrote, is not only the properest of all others, as being the most expressive of true grief; but, as it lies in the first poem, the most delicately finish'd that can be imagin'd. The abrupt Opening, the incoherent yet connected musings, the occasional reflections from the Clock, Moon, & Lark, & lastly the glancings & transitions from accidental words, & hints, as they occur in his Soliloquy, are all Nature, beauty, & perfection. They charm, they move, they warm, they distress, the Reader. Th[e] [Ex]pressions, to use your own [. . .] words, fall powerful from distress unfeign'd, & being natural cannot be unfelt. 'Tis commonly remark'd that grief lessens by communication, like a River cut into many Streams, each of which diminishes the force of the whole by drawing off a part into it's own Channel. In exact proportion to the number of these Streams is the diminution of the parent River, in so much that I have somewhere read of a deep & spacious Stream, which check'd the course of a whole Army, after being deliver'd of 365 of these filial currents, becoming so weak, as to be able to make not the least

[1] "O Treacherous Conscience! while she seems to sleep,
On *Rose* and *Myrtle*, lull'd with Syren Song;
While she seems, nodding o'er her charge, to drop
On headlong *Appetite*, the slackned rein,
And give us up to *Licence*, unrecall'd,
Unmarkt; . . ." Edward Young, *Night the Second*, 1742.

[a] MS: "*reflexion*, is".

Resistance.[2] The application is easy to a tide of Grief, & if there be any justness in it, how far from miserable is the very mourner! What numbers are there who have shar'd his Sorrow! <. . . ,> & felt a portion of his bitter wave flowing into their own Bosoms? But wherefore expatiate on ys. sad Topic, when a sweeter theme invites me? Yes! the fragrance yet hangs on my lips, & the delicious compound relish reminds me, by a lively Emblem, of the happy Composition of the fair, who made it. The Ingredients are costly, & of foreign growth; but to what purpose, had there not been a provident head to direct, & a skilful hand to work, the due mixture of them? Small thanks then to East, or[b] West! their Spices & Delicacies are but so many scatter'd flowers, of little use or entertainment to any but the accidental passenger; and tho' art & Industry may extract their Sweets & bring 'em to the hive, yet 'tis then a luscious Mass of <little> small value till duly temper'd & corrected by the ingenious little Artists. 'Tis thus, Madam, I owe to the goodness & dextrous skill of two Ladies, whom Simonides himself would not have scrupl'd to rank in ye order of his *Bees*,[3] [c] all the welcome Sweetness of your well-made Present. Mr. Macro's Rats won't permit him, he says, to take it into his Custody, & I am only afraid that, if I keep it in my own, my rude Tooth will not treat it with all the distance & complaisance that is due from me to any creature, that come[s] from Mrs. Macro. In plain words, I am extremely oblig'd to you for your exquisitely kind, & good present[;] tho' at first I must own I could not but think it a little hard, that [you w]ould not suffer the least Shadow of an Obligation to [be shew]n[d] you, but that you should repel it, as it were, with such superior advantage the very moment it fell upon your Shoulders. Indeed it is a little insufferable that you should be always heaping Obligations upon others, & never submit to bear one yourself. – I am vex'd to be outdone so.

Yours, & Miss Macro's Employments are elegant & instructive, & I must be angry with the Dr., if he offers to wrest those Instructions out of your hands (tho' I must own they are wanted as little there as any where) till you've entirely done with them. The Leathern Gentry are sent home, as you archly but truly express yourself, to repose in a Dormitory, & therefore for their own Sake when you have 'em give 'em a little more Exercise. This is a place *for*, & not *of* reading, & therefore, good Sir, be not so hasty in sending what we don't want.[4]

But o! let me ask, what the Dr. is doing! He is never in the dirt, I know, but when he's looking for Jewells. What! some new Cargo! some newly-transported freight? Say, good Madam, what is it? There[e] is another precious heap coming to him this next week, while poor I can get nothing – sure times *will* mend.[5]

2 The story occurs in Herodotus, i. 189–90. Cyrus marching to attack Babylon, tries to cross the river Gyndes. In the attempt one of the sacred white horses is swept away, so in retaliation, Cyrus divides the river into 360 channels, thus making it so shallow that even women could cross easily.

3 *Lyra Graeca*, II; Simonides, 57.

4 RH sent Cox Macro books from Cambridge (often from Emmanuel Library). Clearly Mrs Macro and her daughter wished to read them themselves before they were returned.

5 Cox Macro had been negotiating for some of the papers left by Richard Bentley on his death in 1742. (*Macro Letter-book*.) He was also expecting some letters and manuscripts from Thomas Gough. (See *post* To Gough, 9 June 1743.)

b MS: "or" written over "to".

c Written in large lower case letters.

d MS torn: "be shewn" supplied in pencil by an unknown hand.

e MS: "There" written over "Here".

Bless me! at what a rate have I talk'd, & yet I am still for talking. Never talk of female loquacity, or as a certain sly Satirist[6] would call it, impetuous verbosity; a male Tongue for what I see is full as flippant. At least I must acknowledge mine to be so, ev'n without the cause, that may be justly urg'd in the case of some female tongues, their c[er]tain Success in pleasing by 'em. Conscious of this, I'll for once do you the favor of breaking off your trouble, before you come at the bottom of the page, by writing myself at ys. distance from it, Madam, your most Oblig'd, & most Obedt. Servt.

R. Hurd.

P.S.

I am extremely Miss Macro's & the Dr.'s Servant. Mr. Macro is well & desires his proper compliments.

Is one permitted to wonder how Mrs. Macro likes Mr. Whitehead?[7]

Endorsed by Mary Macro: "answerd March ye 20 1742/3".

42 To COX MACRO 5 MARCH 1743

Text: MS BL Add. 32557, ff. 69–70; unpublished.
Addressed: To/the reverend Dr. Macro.

reverend Sir,

I am much oblig'd by your answer to my three Queries. You have set the great Articles of the Fall & Redemption of man in an infinitely clearer light, than I had ever seen them plac'd in; &, to say the truth, have eas'd me of some scruples that hung upon my mind concerning them. However I cannot yet say I am wholly satisfy'd in the point; which I can easily charge upon the shortness of your reply, rather than upon the importance of the reasons, which I am going to offer.

1st then if Mortality, i.e a cessation of being after this life was all that was inflicted upon Adam, I am at a loss to know how it could be properly term'd a Punishment. Immortality is a free gift & as such neither Adam nor any of his posterity could have any right to it. He was not injur'd in it's being deny'd him: 'twas no actual pain or penalty, but a less degree of happiness only.

2. if mortality was the sole punishment intended by the word *Death* what becomes of the distinction betwixt good men & Sinners? The most profligate of men as well as the best had this equal lot to lay down Existence with this life. Now to me it should appear yt. whatever penalty was inflicted it should be such a one as might be proportion'd to the demerits of the several offenders; otherwise what was intended as a punishment for Sin must become the most pow'rful Inducement to it. I know indeed 'tis said that Xst dy'd from a foundation of the world, & that therefore 'tis believ'd rewards & punishments will be distributed in another life to such as liv'd before, as well as after the times of the Gospel, but supposing this, what becomes of mankind in the mean time? They did not I take for granted know this; & if they did not, how

6 Cox Macro. The reference to "impetuous verbosity" was obviously a family joke. RH uses it earlier in To Macro, 3 October 1742.

7 William Whitehead had published *An Essay on Ridicule* on 19 February 1743. (Ralph Straus, *Robert Dodsley. Poet, Publisher & Playwright*, 1910, Bibliography.)

great encouragement must it be to Sinners, that bare non-existence after this life was the whole punishment to be inflicted, especially as it would equally be their portion, whether they acted wickedly & irrationally or not!

3. In regard of original Sin I could wish you to be a little more explicite: viz: whether there be not a corruption of nature deriv'd upon Us[a] by Adam's fall, or how we can otherwise account for that universal depravity, & tendency to vice, in a creature who must have come with other dispositions out of the hands of the Creator. As to man's being born in a state of Sin, so <yt.> as without the Intercession of Xst. to deserve damnation whether he actually commit sin or not, if this be all you understand by Originall Sin, I must entirely agree with you in thinking it too gross & monstrous an opinion to be embrac'd by any reasonable person.

In one word I should be glad to know how the infliction of *mortality* as a punishment for Sin is consistent with the divine abhorrence of it, when it seems to tempt greatly to the commission of Sin; & whether the wilful Disobedience of Adam had not an influence upon the wills & dispositions, & understandings of his Sons.

I shall not be at all surpriz'd if these, or any other queries, which I may trouble you with on such subjects, appear to you who are intimately acquainted with them, weak & insignificant, & therefore I shall always esteem it a mark of your natural goodness, when you condescend to take any notice of them.

Spon I have here sent you.[1] The other books I am so unfortunate as not to be able to oblige you with. Mr. Hubbard & I search'd the University Library for them, but could not find so m[uch as] one that we wanted.[2] Mr. Nevile has, by I know not what means, the 2d. Vol. of Harris' Collection (I am sure I am right now) but no more; if you like to see this I will send it next week.[3] I sent to St. John's to consult their library; but their books are all lock'd up <in order> to be review'd & set in order, & till that is over no book can be had.[4]

Calmet's Dissertations are extracts, it seems, from his Commentary, a work which I have not yet been able to see. Mr. Hubbard has one Vol. of these Dissertations, translated by Tindal, which he bade me say with his humble Service you should be

1 Jacob Spon (1647–86), a celebrated physician, historian, and antiquary. His principal works were a history of Geneva, translated into English, *The History of the City and State of Geneva*, 1687; and *Voyage d'Italie, de Dalmatie, de Grece, et du Levant*, Lyon, 1678.

2 In 1715 the University Library had been presented with the magnificent library of John Moore, Bishop of Ely, which had been bought by George I. This had inspired the university to plan an extension of the library buildings and to create the office of University Librarian. However, as the enthusiasm decreased so did the efforts to organise the new stocks of books, and they were left in disorder till about 1750. Not only was the library difficult to use, in consequence, but large numbers of books were stolen. It was open to all members of the university. (*Cambridge University Gazette*, 10 March 1869.)

3 This is likely to have been the second volume of the two volume work *Navigantium atque Itinerantium Bibliotheca: Or, A Compleat Collection of Voyages and Travels* published by John Harris in 1705. (See *post* To Macro, 26 November 1743, n. 3.)

4 According to Zacharias von Uffenbach, who visited Cambridge in 1710, the books in St John's library were "more tidy" than he had found was the case anywhere else in England. ('Visit to Cambridge by Zacharias Conrad von Uffenbach', 1710, in *Cambridge under Queen Anne*, ed. J.E.B. Mayor, Cambridge, 1911.)

a MS: "Us" written over ?"the".

very welcome to a sight of, if you pleas'd. The work it seems did not take, & therefore there were no more of them translated.[5]

Mr. Macro, Mr. Longe, & I are going to drink Tea this Afternoon with the Master, & then I shall not fail to put in a word about the Papers.[6]

I beg my humble Service to Mrs. & Miss Macro, & am, reverend Sir, your most oblig'd, Humble Servt.

R. Hurd.

Cambridge 5 March 1743.

Mr. Macro sends his compliments, but pleads a cold in [ye] eyes as an Excuse for his not writing.

43 To JAMES DEVEY — 28 MARCH 1743

Text: *Memoirs*, 15.

Emmanuel, March 28, 1743.

Rev. Sir,

A succession of business of one kind or other prevented my answering that part of your letter which desired me to make inquiry about a Popish book called *Charity and Truth.*[1] I have asked Thurlbourn, our great bookseller,[2] if he knew of any answer that had been made to it, and he told me that he had not so much as heard of the book itself. The Popish controversy is so entirely demolished, that we now hear nothing at all of it; at least it seems wholly overlooked at present by the University . . .

5 Augustin Calmet had published a commentary on all the books of the Old and New Testament in 1707. This ran into twenty volumes and was reprinted in 1715 and in 1724. Certain subjects in the commentary had required special attention, and these Calmet had explained in "distinct and Separate Discourses". They were first published separately in 1715, a second edition followed in 1720, and another in 1724 to complement the third edition of the *Commentaire*. Nicholas Tindal began to translate the "Discourses" as soon as they were published in the 1724 edition. His translation appeared in parts from 1724 onwards, and comprised dissertations on the poetry and music of the Hebrews, their history, chronology, money, coins and other subjects. The title of the collection was *Antiquities Sacred and Prophane: Or, a Collection of Curious and Critical Dissertations on the Old and New Testament*. Numbers were issued until 1727, but the book was never completed.

6 Probably a reference to further manuscripts to add to Macro's collection, presumably in the hands of the Master, William Richardson, or belonging to the college.

1 Edward Hawarden, *Charity and Truth: or Catholicks not Uncharitable in Saying, That None Are Sav'd Out of the Catholick Communion*, 1728. Occasional resurgences of anti-Catholic feeling manifested themselves well into the eighteenth century. In the mid 1730s there had been particular concern about conversion to Catholicism. Numerous seventeenth century tracts against popery had been republished by Edmund Gibson, Bishop of London, in his *Preservative against Popery*, 3 vols., 1738; and in 1735 the Archbishop of York had sent queries to all his clergy concerning the numbers of Roman Catholics in their parishes. ('Archbishop Blackburn's visitation returns of the diocese of York, 1735', ed. R. Trappes-Lomax in *Publications of the Catholic Record Society*, xxxii. (1932), 204–388.)

2 William Thurlbourn was the most important bookseller in Cambridge from 1724–68. (Henry R. Plomer, *A Dictionary of Printers and Booksellers*, 1932.) Emmanuel bought all their books through his shop, as well as pens, paper and ink. Most of the books that they wished to have bound were also sent to him. (*Steward's Account Book*, STE. 1. 5.; *Ash Foundation Accounts Book*, SCH. 1. 2.)

44 To MARY MACRO 22 APRIL 1743

Text: MS BL Add. 32557, ff. 53–4; unpublished.
Addressed: To/Mrs. Macro./at/[Norton]

Camb: 22. Apr. 1743.

Madam,

Tho' I have not much to say, nor much time to say anything in, yet I could not answer it to myself, were I wholly silent. The last Ideas that float in the Brain, generally make the strongest Impression, and therefore you are not to wonder at the whimsies, I am going to treat you with, as they are of late date and freshest in the fancy. 'Twas but yesterday in the afternoon (& a troublesome windy afternoon it was) that Mr. Macro & I took a solitary walk, for so we think it when no body else is with us. The chat grew in a little time serious, respecting chiefly the different pursuits of life, and the several requisites to happiness in it. The advantages and disadvantages of a large fortune soon came in play, and after some remarks on both sides, Yes, says my Friend, I'll tell you how an immense fortune might conduce to solid happiness. What! in the opportunity it gives, reply'd I, of gratifying the humane and elegant affections in works of charity and works of Art. Why, yes, there is a good deal in that, but my Scheme is a little visionary, you shall hear. Money, you know, commands learning: suppose then one could spare such Sums, as might induce some of the learnedest and most considerable men in the Kingdom to be always with one! As I mus'd on this thought, and was reflecting who the people might be, that should deserve this honor; Nay, says he, I have fix'd upon my men, nor am I very unreasonable. Dr. Middleton,[1] and Dr. Heberden,[2] to go no further, would content me. Three or four hundreds a year to each should be the gratuity for doing me this favour. In pursuance of this wild Scheme separate houses were contriv'd for each, and the manner of living describ'd with great minuteness. Sometimes Dr. Macro and the two Dr.'s were in close conference upon some point of deeper learning or curious Antiquity, while the young Maecenas listen'd for Instruction. Sometimes the conversation was to turn on classic Elegance, and Middleton was to be his own Tully. Sometimes again the Ladies were introduc'd, for these Literati were to have families, and an Air of mirth and delicacy was to spread itself over the conversation. And bless me, said I, the contrast between Mrs. Middleton and a certain Lady:[3] well! I'd give ever so much to be present at the first Interview; to see how she'd relish the flirts, tosses, flings, & drawls of that half-french'd, English Lady. This occasion'd the discourse to take a merrier turn, but still the Scheme was lik'd, and the several pensions continu'd. But mark the unworthy natures of some folks, however honor'd & oblig'd, and how near your bounteous Son was to throwing away a pretty round Sum on the undeserving. For doing to a Concert in the Ev'ning, we had not sate long, e'er one of these worthies, the highly honour'd

1 Conyers Middleton. See *ante* To Potter, 22 March 1741, n.1, and 27 January 1743, n. 7.

2 William Heberden (1710–1801) was a Fellow of St John's, Cambridge. He had been admitted in 1724, proceeded B.A. in 1728, M.A. in 1732, and M.D. in 1739. He had subsequently established himself as a physician in Cambridge but was also known for his classical scholarship. In 1748 he moved to London where his reputation as an able and distinguished physician was consolidated. He was made a Fellow of the Royal Society in 1749 and honorary member of the Royal Society of Medicine (Paris) in 1778. (*D.N.B.*; Nichols, *Lit. Anecs.*, iii. 71–3.)

3 Mary Macro.

and oblig'd Middleton enter'd, to mock us more, came and sate by us. For, would you think it, the ingrateful creature bow'd to numbers, but look'd with perfect disregard on his Benefactor. Nay ev'n I, who by some means or other in the visionary Scheme above mention'd became a Bishop, was as little minded, tho' the thoughtless Animal might have consider'd it was in <my> a Bishop's pow'r to have serv'd him. Well we were highly vex'd as you'll imagine, and came home with a fix'd resolve not to heap honours ev'n in fancy on a person, whose thankless temper shew'd he so little deserv'd 'em. You see how abrupt I am forc'd to [be] in writing myself, Madam, your most Obed: Humble Servt.

R: H:

Endorsed by RH: "NB: A Single S[heet]".

45 To THOMAS GOUGH — 9 JUNE 1743

Text: MS BEINECKE Osborn Files, 18.429; printed, *Lit. Anecs.*, ix. 361.

Dear Sir,

I have been long wishing to hear from you on the Subject of those letters & other Manuscripts, you were so kind to promise Dr. Macro.[1] You must doubtless by this time have made yourself Master of a pretty large Cargo; which I should gladly have receiv'd from your own hands, but that the short Stay, I make here, will not permit me to see you. Perhaps you might contrive to send them to me at Mr. Budworth's in Brewood within a fortnight or three weeks, from whence I should have the pleasure of being the Bearer of them directly to Norton. The favor of such a present will, I need not say, equally oblige Dr. Macro & Dear Sir, your most faithful humble Servt.

R. Hurd.

Brewood: June. 9. 1743.

46 To MARY MACRO — 22 JUNE 1743

Text: MS BL Add. 32557, f. 55; unpublished.
Addressed: To/Mrs. Macro at Norton to be left at/Mr. Haywood's in the Cook-Row/Bury St. Edmunds/Suffolk./ By London.
Postmarked: SHIFNALL 24 IV

Madam,

The favor of your last, at a time when I was indebted to you for a former letter, is such as I know not well in what terms to acknowledge. Tho', to say the truth, I rather take it as a polite reproof to my Indolence, and yt. your purpose was to shame me out of my Silence by a degree of goodness, I had no reason to expect. You see, Madam,

1 No more is known of these manuscripts. See *ante* To Gough, 6 August 1742, for a previous letter concerning the acquisition of manuscripts for Cox Macro.

how industrious I am to lessen my Obligation to you, or rather how sensible I am of my fault by raising such a Suspicion. But to make something like an Apology for it, you'll permit me to urge a constant round of company, which has engross'd almost ev'ry waking hour for these three whole weeks. Last night I return'd, & this morning soon as sleep had left me, and light & reflection made their way to my Pillow, what should strike my conscience first, but this Omission of thanks for Mrs. Macro's Letters? Alarm'd at the thought, and starting like Virgil's Chief with a God at his Elbow,[1] I immediatly arose; determining with all Speed to discharge myself of a debt, which on ev'ry Recollection lay so heavy upon me. But to turn to your Letters. – What you observe in the first of them of Women in different parts of the World is very Satyrical: but had any of our Sex, after some years Travel, brought back such a remark, your's or some female Wit, would have soon made 'em smart for it. For do the Women indeed cut such odd figures in the several Countries of the World? What Brutes then must the Men be in those several Countries, an obliging conformity to whose Taste is the true cause of that Oddness? What a Monster might not an ill Fancy make of the shapely Fir in your Garden, and could you on such change lay the fault on the Fir? Mistake me not, Madam; I am not for running a degrading Parallel between the Glory of Creation, and a Tree, but if the tender and pliant dispositions of the one, like the Branches of the other, are so form'd as to yield and give way to wrong Impressions, what Woman can help it? Left to themselves, they had rose in all the Elegance of Shape, and shot out into ev'ry lovely tendency and disposition. But there is no resisting Steel & a bad Taste: the distortions, that follow, are easily accounted for, and if their Graces are lopp'd off, there is no doubt about the hand, that did it. See! but the Gall, you have dropp'd in this part of your letter, and which your Pen has convey'd so artfully, that I had almost expos'd myself by taking it seriously, and undertaking a defence of the female world in ys. particular. Well! I find you with milder designs in your next Paragraph, list'ning to the Nightingales, planting for their repast and (could I hope it) wasting a thought on me. For, Madam, whatever be the Cause, to be the Subject of Mrs. Macro's thoughts at the distance of 200 miles, is enough to raise a Vanity, which no consideration of the want of 15 years can easily suppress.[2] And now I am got on this Subject of a Lady's Age, which, permit me to say, you have here represented in a very disadvantageous manner, I shall venture to express my thoughts upon it in a Simile, that just jumps into my Brain, and which I think marks the truth of the case with great Exactness. The illustrious thought comes from Heav'n, and therefore 'twould be degrading it too much not to dress it up in Rhyme. – Be pleas'd then to take it thus:

See! but yon Star, that gilds the brow of Night,
And momentary twinkles to the Sight:
Thus shines in bloom of early youth the Fair
With Eyes all sparkling, and unquiet Air.
But if the Glass it's scatter'd light confine
And thro' it's straiten'd pass the Lustre shine,
The Twinkler's giddy Blaze no more we view,
The Beam falls steady & resembles – You.

1 Virgil, *Aeneid*, iv. 259–83.
2 Mary Macro was actually thirty–one years older than RH.

Your Account of the demolition of the old Tower pleas'd me extremely; but here again you seem a little Satyrical, when you close it with a "What cannot the head & hands of MAN do?" Yes they can raise, as you are candid enough to own in the following lines, a new Edifice with Venetian Ornaments on the Ruins of the other, & will not that restore 'em to favour? Sure you are the only Lady in Suffolk, that would express so tender a concern on a change of Fashion! But I come to your last favour: and here what shall I say to your Account of the Travellers?[3] Envy 'em to be sure I must, not only for their pleasure in viewing the works of Alcinous & Palladio, (by which understand the wonders of Stow)[4] but for steering their course tow'rds[a] Die, & Mrs. Gardiner.[5] Well! what reception had the Dr.? say, good Madam, for I am very impatient, how did the flirts of the one, and forward tossings of the other agree with him? Did the Dr., (but I cannot hope such news) did the Dr. nap a little – or to give me some comfort, was not my friend rather sleepy – O! what did the Creature say of my Stupidity! – and Miss Die – sure she does not still say I am nasty! The truth is, I am in great Agitation about the Event of this journey, but whatever it be, I beg you'll favour me with a minute account as soon as possible. The Curate of Reymerston, I suppose, bears some part in the play & you'll be able to send me at least one Scene about him. I read that part of your entertaining letter, which relates to Mrs. G., to my Father, telling him the occasion of the pleasantry; at which the good old Gentleman laugh'd heartily; and if he could ever think of taking so long a journey, I may venture to add, there is no family he would take a sincerer pleasure in paying his respects to, whether his old Acquaintance were there or not,[6] than the good Family at Norton. He bade me present his humble Service to ev'ry body in it.

What you just mention about a Dome, Columns, Pilasters, Niches, Ballustrade, Stucco-work &c picques my curiosity so much, that I am very inquisitive to know

3 Cox Macro and Edward.

4 Stowe was the seat of Richard Temple, Lord Cobham, who inherited the estate in 1697. He had a great deal of work done on the house and gardens, which by 1730 had the reputation of being the finest in the country. The improvements to the house were begun in the early 1720s and were designed to give a Palladian look to the original tall seventeenth century building. The gardens, however, were the most remarkable feature of Stowe. From 1720 onwards, Cobham poured money into improving them, and employed a succession of leading architects and designers to draw up plans for the landscaping, and for new buildings to be scattered throughout. The first guidebook of any country seat ever produced, was a description of Stowe published in 1744, by Benton Seeley. (*A Description of the Gardens of Lord Viscount Cobham, at Stow in Buckinghamshire*, Northampton, 1744.) In 1750 an even fuller guide was produced by George Bickham (*The Beauties of Stow*), in which the gardens are described as an "unparallel'd Chain of artificial and natural Beauty"; and the whole estate as "the Wonder of our Days, and the most charming Place in all *England*!" (pp. 64, 65). The reference to Alcinous indicates the gardens at Stowe.

5 For RH's own encounter with the Gardiners, see *ante* To Macro, [19 September 1742]. "Miss Die" has not been identified.

6 Edward Macro. In the summer vacations RH and Macro travelled together through Staffordshire and Shropshire, calling on RH's parents during their tour.

a MS: "towrd's".

more;[7] and indeed if I cannot procure a description of them very soon, I shall revenge it upon you by coming in Person to view it with my own Eyes. Oh! that Garden, & those Walks in this lovely Season! – See! but how Sense, & Books are connected with the Idea of Norton, when I cannot leave the mention of it without inquiring if you have read The New Marianne.[8] If you have not, I dare almost venture to say, never was such Nature, such beauty, such passion, such ev'ry thing that is lovely, put together in one piece. Not Pamela itself has Marianne's charm, & delicacy, tho' perhaps it may exceed in variety of Characters. – Twere too great a fall after this to ask, if you have seen the Epistle from Anne Boleyn to H: 8.[9] – After all this prate let me draw your trouble to an end, by desiring my H: Service to Dr. Macro, whose repose I should have invaded e'er now, but that I have only to say, Mr. Gough is alive, and that I have wrote to him on the Subject of those letters,[10] but without receiving as yet any Answer. I am, with compliments to Miss Macro, Madam, your most oblig'd & most obedient Servt.

R. Hurd.

Hatton-Grange: 22. June. 1743.

47 To EDWARD MACRO 22 JUNE 1743

Text: MS BL Add. 32557, f. 56; unpublished.
Addressed: To Mr. Macro.

Dear Sir,

I am glad to find from your's, & Mrs.[a] Macro's letter, that you have been so agreably entertain'd in the Country.[1] My request is, that you would not, like a Miser, keep the whole Satisfaction to yourself, but impart something of it, at least in Description, to your Friend. If I am right in my conjecture you have seen Ld. Cobham's, and then you

7 The Macros made continual alterations and improvements to their house, Little Haugh Hall, throughout the 1730s and early 1740s. RH's references are to work done on the central staircase which is surmounted by a dome, painted by Francis Hayman (1708–76). Below this, on the main landing, there is a large niche surrounded by ornate wood carving, and originally designed to hold a bust (sculpted by Michael Rysbrack) of Tillemans, the Belgian painter, and a close friend of Cox Macro. There is a good deal of stucco-work both around the dome, and in some of the rooms. This work, though, was not carried out till 1745. (See *post* To Macro, 29 August 1745.) The dome was probably built about 1730; the painting of it, however, was for some reason left till much later. Hayman was first approached by Cox Macro in 1741, but a price could not be agreed upon, so instead Macro turned to the German-born Norwich painter, D. Heins. He also refused the work, and the painting seems at last to have been carried out by Hayman about 1743 or 1744. (Norman Scarfe, 'Little Haugh Hall, Suffolk', in *Country Life*, 5 June 1958; Robert Raines, 'An Art Collector of Many Parts', in *Country Life*, 24 June 1976.)

8 *La Nouvelle Marianne; ou les Memoires de la Baronne de ****, Ecrits par Elle-même*, La Haye, 2 vols., 1740. This book was published anonymously by Claude-François Lambert. RH read it in French; it does not appear to have been translated into English.

9 *Ann Boleyn to Henry the Eighth. An Epistle*, 1743, by William Whitehead. The poem was published in May. (Straus, *Dodsley*, Bibliography.)

10 See preceding letter.

1 See preceding letter.

a MS: "Mr's".

cannot but have a large field for curious Observation. Pray let me know too, how the Plan of Norton goes on, for it seems of late to have receiv'd some considerable Improvements, tho' what, or exactly in what manner I am yet to learn.

I can't but felicite (that you know is the fashionable term) Ld. Radnor's Nephew on his being plac'd under the care of Dr. Middleton: 'twas excellently judg'd, & if the young Gentleman has any Parts, he must find his Account in't.[2]

Mr. Whitehead's Epistle from Anne Boleyn to H: 8. I have seen, & must agree with you, that it cannot much advance his Character in Poetry.[3] If I may own my opinion of it to a friend, it is too spiritless, too void of Passion, too heavily imagin'd, to bear any comparison with the lovely, tho' itself perhaps inaccurate Model, on which it was form'd. But I'll say no more: you are already too severe on the Author, in believing, as you say, that he never will *now* shine as a Poet.

Since my last I have made a pretty long Visit to Mr. B.[4] – His suspicions, for I can call 'em nothing else, were extremely trifling, and can be only accounted for from that too natural turn of the unfortunate, which disposes them to be fretful on ev'ry little occasion, and suspect the whole world, & not least their truest friends. We talk'd the matter over for some time; after which conversation flow'd in it's old easy channel, and the same ea[se,] freedom & chearfullness appear'd in his behaviour, as before. I must own I am pleas'd at ys. almost unexpected reconciliation (for when throughly warm'd I knew him to be very resolute) as I cannot bear, that any man, who has done me real favors, should think I use him ill.

But I have troubl'd you already too much on ys. Subject; forgive the impertinence, & believe me, dear Sir, with great sincerity your very affectionate Friend & oblig'd Humble Servt.

R: H:

Hatton-Grange: 22. June. 1743.

2 According to John Nichols in his *Literary Anecdotes*, Middleton "superintended in his own house the education of two or three young gentlemen of rank". (*Lit. Anecs.*, v. 419.) Amongst these was "Mr. Robarts, nephew to the Earl of Radnor", who remained with Middleton from "1745 till his death". (*Ibid.*, v. 420.) Lord Radnor had been a contemporary of Cox Macro at Christ's, Cambridge, and had corresponded with him on the subject of the employment of Francis Hayman to paint the dome surmounting the stairwell at Little Haugh Hall. (Robert Raines, 'An Art Collector of Many Parts', in *Country Life*, 24 June 1976.) Thus the news about his nephew could be presumed to be of some interest to the family.

3 William Whitehead's *Ann Boleyn to Henry the Eighth* was apparently modelled on Pope's *Eloisa to Abelard*, 1717. It was not generally admired, though it was allowed to be "correct". William Mason in his 'Memoirs' of Whitehead judged that the author had "made a judicious use of the Queen's original letter, and, in his own additions, preserved a true characteristic unity with it, yet [the poem] cannot, with justice, be ranked high amongst the numerous productions of this nature. For the truth is, Mr. Pope's Eloisa to Abelard is such a *chef d'oeuvre*, that nothing of the kind can be relished after it." ('Memoirs', prefixed to Vol. 3 of *Poems by William Whitehead*, 1788.) Whitehead was made Poet Laureate in 1757, but was never considered to be a poet of great distinction.

4 Unidentified.

48 To JOHN POTTER 11 JULY 1743

Text: MS NLW 12432E; unpublished.
Addressed: To/the reverend Mr. Potter/at Batcombe near Brewton/ Somersetshire/By London.
Postmarked: SHIFNALL 15 IY

Dear Sr,

Your last did not reach me till about a fortnight ago, when a Gentleman of ys. Neighbourhood brought it from Camb:[1] where it had lain since the beginning of May. This I mention in order to acquit myself of the Suspicion of being negligent in replying to your favors; an imputation I would willingly be very far from deserving!

Your remarks on Dr. Young's Night-Thoughts are too just to leave me any pretence of quarrelling with you.[2] I could only wish you had been more extended on the poetical parts; but that I know your candor prevented, lest you might be sometimes forc'd to blame.

I thank you, Sir, for your pretty enough Version of Adrian's dying Speech;[3] the only objection I have to it, besides it's want of diminutives, [a] fault which must ever attend any translation of it in our [la]nguage, is the calling Adrian's Soul the Harbinger of his Clay; a manner of Expression which I make no scruple of owning I do not understand. But now I am got on the Subject of Poetry, you must give me leave to remind you, that this little piece is the only present I have receivd from your Muse this Spring. Landlords that are us'd to receive a Turkey at Xstmas from their good Tenants, take it hugely ill, tho' they have no strict right to any such thing, if they are disappointed of it: Or to put a case more parallel, the country friend that has been accustom'd to a yearly present of Hare or Partrid[ge] from his wealthy Neighbour, thinks himself ill-us'd, if it chance on any account not to be continu'd. Pray consider how ap[pli]cable these cases are to the present, and let it not be in my power to say, that an old friend, who keeps so good a Muse, is very niggardly in point of Game. Or, if this won't do, to shame you out of it, see here a little present from my hands. [']Twas a thought, I accidentally *started* in my ramblings the other day, and run it down by my own Strength without such an Assistant, as you are bless'd with. Ruminating on Norton gardens,[4] (which you have probably had some account of, either from me or your Brother) –

1 Perhaps James Devey who lived in Beckbury, about two miles from Hatton Grange. He had left Emmanuel on 7 June. (*Residence Book*, TUT. 11. 1.)

2 Four 'Nights' had been published by July 1743; the fifth 'Night' followed in December.

3 "et moriens quidem hos versus fecisse dicitur:

Animula vagula blandula
hospes comesque corporis,
quae nunc abibis in loca
pallidula rigida nudula?
nec ut soles dabis iocas!

tales autem nec multos meliores fecit et Graecos."

Scriptores Historiae Augustae I, Hadrian, xxv. 9–10. This famous dying speech of Hadrian's was much imitated. One of the best known versions is Pope's *The Dying Christian to his Soul*, first published in 1730.

4 These were the Macros' gardens at Little Haugh Hall.

"The Scene, the Master op'ning to my view"
Bless'd Grove (said I) whose fate ordain'd to rise
To shelter Science & protect the wise!
Whose bending branches guard the sacred Stream
Whence ev'ry healing draught of science came;
Infuse the Art, that else were idly sought,
And lend a Shade to deepen learned thought!
Bless'd Grove! in whose imbowring Shades & Cells
All human Wisdom, & all Virtue dwells,
Where contemplation from the world retires
To dress her Lamp, & kindle all her fires,
Thro' Learning's widest field where Pollio flies
Tastes ev'ry Sweet, that ev'ry Art supplies.
Thro' Nature's walk the God, the God explores,
With wonder views, with ecstacy adores,
Man's various Duty weighs in Reason's Scales
Sees, where the *casting* Good, or Ill prevails;
To Heav'n from thence directs th' ambitious ray,
That opens still & opens on the day,
Till thro' Faith's optics, strengthen'd & refin'd,
<. . .> Shines all the Truth, that lightens all the Mind!
Hail! happy Shade, for such a Lord to rise!
Hail! happier Lord, who such a Shade enjoys!
Hail! happy'st Theme, which Such a Muse employs!

See, here what I venture into your hands! Use it as rigorously as you please: I am one of those Adventurers in Poetry, who have no Reputation to lose, but may possibly receive much benefit from being censur'd for it.

Whitehead's paltry Epistle from Ann Boleyn has, I suppos'd, not escap'd you.[5] 'Tis dangerous treading in Pope's Steps: how might it have pass'd but for Eloisa to Abelard!

I know not whether you are yet a French man, but wish you may for the sake of reading Marianne:[6] a Novel of that exquisite Beauty, as never sure was yet equall'd, no not by Pamela itself, full as it is of living Nature. I could expatiate an hour on ys. lovely <Subject> performance, which, tho' I have not been entertain'd with it very lately, yet so entirely possesses my present thoughts, that [it is] with some difficulty I leave the Subject, even to tell you how much I am, dear Sir, your very affectionate Friend & Faithfull Humble Servt.

R. Hurd.

Hatton: 11. July. 1743.

P.S.

I hope to be in Cambridge in less than a fortnight,[7] where I shall ev'ry day expect the pleasure of a letter.

5 See preceding letter n. 3.

6 See *ante* To Mary Macro, 22 June 1743, n. 8.

7 RH was back in Cambridge by 28 July. (*Residence Book*, TUT. 11. 1.)

49 To JOHN POTTER 17 [AUGUST] 1743[1]

Text: MS NLW 12432E; unpublished.
Addressed: To/the Rev: Mr. Potter at Batcombe/n[ear] Brewton/ Somersetshire./By London.
Postmarked: C[AMBRIDGE] 19 AV

Camb: 17. July. 1743.

Dear Sir,

The contents of your last concern me too much to omit answering it by the return of the Post. In regard to your first charge therefore I must have leave to say, you conclude very ill, in supposing me not unwilling to drop a correspondence, on account of one omission, merely because I did not write again immediatly. During my stay in the [cou]ntry, I wrote to very few of my friends: indeed it was [with] difficulty I could find time to do it. Your answer I always guess'd waited for me at College; at least it was from thence I all along purpos'd to write, whether I found [a]n answer or not. This you'll say is gratis dictum: but [how]ever as you cannot any way be sure of the contrary, it may seem a little hasty, to infer I would not. After all, this charge of coolness or neglect, or whatever else it may be call'd, gives me a real pleasure, which I am pleas'd a greater punctuality did not prevent. In short it affords me a new proof of your affection, and is a kind of Jealousy, as in love, which while it seems to loosen, but the more confirms our mutual confidence and regard. You could not have been capable of such Suspicion, but from the warmth of friendship, and that with me makes an ample amends for the injustice of it.

The same friendly concern I have the pleasure to find you witness for me in the freedom you take to lay before me a charge on my Behaviour. This indeed I take very kindly, as it shews the hearty zeal you have for my reputation: but as I make no account of the charge itself, you must be surpriz'd to find me very short in the Vindication. Indeed I should hardly prevail with myself to take any notice of it at all, did not the niceness of your friendship require something from me. You'll excuse me then, if I only say, "yt. the Lecturer's place was obtruded on me for the Service of Mr. Tooke"; "yt. what is c[all'd] a severity w[as] a Gentleness the Society blam'd in me", "and that I shall never suffer a vicious complaisance to carry it with me before a Sense of Duty".[2] I shall only add, that you were very kind to palliate my suppos'd fault, tho'

1 The evidence for dating this letter to August and not to July is the postmark, which is quite clearly a stamped AV, and the entries in the Emmanuel College *Commons Accounts Book*, STE. 15. 9, and the *Residence Book*, TUT. 11. 1. These show that RH was out of college until at least 23 July.

2 This reference remains obscure. In October of this year RH was chosen as a Sub-lecturer (a post he had held from 1739 until the time he left Emmanuel in 1742). At the same time, John Tooke, a Fellow of the college since 1732, was chosen Dean and Greek Lecturer. (*Order Book*, COL. 14. 2.) Whether RH already knew that he was to be elected, and is therefore referring to some arrangements connected with this, or not, cannot be established.

you have my permission[a] another time to own, and defend, it. But enough on this idle theme; which I am very glad to exchange for a little of our old chat. I know not, if it were greater Vanity or Gratitude[b] to own your compliment on my Norton Gardens;[3] the more welcome return for yt. trifle is your own six Stanzas, which I could be pleas'd with, if I did not suppose 'em a transcript of your own case. The conflict & inconsistency of passion is naturally express'd in 'em; but the relief you promise yourself in the close, gives me the greatest Satisfaction.

You have alter'd the Line in Hadrian's speech much for the better.[4]

The Marianne you have seen is not the same I meant: tho' it is the most known, and most generally admir'd: the Marianne I meant is not yet translated: it is wrote by way of Memoirs in two Vols.; has therefore a quite different cast and form;[5] but if for the better or no my ignorance of the other makes me quite incapable of saying.

I am just now piping-hot on my pastoral Scheme; which I am in hopes of bringing to some conclusion before the close of the Summer.[6] You see my wav'ring disposition is at last fix'd, but to what purpose I know not.

I must not conclude without expressing my concern [for] your rupture with Gould; and especially as I had the unhappiness to be the occasion of it. Sure he misunderstood you or you him. I believe I shall see Gould at Bishop Stortford the 30th of this month at the School-feast, where I shall think myself concern'd to look into it.[7]

You'll see by many marks in ys. letter, that I write it in the utmost hurry, and therefore you'll excuse my saying no more at present, than was merely necessary for an Answer to you. Write immediatly, and believe me, dear Sir, your most affectionate friend & faithfull, humble Servt.

R. Hurd.

P.S.

Your Brother is well: I heard from him a few days ago.

3 See preceding letter.

4 See preceding letter.

5 The most popular version of the *Life of Marianne* was that written by Marivaux (*La Vie de Marianne*), which was published in France between 1731 and 1741. It was translated concurrently into English between 1736 and 1742. RH, however, had been reading *La Nouvelle Marianne*, a scarcer work in imitation of Marivaux, by Claude-François Lambert. (See *ante* To Mary Macro, 22 June 1743.)

6 RH probably did not complete his pastoral treatise. The idea had first come to him some years earlier and in 1741 he began writing. (See *ante* To Potter, 19 September 1741.) In this new assault on the treatise he changed the form and by November had written an introductory section. (See *post* To Potter, 25 November 1743.) After this, however, nothing further is heard of the project.

7 A school feast was held at Bishop's Stortford Grammar School each year in August. (Nichols, *Lit. Anecs.*, ix. 165, 730–2.) RH had no direct connection with the school but may have been invited through John Tooke of Emmanuel, the nephew of Thomas Tooke, "Refounder" and Headmaster from 1693. (*Ibid.*, p.165.) Tooke's father, also John, had followed Thomas Tooke as Headmaster in 1721. (*Alum. Cantab.*) Nothing more is known of John Potter's quarrel with William Gould.

a MS: "permision".

b MS: "Gratititude".

50 To MARY MACRO 27 AUGUST 1743

Text: MS BL Add. 32557, ff. 63–4; unpublished.
Addressed: For/Mrs. Macro.

Camb: 27. August. 1743.

Madam,

Were it only to acknowledge the late civilities I receiv'd at Norton, I should think it incumbent on me to use this first Opportunity:[1] But I have besides a dismal Tale to unfold; a tale, which were it as well related, might almost move as much, as the adventures of the distress'd Marianne.

The regret I felt in leaving Norton on Thursday was, you'll imagine, pretty much increas'd by the bad condition of my Steed. The discovery of those wounds gave me, I believe, as much pain, as the wounds themselves did the Horse. However we made shift to amble to Bury,[2] where we staid awhile in order to ease the tortur'd Animal, if possible by a couple of plaisters, apply'd to his Back. In about half an hour we were mounted again, and with much ado crept forwd. as far as Kemfer by six o'clock. But here the Tragedy begins: before we had fairly got quit of the Town, the poor, jaded creature made a full Stop, and notwithstanding all the pungency of a couple of Spurs, and the pretty smart Application of a well-corded whip, remain'd in that Situation for a considerable time. The same fit took him several times afterwards betwixt that place & New-market, which indeed I am much despair'd of getting him to that Night. But see what patience, and resignation does! By suffering him to take wind at several Intervals, as he chose himself, &[a] by indulging him, betwixt those intervals, in a slow sullen pace, we at length reach'd the Town of Races between seven & eight o'clock. But further than there I durst not, with all my patience think of taking him, & was therefore oblig'd to leave him to be brought home by Smith on Friday, and hire another to Cambridge that Night. Well! it was now growing dark, or in the language of Novels, Phoebus had now withdrawn his golden Car, and Night had cast her sable Mantle o'er the face of the Earth, when I was again mounted on a second palfry, and began to try his paces on the heath. But what was my concern to find this as uneasy by his hard, awkward gate, as the other had been by his dullness, & fatigue! However we got on pretty fast, and tho' greatly teiz'd & weary, arriv'd at last at Cambridge betwixt nine & ten. But alass! my troubles ended not yet! Foolish man, in the midst of calamities, is forward to please himself with thoughts of future ease & repose, and questions not, were but the present ill remov'd, that any thing will come to afflict him afterwards. Such were my dreams of happiness, during the fatigue of the Journey, when I should reach home. "We'll refresh ourselves", said I to Mr. Cox, "after this vexation, as soon as we get in, with a little supper, and a pipe after it. The fatigue, we have undergone", continu'd I, "will give uncommon softness to an Arm'd-chair, and a [gla]ss of wine must needs have a better relish for it." Fond imaginations these! – the wine indeed was good, the Tobacco pleasant, & chair easy – but a store of wind, that

1 RH had only stayed with the Macros for a short time. He was still in Cambridge on 17 August and had left Norton on 25 August. This letter was written on the following Saturday.

2 RH's route from Norton to Cambridge lay through Bury St Edmunds, Kentford (which he calls Kemfer), and Newmarket. The distances between these places were ten miles from Norton to Bury; ten miles from Bury to Kentford; four miles from Kentford to Newmarket; and a further thirteen miles from there to Cambridge.

a MS: "himself, & and".

had been collecting within the Stomach on the way, began to exert itself, in proportion as I grew warm, and at last expanded itself in such a manner, as to occasion excessive sickness, and dizziness: which had perhaps remain'd longer with me but for the obliging Industry of Mr. Cox, who administer'd a glass of water & the Specific of Miss Cancellor's Drops.[3] – I love a Tragedy, that ends well, and therefore am pleas'd to conclude this with telling you, that I slept well afterwards, & was the next morning serene, & <well> hearty, as tho' nothing had happen'd. I shall drop the curtain after having made the customary Address of being, Madam, your most obedient humble Servt.

R. Hurd.

P.S.

Miss Macro & the Gentlemen will be pleas'd to accept my Humble Service.

Endorsed by Mary Macro: "answer'd ye 3 of Sept. 1743."

51 To MARY MACRO 17 SEPTEMBER 1743

Text: MS BL Add. 32557, ff. 65–6; unpublished.
Addressed: To/Mrs. Macro at Norton/to be left at Mr. Haywood's/ in the Cook-Row Bury St. Edmunds/Suffolk.
Postmarked: postmark missing.

Cambridge: 17. Sept. 1743.

Madam,

Retirement & Norton are to me inseparable Ideas. I cannot indulge a moment [in] reflexions on the one, without recollecting instantly the other. 'Twas [but] a day or two ago I was rambling in our College-Garden, a spot of ground indifferently laid out, but of variety enough for the compass, & which has I know not what of rude & artless in it, that is very agreable. The walk I had got into was dark & shady; occasion'd by some old Apple Trees, & a Chessnut or two, which so spread their Branches on either side, as to give it a lovely gloom, which was the more delightfull from the heat of the day, & the glare of the Sun all around it. The Scene insensibly led to seriousness & reflexion, & impress'd a kind of feeling on the Soul, which, 'tho one knows not how to express, is exquisitely pleasing. 'Tis in these intervals of stillness & tranquillity the Fancy is most at work, diverting herself with infinite whims & wanderings of thought, & making the freest Excursions into the world of Reverie. Exactly this was then my case. Numberless Images & Ideas danc'd immediatly before me. At one time you might see me treading the Solitary waste with the love-sick Dido; at another hiding myself with Orpheus in hollow caves & sheltring forests; & sometimes wand'ring in the moon-light grove, attentive to Amanda's tender Strain, and the ecstatic Sallies of her Romantic Fido.[1] But this Succession of Images lasted not long; the Vision soon fix'd & charm'd me at once with all the sweets of Solitude in the view of Norton. 'Twas there I had wander'd some time, when strolling at last into one of the thickest

3 No further information concerning this remedy has been found.

1 Amanda and Fido do not seem to be literary characters as Dido and Orpheus are. The name Amanda is used by Addison in a *Spectator* paper (no. 375), but RH seems to use these names to denote lovers in the abstract.

shades (I think it was near the laurel-border'd Pond) & seiz'd with I know not what transport, whether infus'd by the genius, or struck into me by the awefullness, of the Place, I thus, in a sort of rapture, began:

In these still shades, where thought & Silence reign,
Where stirs no tumult & no griefs complain,
Oh! let the Muse her tender Accent try,
And prove her pinion in a Summer's Sky!
Be Solitude my Theme: & whilst I sing,
Ye Nymphs of N–n, your Assistance bring.

The Invocation gave me fresh Spirits, & hurry'd away, as it were, by a secret & instinctive force, the gracious gift of my Patronesses, I thus went on.

O! say, what Magic in retirement charms,
In lonely shades what secret rapture warms?
Why pants the Soul for Solitude's soft hour,
'Midst fortune's glitter, & the pride of pow'r?
Say, is there ought in life's still Scene should please
Like London's noise, and Louis' Palaces?
Yes: You'll unfold this Riddle to the heart:
Nature the Goddess is: the Idol Art.
See! gilded o'er with picture's richest dye
Art's mimic Beauties catch the distant Eye;
But nearer view'd her slighted charms she mourns,
And the tir'd Eye to simpler Beauty turns.
Deep in the Soul the fix'd occasion lies:
Man, fool to Custom, is by instinct wise.
Leave then to Instinct the uncertain Strife,
Or let right reason guide the reins of life,
And half the wise & half the good retreat,
Like happy Pollio,[2] to their country Seat,
E'er life's decline or fortune's gath'ring frown
Remove from Courts, and banish from the Town.

The Name of Pollio inspir'd a kind of awe & respect, which stopp'd my course for awhile, & it was not till after a pretty long pause, that, casting my Eyes on the surrounding grove, I could collect myself enough to go on.[3]

Bless'd grove! whose earliest fate ordain'd to rise
To shelter Science & protect the Wise!
Whose bending branches guard the sacred Stream
Whence ev'ry healing draught of Science came,
Whose look inspires, what else were idly sought,
And lend a Shade to deepen learned thought!
Bless'd Grove! in whose imbow'ring shades & cells
All human Virtue, & all Science dwells!
Where Contemplation from the World retires,
To fix her Lamp, & kindle all her fires;

2 C. Asinius Pollio, a Roman consul in the reign of Augustus, and patron of Virgil and Horace. (*Lempriere's Classical Dictionary of Proper Names.*)

3 See *ante* To Potter, 11 July 1743, for an earlier version of the following verses on "Norton Gardens".

Thro' Learning's widest field where Pollio flies,
Tastes ev'ry Sweet, that ev'ry Art supplies;
Thro' Nature's crowded page the God explores,
With wonder views, with ecstacy adores,
Man's various Duty weighs in Reason's Scale,
Sees or the *casting* good or ill prevail,
To Heav'n from thence directs th' ambitious ray,
Till thro' Faith's Optics pours the perfect Day.
Hail! happy Shade, for such a Lord to rise!
Hail! happier Lord, who such a Shade enjoys!

Here I stopp'd; but a croud of other Ideas pouring in upon me, I had certainly gone on, had not the friendly Muse just then whisper'd in my Ear this soft reproof:

Cease, Trifler, cease, nor fondly hope to raise
Due Trophies to thy favour'd Pollio's praise.
Himself a surer monument shall give:
His own Hand labours, what shall ever live.

Convinc'd with this reproof, I was preparing to change my Theme, & had even gone some way in the attempt to do justice to the Nymphs of the Place, and to an old Friend, who had taken up his residence in that Quarter;[4] but was luckily prevented the hazard of doing it by reflecting with myself, that Goddesses could receive no addition of fame from mortal Encomiums, and that a Friend disclames them all, especially in Poetry.

Permit me to conclude this Rhapsody with being, Madam, with the greatest respect, your most obedient, humble Servt.

R. Hurd.

PS.

Please to make my compliments to the Dr. & Miss Macro, (with whom I beg leave to condole on her disappointment of Bury Fair)[5] &, if there be such a person in being, to Mr. Macro.

I hope the last parcel of Books came safe.

4 The "Nymphs" are Mary and Molly Macro; the "old Friend", Edward Macro, who had been out of college since the middle of May. (*Commons Accounts Book*, STE. 15. 9.)

5 Bury Fair began on 21 September every year and lasted for two weeks. It was the "Rendezvous of the Beau Monde every Afternoon", and the occasion for plays and Assemblies in the evenings. The fair itself consisted chiefly of "several Rows of Haberdashers, Milliners, Mercers, Jewellers, Silversmiths, and Toy Shops". ([C. Caraccioli], *An Historical Account of Sturbridge, Bury, and the Most Famous Fairs in Europe and America*, Cambridge, [1773], pp. 12–16.) Molly Macro may have been prevented from enjoying these entertainments in 1743 by a small-pox scare which broke out in September. Although the authorities tried to allay people's fears by issuing advertisements giving the real figures for the outbreak, there was still a good deal of panic. And, in fact, Bury was not free of small-pox cases for at least a year. (*Suffolk Notes from the Year 1729. Compiled from the Files of the "Ipswich Journal"*, Ipswich, 1883–4, pp. 10–11.)

52 To EDWARD MACRO 19 SEPTEMBER 1743

Text: MS NORFOLK RO; copy in a later hand; unpublished.

Emanl. Coll: 19 Sep 1743.

Dear Sir,

It was Yesterday I recd. your letter, and am now sate down, as soon as Breakfast is over to write an answer to it. I have also taken a whole sheet, that I may have room enough to open my whole mind to you on a Subject, in which I cannot but think myself a good deal concern'd, & which, notwithstanding the air of humour you have thrown into it, has given me some uneasiness. Dear Sir, I could not have imagined that a trifling Irony, that was intended only to laugh you out of a little Indolence in[a] regard to writing, could have been ever construed as a Satyrical Sneer, or have given occasion for the Surmise of my having taken too great liberties with you. But I will not insist much on yt. part, because your good Genius immediately suggests the proper reply to it. What amazes me is, that after so true and natural an account of the matter, a Genius of another sort should, as you express it, return to torture you about it. It represented to you, it seems, that under a pretence of receiving pleasure from your letters lay a nicely conceal'd bait for your Vanity, & that I was ungenerous enough to use that little & unfriendly act in order to secure your respect. The imputation is a little severe; but let us hear the reason of it, why it follows, yt. *I who weigh ev'ry word & sentence with the nicest care, and have a peculiar Sagacity in finding out what it is that pleases the mind (which is novelty only) could not possibly be pleas'd with your thoughts, which were always common, and dress'd in as common language.* I am not of that refining Spirit, as to suspect a Sneer in these words, or that there is any artifice conceal'd in them, and shall only observe that whether the observation be true or false, your conclusion is unjust from it. For be it suppos'd if you will, that your letters contain common thoughts in common language, & that I truly am too nice to relish either, is that a proof that they cannot give me any pleasure? Is a correspondence betwixt friends a mere tryal of wit, & of their skill in composition? Surely upon second thoughts you will not say it. Tell me are not five lines, from a friend of whose affection you are assur'd, & whom you have cause to esteem, tho' penn'd in the most careless manner, more acceptable to you, as a letter, than the best wrote Sheet from an indifferent person! Are there not a thousand little touches in the artless letter of a real friend, that delight & please, tho' there is not perhaps one accurate Sentence in it? I could shew you in the late Collection of Pope's letters[1] some of them, which contain as common things, as ever were said, & in as common a manner, & yet I make no doubt but they were highly acceptable to the persons, for whom they were design'd. Such then, for ought you can possibly know, may be my case: I profess at least (for indeed you have nothing for it but my profession) to have an esteem & affection for you, & I am sure you have the same for me; can you in these circumstances conceive a

[1] Five volumes of Pope's correspondence had been published between 1735 and 1737. (*Mr Pope's Literary Correspondence For Thirty Years; from 1704 to 1734. Being, A Collection of Letters, which passed between him and Several Eminent Persons*). RH may be referring to this edition or to a later edition of the letters which formed Parts I to III of Volume IV of *The Works of Alexander Pope* and were published in 1742. (See Reginald Harvey Griffith, *Alexander Pope: A Bibliography*, University of Texas, Austin, 1 vol. in 2 parts, 1922–7, ii. 454–6.

[a] MS: "in ~~writing~~ regard".

letter from you incapable of affording me any pleasure, unless it were trick'd out in new thoughts & new Expression! You cannot on the least reflexion but see, that 'tis affection & sincerity, either real or suppos'd, that makes the great charm in a correspondence by letter, & so long as this subsists, it must, on any Supposition, be agreable: more particularly at this time to me, when there is not a single Soul in this place, whom I can look upon as a friend, or for whom I have any regard, besides what common Civility exacts from me.

Hitherto I have argu'd on the Supposition of your own figurative evil Genius, that your letters are common both in thought & expression. I am not allow'd, I perceive, to touch the other side of the question, tho' perhaps it were no difficulty to produce some Arguments for it, from the very letter, I am now answering. But I forbear, & will even own, if you please, there are sometimes inaccuracies in your letters, but which are so far from giving my niceness any offence, that they only assure me of the confidence you repose in my friendship, in disregarding such little Slips, as I am sensible a greater care would enable you to prevent.

Upon the whole of this Surmise of the evil Genius I cannot but observe of you, what is common to Politicians, more of whom, I believe, are misled by an over refinement in their views, than a want of discerning. You have some knowledge of Mankind; & 'tis usual with such to suspect the obvious & pretended motives to action, & assign others of a deeper policy which tho' sometimes just enough in their application are, I incline to think oftener wrong. Dear Sir, you have known me for some time. I am not forward to engage in friendships, & indeed have but few acquaintances which I can properly call by that name. The consequence of this is, that I am more than commonly sollicitous in supporting & improving those few. I would extract all the happiness from them, that I can, & perhaps for that reason [am][b] troublesome, when I mean nothing less. I may venture to say, you will do me the justice to ascribe my late importunity for letters to this cause: I must own I did not so much consider your aversion to writing, as the pleasure (it is not flattery) which I promis'd myself from it. If I was unfriendly in this judgement, I thought, that, after such aversion was got over by a little use, it might prove an entertaining, & ev'n no unprofitable Amusement. I was perhaps wrong in this; I will not press it further: only let me [say][c] that tho' I cannot desire an increase of pleasure from your uneasiness yet whenever you find yourself in a disposition for it, nothing but your Company, can give me greater pleasure, than your letters. Thus much for the more concerning part of your letter, which you'll accept with that candour, which is due to a friend, who professes to declare his Sentiments without the least cover or disguise. I must not dismiss the other part without some notice.

I am sorry it is not in my power to debate the first part of your letter, as I have done the last. Your complaint & horror at the spread of vice is natural & just; & 'tis but too strong an Argument of the malignity of that disease, when, as you observe scarce a Clergyman escapes.

Mrs. Rays compliments are too [. . .][d] not to be acknowledg'd, tho' I am afraid not deserv'd. I beg when you see 'em you'll present my Services at Haughley, and

[b] MS: "reason troublesome,"
[c] MS: "only let me that".
[d] MS: "too not".

particularly to Mr. Ray for the favor he design'd me, when in Cambridge tho' I was so unfortunate as not to be at home.[2]

You are very good in taking such care about my piece of Plate,[3] & a very cheap Manager to bring the advance Money so low as three Guineas. Did I tell you in my last that Elliot's plate is come?[4] We are wishing now to secure Chase's money,[5] the Master growing a little impatient, but we hear nothing of him. I enquired for him at Bishop Stratford School feast, & was told he was in Wales. He is not I believe returned.

Yrs &c.

R. Hurd.

P.S.

I have but just room for Services.

53 To JOHN POTTER 11 OCTOBER 1743

Text: MS NLW 12432E; unpublished.
Addressed: [To]/the Rev. Mr. Potter at Batcombe/near Brewton/ Somersetshire./By London
Postmarked: 12 OC

Camb: 11. Oct. 1743.

Dear Sir,

I had great pleasure in the copy of verses, you were so good to oblige me with in your last. The op'ning of it is fancifully pretty, & the main of the poem full of Nature & Passion. It should seem to me, however you may dissemble the matter, that it could not proceed but from a heart, actually feeling the distress, of which it complains. *The melancholly Season, you say, has been long over*: I am glad to hear it, but the description could not have been so strong without reta[in]ing at least a lively Sense of it. If I was with you, I c[oul]d point to some lines, that appear to me inaccurate; tho' that very inaccuracy is in a piece of this kind it's greatest beauty.

I am glad you like Marianne: but I may venture to assure you, that you have lost half the beauty of it in the Translation. I can't suspect you'll think it any affectation in me to say this, when it must be clear to any one that ever read french, that no modern language can possibly come up to the inimitable delicacy of the French-Dialogue.

2 Richard Ray and his wife were friends of the Macro family and lived at Haughley near Stowmarket, Suffolk. Ray had been born in Cambridge and went to Trinity College from 1692–9. From 1702 till his death in 1758 he was Vicar of Haughley. The visit he made to Cambridge which RH refers to, may have been to his family, or possibly to his son, Richard, who was at this time also at Trinity, reading for an M.A. (*Macro Letter-book*; *Alum. Cantab.*)

3 Further information concerning RH's piece of plate has not been discovered.

4 It was the custom for Fellow-commoners to present the college with a piece of silver plate when they went down. James Elliot, a Fellow-commoner since 1739, had taken his name off the books on 24 July 1742. (*Commons Accounts Book*, STE. 15. 9.) He presented Emmanuel with three casters in a stand, engraved with his own and the college arms. (*A Catalogue of the Plate in the Possession of Emmanuel College*, compiled by Joan M. Stubbings, (typescript), 1970–1.)

5 Richard Chase had been a pupil at Bishop's Stortford Grammar School, and was admitted to Emmanuel in 1739. He had taken his name out on 2 June 1743. (*Alum. Cantab.*; *Commons Accounts Book*, STE. 15. 9.)

Had Middleton himself been the Translator, he could not have preserv'd the grace of the french in our Language; for which I can give no other reason than this, that the very Idiom of the french is peculiarly adapted to conversation, & naturally runs into all the graces of it.

You are by y[s]. time a proper Judge of Ann Boleyn: I make no scruple of owning myself to entertain no extraordinary opinion of it, for which I'll only give you two reasons, which you are at liberty to admit or reject, as your better Judgment shall direct you. My first reason is, that the Original letter is infinitely better than his Copy;[1] & would have been so, had Pope himself taken it, it being impossible to preserve in the politeness & accuracy of our present poetry, the native frankne[ss] & simplicity of Anne of Boleyn. My second is, that I have seen Eloisa to Abelard; of which Mr. Whitehead's greatest Admirers must allow this to be a very unequal, in some places, a servile Imitation.[2] The part I admire most is an Allegory wholly added without Authority from the letter: it is that which represents Anna as a flower in life's low vale:[3] a thought obvious enough, & blown upon by ev'ry Scribler, but so finish'd in this place as to have an extreme Beauty. I expect your opinion very soon & very frankly.

The next Paragraph in your letter was particularly agreable, as it inform'd me of my friend's near prospect of preferment.[4] It is not in the power of the most zealous Interest to procure livings, just when it will; & therefore I do not much wonder at <their> your friends not having hitherto be[e]n able to serve you; tho' I doubt not of their doing it for their own credit, as soon as they can. I have just now hear'd, but know not if it be on good Authority, that Gold has got a living in Suffolk.[5] If so, I shall expect to hear soon.

Your account of the Hail-Storm was very terrible: the concern you express for the unhappy chance of the Goldfinch shews a degree of humanity, which I much approve. It would methinks be a pretty Subject for a little poem, which you'd know how to work up in a very agreable manner.

I am going in about a fortnight's time to Reymerston, where I shall pass a week or more with your Brother. He has oblig'd me lately with some good versions of the Episodes in the first Georgic: by the help of a little correction they'll be masterly things. I am told he studys hard, & is much respected in the Parish. He wrote to me lately to use my Interest for a little College living near Norwich; but it was dispos'd of,

1 Ann Boleyn's last letter to Henry VIII is printed before Whitehead's poem (pp. 3–4).

2 See *ante* To Edward Macro, 22 June 1743, n. 3.

3 *Ann Boleyn to Henry the Eighth*, ll. 21–30.

"Why was I rais'd, why bade to shine on high
A pageant Queen, an earthly Deity?
This Flower of Beauty, small, and void of Art,
Too weak to fix a mighty Sovereign's Heart,
In Life's low Vale its humbler Charms had spread,
While Storms roll'd harmless o'er its shelter'd Head:
Had found, perhaps, a kinder Gath'rer's Hand,
Grown to his Breast, and by his Care sustain'd
Had bloom'd a while, then, gradual in Decay,
Grac'd with a Tear had calmly pass'd away."

4 Potter was hoping to obtain the curacy of Pylle, near Shepton Mallet, Somerset. He was successful and was licenced as curate on 26 May 1744. (Somerset RO, Clergy List, D/D/VC87.)

5 See *ante* To Potter, 27 April 1740, n.1.

before his letter came, to Freeman, whom you remember.[6] It is besides a trifling thing; under 30 pounds a year, & as I apprehend impossible to have been serv'd together with his present cures. The living, which was your old Master's, is dispos'd of to one Bentham, a moddest, good-natur'd man, whom it is likely to make happy for life.[7] Excuse my not answering your letter sooner, & believe me, Dear Sir, your's most affectionately

R: H:

Re-addressed by Potter: "To ye. Revd. Mr Potter at Reymerston Norfolk. To be deliver'd to ye. Norwich Carrier at ye. black Bull in Bishop's-Gate-Street London".
A further sentence added, now illegible.

54 To EDWARD MACRO 31 OCTOBER 1743

Text: MS NORFOLK RO; copy in a later hand; unpublished.

Dear Sir,

I have now got so much the better of my Indisposition, as to be able to discharge my promise of answering your last. In doing which I mean to use that frankness which on such occasions becomes a friend, & of which you have giv'n me a very agreable example in your own letter.

I will not dissemble the pleasure it gives me, that I stand so fair in your good opinion: tho' you must allow me to think, without the imputation of an affected Modesty, that you carry that opinion much too far; I mean, when you intimate a kind intention of confining your entire confidence & friendship to me; to me, in exclusion of all others, for this, it seems, is your notion of friendship, that, like love, it can admit of no rival. I will not take upon me to dispute this nice point with you; allowing it to be true, the office, I am charg'd with, is so very important, that with all my little vanity I dare not flatter myself with having merit enough to support it. Kindly as you may endeavour to think of me at present, you must expect in the intercourse of our friendship to observe many foibles, weaknesses, & ev'n faults. Can you overlook, can you forgive 'em, & yet retain that warmth of friendship, which you had before? Or will not your high notions of friendship render you uneasy & disatisfyed with your choice, on remarking such imperfections as will be sometimes, perhaps often appearing in this only friend? Tell me, will such a person seem worthy your whole regard, & will you

6 The living in question was Melton Parva. John Freeman (d.1797), who had been at Emmanuel from 1732–9, was nominated Vicar in 1743. He held the living till 1746, when Robert Potter succeeded him. (*Order Book*, COL. 14. 1.)

7 This was Winsford, another college living, previously held by John Gaylard (d. June 1743). He had been an undergraduate and Fellow of Emmanuel, and was presented to Winsford in 1714. He held the benefice till his death, but was also Usher at Sherborne School from 1723–8; Master of Wells Grammar School from 1728–33; and Headmaster of Sherborne from 1733–43. (NLW, MS 12502E; *Sherborne Register 1550–1950*, Winchester, 1950.) Though there are no records preserved to confirm the supposition, it is most likely that John Potter was educated under Gaylard at Wells Grammar School.
Samuel Bentham, who succeeded Gaylard at Winsford, had just completed six years at Emmanuel, having matriculated in 1737. He retained the living until his death in 1752. (*Alum. Cantab.*)

not repent of having repos'd so entire a confidence in him? Mistake me not: I do not mean to accuse you of fickleness in friendship: you'll be constant in approving such a Character, as was fondly imagin'd in the friend at the time of fixing your choice; but what if that Character should alter! what if some Spots should appear in it which you did not expect! spots perhaps of no very deep dye, but yet such as will diminish something of its lustre? Will such discovery give you little or no offence, & will you, after reposing so high a trust, & centring yt. whole affection in one, content yourself with finding that favrite *one* so imperfect? If you can answer in the Affirmative to these questions, I shall be your friend with much less concern & apprehension, & yourself perhaps will not be much disappointed in me: For as to glaring faults, such as in ye. general sense of Mankind will justify a rupture in friendship, of these it is my hope, & shall be my Endeavour, that you have never any reason to complain.

Of this sort (to come to the point) I will not deny flattery to be one: it is as you observe the bane of friendship, & if clearly prov'd, enough to dissolve it at once. But let me observe to you very freely, yt. this is a point not easily to be done. The language of flattery is the genuine language of true friendship; which is indeed the reason, why flattery has made use of it. The artfull flatterer, & the true friend then you cannot distinguish by their discourse. Give me leave therefore to caution you agst. suspicion from that cause only: actions & not words are the test of friendship, & when you find me a flatterer then, condemn me. I would not revive the mention of a thing, which I know will be disagreable to you, but to prevent any misunderstandings for the future. I will venture to assert therefore, yt. you know not ev'n yet, however inclinable your respect for me might make you to think so, whether I am a flatterer or a friend. I call myself the latter, but so would the flatterer: I endeavor to conduct myself in my addresses to you, & my conversation with you, as a friend,[a] but so would the flatterer. What then is to be done? Why fairly, & only this, if my Actions have not hitherto contradicted my words to presume me to be what I pretend, & whenever they do to determine the contrary. And this I am the most earnest in, as it will free us from another bane of friendship, which is Suspicion. I am sensible indeed that, like Jealousy in love, it arises from great affection; yet I know not how it is they have both of them a tendency to weaken & dissolve it. I will ev'n own that your late Suspicion of me must unavoidably have been attended in some sort with this effect,[1] had you not so generously confess'd yourself to have taken a too hasty Step, & had not one of the franckest, friendliest, & most affectionate letters, that ever was wrote to a friend, made ample amends for it. I wish Mr. B. had taken this method: he suspected me, from trivial reasons, unjustly;[2] he persists in thinking he had sufficient grounds for such Suspicion; & therefore, notwithstanding all the shew & outside of settl'd reestablish'd[b] friendship on his part, I have not, nor can immediately have that warm[c] Affection for him, I once had. I will not set myself to philosophise on yt. Subject, & to inquire into the reasons of this effect of Suspicion, (which whatever they are, must, I believe be fix'd in the human nature) all I shall say further upon it, is, (& I do it with equal pleasure & sincerity) that it has had the quite contrary effect here, The

1 See *ante* To Macro, 19 September 1743.

2 "Mr. B." has not been identified; see also *ante* To Macro, 22 June 1743.

a MS: "friend, ~~& only this~~ but so".

b MS: "reeastablish'd".

c MS: "warm~~th~~".

suspicion has been so circumstanc'd, as even to increase my opinion of your friendship, in discovering to me some qualities, which before I knew not yt you possess'd in so eminent a degree. Much the same you tell me has been the case on your part; so that each of us, emerging as it were out of a Shade, appears but the more amiable in the Eyes of the other. God grant this mutual good opinion to continue, & increase; which it will do, if we continue to be virtue's friends, and are carefull to make advances in the practice of it; it being, as you justly say, one of her sure rewards to make those, who have begun & continu'd their friendship according to her laws, *alternately bless the day, they first saw each other*. I should not have us'd this solemn conclusion, which betwixt friends of our age, is not very fashionable, & which with many would appear to have the Air of Cant, if I had known you[d] to be averse to a serious thought, & if I was not (if I know myself) most affectionately & faithfully, Dear Sir, Your friend & Servant

R. Hurd.

Oct 31, 1743.

P.S.

Before I had finish'd this letter, came Goodwin with the Books,[3] in which I had the pleasure of finding a favor from You, for which I thank you. You are very good in wishing the College Chase's Money, which however entre nous (for it must not be talk'd of, at least as coming from me) I begin to give up. He just called here at the time of Newmarket races,[4] but said not a word of it: & went from hence to the Duke of Ancaster's,[5] who is a great gamester, where he may possibly have occasion for all his Money. Tooke talks of being at Hadnam[6] in a little time, when he expects, if ever, to hear something of it.

Now I have mentioned Tooke it puts me in mind of your accusation of him for not sending at least a compliment to you by letter; his Plea is (for Ben,[7] you know, is not very formal) what a duce signifies sending an insignificant humble Service?

I thank you for your repeated Invitation, & shall not fail using the first opportunity of[8]

3 Edward Goodwin was the carrier between Cambridge and Bury St Edmunds, leaving the "*White-Lyon* in *Silver-street*, on Fr. 8 Morning" and returning on "Sat. 6 Evening". (Carter, *History of the County of Cambridge*, 1753, p. 48.)

4 Newmarket was the resort "of the Court or Nobility . . . Twice a Year for Horse Racing and other Diversions", which also drew to the town "Multitudes of Spectators . . . to see them". (John Kirby, *The Suffolk Traveller: or, A Journey through Suffolk*, Ipswich, 1735, p. 79.)

5 The Duke of Ancaster was Peregrine Bertie (1714–78); he had succeeded his father as third Duke in 1742.

6 Richard Chase and his family lived at Much Hadham in Hertfordshire. The MS spelling is perhaps a scribal error; but could be attributable to RH who makes one or two similar mistakes (e.g. Kemfer for Kentford).

7 Tooke's Christian name was John; RH's reference to him as "Ben" cannot be explained.

8 The copy of RH's letter breaks off at this point without any explanation.

d MS: "(If I had known ~~myself~~) you".

55 To JOHN POTTER 25 NOVEMBER 1743

Text: MS NLW 12432E; unpublished.
Addressed: To/the Rev. Mr. Potter at Shepton-Mallet/in/Somersetshire./By London.
Postmarked: CAMBRIDGE 26 NO

Camb: 25. Nov. 1743.

Dear Sir,

I thank you for your obliging & very ingenious Letter. There are many beautifull things in your Verses, & a vast profusion of fancy. My only Objection to 'em is their Metre, which I must own I am no friend to, & what I take to be the consequence of your choice of this Pindaric or rather Cowleian measure,[1] an over-charging of the Description; as particularly in those lines,

> Huge Trees & broken rocks adown the mountains sail
> In floods of liquid fire, & Seas of melted Hail.

You see how impertinent my assum'd [c]haracter of a Critic makes me. I wish [you'd] revenge it upon me in the severest censure of the following little piece, which I have just been throwing together with the design of making it the introductory part to the first Letter on the Eclogues: (For I have lately alter'd my plan from Essays to Letters, for which I could give many reasons; one of which is that it helps me to the following simple & expressive Title: *Thoughts on Pastoral Poetry; in ten Letters on the Eclogues of Virgil.*) I the rather chuse to send you the following at this time, as it will convince you that I have not laid aside all thoughts of what you so kindly, but too partially, urge me to. – Do not only point out faults, but send me such corrections or additions, as you shall think proper.

Letter. 1.

Sr.

"I am by no means surpriz'd, as you <suppos'd> believ'd I should be, at[a] the pleasure you express in reading the Eclogues of Virgil. A person of your parts will be always pleas'd with *beautifull Nature*, nor can it be any reflexion on your good-sense to have read & admir'd at thirty, what the great Author thought considerable enough to engross his whole <care &> attention at the same Age. I am not insensible indeed of the growing prevalence of a very different humour, & can easily <subscribe> come into your Opinion *that there are but few ev'n amongst the Admirers of polite Letters, that would not esteem such a confession*[b] *soundly ridiculous*. But you have luckily hit upon a person of another character; one who is not perhaps less fond of *rural Representation* than yourself, & who is not ev'n asham'd to own, that he has employ'd a much longer time upon [it]. In the agreable retreat you know I enjoy'd at – the two Pastoral Poets

[1] Abraham Cowley (1618–67), an admirer of the Greek lyric poet Pindar, was one of the first English writers to experiment with the Greater Ode, and the first to win popularity for the form. His 'Pindarique Odes', published in 1656, are an attempt to convey the exalted tone and spirit of Pindar's work. They imitate the irregularity and abruptness of the original form but, in common with later imitations, lack the complex metrical structure which gave unity to Pindar's own works.

[a] MS: "as".

[b] MS: "confesion".

were my fav'rite Entertainment; a choice, which indeed the romantic Air & Situation of the place had naturally drawn me into, if I had not by a sort of Instinct been previously determin'd to it. 'Twas there I found leisure to indulge in a course of rambling remarks on Pastoral Poetry, in which if there be any less obvious, or out of the common road, it will be justice to impute them, rather to a certain natural turn, & bent of disposition, than to any superior Sagacity I would be thought to affect in point of Critique. I should be glad, if these thoughts, which prov'd so amusing to myself, could in any degree answer the Idea y[ou have] form'd of a *proper Comment on Virgil*; which, you think, *should be rather a lively Illustration of the plan & conduct of the Poet, than a dry detail of grammatical Observations on the one hand, or a System of arbitrary laws and precepts on the other*. In this point, it seems, we are agreed; & therefore to you I make no Excuse for following my own wild thoughts, wherever they led me, without troubling myself much to retail the different Sentiments of his numerous Commentators.

What I here send you on the first Bucolic is a Specimen of the whole; in which if there be anything to your taste or that may chance to divert in an hour of leisure & amusement, it will be no great difficulty, from the papers I have by me, to furnish out, in a continu'd Series of letters, a distinct commentary on each Eclogue. The whole will be the properest Answer I can make to your complex & not very easy Question, *What is the true Nature of Pastoral Poetry, & how far observ'd by the two great Masters of it, Theocritus & Virgil?*"

This, Sir, is what I intend for the Introduction, the design of which, you see, is to obviate some common Prejudices agst. the work itself, & the manner in which it will be perform'd. – I shall expect by the first Post your full Opinion of it.

I believe you & I are pretty well agreed as to Whitehead's Ann Boleyn; on wch. presumption I shall have a little farther Talk with the Curate of Reymerston, when I see him; which will be, I hope, this Xstmas at Norton; for I was prevented going, as I talk'd of, to Reymerston by a very severe cold, from which I am but just recover'd.[2]

I wonder I never told you that Mr. Hand had a living & that he was coming to live at Aller in Somersetshire next Spring.[3] It is a living of near 300 pounds pr. Ann:. He is, as you say, a good man. I wish you joy of your new Cure,[4] & am greatly pleas'd to hear of it's being every way better than the old one. A clear 50 pound Curacy is vastly better than a great many of the smaller livings. [Your] next change will therefore, I hope, be to a good Vicarage or Rectory; such as hath lately, & unexpectedly falln to Gould, who has been here lately for Priest-Orders & Institution to the Vicarage of <Hoxne> Hoxen in Suffolk, worth a good 100 a year; to which he was presented by one Mr. Maynard.[5] He talk'd of you, when he was here, with much respect, & said he intended writing to you very soon, as indeed he said he should have done before but for an unsettl'd sort of way he has been in this Summer, which occasion'd a neglect of all his friends.

Give me your Opinion of these Verses.

2 See *ante* To Potter, 11 October 1743. RH had proposed to go to Reymerston at the end of October.

3 Christopher Hand had been at Emmanuel since 1717, first as an undergraduate and from 1723 as a Fellow. He was nominated to Aller, a college living, in 1743. (*Alum. Cantab.*; *Order Book*, COL. 14. 2.)

4 Pylle near Shepton Mallet. See *ante* To Potter, 11 October 1743, n. 4.

5 Charles Maynard (d.1775), afterwards sixth Lord Maynard, who had inherited Hoxne Hall in September 1742, on the death of his cousin.

Verses wrote in a Pope's Essay on Man:[6]

Bound in Morocco & gilt.[7]

What tho' illustrious flames on either side
The purple Radiance of Morocco's pride,
What tho' in Gold the *Back* <was> is seen to glow,
And the rich leaves a golden Edging shew;
Yet is in vain, great Bard, thy worth expres'd;
Yet is thy praise unequally confess'd;
Than purest Gold more solid still thy Sense,
Thy wit out-shining purple Radiance.
Oh! unreveal'd thy worth, thy praise unknown,
Unless these leaves have to the Reader shewn,
How thy own Wit enlivens Sense thy own.

I am, dear Sir, your faithfull Friend & Humble Servant

R. Hurd.

Endorsed by RH: "NB. A single Sheet."

56 To COX MACRO 26 NOVEMBER 1743

Text: MS BL Add. 32557, ff. 67–8; unpublished.
Addressed: cover missing.

Dear Sir,

For this, with all the respect I so justly bear you, must be the manner of my Address, when I am thanking you for your last most obliging Letter. I have not read, or thought enough upon the Subject to determine peremptorily for myself at present, but shall carefully lay up your letter upon it, where I may have recourse to it hereafter, as occasion shall require, in order to assist my thoughts in so important an Enquiry. That you have trusted me with your freest Sentiments on so nice a point is so valuable a Mark of the confidence, you repose in me, that I know not whether there be not more vanity, than gratitude in making this acknowledgment of it. One thing I am sure of, & you may safely depend upon it, that, in return for such favours, I shall always be incapable of being either so imprudent, or so base, as by any means to be instrumental in engaging you in, what you justly express a great aversion to, Controversial Trouble.

I shall not fail to get Graham's Edit. of Fresnoy on Painting;[1] whom I should have

6 Perhaps Warburton's edition, *An Essay on Man: Being the First Book of Ethic Epistles to H. St John L. Bolingbroke. With the Commentary and Notes of W. Warburton*, A.M., 1743.

7 Dark red morocco (tanned goatskin) was used for bookbindings from c.1710 to the mid eighteenth century. It was a more expensive binding frequently decorated with gold-tooling in the Harleian style. The more usual covering for books in the seventeenth and eighteenth centuries was plain calf. (Graham Pollard, 'Changes in the Style of Bookbinding, 1550–1830', *The Library*, June 1956, p. 79.)

1 RH refers to a translation of Charles Alphonse Du Fresnoy's work, *De arte graphica*, 1668, entitled *De Arte Graphica. The Art of Painting, by C.A. Du Fresnoy. Translated into English. Together with an Original Preface containing a Parallel betwixt Painting and Poetry. By Mr. Dryden.* To this is added 'A Short Account of the most Eminent Painters, both Ancient and Modern, By another Hand' (Richard Graham). The first edition of the translation was published in 1695 in quarto. A second edition, "Corrected, and Enlarg'd" was published, in octavo, in 1716.

read before this, as well as other books on the Subject, but for this entangling affair of Pastoral, in which I still find myself ingag'd, and which tho' I only employ myself about by times, yet I know not how it is, it prevents my setting heartily upon other Business. I am in hopes however of dispatching it now in a little time. It will require your utmost candour to acquit me of egregious trifling, when you see it.

The following is a little whim, I took into my head the other day, & which I would beg your Opinion, I mean critical Opinion, of. My design was to write 'em in a blank leaf[a] at the beginning of a *Pope's Essay on Man*, which I have by me in a very plain binding. 'Tis, as you'll see, a kind of Apology to Mr. Pope for not paying his book the complement, which according to the present mode, it might seem to deserve, of Morocco, & Gilding.

Verses:

to be wrote in a Pope's Essay on Man;

bound in plain Calf.

What tho' illustrious flam'd on either side
The purple radiance of Morocco's pride;
What tho' in gold the beaming *Back* had glow'd,
And the rich leaves a golden Edging shew'd;
Yet were in vain, great Bard, thy worth express'd;
Yet were thy praise unequally confess'd;
Than purest gold more solid still thy Sense,
Thy wit out-shines the purple Radiance.
Oh! unreveal'd thy worth, thy praise unknown,
Unless these leaves have to the Reader shewn,
How thy own Wit enlivens Sense thy own.[b]

If your complaisance should hinder your being so severe on this trifle, as it perhaps deserves, be pleas'd at least to devolve that Task upon your Son, who I expect should deal less formally with me, & whom, I know, & Mr. Whitehead can testify, to be no Flatterer.[2]

Excuse these Bagatelles & believe me, with a perfect Respect, Reverend Sir, your most Oblig'd & most Obedt. Servt.

R. Hurd.

Em̃an: Coll: 26. Nov. 1743.

I beg my particular humble Services to your good Family. I had thank'd Mrs. Macro for her last favour, but for want of time. I said there were but two Vols. of Harris.[3]

2 RH had commented earlier on Edward Macro's severity in his opinion of Whitehead's ability as a poet. (See *ante* To Macro, 22 June 1743.)

3 Probably the work by John Harris, *Navigantium atque Itinerantium Bibliotheca: Or, a Compleat Collection of Voyages and Travels*, 1705, referred to in To Macro, 5 March 1743. This collection has sometimes been confused with another collection of voyages printed for Awnsham and John Churchill and issued in four volumes in 1704 (see *NUC* entry under John Harris): hence, perhaps, RH's emphasis on the number of volumes.

a MS: "leaf" written over "leave".

b Line printed for emphasis.

57 To JAMES DEVEY 29 NOVEMBER 1743

Text: *Memoirs*, 17.

Emmanuel, Nov. 29, 1743.

Reverend Sir,

I am at last sate down to answer your kind letter, especially that part of it where you intimate a desire of knowing Dr. Macro's objection to the Life of King David, which, in as few words as possible, is as follows:–[1] Dr. Delany had said, by way of alleviation of David's crime of murdering Uriah, that *he was under a kind of necessity of committing it, in order to protect Bathsheba, and, he thinks, himself, (vol. iii. page 11,) from being punished with death by the Sanhedrim.*[2] But all this the doctor believes to be a mere surmise, in proof of which he urges the silence of Scripture history, which (notwithstanding what Delany says in his notes on the place) he insists upon being a very good argument, because the institution of the Sanhedrim was, as he proves very largely, *an occasional institution, or present expedient for the relief of* Moses, *that by the addition of other rulers (all endued with gifts extraordinary as well as he) the complaints of the people might not fall upon him, but be diverted in part upon others, and that by the joint influence of so many persons, all possessed with the spirit of government, they might either hinder or appease them*. The solemnity, therefore, of the institution, which is the only thing that Delany opposes to the silence of Scripture, proves nothing.[3] As to the Talmudists, Dr. Macro shews that their authority in this case is of little or no weight;[4] *for besides, says he, that they are the worst historians in the world, they cannot otherwise support their traditions, which, they say, were handed down by their great Synagogue, but by asserting the antiquity of the Sanhedrim, and pretending that its original came from the Seventy Elders, &c.* As to Jer. xxxviii. 5,[5] the doctor observes that the power of the princes there mentioned is nothing to the Sanhedrim. *The matter, he adds, is only this, that, in those times of confusion and sedition, the King was not able to protect Jeremiah from the grandees of the court, who were exasperated against him by reason of his threatening predictions*. He concludes with observing, *that not only the sacred writers, but even Josephus, Philo,*

1 Patrick Delany in his *Life of David*, 1740–2, had suggested that King David, having seduced the wife of Uriah, arranges the latter's death in the fear that he will discover his crime and bring it before the Sanhedrim. Cox Macro argued against this that the Sanhedrim (the highest court of justice in Jerusalem) had not yet been established and therefore could not pose a threat to the King.

2 *Life of David*, iii. 11–12. "If the infamy were exposed, it were in all appearance impossible to protect *Bathsheba*: it is not clear, that he could protect himself. An affair of that consequence would doubtless be brought before the supreme council of the Seventy, established by *Moses**: from its nature, the most solemn, and powerful assembly, that sat in judgment in any state!" See also p. 13 where RH echoes Delany's phrasing: "This then I take to be beyond all doubt the truth of *David*'s case. He had committed one great crime; and he was under a kind of necessity* of protecting that, by committing a greater."

3 *Ibid*, p. 11, n*. "Some people infer, from the silence of the Scriptures, that the *Sanhedrim* had ceased under their kings: but they forget how absurd it is to suppose, that a council so solemnly instituted by GOD, and in the continuance of which, every tribe was so nearly interested, should ever cease, tho' perhaps its power might, at certain periods, have been considerably lessened, and possibly was so now."

4 Delany refers to the Talmud for evidence to support his claims that the Sanhedrim had power even over the King. (*Ibid.*, iii. 12.)

5 "Then Zedekiah the king said, Behold, he is in your hand: for the king is not he that can do any thing against you."

Origen, Eusebius, and St. Jerome, who were all well versed in the antient government of the Jews, make no mention of the Sanhedrim in the times we are now upon, and therefore that this universal silence in writers of all kinds is a very good argument, &c. He adds, as a further proof of the institution of the Sanhedrim's being of later date, that the very name is of Greek derivation, *Συνέδριον* Lowth, p. 189,[6] and takes notice, that the senators who were entrusted by the Macedonians with the administration of affairs were called *Συνέδριοι*.

This, Sir, is in substance what the Dr. has advanced, but I have done him great injury in throwing so connected and regular a discourse as he did me the honour to write me into such scraps. But a few hints to you will be enough, and indeed, I could not conclude the whole in a letter of any reasonable compass.

I shall trouble you no further at present than just to add your son's compliments and my own. Your son is very well and very studious; he and I have a little talk in a morning about Locke, in the Hall, when I receive such answers from him as almost persuade me that Mr. Locke will soon gain a new proselyte . . .

58 To JAMES DEVEY 17 FEBRUARY 1744

Text: *Memoirs*, 19.

Cambridge, Feb. 17, 1743–4.

Rev. Sir,

I had the favour of your very obliging letter at Norton;[1] but, through one avocation or other, have till now had no time to answer it. I thank you, Sir, for your just and learned remarks on the case of David: they tend much to confirm the sentiments of my other learned friend Dr. Macro, and have indeed, together with his, convinced me of the weakness of Dr. Delany's supposition. It is plain from your review of the Jewish History that the Sanhedrim, if it existed then at all, was without any great power under David. Indeed it does not appear that they had any power at all, much less such a one as to endanger the life of the prince.

I returned from Norton but last night, so that you see I made a hearty stay with my friends there. Indeed I was less solicitous to return, not only on account of the hearty welcome and obliging treatment I met with, but also as I had all the privileges and convenience for study that I could have had in College. Nay more, for the Dr. himself was so good as to become my instructor in form. I had intimated a desire of knowing something of Italian, as 'tis the next fashionable language after French, and, as I had heard, of no great difficulty. Upon this, the Dr., (who is master of most of the modern languages, and, in particular, had learned Italian of *Altieri*, the famous author of the Italian Dictionary in use,)[2] at once undertook to teach it me; and by the benefit of his

6 William Lowth in *A Commentary Upon the Larger and Lesser Prophets*, 1714–25, third edition, 1730, had written: "The Word *Sanhedrim* is without doubt of *Greek* Original, derived from *Συνέδριον*, which often signifies this great Council in the *New Testament*; and from thence is adopted into the *Jewish* Language, by the Rabbinical Writers, as many other *Greek* Words are." But he concludes that: "the Council may still have been of much ancienter Date, and expressed in the *Old Testament* by *Rulers, Princes*, or *Elders, or Senate of the People*." (p. 190.)

1 RH had been staying at Norton since the end of December. (*Residence Book*, TUT. 11. 1.)

2 See *ante* To Potter, 8 October 1742, n. 5.

instructions I am become a notable proficient . . . Nothing is talked of here but an invasion from the French. The Chevalier is at Paris, and we are to expect him here in a short time. Whatever there may be in this news it seems to have consternated the ministry. The Tower is trebly guarded, and so is Saint James's; and the soldiery have orders to be ready for action at an hour's warning.[3] They are hasting, it seems, from all quarters of the kingdom, to London. I saw a regiment yesterday going through Newmarket. After all, I apprehend very little from this terror; it seems a politic contrivance of the French to give a diversion to our men, and keep the English out of Germany.[4] Let me know what is said in your part of the world . . .

59 To COX MACRO 25 FEBRUARY 1744

Text: MS BL Add. 32557, ff. 88–9; unpublished.
Addressed: To/the Reverend Dr. Macro/at/Norton.

Reverend Sir,

It would be strange if I could easily forget the many obliging instances of your favor & goodness, shew'd to me at Norton. Amongst the rest the Satisfaction I receiv'd in going over some of your own excellent Paraphrases on the Epistles was what made a considerable impression on me, & has, since my coming home, drawn my thoughts & attention so much that way, that you must not wonder if I too am turn'd <an> Interpreter, &, with the rashness of a young Adventurer, have been led a little out of my depth. In looking over the Ep. to Timothy I was particularly pleas'd with your pointing of that verse Ep.2 c.2. v.26. Κὰι ἀνανήψωσιν, ἐκ τῆς τω διαβόλω παγίδος ἐζωγρημένοι ὑπ̓ ἀυτῶ, ἐις τὸ ἐκείνω θέλημα:[1] but could not help observing at the same time that while the Metaphor was beautifully carry'd on in the terms *παγίδος*[2] & *εζωγρημένοι*,[3] it was dropp'd entirely, where one would still expect it in the word *ἀνανήψωσιν*:[4] for what relation has *waking* to *Snares* & *captures*? *ἀνανήφειν* signifies properly to awake out of drunkenness to Sobriety, & tho' it may be us'd figuratively to express a change of life & a return or awaking out of the Sottishness of Sin to Repentance and a sober life, yet that would occasion such a jumble of the Metaphor here, as seems inconsistent with the rules of good writing. My conjecture therefore is,

3 Plans for an invasion of England had been made at the end of 1743 by the supporters of Charles Edward, the Young Pretender (1720–88), and by the French. Throughout January 1744 squadrons from the French fleet were manoeuvring in the Channel, and by 10 February Charles had left Rome and arrived in Paris. According to the February issue of the *Gentleman's Magazine* several "extraordinary Councils" had to be held to discuss the situation, including two on Sunday, 12 February "at St. *James's*, at which Place and the Tower a double Guard mounted". RH treats this news with calm, but the reality of the threat was demonstrated by the outbreak of the '45 Rebellion. Charles landed in Scotland at the end of July 1745.

4 France had been fighting an Anglo-Austrian alliance in the War of the Austrian Succession since 1741, although she did not officially declare war until the spring of 1744. The invasion plans were an attempt to distract Britain from her commitments on the continent.

1 II Timothy 2. 26. (. . . τοῦ διαβόλον . . . αὐτοῦ . . . ἐκείνου) "And that they may recover themselves out of the snare of the devil, who are taken captive by him at his will." RH's abbreviation "ου" to "ω" is consistent with seventeenth century printed usage.

2 Trap, snare.

3 Taken alive.

4 Return to sobriety of mind.

that instead of *ανανήψωσιν* it should perhaps be read *αναπηδῶειν*, which makes an ex[act c]ontinuation of the Metaphor & is not so unlike but that it might be mistaken for it by a Copyist:

ΑΝΑΝΗΨΩΣΙΝ
ΑΝΑΠΗΔΩΣΙΝ

The word is well known to mean to run with joy to a thing, & tho' I cannot recollect at present many Authorities for it, yet I find one in Chrysostom, as it is quoted by Scapula,[5] that seems alone sufficient. 'Tis this, ἀπὸ φαυλοτέρον βίω προι ἐνσέβειαν *μετεπήδεσε*, which is both in sense & manner of expression the same as in St. Paul.

Again: in the Epist. to the Hebrews c. 2. 5. it is wrote, ό*υ* γὰρ ἀγγέλοις ὑπέταξε *τὴν ὀικωμένην* τὴν μέλλωσαν, περὶ ἧς λαλῶμεν:[6] translated thus "for unto the Angels hath not God subjected the *world* to come, whereof we speak". But does *ὀικωμένην* signify *world*, i.e. according as it is here us'd for *dispensation*? or has *ὀικωμένην* in Greek the same ambiguous Sense as *world* in English. This is what I greatly suspect, nor can I find one such Instance in the whole G. T. wherein 'tis always us'd for *τὴν γὴν* the habitable world, not *τόν ἀιῶνα*, the world, or Age. I should imagine therefore the true reading might probably be τὴν *οικονομίαν* μέλλωσαν, the *oeconomy or dispensation to come*, which is much the same sort of Expression with that in Eph. 1. 10. *ὀικονομίαν τῶ πληρώματος τῶν κάιρων.*[7] & *όικονομίαν θεῶ τὴν ἐν πίζει* Ep. 1. Tim. c. 1. v. 4.[8] and this is that whereof the Apostle, as he says, was speaking, viz. the *τὴν σωτηρίαν* v. 3.[9] which began first to be spoken by the Lord &c.

I know not what you'll think of these random Conjectures, but as they were quite fresh to me, & lay uppermost in my thoughts, they would out upon paper: & indeed I might say one thing in their favor, that if they have not the felicity & Acumen of the Bentleian Emendations (to speak in the language of our Orator)[10] they at least come up to 'em in point of boldness; which is one requisite in a Critic's character.

You may expect a parcel of some kind next week. Mr. Wallop[11] is out of College & is not expected till the beginning of next week, so that I have not been able to do my errand there.

I conclude with being, Reverend Sir, your most oblig'd & most obedient Servt.

R. Hurd.

Cambridge. 25. Feb. 1744.

5 *Ioan. Scapulae Lexicon Graeco-Latinum, E probatis Auctoribus locupletatum, Cum Indicibus, Et Graeco & Latino, auctis, & correctis*, Lugduni Batavorum, 1652, p. 1241.

6 Hebrews 2. 5. (... οἰκουμένην ... μέλλουαν ... λαλοῦμεν:) "For unto the Angels hath he not put in subjection the world to come, whereof we speak."

7 Ephesians 1. 10. (... τοῦ ...) "... in the dispensation of the fulness of times ..."

8 I Timothy 1. 4. (... θεοῦ ... πίστει) "... the dispensation which is faith ..."

9 Salvation. The expression does not appear in I Timothy 1. 3. RH is perhaps thinking of Ephesians 1. 13. (... τῆς σωτηρίας ...)

10 James Tunstall (1708–63), Public Orator at Cambridge from 1741 to 1746. (See *post* To Littleton, 21 December 1744, n. 2.)

11 Charles Wallop (1722–?71), third son of John, Earl of Portsmouth. Wallop matriculated at Corpus Christi in 1742, became M.A. in 1743, and M.P. for Whitchurch, Hampshire, in 1747. (*Alum. Cantab.*; *The House of Commons, 1715–1754*, ed. Romney Sedgwick, 1970.) His connection with Macro is not known.

60 To COX MACRO 16 MARCH 1744

Text: MS BL Add. 32557, ff. 90–1; unpublished.
Addressed: To/the Reverend Dr. Macro/at Norton.

Camb. 16. March. 1744

Reverend Sir,

I am much oblig'd by your kind reception of my two Pseudo-Bentleians.[1] You are certainly right in rejecting all corrections of the sacred Text, without either a very great Necessity or some good Warrant from MSS or old Copyes. And as I cannot plead the latter, so you have convinc'd me that the other does not take place in either of the cases I was hardy enough to propose to you. Indeed I was much too hasty in asserting thc Brcak of thc Mctaphor in St. Paul to be a jumble inconsistent with good writing, it being evident to me on second thoughts, that, however scrupulous we may be in that respect, the vehemence of an Eastern Wit is not at leisure to regard such Niceties.

As to a Paraphrase on the Book of Job, which you do me the honor to recommend to me, tho' I cannot but think myself extremely unequal to such a Task (having but little Acquaintance with the Old Scriptures, & being wholly ignorant of the language, in which they are wrote) yet since[a] you needs will have it, that I may be able to do something in that way, I owe that just regard & deference to your opinion & advice, as without further ceremony to set about it.[2] The Difficulties I am to expect in such a work are many & great; as I have in some measure experienc'd from an attempt of the like Nature on the Canticles, which I have finish'd this Morning: When I set about this Song, I expected to find it a tolerably regular Pastoral Drama, wherein there should appear some connection or design, & in which, after a proper Allowance for the Eastern way of thinking, something of a consistent Shape might be found. But after all the pains I have spent upon it, & all the little lights to be borrow'd from the Commentators, I am able to make of it only a Tissue of Love Songs, betwixt which

1 See preceding letter.

2 The interest shared by RH and Macro in the Book of Job and the Song of Solomon became increasingly widespread in the late 1740s. There had been considerable interest in both books in the late seventeenth century and early eighteenth century. The Book of Job had been paraphrased by writers as different as Symon Patrick (seven editions of his paraphrase appeared between 1679 and 1734) and Edward Young, who published just a section. The Song of Solomon had been regularly reprinted, particularly in two versions by James Durham (first edition 1669) and John Mason (first edition 1683). In the 1720s and 1730s, however, interest waned. It was revived in the case of the Book of Job by William Warburton's analysis in *The Divine Legation of Moses Demonstrated, on the Principles of a Religious Deist*, 1738–41 (see vol. II, pt. ii, pp. 482–553), and by the controversy which arose out of this between Warburton and Robert Lowth. (A.W. Evans, *Warburton and the Warburtonians. A Study in some Eighteenth-Century Controversies*, Oxford, 1932, pp. 246–7, 250.) A number of new paraphrases and translations followed: in 1748 a paraphrase by Daniel Bellamy; in 1752 a translation by Leonard Chappelow; in 1756 *An Essay towards a New English Version of the Book of Job*; and in 1764 a paraphrase by Lawrence Holden. A corresponding revival of interest in the Song of Solomon also gave rise to new editions: see John Bland, *A Grammatical version, from the original Hebrew; of the Song of Solomon*, 1750; John Gill, *An Exposition of the Book of Solomon's Song* (containing a translation), 1751, 1757–8; Ralph Erskine, *A New Version of the Song of Solomon*, 1742, 1758; and Thomas Percy's translation published in 1764. At the same time, new editions of John Mason's paraphrase, an early paraphrase by Ralph Erskine, and a sixteenth century translation by Theodore Beza were all reprinted and added to the available versions.

a MS: "sine".

there seems to be little more Connection, <at least not more> than between the Odes of Anacreon or Horace, or than what must necessarily be between several Poetical Pieces of much the same Subject. The Commentators by their perpetual drawing & wresting of it to their Allegory, have in a manner forc'd it out of all Shape & Sense, & made the most unnatural & distorted [. . .] of it imaginable.[3] What is clear & beautifull in the Poetry happens unluckily sometimes to convey an Idea of no great Delicacy, & then the carnal Poetry must be giv'n up for the sake of the Spiritual Sense. On the other hand, what is both decent, & poetical, has also the misfortune sometimes of standing out of the Allegory & then the method is for force to pull it in again. In short this ridiculous way of commenting in one class of the Critics, & a superficial Brevity in all the rest, have left this Piece involv'd in such Obscurity & Difficulty, that a second Solomon, I suspect, were little enough to explane it.

As for my own attempt, I must profess myself entirely dissatisfy'd with it; & should hardly think of troubling you with a Sight of it, if I did not hope you would please to add to it such hints & corrections, as may be of use for the further illustration of it. The prospect of this favor encourages me to transcribe it for your perusal as soon as possible. In the mean time believe me with great respect, Rev. Sir, your most Oblig'd Humble Servant

R. Hurd.

I have got Chandler's Vind:[4] but Goodwin did not go to Bury this week.

61 To JAMES DEVEY — 23 AUGUST 1744

Text: *Memoirs*, 20.

Cambridge, 23 Aug. 1744.

Rev. Sir,

I return many thanks for your accurate letter on Mr. Chandler's tract,[1] which, though long in coming, was extremely welcome. I find that Dr. Macro and you agree in thinking it a clear, spirited, and useful piece, though it may not, as you observe, be without its blemishes. I am glad to hear you have got Mr. Arnald's book,[2] which by this time you must have read, for I know your diligence. In your next, therefore, which

3 The distortion of the Song of Solomon by its commentators was still a cause of remark twenty years later. Thomas Percy, in the 'Preface' to his translation of the Song, published in 1764, says that his aim is "to rescue one of the most beautiful pastorals in the world, as well as the most ancient, from that obscurity and confusion in which it has been involved by the injudicious practice of former commentators. The generality of these", he continued, "have been so busily employed in opening and unfolding its allegorical meaning, as wholly to neglect that literal sense, which ought to be the basis of their discoveries." (Percy, *The Song of Solomon, Newly Translated from the Original Hebrew: with a Commentary and Annotations*, 1764, p. v.)

4 Probably the second part of Samuel Chandler's *A Vindication of the History of the Old Testament, Against the Moral Philosopher*, 1741. The title of this continuation of the *Vindication* was *A Defence of the Prime Ministry and Character of Joseph: In Answer to the Misrepresentations and Calumnies of the Late Thomas Morgan, M.D. and Moral Philosopher*, but it was advertised in the *Gentleman's Magazine* as *A Vindication of the prime Ministry* etc. It had been published in June 1743.

1 See preceding letter, n. 4.

2 Richard Arnald, *A Critical Commentary Upon the Book of the Wisdom of Solomon; Being a*

I beg may be soon, I shall take it a favour if you'll please to send me your thoughts upon it. You see the effects of your good nature; but you know, the way of the world is to trouble those most, who are most obliging. The Vacation is always a dead time with us for literary news;[3] however, there is some little stirring. A countryman of ours, one Mr. Worthington, has lately published a chimerical piece which he calls a Scheme of Redemption,[4] wherein he endeavours to shew that we are gradually advancing towards original virtue and happiness, and that the Redemption of Jesus Christ will not be absolutely complete till His religion shall have freed mankind from every part of the curse, and convert the whole world, both in respect of innocence and pleasure, into a very paradise. Accordingly, he interprets Isaiah and the Prophets in such a manner as to draw them over to his own opinion, and understands all those figurative and poetical encomiums which they have poured out on the Evangelic age, in the exact, literal sense. What you think of this piece in Shropshire I know not, but here it passes with such as have read it for a strangely whimsical and enthusiastic performance. In the end of this famous tract, he has given a new interpretation of the Book of Job, which puts me in mind of another piece of the literary kind, which is much talked of.[5] Mr. Warburton in his Divine Legation took occasion to interpret the Book of Job in a manner very different from that of other commentators; which Dr. Richard Grey animadverted upon in the preface to his late Hebrew edition of that book.[6] Mr. Warburton replied to Dr. Grey, but with so much acrimony as to spirit up the Dr. to fall upon him with a good deal of resentment.[7] The pamphlet is reckoned to be well wrote, and with so much smartness as to be much admired by the enemies of Mr.

Continuation of Bishop Patrick and Mr. *Lowth*, 1744. Arnald had been a Fellow of Emmanuel from 1720 to 1733. His *Commentary* had been supported by the subscriptions of seventeen members of the college, including RH's friend Edward Macro. RH himself did not subscribe to the work.

3 Fewer books were published in England between July and September than during the rest of the year, and August was a particularly thin month.

4 William Worthington (1703–78) was at this time Vicar of Blodwel in Shropshire, but he had been born in the adjacent county of Montgomeryshire. His book, *An Essay on the Scheme and Conduct, Procedure and Extent of Man's Redemption* had been advertised for sale in the *Gentleman's Magazine* in December 1743.

5 'A Dissertation on the Design and Argumentation of the Book of Job'. Worthington interprets Job as an "allegorical" and "philosophical" poem, which, in support of his general thesis, he claims was written to comfort and support mankind by indicating the certainty of final redemption. (pp. 494–8.) The 'Dissertation' appears to have been prompted by Warburton's *Divine Legation* in which the Book of Job is discussed at length (see vol. II, pt. ii, pp. 482–553). Both writers see Job as an allegory, but Warburton had tried to set the book in an historical perspective and interprets it as written specifically for the Jews on their return from exile. It had been intended, he thought, to convince them that "they were no more to expect to be governed by an *extraordinary* and *equal* Providence" but by "an *ordinary* and *unequal* one". (Worthington, 'Dissertation', p. 466; and see the *Divine Legation*, vol. II, pt. ii, pp. 503–6.) Worthington considers this view in his 'Dissertation', but dismisses it, taking Job as having a more general application comprehensible to men of all times.

6 Richard Grey, *Liber Jobi in Versiculos Metrice divisus*, 1742. The edition gives the Hebrew text of Job with a Latin translation and notes. In the 'Praefatio' Grey expresses the opinion that no deeper understanding of the Book of Job can be attained by knowledge of authorship or date of composition. Nevertheless, since many previous critics had debated the possibilities in each case, he gives a summary of the views of the "*chief*" of them. (p. viii ff.) It is in this section of the 'Praefatio' that Warburton's theories are considered. (pp. x–xv.)

7 Warburton was attacked by many writers for his views on Job (see RH's account in *A Discourse, By Way of General Preface to Bishop Warburton's Works*, 1794, pp. 46–7. The *Discourse*, though

Warburton. This, I think, is all the news I have at present. I will beg the favour of you to make my compliments to Mrs. Devey, the young ladies, and your son, and to our family at Hatton. Nor must I forget to thank you for your care in sending me an account of them when you write to me. Sir Edward Littleton[8] is very sober and studious, and gives me the hopes of seeing him one day a scholar and a worthy man. I am, with great respect, good Sir, your obliged humble servant,

R. Hurd.

62 To ANTHONY ASKEW 2 SEPTEMBER 1744

Text: MS BOD MS Eng. Lett. c. 198, ff. 160–1; unpublished.
Addressed: To/Dr. Askew at Mr. Otway's/Apothecary in Panton-Street/ London.
Postmarked: CAMBRIDGE

Dear Sir,

I return many thanks for the trouble you have giv'n yourself to enquire after Spanheim & the Republics; the former of which I have receiv'd together with *Benjaminis Itinerarium*; but you mention the price of neither.[1] I consulted Dr. Macro about the other Republics, you mention'd, but he seems unwilling to give so immoderate a

published separately, is usually found in Warburton's *Works*, 1788). In response, he singled out a few of the "more respectable" from the "gross body" of his assailants, resolving "to quit his hands of them at once, in a general comprehensive answer". This appeared in two parts in 1744 and 1745; RH refers to the first, entitled *Remarks on Several Occasional Reflections: In Answer to Dr. Middleton, Dr. Pococke, Dr. Richard Grey, and others*. Despite having chosen to answer only the more serious criticisms levelled against him, Warburton gives the impression that he regards them and their authors with scorn. In contrast to this, Grey's reply, *An Answer to Mr. Warburton's Remarks on Several Occasional Reflections*, 1744, is written in the form of a friendly, well-reasoned letter, designed to win the sympathy of its readers, as well as to convince them of the truth of his arguments. The controversy died down after this last publication, though it was remarked upon at some length in notes added to the second edition of Worthington's *Essay on the Redemption*, published in 1748.

8 Sir Edward Littleton (see Biography) had been admitted to Emmanuel on 30 April 1744, aged 16. RH was appointed his tutor and both men remained in college throughout the summer. (*Commons Accounts Book*, STE. 15. 9.)

1 The work by Friedrich Spanheim is probably the *Historia Jobi*, Geneva, 1670 (see *ante* To Macro, 16 March 1744, and To Devey, 23 August 1744, for evidence of RH's interest in the Book of Job). A copy of this history, perhaps the same, was acquired by Emmanuel College Library between March 1744 and March 1745. (*Steward's Accounts Book*, STE. 1. 5.) The college paid 1s. for the quarto volume. The other named work for which RH had enquired, the *Itinerarium D. Benjaminis*, is an account of the travels of a twelfth century Spanish rabbi. The most popular version had been published by Constantine l'Empereur in 1633. He edited the original Hebrew text and added a parallel Latin translation and notes. The "Republics" mentioned by RH may have been accounts of the Hebrew republic. Constantine l'Empereur had published one such account in 1641. In 1653 an English translation appeared of a more popular history by Peter Cunaeus, entitled *De Republica Hebraeorum*, first published in 1607; and between 1704 and 1710 a further work with the same title was published by Melchior Leydekker. All three works were printed in the Netherlands.

price as 5 Shills. a Vol. for them. If they can both of them be had for 5 S., the Dr. will think himself oblig'd to you to buy 'em.

I am next to thank you for your two Criticisms on Theocritus, the first of wch I like very much, & think an easy correction, if it be true, as you suspect, that the Antients never rub'd their cups over with wax.[2] But of this I have some doubt, but have not leisure now to examine into it. As to your next Emendation I think it ingenious, but not necessary. You know I am a scrupulous kind of Critic, & am not for admitting corrections without good reason, however the ingenuity of 'em may sometimes please me.[3] Your mistake, I conceive, lies here, (& 'tis an Error enterprizing Critics often fall into) in requiring that minute exactness in a Poet, which one would hardly expect from the Mathematician. Especially to expect it from Theocritus, a pastoral Poet, & one of whose beauties is a certain inaccuracy & negligence, I think unreasonable. Βατοι & ακανθαι, you say, signify pretty much the same thing. I believe they do, & therefore think it very likely, that the Poet might call upon them both to bear Violets: instances of which you will recollect in great Abundance from the Poets. You see I deal very freely with you; but that I know you expect from me. In yr. next I must insist on seeing more of your conjectures; which, whether right or wrong, I shall think an Entertainment.

But I must not conclude without congratulating with you on your Admission to the great Bentley's Remains.[4] Could you not send me some of his Emendations? You know I am particularly curious there; so that such a present would be of great value. And pray write me a copy of his Epitaph, which, however plain, I should take a pleasure in seeing.[5] Sr. Edward Littleton sends compliments; & I am, Dear Sir, your faithfull, humble Servt.

R. Hurd.

Camb: 2. Sept. 1744.

Let me know abt. the Republics as soon as possible.

2 Askew had evidently proposed a different reading of the word "κηρῷ" in Theocritus i. 27: this was usually translated as "beeswax" and still is today. The second emendation suggested by him was of another line in the same poem:

"νῦν ἴά μέν φορέοιτε βατοι, φορέοιτε δ' ἁ'κανθαι".
Bear violets now ye briars, ye thistles violets too. (Theocritus i. 132.)

3 This was a recent development in RH's approach to emendatory criticism. He had been warned against ingenious corrections only a few months previously (see *ante* To Macro, 16 March 1744).

4 Richard Bentley died on 14 July 1742. He had left his library and manuscripts to his nephew Richard. According to James Monk in *The Life of Richard Bentley*, 2 vols., 1833, ii. 415, all the books and papers were transferred from Cambridge to the younger Bentley's home in Leicestershire, with the exception of a few books sold soon after his uncle's death. There is no evidence to show how Askew obtained access either to books or papers.

5 The epitaph, on a small stone in the pavement of Trinity chapel, runs:

H. S. E.
RICHARDUS BENTLEY, S. T. P. R.
Obiit xiv Jul. 1742.
Aetatis 80.

63 To EDWARD MACRO 25 SEPTEMBER 1744

Text: MS BL Add. 32557, ff. 84–5; unpublished.
Addressed: cover missing.

Camb: 25. Sept. 1744.

Dear Sir,

As Mr. Beauvoir[1] tells me, he intends to set out for Bury-fair to morrow, I was willing to take the opportunity of paying my respects to you in a letter. As to your's dated the 12th. Inst. I know not by what fortune it happen'd, but I never receiv'd it, till Saturday last;[2] when Mr. Beauvoir deliver'd it to me together with one from Dr. Macro.

Since my last to you I have read the other Vol. of the life of Sethos,[3] & as I then promis'd, shall now trouble you with my thoughts upon it. Upon the whole then I think it an excellently well wrote book: the plan of it is new & interesting: abundance of Aegyptian learning & Antiquity is curiously interwove in it;[4] and the Adventures are many of 'em singular & affecting. But on the other hand I am apt to suspect, the French[a] loquacity prevails too much in many places;[5] that several parts have too much the Air of wonder & romance to make any great impression; & that in his Characters there is not so much of Nature & of real life as might be wish'd in them. Ev'n Sethos himself is rather a character to be gaz'd at, than imitated. The Knight-Errant is so predominant in his Undertakings; he is always so unerringly right in his counsils, & so perpetually successfull in the execution of them, that for my part I

1 Osmund Beauvoir (1720–89) was at St John's, Cambridge. He had been admitted in 1738, obtained his B.A. in 1743 and was working for an M.A. He later became a Fellow of the College (1746–51) and subsequently Headmaster of his old school, King's, Canterbury. Beauvoir was particularly friendly with Edward Macro who had a large acquaintance at St John's. According to William Cole, the famous Cambridge antiquary, he was "a cheerful companion, sung a good song, and understood music well". (*Lit. Anecs*., ix. 351–9, 810; see also C.E. Woodruff and H.J. Cape, *Schola Regia Cantuariensis: A History of Canterbury School*, 1908, pp. 175–8.)
A letter in the *Macro Letter-book* indicates that Bury Fair was to start on Wednesday 26 September.

2 22 September.

3 Probably the two volume English translation of *Sethos: Histoire ou Vie Tirée des Monumens Anecdotes de l'Ancienne Egypte. Traduite d'un Manuscrit Grec*, 3 vols., Paris, 1731. The work, an account of the life of an Egyptian prince, was written by Jean Terrasson. It had been translated immediately into English and was published in London in 1732, as *The Life of Sethos*. The translator was Thomas Lediard.

4 As the title indicates, *Sethos* is supposedly a "history" of Greek origin, based on Egyptian "Anecdotes". The work is designed to display "a compleat life" and the "actual application of those principles and sentiments, which [the] hero had imbibed in the course of a most excellent education". ('Preface', p. vii.) Like Middleton's *Life of Cicero*, 1741, and Delany's *Life of David*, 1740–2 (works which also appealed strongly to RH), it is not a straightforward, uninterrupted narrative. The author takes advantage of his hero's Egyptian origin and incorporates into the life a number of digressions on Egyptian and Phoenician manners, government and religion.

5 This characteristic is noted in the *Retrospective Review*, 1821. Terrasson, the writer says, becomes "alarmed at his own *lengthiness*, and charitably postpones a part [of an account of Sethos' course of public instruction] to the end of the volume, as 'une preuve et un exemple des egards que l'on a eus pour les lecteurs qui n'aiment pas de details un peu longs'." But Lediard, he remarks, "unmercifully restores this supplementary matter to its original position". (*Retrospective Review*, iii. 86.)

a MS: "french" changed to "French".

could never look upon him, quite thro' the book, but as a mere creature of the Writer's fancy. It will be said perhaps the very design of the Author was to draw a perfect character.[6] It may be so. But I should then be tempted, if it were not too pert, to attack that very design. A perfect character is certainly a Monster in Writing. It is out of nature, we can't even conceive it. Nay it disappoints the use, we might otherwise make of it. For who will set about to imitate a character, which he plainly perceives must be to him inimitable? Besides, this has ev'ry way a bad Effect in the History. It not only, as I said before, leads one to think the whole account unreal; but takes away all the pleasure of Suspense & Expectation, by ensuring to us before-hand the Success of ev'ry Atchievement. I knew he would settle a colony, before he landed; & was sure he would take his towns, before he form'd the Siege. I will only add further, that the concluding Stroke of his resigning the kingdom, & throwing himself into a College of Priests, which were intended to round & finish his character, displeas'd me very much. There is something greatly visionary in all that part; or rather it is an Absurd compliment growing out of the Popish Notion of Heroism & true Greatness. You doubtless observ'd, how very artfull the whole Representation of the Aegyptian Priesthood is, & how carefully ev'ry little incident is improv'd to their Advantage. The Abbot doubtless did not overlook the Service it might do his own Order to draw in so amiable a light a Set of men, to whom in their affected, & mysterious Sanctities they are known to bear so near a Resemblance. The young Dauphin,[7] (for whose use I presume the work was design'd) might by the prejudice of so early an Impression take Paris for Thebes, & the College of the Sorbonne for the Temple of Isis. And in consequence of this who knows but we may one day see the present Sethos of that priestly Nation, after having acquir'd great glory by a life of Arms, resign the lustre of a crown, & as the last & greatest Deed of a brave life, throw himself into the sacred Shade of a Sacerdotal College!

I am, Dear Sir, Your friend, & Servant

R. Hurd.

My compliments.

64 To Sir EDWARD LITTLETON 21 DECEMBER 1744

Text: MS STAFFS RO D1413/1; unpublished.
Addressed: To Sr. Ed: Littleton Bart./at Pipe-Ridware

Dear Sir,[1]

My promise, I think, was to trouble you with a longer letter, than I was at liberty to do last week; & the Sight of this will convince you, that I have kept my word but too

6 The author of *Sethos* did not wish to portray realistic characters. He intended his work to be recognised as a fiction and his aim was to arouse admiration and the imitation of moral virtues. "We might combine and melt down numbers of the great Men in history", he wrote, "and unite the events of many ages; before we should find those materials for wonder and imitation, which a judicious author of a fiction will often produce in but a small part of the life of one single hero." ('Preface', p. iv.)

7 Louis (1729–65), the son of Louis XV.

1 Sir Edward Littleton had left Emmanuel in mid September. He returned to college at the end of January 1745. (*Commons Accounts Book*, STE. 15. 9.)

faithfully. As the news of the Place is naturally the first thing you'll enquire after, I begin with telling you, that Dr. Tunstall is made Chaplain to the Arch-Bishop,[2] & that by this means the Care of an hundred & twenty pupils devolves upon my friend Mr. Powell.[3] As you know the character of this Gentleman, you'll rejoyce to hear of so good fortune befalling him so early. Since the Dr. left us,[4] my L. Burleigh came to St. [John's] & is admitted under Mr. Powell.[5] My Lord seems a good-natur'd, worthy [man] &, if his Parts are none of the brightest, his Sobriety & Diligence, I am told bid fair to make up for the want of 'em.

Sr. John Rouse after all is admitted of Trinity, to the no small Disapointment, I believe, of Mr. Keller.[6] Indeed my Lady Rouse has us'd him scandalously, but the tale is too long to come within the limits of a Letter; & besides 'twill serve to furnish a Conversation, when I see you.

As to literary news, the only thing of consequence, that has hitherto appear'd this winter, is Dr. Middleton's Book of Antiquities:[7] And this, 'tis said, is not so remarkable on account of the novelty of it's remarks, as for the exquisite Latin, in which 'tis wrote. And this praise indeed is so just, that you might pass immediatly from your favourite Tully to him, & scarcely perceive a Difference.[8]

2 James Tunstall, a Fellow of St John's since 1729 and Public Orator to the University from 1741, was appointed Domestic Chaplain to Archbishop Potter in the summer of 1744. From July 1743 he had been one of the two principal tutors at St John's. He resigned this position at the beginning of July 1744, but retained the post of Public Orator until 1746, and his Fellowship till 1748. (R.F. Scott and J.E.B. Mayor, *Admissions to the College of St John the Evangelist in the University of Cambridge*, 3 vols., Cambridge, 1893–1931, ii. 110–13, 372–74.)

3 William Samuel Powell (1717–75) was a contemporary of RH's at St John's, and had been made a Fellow in 1740. Though not close friends, the two men remained in contact till Powell's death, largely through their mutual friend, Thomas Balguy. After a successful career as a Fellow, Powell was elected Master of St John's in 1765. He remained there till his death. RH's assertion that the care of one hundred and twenty pupils was to devolve on Powell appears to be mistaken. Although there were about that number of undergraduates in the college, no one tutor took responsibility for them all. Two tutors accepted the responsibility of the majority of the undergraduates, and the rest (it had been about one sixth of the annual intake) were taken on by other Fellows. Therefore, though in July Powell had gone immediately into the position of a principal tutor, his responsibilities could have been for no more than half the number of undergraduates mentioned by RH. (Thomas Baker, *History of the College of St John the Evangelist*, ed. John E.B. Mayor, 2 vols., Cambridge, 1869, ii. 1042–78; Scott-Mayor, *Admissions to St John's*, ii. 114ff.)

4 Tunstall left college in late April or early May 1745 (*St John's Buttery Books*), but the last pupil allocated to him in his capacity as tutor had been admitted on 5 July 1744. (Scott-Mayor, *Admissions to St John's*, ii. 113.)

5 Brownlow Cecil, ninth Earl of Exeter (1725–93), was admitted to St John's on 9 November. He was Powell's first tutorial pupil. (Scott-Mayor, *Admissions to St John's*, ii. 114.)

6 Frederick Keller (1717–85) was a Fellow of Jesus. He came of a Suffolk family and had been educated at Bury St Edmunds Grammar School (*Alum. Cantab.*); RH may have become acquainted with him through the Macro family. Sir John Rous (1727?–71), the son of Sir Robert Rous, fourth Baronet of Henham, also came from Suffolk. He had been admitted at Jesus *in absentia* on 16 January 1744, and Keller had been appointed as his tutor. (*Jesus College Register*, COL. 1. 2.) This suggests some previous connection between the two men. However, Trinity was a more prestigious college and the realisation of this fact may account for Sir John's migration there in October 1744. Keller was no doubt disappointed at losing a pupil who could have become a valuable patron.

7 Conyers Middleton's *Germana quaedam Antiquitatis eruditae Monumenta* had been advertised for sale in November. (*Lond. Mag.*) The title-page, however, bears the date 1745.

8 This was becoming a cliché in comments on Middleton's works: see RH's previous reference to

But more of this, when I have the pleasure of talking such matters over with you in College. This you tell me shall be very soon; & I will venture to add as a further Inducement to so dutifull a Son of Alma Mater, as Sr. Edward Littleton, that, after an Absence of three-months, She is very impatient to see him.

I must not forget to ask (tho' you know me not very curious in Political matters) how the present face of things is regarded by our Staffordshire Gentlemen. If fame tells true, we are to have a notable Revolution in State-Directors.[9] All the honest men are to come in at once, & now, if ever, is the time for Golden Days, & the prosperity of Old-England. Your friend Virgil (for you'll excuse a Scrap of Latin from a College) has it something differently:– redeunt Saturnia Regna: Iam *nova Progenies* caelo demittitur alto.[10] My Lord Gower is esteem'd by ev'ry one as the Pollio of the Age;[11] & to be sure there can be no doubt about applying the words Regnat Apollo. One might go on to interpret other parts of that famous Prophecy of our own Days; but as the [. . .] way is to wait the completion of an Oracle, before one applies it, I [. . .] hazard no more conjectures at present; but conclude in asserting [wh]at I am quite sure of, that I am, Dear Sir, your most faithfull, humble Servt.

R. Hurd.

Camb: 21. Dec. 1744.

P.S.

Your Venison was the best that[a] has been seen here a great while. Upon this, & other accts. ev'ry body is much your Humble Servant.

Middleton as "our English Cicero" in To Potter, 22 March 1741, and the reference to his *Life of Cicero* as "a Book worthy of Tully himself" in a letter from a Cambridge undergraduate (Hinckesman) printed in Wordsworth, *Scholae Academicae*, p. 315.

9 The political world had been in a state of flux since the end of November 1744, following the forced resignation of John, Lord Carteret, the King's favourite minister and a Secretary of State. In Parliament he had been opposed by the Lord Chancellor, Newcastle and Henry Pelham; but his resignation was welcomed by the public as well, with whom he had fallen out of favour. According to Philip Yorke their dislike arose "from an opinion taken up, that he was desirous of prolonging a war, to the conduct of which he had shewn himself very unequal", and "from the character he had acquired of insincerity and falseness". (*The Parliamentary History of England, From the Earliest Period to the Year 1803*, 36 vols., 1806–20, xiii. (1812) 976.) Nevertheless, once Carteret had been removed, there was some difficulty in forming a new ministry, and it was not until the end of December that an agreement was negotiated which resulted in a coalition. Amongst the opposition leaders who agreed to take office in the new Government was John, Lord Gower, Lord-Lieutenant of Staffordshire and previously a staunch tory. His action in joining the coalition was considered by the predominantly tory Staffordshire gentry as a betrayal of trust, and it created considerable bad feeling in the county. (Josiah C. Wedgwood, 'Staffordshire Parliamentary History (1715 to 1832)', *Collections for a History of Staffordshire*, ed. The William Salt Archaeological Society, 1922.) See Linda Colley, *In Defiance of Oligarchy. The Tory Party 1714–60*, Cambridge, 1982, esp. ch. 9.

10 *Eclogues*, iv. 6–7.

11 This and the following references are all to the fourth eclogue which prophesies a new golden age on the birth of a child in the consulship of Pollio.

"tu modo nascenti puero, quo ferrea primum
desinet ac toto surget gens aurea mundo,
casta fave Lucina: tuus iam regnat Apollo.
teque adeo decus hoc aevi, te consule, inibit,
Pollio, et incipient magni procedere menses;" (ll. 8–12.)

a MS: "thas".

65 To JAMES DEVEY 25 MAY 1745

Text: Memoirs, 23.

Cambridge, 25 May, 1745.

Rev. Sir,

I return abundance of thanks for your last, which gave me every way much pleasure, chiefly as it informed me how exactly my thoughts have coincided with yours concerning Mr. Worthington. For I know not how it happens, but it flatters the vanity of a young man very agreeably, to have his own random notions confirmed by a person of Mr. Devey's experience. Besides this general agreement of our thoughts, I thank you for those particular strictures you have obliged me with on his book, and which I entirely acquiesce in. This Dissertation on the Book of Job is, as you observe, a most strange performance.[1]

The attention of the learned world at present turns entirely almost on the author of the Divine Legation of Moses,[2] who is mowing down his adversaries with as great zeal and success as ever old Bentley did before him.[3] Indeed the superior genius and abilities of that writer gave him a very great advantage over all the gentlemen that have appeared against him, whatever may be determined finally of his cause. A piece he has just now published in answer to Dr. Stebbing and Sykes is very ingenious, but wrote with a severe satiric spirit peculiar to himself and his late friend Mr. Pope.[4] . . . I must add for your and good Mrs. Devey's satisfaction, that your son is very well, and, as usual, very good. The only want of improvement I can discern in him is in point of smoking, which he still continues unacquainted with;[5] and, though I would be very

1 See *ante* To Devey, 23 August 1744, nn. 4 and 5.

2 William Warburton.

3 Warburton's *Divine Legation* had elicited a large and highly critical response. John Disney in *Memoirs of Arthur Ashley Sykes*, 1785, suggests that few learned theological books had been more universally read in their day (p. 269), and by 1745 at least ten volumes (one of them by Sykes) had been written against it. Warburton answered a selection of his critics in two separate publications of 1744 and 1745 (for the first of these, see *ante* To Devey, 23 August 1744, n. 7). They in their turn met a vigorous response. Some readers admired his spirit, but many found his replies offensive. Disney is one of these. Warburton, he says, "most assuredly received much rough language from his adversaries; but he amply paid all convicted, and even suspected offenders, in one common coin, both principal and interest: and it was not seldom that he dealt out, from the same mint, much illiberal abuse upon some of the most learned and respectable characters and scholars of his time, only because they presumed to differ from his system of legislation". (*op.cit.*, p. 264.) In this respect RH's comparison of Warburton with Bentley is misleading. Both men had great intellectual power and were immensely well-read but Warburton relied far too heavily on what was at its best "fire and genius", but at its worst pure abuse. Bentley was a greater scholar and it was his scholarship that won him fame as the victor in the 'Epistles of Phalaris' controversy.

4 Warburton's second defence of the *Divine Legation* had been published in May. (*Gent. Mag.*; *Lond. Mag.*) The title, a parallel to that of the first defence, is *Remarks on several Occasional Reflections: In Answer to the Reverend Doctors Stebbing and Sykes*. It is a longer work than the previous *Remarks* but gives less consideration to points raised by his critics and is more contemptuous of their publications. The similarity of satiric spirit in the writing of Warburton and Pope (who had been friends from 1740 till the poet's death) lies rather in their motivation to satire, than in the execution of their separate satirical works.

5 Smoking was very much the fashion in the university at this time. Thomas Balguy, another of RH's friends, believed it to be one of the staples of college life. "To deprive a Cambridge man of his *Books* & his *Pipe*", he once wrote, "is to leave him hardly any thing in the world worth

cautious of saying anything to the prejudice of so good a lady as Mrs. Devey, yet I must say that I verily believe that the want of this so necessary qualification in her son is wholly owing to her advice and precepts. In punishment of her, I cannot tell whether I may not take a pipe extraordinary myself when I see you.

66 To MARY MACRO 29 AUGUST 1745

Text: MS BL Add. 32557, ff. 96–7; unpublished.
Addressed: To/Mrs. Macro at Norton/to be left at Mr. Hayward's/ in the Cook-Row/Bury St. Edmunds./Suffolk.
Postmarked: postmark missing.

Camb. 29. Aug. 1745.

Madam!

Your last favour gave me much such a Splenatic kind of Satisfaction, as the covetous Man receives from the Sight of a fine Estate,[a] which he wishes in his own possession. The Entertainments of Ipswich, the Conversations of Norton, & let me add, the wonders of your Apelles,[1] were charming enough to contemplate, but how could one help grieving at being shut out from them? The truth is, ev'ry body that comes hither from[b] You seems to be in a conspiracy against me, & to carry on the Design of your Letter.

Mr. Thurlbourn[2] comes with a solemn, book-selling Face, & protests he did not think Norton had been so sweet a place as he found it. The Gardens were as large again as his Expectation, & then they were so snug & pleasant – But this is a trifle. Mr. Du Quesne[3] sets himself up in an Elbow-Chair, & harangues me by the half-hour together. – 'Tis really a sweet place, begins he – that Norton! The new Rooms are so beautifully fitting up, – the carving is so pretty & then the Stucco[c] looks so well, that I was quite delighted.[4] What a lovely place is the little Closet to the Best-Bedchamber! – And then he runs over ev'ry minuter Ornament in it. – Well – & proceeds He, you can't imagine how merry we were, – we did so laugh, & chat, & dance – & then the Gentlemen are so good, & the Ladies so agreable! – Here indeed I could hold out no longer. The other part I bore pretty well, but when he came to insult me with the last particular, I was quite outrageous, & could almost have found in my

keeping: the former being the chief support of solitude, & the latter of society". (Thomas Balguy to Samuel? Hill, 26 March 1749, MS BL Add. 35590, ff. 269–70.)

1 Apelles, the Greek painter of the fourth century B.C. RH's allusion is to Francis Hayman who was painting the dome over the staircase at Little Haugh Hall. A reference in the *Macro Letter-book* makes it clear that he was still working on the dome well into September.

2 William Thurlbourn, the Cambridge bookseller and publisher. See *ante* To Devey, 28 March 1743, n. 2.

3 Thomas Duquesne, a Fellow of King's since 1741. (*Alum. Cantab.*).

4 The stucco work and wood-carving had been going forward for many months. (*Macro Letter-book.*) It is thought that Thomas Ross "sculptor" was responsible for the latter; but it has not been established who undertook the plaster moulding. (Norman Scarfe, 'Little Haugh Hall, Suffolk', *Country Life*, 5 June 1958.)

a MS: "Estate" written over "Estates".

b MS: "from" written over "to".

c MS: "Stuco".

heart to have broke his pipe for him. – But just so Mr. Hubbard[5] also serves me; so that amongst 'em all I have a sad Life, & am ev'ry day put in mind how much happier I should be, than I am, if I was where, I must not be. The only thing[d] I have for it is to get out of the hearing; which I intend to do some time next week, that being the time fix'd upon for our Staffordshire Journey.[6] The first & second week are to be spent amongst forms, & Ceremonials; the <second> third & fourth amongst friends & my good old Parents. I must own I have a pleasure of no small size to come here; & unwilling as I am & backward to move from hence, I never think on this[e] last part of my Design, but methinks I feel a filial fondness push me on strangely. When I turn my Horse from thence, my direct course is back again to Cambridge; from thence to Norton, & from thence to Reymerston.[7] See but what a Scheme I have plann'd for myself: if this does not drive thee, Jaundice, all is lost <with me,>, & thou art triumphant. At present I am much in the State, as when I troubl'd you with an Account of myself last. Not out of order enough to be ill, nor well enough to be in health; not dispirited enough to be hypp'd, nor alert enough to be in Spirits. My Horse trots me into a Complexion by that time I return from the Hills, & I lose it again by the next morning. O! how uncertain were a Lady's conquests, if her bloom & the lustre of her Eye were as changing as mine! – if the delicate Mixture of the white & red in a Lady's cheek <came> was to come & go, like my Yellow! But Venus, & all the Graces forbid it! – Rather wither all the Roses in June! & perish a whole Spring of flowers! – The Ardor of this prayer, & the Subject of it should methinks be some proof of my returning Spirits. And I know not how it is, but I feel a great[er] Alacrity of heart at this instant than I have experien[c'd] for some time. If I were call'd upon for a reason of this change, I should certainly say, it was the Expectation, I please[f] myself with, of an answer to this Scroll, that enlivens my Spirits. After the fatigue of a long Journey, & the formality of I know not how many visits, what a refreshment, think I, would it be to regale on an agreable Packet, prepar'd by Mrs. Macro's hand, & directed to Hatton-Grange-Salop![8] The Thought[g] of this is so flattering, that I must take it along with me; & therefore committing myself to Your Goodness I am, Madam, your most Obedient & most Oblig'd Hble Servt.

R. Hurd.

P.S.

You'll please to present my Hble Service to Miss Macro.

5 Henry Hubbard (1708–78), Fellow and Librarian of Emmanuel.

6 RH left college on 3 September. He was usually accompanied on his summer visits to Staffordshire by Edward Macro.

7 RH returned to Cambridge for a few days in October. He then visited the Macros, and Robert Potter at Reymerston, and was back in college about 9 November. (*Commons Accounts Book*, STE. 15. 9.)

8 The hamlet where John Hurd, RH's eldest brother, lived.

d MS: "think" changed to "thing".

e MS: "the" changed to "this".

f MS: "pleas'd" changed to "please".

g MS: "thought" changed to "Thought".

67 To Sir EDWARD LITTLETON 24 NOVEMBER 1745

Text: MS STAFFS RO D1413/1; unpublished.
Addressed: [To/S]r. Edward Littleton Bart.

[Dea]r Sr. Edward,[1]

The Account you gave me of your Regiment & it's Motions was very obliging, & I will beg the favor of you to complete it by sending a List of your Officers Names in your next.[2] Whoever they are, I perceive, they are not much to your Taste; but it happens luckily, that your Lieu-tenant[3] is so sensible & worthy a Man.

You did certainly right, in not using the Liberty Your Colonel gave You of returning to College.[4] Your Honor, as you justly express it, was too much concern'd, & it was the greatest Satisfaction to me to find, You had so lively a Sense of it. At this important time, when ev'ry thing valuable is at S[t]ake, it is greatly becoming your Rank & Fortune to be employ'd, as You now are; in bearing a part in the defence of the best of Governments, & in contributing all You can to the Service of your King. It shews a fine Spirit, glorious in a young Gentleman, to sacrifice, not your Ease & Diversion, [o]nly, but your Studies to so good a cause, & to hazard ev'n your Person, should there be occasion for it, rather than desert it. To inspire such Sentiments of Honor & Virtue into young Minds is one of the chiefest Ends of those Studies, you are now awhile to neglect;[5] & your conduct on this occasion convinces me of their having already, in concurrence with a good natural Disposition, produc'd this Effect. I remember, in our reading together the Account of Cataline's Conspiracy,[6] the Abhorrence You express'd of that Rebel's Enterprize, & the just Admiration You conceiv'd of the

1 During Sir Edward Littleton's stay in Staffordshire in the long vacation, the "Forty-five" rebellion had broken out. On 23 July Charles Edward, the Young Pretender, had landed in the Hebrides. By September he had mustered enough support to defeat the English army under General Cope at Prestonpans, and on 14 November the Jacobites seized Carlisle. English troops had been recalled from the Netherlands in July, but such was the anxiety aroused by the invasion that fifteen extra regiments and twenty independent companies were raised for the service of the King. The raising of a regiment of Staffordshire men was undertaken by Lord Gower, Lord-Lieutenant of the county. According to a letter of 13 October 1745, he had proposed the levying of troops at the Quarter Sessions held on 9 October. The proposal had been agreed to and Sir Edward Littleton, among others, had volunteered to raise his own company. The regiment was quickly assembled and Gower received orders to send the men to Chester about 13 November. By 19 November they had arrived and been joined by part of another, established regiment (Bligh's), sent to assist with the training of the new troops. (Gower Correspondence, William Salt Library, S.M.S. 520, 521, 522; see also, Katherine Tomasson and Francis Buist, *Battles of the '45*, 1962, passim.)

2 Few papers concerning Lord Gower's regiment have survived and there is no list of officers amongst them. Most of the information about the regiment must now be gleaned from surviving correspondence. Gower's letters give the name of his Lieutenant as Congreve and mention Captains Crewe and Littleton. He notes that all the Captain's commissions were taken by "Gentlemen of Family & fortune in the County". (Gower Correspondence, William Salt Library, S.M.S. 520, 521, 523.) There are other letters addressed to a Captain Eld from his brother, in the Staffordshire Record Office (D798/3/1/1), and some papers relating to a company led by Captain Robins, again in the William Salt Library (H.M. 296/40).

3 Unidentified.

4 Littleton had been away from college since 7 September. The term had begun on 10 October.

5 RH restated this opinion of the ends of education in *Dialogues on the Uses of Foreign Travel*, published in 1764. See, for example, p. 77.

6 RH had probably read Sallust's *Bellum Catilinae* with Sir Edward. It was a text commonly set for the first or second year at Cambridge. (Wordsworth, *Scholae Academicae*, pp. 331, 339.)

Character of the good Consul.[7] You are now copying, as far as your different Sphere & Office will permit, his Conduct & Virtues. Nor think me extravagant in quoting this Instance: the cause you are engag'd in is very like his. 'Tis the cause of all the Good against all the Bad; & the strong Opposition wch. Tully makes betwixt the Adherents & Interests of Rome & Cataline is full as applicable to the present case of England & her Pretender. God grant it may end as happily as that did! I trust, it will thro' the Divine Assistance, & then tho' the Government will lay claim to the Honors of Cicero, & Mr. Wade[8] to those of Petreius[9] (whose character, you know, is not unlike Mr. Wade's, *Homo militaris, quôd amplius annos triginta tribunus, aut praefectus, aut legatus, aut Praetor cum magnâ Gloriâ in Exercitu fuerat*)[10] yet will no small degree of Honor devol[ve] to You, & to ev'ry Gentleman, who, like You, has done his best in procuring so great a Good for us.

The Subject, I find, has betray'd me into a greater Seriousness, than is very common in a Letter; & upon looking back I perceive myself to have been preaching, rather than writing an Answer to your's.[a] This might want an Apology to some: but I am satisfy'd You will not think so. However the rest shall be of a lighter kind, & I will endeavour to recollect all the news we have got here to make up my Paper.

Soon after my return to College Mr. Lyne dy'd of a fever,[11] & since that Mr. Took has left us, a good Estate coming to him by the Death of his Father;[12] So that possibly we may have two new fellows, before you see us.[13] By this means I am to remove soon into the new-Building. It had been lucky, could it have been in your Stair-case.[14]

7 An allusion to Cicero.

8 George Wade (1673–1748) was in command of the troops in the north of England. In early November he had made an attempt to halt the advance of the rebel army but had been unsuccessful. He was now stationed at Newcastle awaiting further developments. (Sir Bruce Seton, 'The Orderly Book of Lord Ogilvy's Regiment', *Journal of the Society of Army Historical Research*, 1923, ii. (Special Number) 12. n. 2; 17. n. 2.)

9 It was Cicero's effective spy system that provided evidence of Catiline's conspiracy; Marcus Petreius led the troops who opposed and broke the rebel army, killing Catiline and many of his men. Such success eluded General Wade whose part in quelling the rebellion remained a minor one. The most successful military commander proved instead to be the Duke of Cumberland.

10 Sallust, *Bellum Catilinae*, lix. 6.

11 Matthew Lyne, a Fellow of Emmanuel from 1729, had died in college on 2 November.

12 John Tooke vacated his Fellowship on 22 November.

13 Only one Fellow was elected before Littleton's return to Emmanuel in April 1746. This was John Gamage: he was made a Fellow on 21 March 1746. Another election took place in July. (*Order Book*, COL. 14. 2.)

14 No record can be found of Sir Edward's accommodation. RH followed Tooke as occupant of rooms on the left-hand side of the Founder's Staircase, second storey. He remained in them until he left Emmanuel in 1757. (*Chamber Rent Books*, STE. 24. 1; STE. 24. 3.)

a MS: "your Letter" changed to "your's".

Mr. Powell's Lectures,[15] as I told you, began on the 12th. Instant, &, as I had then Expectations of seeing you ev'ry day, your Name & mine are amongst the Subscribers. Some Senior Tutors in ys. place, as you know, were not favorable to Mr. Powell's Design, & indeed were rather willing, by insinuations & otherwise, to obstruct & discourage it. But I have the pleasure to tell You, yt. their Malice has had but little Effect, for, instead of twenty or thirty wch. was the largest Number Mr. Powell durs't flatter himself wth. the hopes of raising at the first, there are near eighty Subsc[rib]ers. I know you'll rejoyce with me on a worthy man's findin[g] such uncommon Success.

A few days ago Mr. Thurlbourn sent me for you the long expec[ted] Set of Crevier's Livy.[16] He recd. but three Sets from Holland [. . .] thought, in a short time they'll be invaluable.

This, I th[ink, is] all the news I can recollect worth mentioning. I must add a [. . .] that you'll do me the favor to write immediatly; if you have leisu[re to] do it, & especially if there be any news, I could wish to recei[ve a] Letter from You ev'ry Post,[17] so long as you stay at Chester. [If] this be unreasonable, let me at least hear from you, as often [as] is convenient. Only observe, the oft'ner that is, the more agreable will [it be] to Him, who, with his Prayers & best wishes for your Success & Saf[ety, . . .] with an entire Respect, is always, Dear Sr. Edwd., Your most Faithfull, Humble Servt.

R. Hurd.

Camb. 24. Nov. 1745.

P.S.

Your friend Mr. Manwaring is well:[18]
He, with all here, are at your Service.

[15] Most lectures given in Cambridge in the mid-eighteenth century were intended only for the undergraduates of the college to which the lecturer was attached. But there were also some inter-collegiate lectures given by the University professors and a few courses of lectures run by individual Fellows: Powell was giving one of these. Usually, it seems that the lecturer published a proposal in the form of a programme of the suggested course, with information on the time and place at which the lectures were to be held, and details of cost. All those who wished to attend were to send in their names. Four such proposals, published between 1743 and 1753, may be found in Cambridge University Library. (CUL, UA/UP/1.) These indicate that the usual price for a first course of lectures was two guineas, and for a second, one guinea. At least some of the courses involved attendance every day and they seem to have lasted for five or six weeks. For William Powell's lectures, see also *post* To Littleton, 14 March 1746, n. 2.

[16] Jean Baptiste Louis Crévier's edition of Livy, *Historiarum ab urbe condita libri qui supersunt xxxv*, had been published in six volumes, quarto, in Paris between 1735 and 1742.

[17] Post between Cambridge and Chester had to go by London. There were probably two or three posts a week (see P. Broster, *The Chester Guide*, Chester, 2nd edn, 1782, pp. 60–1, where three posts between London and Chester are listed).

[18] John Mainwaring (1724–1807) came of a Staffordshire family living not far from Pipe-Ridware, and had been admitted at St John's in 1742. He was subject to attacks of asthma throughout his life and his health was a perpetual cause of concern to his friends. (Joseph Cradock, *Literary and Miscellaneous Memoirs*, 1828, i. 189–90; iv. 228–34.)

68 To Sir EDWARD LITTLETON 29 NOVEMBER 1745

Text: MS STAFFS RO D1413/1; unpublished.
Addressed: To/Sr. Edwd. Littleton Bart. Captain in/Ld. Gower's Regiment at the/Assembly-House in/Chester/ By London
Postmarked: cover missing.

Camb. 29. Nov. 1745.

Dear Sir Edward!

In answer to your's of the 16th. Inst. I wrote a great deal of grave Stuff, such as occurr'd to me in the Humour I was then in, & sent it inclos'd in a Letter to Mrs. Littleton.[1] Whether You will receive it by the time this comes to hand I know not, but am willing to take the first Post to answer your last favor, which comes from Chester.[2] I [am] glad to hear You are so strong in yt. City, & that You [are] preparing to make a good resistance to the Rebels, if they think proper to shape their course that way; tho' we incline to think, as You do, that it is not for their Interest to come against You. By an Account wch. came with the same Post, as Your's, from Jack Roper,[3] who writes from Lichfield, & is Major-Brigade under Ligonier,[4] we are in great Expectation of the whole Affair's being over in a little time.[5] If so, we shall have the pleasure to see you <in a short time.> soon. But if anything falls out to protract this Business, & You are detain'd upon Duty from us longer than we imagine, I shall take it as a favor, as I hinted in my last, if you'll oblige me with a Letter ev'ry Post. You are now in the Center of news, & at a Season like this You'll allow us to be very inquisitive after it. For this reason, as also because it inform'd me of your Health & good Spirits I was much oblig'd, & entertain'd by your last; & you must not refuse me the continuance of such favors.

I cannot wonder to hear You have no time for Books. Mars has no fellowship with the Muses; nor I find with Venus according to the Account you give me, for the

1 See preceding letter. Mrs Littleton was Sir Edward's mother, Frances.

2 Lord Gower's regiment had arrived in Chester on 19 November and had since been joined by further troops (see preceding letter, n. 1). The city itself was put in a state of defence and by the end of the month the citizens were "no longer in any Pain about the Rebels". ('Extract of a private Letter from Chester, Nov. 30.', *Cambridge Journal*, 7 December 1745.) Meanwhile the rebel army was marching south and on 29 November passed Preston in their way towards Macclesfield, which they reached on 1 December. Their ultimate goal is uncertain and may well have been Wales rather than the capital, since a promise of support had already come from there. In this case, Chester would certainly have been threatened; but in the event, the army continued south and east to arrive at Derby and advanced no further. (S.A.H. Burne, 'The Staffordshire Campaign of 1745', *Transactions of the North Staffordshire Field Club*, lx. 50–76.)

3 Probably John Rooper of Peterhouse. RH could have met him through Richard Jenoure, an early acquaintance, who had been to the same school (Felsted) and had come up to Peterhouse in the same year (1735). (*Alum. Cantab.*)

4 Sir John Ligonier (1680–1770) had been in command of the British troops withdrawn from the Netherlands at the invasion of England. On his reaching London the Government had dispatched him to form an army of 10,000 men in Staffordshire. They had been assembled by 1 December and were now under the command of the Duke of Cumberland. Ligonier was also stationed in Staffordshire with his regiment. (Seton, 'The Orderly Book of Lord Ogilvy's Regiment', p. 17, n. 1.)

5 The rebels began their retreat on 6 December, but the British army failed to intercept them, and it was not until 16 April 1746 that the Pretender was finally defeated at the Battle of Culloden.

Ladies as well as Learning are fled from Chester. The last indeed is <. . .> a stale, Antiquated Jade, but old D.[6] (as You call him) must surely lament the loss of the former.

I accept your Colonel's *twofold* Reason for Absence, tho' a third perhaps is not very difficult to guess at.[7]

Here is no news to send You, & therefore, without further Impertinence, I am always, Dear Sr. Edward, Your most Faithfull [. . .]

R. Hurd.

P.S.

Mr. Nevile, Manwaring, & Bridgman[8] of Queens [. . .] in desiring Services.

69 To COX MACRO 4 DECEMBER 1745

Text: MS BL Add. 32557, ff. 109–10; unpublished.
Addressed: To/the Revd. Dr. Macro at Norton/to be left at Mr. Hayward's/in the Cook-Row/Bury St. Edmunds./ Suffolk.
Postmarked: CAMBRIDGE

Camb. 4. Dec. 1745.

Reverend Sir,

That I may avoid being tedious at least upon a Subject, about wch. it is not likely I should talk much to the purpose, my Design is to reduce what I have to say on the *Origin of Sacrifices* into as narrow a Compass as possible.[1] The whole Enquiry, I think, is 1. Whether the Scriptures declare 'em to be of Divine Original. 2. Whether, if it be not expressly declar'd, it may not be concluded by fair Inference & Deduction from them; Or, 3. supposing neither to be the case, whether the nature of the thing does not plainly shew it. This, I say, takes in the whole Dispute about the *Divine Original of Sacrifices*. And here

1. As to the first Enquiry, that will receive a very easy Answer, it being evident & agreed on all hands, that the Scriptures no where *in express* words assert the custom of Sacrifices to have been of Divine Institution. How far this Silence & Omission in the sacred History may be constru'd as an Argument in proof of the contrary Opinion is a Question not proper to be debated at present. Especially, since 'tis pretended, that tho'

6 Unidentified.

7 Gower had been obliged to remain in London for some time with important business to transact and an attack of the gout. (Gower Correspondence, William Salt Library, S.M.S. 520, 521, 522.) No further reasons for his absence have been discovered.

8 Henry Bridgeman (1725–1800) of Blodwell, Shropshire. He had matriculated at Queens' in 1744. (*Alum. Cantab.*)

1 The origin of sacrifice had been much debated in previous centuries. In this letter RH gives and refutes the arguments used to prove the "Divine Institution" of sacrifice and asserts that it owes its origin to primitive human reasoning. Various distinguished theological writers had reached a similar conclusion (amongst them Chrysostom, Justin Martyr, Tertullian, Theodoret, Maimonides and Grotius). More recently, William Outram had reviewed and summarised the arguments put forward on both sides, in a Latin work, *De Sacrificiis libri duo*, 1677. In the following letter to Macro (To Macro, 1 January 1746) RH develops his theory on sacrifice and from this point breaks new ground in the discussion.

the Scriptures do not in express words, yet that in effect & by fair deduction they do, affirm it.

2. Now the passages, from whence this is pretended to be infer<r>'d, are, 1, *the short History of the first Sacrifice in Gen. IV.*[2] & 2. *St. Paul's Comment upon it Ep. Heb. XI.*[3] I will examine the Reasonings drawn from each of them. 1st. then it is said in the History of Abel's Sacrifice, *that the Lord had respect unto it,*[4] in the words of the Apostle, *that it was acceptable to the Lo[rd,*[5] from whence] it is concluded, & Mr. Pierce is very sure,[A] that the Original of Sacrifices must have been owing to the Divine Appointment.[6] *Otherwise, says He, it could not have been acceptable at all, according to that plain, obvious, & eternal maxim of all true Religion, "In vain do they worship God, teaching for Doctrines the Commandments of men."* Mark. VII. 7. To wch. I answer, that to suppose no Act of Religion, tho' done with the best & most upright Intention, pleasing & acceptable to God, unless enjoyn'd first of all by his own express will & Authority, is to contradict the notions we have of the Divine Equity & Justice, wch. ever determines according to *what a man hath, & not what He hath not*, & is a remnant of that narrow-soul'd Divinity, wch. confines all favor & mercy to those within the Pale, in exclusion of all the world without. For my part I can never doubt, that, if Abel offer'd *a Sacrifice of thanksgiving* with a pious thought & intention of doing Honor to God & giving glory to his name, tho' the Act by which he did it was uncommanded, & ev'n not dictated by the injunctions of right Reason, yet that a good & mercifull & righteous God would accept it at his hands. Indeed where men will presumptuously lay aside all Attention to the *express will & commands of God*, & rather follow their own Imaginations, or (which is much the same thing), Traditions, than <obey> observe his *reveal'd Institutions*; or if they will presume to add to, or diminish from such express, reveal'd Institutions, from a fond Attachment to any Opinions, or Customs, wch. they have taken up from mere Human Authority, in such cases 'tis plain th[e] Services are no better than Acts of Impiety & Rebellion, & cannot be acceptable to Almighty God. Which shews the Impertinence to the matter in hand of that Text Mark. VII. 7. alledg'd by Mr. Pierce in proof of his Petition; for it plainly respects these later Services, whereby it is true that *men worship God in vain*; but by no means the former, wch. contradicting no reveal'd Laws, are not such *Commandments of Men*, as <the Apo> are there condemn'd, & rejected. But

A See his [note on that line.]

2 Genesis 4. 3–5.
3 Hebrews 11. 4.
4 Genesis 4. 4: "And the Lord had respect unto Abel and to his offering".
5 Paul does not use these words, but they are used in the commentary mentioned by RH in this context (see n. 6). The Apostle, it is stated, "expresly says, as *Moses* said before him, that *Abel's* sacrifice was *acceptable to* GOD".
6 RH refers to a work by James Peirce, *A Paraphrase and Notes on the Epistles of St. Paul*. The first edition, published in 1727, is incomplete. The next edition, published in 1733, had been completed by Joseph Hallett, who supplies the paraphrase and notes to the last three chapters of Hebrews. It is Hallett's notes that RH uses. In the note on Hebrews 11. 4. ('Supplement' p. 12) Hallett asserts that: "it is easy to be *demonstrated*, that sacrifices owed their original to the *will* and *appointment* of GOD. The apostle expresly says," he continues, "that *Abel's* sacrifice was *acceptable* to GOD. But it would not have been acceptable, if it had not been of *divine* institution, according to that plain, obvious, and eternal maxim of all *true* religion, Christian, *Mosaic*, and natural, *In vain do they worship* GOD, *teaching for doctrines the commandments of men*, Mark vii. 7."

Since men had no right to eat flesh before the flood, Abel could not (unless Sacrificing was a divine Rite) see the lawfullness of animal Sacrifices, & therefore wd. not practice it in the worship of God.

Ans. It is by no means clear that Abel's was an animal Sacrifice, some & those the best Interpreters[7] maintaining, that what we render the *firstlings of his flock* &c [is] more properly to be render'd the *Milk of his flock*; an Interpretation wch. might be defended by many Authorities,[a] & Considerations. St. Paul indeed calls it θυσία,[8] wch., 'tis said, necessarily implies an Animal Sacrifice. But that is an Argument of little weight, since, <supposing> allowing that to be the [. . .] sense of the word, St. Paul, whose business it was not here to distinguish betwixt the several kinds of Sacrifice, might very well be suppos'd to use it in a larger Sense, for Sacrifice in general. But ev'n if the Sacrifice was animal, I conceive Abel might lawfully offer up the flesh of a beast to God in Sacrifice (provided he had no Law to <contrad> forbid it, wch. in the present case is not pretended) since it is plain he might lawfully use the Skins of Beasts for clothing. Gen. 3. 21.[9] I know indeed it has been pretended from this very passage, that, because God clothed Adam & Eve wth. Skins, that therefore he had instituted Animal Sacrifices; but surely I have greater right to conclude, that men *might* offer up the flesh of a Beast witht. blame from an *express permission* to use their Skins, than another has to infer an express command to do so (of wch. there is not one word) from the same permission.

These, I think, are all the Argumts. of weight urg'd from the Account of Moses.

2. There is but one of any consequence (besides what has been taken notice of already) to be drawn from St. Paul. And this is taken from the word *Faith*: By *faith* Abel offer'd &c.[10] Where the word *faith*, it is said, in this & the other Instances giv'n in this chapter, always implies a Belief in, & Obedience to, [so]me reveal'd Command; & that therefore Abel's sacrificing *by Faith* implies his *sacrificing* in consequence of an express command to do so. This reasoning is very weak as appears by considering v. 3[11] where we are [said] *to understand that the worlds were created by* God *by Faith: & v.* 6.[12] *where* Enoch's *faith*, & universally that *faith*, wch. is requisite to please God, is made to be that whereby we believe that God *is* &c. In either case it necessarily implies no more than this viz: A *belief of the Existence of a Divine Power, who made the worlds, notwithstanding we have not sensible i.e. ocular proof of it.* And this agreably to the Definition of Faith's being *the Evidence of things not seen*. Exactly in this sense would I understand Abel's offering a Sacrifice *by Faith*; that, with full Assurance of the being & perfections of God, & in consequence of believing in Him as the best & greatest of Beings, he made this offering, as an Act of Gratitude for blessings receiv'd, & to the

7 Amongst them are Josephus and Grotius. The phrase occurs in Genesis 4. 4.

8 Hebrews 11. 4.

9 "Unto Adam also and to his wife did the LORD God make coats of skins, and clothed them."

10 Hebrews 11. 4: "By faith Abel offer'd unto GOD a more excellent sacrifice than Cain, by which he obtained witness that he was righteous, GOD testifying of his gifts".

11 "Through faith we understand, that the worlds were framed by the word of GOD, so that things, which are seen, were not made of things which do appear."

12 "But without faith it is impossible to please him: for he that cometh to GOD, must believe that he is, and that he is a rewarder of them that diligently seek him."

a MS: "Autorities".

honor & glory of his Name. His performing this Act wi[th] a deeper Sense of piety than Cain seems to have constituted the superior Excellence of his Offering.[13]

III. Lastly, as to the Nature of the thing, whence some Writers argue for the Divine Origin of Sacrifices, the plea from thence is very insufficient. For 'tis pretended that the conceit of sacrificing, if taken by itself, is so absurd & contradictory to the reason of mankind, that wtht. a Divine Injunction it cd. never have been practic'd, much less have spread over the whole world. But has no Opinion or custom, wch. cannot be reconcil'd to right reason, generally prevail'd? What think we of *mediatorial Worship* (to mention no other) wch. was universal, as Sacrifice, & yet cannot be shewn to be the result of any rational Enquiry? But this will be further consider'd in my next, in wch. (if You indulge me in this impertinence) it is propos'd to consider, from what Original Sacrifices *did* spring. Let me know, in the mean time, your objections to this part, & whether you think me right in not accounting for them from an Origin Divine.

I am always, Revd. Sr., your most Obedt. Hble Servt.

R.H.

70 To Sir EDWARD LITTLETON 18 DECEMBER 1745

Text: MS STAFFS RO D1413/1; unpublished.
Addressed: To/Sr. Edward Littleton Bart./Captain in Ld. Gower's Regiment/at the Assembly-House/Chester/ By London.
Postmarked: CAMBRIDGE 19

Dear Sr. Edward,

My Epistolary Preachment, I find, had the same fate, as our Pulpit ones generally have with You young Gentlemen, the fate of being laugh'd at. And therefore not to do a second Violence to your Muscles, I shall continue the Style & Manner of my last, in chatting with you on indifferent Occasions.

Your Situation at Chester seems now pretty safe.[1] For I am unwilling to think the Rebels will have it in their power to make good their word of returning to You with Recruits from Scotland: tho' whether they can be hinder'd getting back there seems very uncertain. What is manifest is, that our Young Hero does his utmost to prevent it.

The Scheme of furnishing the Army with Shoes, Stockings, & Waistcoats is excellently contriv'd, & the Soldiery in this cold Season of the Year must find the Advantage of it.[2] We are doing what we can in the University tow'rds forwarding the

13 RH again disagrees with Hallett here. The latter believed that: "*Abel's faith* is not to be look'd upon as an *ingredient* in, or a *part* of, his sacrifice, which render'd it more valuable *in itself* than the sacrifice of *Cain*. For *Abel's*" he says, "was *in itself* more excellent than *Cain's* (abstracting from the consideration of *Abel's* faith) because it was of the *best* and *fattest* of his flock". ('Supplement', p. 13.)

1 The rebel army had been retreating since 6 December. By 18 December it had been reported as marching north from Manchester. (*Cambridge Journal*, 14 December 1745, news from Lichfield, 11 December.) The attempts made to cut off the retreat were ineffectual and it was not until the rebels reached Penrith that they were faced with serious opposition.

2 Many associations were formed in October and November to give support to the King and

same or a like Design by a contribution which is now set on foot for that purpose.[3] And here I must not omit to tell you of a noble Act of our Chancellor,[4] who, being inform'd of the University's having subscrib'd four hundred pounds out of the Common Chest, sent his Agent to the V. Chancellor[5] with six hundred more, with orders for it to be joyn'd to the other four, & the whole to go under the name of the University-Subscription, as being a Sum, he said, more suitable to the Honor & Dignity of such a Body.[6] – You see a Grace in the manner of conducting this Affair very becoming the Blood of the Seymour Family –

All the talk in this part of the world is of an Invasion,[7] which has greatly alarm'd the Government, & indeed makes us less attentive to matters in the North. But a few days I hope will free us from these Apprehensions. In the mean time let me have the satisfaction of knowing what is going forward with You; & should ev'n nothing of any consequence occur, let that be no Excuse for your not writing.

Your Bill for the last Quarter will be made up in a few Days;[8] which I shall send to Mrs. Littleton, unless You give me contrary Orders.

P[oor] Mr. Manwaring is not well; but agrees with me [. . .] Dear Sir, Your most Faithfull, Hble Servt.

Camb. 18. Dec. 1745.

army. (See W.A. Speck, *The Butcher. The Duke of Cumberland and the Suppression of the 45*, Oxford, 1981, pp. 55–8.) Several of these devoted themselves to raising subscriptions to buy necessaries for the army, such as breeches and shirts, woollen caps, stockings, gloves and "spatterdashes", and blankets. In the *Cambridge Journal* of Saturday 14 December, it had been reported that General Wade's men at Wetherby had been issued with "Shoes, Stockings and Flannel Waistcoats" which had been sent up from London.

3 According to a letter of 26 November from Thomas Duquesne to Edward Macro, the university intended to raise £4,000 for the service of the King. "If there shd. be occasion for it", Duquesne wrote, "poor as we are we shall chearfully pay it". (MS BL, Add. 32557, ff. 107–8; Cooper, *Annals*, iv. 252–5.)

4 Charles Seymour (1662–1748), sixth Duke of Somerset. He had been elected Chancellor in 1689.

5 George Henry Rooke (1702–54), Master of Christ's. He had been elected Vice-Chancellor on 9 November.

6 The rest of the £4,000 was to be raised by individual colleges.

7 From the beginning of December there had been reports of the preparations being made by the French for an invasion of the south of England. Anxiety reached a peak on 14 December when the King was reported to have issued a Royal Proclamation "to signify the Danger this Nation is under from the intended Invasion from France". (*Cambridge Journal*, 21 December 1745.) Orders were given for precautionary measures to be taken and the Duke of Cumberland was recalled from his pursuit of the rebels in the north, to organise the troops in the south. He set out on 2 January, but soon after his arrival in London it became evident that the French had lost the initiative and were now unlikely to invade. When Parliament met on 14 January, the King was able to report favourably on the effects of the "seasonable Preparations made for our Defence", and Cumberland returned to the north. (John Marchant, *The History of the Present Rebellion*, 1746, pp. 232–6, 257, 287–302; James Ray, *A Compleat History of the Rebellion*, 1749, pp. 247–8.)

8 Undergraduates' college bills were always sent through their tutors. (D.A. Winstanley, *Unreformed Cambridge*, Cambridge, 1935, p. 271.) See *post* To Littleton, 14 March 1746, for an example of Sir Edward's quarterly payments.

71 To JAMES DEVEY [DECEMBER 1745/JANUARY 1746][1]

Text: *Memoirs*, 24.

Rev. Sir,

I am much obliged to you for Dr. Middleton's Letter, &c.[2] I have read the additions over with much pleasure, and think he has defended his argument, not only against the author of the Catholic Christian, but Warburton himself. Though, if there be any flaw in what regards this last, I doubt not but he'll soon hear of it.

If you have got Veneer upon the Articles[3] I would beg, the favour of you to send it to me. Pray let me know how your son does, and what news, if he sends any, is stirring in Cambridge.

I am, Sir, with service to Mrs. Devey and your son when you write, your obliged humble servant,

R. Hurd.

P.S.

A happy new year to you. Mr. Budworth sends services, and honest Roger twists in a compliment.[4]

72 To COX MACRO 1 JANUARY 1746

Text: MS BL Add. 32557, ff. 111–12; unpublished.
Addressed: To/the Reverend Dr. Macro/at/Norton.

1. Jan. 1745–6. Camb.

Reverend Sir,

As it is generally much easier to object to a receiv'd Hypothesis, than to substitute & support a better in it's Stead, so I shall not be at all surpriz'd, if what I am going to offer upon the *true Original of Sacrifices* be less satisfactory to You, than You have been

1 Kilvert prints this letter without a date although its position in the *Memoirs* suggests that it was written at the end of 1745 or the beginning of 1746.

2 Conyers Middleton's *A Letter from Rome, Shewing an Exact Conformity between Popery and Paganism* had originally been published in 1729. It was his first theological work. The main argument is that Catholic ceremonies are strikingly similar to the forms of paganism, and that the spirit of idolatry pervades both. Middleton also takes the opportunity in the *Letter* to attack "Popish" miracles, a line of argument which he pursued on a larger scale in the 1740s (see *post* To Mason, 7 May 1747). The *Letter* proved popular, a second edition appearing in the same year and a third "with Additions" in 1733. RH refers to the fourth, which was published in 1741. This edition had been more than doubled in length by the addition of a 'Prefatory Discourse' and a 'Post-script'. The former was directed against the anonymous author of *The Catholick Christian instructed in the Sacraments, Sacrifice, Ceremonies, and Observances of the Church*, 1737, who had "thought fit, in a preface to that work, to attempt a confutation" of Middleton's *Letter*. ('Prefatory Discourse', p. i.) The author was Richard Challoner. The postscript was written in answer to a section of the *Divine Legation* in which Warburton had expressed the opinion that Christian Rome had *not* borrowed its superstitions and ceremonials from the pagan city. Warburton did not reply to Middleton's criticism till 1744, and then it was with the respect he felt he owed to their friendship. But Middleton was offended and the friendship cooled. (Leslie Stephen, *History of English Thought in the Eighteenth Century*, 1876, Third Edition, 2 vols, 1902, i. 255–7; Warburton, *Remarks on Several Occasional Reflections*, 1744, pp. 5–12; Evans, *Warburton and the Warburtonians*, pp. 108–10; see also *post* To Warburton, 22 January 1757, n. 20.)

3 [John Veneer], *An Exposition on the Thirty nine Articles*, 1725.

4 *I.e.* your servant. (*O.E.D.*)

pleas'd to say, my Objections were, to the *false*. This however is clear, that in a matter, wherein the Scriptures are wholly silent, Conjectures can do no harm; & I know your Candour will excuse the freest thoughts I may be led into by them.[1]

1. then I observe, that the rite of *sacrificing* in general was of the earliest & most remote Antiquity; certainly, from the Scripture-History, in practice with the first Generation; & probably practis'd by the very first man.

2. It is true, that rude & untutor'd minds in the simplicity of that *infant* State would unavoidably form their Conceptions of the *Divine Nature* from what was felt & observ'd in the *Human*. In other words, men would of course estimate the Divine Dispositions from their own; & ascribe to God the same Attributes & Properties, which they experienc'd in themselves. This is so natural a prejudice, that it subsists to this Day; ignorant, untutor'd minds (after all the improvements of Reason, & the Light of Revelation itself, which cannot but impart some Rays of Instruction to the lowest & least improv'd Capacities), thinking & conceiving of the Deity by the very same rule & in the same manner now. And I fear upon strict Enquiry something of this Infirmity would be found to stick to us all. At least I could point to many able Divines (that would take it very ill to be thought defective in Intellectual Improvements) who yet seem to have measur'd (if one may judge from some celebrated Systems) the divine goodness & mercy from the Defect & Narrowness of their own.

3. The *Human Nature* necessarily appearing to the *persons*, & in the *times*, suppos'd, a mere Compound of *Sense* & *Passion* (their reasoning faculties not being exercis'd enough as yet, nor enabling them to see at all further into it) the *Divine Nature*, or Deity, would (by G. 2.)[2] certainly appear to them in the same light. Hence they would judge of his Inclinations by their own Appetites, & suppose those Sensations most gratefull to him, that were most so to themselves. Now from these Observations put together I ask

4. Why might not *Sacrificing*, (which certainly had it's rise in the earliest Antiquity, when mankind was unpractis'd in reasoning, was wholly conversant about sensible Ideas, & had therefore made but slender progress in the Study & knowledge of God) be the result of Ignorance & Infirmity – be (in softer terms) the genuin Effect of *simple unimprov'd Nature*? In a word, I ask, why *Sacrifices* may not be look'd upon in their original Design & Institution as *Presents*; offerr'd from the same *Motives*, & to the same *Ends*? To make out this point the more clearly (besides the principles already laid down, which make it highly probable *a priori*) let us consider the correspondencies betwixt them. For if these are *striking*, & remarkeable, it will give a strong presumption of their being owing to *one common Cause*.

[1] During the eighteenth century several writers evolved the theory that the origin of sacrifice lay in primitive man's anthropomorphitical notions of God, and hence that sacrifices were originally intended as presents offered to God. The offering of such gifts was interpreted as an imitation of patterns of social behaviour. RH appears to be among the first to explain their origin in these terms. Another early work with a similar approach, worked out in more detail, is Arthur A. Sykes', *An Essay on the Nature, Design, and Origin, of Sacrifices*. This was published a few years later in 1748. By 1774 the anthropological explanation for the origin of sacrifice had gained widespread acceptance (see Joseph Priestley, *Institutes of Natural and Revealed Religion*, 1774, iii. 139–45). RH's analysis is less sophisticated and more literalistic than those that followed. For instance, Sykes and Priestley account for the use of fire in sacrifice by suggesting that it had a symbolic significance for the sacrificers; RH sees it only as a means of cooking the offering and thus making it more pleasing to God. His analysis is also characterised by a reliance on imaginative intuition rather than on historical or theological learning.

[2] Genesis 2.

1. then the *Intention* of *Gifts, or Presents* (in use unquestionably from the very beginning of the world) was:[a] 1. to express a thankfullness for favours receiv'd – whereunto we are prompted by natural Gratitude. Or:[b] 2. to *propitiate*, or *reconcile* the Affections of one, we have offended – whereunto we are prompted by *natural Fear.* Or:[b] 3. lastly to testify an Honor for another; or in order to obtain a kindness, or benefit to ourselves – & to this we are prompted by *natural Reverence,* & *Self-Love.* This Division, I think, takes in all the Ends of *presents*, corresponding to as many natural *Passions*. But in exact Conformity to this is the Division of Sacrifices themselves. When offerr'd to the Deity with the first Intention they are call'd *Eucharistic*: when with the second *Expiatory*:[c] & when with the third *Honorary* & *Precatory*. In this way You perceive I make it a matter of no greater Difficulty to account for the rise of *Expiatory Sacrifices*, than others: And indeed I cannot see that it is. For if men naturally presume, they may attone for faults, which they commit against each other, by the intervention of presents, I see no reason why they might not, & would not (in the circumstances suppos'd) presume the same of faults, committed against God.

2. Agreably to this Theory men would naturally be led to sacrifice to the Gods of such things, as they fed upon themselves. And this perfectly agrees with the *History of Sacrifices*, from whence we learn, that such *Edibles*, as were in chief value & Use amongst men, were also offer'd to the Gods. Accordingly when Vegetables &c. made the *principal* part of Human food (for I do not think it clear, that they were ever the *Sole food*) these chiefly were offer'd in *Sacrifice*; & when afterwards *Animal food* was in frequent Use, *Animal Sacrifices* were more frequent also. Again: if *Sacrifices* were intended as *Presents* it is reasonable to expect (in pursuance of the same Analogy) that of *Vegetables, or Animals themselves* those only should be offer'd to their Gods, which were most agreable to their own palates, & were esteem'd of most exquisite relish amongst themselves. And this we know to have been the case: *Wine, fruits,* & *Milk*, of the *unbloody* kind, & *Sheep, Goats,* & *Oxen* of the *bloody*, were the most usual & noted Sacrifices to the Gods, as they made the most delicious, & exquisite Entertainments of Men. – For the same reason, it should seem, the very best of each *Species* were usually offer'd, & of those *best* only the very nicest & most admir'd *Parts*.

From these corresponding likenesses betwixt *Sacrifices* & *Presents* it seems evident to me, that they had both one common Original; equally springing out of the Simplicity, & natural, Instinctive passions of mankind. And to this I can at present think of but *one* Objection that can with any degree of plausibility be now made. For it will probably after all be said, that however naturally rude & ignorant minds would conceive of the Gods *by* themselves, & therefore however accountable it may be, that they should believe the same Sensations gratefull to them, as to themselves, yet how should they ever think of offering *meats & drinks*, when the Gods were not the Objects of Sight, & Sense, & when they had no way of conveying such presents to them?

I reply in asking, How should they ever think of offering *Praises & Thanksgivings*, when the <Objects> Gods were not the Objects of Sight & Sense & when, as appear'd to them, they had no way of conveying such *Praises & Thanksgivings*? The instance is exactly parallel; & shews us, that when they had once conceiv'd so grossly of the Deity, as to give him Senses, & passions, the other would be no Difficulty with

[a] MS: "was.".
[b] MS: "Or.".
[c] MS: "*Expiatory*.".

them, however important it may seem to us. When they offerr'd *Praises* to their Gods, there is no doubt of their believing them to have the Organs of hearing, & that the Sounds, they utter'd, would (tho' they saw them not) be convey'd to 'em. Just in the same manner they conceiv'd the Gods to have the Organs of *tasting & smelling*, & had no doubt but the *Odors* of *fruits*, *Wines*, or *Herbs*, or the *Steams & fumes* of burning Animals would be convey'd to, & highly gratify (tho' they could not see) them. Their Conceptions in this matter would be facilitated from hence. – Several concurring prejudices leading them to think the Air, or Heavens the seat of Residence of their Gods, & they easily observing that their words mix'd with the Air, & that *Odors*, or *Steams* went up thither, the rest was easy, that such *words*, or such *Odors* ascended to their Gods. So that there is nothing so incredible in this belief, as the Objection supposes. And that this was in *fact* believ'd is plain, since men *did* for many Ages conceive thus of their Gods, & ev'n suppos'd a main part of their happiness to consist in *sensible Regalements*. Moses himself doubtless spoke in agreement to *antient* at least, if not to the *then*, Belief, when speaking of Noah's Sacrifice he says (Gen. 8. 21.) *the Lord smelled a sweet Savour*.

Thus, Sir, I think I have tir'd you sufficiently for the present. There are a few other Reflexions, <which> that may serve to complete & illustrate this Account, wch. I will trouble you with in my next. Your freest Animadversions in the mean time on this part would extremely oblige, Revd. Sir, Your most Obedt. Humble Servt.

R. Hurd

73 To EDWARD MACRO 2 JANUARY 1746

Text: MS BL Add. 32557, ff. 113–14; unpublished.
Addressed: cover missing.

Camb. 2. Jan. 1745–6.

Dear Sir,

The pathetic Account, you give of the ravages of the Rebel Army,[1] & the Disturbance & Tumult they create in private families, is very touching, & I assure you, was felt by me very sensibly. But you are unquestionably right in giving no Encouragement to any gloomy Reflexions of your own, & composing yourself as much as possible amidst the Alarms of others. Rebellions & Invasions are doubtless horrid Sounds, but I trust in God our Ears will not be stunn'd with them much longer.[2] But this being the Subject of hourly talk, & having just now prated a whole Sheet-full on it to Mrs. Macro, I trouble you no farther.[3]

I have Commotions of another kind to write of. The University proceedings in regard of a Subscription &c. have made a good deal of noise; & by some means or other, I perceive, have reach'd Norton; & that in no very advantagious Light, for Mrs.

1 The newspapers had printed many reports in December describing the plundering of the rebels as they retreated northwards. The *Cambridge Journal* in its issue of 14 December, for instance, carried several such accounts and recorded that although the invading army had "behaved tolerably well" in its march southward, the rebels on their return through England had subjected the towns they came to, to "Plunder, Rapine and Robbery".

2 The rebel army was finally routed at the Battle of Culloden on 16 April; danger of a French invasion had already been averted.

3 This letter has apparently not survived.

Macro tells me, Ye have had a very odd Account of 'em.[4] For this reason I shall here send you a true State of the case. In October the Chancellour was consulted about what Steps were proper to be taken by the University in so critical a Season; & his Answer was, that an Association was highly necessary; but yt. as for a Subscription he knew not, if it would be expected. As the Parliament was then sitting, he concluded such Supplies would be granted, as might supersede the necessity of private Contributions.[5] After this, & without a second Application to Him (as he might reasonably expect, if upon maturer thoughts the University thought a Subscription necessary) the V. Chancellor & his Mates,[6] to shew the forwardness of their zeal, & from an ardent passion doubtless for their Country's Service, apply'd themselves to the Duke of New Castle,[7] mentioning the desire they had of testifying their Loyalty by a Subscription & desiring Directions from him, in what manner they should apply the money to be rais'd by it. All this was done by a Junto of Heads, as I before hinted, who had their frequent meetings & cabals about this important Affair, & took care to transact ev'ry thing without consulting at all with, or communicating their Intentions to, the Body. Nay they went further: besides this secret treating with the D. of N., they had their nightly Assemblies in order to agree upon the Sums to be rais'd: they had ev'n settl'd it amongst 'em, not only how much the University should give, but what should be the Quota of each College. – My College, says one Reverend Head-piece, shall pay so much; & mine, quoth a second, so much. – They had also drawn up a Grace,[8] wch. in good time they would condescend to propose to the Senate, in wch. with great modesty they had enter'd their whole Body, for a Committee to <dispose of> manage & dispose of the entire Subscription.[9] This Series of proceedings, as you'll imagine, when it came to be known, gave general Offence. It was evident, their design was to make a Job[10] of the Affair, & <had a mind> to assume the whole merit to themselves. It was manifest too, that they had us'd the University scandalously. Upon this an Agreement was enter'd into, as a fit return for their Insolence, & in order to disapoint, & pique their pride in a point the most tender to them, to stop their Grace for a Committee, & to exclude the greatest part of the Heads out of it. This was but serving 'em right & it was in itself reasonable; the Heads having no more

4 This may be a reference to an account given in a letter from Thomas Duquesne to Edward Macro (see *ante* To Littleton, 18 December 1745, n. 3). The facts given are much the same, but Duquesne presents them in a less favourable light.

5 It had nevertheless been reported in the *Gentleman's Magazine* of November that many subscriptions were being promoted to buy necessaries for the army (p. 614); and by the beginning of December a subscription had been opened in the chamberlain's office, to which numbers of associations had contributed. (*Gent. Mag.*, December 1745, pp. 665, 666, 668; but see Speck, *The Butcher*, pp. 57–9, for a more detailed account of the debate over subscriptions.)

6 George Rooke (see *ante* To Littleton, 18 December 1745, n. 5) and some of the other Heads of Colleges.

7 Thomas Pelham-Holles, first Duke of Newcastle (1693–1768). Newcastle was High Steward of the University (he was to be elected Chancellor in 1748). He was also a Secretary of State and a leading member of the ministry.

8 At Cambridge all decrees forming part of the statutes, or proposed as additions to the statutes, are known as "graces".

9 This is recorded in the *Annals* (iv. 255): "1745–Nov. 26. Grace to give £400. from the chest, for his Majesty's service, with an appointment of Syndics for the disposal of it. Stopt by the Non-Regents, because too many of the Heads were to be made Syndics".

10 A public service or trust turned to private gain or party advantage; a transaction in which duty or the public interest is sacrificed for the sake of private or party advantage. (*O.E.D.*)

Authority in the Senate than other members, & therefore having no claim to be consider'd before them. In consequence of this their Grace was rejected, tho' they had artfully contriv'd, in order to get it pass'd, to joyn to this Grace for the Committee another for the Sum to be subscrib'd, concluding that, as both must pass or neither, the University would rather chuse to vote the former, than incur the Odium of rejecting the later. But they found themselves mistaken: their Grace was thrown out with general Indignation, tho' not till after having propos'd, for the sake of avoiding their intended Odium, to offer each Grace separately. Here then, I conjecture, commences[a] the oddness of the Affair; & the University has been censur'd as opposing a Subscription itself; which I assure you was very far from being the cas[e,] the only point in view being to secure ourselves from being the Dupes of the Heads. In this cause, if it be a disgracefull one, I must freely own myself to have been concern'd, & I will add, with a hearty, good will. For I, who have a most unlimited Aversion to Tyranny, who can half forgive Cromwell, & envy Brutus his Stroke at Caesar, could not refuse my voice against a pack of lordly, insolent, temporizing Heads; who have as little Ability to rule, as they have Authority, & are equally disqualify'd from prescribing to the University by their Heads, as our public Statutes. In short the Dispute lasted with great warmth for a whole week, without coming to any Conclusion, the Heads still persisting in their impudent Designs, & the Body opposing them. At length it was agreed the Vice-Chancellor should be appointed Treasurer, to receive 400 pd.s from the public Chest, & the manner of applying it was prescrib'd by the Senate.[11] During this contest the Kephalarchy[12] (for that was the new Name given to the tyranny of the Heads) gave it out, that such as oppos'd them, oppos'd the thing itself, & did it from a principle of Disaffection – the common, thread-bare Cant of fools, or knaves, when they are not allow'd to have their own way. – As to the Subscription itself, which has been for some time carrying on, I believe it will be so very handsome,[13] as effectually to confute that silly Calumny. – I must not omit a noble thing of our excellent C., who neglected as he thought himself, & indeed really was, sent an Order for 600 pd.s, to be added to the University-Subscription, (& not to pass as a separate one of his own) as together making up a Sum, in his own obliging terms, *more becoming the honor & Dignity of such a Body*. – You see a Grace & Nobleness in this Act worthy the blood of the Seymour family. – Our M–r,[14] by Chance, or some such cause, was on the right Side. Heav'n send you fresh Happiness with this & ev'ry new Year.

Adieu.

[11] RH conflates two separate graces passed on 30 November and 5 December. The first provided that the University should give £400 "without appointing any persons to have the disposal of it". The second was "to impower the Vice Ch. to pay 4 Guineas (out of the £400) to every soldier that should be procured by any member of the Senate, & enlisted among his Majesties forces". (*Annals*, iv. 255.) Many other subscriptions were divided amongst the soldiers in the same way: four guineas was the standard payment.

[12] From the Greek κεφαλη: head.

[13] Thomas Duquesne quotes £4,000 as the proposed sum. (See *ante* To Littleton, 18 December 1745, n. 3.)

[14] The Master of Emmanuel, William Richardson.

[a] MS: first "c" written over ?"b".

74 To Sir EDWARD LITTLETON 9 JANUARY 1746

Text: MS STAFFS RO D1413/1; unpublished.
Addressed: To/Sr. Edward Littleton Bart./at Pipe-Ridware near Lichfield./Staffordshire./By London.
Postmarked: CAMBRIDGE

Camb. 9. Jan. 1745–6.

Dear Sir Edward,

I had this day the favor of Your's, which teaches me I was something too hasty in supposing You'd have left Pipe-Ridware, by the time my Letter to Mrs. Littleton could reach it. However to be sure of catching You now, I have judg'd it proper to write by the return of the Post.

It gives me a Concern upon many Accounts to find this ugly Affair in the North depending so long. Of these You'll allow me to reckon it one, that it robs me of the pleasure of your Company; as I perceive it is no small Uneasiness to Yourself to be so long detain'd from College.[1] And indeed I cannot wonder, a Life so very different from what Your's us'd to be, should appear not quite so pleasant. You could certainly find business or Conversation much more to your Taste here – But whether this should be a reason to determine your immediate return to us, is what, I perceive, you regard as a matter of much Doubt, & for a resolution of which You can certainly apply to no one so proper as Mr. Hill;[2] who will doubtless advise You to such a Conduct, as may best become You at this time, as I am satisfy'd your own Inclination will be to follow any Advice, that shall appear to Him most suitable.

For myself, I need only say, I shall heartily rejoyce at your Return to this Place, whenever it be thought consistent with your other Engagements. Till then You will not attempt it – nor can I wish it, as being always, with great Respect, Dear Sr. Edward, Your most Faithfull, Hble Servt.

R. Hurd.

P.S.

I beg my Compliments to Mrs. Littleton & Mr. Hill.

75 To Sir EDWARD LITTLETON 27 JANUARY 1746

Text: MS STAFFS RO D1413/1; unpublished.
Addressed: To/Sr. Edward Littleton Bart./Captain in Lord Gower's Regiment/at the Assembly-House/Chester./ By London.
Postmarked: CAMBRIDGE

Dear Sir Edward!

I am much oblig'd by your last favour, in which is inserted a Copy of your Letter to my Lord Gower, concerning the Affair of Your Resignation.[1] It is with pleasure I

1 Littleton had left college about 7 September 1745. (*Commons Accounts Book*, STE. 15. 9.)

2 Samuel Hill (1701–58) of Shenstone Park, Staffordshire. Hill was one of Edward Littleton's guardians.

1 On accepting his commission in the Staffordshire regiment, Sir Edward Littleton had made an

observe your Expostulation with my Lord to turn chiefly on the importance of your University-Engagements; & the rather as I have reason to believe it is not a pretence only, but the real, at least the principal reason, that weighs with You. As to the Letter itself, it is very handsomely wrote; unless that perhaps the whole is rather too long, & there are possibly two or three Inaccuracies besides, which however his Lordship's Candor & Good-Sense will readily allow for. Thus much You'll forgive me saying in the Character of Tutor, or rather I know You would expect & require this freedom from me.

For the rest, I am very impatient to know the Success of Your Expostulation, & shall rejoyce to find it answerable to your Wishes;[2] but am assur'd in the mean time, that if it happens otherwise, (as for reasons not known to me it possibly may) You will make Yourself very easy under the Disapointment; & tho' your Life at Chester may not be so agreable, you will however continue it, if requir'd of You, with Chearfullness & Resolution. This I can depend upon from my knowledge of your good Sense; & am always, with an entire Respect, Dear Sr. Edward, Your most Faithfull, Hble Servt

R. Hurd.

Camb. 27. Jan. 1745–6.

76 To Sir EDWARD LITTLETON 14 MARCH 1746

Text: MS STAFFS RO D1413/1; unpublished.
Addressed: To/Sr. Edward Littleton Bart./at Mr. Gunn's Organist/in Birmingham/Warwickshire/By London.
Postmarked: CAMBRIDGE 17 MR

Dear Sir Edward,

I had not omitted thus long to congratulate with You on the Release from your Military Engagements, but that I knew not whither to direct a Letter with any probability of finding You. I shall now ev'ry day expect, as You give me leave to do, the pleasure of seeing You in Cambridge;[1] where, notwithstanding the Disturbance

agreement with Lord Gower that he should be allowed to return to Cambridge as soon as the "impending danger" was over. Littleton had understood that this would mean resigning his commission whilst Gower intended that he should only be granted leave. He was therefore surprised to receive an application to resign made on Littleton's behalf by Samuel Hill and in reply wrote a long letter explaining his understanding of the agreement and suggesting that Littleton should reconsider his position. (Gower to Hill, 18 January 1746, Littleton Correspondence, Staffs. RO, D1413/2.) A note added to this by Sir Edward explains that it crossed with his own first letter of application which must therefore have been written about 18 January. This letter, however, has been lost.

2 Lord Gower had acted upon Littleton's request by 6 February. In a letter written that day to his Lieutenant he sends his compliments to Sir Edward and another Captain and adds a wish that they might be told that he had "obtain'd their dismission from his Majesty". But, he continues, he would be glad if they could "continue wth. their Companys until . . . the Regiment is got into fresh Quarters". (Gower Correspondence, William Salt Library, S.M.S. 523.) Littleton finally returned to college in the middle of April. (*Commons Accounts Book*, STE. 15. 9.)

1 Lord Gower had written a letter to Edward Littleton on 4 March apologising for having

that has [s]pread itself over almost ev'ry other part of the Kingdom, the Muses are yet so happy as to retain their native peacefullness & Serenity. Amongst other Amusements we shall find for You, You will come in good time for Mr. Powell's Lectures in Optics, which do not begin till after Easter.[2]

As the Quarter is just now ended, I take this Opportunity to inclose Your Bill.

Be pleas'd to make my Compliments to Mrs. Littleton & Mr. Hill; & let me have proper notice of your Coming, that your Chambers may be in readiness to receive You.

In the mean time, & with the hopes of this agreable Intelligence by ev'ry Post, I conclude with being always, Dear Sir Edward, Your most Faithfull, Humble Servt.

R. Hurd.

Camb. 14. March. 1745–6.

Sr. Edward Littleton's Bill for Xstmas Quarter. 1745.[3]

Steward	3.	5.	11
Study-Rent	2.	12.	6
Sizar	1.	0.	0
Tuition	6.	0.	0
	£: 12.	18.	5

P.S.

Mr. Nevile, who is remov'd from Jesus hither, sends Compliments.[4]

detained him whilst the regiment was in some disorder and adding that he was now "at liberty to quit" as soon as he pleased. (Littleton Correspondence, Staffs. RO, D1413/2.) The letter, according to a note in Littleton's hand, had been directed to him in Birmingham.

2 A book of notes taken during a course of Powell's lectures in 1746 may be seen at St John's College Library (MS 608). The notes were taken by a Trinity undergraduate, Thomas Sympson, who gives the title of the course as "Lectures in Experimental Philosophy by W.S. Powell A.M." The last paragraph of the introductory section indicates that a discussion of optics probably occupied a considerable proportion of the course. Powell, it is reported, explained that "By Experiments it is that natural Philosophy is brought out of the greatest Obscurity into the clearest Light and this is cheifly owing to the unparallel'd abilities of Sr Isaac Newton who has to his immortal Honour disclosed more truths in his Principles of natural Philosophy and Opticks than are to be met with in all the Voluminous writings of the Antients. To illustrate some of these truths", he concludes, "is the design of this Course."

3 Littleton's bill corresponds in size to his status as a "nobleman". The payment to the Steward was for "commons" and "sizes", i.e. the food and drink consumed in college. The study rent paid for his rooms in the "New brick Building". It was over one pound higher per annum than that of any other undergraduate because of the quality of the rooms and because, unlike many other undergraduates, Littleton did not share accommodation. His bill for a sizar covered the service given by one of the poorer undergraduates at meals. The sizars helped pay for their education by serving at the Fellows' table on which Sir Edward, as a nobleman, was included. The tuition fees were officially set by the University. The last ruling made by the Heads of Houses had been in 1721 when the highest tuition fees, those for Fellow-commoners, were set at £3.0.0. (*Statuta Academiae Cantabrigiensis*, 1785, pp. 507–8.) The next official ruling was not made till 1767 when the further category of noblemen was added and their fees set at £8.0.0 (*Statuta*, pp. 513–14.)

4 Thomas Nevile had been admitted as a Fellow-commoner on 28 January. He remained at Emmanuel until 7 October when he returned to Jesus to take up a Fellowship. John Nevile, a Fellow of Emmanuel, was his elder brother.

77 To COX MACRO 28 APRIL 1746

Text: MS BL Add. 32557, ff. 115–16; unpublished.
Addressed: cover missing.

Camb. Apr. 28. 1746.

Revd. Sir,

My last[1] attempted to account for the Rise of Sacrificing from the *Ignorance & Simplicity of Mankind*. And this after all is perhaps no such Discrediting Original, as it may at first appear. For to what but this *Rudeness & Simplicity of Conception* is owing the Practice ev'n of *Prayer, & Thanksgiving*, I mean, in the manner in which those Duties are understood by the Generality of mankind? For tho' I do not deny, that they may certainly be prov'd to be Natural Duties, that is congruous to the Human Nature, & deducible from the Circumstances, & <Nature> Condition of Man, yet I cannot believe that the first Worshippers had any other Reason for performing those Acts of Piety, nor that Worshippers in general have now, or ever had any other, (except indeed *that* of their being commanded by way of positive Precept, which does not concern the present Subject) than such as arise out of the rude Prejudices, & narrow Conceptions of Men. I need not be particular in tracing the progress of these Conceptions to You, who so thoroughly understand the workings of Humanity. All I will presume to say is, that so long as Men conceive of Prayers & Thanksgivings, as of themselves gratefull & acceptable to God, & of sufficient force to engage the favour <of Heaven &, by their intrinsic Value, to draw down the Blessings>, or avert the impending Judgments of <his Providence> Heaven, so long as such Conceptions are general (and it is submitted to your Experience & Observation of Men, how far they are so) it cannot but be true, that *Prayer & Thanksgiving* are but the Effects of rude thinking, – the Services of weak Reasoners, misled by their own uncorrected Prejudices, & measuring the Divine Nature, & Disposition by their own. And hence it has come to pass, that these & all other Duties, respecting the ritual & external Worship of God, have ever been so grossly abus'd. For conceiving them some way pleasing, & gratefull to God for their own Sake, nor looking on them as *Means* only to a valuable *End*, Men have been led to rest in them, as alone sufficient, neglecting the *End* itself, for which they were ordain'd. This has almost universally been the case in many Ages & Nations, & is ever too much so in all. Now from hence arises an Answer to the Objection You did me the favour to make to my Account, & which You express'd in these Words.[a] "As sacrificing was, probably, practis'd by the very first Man, & as You have laid it's foundation in rude, untutor'd Minds, who, from the narrowness of their Reason, judg'd of God's Dispositions by their own, I ask, if Adam is to be reckon'd of this Number, notwithstanding his coming directly from God's Hands, & his being so constantly favour'd with Divine Intercourses, & Communications?"[a] What has been observ'd of *Prayer & Thanksgiving* afforded, I said, an Answer to this Objection. For these Offices might as well be expected to be forbidden by God in his Communications with Adam, as the Rite of Sacrificing. No – You will say. *Prayer* &c was founded in Reason, the Rite of Sacrificing not. Admitting this in *general*, yet if the Account here giv'n be true, *Prayer* &c was not so founded in the case of Adam, or the greater part of his Posterity. Yet it receiv'd no Prohibition, nor even any Check. But *Sacrificing*, You will say, was the Parent of the most enormous

[1] See *ante* To Macro, 1 January 1746.

[a–a] MS: each new line of quotation prefaced by quotation marks.

Corruptions, & Immoralities – So has *Prayer, & Thanksgiving* falsely understood. Erroneous in their Principle, & pernicious by their *accidental* Consequences, both of them, if either, should have been forbid. But excuse me, if I go on to ask, how far, & in what Respect is the *Rite of Sacrificing* unreasonable? Is it unreasonable to express a thankfullness, & homage to God by setting apart a Portion of his Gifts, as a Memorial of it? Is it unreasonable to endeavour to stir up the like Sentiments of thankfullness & Dependence[b] by making that *Memorial* public, & repeating it at proper Intervals in the Sight of others? This cannot be said. *Sacrificing* thus understood, & confin'd to these Uses is rational as *Prayer*, or any other *mode of Worship*, & productive of the noblest Ends. What is it then, that renders *Sacrificing* unreasonable, & hurtfull? Why the conceiving *wrong* of it, & supposing the Odors of Plants, or Steams off Victims regaling to the Divinity. But this is a Consequence not *necessary*, but *accidental*. And the same, as we observ'd, is true of *Prayer*. God was not therefore concern'd to prohibit the *Rite of Sacrificing*, no more than this of *Prayer*, on account of such *accidental* ill Consequence. And it will fairly be presum'd, that *Sacrifice*, with all it's bad Consequences, was of Use to keep alive a stronger general Sense of the Divine Superintendance in the World, than could have been expected without the Observance of all outward Rites & Ceremonies. And tho' some perhaps might be less liable to Abuse than this, yet if it be not necessarily so, I cannot see that God was <oblig'd> concern'd to forbid it. The Truth is, The Rite of *Sacrificing*, however it may have been perverted to the most abominable Uses, is not in itself *necessarily*, & *essentially* wrong, or unreasonable. What then should render it displeasing in the Sight of God, & induce him to prohibit in Adam (supposing Him the first Sacrificer) the Practice of it. If Adam conceiv'd wrong of the Nature of *Sacrificing*, it is full as likely He would do so of *Prayer*. And therefore if such wrong Conception were a reason for God's forbidding the *former*, it <were also for his for> must also extend to the *Later*. If Adam, from the excellence of his faculties, & as coming immediatly from the Hands of God, be suppos'd to have conceiv'd rightly of Prayer; the same I shall beg leave to suppose in regard to his Conception of Sacrifice. And then, as hath been observ'd, both are rational, & need no Prohibition. I must own, when I drew up my former Letters, I conceiv'd of Adam, as liable to the same Prejudices of Humanity, as we his Sons are, & therefore made no Distinction betwixt the Case of Him, & his Posterity. But if You think the Scripture Accounts make it necessary to ascribe a much greater Perfection to Adam in his unlaps'd State, & yet suppose Him to have offer'd Sacrifices, my Scheme is a little alter'd, & stands thus. Adam was induc'd to *sacrifice* to God, from the sole views of expressing by such a Rite his Dependance upon Him, & of raising such Sentiments of Dependance in the Breasts of his Children; without any Conception of it's being pleasing to God for it's own Sake. Laps'd Man, having his Understanding darken'd & deprav'd, conceiv'd more grossly of the Deity, & at least mix'd other reasons with these; thinking it someway gratefull to God, as, they found, it was to themselves, to receive the Gifts & Oblations of a Dependant. In short the Difference of the Scheme, upon ys. alteration, lies here: that whereas I suppos'd Sacrifice to have had it's first Rise from Simplicity of Conception, the case is, that in reality: [it][c] drew it's first Rise from Reasonable Views & Motives, but upon the Fall, and especially as Men sunk into Barbarity, & Ignorance, their notions grew more sensual, & deprav'd, & they then *sacrific'd* from, some at least, wrong views &

b MS: "Dependendence".
c MS: omitted by RH.

Intentions. The Sum is, *Sacrificing*, as all other Rites of Worship, is liable to great Corruption; but some Rites being usefull & necessary to Mankind, & this, arising either from the Dictates of Reason, or almost naturally growing out of the Prejudices of Men, <had> having a very early Rise, was tolerated at least by God in the Nations of the World, & ev'n adopted by Him into his own especial form of Worship deliver'd to the Jews. With all it's Abuses & bad Effects, it serv'd, it may be, to keep up a Sense of God's over-ruling Providence, &, imperfect as it was, when perform'd with pious Intentions, it became, I doubt not, an acceptable Service to a mercifull & Gracious God. The Xstian Institution has indeed remov'd this & all other carnal Ordinances: but it is not clear to me, that they were always had in <abhorrence of God.> such Dislike. *The Ignorance of Heathen Times God winked at*; & however reasonable it is, that He *should* all times, He did not, if I may so speak, *expect* in those Days to be worshipped in *Spirit & in Truth*.

These are free &, it may be, wild Notions. Such as they are I commit them to your Candour, which I have found ever ready to give a favorable hearing to the [. . .] Revd Sir [. . .]

R. Hurd.

78 To MARY MACRO 22 AUGUST 1746

Text: MS BL Add. 32557, ff. 121–2; unpublished.
Addressed: cover missing.

Camb. 22. Aug. 1746.

Madam,

I had the favour of Your's, which shall be answer'd more at length, as it deserves, in a short time. At present my Intention in writing is to acquaint You with the Event of Mr. Brinkley's Tryal, which I attended, & which I thought You would be desirous to have an early Account of.[1] The Court sate yesterday Morning by seven o' Clock, & the Cause lasted till within a few Minutes of twelve. The main Difficulty lay in accounting for such a wound, as the Deceas'd died of, by the fragment of a Chamber-Pot. For the Shape of it was semi-circular, & as clean or smooth, as if it had been made by the keenest Instrument. Whereas the fragment, which was suppos'd to give it, was of a triangular shape drawn out into a sharp point at top; & being a piece of a Pot would be expected to tear the flesh, instead of clearly dividing it, & so leave the wound jagged. But in order to remove these Difficulties several similar Cases were produc'd: one especially of a young Girl, who fell down upon a Bason, a part of which running into her Neck, & leaving, as the Girl's Mother attested, a smooth wound, occasion'd her Death within a few Minutes; another of a person, falling upon a Pint-Pot, which he was carrying full of Ale across a Street, a fragment of which running into the very place, where Ashton's wound was, the Person died immediatly.

1 John Brinkley (b. 1727) was the son of an attorney living in Bury St Edmunds. His trial was on the charge of murder, following the suspicious death of James Ashton, on 9 March 1745. Both men were undergraduates at St John's and had been on friendly terms since Brinkley's admittance on 18 January. The trial aroused considerable interest and letters attacking and defending the jury's verdict were published in the London newspapers, the *General Evening Post* (6 September) and the *Daily Advertiser* (16 September). These were reprinted in the *Gentleman's Magazine*, September 1746, pp. 466, 469, and give more detailed accounts of the evidence presented in the trial.

This later Case had the greater weight, as coming from a Surgeon, who was sent for immediatly upon the Accident, but who, notwithstanding that he had not above 300 yards to go, came too late. This Surgeon attested also, that the wound in this case was smooth. As to the semicircular form of the wound, Dr. Heberden[2] observ'd (& it was of great Use to the Prisoner) that it was more likely to proceed from a blunt Instrument, than a sharp one; for that he had frequently, since the thing happen'd, attempted to thrust his finger, or some obtuse Instrument thro' Paper or Parchment, & that in so doing the rent was always of that form. He added, that indeed this must needs be the Case, for a blunt Instrument pressing the Skin inwards, & not penetrating the Surface immediatly, would burst it, as it were, & so of course leave that shap'd wound; whereas a sharp Instrument instantly piercing the Skin would not. This Observation, which appear'd just, strongly favour'd the Prisoner. As to the other Circumstances, they were none of them of any great weight, & were more easily accounted for. One indeed seem'd considerable at first, which was, that Brinkley burst open the Door of the deceas'd, in order to come to him that night, which might naturally be constru'd as a Mark of Violence. But it appear'd, that the Door was so slightly fasten'd, that it was the usual way in which the deceas'd came in himself, seldom using a Key, but opening it with a very slight Push. Upon the whole (for I cannot pretend to relate all the Circumstances, which came into Consideration) the Evidence agst. the Prisoner was so slight, & so weakly founded, that the Jury without any Hesitation brought him in unanimously *Not Guilty*.[3] For my part, having attended to the whole tryal with all the Care, I could, I[a] should incline to think, He was quite innocent; which also his intrepid, & secure behaviour all along seem'd to indicate. If anything, He appear'd perhaps too insensible. When the Jury brought Him in *Not Guilty* He discover'd no more Signs of Joy, than he had before of Fear, or Concern: Either case perhaps the Effect of conscious Innocence, but a little Sensibility had touch'd me more. You'll please to accept this hasty Narrative with your usual Candour, & believe me always, with all Respect, Madam, Your most Oblig'd & most Obedt. Servt.

R. Hurd.

79 To COX MACRO 5 JANUARY 1747

Text: MS BL Add. 32557, ff. 125–6; unpublished.
Addressed: To/The Revd. Dr. Macro at Norton/to be left at Mr. Hayward's/in the Cook-Row/Bury St. Edmunds.
Postmarked: CAMBRIDGE

Revd. Sir

I never sate down to write to Dr. Macro under more perplexing Circumstances, than at present, when I am going to own to Him, what I ought not to have conceal'd

[2] William Heberden was a Fellow of St John's and had been called to Ashton's room almost immediately on the discovery of his body. (*Gent. Mag.*, September 1746, p. 466.) He was much esteemed as a physician in Cambridge circles.

[3] A different impression is given by William Cole, the Cambridge antiquary, in his account of the affair. Brinkley, he writes, "was acquitted upon want of proper Evidence: tho' he was much suspected by most People to be ye. Murtherer: He was however not suffered to stay in *College* afterwards". (Cole Collections III, MS BL, Add. 5804, f. 142.)

[a] MS: "I" written over "wd".

thus long, or what I ought always perhaps to have kept secret. For can You pardon it in me, that I have ventur'd to print a Pamphlet, without saying a Syllable to You about it?[1] Or rather can I pardon myself for having done an Act of so much Imprudence & Incivility? But the truth was (for the Confession of the Truth is the only Atonement to be made for an Offence of this Nature) I was dispos'd for once to play the fool, &, like young Fellows determin'd to play the fool in another way, was averse to consult those, who might advise me against it. And thus, agreably to their Custom, I resolv'd to do wrong first & then ask Pardon after; throwing myself entirely, as they are us'd, on your Indulgence & Good Nature. The Pamphlet I speak of is a little Thing in answer to Mr. Weston's Book about the Heathen Rejection of Xstian Miracles,[2] which I propose sending You in the next Cargo & was willing to prepare You for it by this Notice. In the mean time, & till I see reason to the contrary, I must beg of You to keep it quite secret; no body knowing a tittle of it as yet, but such as it was necessary to make acquainted with it.

If You can forgive this Indiscretion in me, 'twill be a singular Mark of your Goodness; & I think I may assure You, You will not find me offending again in this way in Haste.[a] And so, with my good Wishes for your Health & Happiness, I remain ever, Revd Sir, Your most Obedt. Hble Servt

R. Hurd.

Em̃an: 5. Jan. 1746–7.

80 To Sir EDWARD LITTLETON 15 JANUARY 1747

Text: MS STAFFS RO D1413/1; unpublished.
Addressed: To/Sir Edwd. Littleton Bart./at Pipe-Ridware near Lichfield/Staffordshire/By London.
Postmarked: CAMBRIDGE

Camb. 15. Jan. 1746–7.

Dear Sir,

I am much pleas'd with Mr. Manwaring's Compliment of the Deputy-Stewardship of Tamworth, which I suppose to be a Place of some Distinction, & will therefore be a proper Introduction to greater Matters.[1]

1 This work, *Remarks on a late Book, Entitled, An Enquiry into the Rejection of the Christian Miracles by the Heathens*, is RH's earliest publication. It was first advertised for sale in December 1746. (*Gent. Mag.*; *Lond. Mag.*)

2 William Weston, a Fellow of St John's, had published *An Enquiry into the Rejection of the Christian Miracles by the Heathens* in Cambridge in March 1746. Neither it nor RH's *Remarks* relate significantly to the mainstream of debate on miracles (see *post* To Devey, 17 March 1747, n. 3, for some account of this) and both show more interest in classical evidence than theological argument. RH's attempt to refute Weston's claim that the heathens had a low opinion of miracles, met with a sharp rejoinder from the latter, *Observations on some Remarks on a late book, intitled: An Enquiry into the rejection of the Christian Miracles by the Heathens*, published in Cambridge in February 1747. (*Lond. Mag.*) The work is an effective mockery of RH's pamphlet and seems to have discouraged him from joining in further theological debate.

a MS: "in the Haste".

1 John Mainwaring had engaged the patronage of Thomas Thynne, second Viscount Weymouth

Mr. M.s Honesty, not only in consulting the Interest of his Lord, but in frankly owning this to You, is very commendable.[2]

But above all I am vastly pleas'd with your having got the Possession of the Lord Keeper:[3] it is of great Value to You, ev'n if it be a bad Picture; but, if a good one, in[valu]able.

I could be glad to make a Third with You at the Park,[4] when Mr. Hill is to give his Opinion of the Situation, & other Circumstances relating to your Design of building. To make up this Loss, You must not fail to give me a very particular Account of what passes.

All the News that I can think it worth while to write from this Place, is, that Colley Cibber, having <try'd> been trying his Hand for these many Years, but with slender Success, at Poetry, is now at last, as it were in mere Spite, resolv'd to turn Critic, & has accordingly publish'd a Book against Dr. Middleton's Life of Cicero.[5] The curious Design of this Piece is to shew, that, allowing the Doctor's Account of Cicero to be just, yet his Character is not a good one. This, You perceive, is the true Itch of finding fault: & I only mention it to shew Y[ou] that the Censure of Mr. Pope, so much complain'd of by his Admirers, is well merited; & that *Pert & Dull* is like to be the Character of poor Colley for Life.[6]

I know You would not excuse me, if, amongst other Compliments, (which I beg You to make for me at Pipe-Ridware & Shenstone)[7] I omitted to express my desire of

(1710–51), who had been appointed High Steward of Tamworth in 1733. (G.E. C[okayne], *The Complete Peerage, or a History of the House of Lords and all its Members from the Earliest Times, revised and enlarged*, 1910–59.) No other information concerning his appointment has been traced.

2 The nature of Littleton's connection with Mainwaring has not been established.

3 Lord Keeper Littleton (1589–1645) and Sir Edward came of the same Littleton family but were not directly related. Nothing further is known of this picture.

4 Teddesley Park. This was land on which Sir Edward proposed building a new house. The plans must already have been partly formulated in the previous year, since in August 1745 Mrs Littleton had paid for Sir Edward's bed to be taken to Teddesley. (Mrs Littleton to Sir Edward Littleton, Private Accompt, Staffs. RO, Ex. D260/M/T/5/107.)

5 Colley Cibber (1671–1757) had been made Poet Laureate in 1730 and had won fame as an actor and dramatist. He attracted much attention in the literary world, but was regarded with contempt by several major writers of the mid eighteenth century (Johnson, Fielding and Warburton, for instance), as he had been regarded with dislike by Pope. RH's opinion of him appears to be an inheritance of this tradition of hostility, rather than an independent view. Nonetheless his criticism of Cibber's book, *The Character and Conduct of Cicero, Considered*, 1747, is not unmerited. The chief object of the work is to illustrate Cicero's vanity, the "solid Folly of a Man's being so frequently eloquent in his own Praise" (p. 274), and its conclusion is a criticism of Middleton's vindication of this fault.

6 Pope had referred to Cibber thus in *The Dunciad, in Four Books. Printed according to the complete Copy found in the Year 1742*, published in 1743. In a note to Book I, line 109 he commented: "It is hoped the poet here hath done full justice to his Hero's [Cibber] Character, which it were a great mistake to imagine was wholly sunk in stupidity; he is allowed to have supported it with a wonderful mixture of Vivacity. This character is heightened according to his own desire, in a Letter he wrote to our author. 'Pert and dull at least you might have allowed me. What! am I only to be dull, and dull still, and again, and for ever?' "

7 Mrs Littleton lived at Pipe-Ridware and Samuel Hill at Shenstone Park.

seeing You here by the twenty sixth of this Month, when Mr. Powell begins his Lectures.[8]

I am, Dr. Sir, Your most Faithfull Hble Servt.

R. Hurd.

81 To JAMES DEVEY 17 MARCH 1747

Text: Memoirs, 26.

Cambridge, March 17, 1746–7.

. . . I have read over more than once your strictures on Mr. Chandler's Answer to the Moral Philosopher,[1] and am pleased to find that in the main you agree with me in approving that piece. As to what you observe about his notion of human sacrifices, I think that it appears from the quotations you have produced, to be at least disputable whether what Mr. Chandler has advanced about the high antiquity of them can be defended.[2] As the matter, indeed, appears to me at present, I rather incline to your opinion, and am vastly obliged by the learned pains you have taken to confirm it.

As I am so great a gainer by recommending books to you, I will take this opportunity of mentioning another piece, which has lately appeared on the side of religion, and which I believe you will be much pleased with. 'Tis a Defence of the Evangelical History of the Resurrection, by Mr. West, a gentleman who converted himself from Deism to Christianity by his own diligent inquiries, the result of which, so far as respects the Resurrection, which seems to have been a main difficulty with him, he has given us in this book.[3]

8 This was probably another course of lectures in Experimental Philosophy (see *ante* To Littleton, 24 November 1745, and 14 March 1746).

1 Samuel Chandler, *A Vindication of the History of the Old Testament. In Answer to the Misrepresentations and Calumnies of Thomas Morgan, M.D. and Moral Philosopher*, 1741.

2 The question of the antiquity of human sacrifice arises in the seventh section of the *Vindication* (pp. 145–239) on "Abraham's *offering up his Son*". Chandler agrees that "human Sacrifices were both very ancient and frequent amongst the Inhabitants of *Canaan*", but insists that they were only used by the "corrupted and idolatrous *Jews*" (pp. 185, 188). He argued strongly against Morgan's theory that it was "*the common Notion* of Abraham's *Time* that such unnatural Sacrifices were the *most valuable and meritorious Part of Obedience*" to God (p. 186).

3 Gilbert West's *Observations on the History and Evidences of the Resurrection of Jesus Christ* had been published in December 1746. (*Lond. Mag.*) It forms part of the debate upon the authenticity of Christian miracles and is a reply to Peter Annet's *The Resurrection of Jesus Considered: By a Moral Philosopher*, (1743?). The controversy over miracles had been initiated in 1727 by Thomas Woolston and was part of the larger controversy between orthodox Christians and deists concerning the literal authority of the Gospels. Woolston, in a series of six discourses published between 1727 and 1729, had attempted to prove that the New Testament miracles contained no element of historical truth, though they could be interpreted allegorically. He had been opposed by Richard Smalbroke and Zachary Pearce without much effect, before Thomas Sherlock, then Bishop of Bangor (and later of Salisbury), joined in the debate with a powerfully argued work, *The Tryal of the Witnesses of the Resurrection of Jesus*. This proved immensely popular, going into five editions in the year of its publication (1729) and reaching its eleventh edition by 1747. It depends, as West's book does, on the assumption, common to the orthodox and to most of the deists, that the Apostles were sincere in their accounts of the Resurrection. From this the writers prove that the miracle of the Resurrection really did take place and thus that all other miracles were not only possible but highly probable. This position was effective as a defence against deistical thought for a time, but was ultimately undermined by David Hume

The Bishop of Salisbury,[4] who had the revisal of it before it went to the press, says, it is by much the best thing on the subject, which is a great deal for the author of the "Trial of the Witnesses" to say. The first part of this treatise you will find most curious, being a new method of accounting for the seeming inconsistencies in the Gospel narration. But I will not prevent your curiosity, which I think will be agreeably gratified in looking into this piece, and, if so, I shall expect to be favoured with some account of your entertainment.

I beg my best services to Mrs. Devey and the young ladies, who are desired to suspend their displeasure till I come to confront that mischievous knave Mr. Binnel,[5] who, I find, has taken the opportunity of my absence, to dress up such a story as he must expect to be called to an account for. It is a sad thing that Parsons, who are peace-makers by profession, should set folks together by the ears at this rate, and especially where a brother is concerned.

Ds. Devey is well and sends compliments. Pray make mine to friends at Hatton, and Ryton.[6]

82 To WILLIAM MASON 7 MAY 1747

Text: MS HC; printed, *H-M Corr*, 1.
Addressed: To/Mr Mason at the Revd Mr Mason's/[1] in Hull/Yorkshire/ By London. Caxton Bag[2]
Postmarked: CAMBRIDGE

Dear Sir

I am just return'd from a fortnight's ramble into Norfolk;[3] wch must be my Excuse

and Conyers Middleton. West's particular contribution to the controversy is an interesting reworking of available material, but his arguments do not substantially differ from those used before him by Sherlock and others. There seems no authority for RH's claim that he was a convert from deism; both Johnson and later Leslie Stephen emphasise the soundness of his faith. (Johnson, *Prefaces*, 1779–81, x. (West) 3; Stephen, *English Thought in the Eighteenth Century*, 1902, i. 248–9.) For a more extended account of the debate on miracles see R.M. Burns, *The Great Debate on Miracles. From Joseph Glanvill to David Hume*, 1981.)

4 Thomas Sherlock. See preceding note.

5 Robert Binnell (1716–63) was vicar of Sutton Maddock, about ten miles from Shifnal. He had been brought up in Shifnal and after obtaining an M.A. at Oxford in 1739 had been appointed vicar of Sutton Maddock in 1740. He succeeded Devey as rector of Kemberton on the latter's death in 1754. (*Alum. Oxon.*)

6 Ryton lies about a mile from Beckbury on the road to Hatton Grange. RH's acquaintance there have not been identified.

1 William Mason the elder (1694–1753), vicar of Holy Trinity, Hull.

2 Caxton was a stage on the North Road not far from Cambridge. According to *Cantabrigia Depicta* published in 1763, the "*North-Post*, by *Caxton*, Sets out every Night at *Ten*, except *Sunday*: and returns every Forenoon, except *Sunday*". (*Cantabrigia Depicta. A Concise and Accurate Description of the University and Town of Cambridge, and its Environs*, Cambridge, [1763], p. 112.)

3 RH had arrived back in Cambridge about 3 May. (*Residence Book*, TUT. 11. 1.) He had probably

for not acknowledging, so soon as I ought, your present of Musaeus.[4]

This Piece has now had it's fate; & tho' You must have known it long since from other hands, I must have leave to say, that ev'ry body here reads & admires it. Nothing ever pleas'd so generally: It has caught all sorts of Readers from Heads of Colleges down to little Coffee-House Critics. If there be here & there a little Envy, it dares not so much as shew itself in faint praises. Ev'ry one is asham'd not to appear struck, with what charms ev'ry body. Don't suspect me of flattery: I am only making a true & faithfull Report, which I do with the greater pleasure, as I hope this early tast of honest fame, a motive which a Poet may freely avow, & the noblest indeed that can excite to any Undertaking, will engage You without further Scruple to complete your other Imitations of Milton.[5] The success of anything You do hereafter is certain; ev'n if one may suppose it to have much less merit, than Musaeus, which nothing I am sure of Your's can ever have.[6]

I know You are in pain, till I quit this Subject; but You must allow me to say, it gives me the greatest Joy to observe this public testimony to the Merit of a Person, who has hitherto been so unjust to Himself, as by all means to conceal it. And I could not resist the pleasure of persecuting You with some part of the Applause, You fly from, ev'n tho' I follow'd You to that very Hawthorn-shade,[7] which, You hop'd, might secure You from it.

Next to Musaeus, the Thing, that occasions most noise here is a piece of Dr Middleton's, which undertakes to overthrow the Credit of the Fathers.[8] You may not perhaps be much interested in Theological Disputes; but, as a Composition only, it may chance to entertain You.

been visiting Robert Potter (Vicar of Melton Parva since October 1746) and other acquaintances made whilst he was curate of Reymerston.

4 *Musaeus: A Monody to the Memory of Mr. Pope, in Imitation of Milton's Lycidas* had been published in April. (Straus, *Dodsley*, Bibliography.) The poem had been written in 1744.

5 Probably 'Il Bellicoso' and 'Il Pacifico' although these were originally written in 1744. 'Il Pacifico' was published in 1748 in *Gratulatio Academiae Cantabrigiensis*.

6 Nearly half a century later RH was still of the same opinion. In his *Discourse* on the life of Warburton he refers to Pope's death as having "brought on the dawn of Mr. Mason's genius", and adds that *Musaeus* "gave so sure a presage of his future eminence in poetry, and so advantageous a picture of his mind, that Mr. Warburton, on the sight of it, 'With open arms received one poet more' ". (*A Discourse, By Way of General Preface to Bishop Warburton's Works*, pp. 41–2.)

7 *Musaeus* (last canto): "Unseen, unheard, beneath an hawthorn shade".

8 This was *An Introductory Discourse to a larger Work, designed hereafter to be published, concerning the miraculous Powers, which are supposed to have subsisted in the Christian Church from the earliest Ages, through several successive Centuries*. The book had been published in April. Both the *Introductory Discourse* and the full study of Christian miracles that followed it in December 1748 (*A Free Inquiry into the Miraculous Powers*) developed out of Middleton's consideration of "Popish" miracles in his *Letter from Rome* (see *ante* To Devey, [December 1745/January 1746], n. 2). His general thesis is that miracles ceased after the death of the Apostles and that those reported by the Fathers only prove the latter to be fools or liars. In their controversies with the Church of Rome, divines of the Church of England had already denied the continuance of miracles after the fourth century. Middleton applied the same principles of argument in a refutation of Patristic accounts of miracles performed during the first three centuries of the Church. Much of the originality of this approach lies in his sense of historical continuity; but also implicit in Middleton's methodology is the apparent suggestion that the same standards of criticism might be applied to both sacred and profane history. (Stephen, *English Thought in the Eighteenth Century*, i. 264–70; Burns, *The Great Debate on Miracles*, pp. 10–11.)

A Postscript very well exposes an absurd whimsy of Dr Chapman.[9]

Since this Attack upon the antient Fathers, another with equal Violence has been made upon a certain modern one. And to heighten the Surprize, Dux faemina facti[10] – that is to say, the old Lady of Yorkshire[a] has fall'n tooth & nail upon Dr Rutherforth, set on too by Mr Warburton, who leads her to the Ring, & in a short Speech, after the old Homerical Mode of Taunt & Defiance, commits Her to the Engagement.[11] The Short of the story is, that the old Lady writes with a Spirit below her Years tho' 'tis observ'd of Her, that She has reason in her rage & upon the whole seems to have pretty well expos'd that very foolish Book, call'd an Essay upon Virtue.

This is all the literary News I know of worth sending. In return You must tell me, what grove has shelter'd You & the Muse, & what new Designs She has put You upon in your Retirement. Genial Suns & blue Skies are strong Incitements; above all in this fav'rite month, wch no <Poet> Son of the Muses ever let pass without some poetical tribute to it.

Sr Edwd Littleton, (who is just come in from his Journey out of Staffordshire & sends Services & thanks for Your Poem)[12] prevents my saying anything more at

9 The *Postscript* was occasioned by John Chapman's archidiaconal charge, *Popery the Bane of true Letters*, published in August 1746. (*Lond. Mag.*) Chapman believed that the Protestant Church was severely threatened by Roman Catholicism. His belief was founded on his discovery of several plots against the "Cause", the most recent being an attempt to undermine the Protestant faith by spreading the "admir'd Spirit of Incredulity and Free-thinking". (*Popery*, p. 3.) However, the work he singles out as the most dangerous instrument of this "most desperate plot" turns out to be (in Middleton's words) no more than "the stale and senseless whim of a single old Jesuit, formed by no concert or confederacy with any set of men in the world, and published about forty years ago without any other effect whatsoever, than of being laughed at ever since by all men of sense". (*Postscript*, p. 61.) The *Introductory Discourse* and *Postscript* were published as one work with continuous pagination.

10 Virgil, *Aeneid*, i. 364.

11 This attack was made on Thomas Rutherforth's *Essay on the Nature and Obligations of Virtue*, 1744. The critic was Catharine Cockburn (1679–1749), a well known dramatist and philosophical writer. Cockburn (who lived in Northumberland not Yorkshire) had initiated a correspondence with Warburton in 1744 or 1745. Subsequently she sent him the manuscript of her book on Rutherforth's *Essay*, knowing that he had already written against Rutherforth himself, in the second part of his *Remarks on Several Occasional Reflections*, published in 1745. Warburton approved of the book and wrote a preface to it. In it, he reiterates his own idea of moral obligation, explained in the *Divine Legation*; summarises and dismisses Rutherforth's theory of practical morality; and gives his support to Cockburn's confutation. ('Preface' to *Remarks upon the Principles and Reasonings of Dr. Rutherforth's Essay on the Nature and Obligations of Virtue: In Vindication of the contrary Principles and Reasonings, inforced in the Writings of the late Dr. Samuel Clarke. Published by* Mr. *Warburton with a Preface*, 1747; RH, *Discourse*, p. 42.)

12 Edward Littleton had first met Mason in 1745 or 1746, but did not then have the opportunity to improve his acquaintance with him. In the autumn of 1746 he apparently expressed a wish of knowing Mason better in a letter to John Mainwaring. Mainwaring replied with the advice that Littleton should try "to get [Mason] to [his] Room sometimes without any other Visiters, when Ceremony will be banish'd, and Freedoms naturally commence. For this Purpose", he concludes, "You are already enough acquainted with him." (Mainwaring to Littleton, 20 October 1746, Littleton Correspondence, Staffs. RO, D1413/2.) The two men did become better acquainted, but did not develop a lasting friendship. (See *post* To Littleton, 20 February 1748.)

a Note by RHn: "Mrs. Catharine Cockburn".

present, but that I am always, with an entire respect, Dear Sir, Your most Faithfull Friend & Servt

R. Hurd.

Camb. 7. May. 1747.

Endorsed by William Mason: "Answerd May 26".
Endorsed by Richard Hurd, nephew: "May 7th 1747/about Mr. Mason's Musaeus, &c".

83 To WILLIAM MASON 30 MAY 1747

Text: MS HC; printed, *H-M Corr*, 4.
Addressed: [. . .] Yorkshire/By Caxton.
Postmarked: postmark missing.

Dear Sir

I expect with great pleasure your Epistle on Fashion,[1] wch will be sure to find me in College & am glad to hear, yt, notwithstanding the Muse has been bed-rid, She has been able to produce thus much. Tho' You Poets are perhaps not the more lazy, for appearing to be so. Your trade may go on, seu *lectulus* aut vos porticus excepit.[2]

You are very kind in not forgetting Pope's Head,[3] which I want very much to preside over the little band of worthies, which I am collecting for the ornament of my Study.

If You would but, at some leisure time, contrive to give me a Sketch of your own from Hayman's picture,[4] it would complete the Obligation.

This Afternoon I have seen a small Poem of Mr Nevile's (for the fame of Musaeus has kindled up a flame which I thought expiring) call'd an Essay in the Art of writing Tragedy.[5] The Essay-way, You know, has been worn quite thread-bare.[6] But there are some fine passages in it, &, with a little Alteration, would be worth your seeing.

1 'The Birth of Fashion: An Epistolary Tale. Written in the Year 1746, and Sent to a Lady with Hollar's Habits of English Women, Published in the Former Century 1650'. (*The Works of William Mason*, M.A. *Precentor of York, and Rector of Aston. In Four Volumes*, 1811, i. 149.)

2 Horace, *Satires*, I. iv. 133–4. (cum lectulus aut me)

3 This sketch of Pope's head now hangs at Hartlebury Castle. It is inscribed underneath:

Mr. Pope.

E Descriptione J. Richardson. W. Mason Delineavit.

William Gilpin in an account of 'Masters of Portrait' remarks that Richardson "hath left us several heads, which he etched for Mr. Pope, and others of his friends. They are slight; but shew the spirit of a master. Mr. Pope's profile is the best." (*An Essay upon Prints, containing Remarks upon the Principles of picturesque Beauty, the Different Kinds of Prints*, 1768, p. 134.)

4 RH alludes to the vignette on the title-page of Mason's *Musaeus*. This represents Chaucer, Spenser and Milton with Pope, after a design by Francis Hayman. Mason sent him Hayman's original preparatory drawing, now at HC. (*A Candidate for Praise. William Mason 1725–97, Precentor of York*, Comp. Bernard Barr and John Ingamells, York 1973, p. 7.)

5 The poem by Thomas Nevile was never published.

6 D.F. Foxon lists thirty two poems entitled *An Essay* . . . published between 1701 and 1750, nineteen of which were published in the 1730s and 1740s. This sudden revival of interest in the verse essay was obviously accelerated if not initiated by Pope's use of the form: *An essay on man I* was the first of the poetical essays to be published in the 1730s, coming out in February 1733. (D.F. Foxon, *English Verse 1701–1750. A Catalogue*, Cambridge, 1975.) See also the Advertisement to Joseph Warton's *Odes on Various Subjects*, 1746, where Warton speaks of the public being "so much accustom'd of late to didactic Poetry alone, and Essays on moral Subjects".

As You promise to be a better Correspondent for the future,[7] & here are no Compliments, I shall depend on the favour of a Letter very soon.

The Swaggerer[8] & Sr Edward send Services: & I am, Dear Sir, Your most Affectionate Friend & Hble.[a] Servt.

R. Hurd.

Camb. 30. May. 1747.

Endorsed by William Mason: "Ans July 12".
Endorsed by Richard Hurd, nephew: "May 30th 1747 about Pope's Head & Mr. Mason's, &c.".

84 To WILLIAM MASON JULY 1747

Text: MS HC; printed, *H-M Corr*, 6.
Addressed: To/Mr Mason at the Revd. Mr/Mason's in/Hull/ Yorkshire./By Caxton.
Postmarked: CAMBRIDGE

Dear Sir

I am much oblig'd by your favour of Pope's head, which I receiv'd safe & shall value, as it deserves, extremely.

Your letter, instead of bringing the long-expected poem on Dress, puts me off with an Excuse, which has so much ceremony in it, that, for friendship's sake, I could wish You had not made it. You bid me neither "scold nor repeat the Request", which, it must be own'd, are two very reasonable Injunctions, considering that You ought certainly to expect both. However I shall so far conform to them, as to leave it to your own conscience, whether "a want of finishing" should be a pretence for denying me so much pleasure, as ev'rything of Your's gives me.

Your new Canon of Criticism is very ingenious, &, to say the truth, shrewdly urg'd against the Authenticity of the Ode on Eaton.[1] Yet 'tis confidently giv'n out here to be Mr Grey's; & perhaps it may save the honour of your new-invented rule, if we suppose it printed, with the consent indeed of Mr G., but not under his direction. And this, it seems, was the case; for it was the force of friendly importunity, we are told, that drew it from him. And, to shew how little He interested Himself in it's fame, He ev'n suffer'd it to pass with ill-plac'd Capitals & wooden Ornaments.[2]

[7] Mason's failings as a correspondent no doubt arose from his indolence, which was remarked upon disapprovingly by Thomas Gray in a letter to Thomas Wharton, 8 August 1749. (Gray, *Correspondence*, Letter 150.)

[8] Probably Edward Macro.

[a] MS: "Hbe".

[1] Thomas Gray's *An Ode on a Distant Prospect of Eton College* had been published anonymously on 30 May. It was his first publication in English; the earlier printed poems are in Latin. Mason's "Canon of Criticism" has not survived. The two poets were first introduced to each other sometime in 1747. (Gray, *Correspondence*, Letter 144, n. 33.)

[2] It has generally been assumed that Horace Walpole arranged the publication of the *Eton Ode* as he did afterwards for other poems of Gray's. Although he had no hand in its production, Gray seems to have been highly pleased with the appearance of the *Ode* when it was published,

I remember to have just seen it at the Coffee-House, &, if I might presume to criticise so delicate an Author, should pronounce it to be a common thought, indifferently executed.[3]

This is dogmatically said, but I am just come from the reading of the new Edition of Shakespeare by Mr Warburton,[4] a Gentleman, You know, in whose company one does not usually pick up much civility. But what He wants in compliment, He makes up in Sense & Ingenuity, two things, which, as they are very rare, cannot fail of pleasing, in a Critic. My main quarrel agst Him is for his Abuse of our friend Dr Grey, whom, tho' his notes on Hudibras may deserve all, that can be said of them, yet, for his own good nature, one would wish not to see so publicly insulted.[5]

Sir Edward[a] & I stay here much longer, than we intended, wch. is chiefly owing to the noise & fury of Elections.[6] It is, I think, time enough for a young Gentleman to be

describing himself in a letter to Walpole as "much delighted". (Gray, *Correspondence*, Letter 139.) In fact, though the capitals are placed slightly awkwardly and the ornaments not very finely engraved, the overall impression is still very attractive.

3 In his biography of Gray, R.W. Ketton-Cremer records that his *Eton Ode* "aroused little interest anywhere". (*Thomas Gray. A Biography*, Cambridge, 1955, pp. 79–80.)

4 *The Works of Shakespeare in Eight Volumes* edited by Pope and Warburton had been advertised for sale in May 1747. (*Gent. Mag.*) A copy was bought for the library at Emmanuel (RH was Librarian) and RH's own set is preserved in the library at Hartlebury Castle. (*Steward's Accounts Book*, STE. 1. 5.) The edition met with a generally hostile reception (see Warburton's letter to RH, *Prelate*, p. 10), although Johnson in his assessment of Warburton's commentary had praise for the work as well as criticism: "His notes", he wrote, "exhibit sometimes perverse interpretations, and sometimes improbable conjectures; he at one time gives the authour more profundity of meaning, than the sentence admits, and at another discovers absurdities, where the sense is plain to every other reader. But his emendations are likewise often happy and just; and his interpretation of obscure passages learned and sagacious." ('Preface' to *The Plays of Shakespeare*, ed. Johnson, 1765, i. liii.)

5 Zachary Grey, vicar of St Peter's and St Giles' in Cambridge, had published an edition of Samuel Butler's *Hudibras* in 1744, to which Warburton had contributed notes. He had followed this, however, with a sharp attack on Warburton published in 1746, and called *A Word or Two of Advice to William Warburton; A Dealer in Many Words*. In this pamphlet he tells "*Friend W——n*," that his "Remarks upon that profane *Deer-stealer, William Shakespear* [those contributed to Theobald's edition of his *Works*], afford thee no more Credit, than those upon *Pope's Essay*, nay rather take from thee that 'little Reputation which the *Divine Legation* had accidentally bestow'd upon thee' ". (p. 2.) Warburton's reply to this was confined to a sharp reference to Grey's commentary on *Hudibras* as an "execrable . . . heap of nonsense". (*Works of Shakespeare*, i. xxvii.)

6 The July elections of 1747 were held to elect a new Parliament following the dissolution of the previous administration on 18 June. In Staffordshire party feeling ran high and for the first time in a hundred years there was a contest at the polls for the county seats. The division of loyalties

a Note by RHn: "Littleton".

initiated in the Mysteries of Party, which serves to no other end, that I know of, than to corrupt the heart & byass the Understanding. This conduct will, I know, be censur'd by some; but, for my own part, I had rather see any one, I am concern'd with, a candid, rational man, than the staunchest Wig, or honestest Tory in England.

Sr Ed:'s compliments attend You; & I am, Dear Sir, Your most Oblig'd, & Faithfull, Hble Servt

R. Hurd.

Mr Powell is not in College.

Endorsed by Richard Hurd, nephew: "1747 about Mr. Warburton's Shakespeare, &c.".

85 To Sir EDWARD LITTLETON — 17 OCTOBER 1747

Text: MS STAFFS RO D1413/1; unpublished.
Addressed: To/Sir Edward Littleton Bart./at Pipe-Ridware near/ Lichfield./Turn at Coleshill./With Speed.
Postmarked: postmark missing.

Dear Sir Edward,

If You receive this in time, to give me the opportunity of hearing from You by Friday next, I beg the favour of You to inclose three or four of Mr Salmon's Receipts,[1]

had been caused by a change in the politics of the Gower family, previously strong supporters of the "Country Interest" but now allied to the whigs and supporting the Government. Few of the tory gentry followed this move, but the Gower interest in the county was so strong that they were unable to prevent the family's candidate (Lord Gower's brother) from obtaining his seat. Edward Littleton was in a difficult position at the election. As was customary, his tenants looked to him to decide which candidates to vote for; but Littleton had strong connections both with Lord Gower (previously his commanding officer) and with some of the leading tory gentry, three of whom (Samuel Hill, Walter Gough and John Biddulph) had acted as his guardians. Faced with the probability of offending one side or the other, Littleton decided to remain uninvolved and allow his tenants to vote as they wished, without his guidance. Subsequently he followed Gower into the whig camp. RH's suggestion that Sir Edward had as yet no knowledge of party is exaggerated. Although Littleton chose to remain neutral, his correspondence indicates that he made this choice only after considerable thought and discussion of the situation; it was not the result of ignorance or lack of interest. (Littleton Correspondence (1747), Staffs. RO, D1413/2; Josiah C. Wedgwood, 'Staffordshire Parliamentary History (1715 to 1832)', *Collections for a History of Staffordshire*, ed. The William Salt Archaeological Society, 1922.)

1 Thomas Salmon (1679–1767) was an historical and geographical writer. He had been an undergraduate at Christ's College and lived for some time afterwards at Cambridge. (Cole Collections LXXIX, MS BL, Add. 5880, f. 198.) The receipts that RH asks for were to be offered in exchange for subscriptions to a forthcoming work by Salmon. (At this time it was the practice for authors to supply their friends with signed and numbered receipts so that they could collect subscriptions for proposed new works on their behalf; see *Lit. Anecs.*, i. 466.) The work concerned may have been his *New Geographical and Historical Grammar* published in 1749, or possibly a continuation of *The Present State of the Universities and of the Five Adjacent Counties of Cambridge, Huntington, Bedford, Buckingham and Oxford.* The volume on Oxford had been published in 1744, but the rest was never completed.

& to direct to me at Mr Cox's[2] at the Hen & Chickens in Birmingham. These I have wanted very much, upon all occasions, that have offer'd, of solliciting for Him. Tho' nothing, I believe, could have done him much Service with those, I have hitherto met with; who are strongly prejudic'd against the man, either from his party principles, or his Abuses of the University of Oxford.[3] I have yet some prospect at Birmingham & shall therefore, as I said, be glad to receive some receipts there on friday next.

Your Expedition to Chester has, I hear, been not unsuccessful. Mr Fenton,[4] who was here the other day, tells me of some pictures, which You brought back with You,[5] & which I could have been glad of seeing, before my return to Cambridge, if Pipe-Ridware had not lain too much out of the way. I am sorry, there are no Letters.[6]

Busts I hear'd nothing of.[7] But You will give me a more particular account of these things in your letter.

I am, with services to Mrs Littleton & your Brother,[8] Dear Sir, Your most Faithfull, Humble Servt

R. Hurd.

Hatton: 17. Oct. 1747.

86 To Sir EDWARD LITTLETON 15 FEBRUARY 1748

Text: MS STAFFS RO D1413/1; unpublished.
Addressed: cover missing.

Dear Sir

You are certainly right in not omitting any opportunities of attending sales of

[2] Possibly Bayley Cox recorded as a "victualler" at 9 New Street in the Birmingham Directory of 1777. (*Birmingham 120 Years Ago*, ed. Charles E. Scarse, Birmingham, 1896.)

[3] There is no record of the nature of Salmon's party principles. His criticisms of Oxford University appeared in *The Present State of the Universities*, vol. 1. 1744, and seem neither intemperate nor unfairly stated. For example, he remarks on the "Foible" that some members of the University are subject to, of believing that Oxford is "a perfect Paradise" and being offended if all men do not think as they do. But, he adds, "it must be admitted, that *Oxford* is a very desirable Place". (p. 410.) Similarly he observes that there are some "indolent and luxurious Members" of the University; but not before he has praised the "Generality" who are "Men of exemplary Virtue" and "do Honour to their Country, as well as to the University". (p. 412.)

[4] Richard Fenton had been a contemporary of RH's at Emmanuel and was also of a Staffordshire family.

[5] No more is known of these pictures.

[6] It has not been discovered to what this refers. RH had not brought letters from Cambridge, since both men had left college on the same day (15 September).

[7] Littleton became extremely interested in the collection of busts, many of which he later commissioned from Michael Rysbrack. (See *post* To Littleton, 15 March 1755, n. 1.) It is possible that he already had plans to order a bust from the sculptor, as there is evidence that Rysbrack worked for him in the early 1750s (Marjorie Webb, *Michael Rysbrack Sculptor*, 1954, p. 192); however, it is perhaps more likely that he had planned to buy a bust while he was at Chester.

[8] Fisher Littleton (1728–1800), Sir Edward's younger brother, had been admitted to Emmanuel on 30 March 1747. RH had been appointed as his tutor. (*Commons Accounts Book*, STE. 15. 9.)

pictures.[1] Sebastian Bourdon is, if I mistake not, a good name.[2] For Cheron, I do not remember to have hear'd of him.[3] Mr Mason did not do well to desert you at such a juncture. But experience is the best master, as well in acquiring a knowledge of the Arts, as of the World. And if it be true, that that is best, which comes at some expence, the purchase ev'n of some indifferent pieces, on setting out, may in the end be no loss to you.

Mr Macro, who is with me, is much concern'd not to find You in College. He has seen Mr Cowgill's bacchanal;[4] & thinks the colouring & keeping[5] good, but has no opinion of the drawing or expression. On the whole, he scarce believes it deserving a place in a very good collection, & says, that five or six guineas is the full worth of it.[6]

You don't tell me, what pass'd with Mr Lyttelton & Mr Villiers;[7] & whether the

1 The art market in the mid eighteenth century was flourishing. In 1744 Sotheby's had been founded (Christie's was to be founded in 1766) and there were many other auctioneers operating in London. Sales were held at least once a month (perhaps less frequently in the summer) and usually lasted two or three days. (Fritz Lugt, *Repertoire des Catalogues de Ventes Publiques, Interessant L'art ou La Curiosité, Première Periode vers 1600–1825*, The Hague, 1938.)

2 Sebastian Bourdon is one of the artists described in an account of modern painters added to Du Fresnoy's *De Arte Graphica* which RH was proposing to read in November 1743 (see *ante* To Macro, 26 November 1743). Bourdon was born in France in 1619, but went to study painting in Rome, where he "acquir'd so much Reputation by his *Works*, both in *History* and *Landscape*, that upon his Return to *France*, he had the *Honour* of being the *first* who was made *Rector* of the *Royal Academy of Painting and Sculpture*, at *Paris*". He died in 1673. (Richard Graham, 'A Short Account of the Most Eminent Painters, Both Ancient and Modern, Continued down to the Present Times, According to the Order of their Succession', in Du Fresnoy, *The Art of Painting*, Second Edition, 1716, pp. 386–7.)

3 Louis Cheron (1655–1725) was born in France and studied in Italy. In 1695 he came to England where he remained until his death. He produced paintings and engravings in the style of Raphael and was much esteemed for his accuracy of drawing. (*Bryan's Dictionary of Painters and Engravers*, 1816, new edn. ed. George C. Williamson, 1903–5.)

4 James Cowgill was a Fellow at Emmanuel, elected in 1739. Nothing has been discovered of his "bacchanal".

5 "This word implies the different degrees of strength and faintness, which objects receive from nearness and distance. A nice observance of the gradual fading of light and shade contributes greatly towards the production of a *whole*. Without it, the distant parts, instead of being connected with the objects at hand, appear like foreign objects, wildly introduced, and unconnected." (Gilpin, *An Essay upon Prints*, p. 17.)

6 This was a low price for a painting. (Louise Lippincott, *Selling Art in Georgian London. The Rise of Arthur Pond*, Yale University Press, New Haven, 1983, pp. 63–4.)

7 George Lyttelton (1709–73) was a distant relation of Sir Edward, living at Hagley in Worcestershire. He was an active politician and had been the favourite and secretary of the Prince of Wales until 1747 when he accepted an appointment as a Lord of the Treasury in the Broad Bottom administration and thus forfeited the Prince's favour. He belonged to the small but powerful group of whig M.P.s led by Cobham and Pitt. Lyttelton was also a successful author and wrote a variety of literary, historical and political works. He is now best remembered for his *Dialogues of the Dead* published in 1760.

Thomas Villiers (1709–86) was the second son of William, Earl of Jersey. He had returned permanently to England in 1747 after ten years of diplomatic employment abroad, and was immediately elected M.P. for Tamworth (1747). He rose steadily in the following years and was created Earl of Clarendon in 1776. Littleton knew Villiers quite well in the late 1740s and early 1750s. (Wedgwood, 'Staffordshire Parliamentary History (1715 to 1832)', pp. 263–4; Littleton Correspondence, Staffs. RO, D1413/2.) The specific connection between George Lyttelton and Villiers, and the business to which RH refers have not been clarified.

Lord of the Treasury does not mean to resign with the Secretary of State & so leave the Atlas of the government to be supported by the two great Dukes.[8] But perhaps you are as little solicitous about these matters, as I am. What piques my curiosity more is to know, if you have been with Rysbrack a[bout] the Stone for Mr B.s inscription.[9] I think, we agreed, that a plain, neat marble, of an elegant form, & with little or no ornament, was the fittest for the purpose. He will perhaps direct you to a good hand for the cutting: for much, I think, will depend upon that.

I am glad to find your levee is so *largely* attended. I lost much of that importance, which the attendance of so considerable a figure must have giv'n one, by his being out of town, the greatest part of the time, I was there. Pray signify my services to him on your next attack at Nando's.[10]

I scarce believe, you can stay, with comfort, a fortnight longer at George's:[11] & therefore, notwithstanding what you tell me, am in expectation of seeing you somewhat sooner. But, be that as it will, you must not neglect to give me a further account of the other sale, you speak of, & of such other occurrencies, as you think worth committing to paper.

Your Brother is well. Mr Macro sends services & I am always, Dearest Sir, Your most faithful & affect: friend & Servt

R. Hurd.

Camb. 15. Feb. 1747–8.

8 The Secretary of State, Lord Chesterfield, had resigned from office on 6 February. His resignation had been precipitated by the Duke of Newcastle (one of the "two great Dukes"; the other was the Duke of Cumberland) who was opposed to Chesterfield's policy of bringing the war with France to an end. Both Cumberland and Newcastle believed that England could improve her position by continuing the war, whilst Chesterfield was convinced that the financial circumstances of the country rendered peace indispensable. The Lord of the Treasury whom RH mentions was probably George Lyttelton, though he could be alluding to Henry Pelham, first Lord of the Treasury and Prime Minister. Pelham supported Chesterfield very strongly, but there is no indication that he thought of resigning. (William Coxe, *Memoirs of the Administration of Henry Pelham*, 1829, i. 388–92.) The "Atlas" of the Government must refer to the Government itself; RH has unconsciously transferred the image of the supporter to that which is supported.

9 RH and Littleton wished to erect an engraved stone to the memory of their former schoolmaster, William Budworth, who had died in September 1745. Michael Rysbrack (1694–1770), whom they hoped to consult about this, was the most popular sculptor then working in London. Horace Walpole remarks on his "singular industry" and on his "deep knowledge of his art". He was, he writes, "the best sculptor that has appeared in these islands since Le Soeur". (Walpole, *Anecdotes of Painting in England*, 1762–71, vol. iv, 2nd edn 1782, pp. 205–12.) Littleton later commissioned a great deal of work from him (see post To Littleton, 15 March 1755, n. 1).

10 Nando's was a coffee-house in Fleet Street which shared some of the popularity of George's (see n. 11) amongst writers and wits of the day. RH's allusion to a "levee" is probably to a meeting of friends at Nando's. The "considerable" figure has not been identified.

11 George's stood on the south side of the Strand between the entrance to Devereux Court and Essex Street. It was a meeting place for authors and other well-known figures. Shenstone often went there in 1735, finding it to be "economical", and in 1742 Arthur Murphy described it as the regular haunt of the town wits. (Bryant Lillywhite, *London Coffee Houses*, 1963.)

87 To Sir EDWARD LITTLETON 20 FEBRUARY 1748

Text: MS STAFFS RO D1413/1; unpublished
Addressed: To/Sir Edward Littleton Bart./to be left at George's Coffee-house/near Temple-Bar./London.
Postmarked: CAMBRIDGE 2[2]

Dear Sir

I am much pleas'd with your account of A. Philips;[1] which contains some curious particulars, &, in the main, answers to the Idea, I had conceiv'd of him. His vanity in talking of the wits of his time is perfectly natural;[2] &, especially, his imputing the excesses of his youth to Mr Addison is a stroke of that nature, as paints the manners at once & lays open a character entirely.[3] Your opinion of his literary merit seems just. His imagination was too feeble for a Poet, & his judgment too weak & undiscerning to qualify him for the office of a Critic.[4] Yet he had enough of each to set him above the common run of pretenders to tast & letters. This, join'd to an obsequious adulation of some of the first names of those days & (what will always gain the countenance of the great & sometimes ev'n of the wise) an active party-zeal,[5] gave him that figure & reputation in the eye of some very valuable persons & of the public, which, I agree with you, he had better not endanger by any fresh attempt at these years.

The good opinion, You express of Mr Villiers is, I doubt not, what he deserves. If it be true, that he is going to Aix, in the room of Lord Sandwich, his abilities must be unquestion'd.[6] His behaviour was that of a Gentleman & of one inclin'd to shew you a personal regard; & merits that return of candour, which you so handsomely profess in your judgment of him.

I suppose you will judge it proper to make Mr Lyttelton a second visit, as you was so unsuccessful in your first.

I now come to a part of your letter, which gives me the greatest surprize & concern,

1 Ambrose Philips (1674–1749). Edward Littleton may have met Philips at one of the London coffee-houses. He had been employed for some years in Ireland, but returned to England in 1748.

2 Philips had been part of a group of friends led by Addison, who used to meet at Button's between about 1710 and 1719, the year of Addison's death. The coffee-house became well known as a resort of town wits.

3 RH's objection to Philips' claim seems well-founded. Despite Pope's Atticus portrait, Addison's character is invariably given as pleasant and temperate: see, for example, the description of him in Joseph Spence's *Observations, Anecdotes, and Characters of Books and Men*, 1820, ed. James M. Osborn, Oxford, 1966.

4 This opinion of Philips' literary abilities coincides with Johnson's judgment. His "*Letter from Denmark*" (i.e. the 'Epistle to the Earl of Dorset'), he says, "may be justly praised"; his *Pastorals* (1709) "cannot surely be despicable"; and, in his other poems "he cannot be denied the praise of lines sometimes elegant; but", concludes Johnson, "he has seldom much force, or much comprehension". (Johnson, *Prefaces*, viii. 21.)

5 Philips was known to be "a zealous Whig". Johnson records though, that on the succession of George I, when "every Whig expected to be happy, Philips seems to have obtained too little notice; he caught few drops of the golden shower, though he did not omit what flattery could perform". (*Prefaces*, viii. 15.)

6 During 1748 the War of Austrian Succession was brought to an end and a treaty drawn up at Aix-la-Chapelle. Villiers had had considerable experience as a foreign envoy, but he was not chosen as an English delegate to the Congress. According to the *Cambridge Journal*, 12 November 1748, Lord Sandwich and Sir Thomas Robinson were the "Ministers Plenipotentiary" sent over from England.

I mean that which relates to Mr Mason,[7] & the rather, as I had conceiv'd it impossible for him to have behav'd in the manner, you mention. As the matter appears from your account, the suspicion is very strong against him. And yet the knowledge I have of his natural temper & good sense, &, as I thought, of his regard for you, makes it wholly unaccountable, that he should be guilty of so much disrespect tow'rds you. But, be it as it will, you do very prudently to treat him, for the present at least, with your usual civility. For this will not only secure you from the charge of being captious & hasty in your resentment, but, what is more, will give you the opportunity of seeing further into the state of the case, & of informing yourself more perfectly about it. This suspense is no more than is due to yourself, to truth, & the friendship, which hath been betwixt you. But should the affair, in the end, prove, as you suspect, & no tolerable alleviations appear in his favour, you will be right in resenting it, as it deserves, & he will justly forfeit all further notice & regard from you. This is all I can say at present on a subject of such delicacy. You will inform me, if any further light breaks in upon it. I would be the last to interpret the ill usage of a friend, & especially of one, who promis'd to make so valuable a one, as Mr Mason; but the first, when 'tis fully confirm'd, to advise & encourage a proper resentment of it. For of all the good qualities, which I have the pleasure to observe, or which I am sollicitous to inspire & cultivate, in you, there is none I esteem more, than that becoming sensibility to ill treatmt., which you discover on all proper occasions. This, temper'd with candour, is the true spirit of a man & a gentleman, & is the natural result of conscious worth & virtue. Go on in the practice of this & ev'ry other virtue, &, by that means, continue always to be, as you are, most dear to, Sir, Your most Faithful & Affectionate Friend & Servt.

R. Hurd.

Camb. 20. Feb. 1747–8.

P.S.

Mr Macro, Mess. Neviles,[8] & your brother send compliments.

88 To Sir EDWARD LITTLETON 20 APRIL 1748

Text: MS STAFFS RO EX D260/M/T/5/32;[1] unpublished.
Addressed: cover missing.

Dear Sir

That the estate is to be sold, & that no one has been before you in applying for it, are two very favorable circumstances.[2] As to Ld. Gower's having the refusal of it, this,

7 Edward Littleton had written to RH complaining of ill-treatment by Mason. RH is very circumspect in mentioning any details, but it emerges in subsequent correspondence (see *post* To Littleton, 23 February 1749, 2 March 1749, and 21 March 1749) that Sir Edward thought an arrangement had been made for him and Mason to meet. Mason, however, did not turn up, and Littleton seems to have believed that he had made another appointment for the same time and either forgot or neglected to tell Sir Edward of the confusion.

8 John and Thomas.

1 This letter is not included in the main collection of Littleton-Hurd correspondence at Staffordshire Record Office. It forms part of a bundle of papers relating to the sale of an estate owned by Lord Brooke (see n. 2).

2 Edward Littleton was hoping to secure an estate put up for sale by Francis Greville, first Earl

you must see, is but natural, witht. supposing any trick, or sollicitation.[3] But there is no reason to believe, that his lordship will interfere in your making a purchase, which will be so particularly convenient to you. So that I look upon the affair as good as concluded.

You are very obliging to have me in mind abt the prints.[4] I must beg the farther favor of you to send your servt to Elliot[5] some day, to enquire after the watch. His hour, you know, is one o'clock.

Yesterday came another letter from Mr James, which your Brother open'd, not knowing certainly where to direct to you, & yet thinking it necessary to see, if it contain'd anything material. There is, I think, nothing at all of this kind in it, except perhaps the last curious hint about friend Hubert.[6] However, having this oportunity, I send it by Mr. Mainwaring & am, Dear Sir, Your faithful, humble Servt

R. Hurd.

Camb. 20. Ap. 1748.

Your brother is well & sends compliments.

Endorsed by Sir Edward Littleton: "Mr. Hurd 20: April: 1748:".

89 To Sir EDWARD LITTLETON 7 OCTOBER 1748

Text: MS STAFFS RO D1413/1; unpublished.
Addressed: To/Sir Edward Littleton Bart/at Pipe-Ridware near/ Lichfield/Staffordshire/By London.
Postmarked: 8 OC

Dearest Sir

I know not in what terms to express the sense I have of your most obliging letter; which contains the fullest proof of your personal attachment to me, & is, at the same time, the truest picture of a generous heart.[1] It shews, that you know how to give a favour it's full weight & grace; when, to an act of the greatest friendship in itself, you have added the most polite & friendly manner in conferring it.

Brooke, and adjoining his own land in the manor of Penkridge. See also *post* To Littleton, 15 November 1748, n. 9. Further papers relative to the sale have been collected at Staffordshire Record Office; see n. 1.

3 The estate had probably been offered to Gower because he was the greatest landowner in Staffordshire: but Littleton later recorded that he and Brooke had already come to an agreement over the sale of the estate in March 1748 (see *post* To Littleton, 15 November 1748, n. 9). Brooke's negotiations with Gower were therefore most suspicious.

4 RH had an interest in portrait engravings and relied on Littleton to buy prints for him at London sales.

5 Unidentified.

6 Mr James and Hubert have not been identified.

1 RH had asked Sir Edward if he would provide a loan to allow his youngest brother, Thomas, to open a business in Birmingham. Littleton had agreed. The business prospered and in the 1777 *Birmingham Directory* there are two entries under Hurd:

"Hurd and Sons, Merchants, 73, High Street
Hurd, Thomas, Mercer and Draper, ditto".

(*Birmingham 120 Years Ago*, ed. Scarse.)

For my part, I shall have less cause for the future to avoid incurring obligations to one, who has the art of rend'ring them so agreable: &, as an earnest of it, I very willingly accept your kind offer of lending the proposed sum witht int:, which, at setting out in business, must needs be a convenience, for which my brother <. . .> will be exceedingly indebted to you.

I shall have occasion to write again next week, when I will send your account for the last quarter, & shall then reply to the other particulars in your letter. At present I have only time to acknowledge, what I could not think of deferring a single moment, this fresh instance of your singular regard for me, wch makes me more than ever, with the truest gratitude & affection, Dear Sir, Your most oblig'd & most faithfull humble servt

R. Hurd.

Camb: 7. Oct. 1748.

Endorsed by Sir Edward Littleton: "Mr. Hurd [. . .] Octor. 1748:".

90 To Sir EDWARD LITTLETON 14 OCTOBER 1748

Text: MS STAFFS RO D1413/1; unpublished.
Addressed: cover missing.

Camb. 14. Oct. 1748.

Dear Sir

My two last letters were wrote in so much haste,[1] that I could take no notice of your favour of Oct. 1st, which accompany'd the packets.[2] I must now return my thanks for that directed to me, which is somewhat curious in shewing how great men condescend to treat an insignificant correspondent. Your presents to Dr Macro & Dr Grey[3] shall be deliver'd with care, & will, I doubt not, be very acceptable.

At my return to college I found a letter from the last of these gentlemen, full of encomiums on your polite letter of thanks, dated at Huntington, & desiring to know, where he might find you, in order to acknowledge it. He talk'd too of more heads,[4] that he had look'd out for you, so that you may expect a packet from him very soon; especially as I shall write this post to inform him of your late favour. For the packet itself, I believe I must keep it by me till his return from Bedfordshire.

You desir'd me to send the 20th. vol. of the Universal history, which is not yet publish'd.[5]

1 For one of these, see preceding letter. The other has been lost.

2 These appear to have been packets of manuscripts (RH's was clearly a collection of letters) which Littleton had obtained but did not himself want. His own manuscript collection was of the "Signatures of our Princes & famous Personages". (George Lyttelton to Sir Edward, 15 July 1750, Littleton Correspondence, Staffs. RO, D1413/2.)

3 Zachary Grey (1688–1766), the editor of *Hudibras* and Vicar of St Peter's and St Giles' in Cambridge. Grey also held a living (Houghton Conquest) in Bedfordshire where he was now staying.

4 Portrait engravings were commonly called "heads" in the eighteenth century.

5 The first edition of *An Universal History, From the Earliest Account of Time* had been published in folio between 1736 and 1744. Littleton was collecting the second, revised edition, issued in twenty volumes, octavo. It is dated 1747–8, but the last volume was not advertised for sale until

I am sorry, the accidt. of Dr Littleton's illness prevented your journey to Hagley,[6] & the rather, because I take it the family will hardly be there in the spring.

I shall now, as I promis'd, insert your acct,[7] for the last quarter. I am not absolutely sure, that I did not charge the study-rent to Michs. in the bill, I deliver'd to you on leaving college; if so, you must deduct it.

	Midsr. Qr.		
Steward . . .	7.	19.	9
Study-rent . .	2.	12.	6
	£ 10.	12.	3

Having mention'd the study-rent, I must desire you to let me know by the return of the post, if you intend to give up your chamber;[8] which I had no doubt of, & was accordingly going to carry the key to the Master, but was prevented by the uncertainty I find your brother in abt. this matter. It will be proper not to defer your answer to this, because you will otherwise be charg'd with the rent of it till Xstmas.[9]

I am extremely glad to hear by Mr Littleton, that you intend going to town so early this winter. This looks, as if you design'd making a long stay there. We have pitch'd upon St. James' square or somewhere thereabouts for your lodgings,[10] & are sure you are determin'd to throw yourself into a deal of the best company. I have this the more at heart, because I think it is the critical season with you; & because I find some sanguin enough to persuade themselves, you will not make use of it. Tho' this I know is said upon false grounds, being principally conjectur'd from your declining the acquaintance & familiarity of a certain set of men last winter at London. You will from hence make a pretty good guess at my author.[11]

There are others of a different turn, whom I am confident you will not avoid. If I mention Mr Villars, it is to tell you, that he spoke of you with the greatest respect, when I saw him the other day at Ld Jersey's. My Lord too, with whom we spent an entire day at his house in Oxfords., enquir'd of you in the handsomest terms, and said it wd. have given him <. . .> sincere pleasure to have seen you at Middleton.[12]

March 1749. (*Gent. Mag.*) These two sets of the *Universal History* deal with the ancient world. A modern *Universal History* was later published in folio between 1750 and 1765, and in octavo between 1759 and 1766.

6 Dr Charles Lyttelton (later Bishop of Carlisle) was a younger brother of George Lyttelton. Hagley in Worcestershire was their family home. It was famous for its beauty and is described in Thomson's 'Spring'. (*The Seasons*, 1744, ll. 900–58.)

7 Littleton's bill for the Midsummer Quarter covers the long vacation. The tuition fee and payment for a sizar are therefore omitted.

8 Sir Edward had spent about three months of the year in Emmanuel, but his interests and business kept him for long periods in Staffordshire or London. He had not been in residence since 19 July and he finally took his name off the books on 16 November.

9 All college bills were charged by the Quarter.

10 St James' Square was one of the most fashionable areas in London. (Henry B. Wheatley, *London Past and Present. Its History, Associations, and Traditions*, 3 vols, 1891, ii. 302.)

11 Unidentified.

12 Thomas Villiers (see *ante* To Littleton, 15 February 1748, n.7) was the younger brother of William Villiers (d. 1769), third Earl of Jersey. The family seat was Middleton Park in Oxfordshire.

I must not, after this, conclude witht. informing you, that we had the pleasantest journey in the world thro' Oxfordshire & up the Thames to London.[13] We saw abundance of beautiful places & curiosities in every way, especially buildings & pictures, which I could wish you had seen with us. Scot[14] was unluckily not at home & therefore I miss'd seeing your pieces. We saw two or three of his at Ld. Radnor's at Twickenham,[15] that were excellent. Sr. Willm. Stanhope had a very modest whore with him, that did not chuse to be seen, & therefore we were prevented looking into Mr Pope's gardens.[16]

I shall close this rhapsody with Mr Neviles & your brother's compliments, & with desiring min[e] to Mrs & Miss Littleton.[17] There will need little ceremony to assure you, that I am always Dearest Sir, Your most entirely oblig'd & faithful humble Servt.

R. Hurd

91 To Sir EDWARD LITTLETON 27 OCTOBER 1748

Text: MS STAFFS RO D1413/1; unpublished.
Addressed: Sir Edward Littleton Bart./at Pipe-Ridware near/ Lichfield/Staffordshire/By London.
Postmarked: CAMBRIDGE 27 OC

Camb: 27. Oct. 1748.

Dear Sir

I carry'd the key of your chamber to the Master this morning, & intended to have mention'd to him your desire of having your name taken out, but was prevented by a

13 The journey up the Thames presented the traveller with many fine sights, and Samuel Ireland, later in the century, described the approach to London as revealing "such a combination of magnificence, both natural and artificial, as is perhaps not to be equalled in this kingdom!" There were, he said, castles and palaces "proudly vieing with each other in displaying the munificence of their Sovereign; – stately mansions of an ancient and splendid Nobility", and lastly, "rich and costly villas". (*Picturesque Views on the River Thames*, 1792, 2nd edn 1801–2, ii. 1–2.)

14 Samuel Scott (1710–72), an eminent painter of views and sea-pieces. Horace Walpole thought Scott second only to Van de Velde in the painting of sea-pieces; and amongst English artists, he esteemed him "not only the first painter of his own age, but one whose works will charm in every age". (*Anecdotes of Painting*, 1782, iv. 125.) He lived in Henrietta Street, Covent Garden, from 1725 until his death. In the late 1740s, Littleton commissioned a good deal of work from Scott and had been sent notice, in June 1748, of the near completion of some of his pictures. (Scott to Littleton, 28 June 1748, Artists' Letter-book, Staffs. RO, D1178/3.) The correspondence between the men indicates that Scott was prepared to make copies of other paintings (a Hobbema is specifically mentioned) as well as producing his own original work.

15 John Robartes (1686?–1757), fourth Earl of Radnor, owned a fine house adjoining Horace Walpole's Strawberry Hill.

16 Sir William Stanhope (the brother of Lord Chesterfield) had bought Pope's house on the poet's death. The garden in its original state is described by Horace Walpole as "a little bit of ground of five acres, enclosed with three lanes and seeing nothing". But, he adds, "Pope had twisted and twirled and rhymed and harmonized this, till it appeared two or three sweet little lawns opening and opening beyond one another, and the whole surrounded with thick impenetrable woods". Stanhope decided to alter the gardens, opening out the view, according to the "modern taste", cutting down the "sacred groves" and laying gravel walks; but this work may not yet have been started. (Walpole, *Correspondence*, vol. 21, To Mann, 20 June 1760; see also J. Serle, *A Plan of Mr. Pope's Garden, As It Was Left At His Death*, 1745.)

17 Frances Littleton, Sir Edward's younger sister.

message, he gave me to deliver to you on that subject. He said, that as you had been so kind to keep in your name upon his account,[1] & that he began to suspect there would be no occasion for it, he thought himself oblig'd to mention it, <to me> that it might be communicated to you, & that you might do, as you thought proper.[2] He added, that as he had no authority for saying thus much, but went only on his own suspicion, he desir'd it might not be spoken of by either of us, as coming from him, because if afterwards the affair should go forwards, it would be impossible for him after such a declaration, to act in it. This being the case, which I have related to you fully in his own words, & the master taking entirely the keeping in of your name in the light of a favour done to him, I took no notice of the commission, you had sent me; and suppose it would be the handsomer way to write to him yourself, acquainting him with the information I had giv'n you by his direction, & intimating your intention of taking out your name, if it will be of no use to keep it in any longer.

You will excuse my being so particular on this affair, which, tho' of small consequence in itself, becomes a matter of some little nicety, from the obligation wch. the master acknowledges himself to be under to you upon account of it. And I know your intention is to do every thing, that may have the appearance of respect & politeness towards him.

If you send me your resolutions any time this next month, it will be time enough, it being of no moment to take out your name till the End of the current quarter <&> two thirds of <it being> wch. are already expir'd.

I am much oblig'd by your punctuality in putting me in mind of your being prepar'd, as you call it, for my *orders*, which I will therefore give you witht. farther ceremony.[3] If you please then to send a note to *Mr Thos. Hurd at Mr. Walker's in the Square Birmingham*,[4] he will wait upon you to receive the money, at what time & place, you shall think proper to apoint.

I am setting out immediatly for Norfolk [. . .] [s]o have not time to do it now, but will take care to [. . .][5] & send it to you, as soon as I come back. [. . .] must not dismiss this affair witht. renewing my acknowledgments of the favour, you have so obligingly done me in it, and assuring you, that I am with the greatest affection & sincerity, Dear Sir, Your most oblig'd & most Obedt Servt

R. Hurd.

P.S.

You talk of leaving Staff: by the middle of next month. If it wd be convenient to take us in yr. way to town, you might spare yourself the trouble of writing to the master, & be upon the spot to take out yr. name yourself; wch. wd. be rather better, because of the usual treat of wine, wch. is giv'n to the parlour, on that occasion.[6] Your Bro: is well & sends services: Mr Nevile also desires his.

1 No explanation for Littleton's remaining on the college books has been found.

2 Sir Edward kept his name on the books till 16 November. He had not resided in college since 19 July.

3 RH alludes to the arrangements which had to be made for Sir Edward to convey his promised loan of money to Thomas Hurd.

4 Mr Walker's has not been identified.

5 The missing words were probably "execute a bond".

6 The Parlour is the Fellows' combination-room at Emmanuel and the name, like the term "High Table" (the Fellows' table in the dining hall), can be used to denote the Fellows as a body. There are no official records to confirm that it was the custom of departing members of the Parlour to treat their fellows with wine; but it was certainly the custom for the Fellows to have a

92 To Sir EDWARD LITTLETON 15 NOVEMBER 1748

Text: MS STAFFS RO D1413/1; unpublished.
Addressed: cover missing.

Camb: 15. Nov. 1748.

Dear Sir

I have two of your favours now before me. The last, as containing some matters of business, shall be answer'd first.

Immediatly on the receipt of it, I went to Trinity, but found that Dr Vernon[1] was in London, where a letter will find him, directed to him, as minister of Bloomsbury Church; or, if you chuse to stay so long, he will be down here sometime next month & then I will speak with him myself.

Your name is this day taken out.[2] You a little mistake what I mention'd about the treat of wine to the parlour, which is not in the nature of a fee, but means what you call (taking it for another thing) <taking> a decent leave of the college. This, you see, can only be done, when you are present, & therefore I gave your compliments to the fellows, & acquainted them with your design of drinking a glass of wine with them sometime this winter, either in your way to or from London.

There is no ceremony of any kind at the cutting out of your name.

You have been very good in using so much care & dispatch in paying the money to my brother. I have here inclos'd a bond, duly executed; & for the receipt, you need not give yourself the trouble to keep it, as I never mean to make any use of it.[3] Give me leave to put an end to your trouble in this affair with assuring you, that your whole conduct in it has not only laid me under the greatest obligation, but has much confirm'd that unfeign'd affection & esteem I so justly entertain for you. You have convinc'd me, how well you k[now] to enter into the spirit of the philosopher's pulchrum & decorum.

I now return, with a new page, to your other letter, where I find many things worth the noting. First I am to thank you for my A. Philips;[4] & by the way Dr Macro, whom I saw last week, charg'd me with abundant compliments for his epistolary packet: The old Gentleman laugh'd at the high value you would seem to set on the collar of Brawn & is sure it is only meant as a prelude to something better.

I really pity your situation in respect of the Salvator Rosas,[5] which Mr B.[6] ought in

"treat" of wine on the graduating of Emmanuel B.A.s and M.A.s. This was paid for by a levy made on each undergraduate concerned. (*Stewards Account Book*, STE. 1. 5.) Littleton as a nobleman was allowed to use the Parlour and was therefore clearly expected to do more than an ordinary undergraduate on his leaving the college.

1 Edward Vernon (1695–1761) was a Fellow of Trinity and rector of St George's, Bloomsbury from 1731 to 1761. He had been elected a Fellow of the Royal Society in 1723 and was known for his antiquarian interests. Littleton's business with him has not been established.

2 The *Commons Accounts Book* (STE. 15. 9.) gives the date as 16 November.

3 Neither this bond nor any other papers relating to Sir Edward's loan to Thomas Hurd appear to have survived.

4 A letter from Ambrose Philips to a Mr Mainwaring dated 13 September is preserved at Hartlebury Castle.

5 Salvator Rosa (1615–73) was one of the most collected Italian artists in the eighteenth century. He painted landscapes, seascapes and battles. The chief characteristic of his paintings is the wildness and confusion of the scene depicted.

6 Unidentified.

all reason to give up to your impatient curiosity. Tho' a little difficulty at coming at these treasures gives an edge to an Antiquarian's passion.

Our friend Mr P.'s Virgil[7] will, I doubt not, be a master-piece of polite critical learning. Perhaps a conversation between the author & patron, well hit off by your favrite Hogarth, might furnish a very agreable frontispiece. The all-submitting reverence of the critic, & the half-approving glance & nod of his very observant oracle, might afford expression enough for a pleasant picture. But I leave this to your quicker & more Hogarthian imagination, & pass on to a graver subject, which occurs to me from what you say of Mr. Lane's & Sally Fowler's marriage.[8] Your reflexions upon it are but too just. I am as much at a loss to account for Mr Fowler's consent, as I am at the young gentleman's indiscretion. If it was not a down-right love affair, it appears to me altogether mysterious.

I am glad to hear that Ld Brook's estate is to be had at last witht. the drudgery of applications.[9] If it appears, that Ld Gower intended to force you upon them, I shall think very meanly of him.

In following the thread of your letter I am come again at a little business. You refer me to your brother abt. the Study-rent; from whom I learn, that the last rect. was for 2. 12. 6 in easter Qr.; so that the study-rent for midsr. Qr. ending at Michs. last (for in all the college rents we go by the common quarters) is yet to be paid. And it was in relation to this that I put my query to you,[10] having some doubt, that I might have charg'd the whole half year together in the last bill. But this will be set right in your next account.

Mr Littleton excuses his neglect of writing abt. the paper-guards,[11] as also of not

7 This would seem to refer to Christopher Pitt, who had already published a translation of the *Aeneid* in 1740 (second edition, 1743). Pitt had however died on 15 April 1748, although there may have been plans to publish other translations made previous to his death. An edition of the works of Virgil in Latin and English including Pitt's *Aeneid* was subsequently published by Joseph Warton. *The Works of Virgil. In Latin and English . . . The Aeneid translated by . . . Christopher Pitt, the Eclogues and Georgics, with notes . . . by . . . Joseph Warton. With several observations by Dr Holdsworth, Mr Spence, and others . . .*, 4 vols., 1753.

8 No records of this marriage have been traced.

9 RH uses "application" in the obsolete sense of an "appeal" or "petition". According to a note written by Sir Edward in 1749, Lord Brooke's estate had actually been sold to him on 7 March 1748. But the agreement had been verbal and was ignored by Brooke when he discovered that Littleton was not prepared to offer him the price he had expected. Negotiations then began in earnest between Lord Gower and Brooke. When he realised this, Littleton evidently considered the possibility of lodging a petition calling for Brooke to recognise their previous agreement. No formal appeal appears to have been made, however, and by the following spring Gower had withdrawn from the negotiations. Littleton finally secured the estate on 24 May 1749, but was obliged to agree to Brooke's original estimation of its value. (MS Staffs. RO, D260/M/T/5/32.)

10 See *ante* To Littleton, 14 October 1748.

11 Guards are "strips of paper inserted in the backs of books intended for the insertion of plates, to prevent the book being uneven when filled. Also the strips upon which the plates are mounted". (E.J. Labarre, *Dictionary and Encyclopaedia of Paper and Paper-making*, Amsterdam, 1937, revised edn. 1952.) Whole books of guards in which newspapers could be inserted had also been issued since the beginning of the eighteenth century (*O.E.D.*, 'Guard' 16. 1); it may be to one of these that RH alludes.

sending the geography from the absence of Mr Salmon,[12] who is gone to read lectures this quarter in town. He has receiv'd the bill from Mr Cobb.[13]

The Neviles are well & send services; & I am always, with complimts. to Mrs. Littleton, Dear Sir, Your most faithful, humble servt

R. Hurd.

93 To JOHN POTTER 26 DECEMBER 1748

Text: MS NLW 12432E; unpublished.
Addressed: cover missing.

Camb: 26. Dec. 1748.

Dear Sir[1]

Your brother has inform'd me of his safe return to Norfolk, & also of the very handsome legacy your late Aunt has left you.[2] This last is so good a piece of news & gives me such real pleasure, that I cannot defer a moment longer my answer to your last letter, & taking the opportunity, which that gives me, of congratulating with you very heartily upon it. A good living in addition to this, which you are in constant expectation of,[3] would afford your friends the satisfaction of seeing you plac'd, I dare not say above the reach of fortune, but above the apparent danger of it.

We have been very busy here in choosing a new Chancellor upon the death of the D. of Somerset.[4] The papers must have inform'd you of our choice of the D. of Newcastle to succeed him. We have had a most complaisant answer to our compliments & notification of his election; & are told, that his Grace intends us the honour of a visit in person sometime this spring. The ceremony of Installation is expected to be very magnificent. The time is not yet fix'd, but will probably be about Easter.[5]

As one misfortune, they say, seldom comes alone, besides the D. of Somerset, we have also lost our Prof: of Divinity;[6] whose mastership of P.House will this day be fill'd up by Dr. Keene,[7] brother to the Spanish Ambassador.[8] The professorship is expected

12 This may refer to Thomas Salmon's *A New Geographical and Historical Grammar*, although the volume was not actually advertised for sale until July 1749. (*Lond. Mag.*)

13 Large payments had been made to Cobb since at least 1743. In that year he was paid a total of £9.18s. for mourning and "when [Sir Edward] came home", a sum which exceeded every other payment made on Littleton's behalf. In 1744 he received £15.19s. which again exceeded all but the payments made for Littleton's schooling at Winchester. (Mrs Littleton to Sir Edward Littleton, Private Accompt, Staffs. RO, Ex. D260/M/T/5/107.)

1 John Potter was still curate of Pylle, the living to which he had been appointed in 1744. (See *ante* To Potter, 11 October 1743, n. 4.)

2 No further information concerning this legacy has been found.

3 Potter did not obtain a better living until 1754. He was then nominated rector of Badgworth near Axbridge in Somerset.

4 Charles Seymour (b.1662) had been made Chancellor of the University in 1689. He had died on 2 December 1748. Thomas Pelham-Holles (1693–1769), Duke of Newcastle, had been elected in his place on 14 December. He had been High Steward from 1737.

5 The installation was finally arranged for 1 July. (*Annals*, iv. 268–72; see also *post* To Littleton, 8 May 1749, n. 2.)

6 John Whalley (b.1699?) had been elected Master of Peterhouse in 1733, and was created Professor of Divinity in 1742. He had died on 12 December 1748.

7 Edmund Keene (1714–81), a Fellow of Peterhouse, later Bishop of Chester (1752), and then of Ely (1771). He was instituted as Master on 29 December by the Bishop of Ely. (*Cambridge Journal*, 31 December 1748.)

8 Sir Benjamin Keene (1697–1757). He had been appointed Spanish Ambassador in 1727; was

to be giv'n to Mr Green[9] of St John's, whom perhaps you do not remember. This is all the news of the place, except that we are writing verses upon the peace[10] & amongst the rest (as you will see on the back-sid[e o]f this) your most Affect: humble Servt

R. Hurd.

Ode on the Peace.

Be still, my fears, suggest no false alarms;
The poet's rapture & the lyric fire
Are vain: enough that inclination warms;
No foreign influence need the willing muse inspire.
The willing muse, advent'rous in her flight
To thee, lov'd Peace, shall raise her untaught strain;
Her thy fair triumphs & thy arts delight,
Thy festive branch she bears & joins thy social train.
High on some wave-worn cliff she views serene
Safe on the deep the freighted navies ride.
Old Ocean joys to see the peaceful scene,
And bids his billows roll with an exulting tide;
Or, where Augusta's[11] turrets cleave the skies,

recalled in 1739 when war was declared between England and Spain; and had just returned to his post in Madrid.

9 John Green (1706?–79), a Fellow of St John's and later Master of Corpus Christi, Cambridge (1750), and Bishop of Lincoln (1761). (See *post* To Green, 31 January 1762, for RH's letter of congratulation on his elevation.) The *Cambridge Journal* announced the election of a Professor of Divinity for Saturday 31 December. It reported that Green was generally thought to be the best candidate. (*Cambridge Journal*, 31 December 1748.)

10 It was the custom at Oxford and Cambridge for the university to publish a collection of verses on any important occasion when such a volume might be presented to the reigning monarch; after a coronation or a royal death, for instance. In this case, over seventy members of the university contributed verses in English, Latin, Greek, Hebrew and Arabic to a volume compiled to celebrate the end of the War of Austrian Succession and the Peace of Aix-la-Chapelle. This collection, *Gratulatio Academiae Cantabrigiensis De Reditu Serenissimi Regis Georgii II*, is dated 1748, but was not advertised until 1749. RH may not yet have submitted his contribution since there are a number of differences between the version that is given here and the published version, which suggests that he was still revising the poem. The published version is also printed in the *Memoirs* (pp. 27–9). It is the only published poem written by RH with the possible exception of a poem attributed to him and published in 1773: *Discord: A Satire*.
The variant lines in the *Gratulatio* are:

4 No foreign . . . inspire.] No foreign influence needs the willing muse inspire.
14 She mingles . . . band;] She loves to mix with Art's inventive band,
15 Sees Industry . . . arise] Sees Industry in forms unnumber'd rise,
23 Thro' Cam's . . . roves,] Thro' Cam's o'ershadowing bow'rs intranc'd she roves,
30 On these . . . spreads,] On these lov'd bow'rs while Peace her influence sheds,
37 Yet then . . . tell)] Yet then, ev'n then (th'indignant verse shall tell)
38 Was surer . . . foe,] A surer vengeance rose to whelm the foe;
41 But, hark! . . . declare] But, hark! the loud triumphant strains declare,
45–8 Till lo! . . . mute attention stood.]
Till thus the Pow'r, by Freedom's sons obey'd:
"Let blood-stain'd glory swell the tyrant's breast;
"Be mine compassion's healing wing to spread,
"To sheath the wasting sword and give the nations rest:"
49 Then as . . . display,] Then (as the Muse inraptur'd shall display),
52 And lends . . . Peace.] And lends the quick'ning beam to cheer the arts of peace.

11 Augusta was the name given to many Roman provincial towns, including London, and was

She mingles, curious, with Art's learned band;
Sees industry in countless forms arise
To scatter blessings wide & civilize the land;
Or flies, with transport, to <the> her native plain,
Sees corn-clad fields, fresh lawns, & pastures fair,
Sees Plenty vindicate her antient reign,
And pour forth all her charms to crown the various year:
But, chief, the muse to academic groves
Her kindred-train & best-lov'd arts invite
Thro' Cam's imbowring <groves> shades intranc'd she roves,
Whence sacred science streams & Genius spreads his light.
Here will I rest, she cry'd; my laurel here
Eternal blooms; here hangs my golden lyre;
Which erst my Spencer tun'd to Shepherd's ear,
And loftiest Milton smote with genuin epic fire.
And! o! if ought my fond presages shew,
On these lov'd shades while Peace her influence spreads,
Some hand again shall snatch it from the bough,
Wake each high-sounding string & charm the ecchoing glades.
Then shall be sung the glorious deeds of war,
How virtue strove, where envious fortune fail'd,
Expecting fame the conflict view'd from far,
And Britain's valour crown'd, tho' Gallia's host prevail'd.[12]
Yet then, ev'n then (th' indignant muse shall tell)
Was surer vengeance rising on the foe,
When hell-born faction issu'd from her cell,
And on her impious head drew half the destin'd blow.[13]
But hark! the bold triumphant strains declare
How Britain's majesty unrival'd rose,
When all the glories of the naval war
Beam'd round her conqu'ring flag & circled Anson's[14] Brows.
Till lo! her Monarch awfull rais'd his head,
Another Neptune o'er the angry flood,
His pow'rful call the driving storm obey'd,
Contention's waves around in mute attention stood.
Then, as the milder measures shall display,
War's impious roar & faction's murmurs cease,
His gracious eye sheds lustre on the day,
And lends the quick'ning ray to chear the arts of Peace.

adopted by many English poets of the late seventeenth and eighteenth centuries (e.g. Dryden, *Mac Flecknoe*, l. 64; Pope, *Windsor Forest*, l. 336).

12 The combined British and Austrian armies had defeated the French at Dettingen in June 1743, but had been decisively beaten at the battle of Fontenoy on 11 May 1745.

13 An allusion to the uprising of 1745 in support of the Young Pretender which necessitated the withdrawal of troops from the continent.

14 George Anson (1697–1762), vice-admiral in the English navy. He had won great fame in May 1747 by his defeat of a large French fleet and the capture of their treasure. In recognition of his services he was awarded a peerage.

94 To COX MACRO 31 DECEMBER 1748

Text: MS BL Add. 32557, ff. 138–9; unpublished.
Addressed: To/The Revd Dr Macro/at Norton to be left at Mr Hayward's/in the Cook-Row/Bury St Edmunds.
Postmarked: CAMBRIDGE

Camb: 31. Dec. 1748.

Revd Sir

A collection of verses is, you know, expected from this place on ev'ry public occasion[1] & accordingly there is one now preparing on the subject of the Peace. The general fashion has I know not how drawn me into a fit of scribling, the effects of which I take the liberty to send you in the following verses, wch. I commit to your candor without further preface.[2]

Ode on the Peace.

Be still, my fears: suggest no false alarms;
The poet's rapture & the lyric fire
Are vain: enough that Inclination warms;
No foreign influence need the willing muse inspire.

The willing muse, advent'rous in her flight,
To thee, lov'd Peace, shall raise her untaught strain;
Her thy fair triumphs & thy arts delight,
Thy festive branch she bears & joins thy social train.

High on some wave-worn cliff she views serene
Safe on the deep the freighted navies ride;
Old Ocean joys to see the peaceful scene,
And bids his billows roll with an exulting tide;

Or, where Augusta's turrets cleave the skies,
She mingles curious with Art's learned band,
Sees Industry in countless forms arise
To scatter blessings wide & civilize the land;

Or flies with transport to her native plain
Sees corn-clad fields, fresh lawns & pastures fair;
Sees Plenty vindicate her antient reign
And pour forth[a] all her charms to crown the various year.

But, chief the muse to academic groves
Her kindred train & best-lov'd arts invite;
Thro' Cam's imbow'ring shades intranc'd she roves,
Whence sacred science streams & Genius spreads his light.

Here will I rest, she cry'd; my laurel here
Eternal blooms; here hangs my golden lyre,
Which erst my Spencer tun'd to Shepherd's ear,
And loftiest Milton smote with genuin epic fire.

1 The previous collection had been published in 1738 on the death of Queen Caroline.

2 These verses are identical to those in the preceding letter with the exception of ll. 37–8 and l. 52, which read as in the published version, and the variation of the spelling of "awful" (l. 45); in the previous letter "awfull". There are also some differences in punctuation between the manuscript copies and the printed version, but these are arbitrary and do not affect the sense. Capitalisation also varies from copy to copy.

a MS: "fourth".

And o! if ought my fond presages shew,
On these lov'd shades while Peace her influence spreads,
Some hand again shall snatch it from the bough,
Wake each high-sounding string & charm the ecchoing glades.

Then shall be sung the glorious deeds of war,
How virtue strove, where envious fortune fail'd;
Expecting fame the conflict view'd from far,
And Britain's valour crown'd, tho' Gallia's host prevail'd.

Yet then, ev'n then (th'indignant verse shall tell)
A surer vengeance rose to whelm the foe,
When hell-born faction issu'd from her cell,
And on her impious head drew half the destin'd blow.

But, hark! the bold triumphant strains declare
How Britain's majesty unrival'd rose,
When all the glories of the naval war
Beam'd round her conqu'ring flag & circled Anson's brows.

Till lo! her monarch awful rais'd his head,
Another Neptune o'er the angry flood,
His pow'rful call the driving storm obey'd,
Contention's waves around in mute attention stood.

Then, as the milder measures shall display,
War's impious roar & faction's murmurs cease,
His gracious eye sheds lustre on the day,
And lends the quick'ning beam to chear the arts of Peace.

The best amends I can make for having giv'n you so much trouble is by informing you, that you may soon expect a real entertainment of this kind, in a little time, from Dr Nevile, who is preparing some verses on the same occasion.[3] He joins me in compliments to your good family & in wishing you all the enjoyment of many happy years.

I am ever, with great respect, Revd Sir, Your most Obedient, humble Servt

R. Hurd.

95 To Sir EDWARD LITTLETON 23 FEBRUARY 1749

Text: MS STAFFS RO D1413/1; unpublished.
Addressed: To Sir Edward Littleton Bart/at the Wheat-sheaf in Pall-Mall/London
Postmarked: CAMBRIDGE [2]4 [F]E

Dear Sir Edward

I am now to trouble you upon an occasion, which I have been expecting for some time.[1] Mr Mason has at last been inform'd of your resenting something from him, as

[3] Thomas Nevile sent these verses to Cox Macro with a letter of 7 January 1749. (MS BL, Add. 32557, ff. 141–3.) They, also, were printed (with some alterations) in the congratulatory volume.

[1] The whole of this letter is concerned with the misunderstanding between Mason and Sir

he tells me in a letter, which I have just receiv'd from him. He adds, that he is further inform'd, that you tax him with *meaness & ingratitude*; charges which he seems to be particularly uneasy under; but does not say anything of what he suspects to be the occasion of the offence. In answer to this letter, I have this moment been telling him, that I was no stranger to the difference subsisting between you, which however I had never mention'd to him, in hopes that something might happen to set you right witht. coming to a formal eclaircissement: that as to your expressing a resentmt. agst. him to your friends I believ'd it likely; but for the two charges of *meaness & ingratitude*, I ventur'd to tell him, that I could not believe you capable of making 'em. And as a reason for this unbelief, I proceded to assure him that to my certain knowledge, you had shewn no small zeal to do justice to his character on ev'ry proper occasion to persons, in whose opinion he would desire to stand fairest; & this, even since the occasion of your present shyness had happen'd.

After this I let him into the whole ground of offence, such as you represented it to me; & concluded <from> with observing,[a] that, from this representation, he must allow, you had some reason for taking offence at it. I said, I had no doubt, that laziness, forgetfulness or some such cause was at the bottom of the affair, but that I thought him to blame in not excusing himself to you for it. I then took the liberty of hinting to him, that there could sure be no impropriety in his calling upon you at your lodgings, where, I observ'd, an occasion would offer of explaning himself to your satisfaction.

This, Sir, is the substance of my letter to Mr Mason & I am apt to believe, the affect of it will be, that he will think<ing> of paying you a visit, as soon as his health will permit him to stir abroad. But if I might venture to interpose my advice in so nice an affair, I cannot but be of opinion, that you will incline to prevent this visit, in calling upon him first. As you are the person offended & in all appearance with so much <good> reason, & which he is acquainted with too, & as your rank besides sets you so much above him, I think, it would be peculiarly becoming, & an instance of a noble & generous spirit (so far wd. it be from any appearance of meaness & unworthy condescension) to ca[ll] upon him, & open the reason of your disgusts to him. I am confident, such an explanation would settle ev'ry thing at once. But I presu[me] perhaps too much in suggesting this to you. I do it with the sincerest desire of doing the greatest service to you both, I mean that of reconciling differences & promoting friendships between two worthy persons, who cannot but esteem each other, & who, if they were better acquainted, must be, I am confident, the warmest friends. Indeed I could most heartily wish to see a good understanding restor'd betwixt you. When men of few or no virtues fall out, it is of no great consequence, whether they reunite again or not. But such characters, as your's & Mr Mason's (the occasion is too serious to suspect me of flattery) one would not willingly see at variance. I know there is some little difficulty in ys. matter, for you have both a virtuous pride or, as the french term it, *fiertè* in your tempers & which indeed is inseparable from all worthy natures. But

Edward Littleton over an appointment which Littleton believed to have been made, and which Mason had failed to keep. See *ante* To Littleton, 20 February 1748, and n. 7; and *post* To Littleton, 2 March 1749, and 21 March 1749.

a MS: "observining".

from the manner in which Mr Mason speaks of this disagreable event, I know he would be forward to embrace a reconciliation. And if you should think fit to abate something of what you might, in strictness, assume to yourself on this occasion, the rest, I dare say, would be easy.

I write, as you will perceive from many symptoms, in great hast; but you will collect enough from this letter, to shew you, that I most ardently wish to see you again upon good terms: & that I do this from the greatest regard for you both.

I am, dearest Sir, Your most affectionate friend & Servt

R. Hurd.

Camb. 23. feb. 1748–9.

P.S.

Your bro: is retd safe & sends compliments.

Endorsed by Sir Edward Littleton: "Mr. Hurd 23: Feb: 1748:".

96 To Sir EDWARD LITTLETON 2 MARCH 1749

Text: MS STAFFS RO D1413/1; unpublished.
Addressed: To Sir Edward Littleton Bart/at the wheat-sheaf in Pall-Mall/London
Postmarked: CAMBRIDGE 3 MR

Dear Sir

I have receiv'd a letter from Mr Mason, who says, he did not mean to charge you with making those declarations publicly.[1] He does not know, yt. you ever mention'd them to more than one person. He never went to Ld Castlemain's[2] in his life, nor ever went out with Mr Lee[3] but once, when from some circumstances he should conclude, it was impossible for him to have been pre-engag'd. But supposing he was, he thinks it would have been kind, to have mention'd it freely to him. In short he concludes with saying, that as soon as he is able to go so far, he will call upon you.

Thus this matter is at present in so good a train, that I shall expect ev'ry post to hear of ev'rything being adjusted betwixt you. And when you know each other a little better, I may venture to foretell, that nothing can easily happen to disturb your friendship for the future.

Your bro: & all friends are well & send services. I am, Dear Sir, Your most faithful, humble servt

R. Hurd.

Camb. 2. March. 1748–9

1 See preceding letter.

2 Richard Child, Viscount Castlemaine, created Earl Tylney (d.1749). Castlemaine was a friend of George Vertue and a patron of Nollekens and William Kent. He lived in Wanstead in Essex. ([Katherine A. Esdaile, Earl of Ilchester, Sir Henry M. Hake], *Vertue Note Books*, Walpole Society, Oxford, 1930–55, i. 6, 20; iii. 24, 137.)

3 Unidentified.

97 To Sir EDWARD LITTLETON 21 MARCH 1749

Text: MS STAFFS RO D1413/1; unpublished.
Addressed: To Sir Edwd. Littleton Bart/at the Wheat-sheaf in/Pall-Mall/London
Postmarked: CAMBRIDGE 22 MR

Camb: 21. March. 1748–9.

Dear Sir

Your laziness is not to be indur'd any longer. It is quite shameful not to have giv'n me, in all this time, some account of your amusements in town, or of your business; by the latter of which I would chiefly be understood to mean the old affair of prints & pictures.[1] It might look too selfish to say a word of Vandike's heads.[2]

No further intelligence has yet arriv'd concerning the picture at Bury;[3] only that you may be sure, no diligence will be spar'd to secure it.

Mr Cole of King's,[4] to whom I paid a visit the other day, is concern'd, he had not the pleasure of seeing you, when you was here. He inquir'd much of your collection, & desir'd me to mention two places, which perhaps you may have overlook'd, where, it seems, there are many good prints, &, at one of them, he says, many of Nanteuil's heads;[5] out of which he thinks it not unlikely, that you may pick up some, which you want. The places are "Simpson's a Printseller in Maiden lane". & "A French Printshop in Newport Street near St Martin's Lane".[6]

1 Later in 1749 Littleton described some of the purchases he had made during the year in a letter to Edward Macro: "Besides ye two pictures of Mr. Scott wch. I some time since mention'd to you," he wrote, "this last Winter I got a head by Rembrandt, & a large Landscape of Hobima with Figures by A. Vandervelde. Amongst these I dare not presume to mention an excellent history peice by Cheron, wch. I shall hardly give a place to, because it is greatly abused. All I have done in Prints has been to increase ye Nanteuils with 6 or 8 bad plates wch. I had not." (*Macro Letter-book*, Littleton to Macro, 18 September 1749.)

2 Van Dyck's etchings were very popular in the eighteenth century. Mason had remarked in a letter to Jacob Bryant, dated 1747, that they were the "best and cheapest" prints that he knew (John W. Draper, *William Mason. A Study in Eighteenth-Century Culture*, New York, 1924, p. 26); and William Gilpin, in his *Essay upon Prints*, states that although most of Van Dyck's prints "are done slightly", they "bear the character of a master" (p. 128).

3 Edward Macro was trying to secure a picture of the Madonna for Littleton. It appears to have been a private transaction and had not yet been settled by September. (*Macro Letter-book*, Littleton to Macro, 18 September 1749.)

4 William Cole (1714–82) migrated to King's from Clare where he had been admitted in January 1733. He became B.A. in 1737 and M.A. in 1740. Although he subsequently acquired livings outside Cambridge (in 1749 he was made rector of Hornsey, Middlesex), Cole kept in close contact with the University, and from 1767 resided mainly in Cambridge. He is now remembered for his antiquarian collections concerning the city and university. (*D.N.B.*; *Lit. Anecs.*, i. 657–701, and *passim*; W.M. Palmer, *William Cole of Milton*, Cambridge, 1935.)

5 Robert Nanteuil (1623?–78) was the undisputed head of the French school of portrait, and a master of pure engraving. (Arthur M. Hind, *A History of Engraving and Etching*, 1908, 3rd edn. reprinted, New York, 1963, pp. 140, 144, 369.) An examination of a sample collection of art sale catalogues, printed between 1747 and 1750, reveals that of the available portrait engravings, the majority were taken from paintings by Van Dyck. There were about half as many engravings of Rembrandt and Nanteuil portraits, and of these, the Nanteuil were the cheapest. These three artists dominated the market. (Art Sale Catalogues, BL Print Room, A. 1. 3/S.C.)

6 "Sympson" of Maiden Lane, Covent Garden, was a regular buyer at London art sales. His name appears written against the lots he bought. (*Ibid.*) The "French Printshop" has not been identified.

Mr Mason, who is chosen at last fellow of Pembroke,[7] is here. He tells me, he was twice at your lodgings, before he left town, to wait upon you, but did not find you at home. In talking with me upon the affair, he says, it must have been owing to some strange carelessness & forgetfulness, for that he does not remember the particular engagement, referr'd to; but can answer for himself that he could never intentionally be guilty of so much rudeness to any gentleman, much less to you. He further adds, that his engagement with Mr Lee, on the only day he ever went out with him, had been fix'd for several days before, so that he thinks it is impossible he should make a second engagemt. afterwards. But enough of this, till we see you, which some hints from your brother lead me to expect e'er it be very long.

The Comm: &c on Horace[8] goes on very fast. I fancy it is at least half printed off, & will be out, by the farthest, abt. the middle of next month. The plate I am told will be extremely pretty & is put in the hands of the engraver.[9] I could be glad to have it publish'd by the time, you go into the country, because I would in that case take the opportunity of sending a copy to Mr Hill, however unwelcome it may be or unexpected.

James Devie is expected to morrow.

All friends send services & I am, Dear Sir, Your's faithfully & affect:

R. Hurd

98 To Sir EDWARD LITTLETON 4 MAY 1749

Text: MS STAFFS RO D1413/1; unpublished.
Addressed: cover missing.

Camb. 4. May. 1749.

Dear Sir Edward,

All the information I have from Mr Cole concerning the heads is, that the collection is, in his opinion, not only very large, but very excellent, the collector being, as he says, curious in his choice of the impressions.[1] They are handsomely bound in Morocco like your Nanteuil's heads, & in the same form. He talks however of an extravagant price, for he thinks they will not come under 90£; which seems a vast sum for a parcel of English heads, the ingravings of which, must needs be indifferent.

7 Mason had been nominated to a Fellowship at Pembroke in 1747; but the Master had disputed the election, and it was only after more than a year of litigation that he was finally accepted. (Draper, *Mason*, pp. 33–4.)

8 This alludes to RH's edition of the *Ars Poetica*: *Q. Horatii Flacci Ars Poetica. Epistola ad Pisones. With an English Commentary and Notes.* It was published, anonymously, on Thursday 25 May. Advance notice of its appearance was given in the *London Evening-Post*, 20–23 May, and publication itself was announced in the same paper, 25–27 May.

9 The engraving had been designed and drawn by Francis Hayman, and was engraved by Charles Grignion (1717–1810), who had previously worked with Hogarth. (Hind, *A History of Engraving*, p. 234.) It shows Comedy and Tragedy with their masks against a pastoral background of music and dancing, and appears at the top of the first page of the text.

1 Nothing else is known of this collection of engraved portraits. William Cole, RH's adviser, was clearly already an expert in this field of collecting. He was said to be "a collector of portraits at a time when this *trade* was in few hands", and by 1744 had amassed a collection of about 3,000 prints, though not all of these were portraits. (Alexander Chalmers, *The General Biographical Dictionary: Containing An Historical and Critical Account of the Lives and Writings of the Most Eminent Persons in Every Nation*, New Edition, 1812.)

So much for these prints, I have now some better news to acquaint you with, which is, that Mr King's pictures will certainly be sold by auction at Catley sometime in June.[2] You may depend upon this, tho', as to the precise time, it is not yet fix'd. Ld. Mountford[3] will to be sure, be a great bidder, but you can hardly fail of coming in for some.

I will consider what you mention about the too great length of that line in the Epitaph.[4]

I am in constant expectation of the Art. of P. being publish'd,[5] & have giv'n directions for one copy to be sent to your lodgings, which I suppose to be the same, as before.[6] I design'd to have had it bound, before I had sent it you, but as the sheets take some time before they are perfectly dry, it will not bear binding immediatly.[7]

Your bro: & all friends join me in being always, Dear Sir, Your most faithful & affect: Serv.

R. Hurd.

P.S.

Mr Ross' book is coming out & is dedicated to Ld Gower.[8]

99 To Sir EDWARD LITTLETON — 8 MAY 1749

Text: MS STAFFS RO D1413/1; unpublished.
Addressed: To Sir Edward Littleton Bart./at Mrs. De Maye's in Suffolk-street/[1] Charing-Cross/London
Postmarked: CAMBRIDGE 9 MA

Camb: 8. May. 1749.

Dear Sir

The day before I had the favor of your's I directed a letter for you at the Wheat-sheaf,

[2] Catley (now known as Kirtling) is a village about five miles from Newmarket. The pictures referred to were the property of Edward King, whose son Thomas had been admitted at Trinity College, Cambridge, in 1749. RH may have heard of the sale from another Fellow of Emmanuel, William Affleck, who had relatives living in the same parish. (Carter, *History of the County of Cambridge*, p. 140.) No other information concerning the sale has been discovered, but see *post* To Littleton, 7 August 1749.

[3] Henry Bromley, Lord Montfort (1705–55); Fellow-Commoner of Clare College, 1724; M.A., 1726; M.P. for Cambridgeshire, 1727–41; Lord Lieutenant for the county, 1730–42; High Steward of Cambridge from 1741 till his death. (C[okayne], *The Complete Peerage*, ix. 132–3.)

[4] RH and Edward Littleton had composed an inscription to be carved on a stone commemorating William Budworth, who had died in 1745. (See *ante* To Littleton, 15 February 1748, and *post* To Littleton, 7 August 1749; 4 September 1750.) It is not known to which line RH refers.

[5] See preceding letter, n. 8.

[6] Edward Littleton had moved to Suffolk Street. See following letter.

[7] The length of time the printed sheets of a book took to dry could vary from a day to a week according to circumstances. (Philip Gaskell, *A New Introduction to Bibliography*, Oxford, 1972, corrected edn. 1974, p. 143.)

[8] John Ross's edition of *Marci Tullii Ciceronis Epistolarum Ad Familiares Libri XVI* was advertised for sale in June 1749. (*Lond. Mag.*) It is dedicated to John, Lord Gower, for unspecified favours done for the author. Ross was a Fellow of St John's (1744–70), and his book was printed and published in Cambridge.

[1] Suffolk Street was a popular area for lodgings from the late seventeenth century till the end of the eighteenth. Horace Walpole noted that it was particularly favoured by foreigners, which

supposing you to be in your old lodgings. What news I had to inform you of, you will find there.

As to the *time* of the Installation,[2] or the *place*, I can write you no certain acct. of either at present; tho' 'twill most probably be here, & <about> after the rising of the parliament.[3]

I am oblig'd to you for contriving to give me a part of your entertainmt. in the D. of Rutland's pictures,[4] but I have now determin'd not to see London this spring.

Mr Hill is very obliging. His fears, good man, are piteous – & I am perfectly amaz'd, how you could have the *insensibilitè du coeur* to laugh at him.[5]

I am heartily sorry for poor Manwaring. My acquaintance with him was but slight, & yet I feel more on this occasion, than so general a knowledge of him might seem naturally to produce.[6] But his virtues were such, as one could not see witht. loving, nor lose witht. lamenting. I write this, as I did my last to you, in no very good spirits, having been confin'd to my chamber by a very severe cold.

Your Brother & all friends are well.

I am Dear Sir, Your most affect: humble Servt

R. Hurd.

100 To Sir EDWARD LITTLETON 26 MAY 1749

Text: MS STAFFS RO D1413/1; unpublished.
Addressed: cover missing.

Dear Sir Edward

Your last informs me you was packing up, I suppose, for Staffordshire, & therefore I direct this to you at Ridware. Your conference with Mr Villiers was something curious,

perhaps accounts for the presence of Littleton's landlady. (Wheatley, *London Past and Present*, iii. 331–2.)

2 Thomas Pelham-Holles, Duke of Newcastle, had been elected Chancellor of Cambridge University on 14 December 1748, and preparations were being made for his official installation. (D.A. Winstanley, *The University of Cambridge in the Eighteenth Century*, Cambridge, 1922, reprinted 1958, pp. 38–54; *Annals*, iv. 268–72.) The ceremony took place on 1 July.

3 The parliamentary session of 1748–9 was closed on 13 June. (*The Parliamentary History of England*, xiv. (1813) 569.)

4 John Manners (1696–1779), third Duke of Rutland. His fine collection of pictures was housed at Belvoir Castle, Leicestershire. It is described in Gustave Waagen's *Treasures of Art* as consisting "chiefly of excellent pictures of the first masters of the Flemish and Dutch schools, of a moderate number of chefs-d'oeuvre of the best painters of the French and Spanish schools, and, finally, of some good examples of the Italian and German schools . . . The pictures by Murillo, as well as many others," he says, "were collected about 100 years ago by the third Duke of Rutland . . . Many pictures, however, were sacrificed at a fire, among which were several by Salvator Rosa, and eleven by Sir Joshua Reynolds, among which was one of his finest specimens." (Gustave Waagen, *Treasures of Art in Great Britain: Being an Account of the Chief Collections of Paintings, Drawings, Sculptures, Illuminated MSS., &c. &c.*, 3 vols., 1854., iii. 394–402.

5 This reference remains obscure.

6 RH appears to have had mistaken news of John Mainwaring's death. Though often ill, Mainwaring lived to be 83; he died in 1807.

& your management of it shews with what unshaken fidelity you can keep a secret.[1] Yet as I would not be the occasion of bringing you into the like distress for the future, having no reasons for concealing myself so cautiously, as before, I shall very readily release you from all engagements of secrecy on this head: I mean, that you are at full liberty to disclose the matter to such persons, as may think it worth their while to be inquisitive about it, and whom you may think it worth your while to inform of it. I am very glad you receiv'd a copy yourself, before you left town. The commentary you will find very little chang'd from what it was, when you first saw it.[2] The notes, I believe, are for the most part new. As I flatter myself, you will give them a reading, as well as the introduction, it will give me a pleasure to hear your freest thoughts of them. On looking the book over very hastily, I observ'd the following gross blunders, which you will please to correct with your pen. Notes p. 86. 4th. line from the bottom. For *court* read *cart*. P. 89. 5th. line for *poets* read *acts*. P. 91. last line in the notes for *teratur* read *feratur*. P. 103 9th. line for *this purpose* read *the purpose*. There are some others, which you will easily rectify yourself.

You don't say a word of being here in June, or attending the Installation, tho' we expect both. That you may not plead ignorance of the latter, I must acquaint you, that it will certainly be on the saturday before the commencement.[3] The sale of the pictures is not yet fix'd,[4] but you may depend on the earliest information from me.

Mr Taylor & his brother have been here,[5] to whom I was glad to shew any civilities in my power, as well from inclination, as that you did me the favor to request it of me. We manag'd matters so well, as to get the business of his degree dispatch'd in 3 or 4 days.

You will give my service to Mr Tonyn,[6] whom I should be glad to see in Staffordshire, if I come there this summer. But this, at present, is uncertain.[7] One thing you may at all times be assur'd of, that I can want no inducement to come to you, being always, with an intire respect, Dearest Sir, Your most faithful & affect: servt

R. Hurd.

Camb: 26. May. 1749.

My comp. to Mrs. Littleton.
I am delighted to hear of your agreemt. with Ld Brook.[8]

1 Littleton had refused to give RH's name as the editor of the *Ars Poetica*.

2 Sir Edward had been admitted to Emmanuel on 30 April 1744. He could have studied Horace at any time from then on: his works were variously prescribed as first year and third year reading. (Wordsworth, *Scholae Academicae*, pp. 333, 339.)

3 Commencement Day was celebrated on the first Tuesday in July. The preceding Saturday was 1 July.

4 RH alludes to the sale of Edward King's pictures at Catley (see *ante* To Littleton, 4 May 1749).

5 John Taylor (b.1714) came from Courton, Staffordshire. He had a degree from Worcester College, Oxford (B.A. 1734) and was in Cambridge to receive an M.A.

6 Probably Patrick Tonyn (d.1798) who was a Lieutenant in the 6th Dragoons. His regiment was stationed at Shrewsbury and Stafford (after active service abroad) from January to November 1749. (Maj. E.S. Jackson, *The Inniskilling Dragoons. The Records of an Old Heavy Cavalry Regiment*, 1909, pp. 61–2, 260 n. 3.)

7 RH did not go to Staffordshire in the end. Sir Edward mentions that "Mr. Hurd was not there last year" in a letter to Edward Macro of 8 March 1750. (*Macro Letter-book*.) See also *post* To Littleton, 7 August 1749.

8 A final agreement had been reached between Littleton and Lord Brooke on the sale of an estate in the manor of Penkridge (see *ante* To Littleton, 20 April 1748, nn. 2 and 3; and 15 November 1748, n. 9, for details of the negotiations). In the original, verbal agreement Sir Edward had offered a price of £6,143. 7s. 0d. He had to raise this to £6,550 to secure the estate. There is a

101 To Sir EDWARD LITTLETON 5 JUNE 1749

Text: MS STAFFS RO D1413/1; unpublished.
Addressed: address missing.
Postmarked: CAMBRIDGE 6 IV

Camb: 5. June. 1749.

Dear Sir

Within a few days after the writing of last, the author of the Commentary &c on the A. of P. became publicly known. I cannot learn, by what means this was discover'd; nor was I indeed very anxious to trace it, the piece having by that time met with such a reception here, as made it easy for me to own it.

Mr Warburton has since then written me a letter of thanks for my civilities to him in the introduction, in which he speaks in such extravagant terms of the notes, as I am not at liberty to repeat.[1]

You will excuse my vanity in mentioning these things, which I had not done, but from the part I know you take in what concerns my reputation; & indeed from the real interest, which I think you have in it. For such has been the connexion betwixt us, that it is impossible for my credit to suffer, witht. involving your's along with it. On which account I must have leave to say, that the success of my work gives me the greatest pleasure, as it enables you to acknowledge your Tutor without a blush: I will add too, as it justifies in some measure our late friend Mr Budworth, to whose advice & recommendation, it was owing, that I ever stood in that relation to you.

For the rest, I needed not the public favor to assure myself of your's, which you have always giv'n me from our earliest acquaintance, & which I could always have promis'd myself from our mutual friendship. It cannot however but be very agreable to me, when I reflect, that the piece, I have been speaking of, was originally written for your use, & that it will therefore remain with you, a perpetual monument of my zeal for your improvement, as also of some small ability to effect it. As such I consider it, as a kind of cement in our friendship, which tho' I was confident nothing could violate before, yet I know not how this will tend still more to strengthen & confirm it. Ev'ry occasion of doing that cannot but be very agreable to me, for I am always, with great warmth & truth, Dearest Sir, Your most faithful & affect: humble Servt

R. Hurd.

P.S.

Please to let Mr Hill know, when you see him, that I only wait for an opportunity of sending him a present of the comment:

memorandum written by Brooke officially recording the sale in the Staffordshire Record Office. (Ex D260/M/T/5/32.) It is dated 24 May 1749, the day of the sale.

1 RH had concluded the Introduction to his edition of the *Ars Poetica* with the following compliment to Warburton: "I chuse therefore", he writes, "to rest on the *single* authority of a great author, who hath not disdained to comment [on] a like piece of a late critical poet. What was indeed the amusement of his pen, becomes, it must be owned, the *labour* of inferior writers. Yet, on these unequal terms, it can be no discredit to have aim'd at some resemblance of one of the least of those *merits*, which shed their united honours on the name of the illustrious *friend* and *commentator* of Mr. POPE." He followed this up with sending a copy of his work to Warburton who replied with thanks on 1 June 1749. In the letter he speaks particularly highly of the notes which he believed to be "one of the most masterly pieces of criticism that ever was written. I am sure", he continues to RH, "(and I ought to be ashamed to say it) that I should have envied you for it, had I not found you so generous to the Commentator of Mr. Pope." The letter ends with Warburton offering RH his "very unprofitable friendship." (*Prelate*, pp. 1–2.)

102 To Sir EDWARD LITTLETON 7 AUGUST 1749

Text: MS STAFFS RO D1413/1; unpublished.
Addressed: To/Sir Edward Littleton Bart.

Camb. 7. Aug. 1749.

Dear Sir

I am glad to hear of your recovery from your late indisposition, which, indeed, was unlucky on many accounts; amongst others, that it kept you from Catley, where the pictures sold surprizingly cheap.[1] L. Mountford bought very few. I really believe, you might have had all the good pictures in the house for 200 pounds. I bade as far as 8, 10, or 12 guineas for several pieces for you, but durst not go higher, as I had no commission from you. I pick'd up a head of Inigo Jones by Rubens,[2] & a piece of Claro obscuro, which, I know, you will admire, or rather envy. The famous sea-fight of Vandervelt went for 56 pounds.[3]

The part, you take in the little reputation, which the A. of poetry has procur'd me, is extremely kind, & just as I expected. Ev'ry thing has happen'd, in relation to it, exactly to my wishes. I have hear'd of no exceptions to it, but from such persons, as I had long ago persuaded myself, were not much to be regarded. The partizans of ease in writing are disgusted at the stiffness of the style, & others have taken offence at what they call the refinement of the criticisms. I am vain enough to interpret both these censures into compliments.

You will tell me, what is Mr Hill's opinion of it; for I suppose you to have receiv'd the present for him, which was sent by Mr. Muchall.[4]

If you have not yet done it, you must needs send for Mr Ross' Epistles *ad familiares*. The Dedication will divert you.[5] And the notes will be of some assistance to you in reading the epistles. These are, many of them, so exquisitely fine, that I am sure they will give you the highest entertainment. Nothing can equal the address & art, with which they are written.

I have review'd the inscription to Mr Budworth for the last time;[6] of which I send

1 The sale of pictures at Catley (see *ante* To Littleton, 4 May 1749) was probably held at the end of July. RH had gone there with Osmund Beauvoir. (*Macro Letter-book*, Beauvoir to Edward Macro, 7 August 1749.)

2 RH may have been mistaken in identifying the head of Inigo Jones as the work of Rubens; no such portrait is listed in the catalogues of Rubens' works and the majority of engravings listed at the British Museum are taken from portraits by Van Dyck. (Freeman O'Donoghue, *Catalogue of Engraved British Portraits Preserved in the Department of Prints and Drawings in the British Museum*, 6 vols., 1908–25, ii. 656.)

3 This must refer to a painting by William Van de Velde, the younger (1633–1707). He was the best known of the Dutch marine painters and lived in London with his father from about 1673 until his death. (*Allgemeines Lexikon der Bildenden Kunstler*, ed. Ulrich Thieme and Felix Becker, Leipzig, 1907–47.)

4 Thomas Muchall of Brewood, Staffordshire. Muchall had come up to Emmanuel as an undergraduate in the spring of 1747. He had left college for the summer vacation of 1749 in the first week of July, presumably carrying RH's present with him. (*Commons Accounts Book*, STE. 15. 9.)

5 *Marci Tullii Ciceronis Epistolarum ad Familiares Libri XVI*. (See *ante* To Littleton, 4 May 1749, n. 8.)

6 William Budworth had died in 1745. In gratitude for the care he had taken with their education, RH and Sir Edward had decided to erect an inscribed stone to his memory. This plan was first projected at the end of 1747 or the beginning of 1748. (See *ante* To Littleton, 15 February 1748.) The earliest draft or drafts of the inscription have been lost, but RH enclosed a revised

you a copy, & believe, you will think the alterations for the better. I need not be particular in pointing out the reasons of them; they will easily appear to you. You will judge of the fitness of the time yourself: but I should suppose, the sooner the inscription was cut & set up, the better.

It gives me no small concern, that I have no hopes of seeing you in Staff: this summer. The multiplicity of offices, I am incumber'd with this year, makes it altogether impracticable.[7] Tho' one convenience arises from hence, that I can the more easily part with Thumper, for a few months; having no longer journeys to take, than to the hills, whither Peggy's magnified rump will very commodiously bear me.[8] You have promis'd to be very careful of him; & 'tis well you have, for you can't imagine how fond I am of him.

One word about your brother. We have had no relapses into *Sartorism*. His behaviour is perfectly regular. And he continues diligent in his studies. We go on notably in latin. He seems more than ever dispos'd to listen to any advice, I may think proper to give him: & will sometimes sacrifice his own humour to a little company, because I tell him, it is better. This is the main point. You must assist all you can in it. We certainly gain ground; & all means must be us'd to push him forward. 'Tis a work of difficulty & time. But ev'ry thing depends upon it.

If you consider the solitude, I live in here,[9] you will see, how much it concerns me to have the pleasure of hearing from you very often. You must not disappoint my expectations in this matter.

The Mr Neviles are well & send services.

I am, with mine to Mrs and Miss Littleton, Dear Sir, Your most affect: humble servt

R. Hurd.

Gulielmo Budworth A.M.

Huius simùl ac Ecclesiae de Brewood
Nuper Pastori,
Et literarii ibidem ludi
Praefecto:
In utrumque munus,
Innocentiâ vitae, morum comitate,
Humanioribus literis, eloquentiâ simplici,
Instructissimo:
Omnium, quibuscum vixerat familiariter, studioso,
In suos summè officioso;
Ab omni tamen in homines illiberali obsequio,

draft with this letter, and, contrary to his declaration of having done with the inscription, he continued to work on it. Further possible alterations are discussed in To Littleton, 17 January 1750, and 9 March 1750, and another copy (with some alterations) is enclosed with a letter to Littleton of 4 September 1750. The stone was finally placed in the chapel of Shareshill where Budworth had been Perpetual Curate. (*Memoirs*, p. 25.)

7 RH had held the office of Dean and Greek Lecturer (one post) and was College Librarian (appointed 1746). (*Order Book*, COL. 14. 2; *Steward's Accounts Book*, STE. 1. 5.)

8 Riding at Cambridge was, as well as necessary, a popular amusement, but it seems to have been unusual to own horses. (Christopher Wordsworth, *Social Life at the English Universities in the Eighteenth Century*, Cambridge, 1874, pp. 168–9.) Thumper was still in RH's hands in 1755, but was then ready for retirement. (See *post* To Littleton, 3 June 1755.)

9 Comparativly few Fellows or undergraduates remained in Cambridge over the summer, particularly over August. In Emmanuel only 12 of the 51 members of the College were in residence at this date. (*Commons Accounts Books*, STE. 15. 9, 10.)

Potentiorum certe cultu servili,
Alienissimo;
Huic tali viro
Optimo olim praeceptori,
Amico insuper dilectissimo,
Hoc qualecunque amoris et grati animi testimonium
ponendum curavit
Edvardus Littleton Baronettus.

A.D. 1749

103 To THOMAS BALGUY — 18 AUGUST 1749

Text: MS BEINECKE MS Vault Shelves, Hurd; printed in part, *Memoirs*, 41.
Addressed: cover missing.

Camb. 18. Aug. 1749.

Dear Sir[1]

It is in vain to flatter myself any longer with the hopes of seeing you in the north this summer. I find it impracticable on many accounts, which I need not be particular in explaning to you. You will easily believe, that I should not deny myself so much pleasure, if it were not singularly inconvenient. I will beg you to give my compliments to Mr Wright & to tell him, yt. I shall hope to find some other occasion of paying my respects to him.[2] It is not the least of my disappointmts., that I am not able to wast some of these fine days at Rumley.[3]

To enliven, or at least relieve, this solitude, I have taken to my long neglected fiddle.[4] You can't imagine, what pains I am at, & how fast I improve under the forming hand of M. Fischer.[5] Not a grain of tast: but a wonderful exactness of *fingering, bowing* &c. This is the grammar of music. The flourish of rhetoric is to come after. If indeed it ever comes, which, to say the truth, I much doubt. For this fit can never last long. And November & you will furnish better amusements. But 'tis something to keep awake in the mean time. I have said the more on this frivolous subject, to shew you, that, if this indolent summer should turn out ill *pour la santé*, you are not to place

1 Thomas Balguy (1716–95) had been admitted at St John's on 28 May 1734, was made B.A. in 1737, and M.A. in 1741, when he was also elected a Fellow. He held two livings in Lincolnshire and had been installed as a Prebendary of Lincoln Cathedral in July 1748. (See Biography.)

2 Unidentified, but possibly Thomas Wright of London, admitted to St John's a few days earlier than Balguy in May 1734, and said to be a friend of Gray, Mason and Whitehead. (*Alum. Cantab.*)

3 Unidentified, but perhaps a reference to Romiley in Cheshire.

4 There was great enthusiasm for violin playing at Cambridge in the mid eighteenth century. The anonymous author of *The Academic* comments that a "Taste for Musick, modern Languages, and other the polite Entertainments of the Gentleman, have succeeded to Clubs, and Bacchanalian Routs". (*The Academic: Or a Disputation on the State of the University of Cambridge*, 1750, p. 22.) But a writer from Trinity College, Cambridge, whose letter was printed the same year in *The Student* expressed concern that so many students were being "debauch'd by *Sound*, neglecting LOCKE and NEWTON for PURCELL and HANDEL, and instead of *Philosophers* commencing (O ridicule! O shame to common sense!) downright FIDDLERS". (*The Student, or the Oxford and Cambridge Monthly Miscellany*, Oxford, 1750–1, i. 92.)

5 Unidentified.

it to the acct of my books; which you will hereby understand to be quite guiltless.

Your friends at St John's are well & send services. Mr Allen[6] talks of writing, when the affair of Barrow is decided.[7] I would not have you be impatient for this event. For the Seniors gave in their answer only last week. 'Tis, I hear, very long & very learned. What entertainment to see all the logical dexterity of Aristotle's family employ'd on this good occasion. 'Tis not one of those dry disputes, which, because turning on words, some philosophers affect to call frivolous. This, you know, is more than a λογομαχία. Mr Burrow bids me say, that there was no Indictmt. at the Assizes.[8]

A few days ago I receiv'd a packet from Prior-Park. It contain'd, besides a letter, (in which is a curious paragraph, concerning two great persons, altogether *esoteric*,)[9] the mss notes on Mr Pope's Im. of the Ep. to Augustus; sent, as he says, "to convince me, how much a Comment. on that piece of Horace is wanting".[10] You may be sure, it had not this effect. At least I was not to own it. My answer however was drawn in such a way, as to leave me at liberty, either to decline or follow his advice, as I may find myself dispos'd to either.[11] But this is of small moment. You will ask after the notes themselves. They are many of them very curious; especially some, which give us the characters of eminent writers, as Ld Shaftesbury,[12] Bp Sprat,[13]

6 Philip Allen (1723–74), admitted to St John's in 1742; B.A. 1746; M.A. 1749; B.D. 1757; Fellow, 1749–74; Vicar of St Sepulchre, Cambridge. (*Alum. Cantab.*)

7 The living of Barrow, Suffolk, was held in trust by the Master, Fellows and scholars of St John's. On a vacancy arising, the rectory was to be offered under the terms of the trust to any relative or descendant of the benefactor at the college or to the senior divine then a Fellow there. On this occasion a vacancy had occurred and was claimed by John Green, the President of St John's, with a majority of the college voting for him. (Archbishop Herring to William Herring, 7 November 1749, Portland Mss. Nottingham University Library, PWV/120/75.) His right to the presentation was challenged, however, by Thomas Rutherforth "as senior *Divine*, because Doctor, tho' Junior in Admission to the President". (*Ibid.*) The College Visitor, the Bishop of Ely, was consulted and found in favour of Rutherforth; but this so incensed the Fellows that they determined to take the case to court. (Archbishop Herring to Lord Hardwicke, 27 October 1749, BL Add. 35598, ff. 434–5.) Judgment was given on 23 May 1750 by the Lord Chancellor. The case was held to be outside the jurisdiction of the Visitor and Rutherforth was obliged to concede Barrow to Green. (Richard Burn, *Ecclesiastical Law*, Third Edition, 1775, i. 426–7; Cooper, *Annals*, iv. 277.)

8 This allusion remains obscure. William Burrow had been an undergraduate at St John's, and was made a Fellow in 1750.

9 This letter, from William Warburton, is published in *Prelate*, pp. 6–7. It was written on 6 August 1749. The "curious" paragraph mentioned by RH is the first. Warburton commends RH's opinion of Conyers Middleton, whom he esteems "an honest man", an opinion he does not hold of another writer "who is in Politics", he says, "just what [Middleton] is in Divinity".

10 Warburton was preparing an edition of Pope's *Works* for the press (it was published in 1751), and had been working on his imitation of the *Epistola ad Augustum* ('The First Epistle of the Second Book of Horace') throughout the summer. The quotation RH gives from Warburton's letter does not occur in the text of that written in August, but in the letter preceding it, dated 13 June 1749. (*Prelate*, p. 4.) The manuscript notes have disappeared.

11 By January 1750 RH had decided that he would write a Commentary and Notes on Horace's *Epistola*. (See *post* To Littleton, 17 January 1750.) The edition was published in 1751. (See *post* To Edward Macro, 21 May 1751.)

12 Anthony Ashley Cooper (1671–1713), Lord Shaftesbury, is mentioned in a note on l. 108 of Pope's *Imitation*. (*Works*, ed. Warburton, 1751, iv. 159.) The poet refers to the "Mob of Gentlemen who wrote with Ease", and Warburton gives a brief history of "*easy writing*". He concludes with Shaftesbury who, he says, introduced "a new sort of *Gentleman-like writing*", consisting in a "negligence of what is said, but joined to much *affectation* in the manner of saying it".

13 The character of Thomas Sprat (1653–1713), Bishop of Rochester, is outlined in a note to l.

Mr Addison,[14] & Dr Bentley.[15] I am pleas'd with the last, wch. does justice to the great Critic. Two or three notes are purposely brought in to abuse Bps.[16] This delights me, for reasons you will easily guess at. There are besides some ingenious criticisms. On the whole I like the notes extremely, & believe you will, when you see 'em. To inform you more particularly of them, would be to transcribe 'em. He observes in his letter, yt. he has written comments as well as notes on all the *moral* epistles.[17] The Ed. will certainly be clever.

I need not say, how glad I shall be to receive a letter from you, being, as you see, quite desolate, & always, with great truth, Dear Sir, Your most affectionate & faithful humble Servt

R. Hurd.

Not a syllable from Mr Powell.

104 To Sir EDWARD LITTLETON — 22 SEPTEMBER 1749

Text: MS STAFFS RO D1413/1; unpublished.
Addressed: To/Sir Edward Littleton Bart/at Pipe-Ridware near/ Lichfield/Staffordshire/By Lond:
Postmarked: CAMBRIDGE 23 SE

Camb. 22. Sept. 1749.

Dear Sir

I immediately carry'd the Catalogue to Mr Thurlbourn, whose <account> report is, that it is a most excellent collection of books, & of the sort, he apprehends, you wd.

109. (Pope, *Works*, 1751, iv. 160.) Warburton puts him at the "head of the small wits", but on the subjects of his knowledge and ability as a prose writer, he comments dismissively that the bishop's "Learning was comprised in the well rounding a period". He takes his cue from Pope who had catagorised Sprat as one of the "Mob of Gentlemen who wrote with Ease".

[14] Warburton's opinion of Addison was mixed. "He was but an ordinary poet", he says, "and a worse critic. His verses are heavy, and his judgment of Men and Books superficial." On the other hand, he continues, "in the pleasantry of comic action, and in the dignity of moral allegories, he is inimitable. Nature having joined in him, as she had done once before in *Lucian*, . . . the sublime of Plato to the humour of Menander." (*Ibid.*, iv. 178–9.) References to Addison occur in notes on ll. 215, 216 and 217.

[15] The account given of Bentley is a fair one, indicating both his strengths and his weaknesses as a critic. Warburton points out that he had "a strong natural understanding, a great share of penetration, and a sagacity and acumen very uncommon". These qualities made him an excellent critic of "books of science", but betrayed him into "absurd and extravagant conjectures when ever he attempted to reform the text of a Poet". (*Ibid.*, iv. 158.) Pope's criticism of Bentley (in ll. 103–4 of his poem) springs from these attempts at literary criticism.

[16] These notes may have been altered or omitted. Only in one instance could Warburton be said to refer disrespectfully to a bishop in his annotation. The subject of his attack is Archbishop Tillotson, whose argument that it is easier to write satire than panegyric, Warburton disagreed with. The note appears as a comment on l. 405. (*Ibid.*, iv. 198–9.)

[17] "I have indeed wrote comments as well as notes on Mr. P's moral Epistles" writes Warburton in the letter of 6 August 1749. (*Prelate*, p. 6.) The allusion is to Pope's *Moral Essays, in Four Epistles to Several Persons*. (*Works*, vol. 3.) The Commentary does not differ significantly in subject matter from the Notes. Both appear at the bottom of each page along with variations of the text, which are separately noted.

wish to purchase.[1] He advises, that you should, by no means, let it go under 360 pounds. He himself would be glad to give 300 guineas for <them> it. 'Tis, for the size of it, one of the best libraries, he says, he has seen.

Not knowing where to get Franks enough to inclose the Catalogue,[2] I have sent it under cover to Mr Gunn, desiring him to forward it to you, as soon as possible.[3]

I heartily give you joy of this fair beginning of a library, which I one day or other expect to see the completest in the county.[4] You need not be afraid of proceding with vigour, for books are a real ornament to ev'ry gentleman, who is able & willing to make use of them.

I am, with services to the ladies & your brother, Dear Sir, Your most affectionate, humble Servt

R. Hurd.

105 To WILLIAM WARBURTON 25 OCTOBER 1749

Text: Prelate, 13.

Cambridge, October 25th, 1749.

Rev. Sir,

I have read, with great pleasure, the six sheets of your discourse on Julian.[1] The

1 Cambridge was an important centre for book sales and Thurlbourn as the biggest bookseller arranged most of the auctions. The list of books that RH mentions cannot now be traced, and it is not known whether Littleton purchased the library or not. A comparison of reserve prices printed in Thurlbourn's catalogues shows that this collection of books was considerably superior to those generally advertised for sale in Cambridge. (*List of Catalogues of English Book Sales 1676–1900. Now in the British Museum*, 1915.)

2 The cost of postage in the eighteenth century varied not only with weight but according to the number of sheets of paper sent and the distance they had to travel. A catalogue would be expensive to send. Peers and M.P.s were allowed to send letters free and were issued with specially stamped ("franked") covers to enclose them in. There was a weight limit, though, of 2 oz. hence RH's need for more than one cover. (Kenneth Ellis, *The Post Office in the Eighteenth Century*, 1958, pp. 38–40.)

3 Gunn was a Staffordshire tradesman with whom the Littleton family did business. (Mrs Littleton, Private Accompt, Staffs. RO, Ex D260/M/T/5/107.)

4 Edward Littleton's books were valued soon after his death in 1812. Altogether, his library, the books of prints in his study and a collection of printed and manuscript music, amounted to more than 3,000 "Volumes and numbers". Their estimated value was £1,190. 17s. 6d. (Valuation of books, Staffs. RO, Ex D260/M/T/5/110.)

1 RH refers to Warburton's work *Julian. Or a Discourse Concerning the Earthquake and Fiery Eruption, Which Defeated that Emperor's Attempt to Rebuild the Temple at Jerusalem*. The printing of the book had begun in June, though by the end of September Warburton reported that he had got "but six sheets of Julian . . . from under the press". These six (comprising 96 octavo pages) he had ordered to be sent to RH. (*Prelate*, pp. 5, 10.) *Julian* was written primarily in response to Conyers Middleton's work *A Free Inquiry into the Miraculous Powers, Which are Supposed to have Subsisted in the Christian Church, From the Earliest Ages through Several Successive Centuries*, published in December 1748 (dated 1749). Both works were major and provocative contributions to the debate upon the authenticity of (Christian) miracles and the authority of the Fathers. (See Stephen, *English Thought in the Eighteenth Century* i. 228–77; see also *ante* To Mason, 7 May 1747, n. 8, for Middleton's *Introductory Discourse* to the *Free Inquiry*.) Middleton asserts that all the accounts of miracles given by the Fathers are highly unreliable and only the

introduction, which respects Dr. Middleton, is extremely handsome.[2] I agree with you, he ought to be pleased with it. That he will be so, there may be reason to doubt. I suspect your candour hath put a distinction, which the learned Inquirer never thought of.[3] However a fair occasion is offered of explaining himself.

For the discourse itself, you have established the *fact* with uncommon force and perspicuity.[4] The characters of Julian and Marcellinus are very masterly.[5] And the evidence you make the Apostate bear against himself, is one of those happy conjectures, or rather discoveries, peculiar to your genius.[6]

The only thing, that sticks with me at all, is, where you shew, from the *nature* and *end* of Judaism, that the destruction of the temple must needs be final.[7] Your

miracles said to have occurred in the age of the Apostles can be accepted as genuine. Warburton, on the other hand, believed that "*all* the Miracles recorded in *Church-History*, are *not* forgeries or delusions", and to prove this examines a miracle taken from the later period which Middleton considered so full of impostures. His conclusion indicates at least the honesty of the Fathers.

2 In the opening pages of his Introduction Warburton describes how the reputation of the Fathers had progressively deteriorated until they were considered as "fanciful Divines, as bad Critics, and as unsafe Moralists". (p. ix.) Yet, he continues, till of late those critics "who preserved their moderation" would also have agreed that "this would take nothing from the integrity of their Evidence [i.e. their accounts of miracles]: and what we want of them" it is concluded, "is only their Testimony to facts". (*Ibid.*) Middleton is introduced in this context as being unwilling to allow the Fathers even "this small remnant of credit". (p. x.) The validity of such extreme scepticism is questioned by Warburton who argues that we can discern genuine accounts of miraculous facts from those that are false if we bring sufficient knowledge of the age to the examination of the texts. (pp. x–xi.) But his subsequent discussion of the New Testament and later religious writings brings him closer to agreement with Middleton. There is no doubt, he says, that the Gospel writers and their immediate followers the "Apostolic Fathers" convey sacred Truth without any violation of its "integrity", (p. xxiv.) whilst the learned writers of succeeding centuries did sometimes travesty "obscure uncertainties, nay, manifest errors into truth" and seek "in Philosophy and Logic analogies and quibbles to support them". (p. xxviii.)

3 RH probably refers to Warburton's suggestion that the writers of the Gospels and those who came immediately after them were simple men who wrote down plain facts. In contrast, the writers who succeeded them, Warburton says, were later converts among the educated classes who had at first resisted the Word, but when once converted became excessively zealous. (pp. xxv–xxix.) In their desire to spread the faith, he continues, they were prepared to impose upon the people, but with no "*immoral* intention to deceive". (p. xl.) Since therefore they are in a different category from the early Christian writers they must obviously be judged by different criteria and their accounts of miracles interpreted in a different context. This, Warburton believes, undercuts Middleton's arguments for dismissing these accounts as mere fictions.

4 RH alludes to Warburton's establishing the reality of the miracle. This made up the first section of the work. The other parts, as Warburton planned them, were "An Answer to Objections" and "An Enquiry into the *nature* of that evidence which is sufficient to claim a rational assent to the miraculous fact". (*Letters to and from the Rev. Philip Doddridge*, ed. Thomas Stedman, Shrewsbury, 1790, p. 206 (Warburton to Doddridge); *Prelate*, p. 5.)

5 Julian (332–63) is described on pp. 22–32, and the character of Ammianus Marcellinus (c.330–95), the last great Roman historian, is given on pp. 39, and 46–8.

6 In the first part of *Julian* Warburton gives an account of the emperor's efforts to revive paganism in the empire. His attacks on Christianity, he says, would have ended in the destruction of the religion "had it been nothing more than what he affected to think it, a human invention". (p. 23.) The fact that despite this Christianity continued to flourish proves therefore that it is the true religion.

7 Warburton demonstrates that sacrifices constituted the "substance" of Jewish worship and that they had to be performed in "one appointed Temple". (pp. 5–7.) He also shows that the Jewish faith was "preparatory and introductory to another more complete and perfect" religion before

reasoning, as I apprehend it, stands thus. The Jewish worship, as being the *shadow* or figure only of *one* more perfect, was, of necessity, on the introduction of the *substance*, to be done away. The temple was essential to the subsistence of that worship. Therefore the temple itself was also utterly and *finally* to be destroyed. But may it not be said, that all, which follows from the dependence of the two dispensations, is, that the *one* was to *cease*, that is, to be no longer of *obligation*, on the appearance of the *other*? Was any thing more requisite to the establishment of the Christian Institution, than that the Jewish be declared null and void? Or, was the honour of God's providence concerned to defeat, by extraordinary means, and overrule the Jew's perverseness in adhering to his abrogated ritual? The destruction of the temple might, as you observe from St. Chrysostom,[8] be a means *of withdrawing the Jew from the rage of ritual observances*. But was it essentially necessary, on account of the dependence betwixt the two religions, to the subsistence of Christianity. It is very likely, I may misrepresent or misconceive your argument. But you will perceive, I suspect some ambiguity in the term *done away* in the major proposition. And that my doubt is, whether it necessarily means, that the Jewish worship was to be removed, i.e. the *observance* of its ritual to be absolutely prevented, and rendered impracticable, – or that the *law* itself, enjoining such worship, was, simply, to be abrogated, or repealed.

I interest myself the more in the success of this argument, as it renders the miracle, here defended, of the last importance to Christianity, and thereby affords an illustrious instance, among a thousand others, of the momentous use, to which that great work of the D. L. will be found to serve.

On the whole, I can rely on your excuse for the freedom, I have here taken in hazarding these loose thoughts. Whatever else they may fail in, they will, at least, be a proof of the entire confidence I repose in your friendship, when I take a rout of so little ceremony to assure you of the very particular esteem, with which I am, always, Rev. Sir, Your most obliged and most faithful humble Servant,

R. Hurd.

106 To Sir EDWARD LITTLETON 28 DECEMBER 1749

Text: MS STAFFS RO D1413/1; unpublished.
Addressed: To/Sir Edward Littleton Bart/at Tedgely-Coppice near/ Penkrich/Staffordshire/By Lond:
Postmarked: CAMBRIDGE 29 DE

Dear Sir Edward

I am much less surpriz'd, than oblig'd, by your kind letter, wch gives me a fresh proof, if I wanted any, of your very sincere dispositions to serve me.[1]

which it was to give way. (pp. 7–8.) For this reason the Temple had to be destroyed in case the Jews attempted to prolong the life of their faith. RH's objection to this interpretation is valid, but if accepted, would lessen the force of Warburton's account of the miracle. If the Temple as the hub of the Jewish worship was not to be forever abolished, then there was less reason for God to act against Julian's attempt to rebuild it.

8 Warburton translates a passage from a sermon by St Chrysostom (c.347–407). His exact words are ". . . God covertly withdrew the Jews . . ." (pp. 9–10.) (Chrysostom, *Adversus Iudaeos*, Oratio VI.)

1 Littleton had agreed to lend a further sum of money to RH's brother Thomas. (See *ante* To Littleton, 7 October 1748, 27 October 1748, and 15 November 1748, for the previous transaction.)

The delicacy of your generosity wd be as much offended at my large acknowledgmts of this favour, as with any apologies for asking it. I will therefore content myself with returning you my hearty thanks, reserving it to time & opportunity to convince you of the sense I have of it.

I have directed my bro: to wait upon you at Tedgeley, according to your desire, after first of all consulting you, upon what day it wd be most agreable to you for him to do so. He will give you a receipt for the money, & I shall execute a bond to be transmitted to you as soon as possible.[2]

It surprizes me, that the Executors of Mr Levitt shd chuse to parcel out their books, instead of disposing of them at once for the price, you offer'd. Yet I still think, they will not be able to raise the intended sum that way. When the best books are pick'd out, the remainder may hang upon their hands a long time. They must come at last to booksellers, who will give hardly anything for them. I conclude therefore, you have some chance still.

Your brother is well, & returns to us with ye same good disposition to business. But at present I have some struggles with him abt a late regulation, wch the Coll. has made, & wch, for its various uses, I not only assent to, but approve strongly. What I mean are English exercises, wch have been long wanted, & are more especially adapted to the case of fell. Commoners.[3] I apprehended the most difficulty from declamations, wch however he very readily comes into. His greatest dislike is to themes, partly disgusted at the name, wch he thinks something boyish,[4] but principally I guess, (but it is mere surmise) because he has giv'n it out to his acquaintance, yt he will never submit to them. His temper, you know, wd. lead him to make a point of honour in being steady to this resolution.

The former prejudice I think I shall get the better of, by insisting on what I know to be true, yt these themes, or weekly essays on moral subjects, wch is their nature, are so far from being boyish, yt the absurdity lies in setting boys abt them, & that there are not very many, who call themselves *men*, capable of composing them.

The latter, if I find it to be well grounded, I shall attack in some proper way.

On the whole I do not despair of carrying my point, or rather *his*, for it will be of ye greatest use to him. The only obj. to these exercises has been, yt. they were confin'd to latin.

In ye mean time, he must not know, yt I have intimated anything of ys sort to you.

2 This bond has not been located amongst the Littleton family papers.

3 There is no record of this new regulation in the college's Order Book, nor apparently amongst other official papers. RH infers that English exercises were already known in Cambridge, and there is certain evidence that they were in practice at Oxford. Richard Newton in *Rules and Statutes for the Government of Hertford College*, 1747, stipulates that undergraduates should "make a *Theme* or a *Declamation* or a *Translation* every week in full term", and he says that the declamations should be in English during the second and third year, and in Latin in the fourth year. (Wordsworth, *Social Life at the English Universities*, pp. 574–83.) Fisher Littleton was in his second year. The benefit to Fellow-commoners from these exercises was to prepare them for public life, the sphere into which they were expected to move.

4 The word "theme" denoting an English exercise had been more usually associated with school exercises. (*O.E.D.*)

And, as I said, I have the greatest hopes of succeeding with him by my own proper authority.

All friends here send their services. You will give mine to J. Devie.

I am ever, Dearest Sir, Your most oblig'd & affect humble Servt

R. Hurd.

Camb. 28. Dec. 1749.

107 To Sir EDWARD LITTLETON 17 JANUARY 1750

Text: MS STAFFS RO D1413/1; unpublished.
Addressed: To/Sir Edward Littleton Bart/at Tedgely Coppice near/Penkridge
Postmarked: CAMBRIDGE 18 IA

Camb. 17. Jan. 1749/50.

Dear Sir

I have the favour of your very candid criticism on the inscrip. & am so much pleas'd with it, that, if You shd like it better, I wd alter it, thus:

Benevolentiae in omnes perquam studioso;
In suos summè officioso.[1]

The *suos*, as opposed to ye objects of general benevolence, will take in both *friends* & *relations*; & so, as I conceive, express the whole of your design, wch I approve extremely.

If you still think it defective, You must tell me your objections very freely.

To set you an example, I shall give you mine to your motto from Horace, witht. reserve.[2]

The lines are, it must be own'd, very pertinent, as you apply them. But a motto to an inscr. is not only agst. all rule & example, but, in itself, highly improper, as not being of a piece with ye plainess & unpretending simplicity of an epitaph. But my principal argt agst it, is, that very striking pertinency, wch recommended this couplet to you. It wd have stood excellently at the head of a poem or other piece, written, on purpose to vindicate Mr B's character. But if you consult your judgmt., instead of your warm friendship, & affection for his memory, I dare say, you will think the severity of such a motto, unsuitable to the design of an epitaph, wch is meant to give your cool, dispassionate sentiments of his virtues. I lay ye greater stress upon this, because, I think, it will owe a great part of it's effect to it's appearing *dispassionate*.

1 The lines previously ran:

"Omnium, quibus cum vixerat familiariter, studioso
In suos summe officioso".

(See *ante* To Littleton, 7 August 1749.) RH later altered this to,

"In omnes perquam faciliet benevole
In amicos summe officioso".

(See *post* To Littleton, 4 September 1750.)

2 This motto on Budworth's character has not survived.

I'm glad, the workman will soon go upon it, for, as I have taken ye liberty to hint to you, before, ye sooner the stone is put up, the better.[3]

Your bro: shewd me your letter, wch was written with great prudence & address. I believe it has done ye business. But you shall hear more of ys matter, in my next.[4]

I take very kindly your concern abt my collection of Vandykes. I have *Jaspar Gevartius, Theodore Galle, Antonius Triest,* & *Vandyke himself,* more than you suppos'd. But my Vandyke is but indifferent.[5] And as many <. . .> of the others, as you meet with & think worth framing, will be extremely acceptable.

You'll think it a bad return for so much kindness, to provoke your envy, by telling you, there is an honest Gentl. in my study, who is not asham'd to shew his face ev'n before your Rembrant.[6]

I thought, I had quite done with Horace. But Mr Warburton has engag'd me to write a Com: & notes on the Ep. to Augustus. I don't think, it wants much illustration. But he presses it in such a way, yt I must not refuse him.[7]

The new Ed. of Pope's works will be out soon.[8] I have seen some part of it, & think you will be vastly pleas'd with it.

Something is whisper'd of your going to London soon. If this be true, I hope, you will make Camb. in your way; or rather I depend upon it.

Your's most faithfully & affectionately,

R. Hurd.

3 The stone had still not been chosen by the beginning of October. (See *post* To Littleton, 1 October 1750.)

4 What "business" RH refers to has not been established; his "next" letter cannot be traced.

5 RH had reminded Littleton of his interest in collecting Van Dyck's portrait etchings and engravings in March of the previous year. (See *ante* To Littleton, 21 March 1749.) The interest in making up these collections is reflected in the publication of the *Iconographie ou Vies des Hommes Illustres . . . avec les Portraits Peints par le fameux Antoine Van Dyck*, 2 vols., Amsterdam & Leipzig, 1759.

6 No painting by Rembrandt is specifically mentioned in the inventory of Littleton's paintings drawn up in 1812. (Staffs. RO, Ex. D260/M/T/5/110.) But in a letter of 18 September 1749, Littleton mentions acquiring "a head by Rembrandt", and adds in a later letter (both to Edward Macro) that he has some paintings by that "Master yt. [he is] in hopes will do". (*Macro Letter-book*.)

7 Warburton had first suggested that RH produce an annotated edition of Horace's *Epistola ad Augustum* in the previous June. (*Prelate*, Warburton to Hurd, 6 June 1749, p. 3.) In August 1749, after some demurring, RH agreed to begin work on the *Epistola* (*Ibid.*, p. 7), which was published and on sale by May 1751. (See *post* To Macro, 21 May 1751.)

8 *The Works of Alexander Pope Esq. In Nine Volumes Complete. With his Last Corrections, Additions, and Improvements; As they were delivered to the Editor a little before his Death: Together with the Commentaries and Notes of* Mr. *Warburton*. Warburton's edition was in fact not advertised till August 1751 when the date of publication was set as "October next". (*London Evening-Post*, 29–31 August 1751.) In providing a fully annotated edition of Pope, Warburton elevated him to the same category as Milton and Shakespeare, the only other British authors whose texts had been similarly treated. The edition proved highly popular and was frequently reprinted in the next twenty years. (*Pope. The Critical Heritage*, ed. John Barnard, 1973, pp. 23, 366.)

108 To Sir EDWARD LITTLETON 9 MARCH 1750

Text: MS STAFFS RO D1413/1; unpublished.
Addressed: To/Sir Edward Littleton Bart/at Mr Cosgreave's Suffolk-Street/Charing-Cross/London.
Postmarked: CAMBRIDGE 10 MR

Camb. 9. March. 1749/50.

Dear Sir

I perceive you are not philosopher enough to observe a perfect moderation in your good fortune. Tho' a little elation of heart may, I think, be allowed to you, on such an acquisition, as your letter to your brother speaks of.[1] As for A. *Philips*' own originals, tho' they may not be of great value, yet they are worth accepting. And his correspondence, consisting of the great names, you mention, I envy you. To appease this turbulent passion, You must lay aside now & then one for me.

Indeed I am the more inclin'd, as well as oblig'd, to congratulate with you, very heartily, on this treasure, as you take so much pains to enlarge my collection. The *Inigo Jones* is a curiosity, I shall be proud of.[2] And no matter how soon you convey it to me. Perhaps Mr Mainwaring, who, I hear, is expected to morrow, will bring it.

The impudence of Hogarth in setting such a price on his big bellies, is insufferable. I wd <not> scarcely give £200 for all the pictures, the buffoon ever painted.[3]

I have consider'd your objection to *suos*; & cannot meet with any authority, that fully satisfies me. So yt, after all, we must take up with old *Amicos*.[4]

Your brother return'd from Norwich, soon after you left us. And has since exerted

1 Littleton had just acquired a large proportion of the papers of Ambrose Philips; a description of the transaction is included in a letter to Edward Macro dated 7 March 1750. "In making an accidental visit ye other day to a Lady who was a distant Relation of Am: Philip's", Littleton writes, "I found she had the intire custody of all his Papers. This, without doubt, made me think of a second visit, when I most triumphantly brought off as many as two horses cd. drag along in a Coach at twice. There are all his Poems almost intire", he continues, "with several Notes & Commentarys both critical & explanatory upon various Authors; add to these a vast collection of State Papers from many of the Nobility. O! the Carterets, the Baths', & I know not who besides; to omitt ye Swifts', ye Addisons, Steels, &c; &c; &c." (*Macro Letter-book*.)

2 Inigo Jones (1572–1651), architect. The engraved portrait of Jones may have been a contribution to RH's collection of Van Dycks (see preceding letter, n. 5). No other artist appears to have completed a portrait of the architect. (Henry Bromley, *A Catalogue of Engraved British Portraits, From Egbert the Great to the Present Time*, 1793, p. 107.) RH had received the print by the end of March (see *post* To Littleton 29 March 1750); its later whereabouts are not documented.

3 This remark may have been provoked by news of the arrangements being made for the disposal of Hogarth's *The March to Finchley* in its original form as a painting. The print of the picture was advertised for sale by subscription on 16 March 1750, and on 23 April Hogarth placed an advertisement in the *General Advertiser* announcing that the painting was to be offered as a prize in a lottery. It was drawn by the Governors of the Foundling Hospital who were immediately offered £200 for it by the Duke of Ancaster. Hogarth apparently estimated that he had made £300 by the lottery. Littleton's information on the painting probably came from Michael Rysbrack who was a friend of Hogarth's and in frequent consultation also with Sir Edward. (Ronald Paulson, *Hogarth: His Life, Art, and Times*, 2 vols, Yale, 1971, ii. 43, 90–4.) RH's apparent dislike of Hogarth's work is not typical of the general contemporary reaction to his prints and paintings.

4 See previous letter. RH must have used "amicos" as opposed to "suos" in the first draft of Budworth's inscription, now lost.

himself wonderfully in the affair of declaming.[5] His subject was, *the preference of a public to a private life*, on wch he wrote better, & with more ease to himself, than I expected on his first attempt. He was so very eloquent in the praise of patriotism, yt I know not how you will be able to justify your own retir'd resolutions agst him.

He also makes themes very chearfully, & very decently.[6]

The new play is full as good, as I expected.[7] The action, we are told, was inimitable. But you will give me your opinion of these matters.

Since you wrote, I am in hopes, you have had better success at auctions.[8] Mr Macro will be here in a few days, & then, if the *E. of Arundel & his son*[9] be worth your having, I will endeavour to treat with Jacob[10] about it.

All friends send services.

I am, with the truest affection, Dear Sir, Your most faithful humble Servt

R. Hurd.

109 To Sir EDWARD LITTLETON 29 MARCH 1750

Text: MS STAFFS RO D1413/1; unpublished.
Addressed:. To/Sir Edward Littleton Bart/at Mr Cosgreave's in/ Suffolk Street/Charing-Cross/London.
Postmarked: CAMBRIDGE [3]0 MR

Dear Sir

I have the pleasure of two of your letters to acknowledge.

In the first you criticize the new play.[1] You do not express your opinion of it very determinately. But I think, your objections amount to thus much. That there are no marks of great genius in the drawing of his characters. And that, in particular, the Roman Father is drawn with too much humanity.

The first obj. is certainly just. Mr W. is not capable of that sublime, & those strong touches of nature, wch sometimes strike & almost astonish us in the writings of Shakespear. This was not to be expected from him. To excell in this kind is the

5 Fisher Littleton was back in Emmanuel by 24 February. (*Commons Accounts Book*, STE. 15. 9.) He had begun writing declamations in December of the previous year. (See *ante* To Littleton, 28 December 1749.)

6 See *ante* To Littleton, 28 December 1749.

7 William Whitehead's play, *The Roman Father, A Tragedy* had been performed for the first time on Saturday 24 February, at Drury Lane. According to contemporary comment it was "receiv'd with Extravagant applause", and it became part of the company's regular repertory. (*The London Stage 1660–1800. A Calendar of Plays, Entertainments & Afterpieces . . . Part 4: 1747–1776*, ed. George Winchester Stone, Jr., 3 vols., Carbondale, 1962, i. 136, 178–80.) The published work was advertised for sale on 5 March. (*Gen. Advertiser.*)

8 Littleton had just missed one important auction and had been to two others, where, he says, he "was uneasy at finding nothing yt. wd. suit" him. His only buy was a conversation piece by Le Duc. (*Macro Letter-book*, Littleton to Macro, 8 March 1750.)

9 Probably a copy of an etching by Hollar after Van Dyck. The subjects are Thomas Howard, second Earl of Arundel and Surrey, and his son, Lord Mowbray and Maltravers. (O'Donoghue, *Catalogue of Engraved British Portraits in the British Museum*, i. 76–7.)

10 Unidentified.

1 William Whitehead's *The Roman Father, A Tragedy*.

privilege only of first-rate spirits. The world never produc'd but very few of them. It should therefore satisfy us, & indeed may be reckon'd a considerable merit in a writer, if he be able to conduct his subject simply & naturally, if his characters do in the main represent real life, & if there be no gross violations of good sense in their sentiments or actions.[2] And this merit I take the *Roman father* to have. It has the principal beauties of Corneille, witht. his blemishes & absurdities.[3]

Your other obj. is well aim'd, if you take your idea of the *R. Father*, as you ought to do, from the Roman history & manners.[4] Strictly speaking, he shd have been drawn witht. those compassionate relentings. But ye house wd not have endur'd this. Such a severity of manners wd have seem'd incredible & out of nature. That he might not shock his audience, he was therefore oblig'd to soften his character a little. But then this shews (what I take to be certainly the case) that the story itself is, considering our difference of manners, a very improper one for our stage.

Tho' Dr Nevile is no great admirer, as you rightly suppos'd, yet he is more candid, than I expected.

In your second favour you are so obliging, as to press my going with you into Staffordshire, with Mr Macro.[5] I need not say, that this would be very agreable to me, on ev'ry account. But things are so circumstanc'd, yt I cannot, with any convenience, leave college till tow'rds Midsummer. Then indeed I have long promis'd myself the pleasure of spending some agreable days with you at the Coppice. And perhaps that time, may suit Mr Macro full as well. When he comes, I will talk with him & let you know our resolutions.

I am vastly oblig'd to you for Inigo Jones. 'Tis an excellent print.[6]

You have also laid me under fresh obligations by procuring me some others, wch you give me leave to expect soon, & by a promise of some part of your paper-treasure.[7] Mr Mainwaring let drop something of Mr Hutcheson.[8] If one of the letters, you design for me, shd be of his hand, I shall be very happy.

But m[y . . .] obligation to you is for your acceptance of the little [. . .] of *Trag. &*

2 The critics were not unanimous in declaring Whitehead's characterisation to be realistic. In the same month as the play was published (March) an anonymous writer brought out *Remarks on the New Tragedy, Call'd The Roman Father*, an ironic attack suggesting that the characters and their actions were improbable, and the play itself dull.

3 The comparison between *The Roman Father* and Pierre Corneille's *Horace, tragedie* (1640) was often made, and a short work on the subject was published at the same time as the play itself. The volume consists of an exchange of letters between friends and is entitled *A Comparison between the Horace of Corneille and the Roman Father of Mr. Whitehead*. Though praising Corneille for his ability to excite admiration, the writer finally asserts a preference for Whitehead's play because of its power to arouse feelings of love and pity, and to convey what the characters really felt. ([W. Freeman, *pseud.*], *A Comparison*, 1750.)

4 RH had stressed the importance of modelling dramatic characters according to their historical context in the Commentary to his edition of Horace's *Ars Poetica*, 1749. Paraphrasing the original text, he states with approval that Horace had recommended it "as a point of principal concern in the drawing of them [characters], to be well acquainted with the manners, agreeing to the several successive periods and stages of human life". (p. 13.)

5 Littleton had put forward this idea in a letter to Macro dated 8 March 1750. (*Macro Letter-book.*) As enticement, he mentions the possibility of visits to Derbyshire and to Hagley Hall, the home of the Lyttelton family.

6 See preceding letter, n. 2

7 See preceding letter, n. 1.

8 Francis Hutcheson (1694–1747), moral philosopher. No letter from Hutcheson has been preserved amongst RH's collection of autographs at Hartlebury Castle.

Comedy.[9] I have never seen it, & am afraid, 'tis of no great value. But your partiality to the A. of poetry made me incline to flatter myself, that you wd not refuse it.

After so many favours done to myself, I cannot, in mere gratitude, but rejoyce very sincerely with you on your late good success at Auctions. *Trevisiani*[10] is surely a good name. One of Dr Macro's best pictures is, if I remember right, of his hand.[11] Your Ryisdale must be valuable.[12]

I shall write again, when Mr Macro arrives. In the mean time let me know, what pass'd at the Countess of Sunderland's.[13]

Dearest Sir, Your most affectionate & oblig'd humble Servt

R. Hurd.

Camb. 29. March. 1750.

110 To Sir EDWARD LITTLETON 6 APRIL 1750

Text:. MS STAFFS RO D1413/1; unpublished.
Addressed: To/Sir Edwd Littleton Bart/at Mr Cosgreave's Suffolk-Street/Charing-Cross
Postmarked: CAMBRIDGE 7 AP

Dear Sir

An ugly affair has happen'd, which absolutely prevents Mr Macro's coming to town, & I'm afraid, his going with me into Staffordshire.[1] This is a great mortification to him. Tho', if possible, he will make an elopement in August.

He has seen Mr Wrag's picture,[2] & says, it is a tolerable one, & might have a place in a collection, witht. disgracing it. He thinks, however, you should not give much for

9 No work specifically treating of both tragedy and comedy, and published at this time has been traced. But RH could be referring to A *Dissertation on Comedy: In which the Rise and Progress of that Species of the Drama is particularly consider'd . . . By a Student of Oxford* which had been advertised for sale in January. (*Gent. Mag.*) This work contains a discussion of tragedy as well as comedy in the first section.

10 Cavaliere Francesco Trevisani (1656–1746). This picture may be the painting of St Jerome which is recorded in the inventory of Littleton's paintings. (Staffs. RO, Ex D260/M/T/5/110.) Its estimated value then was £80. Trevisani was esteemed for his ability to imitate the style of Old Masters such as Correggio and Parmigiano.

11 Two portraits by Trevisani are listed in a catalogue of Cox Macro's paintings (MS BL, Add. 25473, *Catalogue of the Library etc. of Cox Macro, D.D. 1766.*) They are described as "Our Saviours head. Ecce homo, a very fine one. By Trevisane one of ye best painters in Italy" (no. 36, f. 27r.), and "Mary Magdalen, a very fine picture by Trevisano" (no. 101, f. 28v.).

12 Probably a reference to Jakob van Ruysdael (c.1630–82). At his death Littleton owned a Ruysdael "Sea Piece" valued at £50.

13 This allusion remains obscure. Elizabeth Spencer, the Countess of Sunderland, had become the Duchess of Marlborough in 1733 on the succession of her husband to the Dukedom. RH's use of her earlier title has not been explained.

1 Edward Macro was involved in a court case which came up at the Suffolk Assizes during 1750. Edward Littleton, in a letter of 28 October 1750, condoled with Macro on his defeat, and Osmund Beauvoir, in a letter of 21 April 1751, expressed the expectation that, following the court case, Macro would be chased by the Suffolk ladies. (*Macro Letter-book.*) No further explanatory documentation has been located.

2 Unidentified.

it. Four guineas, he believes, is the full worth of it. You will consider this matter & give me your orders accordingly.

He is vastly more delighted with Mr Finch's[3] landskape, wch he admires exceedingly & says, you should by all means contrive to get it, if possible. In talking with some of the family, he apprehends, there is reason to conclude, it wd not be impracticable. But I rather doubt of this. It's present possessor is too rich to make any attempt upon him. But Mr Macro thinks his avarice might be tempted.

As far as I understand your criticism on the R. Father,[4] we shall not much disagree in our sentiments of it. But I must know the particular scene, & Speeches, you object to, before I can give you my opinion.

Poor Manwaring is very indifferent. He wants to be gone from hence, & set out on his Aix-la Chapelle journey, in hopes that travelling will be some relief to him.[5] I believe, he will return to town in a fortnight; but before that time, we have some expectation of seeing you here. Your brother gives us some hope, of your calling at Cambridge for a few days, when you leave London. I would tempt you by supposing, that this might give you a chance of procuring Mr Finch's picture.

All friends are very much your's, but more especially, Dearest Sir, Your affectionate, humble Servt

R. Hurd.

Camb. 6. April. 1750.

111 To Sir EDWARD LITTLETON 11 JUNE 1750

Text: MS STAFFS RO D1413/1; unpublished.
Addressed: To/Sir Edward Littleton Bart/at Tedgeley Coppi[ce] near/Penkrich/Staffordshire
Postmarked: CAMBRIDGE 12

Camb. Monday. 11. June. 1750.

Dear Sir

I tell you, with great pleasure, yt I intend setting out for Staffords- on wednesday next, but shall not come the direct road. Mr Balguy has seduc'd me with Him thro' Lincolnshire;[1] & 'tis possible I may spend a day or two with a Gentleman in the way. However I can hardly be longer in coming to you than the middle of the next week: probably somewhat sooner.

3 Unidentified; but perhaps of the same branch of the Finch family as Edward Finch, M.P. for Cambridge University 1727–68.

4 See preceding letter.

5 John Mainwaring had reached Aix-la-Chapelle by the middle of July 1750, and wrote to Edward Littleton in much better spirits. He hoped not to return to England that winter, but to continue his travels down to Italy. (Mainwaring to Littleton, 17 July 1750, Staffs. RO, D1413/2.)

1 Balguy held two livings in Lincolnshire and had been made a Prebendary of Lincoln Cathedral in 1748.

My portmanteau will be sent away on Thursday, & if what Hickmans[2] tells me may be depended upon, it will be at the four Crosses by Monday or Tuesday.[3]

Mr Macro desires me to inform you, he has attempted to see Dr Symonds,[4] but witht. success, as he is not at home, & it will be two or three months, before he returns to Bury.

Dearest Sir Your most affectionate humble Servt

R Hurd.

112 To Sir EDWARD LITTLETON 14 JUNE 1750

Text: MS STAFFS RO D1413/1; unpublished.
Addressed: To/Sir Edward Littleton Bart/at Tedgeley Coppice near/Penkrich/Staffordshire/By Lond.
Postmarked: 15 IV

Dear Sir

Since I troubled you with my last, I understand, yt the Chester Coach does not now go thro' Northampton,[1] so yt I shall bring my portmanteau along with me.

I also foresee a possibility of my going as far as Matlock & Chesterfield, before I turn off for Tedgley. A gent.[2] in yt neighbourhood presses it so strongly, that I almost apprehend, I shall be drawn thither.

If this shd happen, & especially as I have been kept here a day or two longer, than I intended, it will be the very end of the next, or the beginning of the following, week, before I shall reach you.

I have talk'd with Mr Wrags about his picture, & believe I shall have it.

Nothing more has been hear'd of Mr Finch's.[3]

I am impatient to be with you, being very truly Dear Sir, Your most faithful & affectionate humble Servt

R Hurd.

Camb. 14. Jun. 1750.

2 Unidentified.

3 The Four Crosses Inn was on the "Great" road from London to Chester, 123 miles out of London. (Daniel Paterson, *A New and Accurate Description of All the Direct and Principal Cross Roads in Great Britain*, 1771, p. 50.)

4 John Symonds (1697–1757), rector of Rushbrooke, Horningsheath and Nowton in Suffolk, and preacher at St Mary's, Bury St Edmunds. (*Alum. Cantab.*) Littleton was hoping to buy a picture by Morel, probably Jean Baptiste (1662–1732), a flower painter, which Symonds had in his possession. (*Macro Letter-book*, Littleton to Macro, 28 October 1750.) It is not known whether he secured the work.

1 RH evidently wished to put his portmanteau on a coach at Northampton to be left at the Four Crosses Inn later on. The latter was on the London-Chester coach road which did not pass through Northampton.

2 Unidentified.

3 Neither Wrag(s) nor Finch have been identified. See *ante* To Littleton, 6 April 1750, for earlier references to them.

113 To Sir EDWARD LITTLETON 20 AUGUST 1750

Text: MS STAFFS RO D1413/1; unpublished.
Addressed: To/Sir Edward Littleton

Dear Sir

My fathers illness,[1] wch has been very severe, prevented my return to Camb. so soon as I intended & indeed kept me in such uncertainty as to ye time of setting out, yt it was not possible for me to give you any notice of it. It has now unfortunately happen[']d yt I am disappointed of ye pleasure of seeing you by your being at the Assizes,[2] wch I did not in ye least suspect, till it was too late to alter my design.

I have inclosed Dr Nevile's Horation epistle,[3] wch, with compliments to you, was sent me some time ago, & Mr W's letter,[4] wch you seemed to have a mind of.

I shall be glad of a letter from you, as soon as your leisure will give leave, in wch I doubt not to hear of your having fix'd upon a stone for poor Mr B's monument.[5] This, I think, was ye most material business we had to transact, in wch, however, you cannot stand in need of my assistance.

I return the more reluctantly from not being permitted to take my leave of you, in a way so much more agreable to my wishes, than this of assuring you, upon paper, how truly I am ever, Dearest Sir Edward, Your most affectionate friend & Servt

R. Hurd.

Brewood 20 Aug. 1750.

114 To Sir EDWARD LITTLETON 4 SEPTEMBER 1750

Text: MS STAFFS RO D1413/1; unpublished.
Addressed: To/Sir Edward Littleton Bart/at Tedgely-Coppice near/Penkrich/Staffordshire
Postmarked: CAMBRIDGE

Dear Sir

How could you resolve to mortify me by reminding me of so many particulars, wch assure yourself I could not forget? But as things fell out, it was impracticable for me to

1 RH's father died in 1755 apparently of cancer. This illness may be linked to his subsequent death.

2 The Assizes were held in Stafford on 18 August 1750. (*London Gazette*, 30 June – 3 July 1750.)

3 Thomas Nevile published a number of verse imitations with parallel text of Horace's *Satires* and *Epistles*. Two epistles (including the seventeenth which was dedicated to Littleton), one satire and an epode were published separately between 1749 and 1756. Others were collected together and issued as *Imitations of Horace* in 1758. The epistle referred to here must have been an unpublished imitation, Nevile's only previous publication being the *First Epode of the Second Book of Horace Imitated*, 1749.

4 An allusion either to a personal letter addressed to RH (see *Prelate*, pp. 23–56 for some letters written to RH by Warburton in 1750) or to *A Letter to the Editor of the Letters on The Spirit of Patriotism, The Idea of a Patriot-King, and The State of Parties, &c., occasioned by the Editor's Advertisement* published by Warburton in 1749. It followed the publication of *Letters on the Spirit of Patriotism* by Henry, Viscount Bolingbroke, which carried a preliminary 'Advertisement' accusing Pope of dishonourable conduct. (Evans, *Warburton and the Warburtonians*, pp. 167–70.)

5 The stone for William Budworth's memorial had still not been selected by the beginning of October. (See *post* To Littleton, 1 October 1750.)

follow my inclination. You had talked so much & so warmly agst the Assize-business, yt I never suspected your going to Stafford, till Mr Slaney[1] put it into my head, wch was ye very day before I set out; when I had actually sent away my portmanteau & was obliged to follow it. Besides cd I have waited your return, I understood the old Counsellor of Hatton[2] & his son intended at yt very time to visit you for some days; so yt my coming wd have been to no purpose. But, indeed, I had so much outstayed my time, yt, for many reasons, I was impatient to get back to college. And I come but just in time to prepare for Sturb. fair, wch begins ys week.[3]

I could have wished indeed to have talked with Mr Littleton about what you mention. But I shall have occasion to send his bill next week[4] & then I shall not omit to give a hint or two, wch you will know how to improve to ye purpose. For ys reason I shall contrive to send a message to you in it, yt you may see ye letter.

But for my own disappointmt, I am extremely glad you went to Stafford. You know I always thought it right for you to do so. And I shall be extremely glad to understand, how notably you bestirred yourself in ys new province.[5]

Nothing could give me more pleasure than ye good news you tell me of Mr Mainwaring.[6] I have made his friends here very happy in communicating it. Pray tell me, how Mr Stafford does![7] It will be a satisfaction to him, at ye worst, to hear yt help is to be had from foreign waters.

Betwixt being very busy & not very well I am prevented adding anything more, but

1 Plowden Slaney of Hatton Grange, who rented out a farm to RH's elder brother, John. RH had frequently stayed at Hatton since the late 1730s, and knew a number of people in the area.

2 Probably a further reference to Slaney.

3 Sturbridge Fair ran from 7 September for three weeks and was considered at this time to be one of the greatest fairs in Europe. (Carter, *History of the County of Cambridge*, 1753, p. 21.) According to Carter, the "shops or booths" were built in "rows like streets, having each their name, as *Garlick-Row*, *Booksellers-Row*, *Cook-Row*, &c. And every commodity", he continues, "has its proper place, as the Cheese-fair, Hop-fair, Wool-fair, &c. And here, as in several other streets or rows, are all sorts of traders who sell by wholesale or retail, as goldsmiths, toymen, brasiers, turners, milliners, haberdashers, hatters, mercers, drapers, pewterers, China-warehouses, and in a word, most trades that can be found in *London*; from whence many of them come; here are also taverns, coffee-houses, and eating-houses in great plenty, and all kept in booths, except six or seven brick houses built many years ago, and in any of which, (except the coffee-booth) you may at any time be accomodated with hot or cold roast goose, roast or boil'd pork, &c." The University was involved in the running of the fair as well as the town, having "the oversight of the weights, and measures thereof . . . and the licencing of all shew-booths, live-creatures, &c." The Proctors of the University kept a court there "to hear complaints about weights or measures, seek out and punish lewd women, and see that their gownsmen commit no disorders". (pp. 22, 26–27.)

4 The Midsummer Quarter of the university year ended at the beginning of September. Undergraduates' bills for rent, food and study were issued soon after.

5 Littleton had attended the Assize Court at Stafford on 18 August (see preceding letter); in what capacity it has not been discovered.

6 A reference to John Mainwaring's recovery from illness. His health had been "very indifferent" in the spring (see *ante* To Littleton, 6 April 1750), but had been improved by a journey to Aix-la-Chapelle, famed as a spa since the days of the Roman Empire.

7 James Stafford (1715–94) was vicar of Penkridge, and had been an undergraduate at St John's from 1738 to 1742.

ye transcript of the Insc. wch you desire, & am, with ye services of all friends, Dearest Sir, Your's most affectionately & faithfully

R Hurd.

Camb. 4. Sept. 1750.

I transcribe ye inscript. from my memory, having somewhere mislaid my copy of it. I believe it is right. But you will compare it with ye copy, you have of it. The Stone-cutter will see from ys rough draught ye manner, in wch it must be engraved.

Gulielmo Budworth A.M.

Hujus simul ac Ecclesiae de Brewoodensis
Nuper Pastori;
Et literarii ludi ibidem habiti
Praefecto:
In utrumque munus,
Innocentia vitae, morum comitate,
Humanioribus literis, eloquentia simplici,
Instructissimo;
In omnes perquam facili et benevolo,
In amicos summe officioso;
Ab omni tamen in alios illiberali obsequio,
Potentiorum certe cultu servili,
Alienissimo:
Huic tali Viro,
Optimo olim Magistro,
Amico insuper dilectissimo,
Hoc qualecunque amoris et grati animi testimonium
Ponendum curavit

Edvardus Littleton Baronettus.

MDCCL.

115 To Sir EDWARD LITTLETON 1 OCTOBER 1750

Text: MS STAFFS RO D1413/1; unpublished.
Addressed: To/Sir Edward Littleton Bart/at his House near/ Penkrich/Staffordshire
Postmarked: CAMBRIDGE 2 OC

Dear Sir

It is just as I expected. There are several faults in ye copy of the Inscription, I sent you. But you have set 'em right. It should be, as your copy has it *Et literarii ibidem Ludi – optimo olim praeceptori – Ecclesiae de Brewood* –[1]

The next news I shall be in expectation of, is, that the stone is pitched upon, and the workman employed in cutting it. Methinks, I could wish to hear of it's being put up, before you go to town this winter.

Your conversation with Mr Seward[2] was pretty curious. It is unaccountable, yt. Mr

1 See preceding letter and inscription, ll. 3, 15, 1.

2 Thomas Seward (1708–90), father of Anna Seward. The family were living at Eyam in Derbyshire.

Lytelton could think so meanly of the Monody.[3] It must proceed from some prejudice he had taken up agst *Imitations*. But what did he say of the original part? I should so far be of a mind with him, that what was purely Mr Mason's own was by much the best in that poem.

On the whole I agree with you, in thinking that Mr L. is no very exact critic.

Mr Mason, who is just returned to College, was with me yesterday. He inquired much after you, and desired services.

The speaking of *criticism* puts me in mind to tell you, yt I have been busying myself, of late, in preparing my papers on the Ep. to Augustus.[4] They are in such forwardness, that I believe I shall get them ready for ye press in a short time. The Ep. itself, you know, is not difficult. So that a continued commentary is not so needful to clear the sense, as it was in the *Art of poetry*. This, wch should seem to shorten my trouble, has, in fact, enlarged it. For, having very little to teach ye reader, I was obliged to study ornament. Which has drawn out the commentary to a greater length, than I expected.[5]

The notes, as those on A. P., are miscellaneous. Some of them explanatory, and immediately respecting the subject of the ep. Others are foreign & digressive.

I have one in wch I speak of Ld. Bolingbroke, that *melter* of all hearts, in a manner, you will not disapprove. It is with an eye to his treatment of Mr Pope.[6]

Perhaps, I may take ye pains to transcrib[e] it for you in my next.[7]

Mr Bourgeois said something to me the other day, about a bill he sent you by Mr

3 William Mason's first publication, *Musaeus: a Monody to the Memory of Mr. Pope, in Imitation of Milton's Lycidas*, 1747. The poem had not been reprinted since 1748, but was the subject of a correspondence in the *Gentleman's Magazine* in 1749. Most critics approved of the poem, though some criticised the extended imitations of Chaucer, Spenser and Milton, incorporated in it. George Lyttelton (of Hagley) may have been amongst these, or he may have disliked the way in which the earlier writers are made to address Pope as if he had excelled them. (Philip Gaskell, *The First Editions of William Mason*, Cambridge Bibliographical Society Monograph No. 1, 1951.)

4 RH had begun work on the *Epistola ad Augustum* in the autumn of 1749. He sent the almost completed work to Warburton in October 1750 and had finished it entirely by the middle of December. (*Prelate*, pp. 47, 48, 52.)

5 The Commentary to the *Epistola ad Augustum* occupies proportionately more space than that accompanying the *Ars Poetica*. The Notes take up 69 octavo pages, however, as opposed to 111 pages accompanying the *Ars Poetica*. The distinction between Commentary and Notes is less clear in the later work.

6 The allusion to Bolingbroke occurs on the third page of Notes (p. 33) in RH's discussion of ll. 13–14 of Horace's *Epistola*. The poet writes:

> "Urit enim fulgore suo, qui praegravat artis
> Infra se positas: extinctus amabitur idem".

But, says RH, he adds "as some consolation to the sufferings of *living* excellence, that its *memory* shall be had in reverence after death: *extinctus amabitur idem*". This does not always happen though, he goes on, as in the "case of a late *sun of glory*; the lustre of whose genius, even to his parting ray, was so insufferable, that a very bosom friend [Bolingbroke], the moment he was *set*, could not help confessing the uneasiness, he had always felt from it. For, though the choicest of his beams were still reserved to gild this idol of his friendship, yet so unequal were his mere mortal powers to the honour of these divine communications, that, like the thunderer's *fires*, in the fable, their misfortune was to *burn*, where they intended to *bless*."

7 RH's next letter is dated 21 December. No correspondence between October and December has survived.

Littleton.[8] I believe, the poor man would be glad to have the money remitted to him immediately.

I am, with the truest affection, Dear Sir, Your most faithful, humble Servt

R. Hurd.

Camb. 1. Oct. 1750.

116 To Sir EDWARD LITTLETON 21 DECEMBER 1750

Text: MS STAFFS RO D1413/1; unpublished.
Addressed: To/Sir Edward Littleton Bart/at Tedgeley near/ Penkrich/Staffords—/By Lond:
Postmarked: CAMBRIDGE 22 DEC

Camb. 21. Dec. 1750.

Dear Sir

I thank you for the favour of your's. What you say of the note on L. B.[1] you may be sure gives me great pleasure. I need not intimate to you, yt I would not have the thing, at present, go any farther.

I shall be much obliged to you for the two landskapes, you speak of. For, tho' they should not turn out perfect masterpieces, they may still deserve a place in my collection.[2]

I am glad you determine to go to town so soon. I shall be there in the latter end of February and shall stay a fortnight or three weeks.

Not a word yet of your brother.

Pray give my service to Captain Tonyn[3] and let him know I am very much out of humour at his passing thro' Cambridge, as he did yesterday, witht giving me the pleasure of seeing him. He must make me amends for this, when he returns.

Dear Sir, Your most affectionate and faithful humble Servt

R H

What news from Mainwaring, who I hear is come to Drayton?[4]

8 M. Bourgeois taught French at Cambridge. He seems to have been well known in RH's circle, and gave lessons to Robert Potter as well as to Sir Edward. (MS BL, Add. 32557, ff. 27–8.)

1 Lord Bolingbroke. (See preceding letter, n. 6.)

2 No further information has been discovered concerning these pictures.

3 Patrick Tonyn of the 6th Dragoons (see *ante* To Littleton, 26 May 1749, n. 6). Tonyn was made a Lieutenant in 1748 and Captain in 1751; this premature reference to him as "Captain" is therefore either polite or an indication that he had been awarded the rank of Brevet-Captain. He eventually became General in Command of the 48th Foot. (Lieut.-Col. Russell Gurney, *History of the Northamptonshire Regiment 1742–1934*, Aldershot, 1935, p. 388.)

4 John Mainwaring had been born at Drayton Manor only a few miles away from Teddesley Park. He had by this time been made a Fellow of St John's (1748) and was evidently returning home for the vacation.

117 To THOMAS BALGUY 19 MARCH 1751

Text: MS BEINECKE MS Vault Shelves, Hurd; printed, *Memoirs*, 44.
Addressed: cover missing.

Dear Sir

I expect to be believed, when I assure you, that no one can possibly be more tender of your reputation, than I am; and that therefore I should never have pressed you to give leave to have your papers inserted in my medley, but that I was convinced, they would be as much to your credit, as to the ornament of my trifling book.[1] Mr Ws strong approbation of them satisfied me, that I was not mistaken in this opinion.[2] And notwithstanding all you say, I must still think, you could possibly suffer no other dishonour from their insertion, than what might arise from the circumstance of their being found in such company. However as <you think otherwise, and> the apprehension you are in of the opinion of the multitude (which surely is more scrupulous, than your great merit needs subject you to) inclines you to think otherwise, I forbear to trouble you any farther about them.

Yet your refusal lays me under great difficulties. I cannot think of dressing up your thoughts in worse language of my own. And to take the merit of so long a note to myself, and especially as given in your own words, is downright impudence. Besides, for want of your last hand to the papers I have (for the new paragraph you have sent is not, I think, so applicable to my purpose, as that I wished you to correct for me) I am reduced to the necessity of omitting a very material part of them, or of injuring your sense by my tampering with them. Yet all these difficulties I am willing to struggle with, in order to shew you that I dare take the *disgrace* of the whole upon myself; which I will do with as little alteration of your words and method, as possible. In hopes that the success of it, of which I have no doubt, will procure your leave for me to give it, in a second edition, to it's rightful owner.[3]

I wish you had seen Mr Allen.[4] He comes up to <my> the notion of my favourites

1 RH was about to publish his edition of Horace's *Epistola ad Augustum*. The first copies were available on 21 May 1751. (See *post* To Macro, 21 May 1751.)

2 Warburton had written to RH on 15 February commenting particularly on his "excellent observations on the Drama". (*Prelate*, p. 56.) These were to form a 'Discourse concerning Poetical Imitation', appended to the *Epistola ad Augustum*. Balguy, Warburton noted, had done well in turning RH's consideration of the drama "from the *object* to the *end*". (*Ibid.*) "Mr. Balguy and you are happy in one another", he continued at a later point. "It was my misfortune when I first set upon scribbling, that I had nobody capable of doing me this service. And as the little I knew, I got without assistance, so I had none to help me in communicating it to others. This is a misfortune too late to retrieve, and almost too late to lament. I am heartily glad our friend has cut out fresh work for you, in the Epistle to Augustus, and on this account I can be content to have the work a little procrastinated." (p. 58.)

3 The second edition of the *Epistola ad Augustum* appeared in a two volume set with the second edition of RH's commentary on the *Ars Poetica* in 1753. No acknowledgement to Balguy is included.

4 Ralph Allen (1693–1764) of Bath. Allen's origins were obscure and his career began at a humble level in the Post Office. However, he won the patronage of General Wade for his assistance in the detection of a Jacobite plot, whilst working in the Post Office at Bath, and subsequently amassed a fortune by his effective running of the recently instituted system of cross-posts for England and Wales. He became proprietor of Combe Down quarries near Bath, and, amongst other projects, built a fine mansion, Prior Park, completed in 1741. His benefactions were numerous (he is said to have given away more than £1,000 per annum), and his reputation

in Q. Elizabeth's reign: good sense in conjunction with the plainest manners – simplex et nuda veritas.[5] I dined with him yesterday, where I met Mr Fielding[6] – a poor, emaciated, worn out rake, whose gout and infirmities have got the better ev'n of his buffoonery.

You lost a great pleasure in not seeing the pictures at Devons. House, which Lord George was so kind to shew me.[7] I mentioned your short stay in town (for I suppos'd it likely he would hear of you) and your indisposition, and your great concern, that you could not wait upon him. He spoke very kindly of you and desired his compliments.

Is this pamphlet with the motto "*Est genus hominum*" &c. from Magdalen?[8] Mr. W.

as a philanthropist has been perpetuated by the portraits drawn of him by Fielding (as Squire Allworthy in *Tom Jones*), and by Pope in the Epilogue to the *Satires of Horace*. He numbered both writers amongst his personal friends, as well as other influential figures such as William Pitt and Bishop Sherlock. (Benjamin Boyce, *The Benevolent Man. A Life of Ralph Allen of Bath*, Cambridge, Massachusetts, 1967; *D.N.B.*; RH, *Discourse*, p. 45.)

5 Lactantius, *Divinae Institutiones*, 3. 1. 3.

6 Henry Fielding had become acquainted with Ralph Allen in 1741 or 1742, and was a frequent guest at Prior Park. By this time he was already suffering from the ill health which was to dog him over the next three years till his death in October 1754. (Boyce, *Benevolent Man*, pp. 126–8, 197, 224.) The dinner must have been in London and not at Prior Park as is suggested by Boyce.

7 Devonshire House in Piccadilly was the home of the Cavendish family. George Cavendish (1728–94) was the second son of William, third Duke of Devonshire. Their collection of paintings, according to Thomas Martyn was "surpassed by very few either at home or abroad". A list of the pictures (largely by seventeenth century Masters) is given in his work, *The English Connoisseur: Containing An Account of Whatever is Curious in Painting, Sculpture, &c. In the Palaces and Seats of the Nobility and Principal Gentry of England*, 2 vols., 1766, i. 41–50.

8 RH refers to *An Inquiry into the Right of Appeal from the Chancellor, or Vice Chancellor, of the University of Cambridge, in Matters of Discipline: Addressed to a Fellow of a College*, 1751, which was published anonymously by Thomas Chapman, the Master of Magdalene. The motto on the title page runs: "Est genus hominum, qui esse primos se omnium rerum volunt, nec sunt". The dispute to which this work contributed was over the authority of the Chancellor's Court in disciplinary matters. In non-disciplinary cases, doctors and masters of arts convicted in the Chancellor's Court had the right of appeal to delegates appointed by the university, and for some years there had been a demand for the right to be extended to all cases. The occasion of the revival of this debate, was the Court's decision to suspend Thomas Ansell from his degree for his part in contravening newly imposed university regulations at the anniversary dinner of the Westminster Club on 19 November 1750, and for his "rude, contemptuous and disobedient behaviour" to the Vice-Chancellor during the hearing of the case. (Winstanley, *The University of Cambridge in the Eighteenth Century*, p. 215.) The impetus for reform and the introduction of new regulations "for restoring good order and discipline in the university" had come from the Chancellor (the Duke of Newcastle), the Vice-Chancellor, and the heads of the colleges. (*Ibid.*, pp. 199–200.) They had encountered strong opposition from the remainder of the university who viewed the institution of a new disciplinary code as an attempt at arbitrary government. The regulations were, however, passed in a modified form and by a narrow margin on 11 May and 26 June 1750. Resistance then lapsed until the attempted enforcement of the regulations on the assembled company of the Westminster Club. Following his conviction Ansell claimed the right to appeal against it, raising once more the issue of appeal in disciplinary matters. His claim was refused in December 1750 although the Vice-Chancellor, Dr Keene, announced his intention of dealing with the question early in the following term. An Association was formed in defence of the right of appeal and a flurry of pamphlets ensued. RH was a member of the Association (see *post* To Balguy, 29 March 1751), which consisted of between 30 and 40 M.A.s, and James Bickham and Thomas Balguy were leading members. The dispute was finally resolved by the decision to put the question to arbitration. Five referees were appointed (Philip Yorke, first Earl of Hardwicke and High Steward of the University, the Archbishop of

says he perceives this is the *bon mot* of the party. From what Mr B.[9] relates of a conversation with Chapman,[10] I pronounce him to be, what I always took him for, an insolent coxcomb.

I am ashamed in the same page to send my services, and name the names of Mr Powell and Mr Allen. Let me hear from you at your leisure and believe me to be your most entirely faithful & affectionate friend & servt

R Hurd.

Inner Temple[11] 19. March. 1750–1

118 To THOMAS BALGUY 29 MARCH 1751

Text: MS BEINECKE MS Vault Shelves, Hurd; unpublished.
Addressed: cover missing.

Inner Temple 29. March. 1751

Dear Sir

How far C's pamphlet[1] is contemptible in other respects, you are much a better judge, than I am. This I clearly see, that it contains many vile and injurious insinuations,

Canterbury, the Bishop of London, Lord Chief Justice Lee, and his brother, Sir George Lee) and three representatives from the heads and the opposition. Bickham and Balguy were chosen as two of the opposition representatives. This conclusion seems to have satisfied all parties and the debate appears to have been abandoned without the referees coming to any definite decision over the matter. (*Annals*, iv. 186, 280–6; Winstanley, *Unreformed Cambridge*, pp. 27–31; Winstanley, *The University of Cambridge in the Eighteenth Century*, pp. 205–22; Wordsworth, *Social Life at the English Universities in the Eighteenth Century*, pp. 65–77, 617–32.)

9 Probably James Bickham (c.1720–85); admitted sizar at Emmanuel, 30 March 1737; B.A. 1741; M.A. 1744; B.D. 1751; D.D. 1774; Fellow, 1743. Bickham remained at Emmanuel till 1762. He was nominated to the living of Loughborough, Leicestershire in August 1761. (*Order Book*, COL. 14. 2; see *post* To Littleton, 14 December 1761, n. 4.)

10 Thomas Chapman (1717–60) had been educated at Christ's from 1734 to 1741 when he was made a Fellow. He was appointed Master of Magdalene in 1746 and became Vice-Chancellor in 1748. William Cole, another Cambridge man, called him "*that pragmatical Coxcomb*" and RH spoke of him at his death as a "vain and busy man", whose ambition was greater than his desire for friendship. (See *post* To Warburton, 22 June 1760.)

11 RH was out of college from late February to 6 April. By Warburton's interest with the Bishop of London, Dr Sherlock, he had been appointed a Whitehall Preacher in May 1750, and was required to preach for one month (March) each year in the Royal Chapel at Whitehall. (*Prelate*, p. 29; John Chamberlayne, *Magnae Britanniae Notitia: or, the Present State of Great-Britain; With diverse Remarks upon the Ancient State thereof*, The Thirty-eighth Edition and the Seventeenth, 1755, Book III, p. 115.) The institution of Whitehall Preachers had been established by Bishop Gibson in 1723. His proposal listed six advantages of such an establishment, amongst them that the "brightest and most learned persons among them will be brought forth from time to time, into ye eye of ye world, and become known to ye Bishops and be better acquainted with them"; and that "Some of these preachers may be thought proper to be made Chaplains to the King: and when the station at Whitehall appears to be a step to that, it will make it a greater mark of favour, and also ye succession at Whitehall will be quicker. In this way a succession of able men and good preachers will be always growing up for ye high offices in ye Church." (Norman Sykes, *Edmund Gibson, Bishop of London 1669–1748. A Study in Politics & Religion in the Eighteenth Century*, 1926, pp. 94, 398.) RH's stay in London also enabled him to meet Littleton, who was lodging in Suffolk Street from mid March, and to make final arrangements with Robert Dodsley for the publication of his Horace.

1 See preceding letter, n. 8.

much courtly sycophancy, and not less *head-like* insolence. On all wch accounts I think it quite necessary, that it be thoroughly exposed. Besides, poor as his reasoning is, yet, as it takes advantage of the reigning prejudices against us, it will certainly impose on the generality, and, from it's being countenanced by such persons as Mr Y.,[2] there is reason to apprehend, it may make an impression on some of great rank and consequence. To all which the opinions of the two lawyers, so much insisted on, will no doubt greatly contribute.[3] Something therefore should and must be done; and, to speak my mind freely, by *You*. There is no one so fitt to undertake this *little Academical lawyer* on many accounts. But principally, because you owe yourself the justice to shew the public, that you are upon no terms with such a fellow. You have had some taste of what you are to expect from him. And nothing can so effectually disarm him of all ability to do you hurt, as to take from him his *mask of friendship*, which I would therefore strip off from him, in the face of the world, without further ceremony.

I would also tell you something more of him. You know how he <. . .> is inclined to represent some persons of our Association.[4] And this unseasonable pamphlet from Oxford, will furnish him with fresh pretences of slander.[5] All this shews, it is high time for you to speak out.

In short, the *Considerations* &c and *the Inquiry into Appeals*, are in ev'ry body's hands; read by all and approved by most. If we are silent, the [Associa]tion must needs suffer in it's credit extremely; a[nd you] as standing foremost in it, will suffer most. [A] sensible and vigorous defence would save all – [. . .] yourself – vindicate the honour of the university, [and] disgrace these reptiles for ever.[6]

Excuse me, if I am warm and pressing on [this] head. I say it again, it concerns your credit, [and] perhaps interest, nearly. And for such a wretch [to] have it to say, that he has done you so much [mis]chief, were an indignity not to be suffered.

Mr W., (who, if possible, is more earnest in this affair than I am) sends his services.[7] I believe it would not be amiss, if you wrote to him.[8]

2 Probably Charles Yorke.

3 Chapman quotes the opinions of "two gentlemen of unquestionable abilities and very great eminence at the bar", to whom the question of the right of appeal had been put. They are identified as "W. N—" and "R. W—", probably the Hon. William Noel, K.C., and Randal Wilbraham, who were called to the bench in 1754 and 1743. (*An Inquiry into the Right of Appeal*, pp. 27–31; *The Records of the Honorable Society of Lincoln's Inn. The Black Books*, 5 vols., Lincoln's Inn, 1897–1968, iii. 356, 329.)

4 See preceding letter, n. 8. A list of the members of the Association has been preserved at Emmanuel. (*Documents concerning the Ansell Case*, COL. 9. 28.)

5 RH refers either to *Considerations on the Expediency of Making, and the Manner of Conducting the late Regulations at Cambridge*, 1751, which had been advertised for sale in February (*Gent. Mag.*) and has been attributed to William King of Oxford; or to another pamphlet, more certainly attributed to King, and advertised for sale in March (*Lond. Mag.*), *A Key to the Fragment. By Amias Riddinge, B.D. With a Preface. By Peregrine Smyth, Esq*, 1751. King apparently involved himself in the Cambridge controversy from a dislike of the Duke of Newcastle's policies generally, and his specific opposition to whig interference in University affairs. (David Greenwood, *William King. Tory and Jacobite*, Oxford, 1969, p. 139ff.)

6 Balguy resisted all suggestions that he should reply to Chapman and King; instead RH himself composed a response, *The Opinion of an Eminent Lawyer, Concerning the Right of Appeal from the Vice-Chancellor of Cambridge, to the Senate*. It was advertised for sale in May 1751. (*Gent. Mag.*)

7 No record of Warburton's opinions has been included in *Letters from a Late Eminent Prelate*.

8 Warburton and Balguy had corresponded since at least November 1750; Warburton had written on 7 February referring to the subject of "Appeals". (University of Texas at Austin.)

I propose being with you sometime next week; but pray let me have the immediate satisfaction to understand, that you will set about this matter directly. I am, with services, Dear Sir, Your most entirely affectionate friend and Servt

R Hurd.

119 To Sir EDWARD LITTLETON 26 APRIL 1751

Text: MS STAFFS RO D1413/1; unpublished.
Addressed: To/Sir Edward Littleton Bart/at Mr Jonquier's in Suffolk-Street/[1] Charing-Cross/London
Postmarked: CAMBRIDGE 27 AP

Dear Sir

I have your obliging letter and have many thanks to give you for your present of Nanteuil[2] and the care you take of the pictures and prints in Matthyson's[3] hands. If you will please to send the box to the Green Dragon in Bishop-Gate-Street to go by Mr Gillam's wagon, it will <be> come safe hither.[4] I must get you to take Matthyson's receipt, when you pay him.

After enriching my little collection with such a rarity, as the best head of Nanteuil, I should be very selfish indeed not to rejoyce with you on the purchase of a first rate *Berghem*; for such I have no doubt it is.[5] I shall be very impatient to see it.

You ask, if I can go into Staff: with you about the middle of next month; but, first, if I can make ye Norfolk tour with you. These questions I cannot resolve at present. I'm engaged so deeply in the business of Authorship (for another project has come across me, since I saw you) that it is most probable, <that> I cannot stir from this place on any acct till June.[6] However I must needs see you here. I have several things to say to you. And if I can contrive matters so as to be at liberty, you may command me as you please. But, as I said, nothing must prevent you making us in your way; whether I am or not. One thing I'll mention now, which I think should determine you.

I think I have hear'd you say that some time or other you intended the college a piece of plate.[7] Would it not be the time to do this, if you are so kind to design us that

1 Littleton lodged with Louis Jonquier or Jonquere again in 1752. (Littleton Ledger, p. 9, Staffs. RO, D260/M/E/116.)

2 This print has not been identified.

3 Littleton's accounts list "Ch Matthyson" as a "Picture Frame Maker". (Staffs. RO, D260/M/E/116.)

4 Almost all stage coaches and carriages to Cambridge left from Bishopsgate, either from the Green Dragon or from the Four Swans or the Bull. The carrier from the Green Dragon left for Cambridge (in 1744) on Wednesdays, Thursdays and Fridays. (*A Complete Guide to All Persons who have any Trade or Concern with the City of London, and Parts adjacent*, Third Edition, 1744, p. 88.)

5 This is probably the picture of "Landscape & Cattle" said to be by Berghem and listed in the 1812 inventory of Littleton's paintings. It was valued then at £200 which estimate was equalled only by a Hobbema. (Staffs. RO, D260/M/T/5/110.) Claes or Nicolaes Pieter Berghem (properly Berchem) was a famous and prolific Dutch landscape artist of the seventeenth century.

6 RH was at work on *The Opinion of an Eminent Lawyer, Concerning the Right of Appeal* (see preceding letter, n. 6); his edition of the *Epistola ad Augustum* was also at press and may have required attention.

7 The *Emmanuel College Plate Book 1731–1913* lists "Sr Edw: Littleton's Dish" on 13 September

favour, before you go abroad? And if so, can you take a fitter time to mention it to the Master, than this?

Your brother too, as I think is partly settled (but this is another important business on which we want to consult you) & is leaving us very soon. Which you will think another reason for using this opportunity.

But be this as it will, I must insist absolutely on your staying some days with us on your return into the country. I have a thousand things to say to you. Mr Afflecks[8] bed and chambers are too at your service. Your brother expects it. All your friends press it. In short I know not what to say, but that I want exceedingly to see you here and that I am, with the truest affection, Dearest Sir, Your much obliged and entirely faithful friend & Servt

R Hurd.

Camb. 26. Ap. 1751.

120 To EDWARD MACRO 21 MAY 1751

Text: Edward Macro Letter-book.
Addressed: cover missing.

Cambridge 21. May. 1751.

Dear Sir

You will think I have exceeded ev'n my usual laziness in neglecting you all this while.[1] But the truth is, I have been kept in constant expectation of this foolish book upon Horace.[2] And I purposely omitted writing, till I could desire your acceptance of it. It is this day published; and on Saturday next I shall send by Smith two copies, one for yourself, and another for the Doctor.

I take for granted, you intend going into Staffordshire very soon. Sir Edward, as I expect, will be here in a fortnight's time, at the farthest. He talked of visiting Houghton;[3] and then proceeding directly for the country. I hope you will be ready to give him the meeting at this place, that we may all set out together.

I had some time ago a letter from Mr Sam: Tatem.[4] It was to recommend to me a young gentleman, Mr Boehm,[5] eldest son to the person, he used to talk so much of. He is a very pretty young man, and a good scholar. He is admitted of Clare-Hall.

Poor Mr Butler[6] is, at present, very ill of his old disorder. I am, as usual, sometimes

1753, and "Sr Edw: Lyttleton's Soop Dish" in 1756, each weighing 123 oz. (COL. 16. 1.) See also *post* To Littleton, 19 February 1755, 3 June 1755, and 18 June 1755.

8 William Affleck, a contemporary and friend of RH; matriculated 1733; B.A. 1737; M.A. 1740; B.D. 1747; Fellow 1739; Rector of North Luffenham, Rutland, 1755–1806.

1 There is no evidence to indicate the date of RH's last letter to Edward Macro. The gap in surviving correspondence extends from 2 January 1746.

2 *Q. Horatii Flacci Epistola ad Augustum. With an English Commentary and Notes*, 1751.

3 RH had himself visited Houghton with Macro in 1742. (See *ante* To Devey, 24 September 1742.)

4 Unidentified.

5 Clement Boehm, admitted Fellow-commoner at Clare, 25 March 1750, matriculated 1751. Boehm was of a London family. (*Alum. Cantab.*)

6 Unidentified.

pretty well and sometimes complaining, but, in all states and in all humours, very much Dear Sir, Your faithful and affectionate friend & Servt

R Hurd.

My compliments to ev'ry body; especially Mrs Macro, to whom I shall endeavour to pay my respects, if it be but for a day or two before I go into Staffordshire. Perhaps I may fetch you hither.

120A To WILLIAM BOWYER 14 FEBRUARY 1752

See Appendix

121 To Sir EDWARD LITTLETON 18 JUNE 1752

Text: MS STAFFS RO D1413/1; unpublished.
Addressed: To Sir Edward Littleton Bart/in Suffolk Street Charing-Cross/London.
Postmarked: CAMBRIDGE 19 IV

Dear Sir Edward

I have the favour of your kind letter of the 6th. It was very friendly what You tell me of Mr Macro's purchase of the pictures: And I give you joy of so considerable an addition to your collection.[1] It would give me great pleasure to see the pictures of yourself which your country painter[2] has drawn, and much greater to spend some time with you at Tedgely. But I'm afraid I must not think of this happiness. I am engaged to Mr Longe (who is high-Sheriff this year) to preach the Assize-Sermon at Norwich.[3] And I have promised Mr Warburton to pass some part of the Summer with him at Prior-Park.[4] So that between these two engagements it will be difficult for me to find time for an elopement into Staffordshire. In the mean time what should hinder your returning into the country thro' Cambridge? I wish I could think of any inducements to draw You this way. This I know, You would find some here would be very thankful for the favour of your company and who would be very proud to pay their respects to Lady Littleton.[5] For as much friers, as we are, You may assure her Ladyship we are not without a due sense of female excellence when it may be seen to such advantage.

1 Macro had bought four paintings for Littleton: "Lot & his daughters", believed by Littleton to be a work by Pietro da Cortona; a "Battle Peice"; a picture by Hondecoeter; and a landscape by Teniers. (*Macro Letter-book*, Littleton to Macro, 6 June 1752.)

2 Unidentified.

3 Francis Longe, the nephew of Cox Macro and patron of Reymerston, had known RH since 1742. His election to the office of High Sheriff of Norfolk had been advertised in the January issue of the *Gentleman's Magazine*. The Assizes were held in July and RH's sermon was given on Wednesday 29 July. It was later published under the title, *The Mischiefs of Enthusiasm and Bigotry: A Sermon Preached in the Cathedral Church of Norwich, at the Assizes*, with a dedication to Longe and other officials of the county. (*Gent. Mag.*, October 1752.)

4 Written evidence of this promise no longer exists, but Warburton acknowledged RH's decision to visit Prior Park in a letter of 9 May 1752. (*Prelate*, p. 79.) RH travelled there in October.

5 In the spring of 1752 Sir Edward had married Frances, eldest daughter of Christopher Horton of Catton, Derbyshire. Their marriage settlement is dated 14 April 1752. (Staffs. RO, D260/M/T/5/129.) The couple had no children and Lady Littleton, having been troubled with

I don't know whether my Lady has not cause to resent your talking of books so soon, and amidst the higher concerns of Milliners and Taylors. But if I receive Mr Davis' catalogue[6] I shall tell You very frankly what of them I think worth your purchasing – The mention of books leads me to ask, if You have receiv'd your Elfrida which was left with Mr Davis, and how You like it.[7] Sir George Littleton, it is said, has expressed a great dislike of it.[8]

My best wishes attend Yourself and my Lady. May Ye live long to enjoy that sincere happiness to which your virtues so well entitle You!

Dearest Sir, Your most affectionate and faithful Humble Servt

R Hurd.

Camb: 18. June. 1752

122 To Sir EDWARD LITLETON 1 JULY 1752

Text: MS STAFFS RO D1413/1; unpublished.
Addressed: To Sir Edward Littleton Bart/in Suffolk-Street Charing-Cross/London.
Postmarked: CAMBRIDGE

Dear Sir

I have put down the few hints I have to give You about the french books in the margin of the catalogue.[1] The best general direction is to order Davis to procure for you the translations of best credit and to have them in the latest editions. There are so few of them that I have looked into, that I cannot say much of their particular merits. When You have got these it will be easy for you to pick up the rest from Sales and Auctions at your leisure.

It gives me great pleasure that you are so forward with your preparations for building and, in particular, that the Ground-plot is fixed by the advice of Mr Gibbs.[2] I

ill-health for most of her life, died in 1781. She too corresponded occasionally with RH. (See *post* To Lady Littleton, 8 August 1759.)

6 Charles Davis (d.1755), a bookseller and publisher, was one of the first to issue priced catalogues of second-hand books. He also sold libraries by auction and was succeeded in his business by a nephew, Lockyer Davis, who was already working with him in 1747. Some sale catalogues produced by the firm survive, but there are none for the years 1749 to 1756. (A.N.L. Munby and Lenore Coral, *British Book Sales Catalogues, 1676–1800: A Union List*, 1977.)

7 William Mason had published *Elfrida, A Dramatic Poem. Written on the Model of the Antient Greek Tragedy* in March. This first edition appeared as a quarto priced 2s. 6d. and was rapidly followed by an octavo edition at 1s. 6d. (Gaskell, *First Editions of Mason*, p. 3.)

8 Lyttelton apparently had little liking for Mason's poetry: his dislike of *Musaeus* is commented on by RH in his letter of 1 October 1750.

1 See preceding letter.

2 James Gibbs (1682–1754), the architect of the Radcliffe Camera, Oxford, and the Senate House, Cambridge, was nearing the end of his distinguished career, but despite illness continued to work on designs for public and private buildings. His style was derived from a synthesis of Italian (both baroque and Palladian) and English architecture and was popular amongst the upper classes. Littleton only consulted with him briefly and there appeared little evidence of his influence in the completed house, which was more severe in appearance than

am so great a novice in these matters that I can only take as a compliment what you say of my opinion about the Situation and ornaments. However I should be very happy to assist at your counsils. Tho', as I said, I'm afraid this cannot possibly be. If Mr Macro be with You, You will scarcely need another person to consult with.

You judge very truly of Elfrida. It is a very classical performance, tho' not witht some defects, of which the author is, I dare be confident, as much aware as Sr George L . The criticism on Vandyke's picture is an ingenious flourish & was intended for no other.[3] Tho' Mr M. has seen that of Lord Townshend.[4]

Mr Christopher Nevile[5] is expected here this ev'ning: I wish for many reasons You could be with us: Or at least I shall wish to be with you. It will make me very unhappy, if neither of these things can take place. But let fortune be as cross as she will she cannot hinder me from being ever, with all truth, Dearest Sir, Your faithful and affectionate humble Servt

R Hurd.

Camb. 1. July. 1752

123 To COX MACRO 28 AUGUST 1752

Text: MS BL Add. 32557, ff. 161–2; unpublished.
Addressed: To /The Revd Dr Macro/at/Norton.

Em. Coll. 28. Aug. 1752.

Revd Sir

I put a line or two into the box to thank you for your late kind civilities and to pay my respects to all of your worthy family. I had a pleasant journey hither, that is, as pleasant as I could expect from Norton to Camb.[1] You will hardly take this for a compliment, especially at a time when the dead vacation makes this place the dullest that can be. Till a day or two ago I had hardly a soul to speak to, when at length Dr Nevile arrived from Tunbridge,[2] in better health and spirits than he left us. After what

the majority of buildings with which he was involved. (Howard Colvin, *A Biographical Dictionary of British Architects*, 1954, new edn. 1978; Stebbing Shaw, *The History and Antiquities of Staffordshire*, 1798–1801, reprint, 1976, vol. 2, pt. 1, Additions II, unpublished plate, no. 2.)

3 *Elfrida* is prefaced by five letters discussing dramatic form, in the fourth of which Mason mentions Van Dyck's painting of Belisarius. (p. xii.) His object is to cap an analogy made in a passage he has just quoted. (p. xi.) The subject under discussion is the importance of having subordinate figures in paintings and plays to reinforce the "passions" felt by their audiences. Mason probably adopted the allusion to Van Dyck's painting at the suggestion of Warburton. (See *Prelate*, pp. 73–4.)

4 Perhaps a mistake for Richard Boyle, Lord Burlington (1695–1753). Warburton mentions the latter as the owner of *Belisarius* (*Prelate*, p. 74), and Thomas Martyn in *The English Connoisseur*, i. 37, confirms this. The painting was housed in Burlington's suburban house at Chiswick.

5 Christopher Nevile (c.1713–58) had matriculated as a Fellow-commoner of Emmanuel in 1731, but did not take a degree. He was known to Warburton who came from the same part of England, and is described by him as a man of good understanding. (*Prelate*, p. 91.)

1 RH was away from Cambridge from 25 July to 14 August, paying a visit to the Macro family. (*Commons Accounts Book*, STE. 15. 9.)

2 Tunbridge Wells was a popular summer resort for people "of every degree, condition, and occupation of life, (if well dressed, and well behaved)". The season began in late May or early

manner, or at least in what temper he passed his time at the Wells, you will guess from the following little Song, which he was gay enough to write upon Miss Bladen,[3] a celebrated beauty, who attracted all eyes, at least, if she captivated no hearts. I snatched it from him last night and told him I would send it Mrs Macro. The thing is no Chef d'oeuvre, but has some common things prettily said in it.

On seeing Miss Bladen at Tunbridge

I

Ye sallow Sons of thought and care
Whose hearts ne'er panted for the fair,
  Whose breasts no passion warms;
Leave your dull labours, and explore
With curious eye all Nature's store
  To match my Caelia's charms.

II

Compare the blooming tints, that streak
With ruby glow her lip, her cheek
  With those that paint the rose;
Her breath sends forth more rich perfume
Than Balm or Aromatic Gum,
  Or sweetest flow'r, that blows.

III.

The Snow, that fleecy melts in Air,
The glossy down that lillies wear
  The Cygnet's velvet vest,
How pleasing to the sight, You cry;
Yet what are these to him, whose eye
  E're glanc'd on Caelia's breast?

IV.

Tell me what Iv'ry can be found
To suit each finger's polish'd round
  That graceful decks her hand?
Her spotless rows of teeth excell
The pearly lining of the Shell
  That glistneth on the Sand.

V

The darkest plume, that shades the crow,
Seen with those Locks, that wavy flow,
  Assumes a dusky hue;
The azure dye, that aether stains,

June and continued to the autumn, reaching its peak in August. Entertainments were as various as at other fashionable spas, the drinking of the waters being interspersed with all the diversions of "social and polished life". (*A General Account of Tunbridge Wells, and its Environs: Historical and Descriptive*, 1771, pp. 6–8.)

3 Unidentified. According to the *General Account of Tunbridge Wells* it was common for the young men of the spa to compose verse. These "*jeux de esprits*", the writer explains, "are various and occasional; but chiefly complimentary to the ladies in general, or to some particular fair one. A copy of them is usually left at the bookseller's shop, and entered into a book there for the inspection and entertainment of the company." (*Ibid.*, pp. 10–11.)

Boasts not the tincture of those veins
  Which streak her skin with blue.

VI.

Ye lifeless, dull, cold Stoic train
For whom Love lights his lamp in vain,
  Whose brows for ever low'r!
If not to senseless statues grown,
Come, look on Caelia's face, and own
  That Beauty has some power.

Mr J. Nevile[4] stays at Tunbridge sometime longer. The waters, he thinks, have done him Service. What rhyming should we have, if beauty should make a poet of him too? In the mean time pray tell Mrs Macro I shall wish to know her sentiments of this gallant Doctor and his sonnet.

I am, with compliments, Revd Sir, Your very obliged and faithful humble Servt

R Hurd.

P. S.

You'll please to give the Account of Wilton,[5] with my Services, to Mr Macro.

124 To THOMAS BALGUY 26 SEPTEMBER 1752

Text: MS BEINECKE MS Vault Shelves, Hurd; printed in part, *Memoirs*, 47.
Addressed: cover missing.

Camb. 26. Sept. 1752

Dear Sir

My excessive laziness has kept me from telling You, what I should have wrote to You a month ago, that Mr Sm[. . .][1] is returned to college and that Mr Bickham is perfectly satisfied about your stay in the country.[2] He adds that, as matters now stand, he is heartily glad his letter was so late in coming to you, since this accident has saved You the trouble of a long journey.

I should say something to hasten your return hither, but that I am preparing to set out for Prior-Park next week. And my benevolence, tho' I verily believe it, in spite of what Lord Bolingbroke prates, to be an innate principle,[3] yet does not act so forcibly as to make me so much concerned for my friends as myself. Tho' you will find Mason

4 John Nevile, a Fellow of Emmanuel, elected at the same time as RH. (*Order Book*, COL. 14. 2.) He was the brother of RH's friend Thomas Nevile, of Jesus. (*Alum. Cantab.*)

5 Probably the work by Richard Cowdry, *A Description of the Pictures, Statues, Busto's, Basso-relievo's, and other curiosities at the Earl of Pembroke's house at Wilton*, dated 1751.

1 Smalley.

2 Bickham's interest in Balguy's whereabouts may relate to business connected with the Right of Appeal, both men having been appointed as representatives of the university opposition. (See *ante* To Balguy, 19 March 1751, n. 8.)

3 Bolingbroke, as a follower of Locke, implied in his writings that moral obligation depended on the divine will, an authoritarian view disagreeable to many in the mid eighteenth century. The prevalent school of thought on the other hand, insisted on man's social nature and his possession of an individual moral sense often categorised as innate benevolence. Two of the most important proponents of this philosophy were Shaftesbury and Hutcheson, both of whom

here who talks of fitting up his *faithful shepherdess* as being in some apprehension that Boyce and Garrick will force it from him.[4] Betwixt ourselves he keeps wretched company. I saw him yesterday speak to Green of Cottenham[5] and S. Jennins Esquire.[6] *And* the morning he owned to me was entirely spent in chit-chat with Daniel Wray.[7] The Devise of the Duke's medal was part of the conversation.[8] Nothing can be more wretched. Granta is to be another Cybele with tour's on her head. She is shewing

influenced RH. In this instance RH is probably responding directly to Bolingbroke's *Reflections concerning Innate Moral Principles*, which was published posthumously in the summer of 1752. On p. 69, for example, Bolingbroke writes that "universal Experience shews, that Education and Custom absolutely determine the general Character of a Nation". Although individuals will be drawn either towards compassion or cruelty this difference results from "the Difference of Constitutions, and will not, in the least, help to prove, that Compassion is innate any more than Cruelty".

4 Garrick wrote to Mason on 14 October 1752 having read his adaptation of *The Faithful Shepherdess*, a pastoral play originally written by John Fletcher. He had been "much pleas'd with ye Poetry," he said, but thought it "not dramatical Enough, to have a good Effect upon the Stage". (*The Letters of David Garrick*, ed. David M. Little and George M. Kahrl, 3 vols., 1963, i. 189–90.) According to a note, Garrick had already considered *The Faithful Shepherdess* as a dramatic production two years earlier, and Mason may have been adapting it at his suggestion. It was never acted or printed. William Boyce (1711–79), composer and organist, had started working for Garrick in 1749, the year in which he had set Mason's *Ode Performed . . . At the Installation of His Grace Thomas Holles Duke of Newcastle* to music. (*The New Grove Dictionary of Music and Musicians*, ed. Stanley Sadie, 1980.)

5 Thomas Greene (c.1711–80) was the eldest son of Thomas Green (1658–1738), successively Bishop of Norwich and of Ely. He held a Fellowship at Corpus Christi from 1732–5, and at Jesus from 1736–8. In 1737 he was given the rich rectory of Cottenham by his father, who also secured him a prebendal stall at Ely. In 1751 he had become Chancellor of Lichfield. Cole describes him as "a finical man always taking snuff up his nose". (*D.N.B.*; *Alum. Cantab.*)

6 Soame Jenyns (1704–87), the poet and miscellaneous writer, came from a landed family near Cambridge and had been an undergraduate at St John's. He was M.P. for Cambridgeshire from 1741–54, and for Cambridge from 1758–80, under the patronage of Lord Montfort and Lord Hardwicke. His manner was good natured and amusing, though Cole speaks of him, too, as "rather of a finical and beauish turn". (*D.N.B.*; *Alum. Cantab.*; *The House of Commons 1754–1790*, ed. Sir Lewis Namier and John Brooke, 3 vols., 1964.)

7 Daniel Wray had been an undergraduate at Queens' but by the 1750s lived mainly in London. He had many friends amongst literary men of the time (including William Warburton), though also some enemies as is indicated by the satirical lines quoted in Nichols' *Literary Anecdotes*:

"but when malignant *Wray*,
Eager in hope, impatient of delay,
A dapper, pert, loquacious, busy elf" . . . (ii. 442.)

(*D.N.B.*; *Gent. Mag.*; *Alum. Cantab.*)

8 The Duke of Newcastle, Chancellor of the University, had founded two gold medals in 1751 to be given annually to two candidates who excelled in Classical learning. The first two awards were made in March 1752. On one side of the medals is a bust of George II; on the other, an allegorical depiction of Cambridge seated as a goddess on a raised throne and pointing to three students, to one of whom Liberality is presenting a medal. The river-god Camus is reclining near the throne and the Senate House is seen in the distance. (RH's reference to Cybele arises from the fact that she is usually depicted wearing a mural crown as does Granta (Cambridge) in this scene.) The full inscription on this side of the medal is: STUDIIS HUMANITATIS LIBERALITAS. T. HOLLES. DUC NOVOCASTR. ACAD. CANCELL. YEO. F. Richard Yeo designed the medals. (*Medallic Illustrations of the History of Great Britain and Ireland to the Death of George II*. Compiled by the late Edward Hawkins . . . edited by Augustus W. Franks and Herbert A. Grueber, 2 vols., 1885, reprint, 1969; *Biographical Dictionary of Medallists . . . B.C.500 – A.D.1900*, compiled by L. Forrer, 8 vols., 1904–30.)

three Bachelors of Arts the way to the Senate-house. And the Motto is Studiis Humanitatis. Voila l'invention & le genie de la Societé des Antiquaires de Londre![9]

The passing from one rarity to another is but natural. My Sermon is expected to come forth this day.[10] I shall punish you so far as to make you wait for it till you come to college. If you never see it all, the misfortune may be supportable. But this I shall be supposed to say *en auteur*.

Garnet is B. of Ferns.[11] I mention this not as a piece of news but as a subject of philosophical meditation. It may furnish much good instruction to us young divines. It must be a pitiable ambition henceforward to be fond of Mitres.

There is talk here of Keene's resigning his Master-ship.[12] Some say Courtail of C. Hall is to be his successor:[13] Others say a clergyman in the North of England, whose name is not mentioned, but which perhaps you will guess at.[14]

If you write immediately on the receipt of this, you will catch me before I enter on my western journey and in so doing will give a great pleasure to, Dear Sir, Your most affectionate friend and Servant

R Hurd.

125 To WILLIAM MASON 29 OCTOBER 1752

Text: MS HC; printed, *H-M Corr*, 9.
Addressed: To Mr Mason Fellow of/Pembroke Hall in/ Cambridge.
Postmarked: 31 OC

London 29 Oct 1752

Dear Mr Mason

I am thus far on my way to Norfolk, for wch I set out to morrow, with hopes of coming to you on Saturday next or very soon after.[1]

9 No connection has been traced between the founding of the medals and the Society of Antiquaries.

10 *The Mischiefs of Enthusiasm and Bigotry: A Sermon Preached in the Cathedral Church of Norwich, at the Assizes*, 1752. (See *ante* To Littleton, 18 June 1752, n. 3.)

11 John Garnett (1709–82) had been admitted to St John's in 1725, but migrated to Sidney in 1728. He became B.A. in 1729, was made a Fellow in 1730 and was Lady Margaret preacher from 1744–52. In 1751 he had been made Chaplain to the Lord Lieutenant of Ireland and was nominated to the united bishoprics of Leighton and Ferns in August 1752. From there he was translated to the diocese of Clogher in 1758 where he remained till his death. He was the author of *A Dissertation on the Book of Job*, published in 1749. (*D.N.B.*; *Alum. Cantab.*)

12 Edmund Keene (1714–81), Master of Peterhouse. As Vice-Chancellor from 1749–51 he was one of the Heads more directly responsible for introducing the new regulations at Cambridge. Horace Walpole described him as "the Duke of Newcastle's tool at Cambridge, which university", he said, he had "half turned Jacobite, by cramming down new ordinances to carry measures of that Duke". (Walpole, *Correspondence*, Vol. 20, To Mann, 11 December 1752.)

13 John Courtail (c.1715–1806); admitted at Clare, 1731; B.A. 1736; M.A. 1739; Fellow, 1736–56. Courtail held a number of livings in Huntingdonshire, Sussex and Kent, and was made Archdeacon of Lewes in 1770. He did not succeed Keene as Master of Peterhouse. (*Alum. Cantab.*)

14 Perhaps a reference to Edmund Law (1703–87), who was at this time Archdeacon of Carlisle (1743–56), and Rector of Great Salkeld, Cumberland (1746–87). He succeeded Keene as Master of Peterhouse in 1754.

1 RH was back in Cambridge by 11 November. (*Commons Accounts Book*, STE. 15. 9.)

You expect to be congratulated on the success of *your* Orator.[2] [a] Tho' I question if the disappointment, tho' it may chagrin for the present, will do the *other* any real hurt. On the contrary I, who hold *that all things work together for good*, I mean for the advancement of such as diligently seek and perfectly *deserve* preferment, am of opinion that it may do him much present credit and recommend him to some future service. At least I seemed to collect thus much this morning from a conversation with one who usually speaks the sense of the great world and was, I found, well informed in the circumstances of the case and the reasons of R's[b] disappointment.[3] But of this not a word, for I come from the schools of Wise men, of whom I have learnt the golden rule of *caution*. To you perhaps I may hereafter explain myself more particularly. But for the present I say no more, and ev'n for this little exact silence.

Mr W.[c] & I laughed at your account of Cs persecuting letters. They will certainly be printed and, it may be said, will do your fame at least as much service as the fond encomiums of F.[4] [d] For both these however I truly pity you. Was not Pope in the right when he preferred a *fool's hate to his love*?[5]

As to the *faithful Shepherdess*, the event, as you say, turns out much to the credit of my divining faculty, the happiness of which arises not from my superior *knowledge of the town and the world*, as you jestingly put it, but from my acquaintance with Garrick's ill taste, and foible as an actor.[6] He is *entre nous* nothing when he is not playing tricks and shewing attitudes, for which You and Fletcher left him little room. Mr W.[e] abuses him for this folly.[7] By the way You must send him your MSS when he comes to town which will be in less than a fortnight. I saw Garrick last night in his element, playing

[2] John Skynner, Fellow of St John's, elected Public Orator at Cambridge, 26 October 1752. He resigned in 1762. (See *post* To Balguy, 3 December 1762.)

[3] The other candidate was John Ross, also a Fellow of St John's, afterwards Bishop of Exeter. Ross lost the election by 75 votes to 85. (C.U.L. Misc. Collect. 36, Journal of Henry Hubbard, Copy of B.L. Add. MS 5852, p. 109ff.)

[4] Pearce and Whibley identify "C." and "F." as William Comber (1726–1810), a Fellow of Jesus, and John Foster (1731–74), a Fellow of King's. (*Hurd-Mason Corr.*) The paragraph as a whole probably refers to critical comments on Mason's *Elfrida* (advertised for sale in March), although the only known published critical work is *Remarks on Mr. Mason's Elfrida, in Letters to a Friend*, which had appeared in May. This, following Alexander Dyce, is usually attributed to Thomas Nevile. (*Dictionary of Anonymous and Pseudonymous English Literature (Samuel Halkett and John Laing)*, New and Enlarged Edition, 9 vols., 1926–62.)

[5] A reference to two lines in *An Epistle from Mr. Pope to Dr. Arbuthnot*, published in January 1735 (but dated 1734):

> "Dear Doctor: tell me, is not this a curse?
> Say, is their Anger, or their Friendship worse?" (ll. 29–30)

The lines were later changed to:

> "What *Drop* or *Nostrum* can this Plague remove?
> Or which must end me, a Fool's Wrath or Love?"

(*The Poems of Alexander Pope (Twickenham Edition)*, ed. John Butt, 12 vols., 1939–69.)

[6] RH refers to Garrick's decision against producing Fletcher's *Faithful Shepherdess* in an up-dated version. (See previous letter n. 4.)

[7] Warburton was nonetheless a good friend of Garrick's and continued so till his death.

[a] Note by RHn: "Rev. John Skynner Fellow of St. John's Public Orator 26 Oct. 1752. He resigned in 1763."

[b] Note by RHn: "Ross' ".

[c] Note by RHn: "Warburton".

[d] Note by RHn: "Fletcher".

[e] Note by RHn: "Warburton".

Jaffier with Mossop whom the town admires in *Pierre*.[8] Write like Otway and You will please. But when You do this, You will at least lose one of your admirers.

I have a deal to say to you on this head and on another of more importance. Have nothing to do with a great Lord in the North.[9] [f] You shall know my reasons when I see you. I have so wretched a pen that writing is uneasy to me. All that You and I want to learn is to be content with a little and then we may be happier than great men, falsely so called, can make us.

All at Prior-Park sincerely esteem you. I cannot be more, than I am, Dearest Sir, Your affectionate friend & Servt

R Hurd.

You must direct to Mr *Brown at Carlisle in Cumberland*.[10]

Endorsed by Richard Hurd, nephew: "Oct 29th 1752".

126 To Sir EDWARD LITTLETON 6 NOVEMBER 1752

Text: MS STAFFS RO D1413/1; unpublished.
Addressed: To/Sir Edward Littleton Bart/at Tedgely Coppice near/Penkrich/Staffordshire./By Lond.
Postmarked: 10 NO

Reymerston Norfolk Nov. 6. 1752.

Dear Sir Edward

This is the first moment's leisure I have had to acknowledge your favour of the 20th past, which I receiv'd but the day before I set out for this place from Prior-Park.

I am not a little perplexed by your kind proposal; which, I can easily perceive, was intended by You as well for my particular benefit as the service of the young gentleman whom You so warmly and, I dare say, so justly recommend to me.[1] It

8 Jaffier and Pierre are characters in Thomas Otway's *Venice Preserved; or, a Plot Discovered*, (1682). The play was acted at Drury Lane on Saturday 28 October, its first appearance for three years. (*The London Stage 1660–1800*, ed. G.W. Stone, Part 4, i. 327.) Mossop is Henry Mossop (1729–74), an actor of great talent who frequently acted with Garrick at this time, but whose career was eventually ruined by his jealousy of the other's success.

9 Charles Watson-Wentworth, Marquis of Rockingham (1730–82). It is not known what office Mason's friends hoped to secure for him, though it may have been related to Rockingham's appointment as Lord-Lieutenant of the North and East Ridings of Yorkshire in the previous year.

10 John Brown (1715–66); admitted sizar at St John's, 1732; B.A. 1736; M.A. 1739; D.D. 1755. Minor Canon of Carlisle; chaplain to the Bishop of Carlisle. Vicar of Morland, Westmorland, 1743–56; Vicar of Lazonby, Cumberland, 1752–63; Rector of Great Horksley, Essex, 1756–60; Vicar of St Nicholas, Newcastle-on-Tyne, 1760–6. (*Alum. Cantab.*) Brown was known to both Mason and Gray (see Gray, *Correspondence*, Letter 144), and had also come to the attention of Warburton, who much admired his poem *An Essay on Satire: Occasion'd by the Death of Mr. Pope*, 1745, and had written to Robert Dodsley to discover the author. (Donald D. Eddy, *A Bibliography of John Brown*, New York, 1971, pp. 5–10.) Brown subsequently published the highly successful *An Estimate of the Manners and Principles of the Times*, 1757, and was the author of, amongst other things, two tragedies produced at Drury Lane: *Barbarossa*, first performed in December 1754, and *Athelstan*, performed in February 1756. (*D.N.B.*; *Lit. Anecs.*, ii. 211–15.)

f Note by Mason: "Lord Rockingham to whom some of my friends (without my knowledge) had recommended me. M".

1 Littleton was hoping to persuade RH into becoming the tutor of his brother-in-law, Walter

therefore gives me pain to decline what You ask of me. And yet I must deal fairly with You. The early affection I had conceived for You and the sollicitations of dear Mr Budworth were inducements I could not resist in your case. And tho' the satisfaction and success I had in your education might be temptations to any other, I find myself much averse to engage in a second care of this nature. You know my way is not to make a sine cure of so important a charge. And to be plain with you, I have always thought the time and attention, requisite to a due discharge of this office, more than it can be usually worth the while of any but professed Tutors, who have a number of pupils and have devoted themselves to this care, to lay out upon it.[2] For my own part, whether it be the indolence of my temper or the undue value I place on my own leisure and amusements, these are my sentiments in my own case.

You say, the young Gentleman's coming to Emmanuel and ev'n to Cambridge depends entirely on my agreeing to this proposal. I am not, You will readily believe, so far prejudiced in favour of either as to press the matter farther than may be for his real service. All I can say therefore is, that, if it shall be thought proper to place the young gentleman in our college (and I need not acquaint You with either the characters or abilities of our tutors) my regard for You and for a person so nearly related to Lady Littleton, as Mr Horton, will determine me to pay a very particular attention to his studies and morals, and to do him all the good offices I can in the way of advice or occasional information. More than this I shall trust your candour to excuse me from undertaking, for the reasons already mentioned. And I am the freer in saying this, because I know how much the partiality of your friendship is concerned in this recommendation. If You, my dear Sir Edward had no reason to be dissatisfied with me in your own case, I am very happy. But I say it with all sincerity, if Mr Horton's design be to consult the real advantage of his son's education, he will be at no loss to find, in either of our universities, at least as diligent and, I ought to think, a much abler Tutor than,

Dear Sir, Your very obliged and affectionate humble Servt

R Hurd.

Please to give my humble Service to Lady Littleton.

127 To Sir EDWARD LITTLETON 1 DECEMBER 1752

Text: MS STAFFS RO D1413/1; unpublished.
Addressed: To/ Sir Edward Littleton Bart./at Tedgeley-Coppice near/Penkrich/Staffordshire.
Postmarked: CAMBRIDGE 4 DE

Cambridge 1. Dec. 1752.

Dear Sir Edward

You are very good to accept my excuse for not engaging in the charge, to wch your

Buswell Horton. RH finally consented and Horton was admitted a Fellow-commoner at Emmanuel on 27 January 1753. He matriculated at Easter in the same year, but died suddenly in October. (*Macro Letter-book*.)

2 It was the practice for two or three Fellows only to devote themselves to tutoring the undergraduates at an average-sized college. Other Fellows might have lecturing or administrative commitments but could otherwise pursue their own research.

partiality had press'd me.[1] But there is one point in which You seem a little to misapprehend me. When I begg'd your leave to decline the office of principal Tutor to Mr Horton, I had no thoughts of engaging in the other relation You mention. Much less did I promise to myself, or would accept, any gratuity for the little services I might do him by what I called *occasional Information.* What I meant was this, and, I think, it would answer your purpose, as well as mine much better, than if I came at once into your proposal.

I entirely agree with You, that a private Tutor would be of singular service, and I have one in my eye of excellent qualifications and who, I dare say, might be engaged by the sum You speak of. This is Mr Richardson, the Master's Son, whose general behaviour and character You know.[2] He is a person of good sense, of an engaging temper and disposition, an excellent scholar, and one who would take great pains with Mr H. both in his public and private lectures. I may further mention as an agreable circumstance that he was educated at Westminster and is no novice in this employment having been for some time private Tutor to a fellow-commoner of the college, Mr Panton.[3] In short I believe he could not be in better hands. And since You think so kindly of me as to suppose that my superintendency might be of service, I should readily assist Mr Richardson with my best advice as to the course of his classical studies and the order and manner of pursuing them. I would further, as I said, be very attentive to his behaviour, which, indeed from what You say of him, will give his friends or tutors little trouble, and shall take a pleasure at all times to converse freely with him on any subject. In this way I think I could do him all the service You propose, and indeed much more than if I took the tuition of him myself, as Mr Richardson would afford him more of his time and attendance, than my affairs would allow me.

Pray think of this scheme and consult with Mr Horton upon it. It would be hard for me indeed to refuse absolutely what You should insist upon. But I had rather a thousand times it should be, as is here proposed. And I persuade myself a little reflexion will reconcile You to it.

I think myself much indebted to Mr and Mrs Horton for the very favorable opinion which they have the goodness to entertain of me, and shall be truly happy if I may discharge some part of this debt by rend'ring any effectual services to the amiable young gentleman, for whose education they are so justly concerned. But however this may be, I must needs have a just sense of their civility and am, with my best services to Lady Littleton, Dearest Sir Edward, Your most faithful & affectionate humble Servt

R Hurd.

1 See preceding letter.

2 Robert Richardson (1732–81) was studying for his M.A. He was subsequently elected a Fellow (1755), and became Rector of Wallington, Hertfordshire, and St Anne's Westminster. He was appointed a prebendary of Lincoln in 1762 and was chaplain-in-ordinary to the King. (*D.N.B.*; *Alum. Cantab.*)

3 Thomas Panton (1731–1808) had been admitted a Fellow-commoner in September 1751. As was usual in the case of Fellow-commoners he did not take his degree, and gained his reputation in later life as an owner of racehorses. (*D.N.B.*; *Alum. Cantab.*)

128 To WILLIAM MASON 20 JANUARY 1753

Text: MS HC; printed, *H-M Corr*, 12.
Addressed: To Mr William Mason at the/Reverend Mr Mason's in/ Hull./Yorkshire./By Caxton.
Postmarked: CAMBRIDGE

Camb. 20. Jan. 1753.

Dear Sir

I suppose You have judged hardly of me for neglecting your letter of the 31st past all this time. But I have a Clerical excuse. I have been preparing for W. Hall.[1] And when I set upon this work of sermonizing, I am in such impatience to get over it that I don't care to be interrupted by other matters. But I am now at liberty again and shall dedicate the first moments of my leisure to your service.

For news, there is little stirring, unless that our *cause of Appeals* [a] is expected to come to a hearing next month.[2] I wish we may succeed. And yet 'tis certain that *we*, I mean the University, do not deserve success. The greater part, as You know, oppose their own reasonable liberty, and the rest, excepting a very few, are ashamed to appear in the vindication of it. You have *one* in your eye,[b] I dare say, whom it much more concerned, than it did me, to assert this cause, and who yet was afraid of being thought to assert it.[3] He is lately charged however with the obnoxious *Fragment*.[4] The Bishops of Ely and Chester openly charged him with it.[5] I told him so. And yet he took no method to clear himself either to them or others. Is not this mysterious? Is he grown indifferent, at last, to his good name? Or is he fearful of giving offence tho' in his own just support? All he has done has been to preach at St Mary's in praise of Candour,[6] which he thinks sadly violated in our times by that outrageous resentment which all men are so forward to entertain against vice and vitious men.

1 Whitehall. RH had been appointed Preacher at the Chapel Royal in May 1750 by Dr Sherlock, Bishop of London. (See *ante* To Balguy, 19 March 1751, n. 11.)

2 The dispute over the Right of Appeal (see *ante* To Balguy, 19 March 1751, n. 8) had gone to arbitration in 1752. Lord Hardwicke (High Steward of the University), the Archbishop of Canterbury, the Bishop of London, Lord Chief Justice Lee and his brother, Sir George Lee, had agreed to act as referees. They were to consider submissions from, on one side, the Vice-Chancellor (Keene) and the Masters of Corpus and Magdalene (Green and Chapman), and on the other, James Bickham of Emmanuel, Smith of King's and Balguy of St John's. (Grace of March 1752, C.U.L. Misc. Collect. 36, Journal of Henry Hubbard.) No information has been found to confirm whether a final decision was made by the referees, although a considerable number of documents relating to the case have been preserved at Emmanuel. (*Documents concerning the Ansell Case*, COL. 9. 28; Winstanley, *The University of Cambridge in the Eighteenth Century*, pp. 220–2.)

3 Possibly William Powell or perhaps Thomas Balguy. RH had urged him to defend the Association in print, but apparently with no success.

4 A *Fragment*, [1750], variously attributed to Henry Stebbing, James Bickham and Francis Coventry. (Wordsworth, *Social Life at the English Universities*, p. 621.) This pamphlet was more concerned with the controversy over the regulations than over the Right of Appeal.

5 Sir Thomas Gooch, Master of Gonville and Caius College, and Edmund Keene, Master of Peterhouse.

6 No printed version of this sermon (preached in the University Church) has been traced.

a Note by RHn: "The Right of Appeal from the Chancellor or Vice Chancellor of Cambridge to the Senate."

b Note by RHn: "[Qu. Mr. Powell]".

But all this I say to You *sub sigillo silentii et amicitiae*.[7]

This last word very luckily connects with what I have next to say to You. You want to hear how our *friend*'s Sermons[c] are relish'd at Cambridge.[8] Why just as You might suppose: Either grossly abused, or faintly commended. *Ross*[9] is clamorous against them: And a friend of your's,[10] [d] whose *taste* is almost as squeamish as his *faith*, joins with him. There is, on the other hand, a junto of friends who like some things, but object to others as not accurate enough and metaphysical. Most agree to censure the *Style* and verily think, Mr W.[e] writes worse & worse. *Ross*[f] was very gay some time since at my room on this last topic but unhappily, for proof quoted a passage which I told him was, in my apprehension, incomparably the most excellent in the whole Volume. It is that (if You have the Sermons by You) about the *African Eloquence*:[11] a passage, the exquisite beauty of which these wretches may well be excused, if they never understand. One of their outcries, as usual, is against *subtleties and Refinements*. In relation to which I will transcribe what Mr W. wrote to me the other day, to whom I had mentioned this stale objection. His answer is just and, in his manner, severe and witty: "*If an Ass could speak, he would call rose leaves such, that pass over his palate unfelt; while he was at his substantial diet of good brown Thistles*".[12] For my own opinion, if You have seen this volume yourself, I need not give it You. If You have not, I will only say they are the only model of Sermons, hitherto published. I am not sure if the cavillers, I have spoken of, have the sense to see their excellencies. If they have, the worst thing I wish may befall their malignity in dissembling it, is the Imprecation of the Poet, in truth a very severe one – *Virtutem videant intabescantque relicta*.[13] And with this punishment on their heads I leave them.

But I have something a little more serious to say to You. The excessive ill usage which the only Great Man of our times (for such he is, let fools and knaves say what they will to the contrary) is constantly receiving, kindles my Indignation, and so, I'm sure, it does Your's. This has put a thing into my head, which perhaps, if I have health and spirits, I may sometime execute. The general plan is such as I have no great doubt of your liking. At least it flatters my Imagination, at this distance, not a little. The design is so laid that it will give me the opportunity of defending ev'ry part of Mr Ws[g] writings and character and yet in a way that will not be controversial nor, if well

7 This does not appear to be a quotation.

8 William Warburton's *The Principles of Natural and Revealed Religion Occasionally Opened and Explained; in a Course of Sermons preached before the Honourable Society of Lincoln's Inn*, 1753. Volume 1 was advertised for sale in December 1752. (*Lond. Mag.*)

9 See *ante* To Mason, 29 October 1752, n. 3.

10 Richard Hurd, nephew, notes that this is George Ashby, the antiquary, of St John's.

11 *Principles*, pp. 191–2. Warburton is discussing what kind of eloquence should have been exhibited by those on whom the "gift of tongues" had been bestowed. Should it have been the "flowing exuberance of Attic eloquence, or the grave severity of the Roman?" he asks. "Or should it have been that African torrent, which arose from the fermented mixture of the other two, and soon after overflowed the church with theological conceits, in a sparking luxuriancy of thought and sombrous rankness of expression?"

12 Warburton to RH, 15 January 1753, *Prelate*, p. 95.

13 Persius, *Satires*, 3. 38.

c Note by RHn: "Mr Warburton".

d Note by RHn: "George Ashby".

e Note by RHn: "Warburton".

f Note by RHn: "of St John's".

g Note by RHn: "Warburton's".

executed (of which I have the most reason to doubt), offensive to the delicacy ev'n of *Rose-leaf* eaters.[14] But of this project I say no more at present, nor ever shall, unless it be executed, and then, perhaps, to no mortal but Yourself. In the mean time, let this general Intimation sleep with You.[h]

What You write of Garnet is very contemptible.[15] But no matter, let him exult in his good fortune. You and I, I verily believe, shall never envy Him. Or, if You have any tendency that way, what will You give me for a *Charm* that will secure You from all danger. I picked it up in an old Ware-house, or rather Lumber-room of cast off goods, and yet there is no *Amulet* of modern date and construction more serviceable. Guess now if You can, from whose honest & plain-dealing pen these Rhymes have been dropped.

Fortune is stately, solemne, prowde, & hye,
And Richesse geveth, to have servyce therefore;
The nedy Begger catcheth an half-peny;
Some manne a thousand pounde, some lesse, some more.
But for all that She keepeth ever in Store
From every manne some parcelle of his wyll,
That He maye pray therfore and serve her styll.[16]

See here the tricks of this sly Goddess, told in honest guise by this rude Enditer. But can You direct me to better sense in sprucer English? I trow not. However let us weigh the matter. Your Bishop would say, "Let *fortune* be as great a baggage, as She will, still

14 RH's nephew notes that this refers to *On the Delicacy of Friendship*, although it cannot be a specific reference since the pamphlet was published as a reply to John Jortin's *Six Dissertations* in 1755. (See *post* To Warburton, 1 December 1755.) RH may subsequently, however, have used some of the material he had prepared at this time.

15 John Garnett. (See *ante* To Balguy, 26 September 1752, n. 11.) Mason's feelings about his elevation to the episcopate were expressed in an epigram, a copy of which is in his manuscript *Commonplace Book*, with a note that it was published in the *London Evening Post*. (York Minster Library, Add. 25, p. 28.)

Epigram
On a late ecclesiastical promotion

Says old Cam to the Bp my Son is it so
Is the Conge d'Elire signd are you sure you shall go
What! must Ireland enjoy all that genius & Knowledge
By my Soul thoudst ha' made a rare head of a College.
"Sir his Grace was so pressing a speedy translation
Besides is Cocksure from my next dedication."
Well Jack! I begin now to smoak thy discernment,
Yet faith I beleivd eer thou got this preferment
That thy hunting so long had quite emptied thy fob
And in all senses made thee as poor as thy Job.

16 Sir Thomas More, Prologue to *The Boke of the fayre Gentylwoman, that no man shulde put his truste or confydence in, that is to say, Lady Fortune*, stanza 36. RH's knowledge of Thomas More's English verse is unusual in the eighteenth century. There were no eighteenth century printings of these poems, and the only source that would have been available to him was the 1557 edition of More's *Workes*, a copy of which is held in the library at Emmanuel. The stanza here occurs in the fourth section of *These fowre thinges*, a section of More's early English verse preceding his more major works. (Stanza 34.)

h Note by RHn: "Pamphlet on the delicacy of Friendship 1755".

She is better than *Poverty*: Of all Spectres let me keep clear of this".[17] Shall we subscribe to this so Episcopal determination, or shall we fetch counsel again from my old Oracle?

Povertee that of Her (Fortune's)[i] gifts wyl nothynge take
With mery cheere looketh upon the Presse,
And seeth how fortune's housholde goethe to wrecke
"Fast by her standethe the wyse Socrates" this verse done *en Critique*.
Aristippus, Pythagoras and many a lease
Of old Philosophers: And eke agaynst the Sonne
Bakyth him poore Diogenes in his Tonne:[18]

And so goeth on enumerating many poor but happy philosophers, from which number however I would willingly have You exempt, whatever may be the fate of one, who yet in all fortunes thinks he cannot fail of being, Dear Sir, Your faithful and affectionate friend & Servt

R Hurd.

Endorsed by Richard Hurd, nephew: "Jan 20th 1753 about Mr. Warburton's Sermons, &c."

129 To Sir EDWARD LITTLETON 12 FEBRUARY 1753

Text: MS STAFFS RO D1413/1; unpublished.
Addressed: To/Sir Edward Littleton Bart/at Tedgely near Penkrich/Staffordshire./By London.
Postmarked: CAMBRIDGE 13 FE

Dear Sir Edward

I have purposely avoided writing to You all this time, because I had a mind to have some taste of your Brother's conduct and disposition, before I gave You my Opinion of Him.[1] I am sensible how dangerous it is, on so slight experience, to pronounce of these young Sparks, who, as they do not know themselves, so neither is it easy for others to have a perfect knowledge of them. However this I cannot help owning to You, how exceedingly taken I am (and indeed so we are all) with what we have hitherto observed of his ingenuous and pretty manner. I find him competently skilled in Greek and Latin, and, what pleases me very much, not unacquainted with the French. He appears, besides, so willing to be directed in what concerns his Behaviour

17 Mason's bishop was Matthew Hutton, Archbishop of York. RH is not alone in suggesting that he had a tendency to avarice. Thomas Wray, in a letter to Dr Ducarel, wrote, "His being a little *ad rem attentior*, I attribute entirely to his having a family, as I have not heard that he ever discovered such a turn in his younger days; and I believe he was above doing any thing little, mean, or dirty." (2 September 1758, *Lit. Illusts.*, iii. 473.) Edmund Pyle, however, asserted that Hutton died leaving "£50,000, which he had saved out of the Church in twelve years, and not one penny to any good use or public charity". (*Memoirs of a Royal Chaplain, 1729–1763. The Correspondence of Edmund Pyle, D.D. Chaplain in Ordinary to George II*, ed. Albert Hartshorne, 1905, p. 76.)

18 Sir Thomas More, *ibid.*, stanza 22, and stanza 20.

i RH uses square brackets.

1 Littleton's brother in law, Walter Horton, admitted on 27 January 1753.

and Studies, that, if he continues in this good way, neither his Tutors nor Friends will have any thing further to desire of Him.

I shall take care to deliver th. books and letters You sent by Mr Horton.

We are much pleased to hear of your preparations for building and adorning the Park.[2] For, tho' You are too much of a Philosopher to place your chief happiness, as great Men sometimes do, in *Palaces and Bowers*, yet must You needs think them very convenient things; and as such, the sooner You get possession of them, the better.

All friends here are very well and desire their best Services. Pray give mine to Lady Littleton and the family at Catton and believe me always, with great truth, Dearest Sir, Your very affectionate and faithful humble Servt

R Hurd.

Camb. XII. Feb. 1753.

130 To THOMAS BALGUY — 14 MARCH 1753

Text: *Memoirs*, 48.

Devereux Court,[1] 14 March, 1753.

Dear Sir,

I thank you for your kind letter. I have the pleasure to inform you that Dr. Heberden is quite recovered from his late illness, which, to the disgrace of temperance, ended in a fit of the gout. Besides its other ravages, it has stripped the doctor of a good deal of that flesh, with which, as you know, his bones were so unmercifully encumbered. He took your compliment, which I reported to him, very kindly . . .

Mr. Warburton has seen a thing against the Newtonian philosophy in favour of Hutchinson by one Horne,[2] of Oxford, and thinks it would be a good employment for some Cambridge Soph[3] to answer it.

Mr. Allen's family is come to town, and betwixt them and my other friends I hardly know when I can make my escape from this place . . .

I am a little of Pope's humour, to love a courtier in disgrace.[4] This, and a little business I had with him, carried me this morning to my Lord Bishop of Norwich.[5] The

2 Littleton had started drawing up plans for his new house in July 1752. It was to be situated in Teddesley Park, a few miles from his parents' house at Pillaton.

1 Devereux Court, Strand, the first turning east after Essex Street. "*Tom's Coffee House* in this court was the resort of some of the most eminent men for learning and ingenuity of the time. Here Dr. Thomas Birch was often to be found; and here Akenside, the poet, spent many of his winter evenings." (Wheatley, *London Past and Present*, 1891.)

2 George Horne, *A Fair, Candid, and Impartial State of the Case between Sir Isaac Newton and Mr Hutchinson. In which is shewn, How far a system of Physics is capable of Mathematical Demonstration; how far Sir Isaac's, as such a system, has that Demonstration; and consequently, what regard* Mr. *Hutchinson's claim may deserve to have paid it*, Oxford, 1753.

3 At Cambridge, an undergraduate in his second or third year.

4 A reference to Pope's friendship with Bolingbroke, who, having risen to be Secretary for War and Secretary of State under Queen Anne, was dismissed on the accession of George I. He was attainted for Jacobite sympathies and fled to France, only returning to England in 1723. (*D.N.B.*)

5 Thomas Hayter (1702–62). Hayter had been appointed preceptor to the Prince of Wales in 1751 but resigned in 1752 because of political differences with other members of the household

oily smoothness of this prelate ran over upon me in all manner of civilities, and I am to eat a bit of mutton with him on Sunday.

The present state of the Theatres confirms my theory of the Drama.[6] A fine old enchanting story of our own, in the *Earl of Essex*, took very much with the town, notwithstanding the clumsy execution of an Irish bricklayer.[7] "*The Brothers*," though an infinitely better play, has worse success.[8] The story, though it reads finely in Livy, is a bad one for a tragedy; and is, indeed, but ill managed. The dresses and other decorations are prodigiously splendid. It was well acted, and yet if this virtuous age had not been fired with a primitive zeal for the propagation of Christianity, nothing, I believe, could have saved it from the poet's hell. The pleading before the King had the best effect in the representation, for which, as well as I remember, great thanks are due to Livy.[9] The character of Perseus is much the best, but outraged, as almost every thing indeed is. This Night Thinker has deepened the horror of some parts so much that the *raven hour of darkness*,[10] to speak in Shakespeare's phrase, does not *smile*, but frown. However, the smile is not lost: it is only transferred elsewhere.

Poor Mason is a wretched politician. He has taken it into his head to serve a friend, but has contrived such a way of doing it as, if the world knew it, would disgrace the very name of poetry. He wrote me a long letter about getting a Commissioner's place of Bankrupts[11] from my Lord Chancellor, which he supposes may be done by a *friend's* asking for it. I referred him, as my Lord Archbishop of York would have done, to parliamentary interest. When will these simple-minded men of Parnassus learn a little prudence?

Speaking of Parnassus puts me in mind to tell you that Mr. Warburton has found in Pope's library an edition of Bishop Hall's Satires, with many expressions of admiration in the margin.[12] The last of those satires, I think, is marked throughout in his own

suspected of Jacobite tendencies. He was refused an audience with the King and his resignation was accepted by the Archbishop. (*Alum. Cantab.*; *D.N.B.*)

6 RH's views on dramatic form are given in 'A Dissertation concerning the Provinces of the several Species of the Drama', appended to his 1753 edition of the *Epistolae ad Pisones, et Augustum*, published in April. (See following letter.)

7 *The Earl of Essex. A Tragedy* was written by Henry Jones, who had been apprenticed to a bricklayer in Ireland before coming to London, and who is referred to in the Epilogue of his play as an "Irish Bricklayer". The tragedy had been revised by Lord Chesterfield and Colley Cibber before being first presented at Covent Garden on 21 February 1753. It was a considerable success, but is, as RH asserts, of poor literary quality. (*The London Stage 1660–1800*, Part 4, ed. G.W. Stone; *D.N.B.*; *Biographia Dramatica; or, A Companion to the Playhouse*, ed. David Erskine Baker, Isaac Reed and Stephen Jones, 3 vols., 1812, ii. 182.

8 Edward Young's *The Brothers* opened at Drury Lane on Saturday 3 March. According to contemporary comment it "went off with Great Applause", but it nevertheless ran only for two weeks whilst *The Earl of Essex* continued to be played throughout the season. (*London Stage*, Part 4; *Biographia Dramatica*, ii. 70.)

9 The pleading of Perseus and Demetrius before their father, Philip, King of Macedonia, is drawn from Livy, xl. 8–16. The scene is depicted in the third and pivotal act of *The Brothers*.

10 Not a direct quotation from Shakespeare, although there are many similar expressions.

11 There were fifty Commissioners of Bankrupts in the Court of Chancery appointed by the Lord Chancellor. (John Chamberlayne, *Magnae Britanniae Notitia*, Part II, Book III, p. 273.)

12 This copy of Joseph Hall's *Virgidemiarum, Sixe Bookes* (published in two volumes in 1597–8), formed part of RH's library up until 1938. It subsequently disappeared, but some information relating to it may be found in the Oxford edition of the *Satyrs*, published in 1753, also at Hartlebury Castle. RH inscribed this with the note: "In a Letter from Mr Warburton to/me/Feb. 24. 1753/are these words–/"You will be pleased to know/that looking into Mr Pope's Library

hand. And Mr. Warburton conjectures he had designed to versify it, as he had done some of Donne's.[13] You may be sure I triumph in this discovery . . .

Ever most entirely yours,

R. Hurd.

131 To Sir EDWARD LITTLETON 3 APRIL 1753

Text: MS STAFFS RO D1413/1; unpublished.
Addressed: To/Sir Edward Littleton Bart/at Mr Bartlet's in the North/Parade/Bath.[1]
Postmarked: CAMBRIDGE 4 AP

Dear Sir Edward

I am much concerned to hear of any occasion forcing You to the Bath; a place, which I dare say neither Lady Littleton nor Yourself have any passion for. I heartily wish her Ladyship all possible benefit from the waters, and shall be very impatient to hear from You that She has found, at least, some good effect from them.

The new Ed. of my pieces on Horace is, at last, ready to be published.[2] You must tell me if I shall send your books to Bath, or order them into Mr Davis' hands to send into Staffordshire. I know You will except this small present with your usual goodness. I thought You had an absolute right to the first Volume, which I have therefore done myself the honour to present to You in a plain Inscription.[3] That I ventured no farther was occasioned rather by consulting your delicacy, than my own Inclination.

The second Volume is addressed to Mr Warburton; and his public character, I thought, would justify a little more freedom, which I accordingly used in hazarding a

I/found an edition of your favorite/Satires of Hall. The first Satire/of his sixth Book he has marked/thus–Sat. opt. and has corrected the versification thru'out. So I/fancy he designed to publish it/as he had done Donne. My favorite is 1 Sat. B. iii."/This edition of Hall's Satires/is not now in Mr Pope's (i.e. my)/Library./R.W." A later note by RH follows this: "I have since met with it. It is now/[July 18, 1801] in Hartlebury Library." (Maynard Mack, 'Pope's Books: A Biographical Survey with a Finding List', *English Literature in the Age of Disguise*, ed. Maximillian E. Novak, 1977.)

13 Pope rewrote the second and fourth satires of Donne. They appeared in a two volume edition of his works published in 1735.

1 North Parade was a fashionable and important street with one of the two Assembly Rooms (Wiltshire's) for balls, card parties and concerts. Facing the houses was the "Parade Coffee-House" (particularly "pleasant" in the spring), also one of the principal places of entertainment in the city. (*The New Bath Guide, or, Useful Pocket-Companion*; . . . Second Edition, with large Additions, Bath, [1762].)

2 *Q. Horatii Flacci Epistolae ad Pisones, et Augustum: With an English Commentary and Notes. To which are added Two Dissertations: The One, On the Provinces of the several Species of Dramatic Poetry: The Other, On Poetical Imitation. In Two Volumes. The Second Edition, Corrected and Enlarged*, 1753. The edition was published sometime between 3 and 12 April. (See following letter.)

3 The one-page inscription reads: "To Sir Edward Littleton, Bt./The following Commentary, &c./on the /Art of Poetry,/First/Written for his Use,/Is now, with all Respect,/Inscribed/By his most Obedient, and/Most faithful Servant,/The Author."

dedication to him.[4] It is not for such a writer as me to think of doing him honour; but I hope You will think the purpose of it such as will do myself no discredit.

Mr Horton is very well and very good. You cannot imagine how fond I grow of him.

All you[r] friends here are much devoted to You and especially, Dear Sir Edward, Your affectionate and your faithful friend & Servt

R Hurd.

Camb. 3. Apr. 1753.

132 To Sir EDWARD LITTLETON 12 APRIL 1753

Text: MS STAFFS RO D1413/1; unpublished.
Addressed: To/Sir Edward Littleton Bart./at Mr Bartlet's in the North-Parade/Bath.
Postmarked: CAMBRIDGE 14 AP

Camb. 12. Apr. 1753.

Dear Sir Edward

I am sorry to hear no better account of Your's and Lady Littleton's Health. Nothing could make me so happy as to be any way instrumental in the recovery of what I so warmly wish. But the truth is, I am a little afraid there may be some impropriety in the application You speak of.[1] I know Mr Allen is very scrupulous in the affair of his *Ride*, and for a plain reason, as the vast resort of people of condition to Bath, who would be constantly desiring that liberty, would deprive him of the pleasure of it. I don't remember all the time I was with him, that any Coaches, except those of the Princess Amelia and her Retinue, had that Indulgence.[2] And this, You know, is no precedent. I think it would be right to inform yourself, as You may easily do, if this liberty be granted to any other persons. If it be, I would write to Mr Allen directly, and have no doubt of his readiness to oblige us. You will judge if what I have hinted be proper. At all adventures, You may depend on my doing in this affair, as You direct me.

As to the *new Edition of Horace*, it has been out some days. So that if I have done wrong, there is now no remedy.[3] I admire as much the good sense as the modesty of all You say of the nicety of dedicating to any but persons of a public character. Those considerations weighed much with me. And the result was, that I thought it most becoming myself, and most respectful to You, to inscribe it, as I have done. But if at last I have judged ill, it will be the greater mortification, since I pretend to be no less concerned for the dignity of your character, than the propriety of my own conduct. As

4 The dedication to Warburton is thirteen pages long. It contains a brief history of literary criticism, attributing great significance to the work of Warburton as critic of Pope and Shakespeare. RH asserts that his own attempts at critical analysis have been modelled on the work of his friend.

1 Littleton wished to take his wife riding or out in a coach in the grounds of Prior Park, Ralph Allen's house on the outskirts of Bath. (Boyce, *The Benevolent Man*, pp. 72–4, 98–117.)

2 Princess Amelia had asked for the use of Prior Park in the summer of 1752. The Allens removed to Weymouth and the Princess stayed at the Park from 7 August for about ten days. (*Ibid.*, p. 205.)

3 The cause of Littleton's dissatisfaction with the inscription addressed to him is not clear. His sense of what was appropriate, however, gave rise to further anxieties concerning subsequent inscriptions. (See *post* To Littleton, 21 July 1755, and 6 June 1756.)

the two Volumes are wholly separate and, in truth, two distinct works I apprehended not the least indecorum in presenting them to two persons. And as to *inscribing* to one, and *dedicating* to another, it was impossible for me to conceive any danger of a misconstruction, both as the two ways are held equally respectful, and as I know the practice is very usual. I have an instance on my own shelves. The first Volume of Mr Balguy's father's Sermons was *dedicated* to the ABp of Canterbury: Mr Balguy *inscribed* the second to the Bp of Winchester.[4]

Indeed if I had inscribed one part to You, and dedicated the other to a person in your Situation, this, perhaps, had looked particular. But as Your's was a private, the other a public character, there could, I thought, be no shadow of an exception.

I mention all this to shew You, that it was not without much caution I resolved on the method, I have taken. And my delicacy in the matter is even so great, that it would not have suffered me to dedicate or ev'n inscribe the second part to any person of less eminent note than Mr Warburton.

After all I find myself in very unlucky circumstances, to be obliged to excuse what, on the maturest consideration, seemed to me the most fit conduct. If I have erred, it was an error of the most unhappy kind; since, if I know myself, my Ambition is to convince You of the entire Respect, with which I am ever, Dear Sir Edward, Your most faithful and most Obedt Servt

R Hurd.

P. S.

I have a set ready bound, which only wait your directions to be sent to You.

133 To WILLIAM WARBURTON 2 JULY 1753

Text: *Prelate*, 105.

Cambridge, July 2d, 1753.

Rev. Sir,

I troubled you the other day with a long letter, the main purpose of which was to draw from you some instructions on a point or two in our history.[1] – Since that I have received your very kind present of the small edition of Pope's works, together with the first part of the D. L.[2] I give you my entire thanks for both. Though my curiosity had

4 One volume of John Balguy's sermons, entitled *Twenty-one Sermons* was published in 1749 with a dedication of sixteen pages to Thomas Herring, Archbishop of Canterbury. Another collection, *Twenty Sermons on the Following Subjects*, was published by Thomas Balguy in 1750, his father having died in September 1748. It carries a one-page inscription to Benjamin Hoadly, Bishop of Winchester. Neither volume has been preserved in RH's library at Hartlebury.

1 RH had asked Warburton for information about leading authorities on the history of the Long Parliament (the original letter has not been traced). Warburton replied on 30 June and 16 August with details of the most important authors. (*Prelate*, pp. 103, 108.)

2 *The Divine Legation of Moses demonstrated, on the Principles of a Religious Deist, from the Omission of the Doctrine of a Future State of Reward and Punishment in the Jewish Dispensation* was first published in three volumes between 1738 and 1741. By 1742 Warburton had prepared a third edition of Volume I and a second edition of Volume II which was in two parts. He was now embarking on new editions of both volumes. The fourth edition of Volume I was expanded into two volumes, published in 1755, and the third edition of Volume II, still in two parts (and two volumes) was published in 1758. Proof sheets of Volume I appear to have been sent to him by his printer, William Bowyer, from December 1751 onwards, and it must be to these that RH refers. (William Bowyer, *Paper-Stock Ledger 1717–73*, Bodleian Library, Ms. Don. b. 4.)

not suffered me to neglect comparing the second edition of Pope in 8vo. with the first, which you gave me. And I had transcribed into it the most material corrections and alterations. But this smaller set is most acceptable to me, both for its being a proof of your kind remembrance of me, and also for the neatness and convenient size of the volume, so proper for that constant pocket use, which such a poet improved by such a critic deserves.[3]

For the *Div. Leg.* I take it most kindly that you give me the pleasure of sharing in the improvements of this new edition so early. I am glad to find them so large as to cause a division of the first vol. into two parts. But of these I shall say no more till I have taken time to consider them, which, with my first convenience, I mean to do with all possible attention. In one of the blank pages I found two *friendly words*,[4] of which I will only say, they give me a pleasure superior to the little movements and self-gratulations of vanity.

Amongst the alterations in Pope, I find you have softened what was said of Hutcheson.[5] I believe you did this to gratify my partiality to that writer, though when I understood how unworthily he had treated you,[6] I was sorry for having troubled you with one word about him. – This experience (and it is not the first I have had) of your readiness to make alterations on such hints as mine, will for the future make me very careful how I presume to give them.

I forbear to trouble you any further. Only, with my best thanks, believe me, Rev. Sir, Your very obliged and affectionate humble Servant,

R. Hurd.

134 To Sir EDWARD LITTLETON 26 AUGUST 1753

Text: MS STAFFS RO D1413/1; unpublished.
Addressed: To/Sir Edward Littleton Bart/at Tedgely Coppice near/Penkrich Staffordshire
Postmarked: BURY 29 AV

Dear Sir Edward

My stay at this place has been somewhat longer than I designed.[1] I believe I shall remove in a few days to college. In the mean time if You will let me know on what

3 Two editions of Warburton's *The Works of Alexander Pope Esq*. were published in nine volumes in 1751, the first a large, and the second a small octavo. The title-pages differ slightly, the earliest edition being described as accompanied by "the Commentaries and Notes of Mr. Warburton", and the subsequent edition as "Published by Mr. Warburton with Occasional Notes". In 1753 a further edition was published with a title-page following that of the first edition, but in small octavo format. RH had apparently been presented with this and the first, but not the second edition.

4 No such manuscript note has survived.

5 In a note to Book IV, l. 487 of the *Dunciad* Warburton had written: "This *Ignis fatuus* has in these our times appeared again in the *North*; and the writings of *Hutcheson*, *Geddes*, and their followers, are full of its wonders." (Pope, *Works*, 1751, v. 278.) This was modified to: "and the writings of *Geddes*, and other followers of *Hutcheson*, are full of its wonders." (*Ibid.*, 1753, v. 225–6.)

6 Warburton had explained his reference to Hutcheson in a letter of 11 July 1751, written in response to RH's original comment on the passage. (*Prelate*, p. 60.)

1 RH had been staying with the Macros at Norton. He was not back in Emmanuel until 22

subject You desire to have my sentiments, with regard to your studies, I shall very readily give them You, tho' I could wish You an abler person to advise with on such an occasion.

What I said to Mr Horton of his Son was in all sincerity. He is an amiable pretty Youth. And there is good reason to believe his diligence will be answerable to the goodness of his disposition.

I write in some hast and therefore shall only trouble You farther with my compliments to Lady Littleton.

Dear Sir, Your most affectionate humble Servt

R Hurd.

Norton 26 Aug. 1753

135 To THOMAS BALGUY 27 SEPTEMBER 1753

Text: MS BEINECKE MS Vault Shelves, Hurd; printed in part, *Memoirs*, 50.
Addressed: cover missing.

Dear Sir

I receiv'd your favour of the 21 of August at Norton from which place I returned last Saturday.[1] I mention this to excuse my neglect of You all this while, as it was not possible for me to give you a satisfactory answer to your queries about your Chambers, till I came back to college. On inquiry I find John Ludlam took care to get the rooms painted before he went out of college,[2] and he now tells me he is taking incredible pains to get the locks cleaned and all other things in readiness for your reception. In short I rely so much on his diligence and punctuality as to have no doubt of evry thing being prepared to your mind in a very short time, and may therefore venture to invite you hither as soon as you please; which, from some hints dropped in your letter, I please myself with supposing may be sooner this year than usual. Don't mistake these for words of form and compliment. I really want you terribly; and am as impatient to draw a chair by your new fire-side as You can be. Besides our friends get together apace. Mr Powel fixes for good next Sunday: Dr Ogden[3] is fixed: Mr Allen only elopes for a fortnight: and Manwaring is with us for the whole winter. – Poor Mason's affliction you have hear'd of. He has lost his father: and since that, two servants have dyed out of the family, and his mother is now ill.[4] All this looks like a contagious fever, which alarms us all exceedingly for him: and besides we fear his situation in

September, possibly delayed by the death of Mary Macro on 31 August. (*Commons Accounts Book*, STE. 15. 9.)

1 22 September. See preceding letter, n. 1.

2 No records of the rooms allocated to Balguy at St John's have been found. RH may have been referring to William Ludlam, a Fellow since 1744, who, Kilvert states, was called 'John' in allusion to his college. (*Memoirs*, p. 99.)

3 Samuel Ogden (1716–78), formerly an undergraduate at St John's and a long-standing friend of RH, had returned to Cambridge in 1753 after nine years as Master of the Free School at Halifax. He had received his D.D. at the Commencement that year. (*D.N.B.*; *Alum. Cantab.*)

4 Mason's father died in Hull on 26 August 1753. His wife, Mason's stepmother, recovered from the fever and lived until 1776. (Draper, *Mason*, p. 42, Appendix C; Gray, *Correspondence*, Letters 180, 181, 182.)

other respects is but indifferent.[5] Pray write a word to him, if you have not already. Advise him to come away from Hull or say any thing else to him that you please. Any thing from a friend on these occasions carries some comfort with it.

I am glad to find that neither the flames of love nor of a fever, be it which it will, can waste your spirits. You cannot tell how much I envy you this disposition, which surely, if it be not health, is something much better. Only with this alacrity of mind I want to see your bodily forces established that you may in earnest apply yourself to some things, which I hold to be in a public as well as private view of great importance.

Mr Warburton is at P. P. from whence I had a letter the other day which speaks an unusual flow of spirits.[6] I had told him of a project Mr Browne had, and with which he wanted to draw me, of taking a trip next Spring to Paris, Berlin and I know not what other great towns of Europe. I had said something betwixt jest and earnest against this humour of sauntering up and down, under the specious pretence of seeing men and manners. And in taking notice of this part of my letter, after a great deal of excellent ridicule of the false taste in travelling, he comes at last to describe the *true*, and bids me instruct our friend of Carlisle in the following manner.– As I have nothing by a thousandth part so good of my own to entertain you with, I will transcribe the whole paragraph. – "This (says he) is enough for any one who only wants to study men for his Use. But if our aspiring friend would go higher, and study human nature, in and for itself, he must take a much longer Tour than that of Europe. He must first go and catch her undressed, nay quite naked, in North-America and at the Cape of Good-Hope. He may then examine how she appears crampt, untracted, and buttoned up close in the strait tunic of Law and Custom, as in China and Japan: Or spread out and enlarged above her common size, in the long and flowing Robe of Enthusiasm, amongst the Arabs and Saracens: Or lastly, as she flutters in the old Rags of worn-out Policy and civil Government, and almost ready to run back, naked to the deserts, as on the Mediterranean Coast of Africa. These, tell him, are the grand Scenes for the true Philosopher, for the citizen of the world, to contemplate. The *Tour of Europe* is like the entertainment that Plutarch speaks of, which Pompey's host of Epirus gave him. There were many dishes, and they had a seeming variety; but when he came to examine them narrowly, he found them all made out of one Hog, and indeed nothing but *Pork* differently disguised". –

This may be called a *Charge* to Travellers, which I thought would entertain and perhaps instruct You more than a late Charge to the Clergy of the Arch-Deaconry of Essex:[7] of which I know no more than that it lays the ignorance and corruption of Churchmen in these times to the account of Pamphlet-Clubs.[8]

5 Financially Mason was in a difficult position since his father had entailed his estate on Mason's half-sister, with a life-interest given to Mrs Mason. He was therefore unable to raise money on the property, at the same time as being deprived of the financial assistance his father had given him during his lifetime. (Draper, *Mason*, p. 43.)

6 *Prelate*, pp. 110–13. The letter is undated.

7 Thomas Rutherforth, A *Charge delivered to the Clergy of the Archdeaconry of Essex at a Visitation Jul. X. XI. XII. MDCCLIII*, Cambridge, 1753.

8 Rutherforth's argument is that there had been an "unusual growth and encrease of infidelity amongst all orders of men" (p. 7), which was attributable to the decay of learning. His contemporaries, he said, "instead of applying with diligence to the true helps of art and learning, have contented themselves with picking up the shreds of it, from translations and

Come soon, and in the mean time write one line that I may know You are coming. Dearest Sir, Your most affectionate and faithful friend and Servant

R Hurd

Camb. 27. Sept. 1753.

136 To WILLIAM MASON 22 OCTOBER 1753

Text: MS HC; printed, *H-M Corr*, 17.
Addressed: To/Mr Mason at George's Coffee-House/near Temple-Bar/London.[1]
Postmarked: CAMBRIDGE 23 OC

Dear Sir

I write a few lines, rather because you seem to expect it of me, than that I have anything of consequence enough to make up a letter.

I had scarcely begun to reconcile myself to the bad news, I had receiv'd from Hull,[2] [a] before I was attacked from another quarter, and in the most sensible manner; I mean with the report of poor Mr Horton's death,[b] which happen'd suddenly, in one of those fits to which he had, for some time, been subject.[3] You did not know Him, and, as it happens, it is very well You did not. For he was, without exception, the most amiable young man, I ever knew, and had a kind of fascination in his behaviour, which won upon all his acquaintance in a wonderful manner. It is some time since the qualities of the head have had but the second, and indeed a very subordinate place with me in my estimation of those few friends, whose acquaintance I care to cultivate. But the person, I speak of, had united these, in a high degree, with the most engaging temper I have ever met with. So that, on all accounts, I cannot but feel his loss very sensibly.

I have been reading much of late in a very contemplative author (tis Bishop Butler)

abridgments, from indexes and general dictionaries, from magazines and monthly reviews; the number of those, who would be thought scholars, has encreased without end; but the number of those, who are so, has diminished to such a degree, that if the next age should go on in the way, which the present age is marking out for it, in the following generation it will almost be forgotten, that there ever was such a character." (pp. 17–18.)

1 George's Coffee House was on the south side of the Strand between the entrance to Devereux Court and Essex Street. It was a popular establishment frequented by the town wits in the 1740s, and by Horace Walpole with his friends in the 1760s. (Bryant Lillywhite, *London Coffee Houses*, 1963.)

2 A reference to the death of Mason's father and the illness of other members of the family.

3 Walter Horton, the brother-in-law of Sir Edward Littleton, had been admitted to Emmanuel in January. (See *ante* To Littleton, 6 November 1752, n. 1.) He died suddenly at his home in Derbyshire. (*Macro Letter-book*, Littleton to Macro, 16 October 1753.)

a Note by RHn: "the death of Mr Mason's Father Rector of Hull".

b Note by RHn: "Mr Edward Horton was of Eman. Coll. & was son of Christopher Horton Esq. of Catton in Derbyshire, whose oldest daughter, Frances, was married to Sir Edward Littleton in 1752".

of this life's being a state of moral discipline and probation.[4] I ev'ry day, more and more, find it to be so. And perhaps it is the best use, which our continuance in such a wretched world as this can serve to. You see by this the temper I write in, and how much it needs the correction of that discipline which the various accidents of life are perpetually furnishing.

But not to trouble You with these uneasy reflexions, which what has so lately befallen yourself must have given but too much room for, let me only say I shall be glad to see You here very soon and much more, if You return to us with those good spirits which You so rightly endeavour to keep up under all your distresses.

You will find all your friends here, except Mr Grey who, as You would hear from himself, was called away, immediately on his coming hither, by the illness of a near Relation.[5]

I gave Mr Warburton some account of You, when I wrote last.

At all times believe me, Dear Sir, Your affectionate humble Servt

R Hurd.

Cambridge 22. Oct. 1753.

Endorsed by Richard Hurd, nephew: "Oct 22d 1753 about the death of Mr. Horton".

137 To Sir EDWARD LITTLETON 7 NOVEMBER 1753

Text: MS STAFFS RO D1413/1; unpublished.
Addressed: To/Sir Edward Littleton Bart/at Tedgely-Coppice near/Penkrich./Staffordshire
Postmarked: CAMBRIDGE 8 NO

Camb. 7. Nov. 1753.

Dear Sir

Your kind favour of the 24th past expresses in a very lively manner the Sense you have of the loss of our late excellent friend,[1] and your usual affection and partiality tow'rds me. I will not trouble You further with any melancholly reflexions on the former of these subjects, and all I shall say on the latter is, that You greatly overpay what You are willing to term services to yourself by your so kind and generous acceptance of them. And I hope You do me the justice to believe I never expected or wish'd any other return for them. – Tho' I cannot forget what effectual care You have

4 A reference to the works of Joseph Butler (1692–1752), Bishop of Bristol and, later, Durham. Butler wrote two of the most important theological works published in the eighteenth century, *Fifteen Sermons preached at the Chapel of the Rolls Court*, 1726, and *The Analogy of Religion, Natural and Revealed, to the Constitution and Course of Nature*, 1736. The *Analogy* was one of the most powerful and effective defences of Christianity against deism, and the *Fifteen Sermons* were a seminal influence on the school of Hutcheson and his followers. Butler's ethical system is primarily psychological, representing the conscience as holding a supreme position amongst the human faculties. His view of the human world extends this system, and shows life to be a probationary state in which man is guided towards virtue and finally rewarded in a future life.

5 On 18 October Gray wrote from Stoke Poges to Thomas Wharton that "as soon as I arrived at Cambridge [on 3 October], I found a letter informing me my Aunt Rogers had had a stroke of the Palsy, so that I stay'd only a single day, & set out for this place". (Gray, *Correspondence*, Letter 183.)

1 Walter Horton. (See preceding letter, n. 3.)

taken not to run in my debt for any inclinations I may have to serve You, by the many favours, and those of a very substantial kind, which You have long since done me.

You ask'd me some time since about the method of prosecuting your Studies. When You have enough recollected Yourself from this loss in your family, and your other affairs will give you leave to resume such thoughts, I hope You will tell me the particulars on which You would have my Opinion. I suppose You mean to confine Your enquiries to *Classics*, *History*, *Ethics*, and *Divinity*: these four being the <four> branches of learning more especially suitable, I believe, to your tast, and certainly most important to one in your rank and condition. I shall very readily give You my thoughts on any or all of these subjects, whenever You think fit to call upon me for them.

Mr Balguy, who is return'd to us, speaks much of the pleasure he receiv'd at Buxton especially from Lady Littleton's and Your company.[2] We are very impatient to receive a better account of my Lady's health, which no doubt must have had a very great shock from so unhappy an accident; tho' Mr Balguy speaks of her Ladyship's resolution and magnanimity in supporting it in terms of the highest approbation.

Pray do me the favour always to assure my Lady of my entire respects and let me further claim the justice of You to believe Yourself that You have not any friend more warmly and affectionately Your's than Your faithful humble Servt

R Hurd.

138 To THOMAS BALGUY [?1753]

Text: MS BEINECKE MS Vault Shelves, Hurd; printed, *Memoirs*, 51.

Addressed: cover missing.

Dear Sir[1]

We had some chat last night at your Chamber about that sort of Characters which for want of a better word I barbarously call'd *mawkish*. On coming home I found a book of *Characters* on my table and, opening it, happen'd to fall on *one* which exactly answers to my idea, tho' I knew not how to express it.[2] Pray shew it to Dr Ogden and tell him if you please (to gain it the greater reverence) that it comes from a Bishop.

My *mawkish* man then "Is one that would fain run an even path in the world and jut against no man. His endeavour is not to offend and his aim the general opinion. His conversation is a kind of continued complement, and his life a practice of manners. The relation he bears to others, a kind of fashionable respect, not friendship but friendliness, which is equal to all and general, and his kindnesses seldom exceed

2 Buxton in Derbyshire was a popular spa in the eighteenth century. Littleton and his wife had spent a good deal of time at various spas during this year. In April, May and June they had paid visits to Bath and Bristol, and in September had travelled to Matlock and Buxton. (*Ledger*, p. 43, Staffs. RO, D260/M/E/116.)

1 No evidence remains to suggest the date of this, or the following letter written to Balguy. Their position in the sequence of manuscript correspondence, and as quoted by Kilvert in his *Memoirs* seems to suggest, however, that they were written towards the end of 1753.

2 The book was John Earle's *Micro-cosmographie, or, A Peece of the World Discovered; in Essayes and Characters*, first published anonymously in 1628. The character is that of a "plausible Man", which in the 1740 edition of the book is described on pp. 99–101. Earle (?1601–65) was Bishop of Salisbury.

courtesies. He loves not deeper mutualities, because he would not take sides, nor hazard himself in displeasures, which he principally avoids. At your first acquaintance with him he is exceeding kind and friendly, and at your twentieth meeting after but friendly still. He has an excellent command over his patience and tongue, especially the last, which he accommodates always to the times and persons, and speaks seldom what is sincere, but what is civil. He is one that uses all companies, drinks all healths, and is reasonable cool in all religions. He considers who are friends to the company, and speaks well where he is sure to hear of it again. He can listen to a foolish discourse with an applausive attention, and conceal his laughter at nonsense. Silly men much honour and esteem him, because by his fair reasoning with them as with men of understanding, he puts them into an erroneous opinion of themselves and makes them forwarder hereafter to their own discovery. He is one rather well thought on than belov'd, and that love he has is more of whole companies together than any one in particular. Men gratify him notwithstanding with a good report; and whatever vices he has besides, yet having no enemies, he is sure to be an honest fellow".

Thus far this discerning prelate who after all, it's probable, was himself a little *mawkish*; at least if Bishopricks were to be got *then*, as some say they are *now*, by a dextrous application of this quality. If you or the Dr call for instances, besides the worthies mention'd last night, I refer you to the master – of ev'ry college, or, excepting the Dr himself and perhaps one or two more, the whole Vestry at St Mary's. You will take notice that I name no names. And so far I may be thought to come myself within the description of an *honest fellow*. But in ev'ry other respect I disclaim the imputation, as being *de tout mon coeur* your sincere friend & Servt

R.H.

Em̄an: Monday morning.

139 To THOMAS BALGUY [?1753]

Text: MS BEINECKE MS Vault Shelves, Hurd; printed in part, *Memoirs*, 51.
Addressed: To/The Revd Mr Balguy/at/St John's.

My most honour'd friend[1]

After my hearty respects and commendations premised.

Our cordial and singular well-wisher, the master of B.,[2] having on the instant signified unto me his loving intention of honouring his poor servant with his company this afternoon, I could not chuse but give you this notice, most earnestly wishing you a part in this my enjoyment, if so be you have not mishaply bounden yourself to any <prior> precedent engagement elsewhere. I will further acknowledge myself indebted to your courtesy for furthering this invitation to our respected acquaintance Mr Powell, provided you think of his discretion in such <. . .> sort, as that he will not be forward to interpose any meddling concerning Bp Fisher's *small scarfe*,[3] or such like

1 See preceding letter, n. 1.

2 "Bennet" was the old name of Corpus Christi. The Master was John Green, formerly of St John's (B.A. 1728; M.A. 1731; Fellow, 1731–50), who had been elected in 1750. He became Bishop of Lincoln in 1761. (See *post* To Green, 31 January 1762.)

3 John Fisher (1459–1535), Bishop of Rochester, was a founder and benefactor of St John's and

unseemly talk before so grave and reverend personage. And so, commending you to your wonted prudence, to determine as seemeth you fit, I rest, in all bounden service, your friend at commandment,

Richard Hurd.

140 To THOMAS BALGUY [?1753]

Text: MS BEINECKE MS Vault Shelves, Hurd; unpublished.
Addressed: To/The Revd Mr Balguy/St John's

Dear Mr Balguy[1]

I am not used to dissent from You in any matter, much less to think ill of You for any thing You do. But I must needs be of opinion that You could not have determin'd worse than You have done on the present occasion. I think You should not have submitted to see Green; Or, if You had, You should by all means have come to an explanation with him. To have done neither, what is it but to give him the double pleasure of insulting You, and of knowing that he has made a Dupe of You? For do You imagine he has not heard by this time of the report, or, which is full as bad, that he will not soon hear of it?

But I say no more. I can reverence the failings of such men as You & Cicero. I know the goodness and warmth of your heart. But it vexes me, that such a friend should give to others, who do not know him so well, a reasonable pretence to think ill of him.

I am with great affection, Dear Sir, Your constant friend & Servt

R Hurd

E.C. Tuesday morning

141 To Sir EDWARD LITTLETON 10 FEBRUARY 1754

Text: MS STAFFS RO D1413/1; unpublished.
Addressed: To Sir Edward Littleton Bart/at Tedgely Coppice near Penkrich/Staffordshire/By Lond.
Postmarked: CAMBRIDGE 11 FE

Cambridge 10. Feb. 1754

Dear Sir Edward

An affair has just happen'd which I beg leave to mention in confidence to You that You may advise me how to behave in it. I believe You hinted to me when I consented to take the care of poor Mr Horton, that I should be desir'd to accept such a matter as 30 Guineas a year as a gratuity for that trouble. Mr Horton has wrote me a very kind letter and inclos'd a bill for that Sum. But as his Son was not with me above half the

Chancellor of the University. The term "scarfe" was sometimes used synonymously for "chaplain", but the origin of RH's reference remains unclear.

1 The placing of this letter follows its positioning in the manuscript sequence, although the indication of hostility between Balguy and Green (probably John Green of "Bennet") makes its proximity to the preceding letter seem unlikely. However, lack of any circumstantial evidence makes more accurate dating impossible. The sphere of reference of the letter remains obscure.

year, I have no pretension to so much. On the other hand I know not how far he may think his civility slighted, if I return what I think I have no right to. As I always consider'd my engagement in this business rather in the light of a little act of friendship tow'rds one I am highly obliged to, than as a bargain with Mr Horton, I should be much dispos'd to accept no part of this offer but that my declining it might perhaps be construed a design to lay the family at Catton under an obligation to me. You have now my whole difficulty before You. Be pleas'd to give me your freest thoughts upon it. As You know both me and the family, you will be able to advise what is most proper to be done in it.

I rejoyce to understand by Mr Horton's letter that Lady Littleton is so much better and that You are so well employed in your projects about building.[1]

You will oblige me with a line immediately, because I shall wait for your answer before I acknowledge Mr Horton's favour.

Dear Sir Ed; Your most faithful humble Servt

R Hurd

142 To Sir EDWARD LITTLETON 22 FEBRUARY 1754

Text: MS STAFFS RO D1413/1; unpublished.
Addressed: To Sir Edward Littleton Bart/at his Seat near Penkrich/Staffordshire/By London
Postmarked: CAMBRIDGE 23 FE

Cambridge 22 Feb. 1754

Dear Sir Edward

You have contriv'd a very polite reason for my accepting Mr Horton's favour which is by taking it as an obligation done to yourself. But this is your way of construing all favours done to your friends. Betwixt You, I leave You to guess what must be [the] sum of my obligation. However on thinking further on the matter, I have determin'd not to decline his civility and shall accordingly write him a letter of acknowledgments this post.

Lady Littleton's better health and your resolution to resume the design of building are two things that give me an extreme pleasure. I have indeed some thoughts of seeing Tedgely this Summer, but whether so soon as April, I cannot take upon me to promise. I wish I may come too late to be at your consultations about the plan. I had much rather be at the laying of the Corner-Stone.[1] By the way I wish You would think well of the project of inclosing.[2] If this will be at any considerable expence of beauty in laying out the Park, I think You should by no means do it. The other is not a consideration for You in executing such a design.

Your accounts and this project will, I suppose, leave You no time or attention for parliamentary concerns. Will You forgive us, if I tell You we could not help a little

1 Sir Edward was still developing plans for his new house, Teddesley Hall.

1 The building of Teddesley Hall itself was actually delayed until June 1759. Meanwhile Littleton had a farm built and laid out the Park. (See *post* To Littleton, 5 July 1759; 8 August 1759.)

2 Throughout the eighteenth century there was gradual encroachment onto common and waste-land both to extend large estates and as part of a process of agricultural improvement. Littleton had evidently been thinking of turning over some of the heathland incorporated in Teddesley Park to provide more available ground for crops. RH feared that this could interfere with the large scale landscaping of the grounds which was favoured at this period.

diverting ourselves here at the abortion of your Lichfield designs?[3] We say there is a sort of fatality attending the policy of your friends. Something or other generally defeats them; and yet it seems your managers were no vulgar politicians and, as Machiavel advises, were resolv'd not to boggle at small matters. Seriously Sir W. Bagot[4] and the old Stagers, who knew how things were carried, must have been greatly to blame. However You will gain something better by this misconduct, than an Election, which is a great deal of experience. Our Mr Nevile is more arch on the occasion than I dare tell You, but bids me say (and I believe very truly) that *whether Whig or Tory he shall always love You.*

Our design of building, I believe, is quite over.[5] So that there can be no impropriety in your pursuing your first thought of obliging the college with a present in another way.[6]

All our Services to Lady Littleton. The Neviles and Mr Mainwaring and Balguy are much Your's; and believe me most affectionately Dear Sir, Your entire friend & oblig'd humble Servt

R Hurd.

143 To Sir EDWARD LITTLETON 29 APRIL 1754

Text: MS STAFFS RO D1413/1; unpublished.
Addressed: To/Sir Edward Littleton Bart/at the Hot-Wells at/Bristol
Postmarked: CAMBRIDGE 30 AP

My Dear Sir Edward

I thank You for your kind letter of the 25th and especially as I was indebted to You

3 Lichfield was the focus of a bitter struggle for political power between the leading county families and an independent tory party. The Gower family had traditionally supported tory interest but altered their allegiance to support the whigs following the Broad-Bottom coalition of 1744. (See *ante* To Littleton, 21 December 1744, n. 9.) From 1747 to 1820 every contest in Staffordshire was an attempt to overthrow the Gower interest which, nevertheless, was established increasingly firmly. The opposing tories gained a brief victory when they won one of the borough's two seats in November 1752. This reversal was challenged by the Gower and Anson families; a petition was made against the result and, on 30 January 1754, the House of Commons ruled that the tory candidate (who had since died) had not been duly elected. Littleton was a supporter of the anti-Government country interest. (Ann J. Kettle, 'The Struggle for the Lichfield Interest 1747–68', *Collections for a History of Staffordshire*, Fourth Series, vi. (1970), 115–35; Linda Colley, *In Defiance of Oligarchy. The Tory Party 1714–60*, 1982, pp. 242–51.)

4 Sir Walter Wagstaffe Bagot (1702–68), fifth Baronet, of Blithfield, Staffordshire. Bagot was M.P. for Newcastle-under-Lyme from 1724 to 1727; for Staffordshire from 1727 to 1754; and for Oxford University from 1762 to 1768. He voted consistently against the Government and participated in the demonstration against the Leveson Gowers at the Lichfield races in 1747. In 1754 he retired in favour of his son, but allowed himself to be persuaded to return to represent Oxford in 1762. (*The House of Commons 1715–1754*, ed. Romney Sedgwick, 1970.)

5 The Master and Fellows of Emmanuel had made a formal decision on 22 June 1752 to rebuild the College Butteries and an adjoining building. This scheme was in the end abandoned (though a considerable sum had been subscribed to fund it) because of disagreement amongst the Fellows. (Robert Willis, *The Architectural History of the University of Cambridge, and of the Colleges of Cambridge and Eton*, ed. John Willis Clark, 4 vols., Cambridge, 1886, ii. 713–17.) It was revived and executed in 1769.

6 Perhaps a reference to a present of plate. (See *ante* To Littleton, 26 April 1751, n. 7.)

for another favour of the same sort which I receiv'd last month at London. But my laziness and my frequent complaints make me a bad correspondent.

It makes me very happy to understand that your prospects from the Bristol waters are so promising.[1] Pray assure Lady Littleton of my entire respects and best wishes. I hope to take a flight into Staffordshire this Summer, and it would complete the satisfaction of such a ramble to find her Ladyship perfectly recoverd, and You busied in your projects of building. I approve your Scheme very much of doing ev'rything handsomely and to good purpose. You consider very rightly that what You design is not for yourself only but your family. It is very likely that I may be with You sometime in July if You return so soon and that Mr Balguy will contrive to give me the meeting from Buxton.[2] He talks of this with great pleasure and sends his compliments to You and my Lady.

As to the civility of Mr Warburton, he is not a man that makes compliments witht meaning. I know he has a true respect for your character from what he has hear'd me say of Your virtue modesty and good sense which make You so different from the profligate, forward, and foolish men of rank and fortune, that are the scandal of our times. He is now in London and will be there, I believe, for some months.[3] I will acquaint him with the sense You have of his civilities and your intention to take some fit opportunity to acknowledge them. Perhaps we shall meet in town e'er it be very long and then it will be easy for You to call upon him at Bedford Row.[4] I should be glad to bring You together and this, I believe, is the way You would like best. He is above ceremony so that You may take your own time and convenience. Only I know he is so much the man You would esteem that You must be acquainted with him.

Mr Macro has so much business in his farms that I a little question his being able to make good his promise of seeing You this Summer.[5] He did his best to serve You in town.[6] By the way Mr Littleton being out of town had like to have put him to difficulties about the money. But this could not be foreseen. My judgment is not worth taking of these things. But so far as my skill goes, I should pronounce the pictures he bought for You very good ones, especially considering the prices. I am of your mind that You ought to look out for a few right good Italian pieces. In the mean time it is convenient to get together a good stock of the Flemish masters, out of which You may

1 In the summer of 1753 the Littletons had moved to Bristol to take the waters, finding that those of Bath disagreed with Lady Littleton. The Bristol waters proved more effective and the Littletons continued to spend time there though in September Lady Littleton is again reported to have benefited little from her treatments. (*Macro Letter-book*.)

2 Buxton spa, Derbyshire (see *ante* To Littleton, 7 November 1753, n. 2).

3 Warburton left London earlier than predicted at the end of May (*Prelate*, p. 115).

4 Littleton's first visit to Warburton was in fact to Prior Park where he stayed two days from Monday 24 June. Warburton found him "a very amiable young gentleman" with "very good sense" and "strong impressions of virtue and honour". Further visits were exchanged in July but the friendship does not appear to have been lasting. (*Prelate*, pp. 116, 117, 119.)

5 Edward Macro had taken over some of the farming land owned by his family in Suffolk in the summer of 1753, and was now attempting to settle down as a farmer. (*Macro Letter-book*, Littleton to Macro, 13 June 1753; Frances Horton to Macro, 19 November 1753.)

6 Macro had advised Littleton on buying paintings, engravings and even manuscripts from 1749. He was used increasingly as an agent when Littleton married and as his commitments grew more extensive. Payment was usually made through Littleton's brother, Fisher, a barrister in London. (*Macro Letter-book*.)

choose the best to preserve and the rest will easily be dispos'd of.[7] There are two pieces of *Rocks and water*, very masterly in the execution, tho' the scenes are not the pleasantest – a rude sort of magnificence however that is not unpleasing. There is besides *an ev'ning Sea-piece* that You will like exceedingly. The *Hondicooter* I did not see but it was highly spoken of. The *head of F. Halles* is truly good but altogether Dutch.[8] This is what I remember of your pictures. We shall criticize them more accurately perhaps at Tedgely.

All things consider'd I think You judge quite right to have little to do with parliamentary affairs. Perhaps our reasons for this judgment may be different. You think there is no good to be done. I think there is no danger of any extraordinary mischief. But if there be any difference in our opinions of these matters, half an hour's conversation would adjust it. Leaving therefore, as we men of the pulpit say, the discussion of this weighty point to some other opportunity I conclude with all our Services and am, with repeated good wishes for Lady Littleton's recovery, Dearest Sir, Your faithful and Affectionate Servant

R Hurd

Cambridge 29 April 1754 –

P. S.

What must be done with your Subscription to *Bower's lives of the Popes*.[9] There is a third vol. just come out. Had not You better lodge it in the hands [of] Mr Davis in L[ond]on who can take in the books and send them to You [. . .] more easily than we can from Cambridge –

144 To Sir EDWARD LITTLETON 21 MAY 1754

Text: MS STAFFS RO D1413/1; unpublished.
Addressed: To/Sir Edward Littleton Bart/at the Hot-Wells near/Bristol
Postmarked: 22 MA

Cambridge 21. May. 1754

Dear Sir Edward

I thank You for your kind concern about my Health. The Bristol-waters are not thought proper for my case. I am got into the fashionable Regimen of Sea-water by Dr Heberden's advice and think I have found some benefit by it.[1] It delights me to hear that the Wells are likely to have their effect on Lady Littleton.

7 RH reflects contemporary preference for collecting works of the Italian painters of the sixteenth and seventeenth centuries. Seventeenth century Dutch painting was highly esteemed but ranked second to the Italian. (*Connoisseur Period Guides*, The Early Georgian Period 1714–1760, 1957; The Late Georgian Period 1760–1810, 1961.)

8 The two paintings named by RH had been bought at the sale of Dr Richard Mead's collection on 20, 21 and 22 March. The Hondecoeter was a picture of "Birds and Beasts . . . Five feet six inches by seven feet". Macro bought it for £30.9.0. The self-portrait by Frans Hals went to Macro for £4.14.6. (*A Catalogue of Pictures, Consisting of Portraits, Landscapes, Sea-Pieces, Architecture, Flowers, Fruits, Animals, Histories, of the late Richard Mead, M.D. Sold by Auction on March 20, 21 and 22,* M.DCC.LIV., 1755, marked copy in the British Library: C28 G 15 [3].)

9 Archibald Bower's work *The History of the Popes, From the Foundation of the See of Rome, to the Present Time* came out in seven volumes between 1748 and 1766.

1 Dr Heberden had moved to London in 1748 but continued to see some of his old patients from

As to Dr Warburton, he is not, I hear, very well and therefore intends to return to Prior-Park sometime next week. I shall run up to town myself, for one night, towards the end of this week, and will then pay your compliments. I will tell him You intend to take the first opportunity, that offers, to acknowledge his Civilities in person. And this will leave it in your power to pay him a visit now, or hereafter at London as You shall choose.

Mr Balguy is much Your Servant. We talk of waiting upon You tow'rds the end of July or the very beginning of August, by which time I suppose there is no doubt but You will be got back to Tedgely.

I am, with compliments to my Lady, very much, Dear Sir, Your faithful humble Servt

R Hurd

145 To WILLIAM WARBURTON 2 JULY 1754

Text: *Prelate*, 117.

Rev. Sir,

I thank you for your kind favour of the 27th past.[1] Sir Edward Littleton thought himself so much honoured by your notice of him, that I knew it could not be long before he found or made an occasion to acknowledge it.[2] I am very happy in your candid opinion of him. He has the truest esteem and veneration of you.

As you give me no hopes of seeing the excellent family here, I shall set forward directly for Shiffnal, in Shropshire, where I propose staying till the end of the month, and shall then return, by the way of Sir Edward Littleton's, to Cambridge.[3]

Mr. Balguy is to meet me there, on invitation, from Buxton. – But if there was not more in the matter, I believe my laziness would find pretences, to excuse me from the trouble of this long journey. The truth is, I go to pass some time with two of the best people in the world, to whom I owe the highest duty and have all possible obligation. I believe I never told you how happy I am in an excellent father and mother, very plain people you may be sure, for they are farmers, but of a turn of mind that might have honoured any rank and any education. With very tolerable, but in no degree affluent circumstances, their generosity was such they never regarded any expence that was in their power, and almost out of it, in whatever concerned the welfare of their children. We are three brothers of us. The eldest settled very reputably in their own way,[4] and the youngest in the Birmingham trade.[5] For myself, a *poor scholar* as you

Cambridge. (Audley Cecil Buller, *The Life and Works of Heberden*, 1879, p. 12.) His writings show him to have had little faith in the effectiveness of the Bath and Bristol waters. He believed that they were soothing when used to treat mild stomach complaints, but otherwise only relieved the symptoms of disease without affecting the cause. Cold, or sea-water bathing he thought more beneficial, recommending it particularly for the treatment of gout, palsy or rheumatism. (William Heberden, *Commentaries on the History and Cure of Diseases*, 1802.)

1 *Prelate*, pp. 115–16.
2 Littleton had paid a two day visit to Warburton that week. (*Ibid.*, p. 116.)
3 RH was absent from Cambridge from 6 July till 23 August. (*Commons Accounts Book*, STE. 15. 9.)
4 John Hurd had been farming in the Shifnal area of Shropshire since the 1730s.
5 Thomas Hurd had established a draper's shop in Birmingham.

know, I am almost ashamed to own to you how solicitous they always were to furnish me with all the opportunities of the best and most liberal education. My case in so many particulars resembles that which the Roman poet describes as his own,[6] that with Pope's wit I could apply almost every circumstance of it. And if ever I were to wish in earnest to be a poet, it would be for the sake of doing justice to so uncommon a virtue. I should be a wretch if I did not conclude, as he does,

– si Natura juberet
A certis annis aevum remeare peractum,
Atque alios legere ad fastum quoscunque parentes,
Optaret sibi quisque: meis contentus, onustos
Fascibus et sellis nolim mihi sumere: demens
Judicio vulgi, sanus fortasse tuo. –[7]

In a word, when they had fixed us in such a rank of life as they designed, and believed should satisfy us, they very wisely left the business of the world to such as wanted it more, or liked it better. They considered what age and declining health seemed to demand of them, reserving to themselves only such a support as their few and little wants made them think sufficient. I should beg pardon for troubling you with this humble history, but the subjects of it are so much and so tenderly in my thoughts at present, that if I writ at all, I could hardly help writing about them.

I shall long to hear that you have put the last hand to the view of Bol.[8] If ever you write above yourself, it is when your zeal for truth and religion animates you to expose the *ignorance of foolish men.*

The subject you mention, and some others you hinted to me when I spent that happy day with you at London, would do excellently for dialogue.[9] But what of this sort my idleness will give my little powers leave to execute, I know not. What I am most confident of, is that I am ever most warmly, &c.

R. Hurd.

Cambridge, July 2d, 1754.

6 Horace recalls how he was sent to the best school in Rome by his parents, instead of the local school, and how this fostered all the best qualities in his character. (*Serm.*, I. 6. 65–82.)

7 *Serm.*, I. 6. 93–98.

8 *A View of Lord Bolingbroke's Philosophy in Four Letters to a Friend* [Ralph Allen] was published in three parts in 1754 and 1755. Warburton had been introduced to Bolingbroke by Pope shortly before the latter's death in 1742. The attempt at uniting his friends proved unsuccessful and their mutual dislike led to further quarrels over the publication of Pope's works following his death. (Owen Ruffhead, *The Life of Alexander Pope, Esq.*, 1769, pp. 219–21.) The *View* was prompted by the posthumous publication of Bolingbroke's *Works*, which indicated his hostility to all forms of revealed religion. Warburton's *View* points out (justifiably) the inconsistencies and contradictions of Bolingbroke's reasoning, and the extravagance of his language. (Evans, *Warburton and the Warburtonians*, pp. 135, 177–82.)

9 Warburton had suggested that "a dialogue between the Chancellor of the Exchequer and his friend Falkland, concerning the clergy of that time . . . would make a fine dialogue in your hands". (*Prelate*, p. 116.) RH later published two volumes of dialogues, *Moral and Political Dialogues* in 1759, and *Dialogues on the Uses of Foreign Travel* in 1764. Neither includes such a dialogue.

146 To Sir EDWARD LITTLETON 2 SEPTEMBER 1754

Text: MS STAFFS RO D1413/1; unpublished.
Addressed: To/Sir Edward Littleton Bart/at Tedgely near Penkrich/ Staffordshire
Postmarked: 4 SE

Eman: Coll: 2. Sept. 1754.

Dear Sir Edward

I have been very long in acknowledging the favour of Lady Littleton's and your civilities. But, besides my usual laziness, I was detained by my friends at Birmingham several days beyond the time that I had intended to pass with them.[1]

One of these days my Brother and I made an excursion to Hagley. Sir George has very magnificent designs. The foundation of his new house is laying. It is 148 feet in front, and 85 deep. The situation is fine, tho' very near the place where the old house stands. I never saw the Park in so good order. After all it is a delicious Spot.[2]

In my way home I call'd at Warwick. The town itself is beautiful, and there are many curiosities worth seeing. But what struck me most was the castle and some improvements which Lord Brook is now making on the river.[3] It will be worth your while to take a ride over on purpose to see them when they are completed.

I have not heard a syllable of Mr Macro.[4] Only I sent him word that if he design'd going to Tedgley after the business of his harvest is over, Mr J. Nevile and I might probably be induc'd to escorte him as far as Northampton, where I think You talk'd of giving him the meeting.

All friends here send their compliments. Pray let Lady Littleton understand how entirely I wish the full establishment of her health, the only thing that is wanting to make You both as happy as You should in reason desire to be.

I am always very truly, Dear Sir, Your faithful and affectionate humble Servt

R Hurd

146A To WILLIAM BOWYER [mid NOVEMBER 1754]

See Appendix

1 RH had only arrived back in Cambridge on 23 or 24 August. (*Commons Accounts Book*, STE. 15. 9.)

2 Sir George Lyttelton had succeeded to Hagley on the death of his father in 1751. The old Hall, now considered out of date, was pulled down and a new house in Palladian style was built nearby. The building was completed in 1760 and cost, with furnishings, £34,000. (*Hagley, Worcestershire, The Official Guide*, Third Edition, c.1958; [Joseph Heely], *A Description of Hagley Park. By the Author of Letters on the Beauties of Hagley, Envil, and the Leasowes*, 1777.)

3 Sir Francis Greville was created Earl Brooke in 1746. No mention of his improvements to the river is made in the earliest Warwick guides. But it is noted that he provided £3,000 towards the building of a bridge over the Avon, eventually completed in 1790, seventeen years after his death. (*The Warwick Guide; containing a concise historical account of the town, and particular descriptions of the Castle*, Warwick, Leamington and Coventry, [?1830]; *An Historical and Descriptive Account of the Town & Castle of Warwick*, Warwick, 1815; *New Guide. An Historical and Descriptive Account of Warwick and Leamington*, Second Edition, Warwick, 1822.)

4 Edward Macro was occupied with his farms in Suffolk. Littleton had written to him in July with expressions of the strongest desire to see him: "I will only say I shall not be quite easy till I see You", he writes. "Your opinion I want greatly on many things to be done in the Park. My building Timber is now allmost sawn out. My Farm yd. will be nearly completed this very year. The Garden Walls I wd. gladly begin on next Spring: but this intirely depends, in good earnest on my seeing You." (12 July 1754, *Macro Letter-book*.)

147 To FREDERICK HERVEY 17 DECEMBER 1754

Text: MS HC; unpublished.

A copy of my Letter to Mr Frederick Hervey[1]

Sir

I understand how greatly indebted I am to your favour for making me known with so much advantage to my L. Bristol. The Proposal* his Lordship is pleasd to make me by Mr Balguy, demands my best acknowledgments. And, if I was perfectly at liberty, there are many considerations, respecting the thing itself and the manner of offering it, that would deserve to have the greatest weight with me. But the truth is, my Situation in many respects is such as will not allow me to think of entering into an engagement of this nature. You will therefore please to present my humble duty and thanks to his Lordship for so great an honour and to believe me Yourself, with a true sense of your kind intentions in the affair, Sir, Your most Obligd and most Obedt Servt

R H.

*of the Chaplainship to his Lps Embassy to Portugal. His L. went to *Turin* (instead of Portugal wch was first intended) & afterwards to *Madrid*.[2]

148 To FREDERICK HERVEY 20 DECEMBER 1754

Text: MS HC; unpublished.

A copy of my 2d letter

Eman: Coll: Camb. 20 Dec 1754

Sir

I am much concern'd You have not receiv'd the letter I sent away by the Post on Tuesday last, according to Mr Balguy's instructions.[1] The purpose of it was to thank You for this obliging instance of your regard, and to <acknowledge to my Lord Bristol the great> express the just sense I have of the honour <of the honour> my Lord Bristol is pleasd to do me in the Proposal; but to acquaint You, which I was careful to do as soon as possible, that my Situation, in many respects, will not allow me to take the benefit of it. If that Letter has miscarried by any accident, I desire this acknowledgment of your favour may be accepted in the room of it. My Lord Bristol will do me the justice to believe that I cannot but be very thankful for the distinction intended

1 Frederick Augustus Hervey (1730–1803) was the younger brother of George William Hervey (1721–75), second Earl of Bristol. He had graduated from Corpus Christi in 1754. Three letters from him to RH are preserved at Hartlebury Castle. The first, dated 18 December 1754, reiterates a proposal that had been made to Balguy and RH that they should accompany George Hervey on his embassy to Lisbon, as his secretary and chaplain. (The nature of Balguy's connection with the Herveys is not known.)

2 George Hervey was issued with credentials and instructions as Envoy Extraordinary to Turin on 22 April 1755, and served there from June 1755 to August 1758. He was made Ambassador to Madrid in June 1758 and took office in September. (*D.N.B.*; *British Diplomatic Representatives 1689–1789*, ed. D.B. Horn, The Royal Historical Society, Camden Third Series, Vol. XLVI, 1932.)

1 In his letter of 18 December Hervey had complained that they had "been a good deal surpris'd at receiving no kind of information by either of the Posts". His next letter of 19 December accounts for the late delivery of RH's reply by "a mistake of the Post:Master at Bury". (MS HC)

me in this appointment. And the terms in which You express yourself in your favour of the 18th are an additional reason for my professing myself, with all respect, Dear Sir, Your most Obligd and faithful humble Servt

R H.

149 To FREDERICK HERVEY 22 DECEMBER 1754

Text: MS HC; unpublished.

A copy of my 3d letter.

Camb. Dec. 22. 1754

Dear Sir

Since my last, I am favourd with two of your kind letters.[1]

I must desire You to believe that your very friendly recommendation of me to my L. Bristol and the intire confidence I had reason to place in his Lordship, left me quite at ease about the Stipend and other profits of the Chaplainship.[2] They were very different considerations that weigh'd with me; such indeed as I could not witht impertinence, were there nothing more in the matter, trouble You with a particular account of. But one thing I may freely own to You, They were not taken from any expectations I have, here or elsewhere of greater advantages; about which, to say the truth, I am apt to be more indifferent than it may be decent for me to profess to You. In one word, You may assure yourself, I could not easily have declined an offer of this sort which promis'd so great advantage & brought me so much honour, if certain private respects had not determin'd me. As it is, I can only repeat my most sincere acknowledgments for this favour, which, whether it be the first or last proof of your friendship, is never to be forgotten by me. Let me add that, tho' I must deny myself the honour of serving my L. B. on this occasion, my obligation is not the less on that account, and that his Lordship shall not find my remembrance of it the less grateful.

I am very truly, what your kindness binds me to be, Dear Sir, Your most Obliged & affectionate humble Servt

R Hurd

1 Dated 19 and 20 December 1754.

2 In his letter of 19 December 1754 Hervey had written: "I can not forbear informing you that the Stipend my Brother propos'd allowing to his Chaplain was fourscore pounds a year wch he did not intend withdrawing even after returning into England 'till some benefice within his Patronage & worthy his Chaplain's acceptance should become vacant, so that if yr tie is onely from yr own College I should think the proffer'd one more Eligible & advantageous." In his third letter of 20 December he says he had been mistaken as to the stipend: "but as the mistake was to the disadvantage of the Chaplain I have gladly undertaken to correct it & as I am strongly prepossess'd by my hopes that your Principal restraint arises from not receiving an Equivalent for quitting yr College, I hope that Bar will be remov'd by my brother's intention of allowing an hundred pounds a year to his Chaplain & continuing this Provision 'till he can give him at least an Equal one in the Church: As to vacating yr Fellowship by non-residence I am inform'd that such an Absence wd be dispens'd with when occasion'd by the King's business." (MS HC)

150 To WILLIAM WARBURTON FEBRUARY 1755

Text: *Prelate*, 133.

Emanuel, Tuesday Noon.[1]

. . .

Sir Edward Littleton is with me, and with his usual kindness hardly cares to stir from me. Yet I got half an hour to read the Apology,[2] which I received this morning, and, as I suppose, am indebted to you for the favour of the present. I cannot be at ease till I have told you, though it be in two words, that if I were capable of honouring you more than I have long done, I should certainly do it on the score of this glorious Apology, which lets me see the bottom of your mind so perfectly. I am sorry for the occasion of it. But you never writ any thing more worthy yourself, or which, in spite of friends or foes, will more endear your memory to the wise and good for ever. Excuse this frank declaration, which comes from the bottom of a heart that is wholly and devotedly yours. . . .

151 To Sir EDWARD LITTLETON 19 FEBRUARY 1755

Text: MS STAFFS RO D1413/1; unpublished.
Addressed: To Sir Edward Littleton Bart./at his Seat near Penkrich/ Staffordshire/By Lond:
Postmarked: CAMBRIDGE 20 FE

Emanl. Coll. 19. Feb. 1755

Dear Sir

I trouble You with two lines to inquire of your arrival at Tedgely, and to tell You that the day after You left us, I receiv'd a letter from Dr Brown,[1] in which are these words: "If Sir Edw. L. is yet with You, pray tell him that I was yesterday two hours at the finishing of Lady Littleton's Picture which is done to my mind, and I think, the most original modern Pourtrait in England."[2] – I thought You would not be displeas'd

---

1 This letter is placed between two letters of 31 January and 15 February 1755. (*Prelate*, pp. 132, 134.)

2 'An Apology for the Two First Letters: which may serve for an Introduction to the Two Last'. Following the publication of the first two letters of *A View of Lord Bolingbroke's Philosophy*, Warburton had received an anonymous but friendly letter from William Murray, Earl of Mansfield (1705–93), a response he had anticipated knowing of Bolingbroke's and Murray's friendship. Murray acknowledged the justification of a critical view of Bolingbroke, but regretted Warburton's descent into railing and abuse. (MS BL, Egerton 1959, ff. 31–4.) Warburton mentioned this to RH in a letter of 15 February 1755 and said that his "provocation perhaps was greater . . . that the accusations in the anonymous letter came from a real friend. Had he made them to me without disguise", he continued, " I could have satisfied him in private". (*Prelate*, p. 134.) This course having been denied him, he printed the 'Apology' in which he rejects the charge of unjustifiable abuse and asserts his moral obligations to expose the true tenor of Bolingbroke's philosophy. (See *ante* To Warburton, 2 July 1754.)

1 John Brown. (See *ante* To Mason, 29 October 1752, n. 10.) His letter has not been traced.

2 Lady Littleton's portrait was being painted by Benjamin Wilson (1721–88), one of the leading portrait painters of the 1750s. Wilson adopted a Rembrandtesque chiaroscuro popular at the time, and he had already been commissioned to paint the portraits of David Garrick, Lord Chesterfield and Lord Orrery. His reputation ranked with that of the young Joshua Reynolds

with this advertisement. – I wonder it did not come into my head, when we talk'd so much about Busts, to suggest to You that the 50 pounds You so kindly intend the College, besides the present of Plate,[3] might perhaps be best laid out in a Bust of one [of] the worthies of our Society, suppose Dr Cudworth, Bp Hall, Sir W. Temple or ABp Sandcroft, as You like best, to be plac'd in the Gallery –[4] Pray think of this proposal. It would be an elegant way of employing that Sum and might prove the beginning of a fine collection of such things, which others might be tempted to carry on by your example.

Mr Balguy and I go for London to morrow Sev'nnight. All friends are much Your's. Your most faithful humble Servt

R Hurd

152 To Sir EDWARD LITTLETON 15 MARCH 1755

Text: MS STAFFS RO D1413/1; unpublished.
Addressed: To/ Sir Edward Littleton Bart/at his Seat near Penkrich/Staffordshire
Postmarked: 15 MR

Dear Sir

You will expect two lines from me before I leave the Town. The first week I was here the weather was so cold that I thought it to no purpose to see Mr Rysbrack.[1]

but he was also known to Littleton through his Cambridge acquaintances, who had met Wilson in 1746. Amongst these William Mason and John Brown made regular visits to his studio, and their appreciation of his work is documented in Wilson's own letters to Littleton. (Ellis Waterhouse, *The Dictionary of British 18th Century Painters in Oils and Crayons*, 1981; Herbert Randolph, *Life of General Sir Robert Wilson*, 2 vols., 1862; Wilson letters, Staffs. RO, D1178/3.) Sir Edward and Lady Littleton were subsequently painted by William Hoare and Thomas Gainsborough. (Staffs. RO, D1178/3 and D260/M/E/117.)

3 See *ante* To Littleton, 26 April 1751, n. 7.

4 Ralph Cudworth (1617–88), Joseph Hall (1574–1656), William Temple (1628–99) and William Sancroft (1617–93) had all been undergraduates and Fellows of Emmanuel; and Sancroft had also been Master. Two portraits, of Temple and Sancroft, had been acquired for the College in 1753 and 1754 (BUR. 8.6.) and portraits of Cudworth and Hall from the same period also exist. One bust, of Sancroft, exists, but it is thought to have been made in the 1690s or early 1700s.

1 Michael Rysbrack (1694–1770), the sculptor, had been working in London since 1720. He was first employed by James Gibbs, the architect, and remained in constant demand until his retirement in 1764. His works include portrait busts and statues (among them Bolingbroke, Pope and George II), decorative sculpture, and monuments, but his reputation was founded on his skill as a modeller in clay. This skill, particularly, offset the formal influences on his style of late Flemish baroque. From the 1740s Rysbrack's popularity was rivalled by that of Louis Francois Roubiliac, a brilliantly innovative sculptor whose work reflected the new taste for the rococo. Littleton, however, thought the latter's work "execrable to ye last degree" and his correspondence with and commissions from Rysbrack lasted until the end of his career. Already in 1748 Rysbrack had been consulted concerning the stone for a memorial inscription to William Budworth (see *ante* To Littleton, 15 February 1748), but Littleton seems to have had no further dealings with him until this time. (M.I. Webb, *Michael Rysbrack, Sculptor*, 1954; Katharine Eustace, *Michael Rysbrack Sculptor 1694–1770*, City of Bristol Museum and Art

When I call'd upon him he said it would be necessary to sit three or four times and that it would take up eight or ten days. As this is longer than I can possibly stay at present I have resolv'd to take another opportunity and shall probably come hither in June for that purpose. He seems to think my bad head will not be disgracd by being turn'd into Stone. And we have almost agreed about the attitude and dress. The head is to turn a little on one side; no cap or wig, but a thin hair upon it – a little loose drapery over the Shoulders. –[2]

I am wonderfully taken with Lady Ls picture. There is no fault unless the colouring be perhaps a little too faint and hardly clear enough. But Dr Brown thinks it quite right and so does Mr Mason. The flowers are certainly inimitable.–[3]

Mr Balguy and I had the pleasure to dine with Lady Littleton who seems pretty well. She looks much better than in the Summer. But Dr Heberden says She is not quite well.

Dr Brown and Mr Balguy send compliments. We set out to morrow for Cambridge, where I shall be glad of a line from You. You seem to mistake my design about the Bust: I only meant one of about 40 or 50 pounds, which Mr Rysbrack tells me is the highest price of a Bust[4] – But the thing is of no consequence, unless You prefer it to any other method of disposing of the Sum, You are so good to intend us.

I write with so wretched a pen that I wish You may read what I have written.

Your's most entirely

R Hurd.

London 15 March 1755.

153 To WILLIAM WARBURTON 23 MARCH 1755

Text: *Prelate*, 137.

Emmanuel, March 23d, 1755.

. . .

It makes me truly happy that I can now, at length, honestly congratulate with you on a preferment, worth your acceptance.[1] The Church has been so long and deeply in

Gallery, 1982; *Rococo, Art and Design in Hogarth's England*, Victoria and Albert Museum, 1984; *Macro Letter-book*.)

2 The conventional form of the portrait bust exhibited the sitter *en negligée* with an open shirt and soft cap to replace a wig. Occasionally the sitter was shown in the classical manner, introduced by Rysbrack in 1723. It is to this style that RH refers. (*Rococo, Art and Design*, pp. 283, 289.)

3 Lady Littleton's picture was frequently viewed during its execution and Dr Brown was one of the most consistent visitors to the studio. By June, Wilson (writing to Littleton) felt that the portrait had been "touched and retouched" sufficiently and "almost every objector of the men is reconciled, since I have given a little strength to the whole work". He could only add to it were he to "proceed upon a different plan and paint the head equally strong with the flowers". The painting was completed in the summer and Littleton expected to sit for his own portrait in October. (Staffs. RO, D1178/3; *Macro Letter-book*.)

4 RH had suggested that Littleton should spend about £50 on a bust in a previous letter. (See *ante* To Littleton, 19 February 1755.) This and the commission for a portrait bust of RH were the first dealings Littleton had had with Rysbrack for a considerable time and he was uncertain about prices. A little earlier he had written to Edward Macro to consult him about RH's bust. "Rysbrack", he said, "recommends it to me to have it done in soft Stone rather yn. in Clay. Quaere? Is not this a Method of his to have it done in Marble". (*Macro Letter-book*, [January 1755].) His anxiety about the expense of these busts lingered some months.

1 In March 1755 Warburton was appointed to a prebend at Durham with £500 a year, through

your debt, that it will seem but common justice if it now pays you with interest. Not that I look upon this Prebend as such payment, which delights me principally, as it does you, from its being given at *this* time and by *such* a person. I have no words to tell you how much I honour the Attorney-General. The nobleness of mind, he has shewn on this occasion, is only to be matched by that which every body takes notice of, in a late *Apologist*.[2] If the world were made acquainted with particulars, it would, methinks, be taken for one of the most beautiful events in both your lives, that he should confer and you receive such a favour at this juncture. – May every circumstance concur to afford you the full enjoyment of this and better things, which your great services have long since merited!

I have been much out of order since my return, or your kind letter had not prevented the thanks I owe you for a thousand favours. I indulge in the memory of the agreeable days and nights I so lately passed with you.[3] The truth is, I am so happy in the share you allow me in your friendship that I have scarce another wish for myself, except for the continuance of it. And this, with all my infirmities, I will not doubt of, so long as I have a heart warm and honest enough to give it entertainment. Mr. Balguy told me he should write this post or the next.

Rev. Sir, Your most faithful, &c.

R. Hurd.

154 To Sir EDWARD LITTLETON 3 JUNE 1755

Text: MS STAFFS RO D1413/1; unpublished.
Addressed: To/Sir Edward Littleton Bart/at his Seat in/Staffordshire/ By London.
Postmarked: CAMBRIDGE 4 IV

Dear Sir Edward

I fully intended running up to town this month about the Bust,[1] but am prevented by Dr Macro, who is come hither to pass two or three weeks with us, in order to

the interest of the Attorney-General, William Murray, with Bishop Trevor. ([P. Mussett], *Lists of Deans and Major Canons of Durham 1541–1900*, Durham, 1974.) He was collated on 21 March and installed by proxy on 11 April 1755. He was already indebted to Murray for his election to the preachership at Lincoln's Inn in 1746, but his appointment to the prebend was a special mark of favour after his attack on Lord Bolingbroke, which had caused Murray some offence. (See *ante* To Warburton, February 1755, n. 2; *Prelate*, pp. 136–7.)

2 Warburton, as author of the 'Apology' appended to the two last letters of his *View of Lord Bolingbroke's Philosophy*. RH was deeply impressed by the 'Apology' and even singled it out in his edition of Warburton's *Works*, published in 1788. "The occasion of the subject", he wrote, "fired the writer. His very soul came out in every sentence, and is no where seen to more advantage than in this Apology; which is . . . at once, the most interesting, and the most masterly of all his works." (Warburton, *The Works . . . In Seven Volumes*, [ed. Richard Hurd], 1788, i. 76–7.)

3 Warburton had expected RH (accompanied by Thomas Balguy) towards the end of February and had told Ralph and Mrs Allen that he [RH] would "come before the first swallow, and bring more to me than the Summer". (*Prelate*, p. 135.) RH was certainly out of Cambridge between 1 March and 17 March. (*Commons Accounts Book*, STE. 15. 10.)

1 See preceding letter to Littleton, 15 March 1755. Littleton was particularly concerned about RH's "head". When informed of his previous visit to London he "immediately gave Mr

rummage Libraries and pick up what curiosities he can beg or lay his hands on. When he leaves us, Mr Balguy and I are under engagement to make a visit to Prior-Park.[2] And from thence in the end of July we propose to set forward for Tedgely, if You shall be there at that time, and to spend a few days with You. You see by this plan of operations we shall have leisure to settle evry thing about the Bust, which must now be deferrd till after my return to college. As to the Horse, You are so good to intend for me and which You have taken care to get in readiness, I shall be oblig'd to You to keep him till I come into Staffordshire. For we go to Bath and shall come round to You in a Post-chaise. However it will be very convenient for me to return upon him to this place. In the mean time what is to become of poor Thumper. As to selling him, I can't think of it. He is grown old and stiff, and utterly unfit for any kind of Service, except little rides. My design was to send him to You, in hopes that You would indulge an old Servant in a quiet retreat in your Park. You know his merits and will incline, I hope, to shew him this regard for old acquaintance sake. But I must have a promise under your hand before I dismiss him. In short his whole dependence is on your generosity. Otherwise I think I shall keep him somewhat longer and let this new horse continue in your hands. But the other way would be more convenient as well as more eligible to honest Thumper. Pray let me know your resolution, and let Thumper and me see on this occasion how far your generosity will go.[3]

I have heard nothing about the Plate but suppose, from what You say, that we shall receive it in a short time.[4]

You are quite right in your notions of *Imitation*. But the Dr had several of these things lying by him and had a mind to make trial of some of them.[5]

I am sorry this obstinate complaint of my Lady's keeps it's ground agst the best Doctor in England.[6] I except only *Time*, wch I doubt not will bring a certain, tho' a slow relief. Pray give all our Services. Dr Macro and your other friends desire to be rememberd to You. Once more take pity of old Thumper and believe me very truly, Dear Sir, Your affectionate humble Servt

R Hurd.

Eman: Coll: 3. June. 1755.

Rysbrack notice of it, & desired him to prepare the Clay immediately, as his Stay wd not excede three Weeks. I am", he wrote, "anxious to ye last Degree about it." (*Macro Letter-book*, Littleton to Edward Macro, 2 February 1755.)

2 RH set out "for ye West" on Friday 27 June. (William Richardson to Edward Littleton, 4 July 1755, Staffs. RO, Ex D1413/2.)

3 In an undated letter written early in 1755, Littleton had mentioned to Edward Macro that he had a horse for RH which he intended to send "soon to Cambridge". (*Macro Letter-book*.) Thumper had belonged to RH since at least 1749. (See *ante* To Littleton, 7 August 1749.) Littleton responded to the plea on Thumper's behalf with his customary generosity and agreed to look after him in his retirement. (See following letter.)

4 See *ante* To Littleton, 26 April 1751, n. 7; and following letter, n. 2.

5 Littleton's "notions of *Imitation*" are undisclosed. They were prompted by Thomas Nevile's anonymous publication in March 1755 of *The First Satire of the First Book of Horace Imitated*. In the following year Nevile published two further imitations of Horatian epistles. RH was not very sanguine as to their success with the public. (See *post* To Mason, 31 December 1755; 30 April 1756.)

6 Dr Heberden.

P. S.

Dr Macro is a perfect Idolater of the Hondicooter You sent him.[7] He thinks it the best of that Master he ever saw.

155 To Sir EDWARD LITTLETON 18 JUNE 1755

Text: MS STAFFS RO D1413/1; unpublished.
Addressed: To/Sir Edward Littleton Bart/at his Seat in/Staffordshire/ By Lond.
Postmarked: 19 IV

Dear Sir

I writ to Mr Payne[1] to tell him that we chose to have the College arms engrav'd here: So that he might send the Plate down directly. But he is so very punctilious that he sends me word he must consult You again about it, before he can venture it out of his hands. By which means I shall probably be gone before it reaches us. However I have giv'n him directions to the Master, who will, I take for granted, acknowledge the favour to You as soon as He receives it.[2]

Thumper and his Master are exceedingly oblig'd to you for the indulgence You promise 'em. I shall find a way to send him to You in a short time.

Mr Balguy and I, when we come to You, can probably form a tolerable guess of the goodness of the Library.[3] But of the value at the market we shall know very little. Could not You send the Catalogue to Mr Davis, who would tell You very honestly whether it be worth the money You speak of?[4] I should think it might pass betwixt You and London very safely.

I thank You for putting me in mind of Mr Hill, whom I shall take care to wait upon, as soon as I get to Bath.[5] I shall remember You to the family. But as to Dr W. I doubt

7 Edward Macro had bought the Hondecoeter at the Richard Mead sale in March 1754 on Littleton's behalf. (See *ante* To Littleton, 29 April 1754.) In July 1754 Littleton wrote to Macro in acknowledgment of the various items he had received from him, and added, "Concerning the Hondikoeyter I believe it a very true Picture. And as your judgement upon it is what I cannot be dubious of, & as, in return for yr. many great favors to me, I cannot have a greater pleasure, than by enriching yr. very valuable Collection by something in its way truly estimable, I desire yr. Acceptance of it." (*Macro Letter-book.*) The painting had cost £30.9.0.

1 Probably John Payne, goldsmith, of the Hen and Chickens, Cheapside. His first mark was entered in 1751 and he subsequently became Warden (1760–2), and Prime Warden (1765) of the Livery Company. (Arthur G. Grimwade, *London Goldsmiths 1697–1837. Their Marks and Lives from the Original Registers at Goldsmiths' Hall and Other Sources*, Second, revised edition, 1982; John P. Fallon, *Marks of London Goldsmiths and Silversmiths. Georgian Period (c.1697–1837)*, Newton Abbot, 1972.)

2 William Richardson, the Master of Emmanuel, wrote to Littleton on 4 July acknowledging receipt of the plate. "I have just now recd a fine peice of Plate, for wc you will please to accept ye Thanks of ye Society . . . I shall imediatly order your Arms, together wt those of ye College, to be engrav'd; and a proper inscription round." (*Macro Letter–book.*)

3 Unidentified.

4 Charles Davis with his nephew Lockyer was one of comparatively few booksellers to deal in secondhand books. (See *ante* To Littleton, 18 June 1752, n. 6.)

5 Samuel Hill (1690?–1758), of Shenstone Park, had been one of Littleton's guardians.

he is too lazy to stir: Tho' I know he had much rather take a journey to see You than Hagley Park or anything that belongs to it.[6]

If You had rather mine should be a soft head than a hard one, it is all one to me, who have no other rule to go by in this matter than your Inclination.[7]

Miss Newton's marriage and Mr Bagot's Legacy are great pieces of News.[8] But what is more to me than both is, that Lady Littleton, You say, grows better. It would be a pleasure indeed if Mr Balguy and I should find her Ladyship perfectly recover'd. Pray give our best Services. Believe me most truly, Dear Sir, Your Obligd and affectionate humble Servt

R H.

Camb. 18 June 1755.

156 To Sir EDWARD LITTLETON 21 JULY 1755

Text: MS STAFFS RO D1413/1; unpublished.
Addressed: To/Sir Edward Littleton Bart/at his Seat near Penkrich/ Staffordshire
Postmarked: 23 IY

Dear Sir

You may make yourself perfectly easy about Dr Nevile's design of printing the Epistle.[1] The thing itself is uncertain. But if he print it at all, it will be under so very different a form from what it was in, when You saw it, and with so much care not to give the least offence to your delicacy (which I entirely approve) that You will have no objection of the sort, You mention, to make to it.

The weather has been but indifferent since we came hither. And yet we have made an excursion or two to see the principal beauties, I should rather say, wonders of this country. One was to Chedder-Cliffs, a place of so romantic a cast, that Mr Balguy says

6 Warburton may not have been welcome at Hagley Park after his attack on Lord Bolingbroke in his *View* of his philosophy. William Murray had warned him in his letter of remonstrance: "Take my word for it, His [Bolingbroke's] illustrious Friend Sr George Lyttelton never will forgive the mention you make of him, tho' flattering, & honourable as long as he lives." (MS BL, Egerton 1959, ff. 31–4.)

7 Littleton was very passionate about RH's bust being of clay. There is, however, no further reference to a "head" in clay or stone in the letters, and no identification of a bust in catalogues of Rysbrack's work. (Webb, *Michael Rysbrack, Sculptor*; Eustace, *Michael Rysbrack, Sculptor*.)

8 The announcement of the marriage between Miss Sally Newton of King's Bromley, Staffordshire, and Sir Lister Holte appeared in the *Gentleman's Magazine* for July 1755. (Lister Holte had been M.P. for Lichfield in 1747 and candidate of the independent tory party supported by Littleton.) Mr Bagot's legacy remains inexplicable; he may be the son of Sir Walter Bagot. (See *ante* To Littleton, 22 February 1754, n. 4.)

1 On 24 June Littleton had received a letter from Thomas Nevile explaining that he intended "the beginning of next winter to print that Horatian epistle, which I some years ago had the assurance to ascribe to you . . . You need be in no fears", he continued, "lest I should disgrace your name by my bad poetry: where any thing personal occurs I shall have recourse to ye expedient of xxxs". (Staffs RO, D1413/2.) The epistle, *The Seventeenth Epistle of the First Book of Horace Imitated*, was published on 10 February 1755. (Straus, *Dodsley*, Bibliography.) It was not apparently welcomed by Littleton. (See *post* To Littleton, 6 June 1756.)

there is nothing in Derbyshire to equal it.[2] We set forward for your country on Monday the 28th of this month; and tho' we shall probably meet with some interruptions by the way, we don't despair of reaching You at the farthest by the end of that Week.

The family here are all well and much at your Service. Mr Balguy bids me give his best respects to Yourself and Lady Littleton. I am at all times Your's and her Ladyship's most Devoted Servant

R Hurd.

Prior-Park 21 July 1755.

P. S.

Mr Hill had left Bath before I reach'd it –

157 To Sir EDWARD LITTLETON 21 AUGUST 1755

Text: MS STAFFS RO D1413/1; unpublished.
Addressed: To/Sir Edward Littleton Bart/at Tedgeley Coppice near/Penkrich

Shifnal 21 Aug. 1755

Dear Sir Edward

I was gone to Brewood, when your Servant was here on Monday.[1] We are all much oblig'd to You for your kind present of Venison. And my Brother sends his particular thanks for your Benefaction to his farming-Library.[2] It was exceeding good in You to think of the poor old folks at Brewood. They are very thankful for your kindness. But my father was unable to taste it. I much doubt if he can eat the Perch You intend him. However I'll thank You to send him one or two (more would be thrown away) at your convenience.

I send the Mare with many thanks. And yet I must beg the favour to have her return'd, if my own be not fit for riding, as by this time I suppose She is. You will receive the remainder of the Paper. Mr Dalton does not return out of Wales this fortnight or three weeks.[3] And my Brother is immers'd in his harvest. So that I design to wait upon You by myself some time next week for a day or two. I mean, if You shall

2 The "romance" of the Cheddar Cliffs was later more fully described by the Rev. Stebbing Shaw in *A Tour to the West of England in 1788*, published in 1789. Near the "small town of Chedder", he says, "are large cliffs of the same name, and a stupendous chasm, quite thro' the body of the adjacent mountain, as if split asunder by some violent convulsion of nature, which exhibits an aweful appearance to strangers. Near the entrance is a remarkable spring of water, rising in a perpendicular direction from the rocky basis of the hill; and so large and rapid is its stream, that it turns a mill within a few yards of its source, and afterwards falls into the river Ax." (pp. 316–37.) Five miles away is the Okey-hole, which Shaw also remarks upon, noting that if it was "as much known as Castleton in Derbyshire, and set off with proper illuminations, a boat, music, &c. no doubt [it] would be greatly resorted to" (p. 316).

1 RH was staying with his older brother, John, at Shifnal. His parents lived at Brewood.

2 No more information on this library has been discovered.

3 William Dalton (c.1720–80) of Over Penn, Staffordshire. Dalton was a contemporary of RH's at St Catherine's, Cambridge, and was made a Fellow in 1742. In 1748 he was instituted vicar of Coton in Cambridgeshire and in 1767 appointed a Proctor of the University. He maintained contact with RH for some years as also with Thomas Nevile. (See *post* To Littleton, 28 July 1758.)

be at home and without company. For the condition, my poor father is in, makes me uneasy in the company of any but my particular friends. On this account I must beg You to excuse me to Mr Horton.[4]

I have only our compliments to add to Lady Littleton, and to assure You that I am very truly, Dear Sir, Your Oblig'd and affectionate humble Servt

R Hurd

P. S.

I did not forget to pay my Uncle for the Paper.[5] He does not make any of the *strong brown packing paper* of wch You wanted a small quantity.

158 To WILLIAM WARBURTON — 13 SEPTEMBER 1755

Text: *Prelate*, 142.

Shifnal, September 13th, 1755.

. . .

Your truly friendly letter of the 31st past, brought me all the relief I am capable of in my present situation. Yet that relief had been greater if the fact had been, as you suppose, that the best of fathers was removing from me, in this maturity of age, by a gradual insensible decay of nature; in which case I could have drawn to myself much ease from the considerations you so kindly suggest to me. But it is not his being out of all hope of recovery (which I had known long since, and was prepared for), but his being in perpetual pain, that afflicts me so much. I left him last night in this disconsolate condition. So near a prospect of death, and so rough a passage to it, I own to you I cannot be a witness of this in one whom nature and ten thousand obligations have made so dear to me, without the utmost uneasiness. Nay I think the very temper and firmness of mind with which he bears this calamity, sharpens my sense of it. I thank God, an attachment to this world has not as yet been among my greater vices. But were I as fond of it as prosperous and happy men sometimes are, what I have seen and felt for this last month were enough to mortify such foolish affections. And in truth it would amaze one that a few such instances, as this, which hardly any man is out of the reach of, did not strike dead all the passions, were it not that Providence has determined, in spite of ourselves, by means of these instincts, to accomplish its own great purposes. But why do I trouble my best friend with this sad tale and rambling reflections? I designed only to tell him that I am quite unhappy here, and that, though its more than time for me to return to Cambridge, I have no power of coming to a

4 RH's father was suffering from what was subsequently identified as cancer. Some weeks later Littleton wrote to Edward Macro and reported that "His Father's extreme Illness, wch. every day makes Him look for his Death, will not permit him to leave Him". (*Macro Letter-book*, 5 October 1755.) John Hurd did not die until November but RH had been obliged to return to Cambridge in late October. (*Commons Accounts Book*, STE. 15. 10.) Christopher Horton was Littleton's father-in-law.

5 Neither a paternal nor a maternal uncle (Evans) has been identified. Littleton has a note in his ledger for 1757: "Tho: Bromwich Paper [paid to] Mr Hurd 2 15 –" (Staffs. RO, D260/M/E/116, p. 190), but no connection has been discovered. There are few surviving records for the paper trade before 1785, and in the only directory of that date which relates to the book and paper trades, no mention of Hurd, Evans or Bromwich can be found. (*The Earliest Directory of the Book Trade by John Pendred (1785)*, Edited with an Introduction and an Appendix by Graham Pollard, The Bibliographical Society, 1955.)

thought of leaving this place.[1] However a very few weeks, perhaps a few days, may put an end to this irresolution.

I thank you for your fine observation on the neglect to reform the Ecclesiastical Laws.[2] It is a very material one, and deserves to be well considered. But of these matters, when I return to my books and my mind is more easy.

I wish you all the health and all the happiness your virtues deserve and this wretched world will admit of. I know of nothing that reconciles me more to it than the sense of having such a friend as you in it. I have the greatest obligations to Mrs. Warburton and the rest of your family for their kind condolence. My best respects and sincerest good wishes attend them. I must ever be, &c.

R. Hurd.

159 To WILLIAM MASON — 31 OCTOBER 1755

Text: MS HC, excerpt made by Richard Hurd, nephew of the writer; published, *MLR* 45 1950, p. 155.

Camb. 31. Oct. 1755[1]

– "In the mean time I create what amusements I can to myself. Among which the scheme of the *Dialogues* is chief at present.[2] I have done nothing all this Summer. But shall now resume it in good earnest" –

1 Apart from academic commitments, RH held the curacy of St Andrew's the Less in Cambridge, a donative then in the gift of "*Jacob Butler*, Esq.", which entailed on him the responsibility of acting as the "*Sturbridge*-Fair preacher". The fair was normally held in the latter part of September and "on the two chief sundays" a sermon was "preach'd from a pulpit placed in the open air, by the minister of *Barnwell*". (Carter, *History of the County of Cambridge*, pp. 20–3.)

2 Warburton had written to RH on 31 August in response to the news about his father. He commends RH's efforts to divert his thoughts from this "calamity" and approves the "design of a dialogue on the effect of *transferring supremacy in religious matters*. A thousand curious hints", he says, "will arise to you as you proceed in contemplation of the subject . . . for instance . . . Could any thing be more absurd than that when the yoke of Rome was thrown off, they should govern the new Church, erected in opposition to it, by the laws of the old"? Warburton's conclusion is that this system was maintained by the monarchy which had greater influence under the canon laws, than it would have done under a body of new ecclesiastical laws founded on the "genius of a free Church and State". (*Prelate*, pp. 140–1.)

1 Originally found between pp. 92 and 93 of RH's *Works*, 1811, Vol.3.

2 RH had been working on dialogues all the year. In January Warburton had received a "packet" containing one such dialogue, which he found charming, as well as the notes, which he said were "original, very happy in their turn and manner, and . . . with a deal of fine satire". In his opinion "a few such dialogues (enough to make a small volume), will be one of the finest works of genius we have in the English tongue". (*Prelate*, p. 132.) In August he approved RH's "design of a dialogue on the effect of *transferring supremacy in religious matters*" (*Ibid.*, p. 140); and in November he was to reiterate his suggestion that a book of such dialogues "must be very taking", though "don't", he added, "engage yourself with a bookseller till we weigh the matter well". (*Ibid.*, p. 146.) At least two of the dialogues indicated in this correspondence appear in *Moral and Political Dialogues*, published in 1759. (See also *ante* To Warburton, 2 July 1754, n. 9.)

160 To Sir EDWARD LITTLETON 1 DECEMBER 1755

Text: MS FOLGER w.a.57(5); printed, *Memoirs*, 57.
Addressed: To/Sir Edward Littleton Bart/at his Seat near Penkrich/ Staffordshire
Postmarked: DE

Camb. 1 Dec 1755

My dear friend

I have your kind letter. By one from Mr Fenton last night I learn that my poor father is at last releas'd from his great misery.[1] I and all his family have reason to be thankful for his deliverance. And yet I feel the loss very tenderly. It is not to be express'd how excellent a man he was, how benevolent and generous in his temper, and how kind ev'n to excess to his family. Such instances of goodness, tho' very rare, cost people in higher life and easier fortunes very little. But his virtues were at the expence of his own ease and other satisfactions. I mention these things to You who have a *heart* and will feel with me, and for me. The generality of mankind know nothing of these matters.

My tears overflow while I write this. God give You ease and content in this life – more is not to be expected even in your fortune – and reward your virtues in another. Your good and generous Lady, I know, will sympathize with me. Remember me to her with all respect and kindness. My dearest friend, Your ever affectionate and faithful Servant

R Hurd

161 To WILLIAM WARBURTON 1 DECEMBER 1755

Text: *Prelate*, 147.

Cambridge, December 1st, 1755.

. . .

I have to tell you that it has pleased God to release my poor Father from his great misery. You will guess the rest, when I acquaint you that his case was cancerous. All his family have great reason to be thankful for his deliverance. And yet I find myself not so well prepared for the stroke as I had thought. I blame myself now for having left him. Though when I was with him, as I could not hide my own uneasiness, I saw it only added to his. I know not what to say. He was the best of men in all relations, and had a generosity of mind that was amazing in his rank of life. In his long and great affliction he shewed a temper which philosophers only talk of. If he had any foible, it was, perhaps, his too great fondness for the unworthiest of his sons. – My Mother is better than could be expected from her melancholy attendance. Yet her health has suffered by it. – I have many letters to write, but would not omit communicating, what so tenderly concerns me, to my best friend.

[1] Richard Fenton had been a contemporary of RH's at Emmanuel and in 1745 had taken over the living at Brewood vacated by the death of William Budworth. John Hurd died on 27 November and was buried on 29 November. (MS HC, "Mem: of my Father's death. & Mother's"; Staffs. RO, Brewood Parish Register, Baptisms and Burials, 1729–1784, D4014/1/4.)

I thank you for your book and your kind letters. Mr. B. and I think much more hardly of J. than you do. I could say much of this matter at another time . . .[1]

162 To Sir EDWARD LITTLETON 13 DECEMBER 1755

Text: MS FOLGER w.a.57(6); printed, *Memoirs*, 58.
Addressed: To/Sir Edward Littleton

Camb. 13. Dec. 1755.

Dear Sir Edward

Let me thank You for the satisfaction I receiv'd from your very affectionate letter of the 6th. The religious considerations You mention are those which have the greatest weight with me. I know they are the only ones that bring us any relief in these distresses of humanity. The dear person I lament was supported by them in all his afflictions. And I should be much asham'd not to feel their whole force, when I consider who it is that recommends them to me. So just a turn of thinking at your years and in your fortune is not very common in our Days. But You have the virtue to begin, where others end, in a true sense of piety and of the emptiness of earthly things.

Assure yourself of my constant affection. Your kindness and your Virtues equally bind me to be, in a particular manner, Dearest Sir, Your most Oblig'd and Entire friend and Servant

R Hurd

P. S.

It was exceeding good in Lady Littleton to favour me with so kind a letter which I have acknowledg'd in a few lines.[1]

163 To WILLIAM MASON 31 DECEMBER 1755

Text: MS HC; printed, *H-M Corr*, 19.
Addressed: cover missing.

Dear Sir

For You who

"In Chiswick Bow'rs your easy hours employ"

[1] John Jortin [J.] had published a volume of *Six Dissertations upon Different Subjects* in November 1755 (advertised in December, *Lond. Mag.*). In the last of these he examines the sixth book of the *Aeneid* as Warburton had done in the *Divine Legation*. Warburton is mentioned as "a learned friend" and certain of his "ingenious" conjectures are considered and refuted. RH and, apparently, Thomas Balguy [Mr. B.] took this as an outright attack. In response RH wrote *On the Delicacy of Friendship. A Seventh Dissertation. Address'd to the Author of the Sixth*, dated "Lincoln's-Inn, Nov. 25, 1755". The pamphlet was published anonymously in December. Warburton himself does not seem to have taken the dissertation as an unfair attack until he received a copy of the pamphlet but thought the latter "a very fine and delicate piece of raillery". (*A Selection from Unpublished Papers of the Right Reverend William Warburton, D.D.*, By the Rev. Francis Kilvert, 1841, pp. 260–1.)

[1] This has not survived.

not to find time to give me a letter is very inexcusable.[1] And if I knew in what way to do it, I should certainly punish You as You deserve. Perhaps the best revenge I can take will be to teaze You into the remembrance of your old friends, if nothing else will do it.

I understand from Dr N.[2] [a] that Dodsley[3] is not over-fond of engaging in this second Imitation.[4] I suppose he is very right in believing that it will not sell. And yet worse things sell ev'ry day. It is true, the sort of writing does not suit the Dr perfectly. Besides other defects, he neither thinks nor speaks exactly enough to excell in the Horatian manner.[5] Yet in all the things he has attempted in this way there are pretty things enough, one would think, to carry off a six-penny pamphlet. But betwixt a want of curiosity and of taste in this our age, an obscure writer has a bad time of it.

You are to know that, as I have no expectation of entertainment from the wits of these days, I mean now You have burnt your Lyre,[6] I am content to seek it in the past ages. And as I know not why I have always conceiv'd high things of the Italian poets, I have been lately trying to get some acquaintance with them.[7] Tho' I cannot boast of

1 Mason had vacated his Fellowship in December 1755 having been appointed domestic chaplain to the Earl of Holdernesse, who for some years "rented a small villa at Chiswick". (Mason, *Works*, 1811, i. 97.) He was staying there at this time. (Gray, *Correspondence*, Letter 212.) RH's reference to "Chiswick Bow'rs" was probably suggested by Mason's *Elegy addressed to Miss Pelham on the death of her father*, which was written in 1754. (*Works*, i. 97.)

"Where D'Arcy call'd to Chiswick's social bower
Mild mirth, and polish'd ease, and decent joy".

2 Thomas Nevile.

3 Robert Dodsley (1703–64), poet, dramatist and bookseller. Originally a footman, Dodsley opened a bookshop at the sign of Tully's Head in Pall Mall in 1735. From there he published works by, amongst others, Pope, Akenside, Young, Johnson and Goldsmith. About 1755 he took his brother into partnership and retired in favour of him in 1759.

4 Nevile's earliest publication *The First Satire of the First Book of Horace Imitated* had been issued in March 1755. He had already written and presented to Littleton a further Imitation, this time of *The Seventeenth Epistle of the First Book of Horace* and wanted this also to be published. (Nevile to Littleton, [letter endorsed "red. June. 24. 1755"], Staffs. RO, D1413/2.) The imitation of the Roman poets had been well established as a literary form since the latter part of the seventeenth century. Pope had popularised the Imitation but it had also been practised by Swift, Johnson and numerous lesser poets. Despite Dodsley's hesitation *The Seventeenth Epistle . . . Imitated* was printed and published on 10 February 1756. (Straus, *Dodsley*, Bibliography.)

5 This criticism was acknowledged by Nevile. In a letter to Littleton he says he has "finish'd the Whole [epistle] with as much exactness as I am capable of – Mr Hurd indeed", he adds, "corrugates his brow at some things; but the truth is, Writers of a mediocre kind must not amuse themselves with vain hopes of polishing up to ye delicate feelings of fastidious Critics of the first class –". (Nevile to Littleton, 29 January 1756, Staffs. RO, D1413/2.)

6 The allusion to Mason's having burnt his lyre is explained in a letter from Warburton to RH of 24 October 1754. (*Prelate*, p. 125.) Before Mason was ordained he called upon Warburton, who impressed upon him that he ought not to go into orders unless he had a resolution "to dedicate all his studies to the service of religion, and totally to abandon his poetry". Mason agreed that this sacrifice was required of him, but it was not long before he resumed his poetical efforts.

7 The study of Italian in the early eighteenth century was not uncommon, but was chiefly prompted by the needs of the traveller and the keen interest in Italian art and opera. There had been comparatively little interest in Italian literature, both contemporary and earlier works having fallen into disfavour towards the end of the seventeenth century as the influence of French canons of criticism and the taste for the Classical tradition grew and spread. Only a few of RH's contemporaries showed a similar enthusiasm for the poetry, among them, Thomas Gray

a Note by RHn: "Neville".

having made any great progress in them, I see enough to convince me that they are above evry thing which is call'd poetry in the other modern languages, except perhaps in our own, which I am us'd to prefer before all others for the force of colouring and height of Invention. Or if this be a prejudice, it is not, I think, to affirm that the french poetry is the tamest poorest thing in the world in comparison of the Italian. One thing that created a presumption in favour of this last, was the observing that Italy was the School to our own poets, and indeed writers of all sorts, at the time when they were the best. It is plain that Milton owed almost as much to the Tuscan as the Greek poets.

In short I'm grown on the sudden such an inamarato of these Italian Bards, that I can almost bear their Sonnets.[8] Yet I wonder that, when they have so many better things to value themselves upon, they should lay such a stress on this elegant indeed, but trifling form of composition. I suspect the folly might arise from a wrong interpretation of the famous maxim – *Difficilia quae pulchra,* which says only that *excellent things are difficult,* whereas they seem to have taken the matter the other way and to have gone on the supposition, that *difficult things are always excellent;* a maxim, which for anything I know might set the discarded french dancers above the best poets.

I reverence that great critic Mr Dodsley prodigiously for his sagacious conjectures about the author of a late pamphlet.[9] However I agree with You that Jortin did not deserve the honour of this ridicule. And I'm persuaded, whoever the writer was, that he was betrayed into it[b] by the weakest of all our passions, an inordinate friendship:[10] In short the very same which makes me run on at this strange rate and pester You with

who had begun learning Italian in 1737 "like any dragon", and was then deep in Tasso; and Joseph and Thomas Warton. RH shared with the Wartons a particular interest in the influence of Italian poetry on English writers. (Gray, *Correspondence*, Letter 37; [Joseph Warton], *An Essay on the Writings and Genius of Pope*, 1756; and Thomas Warton, *Observations on the Faerie Queene of Spenser*, 1754.) It was not until considerably later in the century that the reading of Italian literature grew widespread. (R.W. King, 'Italian Influence on English Scholarship and Literature during the "Romantic Revival"', *Modern Language Review*, 1925, xx. 48–63.)

8 The sonnet had been largely disregarded since Milton's use of it in the 1640s and 1650s, but some renewal of interest was becoming evident. Thomas Edwards had contributed a few sonnets to Dodsley's *A Collection of Poems . . . By Several Hands* published in 1748, and had appended 45 sonnets to the 1758 edition of his *Canons of Criticism*. Mason had obviously experimented with the form and prefaced his 1764 edition of *Poems* with a dedicatory sonnet. It was not, however, until the 1777 edition of Thomas Warton's *Poems* that the sonnet was to attract general literary notice. (E.P. Morton, 'The English Sonnet, 1658–1750', *Modern Language Notes*, xx, pp. 97–8; Clarissa Rinaker, 'Thomas Warton. A Biographical and Critical Study', *University of Illinois Studies in Language and Literature*, Vol. II, no. 1, 1916.)

9 *On the Delicacy of Friendship. A Seventh Dissertation.* (See *ante* To Warburton, 1 December 1755, n. 1.)

10 A more vehement expression of RH's motives is given in a letter apparently sent to a Fellow at another Cambridge college. It is quoted by Warburton in a letter to Charles Yorke, and was written, he says, in response to adverse criticism. "The Author of the Dissertation likewise answered him on this occasion, but in a different strain – 'Since (says he) you have been so free to declare your disapprobation of that piece, I will tell you a secret, which I have told to no other, and which your commendations should never have drawn from me, which is *that I writ it my selfe*; that I writ it in mere indignation at the paltriest & dirtiest Fellow living, not only without any knowledge or allowance of Dr W. but with a fixed resolution that he should never know it' ". (26 February 1756, MS BL, Egerton 1952, ff. 53–4; printed in *Letters from the Reverend Dr. Warburton, Bishop of Gloucester, to the Hon. Charles Yorke, From 1752 to 1770*, The Philanthropic Society, 1812.)

b Note by RHn: "+On the Delicacy of Friendship".

In short the very same which makes me run on at this strange rate and pester You with so long a letter, when I might well have sav'd both You and myself that trouble by leaving You to guess how entirely I am always, Dear Sir, Your affectionate friend and Servant

R Hurd

Camb. 31 Dec 1755

Endorsed by Richard Hurd, nephew: "Dec 31st 1755 about Italian Poetry – the Delicacy of Friendship &c."

164 To WILLIAM MASON — 8 JANUARY 1756

Text: MS HC; printed, *H-M Corr*, 22.
Addressed: cover missing.

Dear Sir

I have your favour of yesterday. And to shew You how punctual a correspondent I am, I mean to those for whom I profess an *inordinate* friendship[1] (for as to others I assure You, I trouble them as little in this way as any body) I will make my acknowledgments to You for it directly.

As to N.'s[a] affair, I will break it to him the first opportunity and will let You know his resolution.[2]

With regard to the letters to D., I can readily believe that they are written with a frankness which to such a man might have been spar'd. But I think there is great reason in what he says. You know Ds[b] brother is Mr A's[c] Servant. And on that account, if on no other, Dodsley should have declin'd having any hand in publishing an abuse on a friend of his, and one of his family. I think You gave him good advice, and I suppose he will take it.[3]

You don't tell me if You have seen Dr Brown.[4] He is in his old lodgings in Tavistock

1 RH is repeating the phrase that he used in the last paragraph of his preceding letter.

2 Richard Hurd [nephew] notes that Nevile is meant, but the allusion is not explained.

3 As Richard Hurd [nephew] noted "D." is Robert Dodsley, "A." Ralph Allen of Prior Park and "a friend of his" is Warburton who had married his niece. It may be inferred that Dodsley was involved in publishing or proposed to publish something, which Warburton considered offensive to himself or to the memory of Pope. Dodsley's brother, Isaac, was gardener to Allen and on that account, RH thinks, Robert Dodsley should not have had any hand in the publication. Warburton had written to Dodsley, who seems to have consulted Mason, who "gave him good advice". See the discussion in *The Correspondence of Robert Dodsley 1733–1764*, ed. James E. Tierney, Cambridge, 1988, pp. 212–17, esp. p. 213, n. 4.

4 Mason did not like John Brown. Gray refers to him as "your Enemy" in a letter to Mason dated 7 September 1757; and Warburton writing to RH on 19 February 1760 commented "Mason rarely sees me. I fancy he is afraid of finding Browne with me". (Gray, *Correspondence*, Letter 248; *Prelate*, p. 221.)

a Note by RHn: "Neville".

b Note by RHn: "Dodsley".

c Note by RHn: "Allen".

here one of these days and then we are to sit upon it. But the Dr is either so lazy or so careless himself, and Garrick is so peremptory in having evry thing his own way, that no great good, I foresee, will come of our criticisms, if they should be ever so reasonable.[7] However the poet may wing his flight for *Gain*, not glory: and if so, it is no great matter, provided it passes upon the Stage, what the few in the closet think of his performance.[8]

I really think, from the little I have seen, that the Italian poets are excellent. They have false thoughts and affected conceits in abundance, it is true. But their allegorical fiction and the brightness of their imagery, the essentials of poetry, make us ample amends for these defects. The french poets are chast and correct. But their invention is poor, and their fancies prosaic. One thing is remarkable enough. Tho' the Italians are sometimes, nay frequently affected, they have, in general, a simplicity which is charming. Don't You think it extraordinary that Milton, notwithstanding the bad taste of his age here at home, and these constant conceits that deform his models, the Italian poets, should yet keep so clear of all these affectations? I can't but look upon this circumstance as a singular proof of the vast superiority of his genius.

You'll think from my saying so much of this subject, that I am quite wild about the Italian poetry. You would think so much more if I was to tell You that I have ev'n gone so far myself as to write a sonnet.[9] I know You laugh at my folly. But your revenge upon me shall go no farther: the rather because, to tell You a secret, You are the

5 *Athelstan. A Tragedy* was first performed at Drury Lane on Friday, 27 February 1756. It was published on Tuesday, 9 March. (*The London Stage 1660–1800*, ed. G.W. Stone, Part 4, ii. 529–32.)

6 Thomas Balguy.

7 David Garrick (1717–79) was at this time at the height of his fame. Nichols in his character of him said that his vanity was "well-known" but added in mitigation that "perhaps no man who had been fed with such excess of praise, would have exhibited fewer marks of self-approbation". He puts a better interpretation on Garrick having his own way and says that there were very few authors who "have not acknowledged themselves greatly indebted to Mr. Garrick for useful hints or advantageous alterations". (*Lit. Anecs.* ii. 317, 319.) Garrick played the leading role in *Athelstan* and wrote the Epilogue.

8 *Athelstan* ran "nine nights to crouded audiences" and "extravagant applause" but was less favourably received by the critics. One reviewer advised Brown to "pocket his 500l. make his bow to Mr. *Garrick*, and depart in peace". The play, he said, was "very deficient in plot, character, sentiment, and diction". (*The Critical Review: or, Annals of Literature, By A Society of Gentlemen*, i. 148–62, 1756.) Unlike Brown's earlier drama *Barbarossa* (still being performed in the 1790s) it was never subsequently revived. There were however three benefit performances for the author at which a total of £420 is recorded as being taken. (*The London Stage*, Part 4, ii. 529–32.)

9 The sonnet is written out in RH's *Commonplace Book*, II. p. 253, from which it is here copied:

Mason, Mr. A Sonnet address'd to him on his
leaving College and going into the family of Lord Holdernesse –

To Mr Mason

Was it for this insidious friendship strove
To clasp our bosoms in it's silken snare,
For this, Thy virtues bloom'd so wondrous fair,
And Fame for thee th' unfading chaplet wove?

Say, will yon Linnet from her Spray remove,
Where sportive She and free from ev'ry care
Warbles at will her softly-soothing air,
And for the glittring cage desert the grove?

subject of it. For You grow so captious, if one offers to give You a little advice (and this sonnet is altogether monitory or rather Vituperative) that, after your treatment of my well intended dialogue, You may be sure I shall avoid this route for the future.[10]

I was very well pleasd with your *Divine* and *Pretty Gentleman's* opinion of a late pamphlet.[11] [d] For if the Irony be too fine for the one, and not fine enough for the other, it is likely to be in that middle way in which the author, I should suppose, intended to write it. But don't conclude from my saying thus much that I have any peculiar tenderness for this nameless offspring. I don't so much as tell You my conjectures. For the knowing ones here pretend to fix the <author> parent, nay to swear to him by certain lineaments which, for anything I know, may be as familiar to You as any other. You don't meddle with Greek in town. Otherwise I could tell You of an awful grammarian who decrees that the concluding Sentence is not to be found in the *Cyropaedia* nor in *Leed's Lucian*, and therefore as he believes in no genuin Greek writer whatsoever.[12] So that the author is likely to have the name, tho' of writing an

Then may'st Thou, sweetest of the tuneful quire,
Thy gentle Muse, the lov'd and loving friend,
The golden competence, the vacant hour,
Celestial blessings, barter for the hire
Of witlings base, and thy free soul descend
To toil for unbless'd gold, and flatter pow'r. R.H. 3 Jan. 1756.

The sonnet, it would seem, was too "monitory" or "vituperative" for Mason, and his relations with his noble patron might have been strained by phrases like "the hire of witlings base". On the same page of his *Commonplace Book*, RH added a revised version, which is headed: "Afterwards, alter'd into the following, corrected by Mr. Mason himself":

A gentle *Linnet* debonair and gay
Whilom had rovd the wood in careless vein,
Perch'd where it pleas'd, and with it's honey'd strain
Had wak'd the Morn and clos'd the eye of Day.

A *Fowler* heard, and o'er her custom'd spray
Inwove of limed twigs the tangling train
And with her fav'rite food bestrew'd the plain:
The wiry cage unseen at distance lay.

Blythe and unweeting to the charmed Tree
The Songster comes, and claps his little wing
Then downward bends to peck the golden fare.

Will no kind hand the struggling captive free?
He yields to fate: he droops: forgets to sing,
Nor greets his Lord with one sweet-warbled air.

The reference in RH's title to Mason's "leaving College and going into the family of Lord Holdernesse" is not easy to explain in connexion with the date "3 Jan. 1756", on which it was written. Mason, according to his own statement (*Hurd-Mason Corr.*, p. xxx), was "instituted to the Living of Aston and appointed Chaplain to the Earl of Holdernesse in November 1754", and he was in attendance on his patron throughout 1755. In December 1755 his year of grace as a Fellow of Pembroke College ran out, forcing him to vacate his Fellowship in he continued to hold the living. His decision to do so meant that he was severing his connection with Cambridge, and this may have been in RH's mind.

10 RH probably refers to the "Political Dialogue" later mentioned in his letter of 7 August 1756.

11 *On the Delicacy of Friendship*. (See *ante* To Warburton, 1 December 1755, n. 1.)

d Note by RHn: "Delicacy of Friendship".

writer whatsoever.[12] So that the author is likely to have the name, tho' of writing an indifferent pamphlet, yet of composing good Greek, which at least will recommend him to the favour of great Scholars.

I say nothing in excuse of all this prate but that I am very truly and affectionately Your's

R Hurd

Camb. 8. Jan. 1756.

165 To WILLIAM MASON 19 JANUARY 1756

Text: MS HC, excerpt made by Richard Hurd, nephew of the writer; published, *MLR* 45 1950, p. 162.

Camb. 19 Jan. 1756[1]

– "You are very logical in your conclusions about the author of a late pamphlet.[2] But tell me honestly, do not you think that Jortin deserved, at least if he had been more considerable, the reprimand that has been given him." –[3]

12 The concluding sentence of *On the Delicacy of Friendship* is a quotation in Greek from the writings of Apollonius of Tyana, given without attribution. (Epistle I appended to the Life of Apollonius by Philostratus.) "The awful grammarian" is John Jortin who though he may not have identified the passage at once had done so by 1758 when he published his *Life of Erasmus*. He too quotes it and gives a translation: "My friendship I bestow upon Philosophers: as to Sophists, little Grammarians, and such sort of Scoundrels and Cacodaemons, I neither have, nor ever will have any regard for them." He then adds: "The man abhors *Grammarians*, it seems; and *Grammars* too, I suppose. But who is the Author of this bit of Greek? An extraordinary person, I assure you; a Projector, a Visionaire, a Linguist by inspiration, a Crack, a Conjurer — in short, APOLLONIUS TYANESIS. He is the man; and the *Grammarians* account it no disgrace to be vilified by a *Mountebank*." (*Life of Erasmus*, i. 604.) Xenophon's *Cyropaedia* and Lucian's *Dialogues* were standard school and university texts. Martin Lowther Clarke, *Greek Studies in England 1700–1830*, Cambridge, 1945.) Edward Leedes was the editor of an edition of Lucian first published in 1678 and reprinted several times thereafter.

1 Originally found opposite p. 257 of RH's *Works*, Vol. 8.

2 *On the Delicacy of Friendship*.

3 The general response to RH's pamphlet is indicated by an article in the *Monthly Review*. The *Dissertation* was agreed to be "written in a very spirited and entertaining Manner", of which some "short Specimens" were given. But whether, the reviewer noted, "Doctor Jortin is liable to any just Censure for not being more liberal of his Praises to his Friend, or whether his Friend deserves those high Encomiums which our Author, and his other Panegyrists, have bestowed upon him with so bountiful a Hand, is not our Business to determine". (*The Monthly Review, or, Literary Journal. By Several Hands*, xiv. (1756) 10.)

166 To WILLIAM MASON 3 APRIL 1756

Text: MS HC; printed, *H-M Corr*, 27.
Addressed: cover missing.

Dear Sir

I send You a Letter from Dr Macro – I have just now receiv'd one from P. P, in which there is a Paragraph relating to You.[1] I transcribe it with the more pleasure because it confirms the judgment which You know I have always passd upon your Poetry.

"Mr Mason was so <good> kind to send us his Odes.[2] They fully support and maintain his character. And this is no slight or vulgar commendation, when it is the common fate of his contemporaries to have ev'ry last production below the preceding.[3] In a word, they charm me much. That on Melancholly is my favourite.[4] You said truly: He compliments his Patron artfully and decently. It is of importance to a man's excelling that he should understand his *fort*, early. The Ode is certainly our Friend's. And if he will indulge himself in Poetry; that is the Province he ought to cultivate.[5] There will be many favorable circumstances, besides his Genius to it, attending it. I will mention only one, That great Repertory of poetical subjects of the Lyric kind, as well as poetical Images, the Bible."[6]

Let me hear from You and let me know which of your court Admirers makes You the happiest compliment.

Your's very affectionately

R Hurd

Camb. 3. Apr. 1756.

Endorsed by Richard Hurd, nephew: "April 3d 1756 about Mr. Mason's Odes".

1 Neither of these letters has been traced. The second letter, from Prior Park (P. P.) was from Warburton.

2 Mason had published his volume of *Odes* on 15 March 1756, probably encouraged by the success of the odes in *Elfrida*, 1752. (Straus, *Dodsley*, Bibliography; Draper, *Mason*, p. 161.)

3 This view is contradicted by the *Monthly Review* which noted the "inferior success [of the Odes] (compared with that of Mr. M's former productions)". The "secret lies", the reviewer continued, "in the pieces themselves: . . . for though the language is, in general, harmonious and flowing, (which, in the opinion of Cowley, often constitutes an excellent Ode) yet are the sentiments neither new nor striking; and, what is worse, there is an obvious sterility of thought; nor do the thoughts themselves always arise from the subjects". (*Monthly Review*, xiv. (1756) 434–5.) The *Critical Review* concurred with these criticisms though stating in mitigation that "Ode-writing" required "a larger share of true creative genius of the divine particular aura" than was necessary for any other mode of writing. (*Critical Review*, i. (1756) 208–14.)

4 'Ode III. *On Melancholy*. To a Friend.' The *Critical Review* did not favour the Ode on Melancholy: such writing, the reviewer said, "can never be disagreeable to the ear; but it is not . . . of that species which can reach the heart". (p. 212). The *Monthly Review* commented, "we cannot see the author of Elfrida in this Ode". (p. 439.) Both critics agreed in pronouncing the second ode, *To Independency*, as the most successful.

5 Mason did publish further odes (Gaskell, *The First Editions of William Mason*), but was better known for his verse dramas and his long poem, *The English Garden*.

6 The Bible had inspired Mason's fourth ode, 'On the Fate of Tyranny', a paraphrase of Isaiah Chapter XIV.

167 To WILLIAM MASON 30 APRIL 1756

Text: MS HC, excerpt made by Richard Hurd, nephew of the writer; published, *MLR* 45 1950, p. 162.

Camb. 30 April 1756[1]

– "I have a mind to know whether this 18th epistle of Horace sells better than the other.[2] Dr. Warburton says 'he is surprized at the force, spirit and harmony of it, and that he shall think it strange if it does not take.' And yet I'll lay a wager beforehand that the *Elegy in an Assembly Room* will outsell it." – [3]

168 To Sir EDWARD LITTLETON 6 JUNE 1756

Text: MS STAFFS RO D1413/1; unpublished.
Addressed: To/Sir Edward Littleton Bart/at his Seat in/Staffordshire
Postmarked: CAMBRIDGE 7 IV

Eman: 6. June. 1756.

Dear Sir Edward

I don't well understand the first Paragraph of your Letter. Yet I think I see in it that You take something amiss of Mr N. with regard to his Imitation of the 17th Ep. of Hor.[1] I do assure You, if there be any part of it not to your mind, it is owing to what he apprehended of your extreme delicacy in such matters. He collected from what You writ to him on this occasion, that to have said more, or to have said it more openly and directly, would not have been at all to your Inclination. On this account he was

1 Originally found opposite p. 151 of Thomas Nevile's *Imitations of Horace*, 1758.

2 Thomas Nevile's *Seventeenth Epistle of the First Book of Horace Imitated* was published on 10 February (Straus, *Dodsley*, Bibliography), and had been favourably reviewed as a poem "not without merit". (*Monthly Review*, xiv. (1756) 259–60.) It had, however, been remarked that the whole poem with the original Latin verse amounted to 160 lines, for which, the reviewer pointed out, "as Horace had no Copy-money for his part of the pamphlet, we humbly conceive the Editor might have charged somewhat less than a shilling". The *Eighteenth Epistle of the First Book of Horace Imitated* (also priced 1s.) was subsequently noticed but not reviewed, the critic merely observing that Nevile maintained "his usual spirit". (*Ibid.*, xiv. 454.) There are no records of the respective sales.

3 *An Elegy written in an empty Assembly-Room* by Richard Owen Cambridge had been published anonymously by Dodsley on 11 April 1756 at 6d. (Straus, *Dodsley*, Bibliography). The *Monthly Review* described the poem as "a mock lamentation, in the stile of Pope's Eloisa to Abelard . . ., in a strain that would have been thought very pretty, had the verses been entirely originals." (xiv. 454.) The poem was obviously popular and two further editions were printed in the first week of May.

1 The source of Littleton's displeasure concerning Nevile's imitation of the *Seventeenth Epistle of the First Book of Horace* is nowhere disclosed. Nevile heard of it immediately and wrote to Littleton apologising, three days after publication, on 13 February 1756. "I don't well know", he confessed, "how to disengage myself of this breach of promise you charge me with: to tell you it slip'd my memory may serve in some degree to lessen the immorality of it, but will leave me expos'd to the full guilt of a shameful neglect." (Staffs. RO, D1413/2.) No substantial changes were made to the first edition (of which there is only one recorded copy at the Houghton Library, Harvard) when the poem was incorporated in Nevile's collection of *Imitations* published in 1758.

scrupulous even of mentioning your name, as for the same reason he avoided mentioning Mr Mason's in the Imitation of the 18th ep. which is meant to be address'd to him.[2]

I could not help saying thus much for our good friend who, I am sure, is warmly your's, has the highest regard for You, and would be hurt beyond measure if he understood that he had been so unhappy as to give You any offence.

If You did not receive the Imitation from himself, it was Dodsley's great fault who, I know, had orders to send You a Present of it, and in the handsomest manner.[3] The other two, I suppose, You receiv'd from him in franks.[4]

Mr Balguy goes to Buxton or at least to Sheffield in the beginning of July.[5] I shall be gone from this place somewhat sooner. I intend to pass the Summer on the coast of Sussex for the sake of bathing and drinking the Salt-water. My chief residence, I believe, will be at Brighthelmston, to which place I am determin'd in some measure by the fame of Dr Russell, the great Sea-water Doctor.[6] But there are many other reasons why I cannot think of travelling westward, as You very kindly propose to me.

I thank You for the offer about Tortoise.[7] But I shall try her at least this Summer. Indeed, She has behavd exceeding well of late; and if She will but keep upon her legs, I have no desire to part with her. She has many qualities that suit me exactly.

You make me very happy in saying that Lady Littleton's health is so much better. I beg my humble Service to her Ladyship and am ever very truly and affectionately, Dear Sir Edward, Your faithful humble Servt

R Hurd.

P. S.

Have You receivd Mr Mason's present of his Odes?

2 The *Eighteenth Epistle* is inscribed "TO A FRIEND", and opens with the line:
" * * ! if one, who knows you, may commend".
The *Seventeenth Epistle* is inscribed "To a Friend in TOWN", and both poems use asterisks throughout in place of names.

3 Nevile had already written to Littleton in January promising him "a book with gilt leaves and gilt covers". (29 January 1756, Staffs. RO, D1413/2.)

4 It is not known where Dodsley obtained franks although there was widespread abuse in their distribution. For a detailed discussion see *Correspondence of Robert Dodsley*, p. 157, n. 6. The maximum weight per letter was 2 oz. but Nevile's two other works (*The Eighteenth Epistle* to Mason, and *The First Satire of the First Book of Horace Imitated*, 1755) would have been sent unbound in their wrappers. (Ellis, *The Post Office*, pp. 39–40.)

5 Thomas Balguy visited Buxton for the spa-water fairly frequently, as did Sir Edward and Lady Littleton. (See *ante* To Littleton, 7 November 1753.) His family originated in Sheffield.

6 Brighthelmstone (later Brighton) was not yet fashionable but had begun to attract attention following the publication in 1752 of *A Dissertation on the Use of Sea-Water in the Disease of the Glands* by Richard Russell, M.D. In the treatise (first published in Latin in 1750), Russell examines the benefits not only of bathing in, but also of drinking sea water. This treatment became so popular that bottled sea water was advertised for sale in London. The dissertation proved equally popular and ran into several editions in the 1750s. (Lewis Melville, *Brighton: its History, its Follies, and its Fashions*, 1909.)

7 RH's horse, a replacement for Thumper. (See *ante* To Littleton, 3 June 1755, n. 3.)

169 To WILLIAM MASON 16 JUNE 1756

Text: MS HC; printed, *H-M Corr*, 28.
Addressed: cover missing.

Camb. 16. June. 1756.

Dear Sir

Your favour of the 8th came hither the day after I was set out on a journey into Norfolk, from which I am but just now return'd.[1] I mention this, because I should otherwise have acquainted You that Dr W. is in town, where he has been ever since the beginning of the month. I think You will do well to write to him immediately.[2]

The public taste has shewn itself to be what I have long thought it, by it's reception of your Odes.[3] It has been so viciated by this long run of insipid Romances that nothing manly or great is at all relish'd.[4] A little easy sing-song, intermixd with what they call *Sentiment*,[5] is the utmost that common readers have any idea of. The sublimer poetry is as unintelligible to them as Coptic. In short, You come too late by half a century to give that pleasure You might reasonably expect to have given, by the finest Odes we have any example of in our language. However the few will still have a juster way of thinking, and to these a good writer must now be content to write to.

I must have a high idea of a young man[a] that could *imitate* L. B. so perfectly.[6] But I

1 RH had been out of Cambridge from 8 to 14 June, probably to visit the Macro family.

2 Warburton had written to RH on 8 May and mentioned that he proposed "to be in town in about ten days time". (*Prelate*, p. 155.) The necessity for Mason's writing to him has not been established.

3 Mason's *Odes* had received a cool response and it was known that although a second edition had been quickly printed the "impressions" had not been "so eagerly bought up as might have been expected". (*Monthly Review*, xiv. (1756) 434; see also *ante* To Mason, 3 April 1756.)

4 The contemporary concept of "romance" was blurred, veering between the established sense of "a tale of wild adventures in war and love" (Johnson, *Dictionary*, 1755) and a looser interpretation reflecting the growing preoccupation with the "Mazes, Windings and Labyrinths, which perplex the Heart of Man". ('Preface' (p. viii) by Henry Fielding to Sarah Fielding's *Adventures of David Simple*, Second Edition, 1744.) In this context RH seems to be referring to the long winter season of novels and "affecting" stories which was drawing to a close. The end of the season was welcomed by at least one critic in the *Monthly Review*. Reviewing a novel characterised by "Poverty of writing, insipidity of narrative, and inutility of design" he gives thanks for "the approach of summer" ensuring that this should be "the last work of the sort, we are like to be troubled with, for some Months, at least". (*Monthly Review*, xiv. 453.)

5 The new use of "sentiment" implying "finer feelings" or a "delicate sensibility" as opposed to "thought" or "opinion" had crept in in the late 1740s. (Susie I. Tucker, *Protean Shape. A Study in Eighteenth-Century Vocabulary and Usage*, 1967, pp. 247–9; Johnson, *Dictionary*, 1755.) Mrs Belfour, a correspondent of Samuel Richardson, was puzzled by the new usage and wrote to Richardson for an explanation. What "in your opinion", she asked, "is the meaning of the word *sentimental*, so much in vogue amongst the polite, both in town and country? In letters and common conversation, I have asked several who make use of it, and have generally received for answer, it is — it is — *sentimental* . . . I am frequently astonished to hear such a one is a *sentimental* man; we were a *sentimental* party; I have been taking a *sentimental* walk . . . I should be glad to know your interpretation of it." (*The Correspondence of Samuel Richardson*, Selected from the Original Manuscripts . . . by Anna Laetitia Barbauld, 1804, iv. 282–3.)

6 Edmund Burke (then only 27) had published *A Vindication of Natural Society: or, A View of the Miseries and Evils arising to Mankind from every Species of Artificial Society . . . By a late Noble Writer* anonymously in May 1756. It was his first work and was intended as a satire on Bolingbroke's theory of "natural" religion. The design was to prove that political truth is no more capable of being rationally explained than religious truth, or, in other words, that "the

a The name "Mr. Burke" is inserted above the line in the hand of RH's nephew.

must still think his Imitation a bad *Irony*. Had the author intended only, in the character of *Sophist*, to mimic Lord Bolingbroke's style and manner and to compose a tract that should pass for his, I should have calld it a happy and most ingenious forgery. But an *Ironist* has quite another office. His business is, *to imitate so as to expose*. When he attempts <his>[b] the *manner*, and much more when he adopts <his>[b] the *principles* of another, he should take care by a constant exaggeration to make <the>[b] his *ridicule* shine thro' the Imitation. Whereas this *Vindication* is everywhere enforcd, not only in the language, and on the principles of L. Bol., but with so apparent, or rather so real an earnestness, that half his purpose is sacrificd to the other. One sees it extremely *like*, but the likeness is not such as excites *ridicule*. 'Tis true, a good Ironist will exaggerate so discretely that all he says may seem not improbably to come from the *person represented*. And when a work of this sort is so managd, we call it a *delicate Irony*. But to personate another witht any exaggeration or with so little as to escape notice, may be thought a *delicacy* indeed, but gives one a strange notion of an *Irony*. In short, if the writer meant to expose Lord Bol. by an *ironical application of his principles* he has miss'd his aim, for he has only rais'd an admiration of his own talents. If he thought the most *serious application of his principles* sufficient to expose him, he has judgd wrong, for as extravagant as his conclusion is, one is half convinc'd of it by his premises. The *Vindication* requires an answer as much, perhaps will not admit so easy an answer, as the *fragments & Essays*.[7]

I am sorry I shall not see You in my passage next week thro' London. I go from thence in the Stage-coach and so shall not have it in my power to stop at Tunbridge, if the road lies thro' it.

Believe me, Dear Sir, Your most faithful and affectionate

R Hurd.[c]

Endorsed by Richard Hurd, nephew: "June 16th 1756 about Mr. Mason's Odes – & on Irony, &c."

late noble Writer was as wild, extravagant, and whimsical in his politics, as in his religious meditations". (*Monthly Review*, xv. (1756) 20.) Some readers were apparently taken in by Burke's parody of Bolingbroke's style and he was criticised for this in the *Review* where the reviewer would have preferred him to be "so candid as to own, that he only wrote in the *manner* of the late Noble Writer".

7 'Fragments or Minutes of Essays' formed the last volume of the collected edition of Bolingbroke's *Works* published by David Mallet in 1754. The previously unpublished fragments continue his arguments concerning "natural" and "artificial" religion.

b Whibley suggests that the alterations in the text were made by Mason. (*Hurd-Mason Corr.*, p. 29.) But although they appear in a slightly heavier hand, it is difficult to make a positive identification.

c At the foot of the letter Mason has added this comment: "My Correspondent was nearly guilty of the same fault, when he wrote his first Dialogue – The Irony was so fine that several readers thought it a grave & serious vindication of *Insincerity*. M". The dialogue referred to is 'On Sincerity in the Commerce of the World: between Dr. Henry More and Edmund Waller, Esq.', published in *Moral and Political Dialogues*, 1759.

170 To Sir EDWARD LITTLETON 19 JULY 1756

Text: MS STAFFS RO D1413/1; unpublished.
Addressed: To/Sir Edward Littleton Bart./at his Seat in/Staffordshire/ By London
Postmarked: 21 IY

Brighthelmston in Sussex 19 July 1756.

Dear Sir Edward

Having a good deal of leisure at this place, I shall presume so much upon your's, as to give You some account of myself since I left Cambridge.[1]

Mr Mainwaring[2] and I came hither in the end of June. We had heard but a very indifferent account of what we were to expect at this fishing-town. But ev'rything is, in truth, very tolerable. We have a fine open country about us, not unlike Canock heath, or rather the Downs about Salisbury.[3] The air is therefore very fine; and the constant Breezes from the Sea make it very delicious in this warm Season.[4] As we got hither pretty early, we have securd one of the pleasantest houses in the place. It is upon the cliff, within forty yards of the Sea, of which we have a constant prospect from our windows. A musical man will perhaps think it something that we are perpetually regal'd by it's murmurs. I have enterd in good earnest into the Regimen of Salt-water. I drink it evry day, and dip ev'ry other. I find both to agree very well with me, and am encourag'd to expect the greatest benefits from this course by the concurring advice of three of the best Physicians in England.[5] So that I shall probably stay here till tow'rds the middle of September.

When we had been here about a week, we took it into our heads to take a flight as far as Portsmouth and the Isle of Wight and so home again by Southampton and Chichester. In this ride we took in the finest part of Hampshire, which is indeed a very agreable Country. The Isle of Wight pleas'd us extremely. It is an epitome of all that is most delicious in England. The town of Newport may vye with the prettiest I ever saw.[6] In rambling upon the hills we had abundance of fine views, and most of

1 RH had left Cambridge about 22 June and was not back in college until 21 September. (*Commons Accounts Book*, STE. 15. 10.)

2 John Mainwaring was a long standing friend of RH and Edward Littleton, with whom he had corresponded. (See *ante* To Littleton, 24 November 1745, n. 18; Staffs. RO, D1413/2.)

3 The healthy situation of Brighthelmstone was often commented on. In the earliest history of the town published in 1761 the surrounding country is described as "open and free from woods, and finely diversified with hills and vallies". Here, the author continues, "the advantage of exercise may be always enjoyed in fair weather: it is ever cool on the hills, and a shelter may be constantly found in the vallies from excess of wind". (Anthony Relhan, *A Short History of Brighthelmston. With Remarks on its Air, and An Analysis of its Waters*, 1761, p. 4.) Cannock referred to by RH was close to Littleton's estate; he had no direct connections with Salisbury at this time but some of his Cambridge acquaintance had livings in Wiltshire.

4 Relhan has a separate section in his *History of Brighthelmston* to discuss the quality of the air. It is, he finds, far superior to the air in many other watering places, "free from the insalutary vapour of stagnant water, distant from the noxious steams of perspiring trees, . . . and every other cause aiding to produce a damp, putrid atmosphere". (*Ibid*., p. 34.)

5 Dr Russel was the foremost advocate of treatment by sea water (see *ante* To Littleton, 6 June 1756, n. 6); Dr Heberden had also recommended it (see *ante* To Littleton, 21 May 1754, n. 1); the third physician has not been identified.

6 Eighteenth century accounts of Newport particularly remarked on the town's neatness. One traveller, J. Hassell, described Newport as "perhaps the pleasantest [town] in this part of the

them were enliven'd by the prospect of the Ocean. We visited Carisbroke castle which is charmingly situated within a mile of Newport, and is memorable, You know, for being the place of Charles 1st's confinement.[7] The very window is still preservd, out of which the King endeavourd to make his escape, when he was prevented by the vigilance of Colonel Hammond.

So much for my travels. I chuse to say nothing of public news, because there is nothing which You or I can hear with pleasure. I'm afraid the rumour is too true, that St Philip's has surrender'd.[8]

When You have half an hour's leisure, I shall be glad to hear that Lady Littleton and yourself are well. You will make my best respects to her Ladyship and to both your families, when You see them. Mr Mainwaring desires that his may be accepted.

I must not forget to tell You that Tortoise behaves incomparably well and is got into favour again as highly as ever. I say nothing of Lords, but You are to understand that few private gentlemen in this place are better mounted than your humble Servant.

Dear Sir Edward, believe me most affectionately Your faithful and entire Servant

R Hurd.

171 To WILLIAM MASON 7 AUGUST 1756

Text: MS HC; printed, *H-M Corr*, 30.
Addressed:. cover missing.

Brighthelmstone 7 Aug. 1756.

Dear Mr Mason

I did not care to press You to a journey which I doubted would not be very agreable to You, but we were much disappointed in not seeing You, especially after Mr Noble had informed us that You certainly intended it.[1] I should have been glad of your

kingdom. The houses are plain and neat; the streets uniform; and, except at the west end, all regularly paved. The church is also a conspicuous and leading feature to its neatness." Few places, he added, "afford better accommodations for genteel people." (J. Hassell, *Tour of the Isle of Wight*, 2 vols., 1790, i. 130–3; see also Richard Worsley, *The History of the Isle of Wight*, 1781, pp. 153–4; J. Albin, *A New, Correct, and Much-Improved History of the Isle of Wight*, 1795, pp. 315–17.)

7 Charles I was confined to Carisbrooke Castle for nearly a year. He had sought refuge with the Governor of the Isle of Wight, Colonel Robert Hammond, who fell into the unenviable position of being under pressure from both King and Parliament. The castle, founded in early Norman times, was now partly ruined, though "very picturesque" and affording "many pleasing views". To Hassell, later in the century, "the fretted Gothic arch; – the nodding battlements" and "the ruined tower" evoked the memory of the "ancient state and splendour of the English barons" (*Ibid.*, ii. 103–4.)

8 The attack on St Philip's in Minorca heralded the opening of hostilities in the Seven Years War. Britain was aligned with Prussia against the newly formed coalition of Austria, France, Russia, Sweden and Saxony. On 6 May 1756 news had been received of the French landing on Minorca, a British possession much valued as a naval base and for the defence of trade in the Mediterranean. War was declared on 18 May. The garrison of St Philip's was besieged for some weeks but capitulated on 28 June. Reports were slow to filter through and the *London Gazette* for 6 to 10 July, for instance, had received no news since the "Advices" of 14 June. Confirmation of surrender with the 'Articles of Capitulation' were printed in the issue of 20 to 24 July 1756. (Marie Peters, *Pitt and Popularity. The Patriot Minister and London Opinion during the Seven Years War*, Oxford, 1980, pp. 46–7; *London Gazette*, 1756.)

1 Unidentified. Noble may have held some post in the household of Lord Holdernesse, whose

company for many reasons; amongst others that I might have known something more of the new scheme You have enterd upon.[2] I rejoyce with You on this project, not only because I dare say it is a good one, but because it will serve to fill up your time and employ your leisure very agreably. I cannot tell how You find it but the best part of my entertainment in this foolish world arises from my own thoughts, which, bad as they are, are a better amusement than any I find in what is calld general conversation. Some of these I should perhaps have troubled You with, if I had seen You here. I told You of my Political Dialogue.[3] It runs out into two parts, each of them pretty long, but the subject, at least if I don't spoil it in the handling, not uninteresting. The first of these is quite finishd, I mean thrown completely into form, so that I might have taken your judgment of it. I must now be contented to wait till we meet next winter at Cambridge, by which time I hope to have finishd the remainder, which is to finish all that I intend of this nature.[4] If You get Caractacus in the same forwardness I promise to repay your criticism, not with the dull civility current amongst authors, but with the free censure of one that takes a greater interest in what You write than in any trash of his own.[5]

I suppose You would learn from Dr Warb that he leaves Durham immediately after the 13th inst. So that You will hardly pay the visit You designd him.[6]

You are very kind in your wishes that I may find the full benefit of this Sea-Regimen. I <cannot> dare not promise myself too much from it. I remember those oracular lines of Pope

> The young disease that must prevail at length
> Grows with his growth and strengthens with his strength.[7]

It is enough if I can but palliate a disorder which comes, like all our woe, by

chaplain Mason was. Gray also mentions a "Mr Noble" in a letter of 19 December 1756. (Gray, *Correspondence*, Letter 230, n. 9.)

2 The "new scheme" is probably the composition of *Caractacus*, A *Dramatic Poem*. Mason had sent Gray his "first idea of Caractacus" in May or early June 1756. (Gray, *Correspondence*, Letter 216, n. 11.)

3 This dialogue seems to have been the basis for Dialogues V and VI, 'On the Constitution of the English Government', published in *Moral and Political Dialogues* in 1759. RH had been discussing his dialogues with Mason (and Warburton) as he wrote them. (See *ante* To Mason, 31 October 1755; 8 January 1756.) The subject of constitutional practice was much debated in the early eighteenth century, although there was general agreement about the nature of the Constitution itself. The discussion of Dialogues V and VI substantiates the contemporary consensus of opinion showing the old tory notion of the sovereignty of the prerogative to be almost completely discredited. (W.A. Speck, 'Politics', *The Eighteenth Century*, ed. Pat Rogers, 1978, pp. 96–102.)

4 RH may have finished all the dialogues for his volume of *Moral and Political Dialogues*, but he did return to the form with a further collection of *Dialogues on the Uses of Foreign Travel*, published in 1764.

5 *Caractacus* and the *Dialogues* were both published in May 1759. (Straus, *Dodsley*, Bibliography; see *post* To Mason, 4 May 1759, n. 2.) In the intervening years RH frequently read and commented on Mason's drama, and it is to him that it is dedicated with a prefatory 'Elegy'.

> "Yes, 'tis my pride to own, that taught by thee
> My conscious soul superior flights essay'd;
> Learnt from thy lore the Poet's dignity,
> And spurn'd the hirelings of the ryming trade".

6 In March 1755 Warburton had been appointed to a prebend at Durham. (See *ante* To Warburton, 23 March 1755, n. 1.)

7 *Essay on Man*, ii. 135–6 (. . . must subdue at length . . .).

inheritance. Happy! if I but inherited the integrity of mind and serenity of temper which made it so easy to him from whom I derivd it.[8]

But I grow too grave even for You. Let me end with telling You that Mr Powell is here with his Sister.[9] They came down on a visit to an Essex family that is here and I suppose will leave us again next week.

Mr Manwaring sends compliments. If this finds You in Town, remember us both to Mr Noble. Believe me most cordially, Dear Sir, Your affectionate friend & Servant

R Hurd

Endorsed by Richard Hurd, nephew: "Augst 7th 1756 about the Dialogues, &c."

172 To Sir EDWARD LITTLETON 20 OCTOBER 1756

Text: MS FOLGER w.a.57(7); printed, *Memoirs*, 59.
Addressed: To/Sir Edward Littleton Bart/at his Seat at Tedgely Park/Staffordshire
Postmarked: OC

Camb. 20. Oct. 1756

Dear Sir Edward

I beg your pardon for neglecting so long to acknowledge your two kind letters to me at Brighthelmstone. But I had a mind to wait the issue of an affair which I knew would give You pleasure as it very much concernd me. One of our college livings became vacant just before I left Sussex. Mr Hubbard has been ever since deliberating about it.[1] He has just now refus'd it. And I shall this day declare to the Society my intentions of taking it.[2] The living, I speak of, lies in Leicestershire, within three or four measurd miles of Leicester. The name is Thurcaston, and the extended value somewhat about 230 pounds a year.[3] Mr Hubbard and I were to see it last week. The Situation is pleasant enough for the country, which You know is no Paradise. The house good enough for a Bishop and in good repair, and the Gardens, which to a bookish man You know is a matter of consequence, quite excellent. But what above all recommends

8 RH's father had died of cancer in November 1755. For some time afterwards RH obviously felt that he was suffering from some similar illness. His words recall the opening lines of *Paradise Lost*:

"Of Man's First Disobedience, and the Fruit
Of that Forbidden Tree, whose mortal taste
Brought Death into the World, and all our woe . . ."

9 William Samuel Powell was at this time a Fellow at St John's. His sister, Susanna, was described as "very like him in person and temper", and perhaps for this reason they could "never agree". (*Lit. Anecs.*, i. 580; *D.N.B.*)

1 The living of Thurcaston in Leicestershire had become vacant on 4 September 1756 by the death of the incumbent, Richard Arnald. Henry Hubbard, Senior Fellow at Emmanuel, had first option on college livings, and following him, RH, as next in seniority.

2 RH's nomination to Thurcaston appeared in the *College Order Book* on 8 November 1756. (COL. 14. 2.)

3 Thurcaston was one of the two richest livings in Leicestershire, both of which were in the gift of Emmanuel. The income of the incumbent had remained stable since the beginning of the century. (John H. Pruett, *The Parish Clergy under the Later Stuarts. The Leicestershire Experience*, University of Illinois Press, 1978, pp. 59, 82; 'Documents relating to Leicestershire, preserved in the Episcopal Registry at Lincoln', ed. W.G.D. Fletcher, *Associated Architectural Societies' Reports and Papers*, xxii. (1894) 350.)

this Rectory to me, is, that it lies within a day's ride or so from my dear Sir Edward. I have calculated the distance. It would be very possible in a long Summer's day to dine at Catton[4] and lie at Tedgeley. But tho' the prospect of this delights me, I shall not go immediately to reside at Thurcaston. It will be near a twelvemonth before my fellowship is vacant.[5] And then I may have some concerns that will keep me here for some time. But I shall be backwards and forwards there at certain seasons, which will give me the opportunity either of meeting You, or of waiting upon You in Staffordshire. In short I am very happy in the thoughts of being brought so near You, and I know Your's and Lady Littleton's kindness to me so well that it will not, I flatter myself, be a matter of indifference to either of You.

Indeed your concern for the ease and happiness of your friend is very extraordinary. I understood your delicate hint in your last letter to me at Brighthelmstone. But your generosity had taken care that I should have no more difficulty in leaving that place than in getting to it.

My dear friend, believe me very sensible of all your favours, of those You intend, as well as of those You do me. Give my most respectful services to your good Lady. Let me hear that She continues in perfect health, that is, that You are both as happy as I wish You.

Dear Sir, Your most faithful and Obligd humble Servant

R Hurd.

173 To WILLIAM WARBURTON 20 OCTOBER 1756

Text: MS BL Eg. 1958, ff. 1–4; published in part, *Memoirs*, 61.
Addressed: To/The Revd Dr Warburton/at his House in Gros'nor Square/London

My truest and most excellent friend,

For so You approve yourself by all titles. I have receivd your most kind letter, written with the tenderness of the Parent I have lost, rather than of what the world calls a friend. Knowing myself so obligd to You as I am, for evry instance of kindness, for your distinction of me, for your constant recommendation, for your effectual services and, for what I value above them all, for your cordial friendship, I am quite confounded with this fresh instance of your goodness to me, so little usual in any, and so much above example in these times. But I should have reason to be much more confounded if I did not return your generosity with the utmost frankness. I therefore embrace your kind favour with the utmost pleasure and at the same time think it but fitting You should know the full value of it.

Let me own to You then that, tho' my little Income, made up of several odd ends, be abundantly sufficient for the wants I have in this place, yet the expences I have been sometimes put to in my attendance on my friends, on some by the calls of duty,

4 Christopher and Frances Horton, the parents of Lady Frances Littleton, lived at Catton.

5 RH was instituted to Thurcaston on 16 February 1757; he was inducted on 25 March, and formally left Emmanuel on 29 September 1757. (MSS HC, Certificate of Institution, Subscription on Institution, Certificate of Induction; Emmanuel, *Commons Accounts Book*, STE. 15. 1.) His name continued to appear in the *College Order Book* until 9 July 1757. (COL. 14.2.) However, he did not immediately leave Cambridge, and his letters are addressed from there until 6 November 1757.

and on others, by civility, but especially in the attendance in my unsettled state of health, have so far run me behind hand in my finances as to render this gratuity of your's doubly welcome. All this indeed I had been a wretch if I had not studiously conceald from You, whose concern or rather sollicitude for my ease and happiness I knew so well. But on such an occasion it was not to be dissembled. And I rejoyce to think it is in my power to make You this return of your kindness, by giving You the pleasure to understand that your present is more reasonable than You perhaps imagind. For as to the reasons You so politely invent to cover this act of generosity, there is but little in them. Mr Arnold died at such a time as leaves the greater part of the last year's profits to his Successor.[1] I dare say, they will be more than sufficient to discharge the usual expences of taking up a living. This last consideration much distresses me in relation to what You mention of Mr Allen's intended bounty.[2] For You are not contented to be a father to me yourself, all your friends must be so too. At least I could wish not to have known of his intention, as it makes it difficult for me to do, what I certainly design'd, to acquaint him with the resolution I was about to take on the receipt of your letter. However I shall write to him immediately, as You advise, tho' I know it will be very awkwardly.[3] When one has to do with such folks as You, one must expect to be exercisd with these difficulties.

But your kindness knows no bounds. You are projecting advantages for me which I never dream't of. I must however say something to each. The preachership at White-hall determines with my fellowship in Emmanuel.[4] So there is an end of that matter. The Master's, I take to be a good life. And tho' I please myself with thinking I am not unacceptable to the people I have so long livd with, yet I have taken no pains to cultivate a peculiar interest with them. And it would be an extraordinary step to prefer a College Clerk to the Mastership, on a vacancy. Besides, Mr Hubbard, who has been Tutor to all the fellows, has a natural claim to it, if it falls in his time. On these accounts I indulge no thoughts or expectations of that nature.[5] For what You mention of the fellowship, if it were to be had in any other of our colleges, (for we have no such thing here) I should most certainly rejoyce in it. Whether such a thing be feasible or not, I have not so much as considerd. However I don't think of quitting Cambridge for the present. The certain Income of my living, at the lowest valuation, will be fully sufficient for this purpose. And if, when I have stayd here as long as I think proper, I afterwards retire to Thurcaston, I have no notion but the profits, with a little good husbandry, will make me quite easy. I, who was born to no hopes, have no large necessities, and have been train'd to philosophy, ought to be ashamd if so decent a provision did not satisfy me.

You see, my dear friend, I have pourd out my whole heart to You. Your uncommon

1 RH had been appointed successor to Richard Arnald as rector of Thurcaston, Leicestershire, a living in the gift of Emmanuel. (See preceding letter.) Income from the living was largely derived from tithe and glebe payments (as well as Easter offerings and surplice fees), and fell due at Michaelmas. Arnald's death on 4 September left RH responsible for their collection. (See A. Tindal Hart, *The Eighteenth Century Country Parson (circa 1689 to 1830)*, Shrewsbury, 1955, pp. 95–114.)

2 No other documentation concerning this suggested gift has been found.

3 This letter has not been traced.

4 The 24 Whitehall Preachers were drawn from among the Fellows of the Oxford and Cambridge colleges; their appointments ceased on the resignation of their Fellowships.

5 The Mastership did not fall vacant until 1775, on the death of William Richardson, who had held it since 1736.

generosity requird no less. And I have done it the rather to relieve You from that anxiety You express for the interests of one You have taken into your bosom. In a word, I accept Thurcaston directly in full confidence that it will make me easy for the time to come. Your goodness has made me so for the present. With all my heart and affections, Dearest Sir, Your most Obligd, and, if there be any such thing in the world as Gratitude, Your most Devoted friend & Servt

R Hurd

Camb. 20. Oct. 1756.

174 To JOHN POTTER 16 NOVEMBER 1756

Text: MS NLW 12432E; unpublished.
Addressed: To/The Reverend Mr Potter/at Axbridge near/Wells in/Somersetshire[1]
Postmarked: 17 NO

Camb. 16. Nov. 1756

Dear Sir

As lazy a correspondent as I am, I could not excuse it to myself if I did not write one word to acquaint you with my Presentation to a college living.[2] It is Thurcaston, near Leicester. A Rectory of between two and three hundred pounds a year. I have seen the Place and think it agreable enough for the country, wch, I need not tell you, is no Paradise. The house is a good one, and in good repair. The Gardens are as pleasant as I have ever seen belonging to a Parsonage. With these temptations however I have no design of settling there immediately. It is probable that I may not go to reside there till Spring twelvemonth.[3] In the mean time I hope your Brother will be no loser.[4] I shall keep Reymerston in my own hands till next Michs. And by that time I believe his Bp will do something for him. Or at the worst, as Mr Hudson is not likely to reside there himself, your Brother will have it in his choice to continue in the Curacy.

I hope to hear a good account of your building, and what concerns me more, of your health, which your Brother tells me, of late has been but indifferent.[5] It is possible I may find time this next Summer to pay you a short visit. But whether I am to have this pleasure or no, let me assure you of my constant good wishes, as being always with great truth, Dear Sir, Your faithful and affectionate friend & Servt

R. Hurd.

P. S.

Pray remember me very kindly to Mrs Potter.[6]

1 John Potter had been instituted Rector of Badgworth near Axbridge, Somerset, on 22 July 1754. (Parish Records, Somerset RO.)
2 See *ante* To Littleton, 20 October 1756.
3 RH moved to Thurcaston in the spring of 1758. (See *post* To Mason, 10 July 1758.)
4 Robert Potter. Potter had taken over the curacy of Reymerston when RH relinquished it on his nomination to a Fellowship at Emmanuel in 1742. (See *ante* To Potter, 27 January 1743.) Robert Hudson had been instituted as Rector of Reymerston, but by an unofficial arrangement, the management and income of the living remained in RH's control. (See *ante* To Potter, 15 April 1742, n. 3; To Macro, 1 May 1742, n. 2.)
5 Badgworth lay in a marshy area, the climate of which consistently undermined Potter's health. (NLW, Potter to an unidentified correspondent, [18] July 1767.) No further reference to building has been found.
6 Potter had married Catherine Conway on 6 February 1755. (Badgworth Parish Register, Somerset RO.)

175 To WILLIAM WARBURTON 30 DECEMBER 1756

Text: *Prelate*, 156.

Cambridge, December 30th, 1756.

Rev. Sir,

I have so many things to thank you for in your favour of the 25th, that I hardly know which to begin with first. I take that which interests me most, I mean your projected Preface to the second vol. of the Legation.[1] If the *former* is to be only displaced, I have no objection. But if you mean to leave it quite out, I cannot easily give my assent. I know that a great part of it was chiefly proper to the time. And Webster you think too insignificant (if, besides, the poor man were not disabused before now) to have this distinction continued to him.[2] Yet, for all this, I shall regret the loss. I think it, in point of writing, one of your master-pieces. The paragraph to the memory of Bishop Hare is so fine in itself, and lets one into so much of your own friendly temper, that I would not part with it.[3] And the concluding page to the Universities flatters me, as a member of one of them, to that degree, that I must needs wish to preserve *that*.[4] 'Tis true, you have been ill recompenced for the noblest compliment that ever was paid them. Many individuals, at least, of both Universities, have shewn how little they deserved this honour.[5] But the rising generation, I trust,

1 The fourth edition of *The Divine Legation* Volume I had appeared in 1755. Warburton had now embarked on preparations for a new edition of Volume II (in two parts) which had last been published in 1742. This revised (third) edition came out in 1758. It was printed with its own Preface and the Preface to the First Edition (to which RH refers), though with some alterations. These new editions of 1755–8 are the only ones held by Emmanuel College Library.

2 Dr William Webster was the first writer to attack *The Divine Legation* on publication of Volume I in 1738. His criticisms appeared in *The Weekly Miscellany* of which he was the editor and were signed 'A Country Clergyman'. They were largely unjust and malicious and particularly misrepresent Warburton's sympathy with Conyers Middleton. In reply, and urged by Bishops Hare and Sherlock, Warburton published *A Vindication of the Author of the Divine Legation of Moses, &c. From the Aspersions of the Country Clergyman's Letter in the Weekly Miscellany of February 24, 1737* [i.e. 1738] advertised for sale in the *Gentleman's Magazine* for April 1738. Webster countered the *Vindication* with four further letters in *The Weekly Miscellany* and provoked Warburton to a sharper riposte in the Preface of Volume II published in 1741. The attack on *The Divine Legation* was opened, he wrote, "by a pretended *Country Clergyman*, but in Reality a Writer of a Weekly News Paper; and with such Excess of Insolence and Malice, as the Public had never yet seen on any Occasion whatsoever". (p. iv.) The references to Webster remain unchanged in the reprinting of the Preface in the third edition. He is not actually named until the fourth edition in 1765. (Evans, *Warburton and the Warburtonians*, pp. 67–70.)

3 Francis Hare, Bishop of Chichester, had died in April 1740. His attention had been drawn to Warburton on the publication of *The Alliance between Church and State* in 1736 and he thereafter acted as critic and friend advising on subsequent publications and endeavouring to assist his promotion. (Evans, *Warburton and the Warburtonians*, pp. 46, 51, 67–70.) The paragraph to his memory is included in the third edition but in a slightly modified form.

4 The compliment to "THE TWO UNIVERSITIES" as "the last Supports of a corrupt declining Age" did not appear in the third edition. Warburton had described "the candid Regard his Book met with" at the Universities as "his supreme Honour. A Writer neglected or condemned by them," he said, "does but vainly struggle to save himself from Oblivion." (*The Divine Legation*, Vol. 2, Part I, 2nd edn., p. xv.)

5 Oxford and Cambridge scholars were among Warburton's many critics and enemies. One of the earliest attacks against *The Divine Legation* came from Oxford in a sermon of 1739 preached by William Romaine and intended to show Warburton's reasoning as "absurd, and destructive of all Revelation". (William Romaine, *The Divine Legation of Moses demonstrated from his having made express Mention of, and insisted so much on the Doctrine of a future State: Whereby* Mr.

will be wiser. I can assure you that the more ingenious and promising of those that are getting up in this place are much devoted to you. Your books are in their hands, and they value themselves upon the esteem they have for them. On this account, I cannot enough rejoice at your editions of our two great Poets.[6] Young people will be reading such things. And the acquaintance, they make by this means with their Commentator, leads them afterwards much farther. I know this by some experience. At the same time, I must own to you, my own case was different; and having this occasion to speak of it, I will tell you what it was.

For the first years of my residence in the University, when I was labouring through the usual courses of Logic, Mathematics, and Philosophy, I heard little of your name and writings. And the little I did hear, was not likely to encourage a young man, that was under direction, to enquire further after either. In the mean time, I grew up into the use of a little common sense; my commerce with the people of the place was enlarged. Still the clamours increased against you, and the appearance of your second volume opened many mouths.[7] I was then Batchelor of Arts; and, having no immediate business on my hands, I was led by a spirit of perverseness to see what there was in these decried volumes, that had given such offence.

To say the truth, there had been so much apparent bigotry and insolence in the invectives I had heared, though echoed, as was said, from men of note amongst us, that I wished, perhaps, out of pure spite, to find them ill founded. And I doubt, I was half determined in your favour, before I knew any thing of the merits of the case.

The effect of all this was, that I took the D. L. down with me into the country, where I was going to spend the summer of, I think, 1740, with my friends. I there read the three volumes at my leisure, and with the impression I shall never forget.[8] I returned to College the Winter following, not so properly your convert, as all over spleen and prejudice against your defamers. From that time, I think, I am to date my friendship with you. There was something in your mind, still more than in the matter of your book, that struck me. In a word, I grew a constant reader of you. I enquired after your other works. I got the Alliance into my hands;[9] and met with the Essay on *Portents and Prodigies*, which last I liked the better, and still like it, because I understood it was most abused by those who owed you no good-will.[10] Things were in this

Warburton's Attempt to demonstrate the Divine Legation of Moses from his Omission of a future State is proved to be absurd, and destructive of all Revelation. A Sermon Preached before the University of Oxford at St. Mary's, March 4. 1739.)

6 Warburton's edition of Shakespeare published in eight volumes in 1747; and his edition of Pope first published in nine volumes in 1751.

7 The second volume of *The Divine Legation* aroused as much controversy as the first. It was published in 1741.

8 The three volumes of *The Divine Legation* (Volume I and Volume II in two parts) were not in fact available until 1741. No record exists in the surviving correspondence of that year of RH's first reading of them.

9 *The Alliance between Church and State, or, the Necessity and Equity of an Established Religion and a Test-Law Demonstrated*, 1736. A copy of this work is amongst the Warburton collection in the Emmanuel College Library.

10 A *Critical and Philosophical Enquiry into the Causes of Prodigies and Miracles, as related by Historians. With an Essay towards restoring a Method and Purity in History* was published in 1727. It was Warburton's second book. Unlike his later works he did not reprint it and it does not appear to have provoked much controversy at the time. RH's enthusiasm for the book abated, so much so that he omitted it from his edition of Warburton's *Works* (1788).

train, when the Comment on Pope appeared.[11] That comment, and the connexion I chanced then to have with Sir E. L. made me a poor critic.[12] And in that condition you found me.[13] I became, on the sudden, your acquaintance; and am now happy in being your friend. – You have here a slight sketch of my history; at least, of the only part of it, which will ever deserve notice. But in giving it, I have wandered too far from my purpose, to which I return.

As I said, I cannot easily bring myself to give up the old Preface. Otherwise, this has the advantage greatly in many respects. T. is a more creditable dunce than W.[14] And the subject is not so personal as the other. As to the manner of introducing it, I can trust your judgment to choose the best. I cannot but think what you mention an extremely proper one. But of this I cannot determine so well, as I have not seen the discourse itself. But, by the way, what do you think to do with the Appendix to this volume against *Tillard* and *Sykes*?[15] I would not lose them on any account. And why might not T. rank with them? After all, keep me but the old Preface in some shape or other, and I will have no dispute with you about the *place*.

You have my best thanks for your observations on the second volume.[16] I need not say how much it flatters my vanity and my laziness to find them so few. But what I have most reason to value myself upon, is in reprobating, as I had done in my own mind, the two notes you lay your finger upon. I am certainly, I begin to say to myself, a

11 *A Critical and Philosophical Commentary on Mr. Pope's Essay on Man. In which is contain'd A Vindication of the said Essay from the Misrepresentations of Mr. De Resnel, the French Translator, and of Mr. De Crousaz, . . . the Commentator*, 1742.

12 RH's third publication, a critical edition of Horace's *Ars Poetica* (1749) with "an English Commentary and Notes", had been prepared partly to assist his then pupil Edward Littleton. His style of editing had been modelled on that of Warburton who is warmly complimented in the final paragraph of the Introduction (pp. xiv–xv.)

13 RH had actually sent a copy of his new publication to Warburton. (See *Prelate*, p. 1, where Warburton acknowledges the present.)

14 Dr John Taylor and William Webster. Taylor had been singled out by Warburton for an hypothesis concerning the persecution of the early Christians suggested in his *Elements of the Civil Law*, Cambridge, 1755 (pp. 578–80). In fact there is no indication that he had any intention of attacking Warburton's theories, but his subsequent defence that "he never read the D.L." is picked up and repeated by Warburton only as evidence of bigoted ignorance. (Preface to Volume II, 1758, p. ii.) The particular prominence the attack on Taylor is given (the whole of the Preface is devoted to it) was explained by Warburton as affected only by the "length" of his "animadversions" which "hindered them from finding a place in the body" of the volume. ('Preface' to the third edition, pp. xxix–xl.)

15 The second edition of Volume II of *The Divine Legation* (1742) had concluded with 'An Appendix: Containing, Some Remarks on a Book, intituled, Future Rewards and Punishments believed by the ANCIENTS, particularly the PHILOSOPHERS: wherein some Objections of the Reverend Mr. Warburton, in his Divine Legation of Moses, are considered.' The author of this work was named in the Advertisement as John Tillard. The Appendix itself was followed by a 'Post-Script' attacking Arthur Ashley Sykes, a consistent opponent of Warburton, for a "couple of random Reflexions" in his book, *The Principles and Connexion of Natural and Revealed Religion Distinctly Considered*, 1740. The third edition does not include this Appendix. Sykes is dealt with in the text and in lengthy footnotes (Volume II, part 2, pp. 111, 118ff., 122ff., 145ff., 475, 486), and the attack on Tillard was dropped in deference to his friendship with Thomas Birch. (See Evans, *Warburton and the Warburtonians*, pp. 105–6.)

16 *Q. Horatii Flacci Epistola ad Augustum. With an English Commentary and Notes. To which is added A Discourse concerning Poetical Imitation*, issued as Volume II with the accompanying edition of the *Ars Poetica*. RH was preparing a third edition of the two volumes which was published in 1757.

no despicable critic, that have so true a judgment in discerning my own faults. You had never given me the least hint of them. Yet they were both in my thoughts when I said there were some things in this second volume to strike out.[17] – You see how arrogant I am in taking the merit of this censure to myself.

The supplement to the discource on P. I. is not, I am afraid, what you would expect from it. – By the way, your hint from Tacitus furnishes a fine example of what I much wanted.[18] – To save myself trouble, and to give it the air of *agrèment*, which the fastidious, you know, look for in these matters, I have thrown it into a letter at the end of the volume; and have addressed it to Mr. Mason, because I had a mind to give him this little mark of my esteem.[19] I fancy you will have no objection to this *form* (and the rather, as the insertion of three or four sheets would hurt the order of the other discourse, which besides is already too long), and for what is wanting in the *matter*, if the *form* will not excuse that defect, I know you will easily supply it. – I am, &c.

R. Hurd.

176 To THOMAS GRAY 7 JANUARY 1757

Text: MS HC; printed, *H-M Corr*, 33; Gray, *Corr*, Letter 231*.[1]
Addressed: To/Mr Gray at/Pembroke-Hall.[2]

Dear Sir

I will beg the favour of your Milton[3] once more. I have considerd your Observations in the Paper You oblig'd me with yesterday.[4] I think them excellent and shall correct accordingly.

17 The 1757 edition of the *Epistola ad Augustum* omitted two notes of historical anecdote and a long digression concerning the Induction of *The Taming of the Shrew*. (*Epistola ad Augustum*, 1753, pp. 60–6, 96–7, 83–91.)

18 RH had wanted an example of a figurative expression which, if used improperly, would give "*pure simple Bombast*". The quotation from Tacitus appears in the Notes on the *Ars Poetica*, p. 75.

19 *A Letter to Mr. Mason; on the Marks of Imitation*. The letter was also published separately. (See *post* To Mason, 17 May 1757, n. 2.)

1 This letter with four others all addressed to Gray is included in *The Correspondence of Thomas Gray*. The originals were in a packet docketed by RH: "My letters to Mr Gray returned to me after his death by Mr Mason". They are now in a bound volume.

2 Thomas Gray (1716–71) was resident at Pembroke College having migrated there from Peterhouse in 1756. There are no indications of when he first met RH but the existence of such mutual friends as Mason and Balguy would have made a casual acquaintance possible for some years. Gray was at this time putting the finishing touches to his two odes *The Progress of Poesy* and *The Bard* which were published in the following year.

3 A copy of Milton, probably the one here referred to, was included in the sale of Gray's books and manuscripts in 1851. It was described as "Milton (John). Poetical works, 2 vol. . ..12mo. Lond. 1730–38. This is a very interesting book; it is interleaved throughout, the interleaving having thereon an abundance of passages in MS. selected from the Scriptures, and from various Authors, Ancient and Modern, wherein a similitude of thought, or expression, to that of Milton, has been considered to be observable by Gray." (*Catalogue of a Most Interesting Collection of Manuscripts and Books of the Poet Gray* . . . which will be sold by auction, by Messrs. S. Leigh Sotheby & John Wilkinson . . . on August 28th, 1851, lot no. 92.)

4 Gray's "observations" relate to the *Letter to Mr. Mason; on the Marks of Imitation* on which RH was currently at work. No copy of them has been traced.

The only one of the least consequence which sticks with me is your hint about the Introduction. And I owe it to your frankness, to tell You my sincere sentiments. I hate the hypocrisy of those men, who think to cover their dullness under the mask of piety, as much as You can do. I know too what is to be said for those who have not devoted themselves to a Profession: And still further for those who read the Poets, not for amusement only, but to contend with the best of them. I honour, in a word, true poetry and true Poets as much as any body. And I think, in particular, with You, that Mr Pope's apologies for himself were very needless. Yet still in my own case I must profess to You with sincerity, that what I say in the Letter is my real opinion.[5] The Profession, I am of, is a sacred one. And tho' it does not oblige me to renounce the poets, my business, I think, should lie elsewhere. I assure You, I take this design to be but a decent one in my circumstances, and, considering the circumstances of the time, an absolute Duty. So that when these things are out of my hands, and the few Dialogues I mentiond to You, I have determin'd long since to pass the remainder of my Life (I mean if in that Remainder I do anything as a writer) in the concerns of my own Profession.

However there are some things in the Introduction put more strongly than they needed to have been, and these I shall soften; principally because what I leave will then be understood, not as words of course, but as my real meaning.

You will think I treat You very formally, in entering into this serious explanation. I do it to shew You on what grounds, and with what reluctance, I deny myself the use of any part of your kind Intimations to me.

I am, Dear Sir Your very Oblig'd humble Servant

R Hurd.

Eman: Friday morning.[6]

177 To WILLIAM WARBURTON — 9 JANUARY 1757

Text: *Prelate*, 161.

Cambridge, January 9th, 1757.

. . .

You may be sure I was not a little pleased with the *home* things you say in your letter to –.[1] I could not resist the temptation of taking a copy of the *first* part of it. You will guess for what reason, and will excuse the liberty. I wonder your correspondent could be so much off his guard as to give you such an opening. It was very indiscreet to bring

5 RH had been nominated to the living of Thurcaston in November 1756 (see *ante* To Littleton, 20 October 1756) and begins his *Letter* with a determination henceforth to renounce the "flowery regions" of poetry. "Yet in saying this", he continues, "I would not be thought to assume that severe character; which, tho' sometimes the garb of reason, is oftener, I believe, the mask of dullness, or of something worse . . . I may recollect with pleasure, but must never live over again

Pieriosque dies, et amantes carmina somnos."

(*Letter to Mr. Mason*, pp. 4–5.)

6 A copy of this letter kept by RH (now at Hartlebury Castle) is dated in his own hand "7. Jan. 1757".

1 Unidentified. The letter from Warburton to which this is a reply is printed in *Letters from a Late Eminent Prelate* (pp. 159–60) but contains no reference to an enclosed letter to another correspondent.

you and his politicians so near together. I honour your frankness in telling him so roundly what you thought of the *latter*.

Your generosity to the Dunciad-hero exemplifies the just observation you make in the letter *to the Editor of the three Letters*, "that excess, though in the social passions, lays us more open to *popular censure* than even the total want of them."[2] I say this the rather because your calumniators, you may be sure, have not failed to buzz about this quondam connexion with a man who so little deserved the honour of it. But the triumphs of such men are ever owing to their dulness or their *meanness*. The *latter* is the case at present. Having no affections themselves, it is no wonder they are not liable to such illusions; and judging from themselves, it is no wonder they condemn in others what they have not *hearts* good enough to understand. For, as the virtuous Cowley said well –

> Th' heroic exaltations of good
> Are so far from understood
>   We count them vice –
> We look not upon virtue in her height,
> On her supreme idea, brave and bright,
>   In the original light:
> But as her beams reflected pass
> Thro' our nature, or ill custom's glass.[3]

And now let your revilers make their best of your acquaintance with M.C. Esq.

But I have more to say to your quondam Authorship. You have a right to undervalue your first attempts in literature as much as you please. The so much greater things, you have done since, are your warrant for so doing. But I should not be very patient of this language from any other. The truth is, and I am not afraid to say it roundly to any man: not *one* of all the wretches that have written or rail against you,

2 *A Letter to the Editor of the Letters on the Spirit of Patriotism, The Idea of a Patriot-King, and The State of Parties, &c. Occasioned by the Editor's Advertisement*, 1749, p. 27. In response to RH's enthusiasm for his *Enquiry into the Causes of Prodigies and Miracles*, 1727 (see *ante* To Warburton, 30 December 1756), Warburton had related the circumstances of its publication: "I was very much a boy when I wrote that thing about prodigies, and I had never the courage to look into it since, so I have quite forgot all the nonsense that it contains. But since you mention it, I will tell you how it came to see the light. I met many years ago with an ingenious Irishman at a Coffee-house near Gray's-Inn, where I lodged. He studied the law, and was very poor. I had given him money for many a dinner; and at last I gave him those papers, which he sold to the booksellers for more money than you would think, much more than they were worth. But I must finish the history both of the Irishman and the papers. Soon after, he got acquainted with Sir William Younge, wrote for Sir Robert, and was made Attorney-General of Jamaica: he married there an opulent widow, and died very rich, a few years ago here in England: but of so scoundrel a temper, that he avoided ever coming into my sight: so that the memory of all this intercourse between us has been buried in silence till this moment. And who should this man be but one of the heros of the Dunciad, Concannen by name." (*Prelate*, pp. 159–60.) Warburton had met Matthew Concanen (1701–49), a miscellaneous writer, in 1726 and remained on good terms with him until he left for Jamaica in January 1732. Some time before this an attack on Pope had led to Concanen's inclusion in the 1729 edition of the *Dunciad* as a competitor in the diving match. (*Dunciad*, ii. 289.) At the time this does not appear to have affected Warburton's friendship for him and there is some doubt as to the accuracy of these later accusations against Concanen. (Evans, *Warburton and the Warburtonians*, pp. 24–6; Nichols, *Illusts*., ii. 192–3.)

3 Cowley, 'Brutus', *Pindarique Odes*, ii. 5–13 (*Poems*, 1656). (. . . vice: alas our Sight's so ill,/That things which swiftest Move seem to stand still./We look . . . our own nature . . .)

and who affect to find great consolation in this first escape of your pen, was ever able in the *acmè* of his parts and judgment to produce any thing half so good. Mr. Balguy and I read it together some years ago, and we agreed there was the same ingenuity of sentiment and vigour of expression as in your other works; in a word, that it was a fine effort of genius, not yet formed indeed and matured, but even in this juvenility portending plainly enough what you were one day to be capable of. I have read it again very lately, and I think of it just the same. So that I almost blame your anxiety about Curl's edition.[4] It was not worth, perhaps, your owning in form. But your reputation was not concerned to suppress it. One sees in it your early warmth in the cause of virtue and public liberty, and your original way of striking out new hints on common subjects. There are many fine observations up and down. Amongst which, that in the Dedication, on the characters of the three great Romans, which you have since adopted in the notes on Pope, is admirable.[5] In running it over this last time, I find I have stolen a hint from you which I was not aware of. It is what I say of the Apes of Plato and Aristotle, in p. 79. of Comm. on Ep. to Aug. taken from what you say in p. 9. on that subject.[6] I should not have said so much on this matter (for I am as much above the thought of flattering you as you are above the want of it) but that I think your shyness in acknowledging this little prolusion of your genius, gives a handle to your low malignant cavillers which you need not have afforded them. I must further request it of you, as a favour, that if Knapton has not destroyed the copies, you would oblige me with half a dozen or so, which you may trust me to dispose of in a proper manner.[7] I ask it the rather, because I could never get one into my own possession. I have tried several times, and now very lately this winter out of Baker's sale, but it was bought up before I could order it.[8] Such a curiosity have both your friends and enemies to treasure up this proscribed volume.

4 According to Warburton, Edmund Curll (1675–1747) bought the rights to the *Enquiry* a "few years" before his death and had intended to publish a new edition. Warburton, however, alarmed at the idea of being published by so notorious a bookseller and reluctant to see a reissue, wrote to his own publisher, John Knapton, and instructed him to buy the book back, which he was able to do. (*Prelate*, p. 160.)

5 Warburton argues in the Dedication that "in describing the Virtues of a great Mind, and tracing out the benign Influences of a moral Constellation, 'tis allowed to display and heighten the bright Side of each glowing Virtue; and strive to reconcile any cross Appearance of an excentric Motion". It is therefore justifiable to call Caesar's "Ambition, the Love of Glory, because joined with Clemency"; Cato's "Pride, an honest Scorn, because arising from the Enmity of Vice"; and Cicero's "Vanity, a conscious Merit, because never spareing in another's Praise". (*Enquiry*, pp. xi–xii.) The three great Romans appear in a less favourable light in Warburton's note to line 215 in Epistle I of Pope's *Moral Essays*. There they are represented as ambitious, proud and vain with no mitigating qualities though without any taint of each other's vices.

6 Admiring imitators (the "Apes") of Plato were said to copy him in making themselves round shouldered, and the imitators of Aristotle pretended to stutter. Both Warburton and RH use this illustration but in different contexts. (*Enquiry*, p. 9; *Epistola ad Augustum*, 1753, p. 79.)

7 One copy of the *Enquiry* is amongst Warburton's works at Hartlebury Castle. It was not published by John and Paul Knapton but they had acquired the copyright on Warburton's behalf from Edmund Curll. (See *Prelate*, p. 160.) Their company had gone bankrupt two years previously in 1755. (*Ibid*., pp. 143–4.)

8 Samuel Baker (d.1778), an eminent bookseller and auctioneer, had been issuing auction catalogues since 1745. Nichols regards this "very respectable *Bibliopole*" as perhaps "the first who brought the practice of selling books by auction into general use". (*Lit. Anecs*., iii. 630.) He was succeeded by his partner George Leigh and great-nephew, Samuel Sotheby, by whose name the company later became known. (Frank Hermann, *Sotheby's. Portrait of an Auction House*, 1980, pp. 2–9.) The catalogue of the sale referred to here has not been traced.

I have thought again of this Preface to the second vol. of the L. I think it not so proper to introduce it before the second part. I am besides afraid of your altering it too much.[9] I will tell you then what has come into my head. When one of these days you make a complete collection of your works, you must by all means put together your controversial pieces by themselves. They will make, I believe, about a couple of volumes. And this Preface may come in amongst the rest, entire, as it now stands under the title of "the Preface to the first edition of the second vol. in 1740." I think this proposal, on all accounts, the best. And then Taylor may stand where you first designed, and where indeed he will figure to most advantage. Pray tell me immediately what you think of this proposal.[10]

I shall perhaps write again in a post or two. For I have other matters to trouble you with in abundance. But I have tired you pretty well for the present.

R. Hurd.

178 To WILLIAM WARBURTON 22 JANUARY 1757

Text: *Prelate*, 168.

. . .

Nothing can be kinder than your two favours of the 12th and 15th.[1] I begin with the last, first.

You are very good to let me have my humour in the little quotation.[2] To say the truth, my only end in it is to gratify my own spleen. I would give a pack of wretches to understand, that your friends can appeal to the Essay as well as they.[3] And when they know this, they will be sensible perhaps of the impotency of their malice, if of nothing else. I like the Speaker's judgment very well.[4] I did not think he had read his Milton to so good purpose.[5]

You are too polite, as well as too kind for me. Since you will have it so, the *Shield*

9 RH refers to the Preface to the first edition of *The Divine Legation*, Volume II. Warburton had intended to substitute a new Preface to the third edition whilst RH had argued for retaining the original. His change of heart may only have been temporary; when the new edition appeared it was with both Prefaces though with some alterations to the first. (See *ante* To Warburton, 30 December 1756.)

10 Warburton replied, "I am glad you consent to my first thoughts of omitting the former short Preface, at present at least. As Cibber supplied the place of Tibbald . . . so shall Taylor take place of Webster." (Warburton to RH, 12 January 1757, *Prelate*, p. 164.)

1 *Prelate*, pp. 164–6, 166–7.

2 Warburton had written "I trust to your judgment about the quotation". (*Prelate*, p. 166); probably a reference to the "Apes of Plato and Aristotle". (See preceding letter.)

3 RH picks up Warburton's phrase "that little Essay" in referring to the *Enquiry into the Causes of Prodigies and Miracles*.

4 Still alluding to the *Enquiry* Warbuton had written "I remember, the Speaker (who had the curiosity to have it bought for him at an auction) spoke to me of it in his bombast way; but I thought no better of it for that, because I imagined the turgidness of a young scribbler, might please his magnificent spirit, always upon the stilts." (*Prelate*, p. 166.) The Speaker (of the House of Commons) had been Arthur Onslow, who held the post from 1727 to 1754.

5 The last paragraph of the *Enquiry* is plagiarised from Milton's *Areopagitica*. (See *The Prose of John Milton* . . . Edited by J. Max Patrick, 1968, p. 324.)

shall pass as my property.[6] I often think of the old fable, so well told in Mr. Allen's picture.[7] What a figure should I make if my feathers were well plucked? 'Tis true, I have this consolation: there would be none but Eagle's feathers found upon me.

You flatter me in saying, I have entered into your idea of the *callida junctura*.[8] I thought, from looking into Dacier, that it wanted explanation. But I never send a hint to you without being a gainer by it. The short dialogue you transcribe from Shirley is incomparable.[9] It will make a fine conclusion to my note, and shall stand instead of the two paltry observations I make on the subject of it. The remark will be *new* too, as well as pertinent.

I doubt you are too indulgent to the hypercritical emendation.[10] It is taking an extravagant liberty with the text. But I take for granted you see nothing absurd, at least, in the conjecture, or you would have mentioned it. So it shall e'en stand where it does, as it will help to enliven a little a very dry note.

I am mightily pleased with your objection to my main principle, and your answer to it.[11] It is a very material consideration; and you may be sure I shall make my best use of it. I understand your polite hint to Mr. Balguy, and shall acquaint him with it.[12]

I come now to your other letter. – I am proud of the liberty you give me of copying

6 Warburton had written "You have so well polished Virgil's Shield, that it is yours of right, and I desire you will give me leave to quote it *from you*." (*Prelate*, p. 166.) He refers to a passage in the Notes on the *Epistola ad Augustum* where RH explains his interpretation of the use of "*double senses*". As an example he takes Virgil's description of the shield of Aeneas, which had already been discussed and explained, he says, "for the first time" by Warburton in *The Divine Legation*. (*Epistola ad Augustum*, 1757, note to l. 97, pp. 67–70.)

7 According to the sale catalogue of the contents of Prior Park (1769) there was a painting of "The Fable of the Fowls plucking the Crow of his borrow'd feathers" in the dining room. There is no notice of the artist. (Boyce, *The Benevolent Man*, pp. 103, 106–7.)

8 "You have so well entered into my idea of the *callida junctura*, that I think it excellent." (*Prelate*, p. 166.) RH was working on a new note for the forthcoming edition of the *Ars Poetica* (1757) defining *callida junctura*. It is, he wrote, "in effect, but another word for *Licentious Expression*" and as "well tempered licence one of the greatest charms of all poetry" (p. 57). In this, he disagreed with Andre Dacier and the R.P. Sanadon, earlier editors of Horace, who define the meaning too narrowly, he says, and fail to show "the whole of what the poet intended by it". (*Ars Poetica*, 1757, note to l. 47, pp. 47–60; *Oeuvres d'Horace, en Latin, Traduites en Francois par M. Dacier, et le P. Sanadon. Avec les Remarques Critiques, Historiques et Geographiques, de l'un & de l'autre*, Amsterdam, 1735, viii. 95–6.)

9 As an instance of the extremes of "*Licentious Expression*" Warburton had sent RH a short dialogue taken from a comedy by James Shirley (1596–1666), *The Changes, or Love in a Maze*, 1632. It appears in the Notes to the *Ars Poetica* at pp. 58–60.

10 In the course of his explication of *callida junctura* RH had proposed an emendation to a line from *Cymbeline* following an earlier alteration made by Warburton. His text ran:

And like the tyrannous breathing of the North
Shakes all our Buds from blowing. Cymb. A.1. S.5.

RH suggested that "shuts" should be substituted for "shakes". (*Ars Poetica*, note to l. 47, pp. 53–5.)

11 Warburton had enclosed some suggested additions to RH's dialogue on the Constitution. He had endeavoured, he said, "to obviate an objection that might be retorted on your main principle. You may venture the freedom of it", he added, "in the mouth of a Maynard". (*Prelate*, p. 167.)

12 In concluding his letter Warburton had been drawn into a discussion of the qualities of vanity and pride. Having analysed these to his own satisfaction he called upon RH to consult Thomas Balguy, for, he said, he "is one of the best judges I know . . . And he has waded very far into the great *Latrina* of humanity, without suffering himself to be defiled in the passage." (*Prelate*, p. 167.)

any of your papers. I promise you, it shall not be my fault, if any improper use be ever made of them.[13]

I am ready to quarrel with you for saying one word of your upbraiders.[14] This was not treating me with your usual goodness. Alas, I understand the condition of these poor creatures so well, that if you would be ruled by me, you should not deprive them of this little consolation of their envy. I know, too, the reason of your former distaste to Mr. P. It was not only his connexions with some you had reason to think ill of, but his *abuse of one you loved.*[15] Was not this the best of reasons? Yet it could not be but that two such men would come at length to understand each other. And when you did, nature had taken care that you should be fast friends for life. But your worthless enemies are as quick at espying contradictions in your life, as in your writings. And the cause is not unlike. They want *hearts* to understand a consistency in moral action; just as their bad *heads* will not let them find out a consistency in rational discourse.

The more I think of it, the more I am satisfied with Taylor's allotted station in the new edition – *Sedet aeternumque sedebit.* – You may be sure I subscribe to your aphorism.[16]

I shall rely on your thinking of me when you see Mr. Knapton.[17] I have a deal of the Speaker's curiosity. I would have every thing that you have ever written in my possession.

Nothing but the love of order (as befits a good critic) could have kept me from touching on the paragraph I now come to, first. You delight me above measure in saying that you are vigorously employed about the *third* volume of the Legation.[18] I do not expect to see all your plans filled up. For, besides that you have many upon your hands, you will always be forming new ones. But this favourite, this capital one must be completed. It signifies little that people clamour for it and expect it. You owe it to yourself, to truth, and to posterity. You think it immaterial perhaps that this

13 RH had taken a copy of part of a letter to another (unidentified) correspondent. (See previous letter, n. 1.)

14 RH had himself raised the subject of Warburton's "calumniators" and "revilers". (See preceding letter.) In reply, Warburton wrote, ". . . Those villains, if any such there be, who upbraid me with my acquaintance and correspondence with the gentlemen of the Dunciad, know I at the same time proclaimed it to the world in Tibbald's edition of Shakespear, in Mr. P. 's life time. – Till his letters were published I had as indifferent an opinion of his morals as they pretended to have." (*Prelate*, p. 164.)

15 Lewis Theobald (1688–1744). Warburton had made Theobald's acquaintance in the late 1720s and had contributed to his edition of Shakespeare, published in 1734. Theobald's attacks on Pope's edition of Shakespeare meanwhile had made the poet his enemy and Theobald became the first hero of the *Dunciad.*

16 John Taylor comes under attack in the Preface to the third edition of Volume II of *The Divine Legation* (pp. i–xl.) Warburton had said of him "*that the most learned Dunce when, or wherever, he exists, remains still the same Dunce in which he came into the world*". (*Prelate*, p. 164; see also *ante* To Warburton, 30 December 1756, n. 14.)

17 RH had asked Warburton for half a dozen copies of the *Enquiry into the Causes of Prodigies and Miracles* if Knapton had any still in stock. (See preceding letter, n. 7.)

18 "You will be pleased when I tell you that I am vigorously engaged both in the second and last vol. of the Divine Legation." (*Prelate*, p. 165.) The first and second volumes of *The Divine Legation* were designed to "explain and discriminate the distinct and various natures of the PAGAN" and the "JEWISH" religions. The third volume was to treat, finally, of the "CHRISTIAN" religion. (Vol. II, Part 2, Third Edition, p. 525.) However, only part of the concluding section, the ninth book, was ever completed. It was printed after Warburton's death in RH's edition of his works.

monument of yourself should be entire. And the *virtuosi*, for any thing I know, might like it the better for its not being so. But who hereafter will be able to throw those lights on *religion* which these preparatory volumes now enable you to throw upon it? And would you envy these lights to the *ages to come*, that are more and more likely to stand in need of them! I only put these questions to shew you that nothing in my opinion deserves so much the whole stretch and application of your parts and industry to finish, as this great work. I dare say you will make great improvements in the other volumes, for you speak of great alterations. But the completion of this last, is your life's *instant business*. And again I must express my delight at your saying, that it *shall not be deferred*.

As for the discourse on *similar rites and customs*, I think it of great importance and curiosity.[19] And what you design upon the subject is fully sufficient. The philosophy of that question will of course be explained in illustrating your instances. The true principle was delivered in that famous paragraph in the D.L. which Middleton in a testy humour bit at, and broke his teeth upon.[20] You love to be complaisant to your friends. But all my wordy dissertation is only a hint catched from you, and applied to a single inconsiderable subject.[21] You will now consider it in a much larger and nobler view. Besides, is it for me to prevent you on any subject by the chance of writing on it first?

I most firmly believe your generous declaration, *that you shall never wittingly advance one falsehood, or conceal or disguise one truth*.[22] And this it is which, besides some tender regards of another nature, makes me so anxiously wish that your health and spirits may hold out with your designs. It is a serious truth, that the brightest visions that were ever painted on the human understanding are liable to many accidents. But your age, your vigorous constitution, but above all your serene and happy life, disturbed by none of those great or little passions which make such ravages in other minds, are so many arguments for the durability of yours. And with this grateful presage I conclude my long letter; for which, though it needs an excuse, I will make none, as knowing the entire indulgence you give to every trouble that comes to you from, dearest Sir, &c.

R. Hurd.

Emmanuel College, January 22d, 1757.

19 The discourse was to consist of "instances of similar customs of a striking nature, which all would judge imitations . . . yet by reason of the distance of place . . . &c. which gave birth to them, we must needs pronounce no imitations". (*Prelate*, p. 165.) It may have been intended as an extension or amplification of Book IV, Sect. 6, but was not subsequently included in this form, and has not been identified elsewhere. (See also n. 20, below.)

20 In the second volume of *The Divine Legation* (first edition), Warburton had stated that our understanding of antiquity was frequently obscured by the mistaken assumption that civil and religious customs were "borrowed" from earlier societies. On the contrary, he asserted, they arose independently in each case, but showed similarities deriving from our "one common nature", either "improved by reason, or debased by superstition". (Vol. II, Part 1, pp. 355–6.) Conyers Middleton had taken exception to this attack on an "established principle". He had just prepared a new edition of his book, *A Letter from Rome, Shewing an exact Conformity between Popery and Paganism; or, the Religion of the Present Romans derived from that of their Heathen Ancestors*, Fourth Edition, 1741; and as he pointed out in *A Postscript* this attack "if it can be supposed to have any force, overthrows the whole credit and use of my present work". (p. 227.) (See also *ante* To Devey, [December 1745/January 1746], n. 2.)

21 RH refers to 'A Discourse concerning Poetical Imitation', appended to *Epistola ad Augustum*, 1753.

22 *Prelate*, p. 165.

January 23d, 1757.

I had written the above letter yesterday, foreseeing that I should not have leisure for it to day. Last night I was favoured with yours of the 18th; which, with the inclosed paper, I shall shew to Mr. Balguy this afternoon, and write you our joint thoughts of it by Monday's post.[23] Once more, adieu.

179 To THOMAS GRAY [MARCH/APRIL 1757]

Text: MS HC; printed, *H-M Corr*, 35; Gray, *Corr*, Letter 237*.
Addressed: To/Mr Gray of Pembroke

Dear Sir

You want amusement at this time. I therefore take the liberty to inclose a translation of Aristotle's Ode, which I have thoughts of printing in the notes on Horace.[1] In the main, it reads easily enough; but You will tell me what it wants of being to your mind. Mr Nevile was so good to turn it for me, and I know will take a pleasure to correct it according to any hints You shall give him. I need not say that the Original is in Diog. Laertius and in the 15th book, I think, of Athenaeus.[2]

Dear Sir, Your faithful humble Servant

R Hurd

Eman: Tuesday.[3]

180 To WILLIAM MASON 15 MAY 1757

Text: MS HC, excerpts made by Richard Hurd, nephew of the writer; published, *MLR* 45 1950, pp. 158, 161, 162.

Cambridge 15. May. 1757.[1]

Dear Mr Mason

– I was hurried down, on the sudden, into Leicestershire, where I stayed about a fortnight, was inducted, and let my tythes.[2] The full value is something better than

[23] Warburton's letter survives (*Prelate*, p. 172); RH's reply has not been traced. The "inclosed paper" was "for a note at p. 484. second vol. D.L. where I [Warburton] enter upon the book of Job".

[1] Aristotle's Ode to Virtue and the translation "from the same hand which has so agreeably entertained us of late with some spirited imitations of Horace" [Thomas Nevile] appeared in the new edition of Horace in a note to l. 219. (*Ars Poetica*, 1757, pp. 159–62.)

[2] *Diogenes Laertius*, v. 7–8; *Athenaeus*, xv. 696.

[3] The letter was endorsed by RH's nephew "Suppose 1757". It was evidently written early in the year since the new edition of Horace was at the press by May. (See following letter.)

[1] Originally found between fly-leaf and back cover of *Poems by William Mason*, M.A., 1764.

[2] RH was instituted to Thurcaston on 16 February and inducted on Ladyday (25 March). The agreements he made to let out his tithes are recorded in his Thurcaston account book, and dated "L.Day 1757". The annual rent comes to a total of £167. 19s. (*Account Book 1756-63*, Leics. RO, DE1416/83.)

200£ a year. The place agreable enough for a Summer Residence. I doubt whether I shall be fond of it in Winter. –

Cambridge 15 May 1757.[3]

– The new edition of Horace has been delayed, for want of paper.[4] We now go on swimmingly. And the whole, I fancy, will be printed off by the commencement.[5] The Letter is to be improved in some respects.[6] After all, it will not be altogether what, on your account, rather than my own, I could wish it." –

Cambridge 15 May 1757[7]

– "I cannot tell whether you read Mr. Hume's Natural History of Religion.[8] If you did, you will be pleased with a pamphlet, this moment come out against it, called *Remarks on Mr. David Hume's Nat. Hist. of Religion: addressed to Dr. Warburton.*[9] It is finely written, in the Warburtonic manner; but in such a way as puzzles us all extremely to guess at the writer. I long to hear what Dr. W. says to it. You must by all means see it directly." –

181 To Sir EDWARD LITTLETON 29 MAY 1757

Text: MS STAFFS RO D1413/1; unpublished.
Addressed: To/Sir Edward Littleton Bart/at his Seat in/Staffordshire.
Postmarked: CAMBRIDGE

Camb. 29. May. 1757.

Dear Sir Edward

I have your favour of the 19th and sent away the Print of Inigo Jones immediately to Mr Hogarth, as You desired.[1] I hope to see a very fine picture made from it, and

3 Originally found opposite p. 29 of Vol. 1 of RH's *Works*.

4 The third edition of RH's Horace was being printed by Joseph Bentham, Printer to the University, for Thurlbourn and Woodyer, the Cambridge booksellers.

5 The Commencement fell in July, but the new edition of Horace seems not to have been published until August.

6 *A Letter to Mr. Mason; on the Marks of Imitation.*

7 Originally found opposite the title-page of RH's *Remarks on Mr. David Hume's Essay on the Natural History of Religion: Addressed to the Rev. Dr. Warburton*, 1757.

8 David Hume, *Four Dissertations. I. The Natural History of Religion. II. Of the Passions. III. Of Tragedy. IV. Of the Standard of Taste*, 1757, advertised for sale in the January/February list of the *London Magazine*.

9 *Remarks on Mr. David Hume's Essay on the Natural History of Religion* was published anonymously in early May 1757. The work was instigated and partly composed by Warburton who was roused to fury by Hume's dissertation. "In a word", he wrote to RH, "the Essay is to establish an Atheistic naturalism, like Bolingbroke, and he goes upon one of Bol.'s capital arguments, that Idolatry and Polytheism were before the worship of the one God. It is full of absurdities." (*Prelate*, p. 175.) He filled the margins of his own copy with his criticisms, and then passed the "skeleton" to RH who corrected and amplified the notes, and added an introduction and conclusion. Although Warburton had proposed that RH should make this his "Summer's amusement", the pamphlet was completed in a few weeks. (*Prelate*, pp. 174–7; Evans, *Warburton and the Warburtonians*, pp. 214–16.)

1 Littleton had commissioned Hogarth to make a copy in oils of Van Dyck's print of Inigo Jones (possibly that given by him to RH in 1750; see *ante* To Littleton, 9 March and 29 March 1750). The copy was completed fairly rapidly as Littleton heard from Benjamin Wilson. "Hogarth", he wrote, "has done the picture of Jones and I like the head very much. Perhaps if you saw the picture you would think some few alterations wo[uld] be necessary. To speak truly and like an

think You do right to employ these great Masters, when they are most at leisure.[2] You do not say one word of your Busts.[3]

I am sorry, your enquiries have hitherto been attended with so little success.[4] If You spend the rest of the Year in Staffordshire, I shall have a chance for the pleasure of passing some time with You. For tho' I have not yet determind of my Summer-months, I fully intend, before they are over, to see my friends in Shropshire, and to return, by way of Tedgely, if You are there, to this place, where I have thoughts of passing the next winter.

Some letters have passed betwixt Mr Horton and me about a Tutor for his Son.[5] I believe I shall send him one about Midsummer, who is so recommended to me (for I have little knowledge of him myself) that I dare say he will be very proper for this charge. He is Brother to Dr Gisborne, of whom I fancy You have some remembrance.[6]

You will do me the favour to present my humble Service to Lady Littleton. All your friends here are well and desire their compliments. I need not say how entirely I am, Dear Sir, Your most Obliged & affectionate humble Servant

R Hurd.

182 To WILLIAM MASON 16 JUNE 1757

Text: MS HC, excerpt made by Richard Hurd, nephew of the writer; published, *MLR* 45 1950, p. 156.

Camb. 16. June 1757.[1]

– "Mr Gray left us this day. He talks of returning in a fortnight, but so uncertainly,

honest man it is rather a little Story. But pray let this go no farther." (Wilson to Littleton, [summer] 1757, Staffs. RO, D1178/3.) Hogarth himself did not write to Littleton until 19 May 1758 when he explained that he had finished the picture a year before but had not notified him assuming that he would soon be in town and would call to see it. A further delay ensued because of problems with the frame and Hogarth's losing Littleton's "directions", but he promised to send the finished work at the end of September [1758]. The painting is now in the Queen's House, Greenwich. (Ronald Paulson, *Hogarth: His Life, Art, and Times*, 1971, ii. 243–4.)

2 This opinion of Hogarth is in marked contrast to the contempt RH felt for him in 1750. (See *ante* To Littleton, 9 March 1750.)

3 During 1755 Littleton had decided to commission a set of twelve busts from Rysbrack for his study. (Littleton to Edward Macro, 5 October 1755, *Macro Letter-book*.) By February 1756 Rysbrack had finished four (Bacon, Locke, Newton and Milton) but more than a year passed before they had been dried and "Burned" ready for display. Littleton received three of the busts at the end of June 1757, for which he paid a total of £61.13.0. (Webb, *Michael Rysbrack, Sculptor*, Appendix One. Letters from Michael Rysbrack to Sir Edward Littleton, pp. 194–97.)

4 No further reference to these enquiries has been found.

5 RH had acted as tutor at Emmanuel to Walter Horton, the eldest son of Christopher and Frances Horton, who had died in 1753. (See *ante* To Mason, 22 October 1753.) A younger son Christopher ("Kitt") was to be tutored at home and did not apparently go to either Cambridge or Oxford.

6 Thomas Gisborne (1726–1806) was a Fellow of St John's and in January 1757 had been appointed Physician to St George's Hospital. (*D.N.B.*) He was a friend of Mason and Gray and also of Thomas Balguy through whom he would have met RH and possibly Littleton. He and his younger brother Francis (1733–1821) were the sons of James Gisborne, Rector of Staveley, Derbyshire. Francis had matriculated at Peterhouse and was made B.A. in 1754 and M.A. in 1757. He became a Fellow in 1758.

1 Originally found between pp. 92 and 93 of Vol. 3 of RH's *Works*.

that I don't expect it. His Odes are so finish'd, that I have little or nothing to object.[2] I hope he will put them to the press directly. I venturd to shew him my first Dialogue between More and Waller.[3] He speaks indulgently, perhaps politely of it, but has hinted two or three things that will much improve it. I am now thinking to prepare the last of them, and to correct them all for the press, before I enter on my Summer ramblings.[4] My intention is to stay here till the end of August." –

183 To Sir EDWARD LITTLETON 3 JULY 1757

Text: MS STAFFS RO D1413/1; unpublished.
Addressed: To/Sir Edward Littleton Bart/at Tedgely Park in/Staffordshire
Postmarked: 4 IY

Dear Sir Edward

I have receivd no letter from Mr Hogarth, but have no doubt of his having the Print which I sent him.[1]

I am glad to hear so good an account of the young gentleman.[2] His tutor is Brother to Dr Gisborne, whom You remember something of. Mr Balguy and I think he will do excellently well. He is a good Scholar, and, what is most material, is a decent, sensible, well-behavd man, and has, besides, the reputation of being so perfectly good temper'd, that there is all the reason in the world to believe he will be very acceptable to his Pupil.

I wish You would let Mr Horton know, that I have spoke with Mr Gisborne about the time of his going to Catton. He finds it necessary, I perceive, to go home to his father in Derbyshire for some days, when he leaves this place; but will certainly be with Mr Horton by the end of this month.

I hope to have the pleasure of waiting upon You in the very beginning of September. What keeps me here so long is the care of a new edition of Horace, which is now in the press. As this is likely to be the standard edition, I have taken the liberty of saying two or three words, and no more, by way of address to You in the entrance of the first volume.[3]

You must excuse this freedom: And another of the same sort which our old friend, Dr Nevile, talks of requesting. It is, that You will give him leave to prefix your name

2 Gray felt that his odes, *The Bard* and *The Progress of Poesy*, were "weakly", but by June was beginning to give way to pressure from his friends to print. On 16 July they went to press (at Strawberry Hill) and by 3 August 1,000 copies had been completed. These were published by Dodsley on 8 August. (Gray, *Correspondence*, Letters 239, 240, n. 2.)

3 'Dialogue I. On Sincerity in the Commerce of the World: Between Dr. Henry More and Edmund Waller, Esq.' published in *Moral and Political Dialogues*, 1759.

4 The dialogues were completed "after a sort" by the middle of August. (See *post* To Gray, 16 August 1757; To Mason, 17 August 1757.) They were not published, however, until May 1759.

1 See *ante* To Littleton, 29 May 1757, n. 1.

2 Christopher Horton. (See *ante* To Littleton, 29 May 1757, nn. 5, 6.)

3 The third edition of RH's Horace is dedicated to Littleton in three brief paragraphs. RH assures him that he has "nothing to fear from that offensive adulation, which has so much dishonoured Letters". Indeed, he continues, "Your extreme delicacy allows me to say nothing of my obligations, which otherwise would demand my warmest acknowledgments. Permit me only to expect, that the following tract, composed originally for your use, will be accepted with candour." The second edition had been prefaced by a one-page inscription to Littleton.

in form to the epistle which he printed some time since and which was designed to be address'd to You.[4] The case is, he thinks to add several new Imitations to his old ones, and to put them together next winter into a small pocket volume.[5] On this occasion he is desirous to pay his respects to two or three of his friends. He will needs pay a compliment of this sort to me: And I fancy You will have no scruple to indulge him in the same way; and the rather, as no body more sincerely loves and honours You than our good friend.

Evry body here is much your Servant. You will do me the favour to present my best respects to Lady Littleton, and to believe me very affectionately, Dear Sir Edward, Your faithfull humble Servant

R Hurd.

Cambridge 3. July. 1757.

184 To Sir EDWARD LITTLETON 12 JULY 1757

Text: MS STAFFS RO D1413/1; unpublished.
Addressed: To/Sir Edward Littleton Bart/at Tedgely Park in/ Staffordshire
Postmarked: 13 IY

Camb. 12. July. 1757.

My Dear Sir Edward

You are much too severe to yourself and us. I confess, that public persons are the fittest for dedications in form. But I went too far in supposing that an address to a private friend is, in all cases, improper. I think the present is one of these cases; and You will find I have not misused the liberty I have taken.[1]

As to Mr Nevile's request, He would only beg leave to prefix your name to that Epistle.[2] It is to be corrected indeed; but there are no additions; none of those fine things, at least, which You are so much displeas'd with. He wishes from the real and old affection he bears You to pay You this little mark of his respect: And You must not be so rigid as to deny him. I say this, because I know he thinks to write to You himself: and You can't tell how it would mortify him to receive your refusal.

Mr Gisborne is just gone to his Father's. He will certainly be at Catton by the end

4 *The Seventeenth Epistle of the First Book of Horace Imitated* [by Thomas Nevile] had been published on 10 February 1755. (Straus, *Dodsley*, Bibliography.) It had been headed 'To Sir ** ***, Bart.' and Littleton refused again to have his full name published.

5 Nevile had published, anonymously, three separate imitations of Horace, one satire and two epistles, in 1755 and 1756. (See *ante* To Mason, 31 December 1755, n. 4, and 30 April 1756, n. 2.) His volume of *Imitations of Horace* was to contain eleven more poems (all with parallel Latin text) and was announced as "speedily" to be published in an advertisement leaf following RH's *Letter to* Mr. *Mason* (the first issue). The book was finally published on 23 March 1758. (Straus, *Dodsley*, Bibliography.)

1 A reference to the dedication (to Littleton) of RH's Horace. (See preceding letter, n. 3 and *ante* To Littleton, 12 April 1753, where the appropriate use of dedications and inscriptions is discussed.)

2 *The Seventeenth Epistle of the First Book of Horace Imitated.* Minor, mainly typographical, alterations were made to the epistle for its inclusion in the 1758 edition of Nevile's *Imitations of Horace*. The inscription was altered from "To a Friend in TOWN", to "To Sir ** ***, Bart."

of the month. I have not the least doubt of his making the young Gentleman a very good Tutor.[3]

I am mistaken if You will not be pleas'd with him on a little acquaintance, and I took the liberty to say he might depend on the pleasure of being known to You, and on your readiness to show him any civilities.

My Dear friend, You are a very Stoic, but under all characters You are sure of the affectionate regard of Your faithful humble Servt

R Hurd.

185 To THOMAS GRAY 16 AUGUST 1757

Text: MS HC; printed, *H-M Corr*, 36; Gray, *Corr*, Letter 245*.
Addressed: To/Thomas Gray Esqr/at Mrs Rogers' at Stoke/ near Windsor/Bucks[1]
Postmarked: 16 AV

Dear Sir

I give You many thanks for the favour of your Odes, which I have received after a tedious expectation.[2] You may be sure the title-page amused us a good deal, but Mr Brown has explained it.[3] It is not worth while to tell You how they are received here. But every body would be thought to admire. 'Tis true, I believe, the greater part don't understand them.

I have been amusing myself in my way, since You left us. The Letter to Mason is printed off, and I shall send You a copy very soon to Dodsley's.[4] The dialogues too are all finished after a sort; so that I shall have work enough for you against our next meeting in November.[5] I should be better pleased, if You would find work for me. And I hope You don't forget, among your other amusements this summer, your design for a history of the English poetry. You might be regulating your plan, and digesting the materials You have by You.[6] I shall teaze You perpetually, till You set about this project

3 See *ante* To Littleton, 29 May 1757, nn. 5, 6.

1 Gray's uncle, Jonathan Rogers, had lived at West End Cottage, Stoke. On his death in 1742 Mrs Gray and her sister, Mary Antrobus, retired there to live with his widow. (Gray, *Correspondence*, Letter 110, n.1.) Gray often stayed there with them.

2 Gray's *Odes* were published on 8 August. (See *ante* To Mason, 16 June 1757, n. 2.)

3 This has been generally taken as a reference to the motto from Pindar on the title-page, **ΦΩΝΑΝΤΑ ΣΥΝΕΤΟΙΣΙ** which Gray renders as "*vocal to the Intelligent alone*". (Gray, *Correspondence*, Letter 367.) Writing to Thomas Wharton a day later Gray noted that "the great objection [to the odes] is obscurity, no body knows what we would be at . . . in short the Σμνετοί appear to be still fewer, than even I expected". (Letter 246.) The Brown who provided illumination was James Brown (1709–84), President (i.e. Vice-Master) of Pembroke and a longstanding friend and admirer of Gray.

4 RH may refer to the separate edition of *Letter to Mr. Mason* or to the reprinting of the *Letter* to follow the new edition of Horace. (See *post* To Mason, 17 August 1757.)

5 Gray had expected to be back in Cambridge in November but did not in fact return until the first week of December. (Gray, *Correspondence*, Letter 256, n. 10.)

6 In the 'Advertisement' prefixed to his poem *The Fatal Sisters* published in the 1768 edition of his poems, Gray wrote: "The Author once had thoughts (in concert with a Friend) of giving *the History of English Poetry* . . . He has long since drop'd his design, especially after he had heard,

in good earnest. It is a wonderful favourite with me, and will, I am certain, in your hands be a work of much use as well as elegance.

Mason has never once writ in all this time, which I take prodigiously ill, and desire You will tell him so. Dr Warburton sends me word too, he did not keep his appointment with him of going to Durham. So that I can only conclude he is laid up of a fit of the Muse, or perhaps is gone to pay a visit to his Druids at Mona.[7]

If You give me the pleasure of hearing from You, You must write very soon.[8] For I grow sick of this place, and set out on the 29th on my summer rambles. It will be a satisfaction to hear that You are well. I am sollicitous for nothing else. For You can never want the best sort of amusements. Once more, let me thank You for the Odes, which I like the better upon every reading. Mr Nevile too desires me to make his acknowledgments in full form. He is mightily flatter'd with the present You was so kind to make him.

I am, Dear Sir, Your very affectionate humble Servant

R Hurd.

Eman: Col: 16. Aug. 1757.

Endorsed: "16 Aug. 1757."

186 To WILLIAM MASON 17 AUGUST 1757

Text: MS HC, excerpts made by Richard Hurd, nephew of the writer; published, *MLR* 45 1950, pp. 161, 156.

Camb. 17 Aug. 1757.[1]

– The Letter to You is printed off, and I shall send a copy for you to Dodsley's, reserving a better and a finer for the winter, when the books will bear binding better. –[2]

that it was already in the hands of a Person well qualified to do it justice, both by his taste, and his researches into antiquity." The friend was Mason, to whom Warburton, in July 1752, had sent Pope's scheme for such a history. (See *Prelate*, p. 89.) In his *Memoirs* of Gray, Mason mentions the proposal and the preparations Gray had made for the work. (Mason, *The Poems of Mr. Gray. To which are prefixed Memoirs of his Life and Writings*, York, 1775, pp. 337–8.) It is again referred to by Walpole in a letter to George Montagu of 5 May 1761 as a "history of English bards". But of the two compilers he wrote that "the former [Mason] has not writ a word yet" and "the latter [Gray], if he rides Pegasus at his usual foot-pace, will finish the first page two years hence". (Walpole, *Correspondence*, Vol. 9, To George Montagu, 1736–61.) It is not known exactly when the design was abandoned; the "Person well qualified" who did complete a history was Thomas Warton.

7 Warburton had written to RH from Durham on 9 August mentioning that "Our friends M. and B. could not agree to come here in time, so they agreed not to come at all". (*Prelate*, p. 183.) As a prebend of Durham cathedral he had been "feasting" there. Gray also complained he had not heard from Mason for two months. (Gray, *Correspondence*, Letter 247.) It seems likely, as RH surmises, that Mason was working on his new tragedy *Caractacus* which he had started in 1756 and which is set in Mona (Anglesey). He had returned to Cambridge, however, by 28 August. (See *post* To Gray, 28 August 1757.)

8 Gray replied to RH's letter on 25 August. (See Gray, *Correspondence*, Letter 247.)

1 Originally found opposite p. 29 of Vol. 1 of RH's *Works*. This excerpt is erroneously dated 17 May 1757 in M.L.R.

2 The *Letter to Mr. Mason; on the Marks of Imitation* was printed and published as a separate work (collation A–E8); and as part of the third edition of RH's Horace (collation O–R8,S6). (See *ante* To Gray, 16 August 1757.) Both issues are dated "15 Aug." at the end.

Camb. 17 Aug. 1757.[3]

– The Dialogues too are finished, and are almost trifling enough to go thro' as many editions as the Estimate –[4]

– I mean to pass the winter here, unless the printing my dialogues carries me to London. –[5]

187 To WILLIAM WARBURTON 27 AUGUST 1757

Text: *Prelate*, 185.

Cambridge, August 27th, 1757.

. . .

I write one line, before I set out, to tell you how tenderly affected I am by your goodness to my poor Mother.[1] The honour of such a visit was best acknowledged by the language of the heart. And this, I am persuaded, would not be wanting, however she might be unable to express her sense of it in any other manner. Nothing, I know, can exceed her gratitude for your constant favours to me. And if they make me happy on other accounts, think how they rejoice me when I see them contribute, as they do, to make her happy, who is so dear to me.

I must have more than the bias of filial piety in my mind to be mistaken in thinking, she is all you so kindly conceive of her. My poor Father was just such another. The same simplicity of mind, and goodness of heart, with an understanding that dignified both. In a word, my dear Sir (for though I spoke of writing but one line, I could fill my paper on this subject), it has pleased heaven to bestow upon me two of its choicest blessings, the best of parents, and the best of friends. While I live, I must retain the warmest sense of such mercies, and of course be more than I can express, &c.

3 Originally found between pp. 92 and 93 of Vol. 3 of RH's *Works*.

4 John Brown's treatise, *An Estimate of the Manners and Principles of the Times*, was first published on 31 March 1757. By 1 September it was into its sixth edition. (Eddy, *Bibliography of John Brown.*) RH, with Warburton, had a rather low opinion of Brown. On 19 September, Warburton wrote to RH, "Browne is here. I think rather perter than ordinary, but no wiser . . . It seems he said something to them of *another estimate*. My wife told him, he must take care of carrying the joke too far." (*Prelate*, pp. 188–9.)

5 RH had intended to have his new work, *Moral and Political Dialogues*, printed and published in London by Andrew Millar. They went to press later than expected and the book was not published until May 1759. (See *post* To Mason, 26 January 1758, 14 August 1758, 4 May 1759, n. 2).

1 In passing through Birmingham on his way from Durham to Prior Park, Warburton had called on RH's mother who now lived there with her youngest son, Thomas. (*Prelate*, pp. 183–5.)

188 To THOMAS GRAY 28 AUGUST 1757

Text: MS HC; printed, *H-M Corr*, 38;
Gray, *Corr*, Letter 247*.
Addressed: To/Thomas Gray Esqr/[at Stoke near Windsor/Berks.][a]
Postmarked: 30 AV

Camb. 28. Aug. 1757.

Dear Sir

I write this to be conveyed to You by Mr Mason. We were together, when your favour of the 25th arrived, and laughd very heartily at the judgments of your great men and great women.[1] Poor people, it is not for them to understand what You write. But without understanding, they will learn to admire, of their Betters. Evry body here, that knows anything of such things, applauds the Odes. And the readers of Pindar dote upon them.

I am truly concernd for what You tell me of your indisposition.[2] You must abstain from books for the present, and use all the exercise You can. I should fancy, if You took a Post-chaise and went to dine with Mason at Kensington, it would be a relief to You.[3] His Caractacus mends daily, and will come to good in the end, in spite of Lords and Ladies, who will not like it.[4]

I set forward on my journey to morrow. If I find a day of leisure, or rather of *enui*, I may attempt to enliven it by writing to You again. In the mean time, take care of your health and believe me, Dear Sir, Your very affectionate friend and humble Servant

R Hurd

P. S.

Mr Brown, to whom I shew'd the paragraph in yr Letter, sends compliments.[5]

189 To CHARLES YORKE 20 OCTOBER 1757

Text: MS BL Add. 35635, ff. 57–8; unpublished; copy, HC.
Addressed: cover missing.

Sir,[1]

I understand from a Letter, which this moment comes to my hands, how extremely

1 Gray's letter is printed in his *Correspondence*, Letter 247. He remarks on how few people can understand his *Odes*, citing in particular, a "very great man", a "peer", and a "lady of quality".

2 His health, Gray wrote, was "not extraordinary . . . It is no great malady, but several little ones, that seem brewing no good to me."

3 Mason had been appointed as a Chaplain to George II on 2 July 1757. (Scott-Mayor, *Admissions to St John's*, ii. (Part 3) 531.) He took over from Thomas Green and was required to preach during August each year. (Chamberlayne, *Magnae Britanniae*, 1755, Book III, p. 114.)

4 *Caractacus* was published on 30 May 1759 after much polishing and consultation with friends. (Straus, *Dodsley*, Bibliography.) Four odes are incorporated in the drama.

5 Gray had added a postscript to his letter to RH. "If Mr. Brown falls in your way", he wrote, "be so good to shew him the beginning of this letter, and it will save me the labour of writing the same thing twice." His first paragraph included the remarks that had been made on his *Odes*. Brown is James Brown, President of Pembroke.

a [ ] In another hand, presumably that of W[illia]m Fraser who endorsed the letter "Free", with his name. (See *post* To Mason, 1 June 1759, n. 13.)

1 Hon. Charles Yorke (1722–70), second son of the first Earl of Hardwicke; Solicitor-General,

honour'd I am by your kind expressions and intentions concerning me.[2] I beg leave to make my humble acknowledgments to You for this great favour; which is solely occasioned by your usual generosity to those You are pleas'd to think well of, or rather by your partiality to those who come recommended to You by any degree of connection with your excellent friend of Gr. Square.[3]

A learned and worthy man can be but ill spared at any time, and least of all when so few, as they say, are at hand to repair the loss. I cannot flatter myself that I have the least pretensions to be put in that number. But this consideration only enhances the favour You are pleas'd to do me in being ready to risque your own credit by the recommendation of one, so little deserving of it, as, Sir, Your most Obliged and most Obedient Servant

R Hurd.

Camb. 20. Oct. 1757.

190 To Sir EDWARD LITTLETON 21 OCTOBER 1757

Text: MS STAFFS RO D1413/1; unpublished.
Addressed: To/Sir Edward Littleton Bart/at Tedgley Park in/ Staffordshire
Postmarked: 24 OC

Camb. 21. Oct. 1757

Dear Sir Edward

I am just returned from Norton.[1] I acquainted Mr Macro with your generous offers to serve him, which struck him in the manner You would suppose. What You are so good to propose, he says, will make him perfectly easy. He chuses on many accounts to continue his farming.[2] As to the sum, he wants, I find he would wish to take up £500,

1756–61; Attorney General, 1762–3, 1765–7; M.P. for Cambridge University, 1768–70; Lord Chancellor, as Lord Morden, 1770. Yorke had met Warburton in the 1740s and corresponded with him until his death. (*Letters from the Reverend Dr. Warburton . . . to the Hon. Charles Yorke, From 1752 to 1770*, 1812, Introduction.) Through him he became acquainted with RH who had sent him a copy of his 1753 edition of Horace. Their correspondence continued intermittently until 1770 and 30 letters (some copies) are preserved at Hartlebury Castle.

2 Warburton had written a short letter to RH on 15 October 1757. "Dr. Foster lies dangerously ill", he said, "and Mr. Yorke was with me this morning, and, of his own mere motion, told me he intended to write to the Master of the Rolls to recommend you in case of a vacancy. He does not know the force of his interest, but that he shall push it in the warmest manner. Let the event of Foster's illness be what it will, it will be proper for you to return your thanks to Mr. Yorke." (*Prelate*, p. 190.) Yorke had already helped to obtain promotion for two of Warburton's friends, John Brown and William Mason. (Nichols, *Lit. Anecs*, ii. 211, 239.) On this occasion he was unable to secure an appointment (to the Preachership of the Rolls) but his influence gained RH the Preachership of Lincoln's Inn in 1765. (See *post* To Charles Yorke, 6 November 1757.)

3 Warburton. He rented a house in Grosvenor Square from 1757 till his death.

1 Since becoming part of the circle at Prior Park, RH had spent less time with the Macros at Norton, and his correspondence with them dwindled. Mary Macro had died in 1753 and Cox was now 74.

2 Edward Macro had been managing farms belonging to his family since 1753. (*Macro Letter-book*, Littleton to Macro, 13 June 1753.)

only for this reason that he may pay off two or three small sums, which he takes to be in no good hands.[3] In a word, with this money, taken of somebody who will not recall it in hast, he thinks he shall be quite at ease for the rest of his life. But all this You will hear from himself. I have only to congratulate You on this noble pleasure of relieving the distresses of worthy men: a pleasure so much to your taste, that I ought not to conceal from You that your generous bounty to my Brother at Birmingham, some years ago, has put him in so good a way, that there is all the appearance in the world of himself and family doing extremely well.[4] But even this is a small part of the obligations I have to You.

Thro' the stupidity of my Boy, and some neglect of my own, one roll of paper was left behind us. I desir'd your Servant would see it carried back to Tedgley, from whence I can have it conveyed in the Spring to Thurcaston, when my Brother sends my new horse.[5]

Lady Littleton gave me leave to expect the honour of a line from her, when She receives an answer from Colchester.[6] I beg my humble Services to her Ladyship, and am ever with the warmest sense of your constant favours to me, My Dear Sir Edward, Your faithful & affectionate humble Servant

R Hurd.

P. S.

You will tell me in what way I may send your Horace one of these days.[7]

191 To COX MACRO 27 OCTOBER 1757

Text: MS BL Add. 32557, ff. 192–3; unpublished.
Addressed: To/The Revd Dr Macro/at Norton to be left at/ Mrs Lambert's in the Cook-Row/Bury
Postmarked: postmark missing.

Revd Sir

I send You Mr J.'s receipt for the money.[1] He promises to get a discharge in form for You from Mr Pitkin.[2]

I mistook in saying the Edict agst tobacco was K. James'. It is a decree of the Heads, entitled "A Decree agst excessive drinking, Drunkenness and taking Tobacco": And dated 1607. The clause I spoke of is this – "And it is further ordered by the advice and

3 Littleton had already lent Macro more than £200 in 1755 and 1756. In 1759 he was called upon to act as surety on a loan of £250 and again in 1761 and 1762, as Macro, despite all assurances, fell increasingly into debt. (Staffs. RO, D260/M/E/129A.)

4 Thomas Hurd had received loans from Littleton in 1748 and 1749. (See *ante* To Littleton, 7 October 1748; 28 December 1749.) He was now prospering as a draper in Birmingham.

5 John Hurd, a farmer in Shropshire.

6 This reference remains obscure.

7 The third edition of RH's Horace had been published in August.

1 Unidentified.

2 Unidentified.

consent aforesaid, that if any Student of this University of what condition or degree soever shall *take Tobacco in St Mary's Church in the Commencement time*, or in the Schools in Lent Acts, or at any other time of exercise of learning in the said Schools; or in any dining Hall of Colleges, or at any other time or place of Comedies or publique University tragedies, Shews or Assemblies" – in all these cases the offender "to be fined, if adult; if not adult, to be corrected in the Schools by Rod."[3]

You see *St Mary's Church in the Commencement time* is only mentiond. The reason is, that the publique exercises were performed there.[4] It was not usual, I suppose, for the most abandoned of those days to take tobacco at St Mary's during the Sermon or at other times, but only during the exercises of the Commencement and in that season of festivity. And this prophanation, You see, the Decree is levelled agst.

What You inquired of Reland is no more than a short hint in a Dissertation of his "*De Reliquiis veteris linguae Persicae*."[5] His notion is this, That the *Shekel* spoken of in 2. Sam. 14. 27 is not the Jewish but Babylonish Shekel. His words are these, "Siclus ille, Babylonicus dictus, multo minor erat Hebraeo, et pondere suo tantum octo obolos Atticos aequabat. Et sine dubio hos siclos intelligit scriptor sacer, affirmans lib. 11. Sam. c. 14. v. 27 capillos capitis Absalomi ponderasse ducentos siclos pondere Regio; Regis nempe Babylonici, sub cujus imperio erant Judaei eo tempore quo libri Samuelis et Regum conscripti videntur. Atque ita pondus capillorum Absalomi fuisset circiter 31 unciarum, quod pondus eximium quidem est (et propterea in Sacro Codice memoratur) at non adeo stupendum, quam si Siclos Hebraicos, quorum singuli unciae pondus habebant teste Hieronymo in quaest. Hebr. p. 161, intelligamus, quale pondus capillorū hominis vix concipi potest, unde quidam ipsum textum Hebraicum sollicitare et mutare aggressi sunt. Quae difficultas plane tollitur, si siclos Babylonicos intelligamus."[6] This is all he says upon the subject.

I hope You receivd Mr Beauvoir's MSS very safe.[7]

I returnd hither very well, after the pleasant days I passd with You at Norton. I am with many thanks for your kind civilities, and with my best respects to your worthy family, Revd Sir, Your most Obedient humble Servant

R Hurd

Cambridge 27. Oct. 1757.

3 Cooper, *Annals*, iii. 28: *Statuta Academiae Cantabrigiensis*, Cambridge, 1785, pp. 475–7.

4 An account of the Commencement "exercises" at St Mary's was written in 1636 for a proposed visit of Archbishop Laud. It recorded that: "St Mary's Church at every great Commencement is made a Theater and the Prevaricatours Stage, wherein he Acts and setts forth his prophane and scurrilous jests besides diverse other abuses and disorders then suffered in that place". (Edmund Venables, *Annals of the Church of St. Mary the Great*, Cambridge, 1856, p. 23.)

5 'Dissertatio de Reliquiis Veteris Linguae Persicae', in *Dissertationum Miscellanearum. Pars Altera, Trajecti ad Rhenum*, 1607, by Adrian Reland.

6 Reland, *Dissertationum*, p. 237 ('Siclus').

7 Osmund Beauvoir (see *ante* To Macro, 25 September 1744, n. 1) was for many years a correspondent of the Macro family and visitor at Norton. He was a collector of manuscripts and supplied Cox Macro with many samples. (*Macro Letter-book*, Beauvoir to Macro, 24 January 1758.)

192 To CHARLES YORKE 6 NOVEMBER 1757

Text: MS BL Add. 35635, ff. 63–4; unpublished; copy, HC.
Addressed: cover missing.

Camb. 6. Nov. 1757.

Sir,

I have your obliging Letter of the 3d and beg leave to return You my sincere thanks for the very warm and generous manner in which You were pleas'd to recommend me on the late occasion to the Master of the Rolls.[1] The Dean of Bristol was so good to acquaint me with the particulars;[2] of which I will only say, that I should be still more undeserving of your favour, than I am, if the honour of such a Recommendation were not more to me than the success.

You flatter me very much by your kind acceptance of the trifle on Imitation.[3] We, that write, are always ambitious of the good word of our Readers. This is often ridiculous enough. But when those Readers are Judges too, our ambition cannot be ill placed.[4]

I am, with the greatest respect and gratitude, Sir, Your most Obliged and Obedient humble Servant

R. Hurd

193 To WILLIAM MASON 30 NOVEMBER 1757

Text: MS HC; printed, *H-M Corr*, 40.
Addressed: cover missing.

P. P. 30. Nov. 1757.

Dear Sir

We have read over Caractacus together, and the inclosed brief notes, if You can

1 Charles Yorke had written to RH on 3 November in reply to his letter of 20 October. Dr Foster (or Forster), the Preacher of the Rolls, had died on 20 October, and Yorke had recommended RH as his successor. He had considerable interest with Sir Thomas Clarke, the Master of the Rolls, who had himself benefited from the patronage of Lord Hardwicke. However, the Duke of Newcastle had also proposed a candidate, and his interest proved the more powerful. Clarke explained this in a letter of 22 October (MS BL, Add. 35635, f. 59), making clear he would have to concede to Newcastle's wishes. In his own letter to RH, Yorke said that he had "prest" his case "by Letter and in conversation with all the weight I could, to convince his Honour the Master of the Rolls, that I acted from opinion; and that if I had not been satisfied you would have become the Station better than any man, who could be named, and given him more satisfaction in your manners and deportment, even the friendship I have for you should not have moved me to ask his favour". The letter is preserved at Hartlebury Castle.

2 *Prelate*, pp. 191–2. Warburton had been made Dean of Bristol in September. (See *Prelate*, pp. 188–9; Evans, *Warburton and the Warburtonians*, p. 218.)

3 RH had sent Yorke a copy of *A Letter to Mr. Mason; on the Marks of Imitation*. Yorke had read it "twice over", and complimented RH on the "new" things he had to say. Ancient and modern critics, he remarked, had treated the subject "as sophists and teachers merely to form the taste of youth, . . . you, as a real critic, to do justice to Writers of original genius, and to tell us, how we may know them with certainty". It was, he thought, "an Enquiry of a more difficult & refined nature, and which, well-explained & understood, is enough to bury half the comentaries on great Authors in oblivion". (MS HC, Yorke to RH, 3 November 1757.)

4 The reference to "Judges" plays on Yorke's high standing in the legal profession; he was Solicitor-General at this time.

read them, will let You into Dr W's judgment of it.[1] He lays an exceeding great stress on the affair of human Sacrifices.[2] This is the main point. In evry other respect, he applauds your play extremely. Thinks it will be a prodigiously fine thing, vastly above Elfrida.[3] You would probably have had all this and more, to greater advantage, under his own hand. But his business calls him away to Bristol, and, to lose no time, I engaged to give You this hasty account of his censures, in his absence.[4]

I forgot to tell You, in the notes, that *Evelyne's* prayer of *One and All* struck him exceedingly.[5] Your Ode charms him.[6] In short, evrything is as I could wish.

As to my own judgment, I agree in all the points here mentiond in the inclos'd papers. I have besides, it may be, some additional criticisms of my own to make. But I defer giving You this trouble, till I look it over with You, more at our leisure, in London. Your letter by to day's post presses for it. And I shall send it with the books directly. I thank You for the receipt of the first fruits.

I have one word of advice, entirely from myself. I take for granted, You will not print this winter. I think You should keep it by You, one year more.[7] So promising a thing, which will establish your reputation, should be quite perfect. For the like reason, I am not for your shewing it about till the Odes are finishd and inserted, and evry thing done to your satisfaction. I don't know whether Lord H. can be put off, I mean from shewing it directly where You said.[8] If he can, I should be glad. You see I am frank in my way. But I am so out of an extreme sollicitude for your reputation, and

1 These are not with the letter.

2 Warburton objected to a passage in which Caractacus addresses six Roman soldiers captured by the Britons and promises them death by sacrifice rather than the slavery of chains.

"Does there breathe
A wretch so 'pall'd with the vain fear of death
Can call this cruelty? 'tis love, 'tis mercy". (*Caractacus*, p. 74.)

Mason was reluctant to alter the passage and resisted the combined persuasion of RH and Warburton. (See *post* To Mason, 1 June 1759; 25 June 1759.)

3 The critical response to *Caractacus* on its publication was mixed. (See *post* To Mason, 1 June 1759, n. 3.) Much of the poetry was thought "excellent" but the piece as a whole was considered to lack dramatic energy. With the public it never achieved the popularity of *Elfrida* which was reissued at least ten times during the eighteenth century. (Gaskell, *First Editions of William Mason*, pp. 3, 7; Draper, *Mason*, pp. 179–94.)

4 Warburton had been appointed Dean of Bristol in September. (See preceding letter, n. 2.)

5 *Caractacus*, p. 66.

"Nor yet unheard let Evelina pour
Her pray'rs and tears. O hear a hapless maid,
That ev'n thro' half the years, her life has number'd,
Ev'n nine long years has drag'd a trembling being,
Beset with pains and perils. Give her peace;
And, to endear it more, be that blest peace
Won by her brother's sword. O bless his arm,
And bless his valiant followers, One, and all".

6 There are four odes in *Caractacus*.

7 Mason continued working on the poem for more than a year; it was first published on 30 May 1759. (Gaskell, p. 7.)

8 The reference is probably to Pitt who was working quite closely with Lord Holdernesse at this time. In a note to his 'Ode XIV. To the Hon. William Pitt', Mason says, "The Poem of CARACTACUS was read in MS. by the late Earl of CHATHAM, who honoured it with an approbation which the Author is here proud to record." (Mason, *Works*, 1811, i. 69.)

the credit of a play, which, when it has your last hand, will disgrace all the Athelstans, and Douglasses of our times to that degree, that no man will bear to hear of them.[9]

Let me hear from You very soon. All here are much Your's. Dear Mr Mason, Your most affectionate

R Hurd

P. S.

Remember me to Mr Gray, if he be still with You. His british Ode, and the conclusion of his other, are wonderfully admir'd by Dr W.[10]

194 To WILLIAM MASON — 21 DECEMBER 1757

Text: MS HC; printed, *H-M Corr*, 42.
Addressed: To/The Revd Mr Mason

Prior-Park 21 Dec. 1757.

Dear Sir

We are perfectly satisfied, or rather delighted with evry part of your and Mr G.s conduct, with regard to the Lawrell.[1] It could not be for the credit of either of You to accept it. And, to tell You my plain mind, it should not have been offerred. But great men never think greatly.

As to W. we hope he will succeed, and are of opinion that the thing is more suitable to his situation and character.[2] He has lost his dignity long since by throwing himself

9 John Brown's *Athelstan. A Tragedy* had been published in March 1756. (See *ante* To Mason, 8 January 1756, nn. 5 and 8.) *Douglas: A Tragedy* by John Home was first performed in Edinburgh in December 1756 and in London in March 1757 when it was published. Both dramas were set, like *Caractacus*, in early Britain.

10 In October Gray wrote to Thomas Wharton, "Dr Warburton is come to Town, & likes them [the *Odes*] extremely". (Gray, *Correspondence*, Letter 251.) The "british Ode" is *The Bard* and the "other", *The Progress of Poesy*. They are untitled in the first edition of the *Odes*.

1 On 12 December the office of Poet Laureate had fallen vacant by the death of Colley Cibber. According to Mason, this "place the late Duke of Devonshire (then Lord Chamberlain) desired his brother to offer to Mr. Gray; and his Lordship had commissioned me (then in town) to write to him concerning it." (Mason, *The Poems of Mr. Gray. To which are prefixed Memoirs of his Life and Writings*, York, 1775, p. 258.) Gray refused the position in a letter probably written circa 15 December. (The correspondence has not been preserved, but see Gray, *Correspondence*, Letters 258*, 258**, 258***.) On 19 December he wrote to Mason giving his reasons. "[In sh]ort", he concluded, "the office itself has always humbled the Pos[sess]or hitherto (even in an age, when Kings were somebody) if he were a poor Writer by making him more conspicuous, and if he were a good one, by setting him at war with the little fry of his own profession, for there are poets little enough to envy even a Poet-Laureat." (Gray, *Correspondence*, Letter 259.) From Mason's own account it seems unlikely that the post was offered to him. In his 'Memoirs' of William Whitehead he wrote, "I was not myself overlooked on the occasion; so far from it, that a previous apology was made to me by Lord John Cavendish, couched in these or very similar terms, 'that being in orders, I was thought, merely on that account, less eligible for the office than a layman'." (Whitehead, *Poems, Vol. III . . . To which are prefixed Memoirs of his Life and Writings*, York, 1788, p. 87.)

2 William Whitehead (1715–85) was appointed Poet Laureate on 19 December. Since 1745 he had acted as tutor to Viscount Villiers, the son of the Earl of Jersey, and had vacated his Fellowship at Clare Hall since retaining it would have obliged him to take orders. He also held the positions of Secretary and Registrar of the Order of the Bath, secured for him by the influence of Lady Jersey. RH had never had a very high opinion of his poetry (see *ante* To

into a dependance, without a Profession. Besides You know my opinion (tho' I have the greatest esteem and value for his other virtues) that he has no great poetical dignity to sustain. On the whole, tho' I would not for a Bprick have seen your temples entwind with this tarnishd lawrel, I shall rejoyce to see it flourish on his head. The salary will be a pretty addition to the little things he has got: and 'tis bad trusting, in his case, for others of more credit or value.

It is entertaining, as You say, the prudery of Garrick: As if one player were not as fit stuff to make a Laureate of, as another!

You will pick up many things, I dare say, for your purpose out of the Druidical books, the Dean sent You.[3]

We return to town in January. I believe I must be in Grov'nor Square. Dr W. is so kind in pressing me to be with him, and my inclinations, You may be sure, draw so strongly that way, that I shall not go about to excuse myself from giving him that trouble.

The dialogues, I believe, will go to the press. But to be at leisure to attend to the printing and revision of them, I shall in all likelihood withdraw pretty soon to Cambridge.

The family are much Your's. Dr W. is always talking to me about Caractacus. The fame of this play, when made what You will make it, is the only true Lawrel for your wearing.

Believe me, my dear friend, Your's most inviolably

R Hurd

195 To Sir EDWARD LITTLETON 27 DECEMBER 1757

Text: MS STAFFS RO D1413/1; unpublished.
Addressed: cover missing.

Dear Sir Edward

I have your favour of the 3d and am glad to understand that Mr M. is made perfectly easy, as I know he will be, by this great instance of your friendship.[1] I think it very likely that I may find him in town, when I return thither tow'rds the latter end of January; and if so, I can attest the execution of the bond very conveniently.

Tho' I do not see any reason for your declining our friend's compliment, yet it is fit your inclination should be complied with. And I dare say that on receiving the least hint from You, he will determine accordingly.[2]

Edward Macro, 22 June 1743) and like Mason and Gray he despised, or affected to despise, the post of Poet Laureate.

3 Mason was still researching the early British background for *Caractacus*, and Warburton had sent him two volumes of Simon Pelloutier's *Histoire des Celtes*, published at The Hague in 1740. A third volume not yet published was "to contain their ceremonials wch", wrote Mason, "is all I want". (Gray, *Correspondence*, Letter 263.)

1 Littleton had agreed to lend Edward Macro £500 to help pay off his debts. (See *ante* To Littleton, 21 October 1757.) A bond was issued on 25 November 1757. (Staffs. RO, D260/M/E/129A.)

2 Thomas Nevile was preparing his *Imitations of Horace* for the press. The 'Seventeenth Epistle' is addressed to Littleton and Nevile wished to insert his name in full. Littleton had objected to this and the poem was printed without it. (See *ante* To Littleton, 12 July 1757.)

Lady Littleton and You are very polite in apologizing for so agreable a present, as that You give me leave to expect from You. If my resolution holds, I shall be in Leicestershire about Lady Day.[3] My intention is to spend the summer there, to do something towrds fitting up my house, and to return in the following winter to Cambridge.[4] You see with what reluctance I part from that delightful scene, in which the best part of my life has been pass'd, and which I must always think of with great pleasure.

My leisure here is employed in revising some papers for the press, which will probably make their appearance this Spring.[5] You shall know one of these days, what they are. At present I will only say that they will be, not only for Your's, but Lady Littleton's reading.

This employment must be my excuse for not sending You the other paper, You requested of me, on your course of Studies. Tho' indeed I have another reason. I forgot to bring with me a little account, I had drawn up some time ago, of the books I judged most proper to recommend to You. When I get back to college You may be assured I shall not be unmindful of this matter. –[6]

By the way, You forgot to tell me if You have any Bookseller in town to whom I may direct your set of Horace, which has been bound some time and only waits for your further orders.

All the family here are well, and desire their humble services to Yourself and Lady Littleton.

You will please to present mine to my Lady, and to believe me very affectionately, Dear Sir Edward, Your most Obliged and Obedient Servant

R Hurd

Prior-Park 27. Dec. 1757.

196 To WILLIAM MASON 26 JANUARY 1758

Text: MS HC, excerpt made by Richard Hurd, nephew of the writer; published, *MLR* 45 1950, p. 156.

Prior Park 26. Jan. 1758[1]

– Millar and Thurlbourn are, between them, to take care of the Dialogues.[2] They are just now sent to the Press: tho' perhaps we shall not publish till next winter.[3] My

3 According to a note by Richard Hurd, nephew, RH moved into the parsonage at Thurcaston on 9 May 1758. (M.*L.R.*, xliv. (1950), p. 158.) Ladyday is 25 March.

4 There is no evidence to show whether RH visited Cambridge or not. He spent some time at Prior Park, in London and in Leicester and seems not to have taken up permanent residence in Thurcaston again until April 1759. (See *post* To Littleton, 17 April 1759.)

5 *Moral and Political Dialogues*. They were not published until May 1759.

6 These notes have not been traced.

1 Originally found between pp. 92 and 93 of Vol.3 of RH's *Works*.

2 Andrew Millar in the Strand, London. W. Thurlbourn and J. Woodyer at Cambridge.

3 The bulk of *Moral and Political Dialogues* was printed by the end of November. Warburton wrote to RH telling him that he had taken with him "all that you had printed to the 208th page". (*Prelate*, p. 201.) There were 311 pages in the completed work.

prefatory Dialogue is to be a master piece of true humour.[4] Take notice of that. Nay, and the whole is to be almost as popular as the Estimate. –[5]

197 To Sir EDWARD LITTLETON 4 FEBRUARY 1758

Text: MS STAFFS RO D1413/1; unpublished.
Addressed: To/Sir Edwd. Lyttleton Bart:/at Teddesly Park/Staffordshire
Postmarked: 6 FE

Dear Sir Edward

You may be sure I condole most sincerely with You for the loss of our worthy friend.[1] I fear'd, he was in no good way when I left him in November. But he himself apprehended his danger so little, that none of us could prevail upon him to call in a Physician. His case was singular and very unhappy. It seems the Cartilages of his breast were ossified to that degree that they would not give room for the Lungs to play. This occasiond his illness to be very painful. Poor man, he had many excellent qualities, which his friends will not easily forget. His Brother of Jesus feels very tenderly on the occasion.[2] Indeed there was always the most entire affection between the two Brothers.

Many reasons have concurred to keep me here in this obliging family much longer than I designd.[3] I am now to be on the wing in a few days. I shall probably stay in London some weeks; after which I propose seeing Mr Macro in Suffolk, if he resolves not to come up to town.

You are very good to think of obliging me with a cast of your Bust.[4] I need not say that I shall esteem this favour very highly. I have a place in my eye that will do excellently for the reception of such an ornament.

4 The prefatory dialogue purports to be a conversation that had taken place between the "Editor" of the dialogues and his bookseller. The "Editor" calls for a print run of 2,000 copies instead of the more usual 250 copies. He is opposed by the bookseller who casts doubt upon the originality of the dialogues and upon the likelihood of their selling well. The "Editor" counters these arguments and a compromise of 500 copies is arrived at. The preface was not liked by reviewers. The critic in the *Monthly Review* remarked of the author that "in the *preface* particularly, he sinks greatly beneath himself"; and the *Critical Review* wished that the preface had been "spared". (*Monthly Review*, xxi. (1759) 36; *Critical Review*, vii. (1759) 471.) It was omitted in the third edition of 1765.

5 *An Estimate of the Manners and Principles of the Times* by John Brown had been published in March 1757. Six editions had already appeared and a seventh was in preparation. RH makes the same reference in an earlier letter to Mason. (See *ante* To Mason, 17 August 1757.)

1 John Nevile, a contemporary of RH and Fellow of Emmanuel since 1742. He died on 19 January. (*Commons Accounts Book*, STE. 15. 10.) Osmund Beauvoir who saw Nevile a few days before he died said that he "seemed, if any Man, as well prepared to die as live". (Osmund Beauvoir to Edward Macro, 24 January 1758, *Macro Letter-book*.)

2 Thomas Nevile.

3 The Allens.

4 Littleton had decided to present both RH and Edward Macro with a copy of a portrait bust made for him by Rysbrack. To Macro he wrote, "I have ordered Rysbrack to send You a Cast of my Head, & another to Mr. Hurd. If you don't think it like, you can but break it, for tis of no great Consequence." (17 February 1758, *Macro Letter-book*.)

The Dean and Mrs W. are gone to town.[5] The rest of the family charge me with their best respects to Lady Littleton, and Yourself.

My domestic matters are in a fair way to be settled to my satisfaction. But I shall be able to say more of this, when I get to London.

I beg my humble service to Lady Littleton and am ever, Dear Sir, Your most faithful and affectionate Servant

R Hurd

P. Park 4. Feb. 1758.

198 To WILLIAM MASON 10 JULY 1758

Text: MS HC, excerpt made by Richard Hurd, nephew of the writer; published, *MLR* 45 1950, p. 159.

Thurcaston 10. July. 1758.[1]

I intended not to trouble you with a Letter, till I could invite you to come and see how I live here. But I have no patience to hold out so long. I have been here more than two Calendar months and yet I am so far from being settled, that it will probably be a month or six weeks before I get the workmen out of the house.[2] You will conclude perhaps that I am rebuilding, or at least completely furnishing, a large house. No such matter. I would only do some necessary repairs, and provide three or four rooms for the convenience of myself and my friends. The plain truth is, these Leicestershire workmen are insufferably tedious, not to say stupid. And the consequence is likely to be, that I shall lose the best part of the Summer, before I can live in this retirement as I would do.[3] In other respects, I have no complaints. The place is perfectly to my mind; pleasant enough, and so retired, that when you favour me with a visit, you will find it no easy matter to make your way to me. –

– how long do you think of staying in the North?[4] Will you take me in your way to

5 Warburton had married the niece of Ralph Allen, Gertrude Tucker, in 1746. (Evans, *Warburton and the Warburtonians*, p. 131.)

1 Originally found between flyleaf and back cover of *Poems by William Mason*, M.A., 1764.

2 Richard Hurd junior notes that RH "Came to Thurcaston to reside IX May 1758". (MS HC, Extracts of Letters from the Rev. R. Hurd to Rev. W. Mason, p. 7.

3 RH was at some pains to improve the parsonage at Thurcaston although at first sight he had thought the house "good enough for a Bishop and in good repair". (See *ante* To Littleton, 20 October 1756.) Contemporary opinion of the work, however, was not always kind. Two comments are recorded in the John Mitford Notebooks at the British Library, apparently taken from letters of Warburton to Mason. "Pray observe", he says, "how Mr *Hurd* has fitted out his Apartments in all respects. He talks magnificently of his doings, and yet I suspect him for a braggadocio & that he does things in a pitiful way. But this *inter nos*.!" And ". . . our friend Mr Hurd is busy at Thurcaston, in making *a very convenient & no inelegant retirement*. I use his own words, which with me are Gospel". Both quotations are dated 1758. (Mitford, *Notebooks*, Vol. 5, Add. 32563, f. 21.)

4 Mason had been instituted Rector of Aston, Yorkshire, in November 1754 on the presentation of the Earl of Holdernesse. (See *Lond. Mag.*, xxiii. 531; and 'Memorandums or Dates of the Principal events relative to Myself', *Hurd-Mason Corr.*, p. xxx.) He had been given a year of grace after his institution, to continue holding his Fellowship, and on giving it up in December 1755, was elected to a Bye Fellowship in March 1756. He therefore divided his time between Cambridge, Aston and London (when acting as King's Chaplain).

London? Or shall we meet again for a few weeks at Cambridge?[5] I sometimes think to return thither in the winter. And yet I know not whether I shall keep this resolution. I hate moving about from place to place. And I can live with satisfaction here or anywhere. In short let me hear of your motions, and they perhaps may determine mine. If it were not for one or two persons in the world, I would never stir from Thurcaston. –

199 To Sir EDWARD LITTLETON 28 JULY 1758

Text: MS STAFFS RO D1413/1; unpublished.
Addressed: To/Sir Edward Littleton Bart/at Teddesly Park near/ Penkrich/Staffordshire
Postmarked: postmark missing.

Dear Sir Edward

I have your favour of the 21st this moment, and write immediately to thank You for your obliging Invitation to Scarborough.[1] You will easily believe that nothing could be more agreable to me than to attend Yourself and Lady Littleton to that place. But my workmen are still in the house; and, when they leave me, I have so many little matters to adjust, that I cannot possibly be from home at this time. I am sorry for the occasion of my Lady's journey, but am in hopes She will receive much benefit from it. Pray present my best wishes to her Ladyship, with many thanks for the honour of her kind Letter.

I am sorry for Mr Littleton's indisposition. I beg my Services to him, and the good family at Ridware.[2] Nothing, I hope, can possibly hinder me from passing some weeks with You before the winter, when it is probable I may return to Cambridge. But I now think it can hardly be sooner than October. I ev'ry day expect Mr Dalton here, and some other friends talk of passing some time with me in September.[3] In short, I seem

[5] There is no evidence that RH revisited Cambridge for any length of time this year, or that he met Mason there.

[1] Scarborough had become increasingly fashionable as a spa in the 1730s. It had a special attraction as providing good sea-bathing as well as the spa-water which was held to be particularly effective. The water is described as being impregnated with five minerals, "Vitriol, Alum, Iron, Nitre, and Sea-Salt", and, being "hot and dry in Operation . . . corrects cold and moist Bodies, and cures Diseases arising from an Excess of these". (Thomas Short, *The Natural, Experimental, and Medicinal History of the Mineral Waters of Derbyshire, Lincolnshire, and Yorkshire, Particularly those of Scarborough*, 1734, pp. 116, 118; *A Journey from London to Scarborough, in Several Letters from a Gentleman there, to his Friend in London . . . with a List of the Nobility, Quality, and Gentry at Scarborough, during the Spaw Season, in the Year 1733*, 1734.) Sir Edward and Lady Littleton frequently visited different spas trying to secure some improvement in Lady Littleton's health. She stayed at Scarborough for seven weeks. (Staffs. RO, D260/M/E/27, p. 71.)

[2] Mrs Littleton and her daughter Frances lived at the old family house at Pipe Ridware, Staffordshire. Fisher Littleton, Sir Edward's brother, appears to have divided his time between Staffordshire and London.

[3] William Dalton, Fellow of St Catherine's, Cambridge, and Vicar of Coton in Cambridgeshire. (See *ante* To Littleton, 21 August 1755, n. 3.) Thomas Nevile writing to Edward Macro on 9 August mentions the projected visit. "Mr Dalton", he says, "is meditating a short visit to Mr Hurd, who, we are told, from a Critic & a Wit is sinking (or shall I say *rising*?) into the calm character of a Parish Priest." (*Macro Letter-book*.) The other friends have not been identified.

necessarily confined here for a couple of months at the least. The moment I am at leisure, and find it convenient, I shall fly to You.

Believe me, with the warmest affection, Dear Sir, Your most faithful humble Servant

R. Hurd

Thurcaston July: 28. 1758.

200 To COX MACRO 13 AUGUST 1758

Text: MS BL Add. 32557, ff. 199–200; unpublished.
Addressed: To/The Revd Dr Macro/at Norton near/Bury St Edmunds/ Suffolk
Postmarked: postmark missing.

Thurcaston near Leicester Aug. 13. 1758

Dear Sir

I purposely omitted troubling You with a Letter, till I could give You some tolerable account of my being settled at this place. After a good deal of expence and trouble I have at last got three or four rooms fitted up for my convenience. I have a Curate and his family in the house with me.[1] So that I can be absent from hence at any time that I think proper. But the country about us is so tolerable, and the place itself pleases me so well, that I believe I shall soon resolve to reside here pretty constantly.

I hope your health and spirits continue as good as when I saw You, and that therefore You are going on with your excellent work on the Old Testament.[2] It is full time for me, You will think, to devote myself entirely to these studies. And I <fully> intend doing it, as soon as I have finished some papers that are now underhand. The thing is a sort of secret, and must be so for a reason You will see, when I tell You that they are a set of moral and political Dialogues, pretended to have passed between several eminent persons of the past and present age. Accordingly I only take to myself the title of Editor, not author of them.[3] They will make a pretty sizable volume, calculated for entertainment rather than use; and with this, I think I shall most probably conclude my Publications.[4]

You will perhaps not dislike to know the subjects of these fictitious conversations, and the persons employed in them. They are these.

1. *On Sincerity in the commerce of the World*; between Dr Henry More & Mr Waller, the Poet.
2. *On Retirement*: Dr Sprat & Mr Cowley.

[1] In 1757 and 1758 RH was assisted by a curate, George Jolland, whose name regularly appears in the parish register of marriages and banns. (Leics. RO.) By 1759 Jolland had found a better post and RH was for some time left without a curate. (See *post* To Littleton, 29 October 1760.)

[2] This was probably a commentary. Some manuscript material by Macro survives but he published nothing.

[3] See *ante* To Mason, 26 January 1758, n. 4.

[4] *Moral and Political Dialogues* was not the last of RH's publications. In 1762 he followed it with *Letters on Chivalry and Romance* and continued to publish works of literary and theological interest until his death. His edition of Addison was published posthumously in 1811, with, in the same year, an edition of his works. (See Bibliography.)

3 & IV. *On the golden Age of Q. Elizabeth*: Mr Digby, Dr Arbuthnot, & Mr Addison.
5 & 6th. *On the Constitution of the English Government*: Sir J. Maynard, Bp Burnet & Mr Somers.

You will think me, I doubt, very presumptuous to undertake to speak for these great men. I have reason, indeed, to fear that the design is too much for me. All I can say is, that they have lain by me some years, and that I shall finish them as carefully as I can.

I am, with compliments to the Ladies,[5] Dear Sir, Your much obliged and faithful humble Servant

R. Hurd

201 To WILLIAM MASON 14 AUGUST 1758

Text: MS HC, excerpts made by Richard Hurd, nephew of the writer; published, *MLR* 45 1950, pp. 156, 159.

Thurcaston Aug. 14. 1758[1]

– I have been too idle, or rather too much employed here, to think of the Dialogues till very lately.[2] The third and fourth on the age of Elizabeth are just gone to the Press. The two last I am polishing at my leisure. The Volume is to conclude with a Dissertation on the *Rise and Genius of Chivalry*, which I explain very learnedly on Gothic, that is on Feudal Principles.[3] Dr. Warburton has given his consent to this addition. And I flatter myself that you will not be displeased with it. –

Thurcaston Aug. 14. 1758.[4]

The trouble and delays of workmen, I believe, had seized me when I writ last; Or, you are not to think that I am at all dissatisfied with my retirement at Thurcaston. I even like it so well that I am almost determin'd to return to Cambridge no more.[5] Not but the *habitude*, you speak of, is of the greatest use to reconcile one to any situation. It is one of the kindest provisions of nature. The very slave in the mines feels the benefit of it. And, if a poet's word be taken, it even makes the shackles of matrimony delightful:

> Quod superest, consuetudo concinnat amorem,[6]

as sings the philosophical as well as tuneful Lucretius.

5 Mary Macro had died in 1753, but following her death one of Cox Macro's sisters had come to live at Norton with him and Molly. (See *ante* To Littleton, 26 August 1753, n. 1; *Macro Letter-book*.)

1 Originally found between pp. 92 and 93 of Vol. 3 of RH's *Works*.
2 The first two dialogues and the prefatory discourse had been sent to press in January. (See *ante* To Mason, 26 January 1758.) Since then RH had been concentrating on improvements to the parsonage.
3 The dissertation did not appear with *Moral and Political Dialogues*. It was altered and amplified over the next three years and published separately in 1762 as *Letters on Chivalry and Romance*. RH's early interest in chivalry had a strong historical bias deriving partly from his examination of the feudal system in the dialogue 'On the Constitution of the English Government'. The emphasis, however, altered from the historical to the literary in the intervening years.
4 Found between flyleaf and back cover of *Poems by William Mason*, M.A., 1764.
5 RH had at first proposed living in Cambridge during the winter and at Thurcaston only in the summer. (See *ante* To Littleton, 27 December 1757.)
6 Lucretius, *De Rerum Natura*, iv. 1283.

– Let me take my leave of you with a stanza of your own Spenser, so suitable to both our situations.

> To them, that list, the world's gay shewes I leave
>   And to great ones such follies do forgive,
> Which oft thro' pride do their own peril weave,
>   And thro' ambition downe themselves do drive
>   To sad decay, that might contented live.
> Me, no such cares nor cumbrous thoughts offend,
>   Ne once my mind's unmoved quiet grieve;
> But all the night in silver sleep I spend,
>   And all the day, to what I list, I doe attend.[7]

Yours most affectionately,
R H.

202 To Sir JOHN DANVERS 20 AUGUST 1758

Text: MS LEICS RO DE1416/29; unpublished.
[Draft or copy]

Thurcaston. 20. Aug. 1758

Sr[1]

I am not sensible that any timber has been cut down, but what stood in the fence of my own close. If by mistake any has, I am very ready to make a reasonable satisfaction for it.[2]

I am, Sir, Your Humble Servt

R.H.

203 To Sir JOHN DANVERS 27 AUGUST 1758

Text: MS LEICS RO DE1416/29; unpublished.
[Draft or copy]

Thurcaston. 27. Aug. 1758

Sir

The proposal You make to me is a very fair one.[1] And if You please to let me know whose opinion You chuse to take, I will immediately appoint another, and have no doubt but they will easily settle the affair betwixt us.[2]

7 Spenser, *The Faerie Queene*, VI. ix. 22.

1 Sir John Danvers (d.1796) of Swithland Hall was the principal landowner in the vicinity of Thurcaston. (John Nichols, *The History and Antiquities of the County of Leicester*, 1795–1811, vol. iii, part 2, p. 1048.)

2 Danvers' original complaint concerning the felling of timber on what was supposedly his land has not been traced.

1 Danvers wrote to RH on 27 August to request that he "would not remove the Wood in dispute, till it is settled, which I think may be done by the Opinion of two capable and honest men, one chose by You, and the other by your humble Servant". (Leics. RO, DE1416/29/3.)

2 See *post* To Danvers, 17 September 1758, n. 1, for Danvers' reply and nomination.

I take for granted You know that the wood was remov'd to my house some time after it was taken down. But none of it has been us'd, nor shall be, till the matter be inquir'd into.
I am, Sir, &c

204 To Sir EDWARD LITTLETON 3 SEPTEMBER 1758

Text: MS STAFFS RO D1413/1; unpublished.
Addressed: To/Sir Edward Littleton Bart/at Teddesly Park/near/ Penkrich/Staffordshire
Postmarked: LEICESTER

Thurcaston Sept. 3. 1758.

Dear Sir Edward
Your kind favour dated the 21 of last month (I do not know by what mischance) did not reach me till last night. And I write in all haste this morning to tell You how extremely obliged I think myself to You for your intention of seeing me here in this dead retirement. My Cambridge friends have left me,[1] and if You will excuse some things that are not to my mind, nothing can make me happier than the pleasure of receiving You at my parsonage. I have but a moment to write in, but will just add that my Brother of Hatton talks of coming hither for a day or two and I fancy, if You will send over a Servant to acquaint him with your time, will certainly wait upon You.[2] Accordingly I write one word to him by this post to prepare him for your message. You are to take notice that I have two beds at my command, besides one for a Servant. So that You will put me to no inconvenience. You need not write to advertize me of your coming, for I am always at home, and always most entirely, Dear Sir, At Your Service

R Hurd

205 To Sir JOHN DANVERS 17 SEPTEMBER 1758

Text: MS LEICS RO DE1416/29; unpublished.
[Draft or copy]

Sir
I have the favour of your Letter, in which You appoint W. Johnson of Newtown to arbitrate in this affair between us.[1] I could not with propriety fix on a Referee for

1 William Dalton was probably of this number. (See *ante* To Littleton, 28 July 1758, n. 3.) The identity of the other friends is not known.
2 John Hurd, RH's older brother, was well known to Littleton.

1 Danvers had written to RH on 16 September. He nominated William Johnson "Carpenter and Woodmonger" as his referee "in the Doubt between us", and asked to be informed "by the Bearer who you have fixed upon for yours, and when he can meet mine". (Leics. RO, DE1416/29/4.)

myself, till I knew the person You had nominated. But I will now make my choice immediately, after which You shall hear again from, Sir, Your very humb. Servt

RH.

Thurcaston. 17. Sept 1758

206 To Sir JOHN DANVERS 23 SEPTEMBER 1758

Text: MS LEICS RO DE1416/29; unpublished.

Copy of my Letter to Sir J. Danvers. 23. Sept. 1758

Sir

I have appointed Mr Daniel Glover of Ansty, in this county and neighbourhood, to be my Referee in the affair of the timber. He is an entire stranger to me, but I hear so good a character of him that I believe You will have no more objection to him, than I have to Mr Johnson.[1]

He is ready to do his part in the arbitration, whenever You please; And, if You think proper, I will give him directions to see Mr Johnson, and to fix the earliest day for that purpose.

I am, Sir, &c

207 To Sir JOHN DANVERS 2 OCTOBER 1758

Text: MS LEICS RO DE1416/29; unpublished.

My Answer to Sir J.D's note of 1. Oct. 1758.

Sir

<. . .> You must have been misinform'd about Mr Daniel Glover of Ansty. He is not my tenant, nor has the least connection of any kind with me, except that of living within one of my Parishes. If You think <. . .> this an objection to him, I will <. . .> look out for some other. For I had no reason for recommending Mr Glover, but that He was the first disinterested and sensible man that I could hear of.[1]

I am, Sir, Your Humble Servt

RH.

Thurcaston 2. Oct. 1758.

[1] Danvers objected to Glover in a letter of 1 October 1758 on the grounds that he was "Mr: Hurds Tenant", and desired RH to "appoint a man with whom he has no Connections as Sir John has done, according to Proposall". (Leics RO, DE1416/29/6.)

[1] Danvers replied, "If you have no Connections with Glover, I agree he shall be your Refferree, I will appoint a Day for their Meeting and let you know". (Leics. RO, DE1416/29/8.) The outcome of their dispute over timber is noted in a letter to Littleton, 17 April 1759.

208 To Sir EDWARD LITTLETON 3 FEBRUARY 1759

Text: MS STAFFS RO D1413/1; unpublished.
Addressed: To/Sir Edward Littleton Bart/at his Seat near Lichfield/ Staffordshire
Postmarked: 3 FE I·G

London 3. Feb. 1759

Dear Sir

I have your two favours of the 22d and 31st past, the former of which was sent to me from Prior-Park.[1]

I have this day deliver'd your Print into the hands of Mr Davis,[2] and took the liberty to say to him that I fancied, when he sent a parcel to You, he might venture to include *Robertson's new history of Scotland* in it.[3]

It is extremely well-written, and will give You a pleasure of another sort from the Life of Erasmus.[4]

Jortin's book is chiefly valuable for a great number of curious facts, that illustrate one of the most memorable aeras of modern history. In this view, your Library cannot be without it. In other respects, as You say, the work is of no great value.[5]

I think all You say of our Suffolk friend's affairs so just and prudent, that, when I get home, I shall venture to say the whole of it to him, as from myself.[6] Mrs Ewan[7] uses him vilely. But what other usage can a man expect in his situation? He wrote me word himself that he should not come to town. And You may be sure I shall be far from pressing him to it.

1 RH had made a short stay at Prior Park over Christmas. Two letters to him from Warburton dated 14 December 1758 and 30 January 1759 define the outside limits of his visit. He was now in London and, according to Warburton, planning to stay "till the 5th" of February. (*Prelate*, pp. 201–5.)

2 Lockyer Davis (1719–91), bookseller and publisher, nephew and successor of Charles Davis. Nichols describes him as having been intimate with "those of the first rank in life and literature" and known as a tradesman of integrity, a scholar and a man of "politeness" and "amiable manners". (Nichols, *Lit. Anecs.*, vi. 436–7.) His uncle had been one of the first to issue "marked Catalogues" of works for sale and Lockyer Davis continued this practice and was considered amongst the foremost of the booksellers who advertised their stock in this manner. (*Lit. Anecs.*, iii. 624–5.) It is not known why RH was delivering a print to him.

3 William Robertson, *The History of Scotland, During the Reigns of Queen Mary and of King James VI. Till his Accession to the Crown of England*, 2 vols., 1759. Warburton had written to RH on 30 January, "Robertson's history is I think extremely well written". (*Prelate*, p. 204.) The work was generally admired.

4 *The Life of Erasmus* by John Jortin published in two volumes in 1758 and 1760.

5 Jortin's *Life of Erasmus* met with a favourable response in the *Monthly* and *Critical Review*. (*Monthly Review*, 1758, xix. 385–99; *Critical Review*, vi. 265–80.) The biography was considered to make "ample amends" for a succession of inadequate biographies that had preceded it (*Critical Review*, p. 265) and Jortin's observations and notes were said to contain an "abundance of curious matter for the entertainment of the Literati". (*Monthly Review*, p. 387.) Mason, on the other hand, thought the book "lumbering" and "Slovenly" (Gray, *Correspondence*, Letter 288), and the *Monthly Review* added a reservation on the "want of perspicuity in some parts, occasioned by the digressions which the Author too frequently makes". (p. 399.)

6 Perhaps a reference to Macro's financial problems. (See *ante* To Littleton, 21 October 1757, n. 3.)

7 Unidentified.

I forgot my Scotch poems, as You say, which may be sent to me, when my mare comes over. I did not however bring the Catalogue with me.

As to the Leicestershire worthies, I can only say that the person, I recommended to Mr Horton, was a friend of one of our fellows, who importuned me very much in his behalf. I did not so much as ask, whether he were Whig, or Tory.[8] However this captious spirit of the faction is a fresh reason with me (and I had a hundred before) not to sollicit their favour. I believe there are honest men in all parties, but I love this so little, that I shall content myself with the few of that character, I can find out of it.

I din'd one day with Mr & Mrs Littleton, who are pretty well.[9]

I leave this filthy town, as You well call it, both in a natural and moral sense, on Wednesday next, and am preparing for a long residence at Thurcaston.

I beg my humble Service to Lady Littleton, and am ever most faithfully, Dear Sir, Your affectionate humble Servant

R Hurd

209 To WILLIAM MASON 14 MARCH 1759

Text: MS HC, excerpt made by Richard Hurd, nephew of the writer;[1] published, *MLR* 45 1950, p. 159.

Leicester[2] 14. March 1759

– I envy you such a neighbour as Mr Wood, who will make your retirement, not only easy, but delightful to you.[3] I want but such a next-door man, to be perfectly happy at Thurcaston. By the by, you will find evry thing to your mind, when you come again this way, except my old Barn, and my Garden: tho' this last is gradually *brightening*, as Middleton said to Lord Hervey, by the Strokes of your Pencil. –[4]

8 These references remain obscure.

9 Fisher Littleton (Edward's brother) and his wife, Mary.

1 Originally found between flyleaf and back cover of *Poems by William Mason*, M.A., 1764.

2 According to Warburton, writing on 17 February, RH was staying with a Mrs Arnald in Leicester "till the settled Spring invites you to Thurcaston". (*Prelate*, p. 206.)

3 John Wood was appointed as Mason's curate at about this time (his signature first appears in the Aston parish register on 3 June 1759). He was the son and heir of John Wood, Gentleman, of Stanwick, Derbyshire, and had matriculated at St John's in 1744 where he met Mason. He graduated LL.B. in 1747, was ordained deacon in the same year and priest in 1749. (*Alum. Cantab.*) Mason's enthusiasm over his appointment was also communicated to Gray, who replied: "I half envy your situation & your improvements (tho' I do not know Mr Wood)". (Gray, *Correspondence*, Letter 292.) Wood appears to be the friend addressed in Mason's 'Elegy II. Written in the Garden of a Friend', dated 1758 and published in his volume of *Elegies* in 1763. (Gray, *Correspondence*, Letter 263, n. 7.)

4 Conyers Middleton prefaced his *History of the Life of Marcus Tullius Cicero*, 1741, with a Dedication to Lord Hervey in which these words appear. "I cannot forbear boasting," he wrote, "that some parts of my present work have been brightened by the strokes of Your Lordship's pencil." (Dedication, p. v.)

210 To Sir EDWARD LITTLETON 9 APRIL 1759

Text: MS STAFFS RO D1413/1; unpublished.
Addressed: To/Sir Edward Littleton Bart/near Lichfield/ Staffordshire
Postmarked: LEICESTER

Leicester IX. April. 1759

Dear Sir

After much puzzling and inquiry we have found the Bust at last, not at the Carrier's Inn, but at the Cranes in this town.[1] The Box is sent to Thurcaston, but as things are now there in much confusion, it is not yet open'd.[2]

In answer to my grave epistle to Mr M. I have received a very chearful one, in which he speaks high things of your generosity, bids me be quite easy as to his affairs, and says if You are contented, he is quite so.[3] He even talks of meeting You some time or other at Thurcaston: which I hope will be put in execution.

But the main business of this letter is to tell You, that I send over trusty Thomas in Easter week for my mare.[4] The day is not fixed, but I believe it will be towards the middle of the week. As soon as he returns, I propose getting into my house as soon as possible.[5]

I desire my humble service to Lady Littleton, and am always Dear Sir, Your most faithful and Affectionate Servant

R Hurd

211 To Sir EDWARD LITTLETON 17 APRIL 1759

Text: MS STAFFS RO D1413/1; unpublished.
Addressed: To/Sir Edward Littleton Bart/at/Teddesly-Park.

Thurcaston[1] 17. April. 1759

Dear Sir

Having troubled You with a Letter so lately[2] I doubt I should have been too lazy to write at this time by Thomas, but that I had a mind to acquaint You, that Sir J. Danvers has at length relented, and sent me last week his final determination about the trees.[3]

1 Littleton had had two casts taken of a portrait bust of himself to give to Edward Macro and RH. (See *ante* To Littleton, 4 February 1758.) On 16 December 1758 Rysbrack wrote to inform him that the casts had been packed up and "sent to the Inns properly directed, which I hope will arrive safe". (Webb, *Rysbrack*, p. 202.)

2 RH had been staying in Leicester since early February.

3 RH's "grave epistle" had been prompted by Littleton's view of Edward Macro's affairs. (See *ante* To Littleton, 3 February 1759.) Littleton had recently agreed to lend Macro £300 which in common with previous and subsequent loans was not repaid.

4 Littleton regularly supplied or looked after horses for RH. Easter Sunday fell on 15 April.

5 RH apparently returned to Thurcaston during the week beginning 23 April. (See following letter.)

1 The last paragraph of this letter makes it clear that RH was still living in Leicester.

2 Probably the previous letter.

3 See *ante* To Danvers, 20 August 1758 *et seq*.

It is, that, in consideration of their being but of small value, he shall trouble himself no farther about them, and that I have his leave to make what use I please of them.

This, You see, is very gracious, and I dare say in his very politest manner. However it is a satisfaction that there is an end of this trifle, and that he has thought fit to give me this proof, at least, of his civility.

I remove to my house from Leicester next week, and shall be very happy if a little exercise may tempt You one of these days to see what housekeeping there is at Thurcaston.

Ever, my Dear Sir Edward, Your Obliged and Affectionate Servant

R Hurd

212 To WILLIAM MASON 4 MAY 1759

Text: MS HC, excerpts made by Richard Hurd, nephew of the writer; published, *MLR* 45 1950, pp. 156, 159.

Thurcaston 4 May 1759[1]

– Notwithstanding the reasons I have to the contrary, I believe the Dialogues will be out this spring.[2] I have just received Bowyers proof Sheet,[3] which by mistake of the people of the post office went to *Lincoln*, instead of Leicester.[4] Three or four Sheets more, I fancy, will finish all. For I withdraw the *Dissertation on Chivalry*, and shall print a short Postscript in it's room against Hume's history of the Tudors.[5] I have pleased myself much in this thing. –

1 Originally found between pp. 92 and 93 of Vol. 3 of RH's *Works*.

2 Progress in printing *Moral and Political Dialogues* had been slow. The first two dialogues and the preface had been delivered to the printer in January 1758. By November two thirds of the book had been printed and Warburton hoped it could be published before Christmas. (*Prelate*, p. 200.) All work was halted however by the loss of the proofs of the last section (see below). Printing was finally resumed in May 1759 and between 28 May and 1 June 1,011 copies of the book were delivered to "Mr Freer, a Bookbinder". (William Bowyer, *Paper-Stock Ledger 1717–73*, Bodleian Library, Ms. Don. b. 4.) The book was advertised for sale in the *London Chronicle* on 2 June.

3 William Bowyer (1699-1777), the "learned printer", regularly worked for Andrew Millar. He had printed much of Warburton's work and continued to print later works by RH.

4 The loss of some part of RH's *Dialogues* in the post was much talked about, particularly as it was said that he had "nothing but a few loose notes left to help him to restore it". (Mason to William Whitehead, 12 March 1759, Beinecke, MS Vault Film, Sect. 16.) The proofs had been posted in London in December or early January. In February Warburton advised RH to advertise offering a small reward (*Prelate*, p. 205); and in due course the papers were returned to Bowyer "by an unknown hand". (Nichols, *Lit. Anecs*., ii. 327.)

5 RH had been working on a "Dissertation on the *Rise and Genius of Chivalry*" in August 1758. (See *ante* To Mason, 14 August 1758.) The essay formed the basis of what was to become *Letters on Chivalry and Romance* published in 1762. In its place he substituted an eight-page 'Post-script' attacking David Hume's *History of England, under the House of Tudor* (part of his six volume *History of England*) advertised for sale in March 1759. Warburton had already procured and read a copy by 3 March and was incensed at what he saw as Hume's "contempt of religion". Moreover, he added, "Hume carries on his system here, to prove we had *no Constitution* till the struggles with James and Charles procured us one . . . Should you not take notice of this address?" (*Prelate*, p. 207.) Prompted by this suggestion RH drew up the 'Post-script' which was sent to Warburton for approval and thence on to Bowyer by 17 May. (*Prelate*, p. 210.)

Thurcaston 4. May. 1759[6]

– I wish you could be with me here for some time. There is wanting but that to make me enjoy myself most perfectly in the shades of *low* Thurcaston. I tell you truly, I think the days short. Yet I rise early, and have scarcely seen a human face since you left me. But thank God for some little use of Letters. *Sibi vacare et Musis* is after all the highest luxury.

This has been said a thousand times. But no matter for that It comes from the heart of, Dear Sir, Your most truly affectionate

R. Hurd

213 To WILLIAM MASON 26 MAY 1759

Text: MS HC, excerpt made by Richard Hurd, nephew of the writer.[1]

Thurcaston 26 May 1759

– I ought to send you a present of my things.[2] But I only order three or four copies in form to some particular persons. And if you will excuse the ceremony, it will make it the easier for me to take this liberty with every body else. And it is of the less consequence, as there are no books upon large paper; and if it comes to a second edition, I will provide that the book shall be printed in such a manner as to make it more worth making you a present of.[3] –

214 To WILLIAM MASON 1 JUNE 1759

Text: MS HC; printed, *H-M Corr*, 44.
Addressed: To/The Revd Mr Mason

My Dear Mr Mason

I thank You for your welcome present of Caractacus.[1] And, formality apart, let me frankly own to You the pride & pleasure I take in seeing myself adorned by You in this fine prelude to the finest of your poems.[2] My vanity is, no doubt, indulged on this occasion; but what makes your partial encomiums truly acceptable to me, is, that I love the person & honour the virtues of the encomiast. This last consideration, I think, more than our kindred studies, has linked our hearts together; a connection, of all others the most firm & indissoluble.

But enough of this. What the public reception of your work will be I know not.[3] A

6 Found between flyleaf and back cover of *Poems by William Mason*, M.A., 1764.

1 This excerpt has been omitted from James Nankivell's 'Extracts' (*M.L.R.*, xliv (1950)).
2 *Moral and Political Dialogues*. See preceding letter, n. 2.
3 The second edition was printed in 1760 with "rather better" print and paper. (See *post* To Mason, 27 Feb. 1760.)

1 *Caractacus, A Dramatic Poem: Written on the Model of the Ancient Greek Tragedy* was published on 30 May. (Straus, *Dodsley*, Bibliography.)
2 Mason prefaced his poem with an 'Elegy' dedicated "To the Revd Mr Hurd" and dated 20 March 1759. It was reprinted in the *London Chronicle*, the *London Magazine* and the *Annual Register*.
3 The public and reviewers of *Caractacus* qualified their admiration for Mason's poetry with regret

better age, as You say, must do You justice in that particular. But for the present I must think You have consulted but ill for yourself by sacrificing to friendship, instead of Greatness.[4] You have softened very properly one obnoxious passage in the elegy, but there are who will not easily forgive so insulting a preference.

I will do as You desire with regard to the omission of the human-sacrifice apology.[5] But to me human sacrifices, and the belief of the Unity are incompatible. I see how difficult it was to make your chorus *favere bonis* in this instance. Yet they might have dropped one word of disapprobation.[6] I doubt our critical friend will not be easily satisfied, especially as I happen'd to say to him the other day that You *had corrected the whole play by the hints which he had sent to You by me from P. P.* [7] This of the Sacrifices was what he pressed most. So that I think You should take some notice of it, when You write to him. You may say that You had designed an alteration, (and it may be right to send it him) but that every body objecting to it as cold & uninteresting in that place, You had left it out. You may further say, as You do to me, that the Chorus give no sanction to human sacrifices, & that the proposal may the rather be indulged as suiting the fierceness of his character. Something of this sort, at least, I shall say to him. For Caractacus is such a favourite with him that I would not have him indisposed towrds it by this omission.

I have read the printed sheets once over, and think You have improved many

that the poem lacked dramatic power. The *Critical Review* found it an "irksome, unpleasing task, to review a work of great merit" that was "dashed with faults almost as conspicuous as its beauties". (*Critical Review*, viii. 11.) Mason's poetical embellishments and obtrusive learning were criticised by both the *Critical* and *Monthly Review* but the reviewers agreed that where he gave "genius" a free rein the poetry was "fine". (*Critical Review*, viii. 11–16; *Monthly Review*, xx. 507–12.)

4 Lord Holdernesse, Mason's patron, might have been a more obvious choice as dedicatee.

5 Human sacrifice is the subject of a speech made by Caractacus to his Roman captives. "Barbarians tho' you call us", he says to them,

"We know the native rights, man claims from man,
And therefore never shall we gall your necks
With chains, or drag you at our scythed cars
In arrogance of triumph . . .

True ye are captives, and our country's safety
Forbids, we give you back to liberty:
We give ye therefore to the immortal gods,
To them we lift ye in the radiant cloud
Of sacrifice. They may in limbs of freedom
Replace your free-born souls, and their high mercy
Haply shall to some better world advance you;
Or else in this restore that golden gift,
Which lost, leaves life a burden." (*Caractacus*, p. 74.)

Warburton had protested against this glorification of sacrifice and had put some pressure on Mason to alter or omit the passage. Mason had resisted all suggestions and was supported by Gray who said that human sacrifice was "quite agreeable to my way of thinking, since Caractacus convinced me of the propriety of the thing". (Gray, *Correspondence*, Letter 291.)

6 No alteration to the text was made until the 1796–7 edition of Mason's *Poems*, the last to be published before his death. In this edition a speech by the Druid Chorus is incorporated rebuking the king for his suggestion that "such deeds of horror" (human sacrifices) had ever been perpetrated on Mona. (*Poems*, i. 254–5.)

7 Warburton had sent Mason some notes on *Caractacus* in 1757. (See *ante* To Mason, 30 November 1757.) "P. P" is Prior Park.

places, especially the part of the chorus towards the conclusion.[8] I shall read it again more critically.

The Heb. society are pleasant people.[9] The truth is, I find myself every day more indifferent to the reputation of a good writer; but I should not enjoy myself in this *sequesterd bower*,[10] as I do, if my heart were not attuned to Your's in every virtuous affection.

My dear Sir, Most inviolably Your Obliged friend & Servant

R Hurd

Thurcaston 1. June. 1759.

P. S.

Could not You send me *Optime*,[11] & *the Letter from a Blacksmith*[12] under Mr Fraser's covers?[13]

Endorsed by Richard Hurd, nephew: "June 1st 1759 about Caractacus".

215 To WILLIAM MASON 25 JUNE 1759

Text: MS HC; printed, *H-M Corr*, 47.
Addressed: cover missing.

Dear Mr Mason

You don't write, and yet You know I am quite alone, and You know too how much I depend on your Letters for the relief of my solitude.

I thank You however for sending me the two pamphlets, I spoke of.[1] There is much truth, but no great wit or humour in the Letter from the Blacksmith. If the writer of

8 Gray concurred in this opinion. The "last Chorus", he wrote to James Brown, "& the lines that introduce it, are to me one of the best things I ever read, & surely superior to any thing he ever wrote". (Gray, *Correspondence*, Letter 294.)

9 Richard Hurd, nephew, wrote "Heberden" above the line. The allusion may be to Dr Heberden and his friends in town.

10 RH quotes from Mason's 'Elegy': "While in low Thurcaston's sequester'd bower". (*Caractacus*, p. vii.)

11 *Candide, ou l'Optimisme. Traduit de l'Allemand. De Mr. le Docteur Ralph* [François Marie Arouet de Voltaire], 1759. *Candide* first appeared in January or February 1759, published almost simultaneously in a number of European cities. Within weeks it had been banned and all available copies were seized; but such was the book's popularity that police action proved ineffective. In 1759 alone about twenty further editions appeared and in London two separate translations were already advertised for sale by May in addition to the earlier issue in French. (Voltaire, *Candide*, ed. J.H. Brumfitt, 1968, p. 11; *Lond. Mag.*; *Gent. Mag.*)

12 A *Letter from a Blacksmith, to the Ministers and Elders of the Church of Scotland. In which the Manner of Publick Worship in that Church is considered; its Inconveniences and Defects pointed out; and Methods for removing them humbly proposed*, 1759, variously attributed to John Witherspoon and Henry Home, Lord Kames. One issue of the *Letter*, which is dated "May 8th, 1758" is recorded for that year, printed for J. Rivington and J. Fletcher (*N.U.C.*); but the *Letter* became more generally available in 1759 printed for J. Coote.

13 William Fraser, an official under Lord Holdernesse, at this time Secretary of State. Fraser was subsequently for many years (from 1760) Under-Secretary of State and eventually (1782) Under-Secretary for Foreign Affairs. He often franked letters for Gray and Mason.

1 Voltaire's *Candide* and A *Letter from a Blacksmith*. (See preceding letter.)

Douglas be the author, I am much scandalized with the indecency of such a satyr on the established church of Scotland, from a member and a minister of it.[2]

But this is nothing to the licence and effrontery of the other man of wit, who has not learnd that Lesson, which even Dunces ought to learn – *not to scorn his God*. Voltaire is the most infamous writer of his age, and in nothing discovers the littleness of his genius more than in writing to the level of the most infamous part of his readers.[3] The *mens divinior* never stoops so low. Even the Atheist Lucretius is always *moral*, which the author of *Candide* is not. Besides Lucretius had a celebrated sect of philosophers on his side, amongst whom were some of the most virtuous men at Rome.[4] Our poet's sect is only the rabble of corrupt men in shameless courts and debauch'd cities. And so much for *L'Optimisme*.

Dr Warburton says he has receivd your Letter, and intends to write to You, I believe to scold You for your human Sacrifices. I confess, I wish this only blemish were remov'd from your tragedy, as I hope it will be in some future edition.[5] Dr Balguy would tell You the fine things our friend says of your odes.[6] Let me know if so much as one fashionable reader about the court, be of the same opinion. The Ladies, I doubt, will give You up as too refin'd and too learned for them.

You talk'd of returning soon to Aston. May I expect the pleasure of seeing You here on your way? I stay here till the end of July, and then remove most probably to Weymouth.[7] Send me a Bushell of news about Caractacus, and say for pity if You have found one reasonable creature that speaks well of the Dialogues.[8] I have much to apprehend. For even You are a little squeamish about the Notes, and Millar makes no scruple to condemn the Preface.[9]

People are so silly as to encourage my vanity by writing me compliments, from all quarters, on your Elegy.[10]

2 John Home was the author of *Douglas: A Tragedy*. RH is incorrect in supposing him still a minister of the Scottish Kirk. The production of *Douglas* in Edinburgh in December 1756 had been regarded as an outrage by the ruling party in the kirk and parts of the play were denounced as profane. Home was summoned to appear before the presbytery but delayed doing so and in June 1757 resigned his living.

3 RH's opinion of *Candide* contrasts with Gray's view of Voltaire as an "inexhaustible, eternal, entertaining Scribler" (*Correspondence*, Letter 390) and with Warburton's opinion. In a postscript to a letter of 8 July 1759 he wrote: "The real design of the Candide is to recommend *naturalism*: the professed design is to ridicule the *Optimisme* not of Pope, but of Leibnitz, which is founded professedly in fate, and makes a *sect* in Germany. Hence M. Ralf, a German, is called the author . . . You will wonder perhaps, the translation was made at my recommendation." (*Prelate*, p. 213.)

4 Lucretius was a follower of Epicurus.

5 The reference to human sacrifice appears in *Caractacus* (p. 74). It remained unaltered until the issue of the 1796–7 edition of Mason's *Poems*. (See preceding letter, n. 6.)

6 Four odes are incorporated in *Caractacus*. The "friend" mentioned here has not been identified.

7 Weymouth was not a fashionable resort but had attracted the patronage of Ralph Allen with whom RH was to stay. In subsequent years Allen's recommendation helped to convert the town into the "resort of the first company from every part of the kingdom". ([Peter Delamotte], *The Weymouth Guide: Exhibiting the Ancient and present State of Weymouth and Melcombe Regis*, Third Edition, Weymouth, [1790], pp. 41–2.)

8 *Moral and Political Dialogues*, published at the end of May.

9 See *ante* To Mason, 26 January 1758, n. 4.

10 *Caractacus* is prefaced by an 'Elegy' dedicated to RH.

If You did not think to do it, pray send a copy of Caractacus to your great admirer, Dr Macro.

Dear Mr Mason, Your's eternally

R Hurd

Thurcaston 25. June. 1759.

* It must be directed to him at Norton to be left at Mr Lambert's in the Cook-Row Bury

Endorsed by Richard Hurd, nephew: "25 June 1759 Caractacus &c."

216 To Sir EDWARD LITTLETON 5 JULY 1759

Text: MS STAFFS RO D1413/1; unpublished.
Addressed: To/Sir Edward Littleton Bart/at Teddesly Park near/ Penkrich/Staffordshire
Postmarked: IY

Dear Sir Edward

I have been disappointed of the journey, I spoke of in my last, and shall now in all probability continue here till the end of the summer.[1] I will write to Mr Macro and engage him, if I can, to come hither in September, when his harvest is over, as that will probably be as convenient a time for You as any other.

I am quite glad, your foundation is laid, and I know how much of your time and attention this great work will take up; [2] tho' if You could slip away for a day or two this month, You would find Mr T. Nevile and Mr Dalton here, who promise to be with me in the beginning of next week, and to stay with me till the end of the month.[3]

Your Bust is a very fine one, and will be a great ornament to my house.[4] Tho' I know not yet where to put it up, and shall not perhaps do it, till I have the pleasure to see You.

I order'd a copy of the *Dialogues*, which are published, to be sent to You from Mr Davis', and hope You have receiv'd it.

I heartily wish You all success of your great undertaking, and with my humble service to Lady Littleton, am ever, Dear Sir, Your most faithful humble Servant

R Hurd

Thurcaston 5: July. 1759.

1 RH had planned to join the Allen family in Weymouth.

2 In March Littleton had contracted with William Baker to begin construction of his new house at Teddesley Park. (Arthur Oswald, 'William Baker of Audlem, Architect', *Collections for a History of Staffordshire*, 1950–1, pp. [107]–35.) Work began about 18 June and a week later Littleton wrote to Edward Macro to tell him that they had laid "near 84,000 of Brick", which, he said, had brought the house about "12 Course of Bricks high all round". (*Macro Letter-book.*) The building took more than ten years to complete.

3 Thomas Nevile and William Dalton were regular visitors at Thurcaston.

4 See *ante* To Littleton, 4 February 1758, and 9 April 1759.

217 To WILLIAM MASON 29 JULY 1759

Text: MS HC, excerpt made by Richard Hurd, nephew of the writer; published, *MLR* 45 1950, p. 156.

Thurcaston 29. July 1759.[1]

– Whatever fate attends the *Dialogues*, I have so much of the author in me as to be perfectly satisfied with them myself. If there be a grain of humour in them, it depends solely on my *pretending*, not *seriously intending* to pass them on the courteous reader for originals.[2] And he that does not see this, is not in a condition to see any thing, as he should. –

218 To Sir EDWARD LITTLETON 8 AUGUST 1759

Text: MS STAFFS RO D1413/1; unpublished.
Addressed: To/Sir Edward Littleton Bart

Dear Sir Edward

I rejoyce to find by your favour of the 20th, that your great work is at last begun, and proceeds so prosperously.[1] I do not wonder, You find your attention to your workmen so necessary. Even in my little concerns here, if I had not overlooked the workmen very carefully, it is not to be imagined what gross blunders they would have committed.

However it pleases me very much, and I hope no mischief will come of it, that You are so good to promise me a few days next month. I have upon this assurance, written to Mr Macro, and am in hopes that he will not fail to give You the meeting at that time.[2]

You may be sure, we gave ourselves the pleasure to remember You very oft, during the stay of our Cambridge friends, which was but very short, a bare fortnight being all that I could obtain of them.[3] They both of them charged me at parting with their very particular compliments to Yourself and Lady Littleton.

I take for granted You must have seen, as busy as You are, the continuation of L. Clarendon's history.[4] It is very curious and entertaining, but a melancholly proof of the little service a good and wise minister can be of, in a court like that of Charles the

1 Orignally found between pp. 92 and 93 of Vol.3 of RH's *Works*.

2 RH refers to the Preface and Notes to *Moral and Political Dialogues*. (See *ante* To Mason, 26 January 1758, n. 4.) They were not generally liked.

1 The construction of a new hall at Teddesley had begun in June. (See *ante* To Littleton, 5 July 1759.) Littleton had been planning the building for several years.

2 Edward Macro was unable to visit Thurcaston in September. (See *post* To Littleton, 30 August 1759.)

3 Thomas Nevile and William Dalton. (See *ante* To Littleton, 5 July 1759.)

4 Edward Hyde, Earl of Clarendon, *The Life of Edward Earl of Clarendon, Lord High Chancellor of England, and Chancellor of the University of Oxford. Containing, I. An Account of the Chancellor's Life from his Birth to the Restoration in 1660. II. A Continuation of the same, and of his History of the Grand Rebellion, from the Restoration to his Banishment in 1667*. Written by Himself. Printed from his Original Manuscripts, Oxford, 1759. Two editions of Clarendon's *Life* were published in 1759, in one volume folio and three volumes octavo. Future references are to the folio edition. RH obtained his copy from Warburton. (*Prelate*, p. 213.)

second. There is some further mention made of the Lord Keeper Littleton, but in a kind way, and agreably to that respect which he appears to have had for him.[5]

I am very faithfully, Dear Sir, Your most affectionate humble Servant

R Hurd

Thurcaston 8. August. 1759.

219 To Lady FRANCES LITTLETON 8 AUGUST 1759

Text: MS STAFFS RO D1413/1; unpublished.

Madam

I have many thanks to pay to your Ladyship for your favour of the fruit-plates, which are extremely pretty, and came in good time for the uses my Garden allows me to make of them this year. We have a great scarcity of other fruit; but my Strawberries and Rasberries, to say nothing of gooseberries & Currants, made a tempting appearance, when serv'd up in these green dishes.

I desire Your Ladyship to believe that I am very proud of this agreable present; and still more so, of the part it shews me to have the honour of preserving in your kind remembrance.

You will excuse the impertinence of my saying one word of my domestic matters, wth which this table-furniture has so near a connexion. I have had the fortune to meet with a couple of servants, that for the present, at least, give me entire satisfaction. And by their means, the affair of housekeeping is as easy and pleasant to me, as a Batchelor can have any reason to expect, or wish for.

It is not certain, whether I shall be able to see your fine improvements at Teddesly this summer, or at least at what time. All I can positively answer for, is, that I shall embrace the first convenient opportunity of doing it with much pleasure, and that I cannot but be, with the utmost regard, Madam, Your much Obliged and most humble Servant

R Hurd

Thurcaston 8. August. 1759.

220 To WILLIAM MASON 26 AUGUST 1759

Text: MS HC, excerpt made by Richard Hurd, nephew of the writer; published, *MLR*, 45 1950, p.157

Thurcaston 26 Aug. 1759[1]

– Mr Mountague pretends to like the Dialogues, save only the obnoxious parts you

[5] Both Lord Keeper Littleton (1589–1645) and Sir Edward Littleton were descended from Judge Thomas Littleton, Sir Edward by direct descent and the Lord Keeper by a collateral line. Littleton was a friend of Clarendon and had been supported by him when early in his office as Lord Keeper he had fallen out of favour with the king. The incident is described in Clarendon's *Life*, pp. 59–64. (See also Andrew Kippis, *Biographia Britannica*, Second Edition, 1778–93.)

[1] Originally found between pp. 92 and 93 of Vol. 3 of RH's *Works*.

wot of:[2] But now I mention the Dialogues I must tell you how well they are receiv'd by Mr Yorke. He thinks nobody has ever catch'd the manner of Cicero so happily, as in the *four* last. The *first* he takes to be in the manner of Fontenelle.[3] Still not a word of the *Notes & Preface*. Under this mortification I turn'd them over yesterday, with some care. And tho' you will laugh at the vain perverseness of an author, I profess to you that on the severest judgment I can form of them, I do not see one paragraph, no nor one sentence, that should give any reasonable disgust. I know, they were composed at first with more care, & in my own opinion, they are in themselves more finish'd and better in their way, than the Dialogues themselves. After all this, such is my natural docility, & so implicit the deference I pay to the public, that I am sure they are not worth a pin, &, if I find this opinion of them so general, as I begin to apprehend it is, I will certainly withdraw the whole in another edition, & give you leave to insult me for want of taste & humour, as long as I live. –[4]

221 To WILLIAM WARBURTON 26 AUGUST 1759

Text: *Prelate*, 216.

Thurcaston, August 26th, 1759.

. . .

Coming home this week from a short visit to Mr. Mason, and Mr. Wright,[1] of Romely, I received your two favours of the 14th and 19th, together with the inclosed letter of Mr. Yorke;[2] which had the effect, you kindly intended by it, to afford me much pleasure. It was impossible not to sympathize with him in his pathetic lamentations for his late loss;[3] and not to esteem the vein of pious reflection with which he supports it. Humanity is but a poor thing at best; but in certain situations is capable of becoming so wretched, that, let proud philosophy say what it will, it is not to be endured without the aids and hopes of Religion.

For his obliging compliment on the *Dialogues*, it was perhaps the more acceptable, as the general opinion of them, as far as I can collect it, is not the most favourable. The Dialogues themselves, it is said, might pass but for the *Notes and Preface*.[4] It is true, I have heard of no good reason, why this playful part of my book should be so particularly disrelished. But there is no disputing about tastes; and if such be that of

2 Probably Frederick Montagu (1733–1800) of Popplewick, Nottinghamshire, a friend of Mason and Gray. (See Gray, *Correspondence*, Letter 216.)

3 Bernard le Bovier de Fontenelle revived the Lucianic style of dialogue in his *Nouveaux Dialogues des Morts*, 1683. RH acknowledges Lucian as his own model for the first dialogue, in the new Preface to the third edition of *Moral and Political Dialogues* (1765) but does not consider Lucian's dialogues to be of "the noblest and the best". (Preface, pp. xxxii–iii.) The remaining dialogues are examples of other styles but owe much to the influence of Cicero.

4 The Notes and Preface were not withdrawn until the third edition of 1765.

1 A friend or acquaintance of Mason's mentioned in Mason to Whitehead, 12 March 1759, Beinecke, MS Vault Film, Sect. 16.

2 *Prelate*, pp. 214–15. The letter from Charles Yorke appears not to have survived.

3 Charles Yorke's first wife, Catherine, had died on 10 July. (Arthur Collins, *Collins's Peerage of England; . . . Greatly Augmented, and Continued to the Present Time by Sir Egerton Brydges*, 1812, iv. 496.) His younger daughter had died on 8 July. (*Lond. Chron.*, 10–12 July.)

4 See *ante* To Mason, 26 January 1758, n. 4.

the public, I have that deference for its decisions which *Fenelon* had for the Pope's, and will myself retract, that is, withdraw, them in another edition.[5] What particularly pleases me in Mr. Yorke's compliment, is, that he finds *an extraordinary reach of thought in some passages*. For it would have been mortifying indeed, if my pen had so far disguised the excellent hints you gave me for the two last Dialogues, as not to be taken notice of by a capable and attentive reader.

The composition of the characters in L.C.'s *Continuation* is, as you truly observe, its chief fault:[6] of which the following, I suppose, may be the reason. Besides, that business and age and misfortunes had perhaps sunk his spirit, the *Continuation* is not so properly the history of the first six years of Charles the Second, as an anxious Apology for the share himself had in the administration. This has hurt the composition in several respects. Amongst others, he could not with decency allow his pen that scope in his delineation of the chief characters of the Court, who were all his personal enemies, as he had done in that of the enemies to the King and monarchy in the grand Rebellion.[7] The endeavour to keep up a shew of candour, and especially to prevent the appearance of a rancorous resentment, has deadened his colouring very much, besides that it made him sparing in the use of it. Else, his inimitable pencil had attempted, at least, to do justice to Bennet, to Berkley, to Coventry, to the nightly cabal of facetious memory, to the Lady, and, if his excessive loyalty had not intervened, to his infamous master himself.[8] That there was somewhat of this in the case, seems clear from some passages where he was not so restrained; such, for instance, as the additional touches to Falkland's and Southampton's characters.[9] With all this, I

5 In 1697 François de Salignac de la Mothe Fenelon, Archbishop of Cambrai, had published an *Explication des Maximes des Saints sur la Vie Interieure*, a work that became the focus of a dispute with Bossuet, Bishop of Meaux, over the religious beliefs of Madame Guyon. The book was investigated at Rome and after 18 months was condemned by the Pope, Innocent XII. Fenelon submitted without hesitation, but was nevertheless confined to his diocese until his death in 1715. ([Andrew Ramsay], *The Life of François de Salignac de la Motte Fenelon*, [Translated into English by N. Hooke], 1723, pp. 115–36.)

6 Warburton had commented: "The truth is, in one circumstance (and but one), but that a capital, the *Continuation* is not equal to the History of the Reb. and that is, in the composition of the characters. There is not the same terseness, the same elegance, the same sublime and master touches in these, which make those superior to every thing of their kind." (*Prelate*, p. 214.)

7 RH refers to Clarendon's three volume work, *The History of the Rebellion and Civil Wars in England, Begun in the Year 1641*, Oxford, 1702–4.

8 Henry Bennet, Earl of Arlington (1618–85), member of the Cabal ministry; Secretary to the Duke of York, 1648–57; Keeper of the Privy Purse, 1661–2; member of the Privy Council, 1662–d.; Lord Chamberlain, 1674–d.
Sir Charles Berkeley (1630–65); an intimate of the royal family in exile and a favourite of Charles and James; Groom of the Bedchamber to the Duke of York, 1656–62; Keeper of the Privy Purse, 1662–d.
Sir William Coventry (1627–86); Secretary to the Duke of York, 1660–7; elected M.P. for Great Yarmouth, 1661; Commissioner for Trade, 1660–9; Commissioner for the Navy, 1662–7; member of the Privy Council, 1665–9; Lord of Treasury, 1667–9.
Bennet, Berkeley and Coventry were close associates and determined to overthrow Clarendon. Only Bennet was a member of the Cabal ministry which succeeded that of Clarendon, but all were instrumental in engineering his impeachment and exile. The "Lady" is probably a reference to Lady Castlemaine, a mistress of Charles II and friend of Henry Bennet. (*The House of Commons 1660–1690*, ed. Basil Duke Henning, 1983.)

9 Lucius Cary, second Viscount Falkland (1610?–43) and Thomas Wriothesley, fourth Earl of Southampton (1607–67). Falkland and Southampton were close friends of Clarendon and both

am apt to think there may still be something in what I said of the nature of the subject. Exquisite virtue and enormous vice afford a fine field for the historian's genius. And hence Livy and Tacitus are, in their way, perhaps equally entertaining.[10] But the little intrigues of a selfish Court, *about carrying, or defeating this or that measure, about displacing this and bringing in that minister*, which interest no body very much but the parties concerned, can hardly be made very striking by any ability of the relator. If Cardinal de Retz has succeeded, his scene was busier, and of another nature from that of Lord Clarendon.[11] But however this be, and when all abatements are made, one finds the same gracious facility of expression; above all, one observes the same love of virtue and dignity of sentiment, which ennobled the *history of the Rebellion*. And if *this* raises one's ideas, most, of the *writer*, the *Continuation* supports and confirms all that one was led to conceive of the *man and the minister*.

I return Mr. Yorke's letter, by this first return of the post, with many thanks, and am ever, &c.

222 To Sir EDWARD LITTLETON — 30 AUGUST 1759

Text: MS STAFFS RO D1413/1; unpublished.
Addressed: To/Sir Edward Littleton Bart/at his Seat near/ Lichfield/Staffordshire
Postmarked: LEICESTER

Dear Sir Edward

I have just now receiv'd a Letter from Mr Macro, who says, he cannot possibly come hither in September. This however, I hope, will not prevent your giving me that pleasure. You may depend upon finding me at home in any part of the month, except for a few days between the 10th. & 15th, when I shall most probably be out of the way of our Leicester Races.[1]

Mr Macro promises to see me at some other time. Whenever it is fix'd, You shall receive the earliest notice of it. But I guess, from some engagements of my own, that it probably will not be till after Christmas.

served Charles I. Southampton returned to the court following the Restoration and acted as Privy Councillor and Lord High Treasurer, though hampered by ill health and his dislike of the court's extravagance. Like Clarendon he was opposed by Bennet and Coventry, but without result. (For Falkland see *Life*, pp. 19–23, 47–8, and 84–5; for Southampton see 'Continuation', pp. 411–16.)

10 Warburton had written: "Do not you read Tacitus, who had the worst, with the same pleasure as Livy, who had the best Subject?" (*Prelate*, p. 214.)

11 Jean François Paul de Gondi, Cardinal de Retz (1613–79). A large part of the extant sections of Retz's *Memoires*, first published in 1717, cover the unsettled years of the Fronde.

1 The "Leicester Races" had been advertised for Wednesday 12 September (when the "Burgesses Purse of FIFTY POUNDS" was to be run for) and Thursday 13 September. In addition to this entertainment there was to be a "Cocking at the Cranes each Morning, and an Assembly for the Gentlemen and Ladies each Evening at the New Assembly Room". (August issues of *The Leicester and Nottingham Journal*; see also Reginald Heber, *An Historical List of Horse-Matches Run . . . in Great Britain and Ireland, in 1753, 1754*, 1754, 1755.)

Dear Sir, present my humble Service to Lady Littleton, & believe me ever Your's most faithfully

R Hurd

Thurcaston 30. Aug. 1759.

223 To THOMAS BALGUY 6 SEPTEMBER 1759

Text: MS BEINECKE MS Vault Shelves, Hurd; printed in part, *Memoirs*, 76.
Addressed: cover missing.

Thurcaston 6. Sept. 1759

Dear Sir

The moment almost I had sent away my last letter, I receiv'd your favour of the 26th past, together with two sheets of observations on the subject of the last Dialogues.[1] All You say on the difference betwixt the Imperial & Norman feuds is very curious, & will serve to correct many mistakes & to supply many deficiences in my account of the feudal constitution. Shall I be fairer than authors usually are, & confess a shameful truth to You? It is, that, tho' in almost ev'ry thing I advance, I have the authority of one or other of our best Antiquaries & Lawyers, yet my laziness would not suffer me to take the pains, wch You have done, of tracing things to their original. The consequence is what You see. But if I ever give a complete edition of the Dialogues, I will reform the whole by your advice & assistance.[2] And then I am sure, tho' I may omit a great deal of what might be said, I shall say nothing but what will bear the strictest examination. In the mean time, accept my best thanks for this friendly trouble, & believe that You could not have given me a more welcome proof of your regard and affection.

Your account of *Gianone* excites my curiosity very much; but where shall I be able to find the book in this obscure corner, & at so great a distance from Libraries?[3]

Mr Warton & his Oxford friends are very indulgent to the Dialogues.[4] – The

1 These have not been traced.

2 *Moral and Political Dialogues* ran into six editions but the last two dialogues 'On the Constitution of the English Government' were not substantially revised. When revising the dialogues in 1763 RH said that his authorities were Selden and Spelman. He was using Balguy's notes but did not intend altering the dialogue "On the Constitution" since his purpose was to give a "true . . . but only a general account of the Norman feuds". (To Balguy, 20 October 1763, *Memoirs*, 90–1.)

3 Probably Pietro Giannone (1676–1748), an Italian historian whose important work *Dell'istoria Civile del Regno di Napoli* was published in 1723 and translated into English from 1729–31. The history was put on the *Index* as espousing the side of the civil power in its conflicts with the Roman Catholic hierarchy.

4 Thomas Warton (1728–90), younger son of Thomas Warton, the elder, and brother of Dr Joseph Warton, Head Master of Winchester; entered Trinity College, Oxford, 1744; B.A. 1747; M.A. 1750; Fellow, 1751; Professor of Poetry at Oxford, 1757–67; Camden Professor of Ancient History at Oxford, 1785–90; Poet Laureate, 1785–90; author of the *History of English Poetry*, 1774–81. RH was not yet acquainted with Warton but had entered into correspondence with him by 1762. (See *post* To Warton, 14 October 1762.) Balguy had also written to Warburton giving him some account of Warton's remarks; this section of the letter is quoted by Warburton in a letter to RH of 12 September 1759. (*Prelate*, pp. 218–19.)

misfortune of Mr Addison's character is, <only,> this.[5] He is known only to most readers, at least to most Scholars, as a man of the gentlest manners, & as a polite writer. Under the last idea, we admire the elegance of his mind, the softness of his ridicule, the beauty of his moral sentiments, & the graces of his imagination. But he had another, & very different character. He was a keen party-man; & when heated in political controversy, he could be as *declamatory*, & more *vehement* than I have thought fit to represent him. In proof of this, I refer You to all his political writings, but more especially to his *Whig-Examiner*, written with a poignancy & severity which could hardly have been expected from Mr Addison.[6] This then was his *political* character, & as such I have drawn it, tho' with many softenings, in the Dialogues. Still I was aware of the prejudice that would arise against this representation, from his *general* character. And to obviate that, I have purposely contriv'd to lead the reader into my design by what Dr Arbuthnot is made to say of his *vehement declamation* over the ruins of Kenelworth, in the opening of the Dialogue – "that *his* (Mr Addison's) *indignation was not so much of the moral, as political kind*".[7] This, I thought, was going as far as the decorum of such things would permit. But it is ill trusting to the sagacity of one's readers. And because these words were not printed in great Church Letters, no body, I suppose, has taken notice of them.

You will perceive by what I have said, that I am of your mind with regard to the *characteristic failing* of the present age. The want of attention & understanding must be lamentable indeed, when there is not enough of either in the present race of critics to comprehend the obvious sense and purpose of these Dialogues.

But let me call a better subject. You have observ'd the great and only defect of Lord Clarendon's new history.[8] It's being a mere apology for himself has hurt the composition in so many respects that I am willing to believe he intended it only, as he says, for the use & inspection of his own family.[9] As a general history of his own administration, he could not but foresee that his minute account of some particular events must be very tedious to the reader. But the greatest misfortune of all, is, that writing in this view of an Apology, he could make little or no use of his supreme talent at drawing characters; that talent, in which he reigns witht a rival, and in the display of which in his history of the Rebellion he so far surpasses ev'ry other writer. The persons of the court, except two or three whom he had made us acquainted with in his other

5 Addison is a participant in the third and fourth dialogues 'On the Golden Age of Queen Elizabeth'.

6 Five numbers of the *Whig-Examiner* were published between 14 September and 12 October 1710. They were designed to "censure the Writings of others, and to give all Persons a rehearing, who have suffer'd under any unjust Sentence of the *Examiner*. As that Author has hitherto proceeded, his Paper wou'd have been more properly entitled the *Executioner*." (*The Medleys for the Year 1711. To which are prefix'd, The Five Whig-Examiners*, 1712, pp. 9–10.)

7 *Dialogues*, p. 100.

8 *The Life of Edward Earl of Clarendon . . . Containing, I. An Account of the Chancellor's Life from his Birth to the Restoration in 1660. II. A Continuation of the same, and of his History of the Grand Rebellion* . . . Written by Himself. (See *ante* To Littleton, 8 August 1759, n. 4; and To Warburton, 26 August 1759.)

9 The nature of his history was such, wrote Clarendon, "as must be as tenderly handled, with Reference to Things and Persons, as the Discovery of the Truth will permit; and cannot be presumed to be intended ever for a publick View, or for more than the Information of his Children of the true Source and Grounds from whence their Father's Misfortunes proceeded, in which nothing can be found that can make them ashamed of his Memory." ('Continuation', p. 2.)

history, were all his personal enemies: And to preserve a shew of candour tow'rds these, his inimitable pencil was restrained from expatiating, as it could have done, in the draught of their characters. Hence Arlington, Buckingham, Berkely, & the rest of that crew of miscreants escape.[10] It did not fare thus with the enemies to the King & Monarchy. After all, what I regret most, is, that his superstitious loyalty would not suffer him to give us a just picture of his infamous Master: a picture, by wch he might have revenged himself at once for all the injuries he had receivd from the politest, if You will, but the meanest and most contemptible of all our Princes.

The Chancellor's reserve does not give me much offence, and was in part owing, I suppose, to the Apologetical design of his memoirs. For his own temper it was high enough, yet I can allow a great deal to his superior sense, and to *the pride*, as he finely calls it, of *a good conscience*.[11] He was, besides, too arbitrary in his notions of Government; and I cannot, You may be sure, forgive his vindictive persecution of the poor coffee-houses.[12] Yet withall, he was one of the ablest, and witht doubt the most incorrupt & virtuous Minister we have ever seen (till *lately*) at the head of the British counsils.

These and a thousand other things I could talk over with You with much more pleasure, than write them. But for the reasons I gave You, I must not see Winchester this year. I am glad You settle there for good next <. . .> Spring. I can then take my own time to give myself that pleasure. And be assurd I shall think it very long till I tell You in your own Prebendal house,[13] how entirely I am ever, Dear Sir, Your affectionate humble servt

R Hurd.

P. S.

I wish, instead of an Archdeacon,[14] You were a Bp, that I might not put You to the expence of this double Letter.

10 For Arlington (Henry Bennet) and Berkeley, see *ante* To Warburton, 26 August 1759, n. 8. George Villiers, second Duke of Buckingham (1628–87), Gentleman of the King's Bedchamber, 1650–7, 1661–7; member of the Privy Council, 1650, 1662–7; Lord Lieutenant of the West Riding of Yorkshire, 1661–7; member of the Cabal ministry. Buckingham was a declared enemy of Clarendon and constantly plotted his overthrow.

11 "The Truth is; the Chancellor was guilty of that himself which He had used to accuse the Archbishop *Laud* of, that He was too proud of a good Conscience." ('Continuation', p. 428.)

12 Charles II had complained to Clarendon about the "License that was assumed in the Coffee-houses, which were the Places where the boldest Calumnies and Scandals were raised, and discoursed". Clarendon suggested that " 'it would be fit, either by a Proclamation to forbid all Persons to resort to those Houses, and so totally to suppress them; or to employ some Spies, who, being present in the Conversation, might be ready to charge and accuse the Persons who had talked with most License in a Subject that would bear a Complaint . . .' The King liked Both the Expedients." ('Continuation', p. 357.)

13 Balguy had been collated to the 11th Prebendal Stall in Winchester Cathedral by Bishop Hoadly on 1 November 1757. (*John Le Neve, Fasti Ecclesiae Anglicanae 1541–1857. III Canterbury, Rochester and Winchester Dioceses*. Compiled by Joyce M. Horn, 1974, p. 105.)

14 Balguy had been appointed Archdeacon of Winchester on 23 July 1759. (*Fasti*, p. 87.)

224 To WILLIAM MASON 28 SEPTEMBER 1759

Text: MS HC, excerpt made by Richard Hurd, nephew of the writer; published, *MLR* 45 1950, p. 157.

Thurcaston 28 Sept. 1759.[1]

– I am glad you did not say a word more of the Dialogues. At least, I am much ashamed in having said so much of them myself. After all the clamours, Millar presses for a new edition, who shall do as he pleases, & I will not alter a single word.[2] As to the Preface, there seems a propriety in withdrawing that, as it refers solely to the first edition.[3] But if I do, I have something to substitute in it's stead, which will be liked no better. The conclusion is, I will write to the best of the little judgment God has given me, & let the public, as it is called, commend or censure as it sees fit. By the way, I have discover'd that both my book, & your Elegy[4] have made some folks uneasy, for which I have ill nature enough to be very glad. –

225 To THOMAS BALGUY 2 NOVEMBER 1759

Text: MS BEINECKE MS Vault Shelves, Hurd; printed in part, *Memoirs*, 79.
Addressed: cover missing.

Dear Mr Balguy

After the frequent letters I pester'd You with a month or two ago, I had a mind to give You some respite, till your return to college. You give the best reason in the world for your continuance at Camb.[1] For if what we hear be true, tho' it may remove our friend from his fellowship, it will hardly take him from college.[2] I rather hope, & believe it will facilitate something else. However that be, I desire You will assure him of the extreme pleasure I take in the news of his good fortune.

It would be endless to say all that comes in my head, in answer to the several things mentiond in your last Letter. But as to L. Clarendon, I must tell You, it would cost You many a pipe of tobacco, & as much wine as your Archdeaconry is worth, to talk me out of my good opinion of that man & minister.[3] I know You think his fine pen seduces me into an admiration of him. But it has a higher source. I believe no very

1 Originally found between pp. 92 and 93 of Vol. 3 of RH's *Works*.

2 The paper for a second edition of *Moral and Political Dialogues* was delivered to the printer, William Bowyer, in December 1759. On 19 April 1760, 200 copies of the new edition were dispatched to Millar. A further 133 were delivered on 29 April and 120 on 27 November 1760. This apparently satisfied the demand. However, in January 1762, Bowyer recorded a delivery of another 556 copies to Millar, bringing his total for the second edition "with the waste" to 1,056. (Bowyer, *Paper-Stock Ledger 1717–1773*.)

3 The Preface was retained unaltered.

4 Mason's dramatic poem *Caractacus* is prefaced by an 'Elegy' dedicated "To the Revd Mr Hurd", which was widely reprinted. (See *ante* To Mason, 1 June 1759, n. 2.)

1 Balguy had been appointed Archdeacon of Winchester in July 1759, but remained temporarily in Cambridge.

2 This reference remains obscure.

3 RH had already written to Balguy about Lord Clarendon on 6 September.

ambitious man was ever half so honest. And it has never been my fortune to meet with an honest minister, half so able. But alass, what could honesty & ability in conjunction do, in such times, & under such a master? To shew You, that I require something more than ability even in a writer, I must tell You that *Davila* whom I amuse myself with at this time, is not half the favourite with me as L. Clarendon.[4] Not, that he does not excell supremely in all the arts of historical composition.[5] But he does not *feel for <virtue> goodness*, like Lord Clarendon. And without this seasoning, a common Newspaper would be almost as agreable reading to me, as a page of Livy. This Davila is a very politician, & we may truly say with the poet, I mean as interpreted by Lord Shaftesbury, *rarus communis sensus in illâ Fortunâ*[6] – Hence he is perfectly enamourd of that She-monster, something between a fox & an Hyaena, the Q. Mother.[7] And hence he can relate the horrid Bartholomew Massacre in a stile that shews he regrets nothing in that affair, but it's want of success, or at most it's defects in point of policy.[8] I confess to You, I had much ado to bring myself to read any more of this accomplish'd historian.

I don't wonder at your observation, that You have generally found yourself disappointed in the characters You have most admired in history. The reason is, none but very ambitious men figure <. . .> there, & their circumstances must be very happy, if very ambitious men can afford, for any length of time, to be very honest. Hence these characters are such rarities, when they occur, I mean the characters of ambitious men, not infamously wicked. But it would be misanthropy indeed, to take one's measure of mankind, from historic characters.

After all the clamours agst the Dialogues, they are now reprinting, & I do not submit to make a single alteration, not so much as to withdraw the Preface. You see how very an author I am at bottom.[9]

4 Enrico Caterino Davila (1576–1631), Italian historian. Davila spent most of the early part of his life in France attached to the court, and to Catherine de Medici in particular. In 1594 he joined the army and fought in the Civil Wars until the peace of 1598. He then returned to Italy and resumed his studies. In 1606 he raised a body of infantry to fight for the Republic of Venice against Pope Paul V and thereafter remained in the service of the Republic, often acting as Governor in troubled districts. His account of the Wars of the Huguenots, the *Historia delle Guerre Civili di Francia* was published in 1630. It was constantly reprinted and both an Italian and an English edition had recently been published in London. (*Historia delle Guerre*, 2 vols., 1755; *The History of the Civil Wars of France*, A New Translation . . . by Ellis Farneworth, 2 vols., 1758.)

5 According to the Preface of Farneworth's translation, Davila had "been compared by Lord *Bolingbroke* to *Livy* in some respects . . . and by others . . . to *Guicciardini*". (p. iii.)

6 Juvenal, 8. 73. (rarus enim ferme sensus communis in . . .). Anthony Ashley Cooper, third Earl of Shaftesbury, had published *Sensus Communis: An Essay on the Freedom of Wit and Humour. In a Letter to a Friend* in 1709. He quotes Juvenal on p. 60 and examines the justice of his satirical comment on the court, concluding that he is not "immoderate in his Censure". (p. 62.)

7 Catherine de Medici (1519–89), Queen of France, wife of Henry II, and mother of Francis II, Charles IX, and Henry III.

8 The Massacre of St Bartholomew's Day (1572), said to have been instigated by Catherine de Medici, is described in Volume I of the *History of the Civil Wars*, pp. 309–13. Davila documents the events without emotion, but adds: "Many stories, dreadful and lamentable indeed, might here be recited: . . . but the rule I have hitherto observed, of relating things in as clear and concise a method as possible, will not suffer me to digress, in giving a tragical narrative of those events". (p. 313.)

9 The printing of a second edition of *Moral and Political Dialogues* did not actually begin until December 1759 at the earliest. See preceding letter, n. 2.

Having by just transition come to that grateful subject, *self*, I must tell You that I lead a life here, which You will think pitiable, & most men, wretched. I am so entirely alone that for weeks together I see no human face, but that of my own Servants, & of my parishioners at Church on Sundays. Yet with all this, one day slides after another so easily & insensibly, that I have no complaints to make of my situation.[10] 'Tis true I should be happier far with You, & others of my friends, but *use*, that great friend to human life, reconciles me to my lot, & keeps me from being positively unhappy. My chief amusement is in my books, & the correspondence of my friends. When You write (& perhaps in this consideration, You will write to me very often) let me know, what books You meet with, new or old, that You think will give me entertainment. You know my taste pretty well; & I am so well acquainted with Your's, that I am sure I shall be pleasd with any thing You think fit to recommend to me.

Adieu, my good friend. And believe me ever most sincerely & affectionately Your's

R Hurd

Thurcaston 2. Nov. 1759.

226 To WILLIAM MASON 6 NOVEMBER 1759

Text: MS HC, excerpt made by Richard Hurd, nephew of the writer; published, *MLR* 45 1950, p. 161.

Thurcaston 6. Nov. 1759[1]

– But what I want to know much more, is the time of your return, & when I may expect you here. The season is now come in for planting, & I want you exceedingly to superintend some improvements of my garden.[2] I wish to consult you in a hundred things, & in short can do nothing without you. Some business will keep me here till after Xtmas, so that come when you will, I shall be at home. But if you have any sort of consideration for me or my garden, you will come directly. –

227 To CHARLES YORKE 13 DECEMBER 1759

Text: MS BL Add. 35635, ff. 325–6; unpublished.
Addressed: cover missing.

Prior-Park Dec. 13. 1759

Sir

The Dean of Bristol must be answerable to You for this trouble, which he will needs have me give You on occasion of his nomination to the See of Gloucester.[1] Tho' the

10 RH had evidently written to Warburton, also, of his solitude. (See *Prelate*, p. 220.)

1 Originally found between flyleaf and back cover of *Poems by William Mason*, M.A., 1764.

2 Mason had a considerable talent for garden design and was frequently called upon for advice by his friends. (See Mavis Batey, 'William Mason, English Gardener', *Garden History. The Journal of the Garden History Society*, i, 2 (Feb. 1973), 11–25.)

1 Warburton, the Dean of Bristol, was officially nominated to the see of Gloucester on 22 December 1759. ([P. Mussett], *Lists of Deans and Major Canons of Durham 1541–1900*, Durham, 1974.) He was consecrated on 20 January 1760. (*Handbook of British Chronology*, 1961, p. 228; Evans, *Warburton and the Warburtonians*, p. 223; Boyce, *Benevolent Man*, p. 253.)

Preachership of Lincoln's Inn be that of all his Preferments which he values most, his extreme kindness to me inclines him to think of resigning it in my favour, if the Society should be dispos'd to honour me with it.[2] Under this encouragement, I would lose no time to acquaint You with his kind intentions. And the constant experience I have had of your favour makes me ready to believe that your countenance & recommendation in this affair will not be wanting to me.[3]

I am, with great respect, Sir, Your much obliged & most humble Servant

R Hurd.

228 To CHARLES YORKE 17 DECEMBER 1759

Text: MS BL Add. 35635. ff. 327–8; unpublished.
Addressed: cover missing.

Prior-Park 17. Dec. 1759

Sir

I beg leave, by the first Post, to return You my sincere thanks for your very kind & obliging favour of the 15th, which I had the pleasure to receive this morning.[1]

As You have seen the Dean of Bristol before this, he would tell You more of his intentions about the Preachership, than I had time to mention to You in my short & hasty Letter.[2] I only wish that, to second your generous dispositions tow'rds me, I had those pretensions, which may be expected in one who aspires to so considerable a preferment, & who has the ambition to engage your interest in his favour.

As it is, my best plea, is the partiality of my friends: Tho', to say the truth, the sollicitude You was pleas'd to shew for my success in the Preachership of the Rolls, made me presume a little upon myself, & that You would allow me to request your favour, on a like occasion indeed, but one of much more importance.[3]

I have the commands of the family to acknowledge your kind compliments & congratulations.[4] We are all happy, as You are, for this distinction of our excellent friend, & that the course of his Dignities, so happily begun in the church of Gloucester, has brought him round again to that place.[5]

I desire You to believe that, with the greatest sense of your kindness, I am, Dear Sir, Your most Obliged & most humble Servant

R Hurd

[2] Warburton had been elected Preacher of Lincoln's Inn on 16 April 1746. (*The Records of the Honorable Society of Lincoln's Inn. The Black Books Vol. III. From A.D. 1660 to A.D. 1775*, Lincoln's Inn, 1899, p. 337; see also pp. xxiii, 34, 315–16, 371, for details of the duties of the Preacher.)

[3] In his reply to RH's letter, Yorke promised to "do whatever is in my power" and to "canvass as well as those who *eat* as those who do *not*; I mean, who feed chiefly on the *black* Letter of the Law-books". (MS HC, Yorke to RH, 15 December 1759.) RH was not elected to the Preachership until 1765.

[1] MS HC, Yorke to RH, 15 December 1759.

[2] i.e. preceding letter.

[3] See *ante* To Yorke, 20 October 1757, n. 2, and 6 November 1757, n. 1.

[4] The Allen family.

[5] Warburton had been made a prebendary of Gloucester in April 1753, but had resigned in 1755 on his appointment as a prebendary of Durham. See preceding letter, n. 1, for his nomination and consecration as Bishop of Gloucester.

229 To THOMAS BALGUY 8 FEBRUARY 1760

Text: *Memoirs*, 81.

Thurcaston, Feb. 8, 1760.

. . . Browne and I are all to pieces, on a suspicion he has taken up, that part of my preface to the Dialogues was a disguised ridicule of him.[1] I condescended to deny the charge, first by a common friend, and afterwards in a letter, which I writ to himself: all to no purpose, I believe; for, after an exchange of one or two letters, he appeared not satisfied, and so the affair rests.[2] See the uncertainty, the *caducity*[3] I should say, if I durst use that word, of modern friendships. Some fate snatches away; some the world takes from us; some die of I know not what brain-sick suspicions; and some again, without any violent means, die of themselves. I could moralize all my paper away upon this chapter. But all the use I should make of these profound meditations would be, only to cleave the closer to those few friends that should haply be left . . .

230 To Sir EDWARD LITTLETON 17 FEBRUARY 1760

Text: MS STAFFS RO D1413/1; unpublished.
Addressed: To/Sir Edward Littleton Bart/in New Bond-Street/ London
Postmarked: LEICESTER 20 FE

Dear Sir Edward

I have receiv'd your favour of the XIth, & am very unfortunate that my occasions should drive me to this place, just at the time that You & Lady Littleton came to London. I am greatly pleas'd to hear of my Lady's good health, & wish You both all the amusement & satisfaction You propose to yourselves by this excursion to the capital.

Before I went from home, Mr Macro had promis'd, on my invitation, to come & see me at Thurcaston. My sudden journey to Prior-Park interrupted this kind intention;[1] but I have renew'd my request to him, since I return'd, & am not without hopes that he will be with me in a short time. 'Tis true, he will want one great inducement; for I had intended to beg You to give him the meeting here, which I doubt now is not to be expected.

You would take a pleasure to see Dr. W. in his new situation of Bp of Gloucester, for

1 John Brown may have resented the discussion of patronage at the end of the Preface to the *Dialogues* in which the practice of dedicating works with an eye to material gain is called into question. (pp. xi–xii.) His own career derived little benefit from the compliments and dedications of his printed works and his resentment was magnified by bouts of depression which increased at this time and led to his suicide in 1766. (Kippis, *Biographia Britannica*, 1778–93; *Prelate*, p. 221.)

2 No correspondence relating to this misunderstanding has been traced.

3 This is an early use of "caducity". The first instance cited in the *O.E.D.* is dated 1793.

1 RH had arrived at Prior Park by 13 December. (See *ante* To Charles Yorke, 13 December 1759.) He had returned to Thurcaston by 8 February. (See preceding letter.)

his own sake, & that of the Public.[2] You have learnt from the public papers, that his Lordship has done me the honour to appoint me his Chaplain.[3]

Mr H. is very ill advised by his friends to stir any more in this affair.[4] He had done much better to sit down by his first disgrace at Stafford, or rather in his own Parlour. To speak in the stile of Chivalry, I take You for a Knight Errant, & him for a base Groom.

Pray present my humble Service to Lady Littleton, & accept, Yourself, the faithful respects of, Dear Sir, Your most affectionate humble Service

R Hurd

Thurcaston 17. Feb. 1760

231 To WILLIAM MASON 27 FEBRUARY 1760

Text: MS HC, excerpts made by Richard Hurd, nephew of the writer; published, *MLR* 45 1950, pp. 157, 160, 163.

Thurcaston 27. Feb. 1760[1]

– You heard me speak of an *Apology* for the Dialogues.[2] But upon maturer consideration, I suppress it. So that the new edition will be exactly the same, as the former, except that the Print & Paper will be rather better.[3] When I have gratified my pride in this instance, I may perhaps, at some other time, take your advice, & reform the whole according to your Idea. –

Thurcaston 27. Feb. 1760.[4]

– It is a saying of somebody, Cicero, I think, *Qui secum loqui didicit roermorem alterius non requiret*.[5] I doubt this is not my case; yet, whatever be the reason, I enjoy myself perfectly in this solitude. The chief want, I experience, is that of books. So that, if any thing new comes out, which you think I should like to see, you will do well

2 Warburton had been consecrated Bishop of Gloucester on 20 January. (*Handbook of British Chronology*.)

3 RH's appointment was noted in the preferments reported in the *Universal Chronicle and Westminster Journal* for 2–9 February 1760.

4 Edward Littleton had been involved in a lawsuit brought against him by Samuel Hellier ("Mr H.") in 1758. Littleton had horsewhipped Hellier for what he considered dishonourable conduct and was fined £100 for assault. Hellier then brought a civil action against him for damages which was not concluded until 1761. (Staffs. RO, D260/M/F/4/11; excerpts from the papers and letters are published in M.W. Farr, 'Sir Edward Littleton's Fox-hunting Diary 1774–89', *Collections for a History of Staffordshire*, Fourth Series, vi, 1970, pp. 137–38.)

1 Originally found between pp. 92 and 93 of Vol. 3 of RH's *Works*.

2 RH had mentioned a substitute for the Preface to the *Dialogues* on 28 September 1759.

3 Quality of paper and print was important to RH. In one of the few surviving letters to his printer, William Bowyer, he comments facetiously: "It is a strange thing that I must instruct you in your own art; but stranger still, that you should not have observed that the success, that is, the *sale* of a book, depends more upon *your* art than upon *mine*!" (RH to Bowyer, 1765, Nichols, *Lit. Anecs.*, ii. 453.) The paper used for the second edition of *Moral and Political Dialogues* is heavier and of a higher quality than that previously used; the typeface does not materially differ, but the text is more generously laid out.

4 Found between flyleaf and back cover of *Poems by William Mason*, M.A., 1764.

5 Cicero, *Tusculanarum Disputationum*, V. xl. 117.

to send it. I insist upon it, I am a greater Philosopher, than you are, yet you will put my philosophy to a hard trial, if you don't contrive to call upon me in your way to Aston . . .[6]

Thurcaston. 27 Feb. 1760.[7]

. . . Our excellent Bishop's (Warburton) only defect or rather excess, is, to be too warm and too friendly: and this inclines him, as he did his friend Pope, to think better, and sometimes no doubt, to think worse of people, than they deserve . . .

232 To WILLIAM WARBURTON 4 MARCH 1760

Text: *Prelate*, 222.

My Lord,

I had your favour of the 19th past, and about the same time received the confirmation of Mr. Allen's recovery, under his own hand.[1] I hope, this fit is now over. But it affects me very much to think that the declining years of this good man are likely to be rendered so uneasy to him, as they must be, by the frequent returns of this disorder.[2]

Mrs. Warburton is always extremely kind. From a letter, she did me the favour to write to me after her interview with Mrs. J. I find she is intent on dignifying all your Lordship's domestics, as well as your footmen.[3] For whereas the Chaplains of other Bishops, and even Lambeth-Chaplains, are usually thrust, with the other lumber of the family, into any blind corner, she invites me to repose in state, in *the Abbot's apartment*, at Gloucester.[4] – You will judge, after this, if I can have the heart to say one word against the *shoulder knots*.[5]

Your early intelligence of the success of Dr. R. was very obliging.[6] I am glad of it,

6 Mason had been instituted rector of Aston, Yorkshire, in 1754 on the presentation of the Earl of Holdernesse.

7 Found between flyleaf and back cover of Vol. 5 of RH's *Works*. This manuscript extract has not been traced.

1 For Warburton's letter see *Prelate*, p. 221; Ralph Allen's letter has not been traced.

2 Allen had just recovered from an attack of gravel. He had had a similar attack in July, the previous year. (Boyce, *Benevolent Man*, p. 251.)

3 Gertrude Warburton had been in Gloucester to decide on furnishings for the Bishop's Palace. She had consulted with Mrs Johnson, the wife of the departing bishop, and according to Warburton had agreed to "lay out . . . about £50 for what she calls fixtures, but what they are", he added, "I know not". (*Prelate*, p. 221.)

4 The Bishop's Palace at Gloucester had originally been used as the Abbot's Lodging before the dissolution of the Abbey and its conversion into a bishopric. (Thomas Dudley Fosbrooke, *An Original History of the City of Gloucester, almost wholly compiled from New Materials*, 1819, pp. 198–200.) It is not clear which particular room RH refers to.

5 Warburton had written, "You will see what she says of your sagacity in the inclosed scrap. But you won't forgive her *silver shoulder knot* for all that." (*Prelate*, p. 221.) The allusion may be to Swift's play on shoulder-knots in Section II of *A Tale of a Tub*.

6 Warburton had written a short note on 26 February to give "the early news (in two words) that Dr. Richardson is come off victorious in the appeal". (*Prelate*, p. 222.) William Richardson, the Master of Emmanuel, had been in dispute over an option to the precentorship of Lincoln bequeathed in the will of Archbishop Potter. His claim was opposed by John Chapman, Archdeacon of Sudbury, whose case had been upheld by the Lord Keeper. On the advice of Charles Yorke Richardson had appealed to the House of Lords and after a hearing of three days

because I know it will make him very happy; and because a piece of justice is done at last upon a man, who had no regard to the decency of his own character.

Your Lordship is always so good to me, that you will be pleased to hear of the health, and usual cheerfulness of my Mother. She is in a disposition rather to beg your blessing, than pay compliments. Though to conceal nothing, I must tell you her infirmity, that she takes all Bishops for such as she reads in her Bible, they should be. So that 'tis only by accident, she does not misapply the veneration she professes for your Lordship.

I resolve to have your Sermon, though at the expence of *six-pence*;[7] which your Lordship will consider as one argument, amongst others, of the regard, with which I am ever, &c.

Thurcaston, March 4th, 1760.

233 To WILLIAM MASON 11 APRIL 1760

Text: MS HC, excerpt made by Richard Hurd, nephew of the writer; published, *MLR* 45 1950, p. 157.

Thurcaston 11 April 1760[1]

– I suppose my Dialogues are coming forth but exactly in their former state, Notes & Preface and all, with the single difference of better paper & print: for which reason I send you no present of them. –[2]

234 To Sir EDWARD LITTLETON 14 JUNE 1760

Text: MS STAFFS RO D1413/1; unpublished.
Addressed: To/Sir Edward Littleton Bart/at his Seat near/Lichfield/ Staffordshire
Postmarked: LEICESTER

Dear Sir Edward

I have nothing to plead, but laziness, the worst excuse in the world, for neglecting so long to acknowledge to You and my Lady, your kind civilities to me, when I was with You in Staffordshire.[1]

Since I came home, I have had the pleasure of a short visit from Mr Mainwaring,

the Keeper's decision was overturned. (Richard Burn, *Ecclesiastical Law*, 2 vols., 1763, i. 172–8.) Accounts of the case suggest that Chapman did not act entirely honourably.

7 Warburton, *A Sermon Preached before . . . the Lords . . . in the Abbey Church, Westminster, on Wednesday, January 30, 1760*, 1760. The sermon was advertised for sale in the *London Magazine* in March (price 6d.)

1 Originally found between pp. 92 and 93 of Vol. 3 of RH's *Works*.

2 See *ante* To Mason, 27 February 1760, n.3. According to his letter of 26 May 1759 to Mason, RH had not made him a present of the first edition of the *Dialogues* either.

1 There is no other record of this visit which must have taken place in April or May.

who flew down to me in the Leicester coach in one day, & returnd in the same hasty manner, after staying with me but just long enough to give me a glymse of him.[2] We talk'd much & often of You. I think him better in his health, & something less like a Shadow, than he was formerly.

Have You seen these new Dialogues of the Dead by Lord Littleton?[3] Tho' he does me the honour to mention mine with approbation, I cannot with a good conscience return the compliment.[4] You will find them very puerile, & composed with less elegance than one expects in such things.

The three last by another hand, suppos'd to be Mr C. Yorke, are something better, but not good enough to rank with Fontenelle's, and Lucian's.[5]

What the public resents most in Lord L. is the liberty he has taken of reflecting, in more places than one, on his old friend, Mr Pitt.[6] A pamphlet has just appear'd on this subject, under the name of *an additional Dialogue*, in which Mr P. is vindicated.[7] I take it to be Dr Browne's, tho' in saying this I go entirely upon conjecture. It is but just good enough to be an answer to Lord Lyttleton.

Dear Sir Edward, pray present my humble Service to Lady Littleton, & believe me ever, with all sincerity, Your most affectionate humble Servant

R Hurd

Thurcaston 14. June. 1760

235 To WILLIAM WARBURTON 22 JUNE 1760

Text: *Prelate*, 226.

. . .

Though your Lordship can never come sooner to me, than I wish, I confess the time of your moving Northward is earlier than I expected.[1] I should otherwise have

2 John Mainwaring was a Fellow of St John's and Rector of Church Stretton, Salop. RH had known him for fifteen years.

3 *Dialogues of the Dead* was published anonymously by George Lyttelton on 17 May.

4 In his Preface to the *Dialogues* Lyttelton acknowledged RH's earlier work as "very ingenious and learned", but of a different nature from his own dialogues as being "supposed to have past between *living Persons*". His own work he believed was of "a much greater compass", bringing before the reader "the History of all Times and all Nations". (pp. iii–iv.) There are 28 dialogues, skilfully argued, but inevitably less elaborate than RH's *Moral and Political Dialogues* and lacking the subtlety of effect.

5 The last three dialogues were contributed by Elizabeth Montagu (1720–1800).

6 Lyttelton had family connections with Pitt and together with the Grenvilles they had formed a small but powerful party known as the "Cobhamites" and subsequently the "Grenville cousins" or the "cousinhood". A breach in their friendship, however, had occurred in 1754 and was openly avowed by 1756. The critical references to Pitt occur in Dialogue XXIII (pp. 241–59) and are noted by the critic of the *Monthly Review* as "some oblique though gentle inuendoes" indicating the author's disapproval of "some late measures" and his disagreement "with the public in holding a certain great Man in such high estimation". But, the reviewer adds, the author "mixes none of the malice or asperity of party in his censure, but gives his sentiments, in regard to the public Favourite, with temper and moderation". (*Monthly Review*, xxii. 410.)

7 *An Additional Dialogue of the Dead, between Pericles and Aristides: Being a Sequel to the Dialogue between Pericles and Cosmo*, [by John Brown] was published anonymously on 3 June. (Eddy, *Bibliography of John Brown*, p. 85.)

1 Warburton had written to RH on 17 June to inform him that he proposed to set forward

made some enquiries after Mrs. Warburton's and my little friend's[2] projected flight along with you, which I have been feeding upon in imagination this good while, but which I am afraid, is now laid aside by your Lordship's mentioning nothing at all of it. As there is now so little time to deliberate upon the matter, I will only say that I shall be at home and alone at the time you mention; for I hope I need not say that my little house, with the best accommodations it can afford, are always wholly at Mrs. Warburton and your Lordship's service.

The roads are so uncommonly good after this dry Spring, that there will be no difficulty in coming hither in your chaise. However my servant shall be in waiting for you at the Cranes, in Leicester, on Tuesday morning, either to shew you the best way for a carriage, or to have my horses ready, if your Lordship should prefer riding.

Remorseless death has cut down poor Chapman in the flower of his life and fortune.[3] I knew him formerly very well. He was in his nature, a vain and busy man. I found, he had not virtue enough to prefer a long and valuable friendship to the slightest, nay almost to no prospect of interest. On which account I dropped him. But the rebuff he afterwards met with in the career of his ambition, might help, and I hope did, to detach his mind from the world, and to make him know himself better.[4] – His preferments, I suppose are flying different ways. An acquaintance of mine at St. John's is, I hear, besieging the great man for his little Government of Magdalen.[5]

I have only to add my humble service to Mrs. Warburton and the family, together with my best wishes for your Lordship's good journey to *Thurcaston*; which has long prided itself in having given birth to one good Bishop, and will not be insensible to the honour of being visited by another.[6] At least, I can answer for its Rector, who is ever, with all devotion, &c.

Thurcaston, June 22d, 1760.

"towards the North the last day of this month", arriving at Thurcaston on the morning of 2 July. (*Prelate*, p. 225.)

2 Ralph Allen Warburton, Warburton's four year old son.

3 Thomas Chapman (1717–60), Master of Magdalene, had died on 9 June. Gray gave several accounts of his death attributing it to the consumption of "five huge mackrell (fat & full of roe) at one dinner", followed by, a week later, "the best part of a large Turbot, wch he carried to his grave". (Gray, *Correspondence*, Letter 321.)

4 From his first appointment as Master of Magdalene, Chapman had cultivated the patronage of the Duke of Newcastle, Chancellor of the University. He was appointed King's Chaplain in 1748, Rector of Kirkby Overblow, Yorkshire in 1749, and in 1750, prebendary of Durham. The "rebuff" RH mentions may refer to Chapman's application to exchange his own prebend at Durham for that of Bishop Benson at the latter's death. He had written to Newcastle in the hope of securing the exchange, but was unsuccessful. (Chapman to Newcastle, 25 August 1752, MS BL, Add. 32729, ff. 184–5.) Both RH and Chapman were involved in the controversy over the Right of Appeal from the Vice-Chancellor, and published pamphlets supporting the opposing factions. (See *ante* To Balguy, 19 March 1751, nn. 8, 10; 29 March 1751.)

5 Samuel Ogden (1716–78) of St John's was one of several candidates for the vacancy at Magdalene who applied to Newcastle (the "great man"). (Winstanley, *The University of Cambridge in the Eighteenth Century*, pp. 318–19.) They were all unsuccessful and the "Headship" went to George Sandby of Merton, Oxford, who was appointed by the College Visitor, Lady Portsmouth. (Edward K. Purnell, *Magdalene College*, 1904, pp. 167–8.)

6 Hugh Latimer (1485?–1555), Bishop of Worcester, had been born in Thurcaston.

236 To WILLIAM MASON 27 SEPTEMBER 1760

Text: MS HC, excerpt made by Richard Hurd, nephew of the writer; published, *MLR* 45 1950, p. 160.

Prior Park 27 Sept. 1760[1]

– I leave this place next week, & propose being at Thurcaston all the winter. The prospect of dark days, & long lonely nights gives me no disquiet. Yet if you could make me in your way, as you return from town, I should be happier a great deal, & the longer you stay with me, still the happier. –

237 To WILLIAM WARBURTON OCTOBER 1760

Text: *Prelate*, 228.

. . .

I thank God for the prospect of Mrs. Warburton's recovery from her late disorder, which has been more severe, than I had any apprehension of, when I left you.[1] It will be a sensible pleasure to hear that she is now in a fair way of being perfectly re-established.

On my road hither I chanced to pick up Dr. Atterbury's book on the English Convocation, which has been my principal amusement ever since.[2] It has given me a higher idea of the capacity, as well as industry of this writer, than I had entertained before, from what I had seen of his productions.[3] The main question, he discusses, *whether the Convocation, on their legal meeting, have a right to debate and consult together on matters within their sphere, without a previous license from the crown*, seems unanswerably cleared, and his determination very justly made, in their favour.[4] And yet I

1 Originally found between flyleaf and back cover of *Poems by William Mason*, M.A., 1764.

1 RH had been staying at Prior Park until the end of September. (See *ante* To Mason, 27 September 1760.) On his return to Thurcaston he had received a letter from Warburton with the news that his wife had had "another bad return of her cholic". Warburton to RH, 9 October 1760, *Prelate*, p. 227.)

2 [Francis Atterbury], *The Rights, Powers, and Priviledges, of an English Convocation, Stated and Vindicated. In Answer to a Late Book of Dr. Wake's, Entituled, The Authority of Christian Princes over their Ecclesiastical Synods asserted, &c.*, 1700.

3 Emmanuel Library holds thirty works by Atterbury (including separately published sermons) to which RH would have had access.

4 The powers of the Convocations of Canterbury and York had been significantly reduced by the end of the seventeenth century. They had lost much of their autonomy and legislative power and were further seriously weakened by a split between the majority of the clergy who were high churchmen and a bench of bishops with whiggish sympathies. In 1697 when the lower house of the Convocation of Canterbury was in fierce opposition to the court and whig bishops, William Wake published *The Authority of Christian Princes over their Ecclesiastical Synods asserted: with particular respect to the Convocations of the Clergy of the Realm and Church of England*, in defence of the royal supremacy. In 1700 Atterbury had replied making the focus of his argument Convocations' "*Right (when Met) of Treating and Deliberating about such Affairs as lie within their proper Sphere, and of coming to fit Resolutions upon them, without being necessitated antecedently to qualify themselves for such Acts and Debates by a License under the Broad Seal of England*". (*The Rights of an English Convocation*, p. 78ff.) For a detailed account of this controversy see Atterbury's Life in Kippis, *Biographia Britannica*, 1778–93, i. 335–7. The best

perceive much more was afterwards written in the controversy. Dr. W. as I guess, writ another book, and Bp. Burnet mentions one by Kennet, as a complete confutation of Atterbury's.[5] Whether there was any thing more than prejudice in this fancy of the Bp.'s, your Lordship will tell me. However that be, I could wish that Atterbury had considered the *expediency* of this practice, as well as the *right*. There is no doubt, but the Church has lost very much of her dignity and authority, by this disuse of her convocations; and by this means, religion itself may have been considerably disserved. But in other respects I have not light enough at present to determine for myself, whether these church synods would be of all the benefit to religion, which Dr. Atterbury supposes. It requires a very extensive knowledge of the history of the church, to judge of the argument from *fact*:[6] and even with that knowledge, it might be something difficult to say, whether the mischiefs or the advantages be greater. Respecting the *reason* of the thing, I see there are some material benefits, resulting from these councils, the principal of which, as I imagine, is, that any *abuse* or *grievance*, which it concerned the ecclesiastical state to take notice of, might be represented with more weight and effect to the legislature. But then, on the other hand, have not the Bishops authority enough to regulate all material disorders within their dioceses? Or, if they have not, does not their seat in Parliament, and the easy opportunity they have of meeting and conferring together every year during the session of Parliament, enable them to consult and provide for the rectifying of all disorders, either by procuring new laws, or more effectually enforcing old ones? And as to that part of the Convocations' office which is supposed to consist in watching over the *faith and principles* of the people, I should question if it would have any good effect. Bad books might be censured, good ones might too. *Burnet's Exposition* I find was fulminated:[7] and had the Convocation been as busy twenty years ago, as Dr. Atterbury would have it, I should have been in pain for the *Divine Legation*.

But suppose their censures ever so just and reasonable, would they do any good? I doubt, in such a country as our's, they would but whet the appetite of readers, and be the means of circulating them into more hands. In short, I do not see that much service could arise to religion from the authoritative condemnation of books, unless

modern account is G.V. Bennett, *The Tory Crisis in Church and State 1688–1730. The Career of Francis Atterbury Bishop of Rochester*, Oxford, 1975.

5 William Wake published *The State of the Church and Clergy of England, in their Councils, Synods, Convocations, Conventions, and other Publick Assemblies; Historically Deduced from the Conversion of the Saxons, . . . Occasion'd by a Book, Intituled, The Rights, Powers, and Privileges of an English Convocation, &c.* in 1703; in 1701, White Kennett had published *Ecclesiastical Synods and Parliamentary Convocations in the Church of England Historically Stated, and Justly Vindicated from the Misrepresentations of Mr. Atterbury*. Part I (all published). Kennett's reply to Atterbury is described by Gilbert Burnet in his *History of His Own Time*. "Dr. *Kennett*", he said, "laid him [Atterbury] so open, not only in many particulars, but in a thread of ignorance that ran thro' his whole Book, that if he had not had a measure of confidence peculiar to himself; he must have been much humbled under it." (*Bishop Burnet's History of His Own Time*, 1724–34, ii. 280–1.)

6 Atterbury, as Warburton pointed out, had argued his case "upon *principles*" (*Prelate*, p. 232); Wake's reply is a detailed historical analysis, in folio, approximately 750 pages long.

7 Gilbert Burnet's *Exposition of the Thirty-nine Articles of the Church of England*, 1699, had been censured in the lower house of Convocation in 1701, as containing "many Passages contrary to the true meaning of the Articles", and "some things . . . of dangerous consequence to the Church". (Burnet, *History of His Own Time*, ii. 284–5; *Synodalia. A Collection of Articles of Religion, Canons and Proceedings of Convocations in the Province of Canterbury, From the Year 1547 to the Year 1717*, ed. Edward Cardwell, 2 vols., Oxford, 1842, ii. 703–4.)

where great penalties were to follow, which cannot be, except in the case of writers who strike at the very foundations of government. And against books of this malignity the state will always exert itself, to purpose.

I put the question, whether *much real service* can be done religion by these synods, which could not as well be done without them. Because if this be so, there are manifest inconveniences to be apprehended from their meeting. The same inconveniences no doubt, or greater, may be apprehended from Parliaments. But these are unavoidable, so long as Parliaments have a right to dispose of money, and must therefore be submitted to, on all sides, on that consideration. But a government would not have more of these inconveniences, than it needs must, or which are necessary to be endured for the most important ends and purposes.

The conclusion is, the Convocation by giving up their old right of taxing themselves, seem to have given up their right of meeting and debating.[8] At least 'tis no wonder, the government should incline to this side. For let what will be said for freedom of debate in popular councils, no government, I doubt, is heartily for it, but where it cannot with any safety or convenience, be avoided.

After all, I find myself, as I said, very much in the dark as to the *expediency* of these convocational meetings. Your Lordship, who comprehends the subject perfectly, will perhaps instruct me to think better of them.[9] Though it will be goodness enough in you I believe, to forgive my impertinence in saying so much, on a subject which I profess to understand so little . . .

238 To Sir EDWARD LITTLETON 29 OCTOBER 1760

Text: MS STAFFS RO D1413/1; unpublished.
Addressed: To/Sir Edward Littleton Bart/at Teddesly Park near/ Lichfield/Staffordshire
Postmarked: LEICESTER

Thurcaston 29 Oct. 1760

Dear Sir Edward

I have been return'd to this place about a month from Weymouth, where I passed some weeks very agreably with Mr Allen's family.[1] It seems likely that I shall be confined here the rest of the winter, having at present no Curate; the Gentleman You remember to have seen with me, & to whom You was so kind, having got a better thing, than my Curacy, in the neighbourhood. Mr. Jolland.[2]

You will believe how much I was shocked with the news of poor Mr Fenton's

8 One of the most important functions of Convocation had been to set the rates of taxation levied upon the clergy. This right had been relinquished in 1664. Thereafter, in Burnet's view, they had "nothing to do; so they sate only for Form's sake". (*History of His Own Time*, ii. 281.)

9 Warburton's interest in the balance of power between church and state had been demonstrated in his early work *The Alliance between Church and State*, published in 1736. (p. 85ff.)

1 The Allens visited Weymouth each summer. (See *ante* To Mason, 25 June 1759, n. 7.)

2 George Jolland had acted as RH's curate in 1757 and 1758. (See *ante* To Macro, 13 August 1758, n. 1). On 24 February 1759 RH had noted that he had "Pd Mr Jolland ¼yr's Salary unto Feb. 10 1759 when he left me [see his account] 7–10–0". (*Account Book 1756–63*, Leics. RO, DE1416/83, p. x.) Another assistant, "Mr Abbot", was also paid in February 1759 for the preceding December and had acted as curate to RH during the summer of 1760. But on 5 July 1760 RH noted that he had "Pd Mr Abbot to 21st of June, when he left my Curacy". (p. 20.)

death.[3] He was one of the honestest & worthiest men I ever knew, & so friendly that, even on my own account, I have great reason to lament the loss of him. It seems, his only child died before him, & without doubt hasten'd very much his own fate. I have the greatest pity for Mrs Fenton, to whom this double Stroke must be very grievous.

But enough on this melancholly subject. I had the pleasure to be informed some time ago of the alliance between Yours & Mr Wallace's family.[4] I know the satisfaction You will receive from this event, & beg leave to congratulate both with You & them very sincerely.

I expect a very particular account of the progress of the new house. The summer, as I take it, has been favourable to You.[5]

Be pleas'd to present my humble service to Lady Littleton, & to believe me always, with all affection, Dear Sir, Your most faithful humble Servant

R Hurd

239 To WILLIAM MASON 30 NOVEMBER 1760

Text: MS HC; printed, *H-M Corr*, 49.
Addressed: cover missing.

Thurcaston Nov. 30. 1760

Dear Sir

I have receiv'd your pitiful Letter of the 19th from Cambridge, & don't care to tell You, at this moment, what I think of You. Your best way will be to send me your Poem directly.[1] It may be, *Mactata veniam lenior hostia*.[2] Tho' I tell You beforehand, if your poem be not excellent, I am determin'd to dislike it. You think to bespeak my favour by the opinion of Mr Gray.[3] As if I car'd for twenty of your own trade. You must turn to your Horace, for a proper idea of a Critic,

Impiger, iracundus, inexorabilis, acer.[4]

After all, to shew You how well prepar'd I am for a piece of Poetry, I just now come from the reading of Tasso's *Gierusal. Liberata*;[5] in which it is my odd fortune to dislike ev'rything which Voltaire, & such critics as He, commend, & to admire evrything

He then served his churches alone until a "Mr Green" took over for five months from 1 May to "Michs. 1761". (p. 30.)

3 Richard Fenton held the living at Brewood and had been a long-standing friend of the Hurd family. (See *ante* To Littleton, 1 December 1755, n. 1.)

4 Edward Littleton's sister, Frances, had married Moreton Walhouse (by licence) on 28 July 1760. (Pipe Ridware Parish Register 1724–97, Staffs. RO, D4190/1/2.)

5 On 4 July 1760 Littleton had written to Edward Macro, "The House goes on notably. We are advanced higher than to the Top of the Parlour Windows, & shall cover in ye whole in good Time." (*Macro Letter-book*.)

1 'On the Death of a Lady' [Lady Coventry], printed in *Elegies*, 1763.

2 Horace, *Odes*, I. xix. 16. (. . . veniet . . .)

3 Gray had already seen Mason's *Elegy* (they were both in London in November) and had marked some passages for correction. (Gray, *Correspondence*, Letters, 326, 327, 329.)

4 Horace, *Ars Poetica*, l. 121.

5 This may be the 1617 edition, *La Gerusalemme Liberata di Torquato Tasso. Con le annotationi di Scipion Gentili, e di Giulio Guastavini, Et li argomenti di Oratio Ariosti, Stampata per Giuseppe Pavoni ad instanza di Bernardo Castello, in Genova L'Anno* MDCXVII. A copy of this work is in the library at Hartlebury Castle.

which they censure.[6] As a Copyist of Virgil & the antients, He is but feeble, & passable at the best. As an original painter of the world of Magic & Enchantments, he is inimitable. On the whole, no french man is capable of entering into the merits of this extraordinary poem. With all it's blemishes, it will live when a hundred *Henriades* are justly forgotten.[7]

You don't say a word of new books. Yet somebody spoke to me the other day of a history, by this Voltaire, of *Peter the Great*.[8] His taste for this sort of writing is as singular, as for Epic poetry. He has Written, I think, three histories,That of Louis XIV, of Charles the XII, & now of Czar Peter:[9] i.e. Of a Swaggerer, a Madman, & a Savage. The only book he ever writ, that reads like a history, & is indeed a fit subject for one, is his Epic Poem.[10]

The Bp, You say, is much pester'd with business.[11] I believe, he is; yet I have rarely been a week without receiving a Letter from him. This raises my ideas prodigiously of your late engagements.

I desire to be remember'd to Mr & Mrs Wood,[12] & am more than You deserve Your affect. friend & Servant

R Hurd

240 To CHARLES YORKE 1 MARCH 1761

Text: MS BL Add. 35636, ff. 23–4; unpublished; copy, HC.
Addressed: cover missing.

Dear Sir

I just now understand that the Bishop of Gloucester has resign'd the preachership of Lincoln's Inn;[1] & I have long ago understood that a majority of the Society are engaged for Dr Ashton.[2]

6 Voltaire discusses Tasso in *An Essay upon the Civil Wars of France, Extracted from curious Manuscripts. And also upon the Epick Poetry of the European Nations from Homer down to Milton*, 1727, pp. 77–92. "No man in the World", he wrote, "was ever born with a greater Genius, and more qualify'd for *Epick* Poetry". (p. 77) But his praise for the "Jerusalem liberata" is tempered by criticism of the moments of "wild Excess". (p. 85) Tasso, he concluded, "could not be unsensible that such wild fairy Tales, at that Time so much in Fashion not in *Italy* only but in all *Europe*, were altogether inconsistent with the Gravity of *Epick* Poetry" (p. 90).

7 *La Ligue ou Henry le Grand*, Voltaire's own attempt at the epic, was first published in Geneva in 1723. On its publication in England in 1728 the title was altered to *La Henriade*.

8 *Histoire de l'Empire de Russie sous Pierre le Grand, Par l'Auteur de l'histoire de Charles XII*, [Geneva], 2 vols., 1759, 1763.

9 *Le Siecle de Louis XIV. Publié par* M. *de Francheville conseiller aulique de sa Majesté, & membre de l'academie roiale des sciences & belles lettres de prusse*, Berlin, 1751; and *Histoire de Charles XII. Roi de Suède. Par* Mr. *de V****, Basle, 1731.

10 The subject of the *Henriade* is Henri of Navarre, later Henri IV of France. The poem describes incidents in his life and events in France during the troubled years at the end of the sixteenth century.

11 Warburton was in London from the end of November.

12 John Wood was Mason's curate. (See *ante* To Mason, 14 March 1759, n. 3.)

1 Warburton had signified his intention of resigning the Preachership of Lincoln's Inn in a letter presented to a council meeting of 23 January 1761. His resignation was accepted and the Benchers agreed to elect a new Preacher on the first day of the following term. (*Records of Lincoln's Inn. The Black Books Vol. III*, p. 370.)

2 Thomas Ashton (1716–75); admitted at King's, 1733; B.A. 1738–9; M.A. 1742; D.D. 1759;

I therefore take this early opportunity to return You my sincere thanks for the most obliging pains You have taken to serve me in this affair; & to assure You at the same time that the honour of having been so warmly sup̄orted by Yourself & the Bishop makes me full amends for the want of success, & obliges me to be, with the utmost respect & gratitude, Dear Sir, Your most Obedient & most Humble Servant[3]

R Hurd

Thurcaston March. 1. 1761

241 To Sir EDWARD LITTLETON 6 MARCH 1761

Text: MS STAFFS RO D1413/1; unpublished.
Addressed: To/Sir Edward Littleton Bart/at his Seat near/ Lichfield/Staffordshire
Postmarked: LEICESTER

Thurcaston 6. March. 1761

Dear Sir Edward

I am glad to find by your kind favour of the 17th, that your new house is in so great forwardness, & is so much to your satisfaction.[1] I shall be very impatient for an opportunity of seeing it.

You are very happy, as You say, in having no disturbance in your county about the approaching Election.[2] From the little I have the honour to know of Lord Grey, I cannot but conceive very favorably of him, & shall be much surprized if he do not approve himself very deserving of the honour which, I find, is intended him.[3]

Fellow 1737; Fellow of Eton College, 1745; Rector of Aldingham, Lancashire, 1742–9; Rector of Sturminster Marshall, Dorset, 1749–52; Rector of St Botolph, Bishopsgate, 1752–d. Ashton was officially appointed to the Preachership of Lincoln's Inn on 8 April 1761. (*Records of Lincoln's Inn. The Black Books Vol. III*, p. 371.)

3 Yorke replied to this letter on 24 March and explained that he had enquired into "the State of the matter last Christmas was twelvemonth; but soon found that the early assiduity & importunity of Dr. A. . . had made a considerable progress before I heard of the Bishop's intention to resign, or of your inclination to the preachership". (MS HC, Yorke to RH, 24 March 1761; see also Warburton to Yorke, 20 October 1760, *Letters from Warburton to Yorke*, pp. 39–40.)

1 Edward Littleton's letters to Edward Macro are the source of much background information on the building of Teddesley Hall but were not preserved after 1760. No further correspondence has been traced and there remain no other detailed accounts of the construction of the building. Some indication of progress, however, is given in Littleton's monthly accounts (Staffs. RO, Day Books, 1752–1811, D260/M/E/27–9; Ledgers, 1752–1808, D260/M/E/116–9a) and it is clear from correspondence addressed to him that Littleton moved into the Hall in 1769.

2 Parliament was dissolved on 20 March 1761 for the general election. There was no organised opposition in the House of Commons and no political issue to divide the electorate and distinguish the candidates. In Staffordshire, election to the county seats had been uncontested in 1754 and was to continue so until 1790. One seat went to the Leveson-Gower interest and the other usually to a county gentleman. (*The House of Commons 1754–1790*, ed. Namier and Brooke.)

3 George Harry, Lord Grey (1737–1819) was the eldest son of Harry, fourth Earl of Stamford, a close friend of Lord Gower. He was returned unopposed for Staffordshire in 1761 as the Leveson-Gower candidate. In 1768 he was again elected without a contest but was called to the

I cannot tell whether You have heard of late from Mr Macro. He wrote to me some time since from London where he is in lodgings at one Mr *Street's a confectioner in Old Bond-Street.*[4] He tells a lamentable story of himself, that His father & He have quarrell'd, that his farms are taken from him, & in short, that he is turnd out of doors.[5] He mentions no particulars of this misunderstanding, only intimates that it was owing to the intrigues of his Sister.

I was greatly shocked at this account, & press'd him to leave London & come hither to me, till some means could be found to make up this unhappy quarrel with his father. But he declines this, & says he has taken lodgings for a twelvemonth, where he is. I find besides that since he has been in town, he has involv'd himself in fresh difficulties. He talks of a challenge, & of his having behav'd in it in such a manner that all London rings with his fame, with other wild things of the same nature; but witht saying a word of what has been the occasion of all this bustle.

Can You imagine what all this will end in? For my part, I am truly sorry for him, & think it will be a great mercy, if his ungovern'd violence of temper & above all his vanity do not turn his head.

What You mention so kindly of the Officialty, tho' it be a small matter, deserves my sincerest thanks, because I know, if it had been the Chancellorship of a large Diocese, You would have offerr'd it to me as readily, & with still more pleasure.[6]

I believe the conclusion of the L's. Inn affair will be just, as You have heared.[7] You do me justice in supposing that it will give me no concern.

I desire my humble service to my Lady & am always, Dear Sir Edward, Your most faithful & affectionate Servant

R Hurd

242 To WILLIAM WARBURTON — 18 MARCH 1761

Text: *Prelate*, 237.

. . .

I see the reason why you thought of printing the *Discourse on the Holy Spirit* by itself, as you did the Discourse *on the Sacrament.*[1] It was on account of that part which exposes

House of Lords later that year on the death of his father. (*The House of Commons 1754–1790*, ed. Namier and Brooke.)

4 Bond Street was a fashionable place to lodge. No reference to Mr Street has been found in contemporary directories of London. (*Kent's Directory for the Year 1759. Containing an Alphabetical List of the Names and Places of Abode of the Directors of Companies, Persons in Publick Business*, etc., 1759; *A Complete Guide to all Persons who have any Trade or Concern with the City of London, and Parts adjacent*, 1760.)

5 Edward Macro and his father were never reconciled. Edward died in April 1766 and almost nothing is known of his last years. Cox Macro died in 1767 leaving his daughter Mary (Molly) as sole heir.

6 In the Church of England the presiding officer or judge of an archbishop's, bishop's or archdeacon's court was styled the "official". The exact nature of the office offered to RH is not known.

7 See preceding letter.

1 Warburton had begun revising his printed works and in January 1761 had published *A Rational Account of the Nature and End of the Sacrament of the Lord's Supper* based on a sermon, 'The Nature and End of the Lord's Supper', printed in Vol. II of *The Principles of Natural and Revealed Religion occasionally opened and explained; in a Course of Sermons preached before the Honourable*

the pretences of our modern enthusiasts. So that this Sermon would be as seasonable a reproof of the *Methodists*, as the other was of the *Prostitutors of the Lord's Supper*.[2]

If this was your Lordship's idea, my objection comes to nothing; all that part of the Discourse being easy and popular, and such as would be readily comprehended by most readers. But then I should be for printing that part *only*, I mean from p. 255 to the end, and under some such title as this, *The trial of the Spirits of our modern Pretenders to Inspiration*.[3] It would make an admirable tract on the subject. But the inconvenience is, that the Methodists would say your Lordship had written against them; an honour, which, for their own sakes, one would not wish them.[4]

Your Lordship mentioned something of changing the *method* of this Discourse. And now I have presumed thus far, I will tell you a thought that comes into my head about reforming the order of this long Sermon, which from end to end is most excellent. It may easily be done, if you approve the idea, in some future edition of these volumes. Though the method, as it now stands, be regular, yet the unusual length of the Discourse, the abundance of matter it contains, and above all the disproportion of some parts to the rest, make the order of the whole appear neither so clear, nor so elegant as it might be. I would then propose to detach the following parts from it, *Of the Style of Scripture – Of the Inspiration of Scripture – Of the Trial of the Spirits*. These would make so many distinct discourses of a proper size, for which suitable texts might easily be found: for instance, *not in the enticing words of man's wisdom*, for the first: *All Scripture is given by inspiration*, for the second: and, *Try the Spirits*, &c. for the third.[5]

Society of Lincoln's Inn, 1753–4, pp. 41–105. He had now turned his attention to another sermon on 'The Office and Operations of the Holy Spirit' printed in Vol. I, pp. 171–281.

2 RH explained in the Preface to Warburton's works that the Lord's Supper was a subject "which had been so embroiled by two eminent writers of opposite principles, that it became necessary to take it out of their hands, and to guard the publick from being bewildered and misled, either by a Popish or Socinian comment. In a moderate compass", he continued, "[Warburton] has refuted the system of either party, and explained his own notion of the sacrament (which was, also, that of the great Cudworth) in so clear a manner, that few men of sense and judgement will now question where the truth lies." (*A Discourse by Way of General Preface*, p. 90.) RH's reference to the "*Prostitutors of the Lord's Supper*" echoes Warburton's last paragraph in the sermon: ". . . by the prostitution of it [the Sacrament] to CIVIL PURPOSES . . ." (*Principles of Natural and Revealed Religion*, ii. 105.)

3 The first part of the sermon on 'The Office and Operations of the Holy Spirit' is an explication of the "GIFT OF TONGUES" and the language and style of Scriptural writings. (i. 175–209.) Warburton then explains the "TRUE NOTION OF SCRIPTURE INSPIRATION" (pp. 216–34) and is led on to the subject of "FANATICS", who, he says, "pretend to as high a degree of divine communication as if no other *rule of faith* were in being". (p. 252) At p. 255 he writes: "But the continued claim to this primitive abundance of the spirit, by Fanatics of all times, may make it expedient to examine their pretensions yet more minutely. And Scripture itself exhorts us to this inquiry where it bids us to TRY THE SPIRITS; and, in another place, directs us how this trial should be made." From p. 264 to the end the commentary is largely directed against the Methodists. The revised version of the sermon was published in 1762 (dated 1763) with a new title, *The Doctrine of Grace: or, the Office and Operations of the Holy Spirit Vindicated from the Insults of Infidelity, and the Abuses of Fanaticism: Concluding with some Thoughts (humbly offered to the consideration of the Established Clergy) with regard to the right method of defending Religion against the attacks of either Party*, 1763. The early sections which RH suggested omitting, were retained.

4 Warburton did not share this view and before publishing the revised and enlarged version of his sermon on the Holy Spirit he sent the manuscript to John Wesley for corrections. Wesley's reply is printed in *The Letters of the Rev. John Wesley*, A.M., ed. John Telford, 1931, iv. 338–84.

5 1 Cor. 2. 4*; 2 Tim. 3. 16; 1 John 4. 1.

The rest might be one discourse under the present subject. Or, because the last head, of the continuance of the powers of inspiration, does not perfectly correspond to the general title *Of the Office and Operations of the Holy Spirit*, the *two* first heads might make a sermon by themselves; and the *third*, a distinct one, *on the Continuance of the miraculous Powers*. There would be matter enough for this division, and I imagine that what I now propose was something like the method, in which these discourses were first written and delivered.[6] – Your Lordship sees I am a furious critic, when I set on, but this VIth Discourse[7] is throughout so curious and important, that each part deserves to be seen distinctly, and by itself. And I should wish to know what your Lordship thinks of the proposal.

I am sorry for Dr. Brown. – It is very painful, as I have heard Mr. Allen say, with his usual tenderness and humanity, to hear these things of one, whom one has known and esteemed. But whatever inclination his spite to the family, rather than the value of the thing itself, might give him to hold the living, he must needs think himself obliged by the good advice of his friends. When he comes to cool a little, he cannot but perceive that both his ease and his honour required him to resign Horksley, after what had passed between him and his patron.[8] But why is this deduction at Newcastle? It is impossible he should have disgusted the Corporation, already.[9]

6 In Warburton's reply to RH he agreed that his sermon "had originally the form, in a good measure, which you now prescribe. It was in several discourses;" he said, "and how I came to jumble them together I don't know." (*Prelate*, p. 240.) He also agreed to reform it by RH's direction, though this was not finally effected.

7 The sermon was printed as the sixth in the first volume of *The Principles of Natural and Revealed Religion*.

8 John Brown had been offered the living of Newcastle upon Tyne in the summer of 1760. Advertisements were carried in the newspapers and in August 1760 Brown had written to his patron, Lord Royston, to inform him of his intention of resigning the living of Great Horksley to which he had been presented in 1756. Royston had subsequently offered the disposal of the living to Thomas Birch. (Birch to the Bishop of Carlisle, MS BL, Add. 4320, f. 190ff.) But on 17 September, Brown wrote to Royston to say that a circumstance had occurred which rendered it "in some Measure doubtful whether I shall be put in Possession of the Vicarage of Newcastle, or not". (Add. 35606, f. 329.) On 4 October however he wrote again to both Royston and his brother Charles Yorke to say that he would after all accept Newcastle and would therefore vacate Horksley in November. (Brown to Yorke, Add. 35635, f. 434.) Institution and induction were accordingly arranged for November. When the date approached though, Brown asked for more time and on 2 December wrote to Birch to inform him that "a very unexpected Overture has been lately made, which will . . . prevent any final Determination concerning the Vicarage of Newcastle, for some little Time". (Add. 4308, f. 218.) At this point Lord Royston intervened and called upon the Bishop of Durham, who had been responsible for allowing Brown a further extension of time to decide on his acceptance of Newcastle. The Bishop consulted Warburton and Warburton confronted Brown on 4 December. Brown then confessed that he was "in a sort of negotiation for an exchange of Newcastle", to which Warburton replied that "he had carried his declared resignation of Hawkesly too far to retract; and that he would dishonour himselfe by such a proceeding". (Warburton to Birch, 5 December 1760, Add. 4320, f. 188.) This point was disputed by Brown but by 9 December he had capitulated and on 10 December he was instituted to Newcastle. (Add. 35635, f. 473.)

9 The connection between the corporation of Newcastle and the vicar of the parish is explained in a transcript of an "Extract of a Letter from Newcastle" dated 10 October 1760. The "Place of Vicar", it states, is "in the Gift of the Bishop of Carlisle. The Corporation has little to do with it; only they give Him a Compliment of 100£ or so a Year." (MS BL, Add. 35606, f. 331.) No further evidence of Brown's dealings with the corporation has been found.

If Dr. Ayscough thinks a Bishoprick, at his time of life, and in his bad state of health, worth the having, it seems but fit and decent, that he should have the offer of it.[10]

How would your Lordship be disgraced if it were known that your Chaplain was permitted, or, which is much the same thing, that he presumed to entertain your Lordship with accounts of Romances? Yet I must just say, that the *New Heloise* has afforded me much pleasure.[11] There are many exquisite beauties in this odd romance: so odd, that one may be sure the story is two-thirds *fact* for one of *fiction*.[12] But to make amends for this defect, the sensibility of the passionate parts, and the sense, the nature, and the virtue of the rest is above every thing we find in the Crebillons and Voltaires, those idol beaux-esprits of London and Paris.[13] – I wish I could say half so much of our Yorkshire Novelist.[14] Not but the humour of his fourth vol. makes up for the dulness of the third. The worst is, one sees by both, that he has not the discretion, or perhaps the courage, to follow the excellent advice that was given him, *of laughing in such a manner, as that priests and virgins might laugh with him*.[15]

10 Francis Ayscough, D.D. (1700–63), Fellow of Corpus Christi, Oxford and Rector of Northchurch, Berkhamstead. Ayscough had been tutor to George Lyttelton at Oxford and through his interest had become preceptor to George III before his accession and to his brother, the Duke of York. He and Samuel Squire, Dean of Bristol, were in competition for the bishopric of St David's, which had fallen vacant on 16 January. (See Gray, *Correspondence*, Letter 330.) Squire was appointed and Ayscough made Dean of Bristol in his place.

11 *La Nouvelle Heloise* by Jean-Jacques Rousseau was first published as *Lettres de Deux Amans, Habitans d'une petite Ville au pied des Alpes. Recueillies et publiées par J.J. Rousseau*, 1761, and had gone on sale in London on 20 December 1760. (Theophile Dufour, *Recherches Bibliographiques sur les Oeuvres Imprimées de J.-J Rousseau*, Paris, 1925; M.M. Rey to Rousseau, 31 December 1760, *Correspondance Complète de Jean Jacques Rousseau*, ed. R.A. Leigh, Geneva & Oxford, 1965–86, vii. 380–1.)

12 Warburton replied: "You judge truly, and you could not but judge so, that there is more of fact than fiction in it. There would never else have been so much of the domestic part. But above all, the inartificial contexture of the story, and the not rounding and compleating its parts, shews the author had not a fiction to manage over which he was an absolute master. The truth, they say, is, that an intrigue with a fair pupil of family, forced him to leave Swisserland." (*Prelate*, p. 240.) Rousseau gives his own account of his writing *La Nouvelle Heloise* in Book IX of the *Confessions*.

13 Claude Prosper Jolyot de Crebillon (1707–77) had published several popular but licentious novels in the 1730s and 1740s. Gray and Walpole admired his writing, particularly *L'Écumoire*, 1734, and *Le Sopha, conte moral*, 1742.

14 Laurence Sterne (1713–68), Prebendary of York. The first two volumes of *The Life and Opinions of Tristram Shandy, Gentleman* had been published anonymously at York in 1760. The third and fourth volumes were printed and published in London and had been advertised for sale in January 1761. (*Lond. Mag.*)

15 The origin of this advice has not been discovered. Sterne responded to it in Volume V, Chapter 20: "Trim", he wrote, "made a shift to tell his story so, that priests and virgins might have listened to it."

I must not conclude this long letter without telling your Lordship that Mr. Sutton did me the favour to steal away from his companions on the circuit last week, and to spend a day with me at Thurcaston.[16] He seems intent upon his profession. But what pleased me most, was, to find the same sweetness of temper, and simplicity of manners, which he carried out with him, when he made the grand tour. I took this short visit very kindly, and the more so, as he promises to repeat it as oft as he comes to Leicester.

Thurcaston, March 18th, 1761.

243 To WILLIAM MASON 30 MARCH 1761

Text: MS HC; printed, *H-M Corr*, 51.
Addressed: To/The Reverend Mr Mason/at the Right Honble the Earl of Holdernesse's/Arlington Street/ London
Postmarked: 1 AP

My dear Mr Mason

I am not one of those who condole with You on the resignation of Lord H.[1] Because I think he will be full as able to serve You now, as when he was in place. Then the D. N. disposed of everything.[2] Now there is a chance at least for this department's falling into other hands. You see the difference. But whatever comes of this, You do right to stay in town for some time, for the reasons You mention. If, after all, things do not succeed, as your friends wish, by all means come hither to me.[3] We are made to comfort each other, or rather we are made to be happy in each other, witht standing in need of any comfort, under such petty disappointments as these. Take my word for it, my dear friend, we are neither of us fated to be rich. <. . .>[a] For I hold we were born under the same stars, tho' their various influence destined You to be a great poet, & me, to be a poor critic. But, courage, my friend: we will be happy in spite of our starrs, I mean your poetry, & my criticism. Heaven has given us an equivalent for this curse, in the blessing of an equal mind. It has done more. It has given us, <. . .> what no fortune could have done, the love & friendship of each other. I have said all in saying this. Let preferments go which way they will. You & I can do very well in our country parsonages.

16 Richard Sutton (1733–1802), son of Warburton's patron, Sir Robert. Sutton had been admitted at the Middle Temple in 1754, and was appointed Under Secretary of State in 1766. (*Alum. Cantab.*; William Betham, *The Baronetage of England*, 1801–5, iii. 397.)

1 Lord Holdernesse had been dismissed from his office as secretary of state for the southern department on 13 March to make way for the king's favourite, Lord Bute. (Walpole to Mann, 17 March 1761, *Walpole Correspondence*, Vol. 21; Newcastle to Devonshire, 13 March 1761, MS BL, Add. 32920, f. 166.)

2 By the mid 1740s the Duke of Newcastle had acquired almost total control over ecclesiastical patronage of the crown. (Stephen Taylor, ' "The fac totum in ecclesiastic affairs"? The Duke of Newcastle and the Crown's Ecclesiastical Patronage', *Albion*, xxiv (1992), 409–33.)

3 The allusion is probably to Mason's hope of a canonry. (See *post* To Mason, 3 May 1761, n. 3.)

a Twelve and a half lines obliterated.

Vive sine invidia; mollesque inglorius annos
Exige: amicitias et tibi junge pares.[4]
Dixi.

I charge You, get this Distich engrav'd in Church Letters on ye front of your new building towrds the Garden, immediately. – Let Mr Wood get it executed agst You come home. Mr Wood & I, for want of better, will stand for the *pares*.

I am not surprized that Mr Gray & other fine readers should dislike *Nouvelle Heloise*.[5] I see a hundred reasons for this. The admirers of *Crebillon*, are out of their element here.[6] To tell You my opinion in one word, this is the most exquisite work of the kind that ever was written. I have read it a second time, & could read it twenty times, with fresh pleasure. The reason is, the <man> author is a man of *virtue*, as well as genius. This *last* indeed is so transcendant in him, that it makes one overlook the most improbable, & worst contrived story that ever was.[7] <And> But, if he had totally wanted Genius, the magic of his *Virtue* is enough to charm evry reader, who is not wholly devoid of it, himself. The part I like least is the character of Lord Bomston & his Italian amours.[8] But the rocks of Meillery, & the domestic transactions of Clarens are above everything that is extant in the world, of that kind.[9] – The age must be very different from what it is, before such a work as this can be relished at London & Paris. Let them dote on *Crebillon & Voltaire*, as usual: this homely Swiss, for my money. In short, I am of the author's mind: men & women may speak ill of it, and welcome:[10] But let no man or woman speak ill of it to me: I am confident I could never esteem such a person, as long as I lived.

4 Ovid, *Tristia*, III. iv. 43–4.

5 J.-J. Rousseau, *La Nouvelle Heloise*, 1761. (See preceding letter, n. 11.) Gray was "cruelly disappointed" by the book. "Rousseau's people", he said, "do not interest me; there is but one character and one style in them all, I do not know their faces asunder. I have no esteem for their persons or conduct, am not touched with their passions; and as to their story, I do not believe a word of it – not because it is improbable, but because it is absurd." (Gray, *Correspondence*, Letter 328; see also Letter 330.)

6 See preceding letter, n. 13.

7 *La Nouvelle Heloise* is the story of the passionate love of Julie d'Étange and her tutor, Saint-Preux, their separation and her marriage with M. Wolmar. Each of the protagonists is supported by a friend and confidante, Julie by her cousin Claire, and Saint-Preux by an English friend, Lord Bomston. The story ends with Saint-Preux, having overcome his passion for Julie, living with her and Wolmar in domestic tranquillity.

8 Lord Bomston's "Italian amours" are explained in Letter CLIII.

9 Saint-Preux, having agreed to leave Julie, had travelled to Meillerie on the opposite shore of Lake Geneva. There, he said "je cours, je monte avec ardeur, je m'elance sur les rochers; je parcours a grands pas tous les environs, & trouve par-tout dans les objets la meme horreur qui regne au dedans de moi. On n'appercoit plus de verdure, l'herbe est jaune & fletrie, les arbres sont depouilles, le sechard & la froide bise entassent la neige & les glaces, & toute la nature est morte a mes yeux, comme l'esperance au fond de mon coeur." (Letter XXVI.) The "domestic transactions of Clarens" are those of the Wolmar household: Julie, her husband and their children. They are described by Saint-Preux at length in Letters CXXIX, CXXX and CXXXVI.

10 This view is expressed by Rousseau in the Preface to *La Nouvelle Heloise*. In the concluding paragraph he says: "Qu'un homme austere en parcourant ce recueil se rebute aux premieres parties, jette le livre avec colere, & s'indigne contre l'Editeur; je ne me plaindrai point de son injustice; à sa place, j'en aurois pu faire autant. Que si, après l'avoir lu tout entier, quelqu'un m'osait blamer de l'avoir publié; qu'il le dise, s'il veut, à toute la terre, mais qu'il ne vienne pas me le dire: je sens que je ne pourrois de ma vie estimer cet homme-la."

It is as violent a transition as any in your Odes to pass at once from *Rousseau*, to *Stern*. Yet in speaking of Romances, I must tell You my mind of his. The 3d Vol. is insufferably dull & even stupid. The 4th is full as humorous as either of the other two. But this broad humour, even at it's best, can never be endured in a work of length. And he does not seem capable of following the advice which one gave him – *of laughing in such a manner, as that Virgins & Priests might laugh with him.*[11] <. . .>[b]

To return to *Rousseau*, pray read him again & again. You will think evry other Romance-writer (I had almost said, not excepting Cervantes himself, but his manner is too different to be compared with Rousseau's) poor & contemptible to him. Pick up what You can in relation to his history, situation, & private morals. I have an extreme curiosity to be better acquainted with him. I say, do all this, & let me see You here as soon as You can. With or without a Prebend is nothing either to You or me.

With all affection, my dear Sir, Most faithfully & for ever Your's

R Hurd

Thurcaston 30 March 1761

Endorsed by Richard Hurd, nephew: "March 30th 1761".

244 To CHARLES YORKE 8 APRIL 1761

Text: MS BL Add. 35636, f. 49; unpublished; copy, HC.
Addressed: cover missing.

Thurcaston Apr. 8. 1761

Dear Sir

I beg leave to trouble You with one word of acknowledgment for your very obliging Letter of the 24th past, wch I have this moment receiv'd under Mr Allen's cover from P. Park.[1]

The only circumstance, that gave me any concern in the late affair, was the disagreable trouble it occasioned to my friends, & of which You were pleas'd to take to Yourself so great a share.[2]

I should be sorry, for the sake of the Society, that their Preacher should be made uneasy by the strictness of their regulations.[3] Without doubt, they will see fit to abate of them when they reflect that such a station should be render'd as eligible, as it may be, in order to invite such persons to serve them in it, as are most likely to do them

11 See preceding letter, nn. 14 and 15.

b Section cut from letter (approx. three lines).

1 MS HC, Yorke to RH, 24 March 1761.

2 RH alludes to the attempts made to secure his appointment as Preacher of Lincoln's Inn. The position had gone to Thomas Ashton. (See *ante* To Yorke, 1 March 1761.)

3 Commenting on Ashton's appointment, Yorke had said that he was "doubtful, whether Dr. Ashton will hold the preachership long. The Benchers", he explained, "have made some strong orders at one or two late meetings about the attendance of their preacher, not very consistent with the Dr.'s other engagements; which will tend to create ill blood. But this is only for your Ear."

honour. But if an opening should hereafter happen by this or any other means, I am obliged, by your kind offer, to tell You my mind of that matter very frankly.

Having had leisure of late for much of that Self-converse, which Lord Shaftesbury recommends,[4] I do not find in myself those talents for Preaching that should make me ambitious of succeeding Dr Ashton in the office of lecturing so learned a Society as that of Lincoln's Inn. So that on the whole I ought to think it an escape to my reputation, that I have not been put on the trial of them. And I do, indeed, think this so sincerely, that instead of presuming to ask the continuance of your favour, in case of another vacancy, I am firmly resolved not to expose myself, again, to the same hazard.[5]

I pride myself, as I have reason, in the honour of having been thought not unworthy your countenance in pretending to such an office. But I shall envy no man the honour of filling it.

I am with the most perfect esteem & gratitude for all your favours, Dear Sir, Your much obliged & most Obedient humble Servant

R Hurd

245 To Sir EDWARD LITTLETON 12 APRIL 1761

Text: MS STAFFS RO D1413/1; unpublished.
Addressed: To/Sir Edward Littleton Bart/at his Seat near/ Lichfield/Staffordshire
Postmarked: LEICESTER

Dear Sir Edward

I have the favour of Your's, by which I perceive what prudent & excellent advice You have given Mr M.[1] But what is advice, to a person whose passions will not suffer him to take the benefit of it.

I know not what to say to this sad story, only that I could be glad to talk it over with You here, & to contrive, if possible, with You some way of making up matters with his father. Unless this is done, & indeed speedily, I see nothing but ruin before him.[2]

In civility, & indeed in reason (for I am a much idler man than You) I ought to wait upon You at Teddesly. But You know how bad a traveller I am, & besides I cannot be from my Churches on a Sunday.[3] If You can oblige me with your company for two or three days, You may take your own time, for I am always at home, & I know of nobody

4 [Anthony Ashley Cooper, third Earl of Shaftesbury], *Soliloquy: or, Advice to an Author*, 1710, pp. 5–16.

5 The Lincoln's Inn Preachership fell vacant once again in June 1765 and despite his present determination RH agreed to stand. He was unanimously elected Preacher on 6 November. (*Records of Lincoln's Inn. The Black Books Vol. III*, p. 384.)

1 Littleton's advice to Edward Macro has not survived.

2 Little more is known of Macro's career. He is occasionally mentioned in RH's letters and in 1763 is said to be "well employed" in London. This is the last reference to him; his death in 1766 is not recorded in RH's surviving correspondence.

3 RH had been without a curate since the autumn of 1760. (See *ante* To Littleton, 29 October 1760.)

that is likely to break in upon us. Pray think of this, & let me know your resolution as soon as may be.

I have not the courage to say a word more of this unhappy man, till I see You. God send, as You say, that this may be the last of his misfortunes. But when a man has no *self-government*, what can this life be but one continued misfortune?

I am, with all affection, My dearest Sir, Your most faithful humble Servant

R Hurd

Thurcaston Apr. 12. 1761

246 To THOMAS BALGUY 1 MAY 1761

Text: *Memoirs*, 81.

Thurcaston, May 1, 1761.

. . . I know not whether I should condole with you for the loss of your patron.[1] He is gathered to his fathers in a good old age, and has left you in possession of two of the best things in the world, a *competency* and *liberty*. God send you health to enjoy these, and then you have all the happiness a reasonable man ought to look for.

I shall not dispute with you about the merits of Tristram; but I require you, upon pain of my displeasure, to retract your opinion of Rousseau.[2] The New Heloise, I do not say as a romance, but as a moral composition, is incomparable. I do not care what you and Mr. Gray in the pride of criticism may pretend to the contrary. I appeal not to your taste, but to your *moral sense*.

The Bishop of Gloucester and you are severe on my Lord elect of ——.[3] I think I could take upon me to make his apology against both of you.

I would begin with observing that the Duke of Newcastle himself could not possibly look for *gratitude* in his dependants. What virtue, pray, did he ever observe in them? And does he think that so big a virtue as gratitude can have room to expatiate in a mind that was too narrow for the entertainment of any other.

I would further ask, when the subjects he preferred had by accident any virtues, whether his Grace preferred them on that account, or from any generous esteem of their virtuous qualities? If not, gratitude, which respects the disposition of the heart,

1 Benjamin Hoadly (1676–1761), Bishop in succession of Bangor, Hereford, Salisbury and Winchester. Balguy had been appointed Archdeacon of Winchester by Hoadly in 1759 and in his account of the life of his father in *Biographia Britannica* mentions that he owed "his Archdeaconry, and all his other preferments, to the favour and friendship of Bishop Hoadly". (Kippis, *Biographia Britannica*, 1778–93, i. 549.) Hoadly had died on 17 April.

2 [Laurence Sterne], *The Life and Opinions of Tristram Shandy, Gentleman* (Vols. I–IV); Rousseau, *Julie, ou La Nouvelle Heloise*. (See *ante* To Warburton, 18 March 1761, and To Mason, 30 March 1761.)

3 Samuel Squire (1713–66), Bishop elect of St David's. Squire had been an active supporter of the Duke of Newcastle's candidature for the Chancellorship of the University in 1748. After his election he had been appointed chaplain to the Duke and had acted as his university secretary. Further preferments had followed but by 1760 Squire had become dissatisfied with Newcastle's patronage and had transferred his allegiance to Bute. On his appointment to the bishopric, Newcastle was at pains to point out that he had had no hand in the promotion. (*Notes & Queries*, First Series, i. 65–7.)

and not the outward act, has properly no root to spring from, and could not, therefore, be expected without absurdity.

Next, I would say, that if haply any one had a mind naturally turned to the cultivation of gratitude, the air of a court, or, which is all one, of Newcastle House, was so baleful to the growth of this virtue, that it could never come to any size or maturity. Rousseau would say that it has seldom or never been heard of since the *golden age*, by which he would mean the savage life, and that it is in a manner inconsistent with the state of men in cultivated society.[4]

I would then urge in his behalf, that preferments, when conferred by the great on their dependants, are not so properly favours as *debts*; that a course of years spent in servitude is the price they pay for such things; and that when promotion comes at last it comes in the way of recompense, and not of obligation. Would not any one laugh to hear of a slave's gratitude to his master?

Further, one might plead that words have not the same meaning in all places, and on all occasions. *Gratitude* is, no doubt, expected from a great man's tool; but by gratitude, when so applied, is only meant an attachment to him so long as he seems likely to serve oneself. When carried further, it means what in common language we express by the name of *folly*.

Lastly, to make short work, and to omit abundance of reasons as good as these, I would plead the example of the great man himself. Where was his gratitude in undermining and jostling out of his place his own patron, – I mean Sir Robert of famous memory, as he and his brother did, as soon as there was a reasonable prospect of getting into it themselves?[5]

All these reasons taken together, and set in a good light, would, methinks, make a handsome apology for *ingratitude*; and when made might possibly be as serviceable to the rest of the duke's dependants in their turn as to Dr. S. . .

247 To WILLIAM MASON 3 MAY 1761

Text: MS HC; printed, *H-M Corr*, 54.
Addressed: To/The Reverend Mr Mason/at the Right Honble the Earl of Holdernesse's/Arlington Street/ London
Postmarked: LEICESTER 6 MA

Dear Sir

You are an impudent bard, that You are, to satirize two Lords at once, & certainly fall under the Statute of *Scandalum Magnatum*, in the proper sense.[1] However it is my

[4] This reference suggests that RH had read Rousseau's *Discours sur l'Origine et les Fondemens de l'Inégalité parmi les Hommes*, Amsterdam, 1755.

[5] Newcastle and his brother, Henry Pelham, rose to power as Sir Robert Walpole began to lose his ascendancy, but Walpole had not been directly instrumental in promoting Newcastle's rise.

[1] In Mason's *Commonplace Book* there is an "Epigram occasiond by Lord Hardwicks & Lord Lytteltons Verses to one another", with a note "Printed in the St James's".

While evry Freeman in the nation
Burgess & *Cit* of each vocation
In Pitts just Praises join

weakness to approve all You do. The Epigram is not without it's salt. Tho' what You mean by writing such lawless things, at the time You are solliciting preferment, I cannot imagine. Learn of Dr Squire or Dr Pyle, to correct your style & manner, or I denounce the pains of poverty & poetry upon You, as long as You live.[2]

Your thought of meeting me at P. Park is excellent. The Bp visits sooner than I expected, so that I shall be with him, I hope without fail, before the end of the month. Your being there to receive me, will give me fresh spirits for this long journey. I charge You, don't disappoint me. I shall <. . .> accept no excuse, unless it be the Residentiariship of York.[3]

Your present of the Dialogue was very welcome & unexpected.[4] I had hear'd nothing of it. It shews me, what my vanity would not let me see before, I mean the reason why my Dialogue of famous memory was so ill received by You judges.[5] It was not the *form*, as you flatterers pretended. It was the *execution*, that did all the mischief. If I had known how to write like Rousseau, it's success had been certain. But to have done with this fond subject, myself, & to say a word of *the Citizen of Geneva.*

His *entretien* is excellent. Yet how Mr Gray should like it so much, after liking the *Letters* so little, I cannot imagine.[6] It looks as if he began to be ashamed of his former judgment. There is nothing in the Dialogue but what he had said, or at least intimated up & down in his work.

I repeat it, Mr Mason, the man that does not approve the N. Heloise, cannot cordially be approved by me. And I have accordingly required Dr Balguy (who by the way is at Bath, & will be there till tow'rds the end of this month) to retract his opinion of it, on the pain of my utmost displeasure.[7]

Thy Meagre Virtue Modest Peer
Hangs dangling by a single hair
  In Hardwicks hitching Line

Indeed My Lord you're much to blame
To risk so rashly your good name
  'Tis true, his Rhymes are terse
Yet Honest folks your Lordship knows
So seldom trust a Lawyers prose
  Theyll ne'er believe his verse

(York Minster Library, *Commonplace Book*, p. 28.)
The epigram appeared in the *St. James's Chronicle* for 25–28 April 1761, without attribution. Penalties for the offence of scandulum magnatum were provided by 2 Ric. II, stat. 1, c. 5.

2 Samuel Squire, Bishop elect of St David's. (See *ante* To Warburton, 18 March 1761, n. 10, and To Balguy, 1 May 1761, n. 3.) Edmund Pyle (1702–76) was appointed Archdeacon of York in 1751. Both men were colleagues of Mason as Court Chaplains.

3 Mason had been promised the stall of a Residentiary Canon at York when it should fall vacant. The present incumbent was William Herring, Chancellor of the diocese of York. He died in January 1762. (See post To Balguy, 29 January 1762; Gray, *Correspondence*, Letters 352, 353; *Gent. Mag.*)

4 Mason had sent RH a copy of Rousseau's *Preface de la Nouvelle Heloise: ou Entretien sur les Romans, entre l'Editeur et un Homme de Lettres*, published in February 1761.

5 RH refers to the Preface to *Moral and Political Dialogues*. (See *ante* To Mason, 26 January 1758, n. 4, and To Mason, 25 June 1759.)

6 See Gray, *Correspondence*, Letters 328, 330. *La Nouvelle Heloise* was first published as *Lettres de Deux Amans*. (See *ante* To Warburton, 18 March 1761, n. 11.)

7 See preceding letter.

I have just finish'd a trifle in 12 short Letters, which You & one or two more will perhaps take the trouble of reading, & which no body else will.[8] I may perhaps take the fancy to bring it with me to Prior-Park.

You are a pitiful philosopher. Talk of pique & I know not what, because great men take no notice of You! Do You know, that if You deserved their countenance & preferments, I should not esteem You half so much as I do? Be content with my esteem, witht a prebend. I can tell You, it is not lavished away upon so many, as that it should seem a trifle to You.

I quit this magnificent style to tell You, I expect a Letter from You forthwith, whether You go to Prior-Park or no.

God bless You, my dear Sir; Accept this benediction from my Lord Bp of Gloucester's unworthy Chaplain, & from your assured friend

R Hurd

Thurcaston May. 3. 1761.

Endorsed by Richard Hurd, nephew: "May 3d 1761".

248 To THOMAS BALGUY 26 JULY 1761

Text: MS BEINECKE MS Vault Shelves, Hurd; printed in part, *Memoirs*, 83.
Addressed: cover missing.

Dear Sir,

I have your favour of the 9th, which I sit down to acknowledge, before I leave this place.

The Bp & I have traversed the finest parts of this County, some of them indeed extreamly fine. Evry thing passed well & smoothly in the visitation, &, I have reason to think, with perfect satisfaction to the clergy.[1] Among the rest Pat Weston was so mollified by the Bp's civilities, that he is one of the most observant & dutiful of the

[8] This was to be published as *Letters on Chivalry and Romance* in May 1762.

[1] Warburton had been consecrated Bishop of Gloucester in January 1760. (See *ante* To Yorke, 13 December 1759, n. 1.) This was his first visitation; the itinerary, recorded in the liber cleri compiled at the time, was as follows:

Date	Church	Deanery
16 June 1761	Chipping Sodbury	Hawkesbury
18 June	Dursley	Dursley
19 June	Stroud	Stonehouse
23 June	Cirencester	Cirencester & Fairford
25 June	Stow	Stow
26 June	Chipping Campden	Campden
30 June	Cheltenham	Winchcombe
1 July	Newnham	Forest
2 July	Gloucester	Gloucester

(Gloucs. RO, GDR 297A)

whole flock.[2] He preach'd at Campden a reasonable Sermon, which ended with a short & decent compliment to his Diocesan.[3] He owned to me, he had much mistaken the character of the Bp of Gloucester, & applied that verse (which he also said was applicable to his Chaplain) – *lasciva pagina, vita proba.*[4] In short, you must not think it strange if this mercurial man be henceforward of our Party, I mean a friend to the fame & virtues of our excellent Bishop.

But I know you expect one word, about the Charge.[5] It was an exhortation to the study of Letters, more especially of Divinity; very lively & entertaining in the manner, & full of admirable things. It will not be printed at present, but will appear hereafter as an Introduction to a small volume, which he promised to his clergy, under the name of *Directions &c on the Study of Theology*.[6] You will guess that a work of this sort will, under the Bishop's management, be very curious as well as useful: And I believe, we shall not wait very long for it.

Here is an excellent Episcopal house, & elegantly furnished.[7] What company the place affords, we see; & when there is no company, we are still happier in our private amusements & conversation. In short the time passes here so deliciously, that it is with regret almost, I hear of shifting the scene even to Prior Park. I return to that place, with the Bp, in the very beginning of August; but, for one week only; this dirty business of the Inclosure calling me directly into Leicestershire at a time, when my inclination would lead me to You & Winchester.[8]

I wish You a long & happy enjoyment of your new house & agreable situation. If Dr Powell be with You, pray give my kindest respects to him. With compliments to Miss Drake, let me assure You how faithfully I am ever, Dear Sir, Your affectionate humble Servant

R Hurd

The Palace at Gloucester July 26. 1761.

2 William Weston, known as "Pat" in Cambridge. (Scott-Mayor, *Admissions to St. John's*, ii. (Part 3) 416.) Weston was Vicar of Campden and the author of *An Enquiry into the Rejection of the Christian Miracles by the Heathens* to which RH had replied in 1746. (See *ante* To Macro, 5 January 1747.) Warburton, in a letter of 10 February 1750, had referred to Weston as "that egregious coxcomb". (*Prelate*, p. 29.)

3 This appears not to have been published.

4 Martial, *Epigrams*, I. iv. 8.

5 'A Charge on the Study of Theology. (Unfinished.)' was published in *A Selection from Unpublished Papers of . . . Warburton*, ed. Francis Kilvert, 1841, pp. 358–68.

6 *Directions for the Study of Theology* was not published in Warburton's lifetime but the first part, probably all that was written, was included in the supplementary volume of his works. (*A Supplemental Volume of Bishop Warburton's Works*, 1788, pp. 427–54.)

7 Gertrude Warburton had supervised the furnishing of the Bishop's Palace at Gloucester. (See *ante* To Warburton, 4 March 1760, nn. 3 and 4.)

8 RH had proposed the enclosure of Anstey Fields, an area of land allotted to him as Rector of Thurcaston and trustee of Brewood Grammar School. The original proposal was made in November 1759 and presented to his bishop, John Thomas, of Lincoln, for approval. His reply indicates that RH wished to accept "evry seventh Acre of the intended Inclosure in Lieu of Tythes" and "2 sh per Acre for the Old Inclosure". (Leics. RO, DE1416/60/1.) Warburton, in a letter of 2 November 1759, wrote "Of the inclosed, you say right: £20 gained thus, is worth twenty times the sum got by Levee-hunting." (*Prelate*, p. 220.)

249 To Sir EDWARD LITTLETON 30 AUGUST 1761

Text: MS STAFFS RO D1413/1; unpublished.
Addressed: To/Sir Edward Littleton Bart/at his Seat near/Lichfield
Postmarked: BIRMINGHAM

Birmingham Aug. 30. 1761

Dear Sir Edward

I am thus far on my way to Hatton, where I think of staying a fortnight or three weeks.[1] On my return into Leicestershire I propose to give myself the pleasure of passing some days with You, unless You acquaint me in the mean time that You are running to the Coronation, which I do not much expect.[2]

Perhaps, during my stay at Hatton, You may do us the pleasure of riding over thither. Methinks we could make a pleasant day of it in paying another visit together at Eudness Wood.[3]

I beg my humble service to Lady Littleton, to whom I wish all imaginable entertainment from the fine Shew, which is so near at hand, & which her Ladyship cannot well be excus'd from taking a peep at.[4]

Dear Sir Edward, oblige me with one line directed to me at Hatton, & believe me always Most faithfully & affectionately Your's

R Hurd

250 To WILLIAM MASON 28 OCTOBER 1761

Text: MS HC; printed, *H-M Corr*, 57.
Addressed: To/The Reverend Mr Mason/Rector of Aston near/ Chesterfield/Derbyshire
Postmarked: postmark missing.

Thurcaston Oct. 28. 1761.

Dear Mr Mason

I had your flying Letter from the North-road, & was much disappointed in your not coming this way, as it was amongst the principal pleasures I had promis'd myself this winter. You may go on with your press-work, & send me the sheets when You please.[1] I shall have nothing better to do, than to attend to them.

You hear what a clamour there is about Mr Pitt's accepting the King's acknowledgments of his late services.[2] Such a monster, is this many-headed beast. But You, who are not of this spirit, have methinks a fine opportunity to do something in your own

1 RH's brother John farmed at Hatton.
2 The coronation of George III was to take place on 22 September.
3 This area of woodland has not been identified.
4 No records documenting the coronation celebrations in Staffordshire have been traced.

1 Mason was preparing his *Elegies* to go to press. The first edition was published on 7 December 1762 and a second edition followed exactly three weeks later. Both were dated 1763. (Gaskell, *First Editions of William Mason*, pp. 8–9.)
2 Pitt had resigned on 5 October 1761 following his defeat in the Cabinet on the issue of declaring war on Spain. A few days later he accepted a pension of £3,000 p. a. and the title of Baroness Chatham for his wife. (See Walpole to Mann, 6 October and 10 October 1761, *Walpole Correspondence*, Vol. 21; Peters, *Pitt and Popularity*, pp. 202–11.)

way by planning an Ode on this famous Resignation.[3] It would take in all the glories of his ministry: a subject, worthy of your pen, & perhaps the only one of the kind which our times are likely to furnish. There would be a dignity in such a panegyric at this season, & besides it would mortify certain great men. 'Tis true, of the prudence of this project I can say nothing.

I have just been reading *Crevier's history of the University of Paris*.[4] I can by no means recommend it to You. What would You think of a history, in form, of our famous University of Cambridge? And yet our never to be forgotten squabbles about Appeals would make as shining a chapter, as any You will find in these labour'd volumes. I sent for them on the supposition of their being a *literary* history. Alass! they are only an *Academical*.

But I have a higher entertainment than this in view. To say nothing of Hume's abridged English history from Julius Caesar to Henry VII (just now publish'd) wch, I suppose, like his other things will be just worth the reading,[5] I have got the best Paris Edition of *Plutarch's* works, & these I depend upon for my winter's amusement.[6]

In fact, anything is better than turning one's thoughts on the men & things of these times. Yet I shall always be attentive to anything in which You are interested.

Let me hear a word of your Stall at York;[7] or at least that You are well & easy out of it.

Dear Mr Mason, Your most affectionate friend & Servt

R Hurd

Endorsed by Richard Hurd, nephew: "Oct 28th 1761".

251 To Sir EDWARD LITTLETON 22 NOVEMBER 1761

Text: MS FOLGER w.a. 57(8); unpublished.
Addressed: To/Sir Edward Littleton Bart/at his Seat near/ Lichfield/Staffordshire
Postmarked: LEICESTER

Nov. 22. 1761. Thurcaston.

Dear Sir Edward

My Brother Tom[1] from Birmingham just now informs me (& 'tis the first Intelligence

3 Mason's opinion of Pitt's conduct in accepting a pension and a peerage was not favourable. (See *post* To Mason, 27 November 1761; Gray, *Correspondence*, Letters 345, 347.) He did not publish an ode to celebrate the occasion.

4 Jean Baptiste Louis Crevier, *Histoire de l'Université de Paris, Depuis son origine jusqu'en l'année 1600*, 7 vols., Paris, 1761.

5 David Hume, *The History of England, from the Invasion of Julius Caesar to the Accession of Henry VII*, 2 vols., 1762, advertised for sale in the *London Magazine* in November. These two volumes completed Hume's six volume *History of England*, the first volume of which had been published in 1754. RH had already publicly attacked Volumes 3 and 4 (see *ante* To Mason, 4 May 1759, n. 5) and was not enthusiastic about these last two volumes. (See post To Mason, 27 November 1761.)

6 Probably *Les Oeuvres Morales de Plutarque, translatées de grec en françois, reveves et corrigées en plusieurs passages par le translateur*, J. Amyot, 2 vols., Paris, 1603. A copy remains at HC.

7 Mason was expecting to be appointed a Residentiary Canon at York. (See *ante* To Mason, 3 May 1761, n. 3.)

1 Thomas Hurd. See *ante* To Littleton, 7 October 1748, n. 1.

I have receiv'd of it) that You are appointed High Sheriff for the following year.[2] In this case he supposes that You will be applied to by several persons to furnish You with Liveries; and among the rest he presumes that I have credit enough with You to be allowed to mention him, who for some years past has dealt pretty largely in Mercery. You know me so well as to believe that I take this liberty only, as I am requested to do it by a person so near to me, & not with a view to press You farther than may be perfectly convenient to You. I should be glad, no doubt, to procure him this advantage. But there may be many reasons why You cannot favour him. You will excuse, however, my saying just thus much, & will determine as freely as if I had not said a word of the matter. Whatever You determine, I know, will be right.

I beg my compliments to Lady Littleton & am, Dear Sir, Your most affectionate humble Servant

R Hurd

252 To WILLIAM MASON 27 NOVEMBER 1761

Text: MS HC; printed, *H-M Corr*, 59.
Addressed: cover missing.

Thurcaston 27. Nov. 1761

Dear Mr Mason

Tho' You affirm roundly, You are quite mistaken, at least in this instance, in thinking that my opinion of Mr P. was determin'd by that of our friend.[1] I did not at that time so much as know what was his Opinion.

I consider'd the case in this view.

A pension & peerage were, I own, suspicious circumstances. But when I understood that these were not bargain'd for, nor so much as ask'd, it seem'd to me that they could not be refus'd without indecency, without reflecting upon the K., nor indeed without an evident degree of faction. It is very true, & Mr P. could not but be aware of it, his popularity was likely to suffer by his acceptance of these favours. But this I make a fresh argument for Mr P's honesty, who sacrific'd what was most dear to him, to his loyalty & his Duty. I could say much more, but am contented to rest the matter upon his future Conduct, if his past do not satisfy You. In the mean time forgive me this candour: I may not, perhaps, offend in the same sort again very speedily.

2 No manuscript record of Littleton's nomination as sheriff of Staffordshire has been found. He is, however, listed as being appointed on 15 February 1762, probably the date at which his period of office commenced. ([Josiah C. Wedgwood], 'The Staffordshire Sheriffs (1086–1912), Escheators (1247–1619), and Keepers or Justices of the Peace (1263–1702)' in *Collections for a History of Staffordshire*, 1912.

1 RH alludes to Pitt's resignation and acceptance of a pension and a peerage for his wife. (See *ante* To Mason, 28 October 1761, n. 2.) The friend is Warburton whose recent promotion to the bench had been secured by Pitt, and to whom Pitt had written, according to Warburton, "in vindication of his conduct". (Norman Sykes, 'The Duke of Newcastle as Ecclesiastical Minister', *English Historical Review*, lvii (1942), 70–2; Warburton to Yorke, 24 October 1761, *Letters to Charles Yorke*, p. 42.)

Hume's history is entertaining.[2] He says a great deal, & very pertinently on the feudal System; but nothing that contradicts me, tho' he may possibly be of that opinion.[3] What I did not expect, is, That I receive no new light from him upon this subject.

Now this work is completed, I will tell You my sentimts of it in few words.

His Libertinism on many occasions is *detestible*: his bigottry to the Stuart family, which occasion'd his political follies, *pernicious*: & his bias to the french taste & manners, which appears thro'out his work, *ridiculous*.[4] Otherwise, this is the most readible General history we have of England. The faults of his *Composition* are, a too frequent affectation of philosophical disquisition; & an incorrect, & sometimes an inflated style. The *former* is unsuited to the general nature of history: And the *latter* is a capital blemish in a work that pretends to be nothing more than a Compilation.[5] With these defects, his work will be read & admird: and which is still worse, the mediocrity of this history will prevent an able writer from undertaking a better.[6] *Dixi*.

As to your Odes, print what You will, provided it be excellent in it's kind. I like the *Water-nymph* as much as You do: –[7] I am not for a good writer's *condescending* – & that is my answer to Manwaring's sophistical Letter.[8]

. . .

2 David Hume, *The History of England, from the Invasion of Julius Caesar to the Accession of Henry VII*, 2 vols., 1762. (See To Mason, 28 October 1761, n. 5.)

3 Hume had added an Appendix on "The Feudal and Anglo-Norman Government and Manners" to the end of the first volume of his *History*. No reference is made to RH's account of the feudal constitution in *Moral and Political Dialogues* (pp. 195–217) and Hume's comments on him in his letters are all dismissive. (See Hume to Adam Smith, 28 July 1759, *The Letters of David Hume*, ed. J.Y.T. Greig, 1932.) A further account of the feudal constitution appears in the second letter of *Letters on Chivalry and Romance*.

4 Hume acknowledged that a "few Christians . . . think I speak like a Libertine in religion" (Hume, *Letters*, i. 189) and was aware that his volume on the early Stuarts was "rather more agreeable to those they call Tories" than to the whigs. (*Letters*, i. 214.) Reviewing what he had already published in ?1756, he wrote, "I am convinced that whatever I have said of religion should have received some more softenings. There is no passage in the History which strikes in the least at revelation. But as I run over all the sects successively, and speak of each of them with some mark of disregard, the reader, putting the whole together, concludes that I am of no sect; which to him will appear the same thing as the being of no religion. With regard to politics and the character of princes and great men, I think I am very moderate. My views of *things* are more conformable to Whig principles; my representations of *persons* to Tory prejudices. Nothing can so much prove that men commonly regard more persons than things, as to find that I am commonly numbered among the Tories." (*Letters*, i. 237.)

5 Hume commented on these two aspects of his history in a letter to the Abbé le Blanc, dated 12 September 1754. "If you consider", he said, "the vast Variety of Events, with which these two Reigns [James I and Charles I], particularly the last, are crowded, you will conclude, that my Narration is rapid, and that I have more propos'd as my Model the concise manner of the antient Historians, than the prolix, tedious Style of some modern Compilers. I have inserted no original Papers, and enter'd into no Detail of minute, uninteresting Facts. The philosophical spirit, which I have so much indulg'd in all my Writings, finds here ample Materials to work upon." (*Letters*, i. 193.)

6 Hume's work remained the standard history of England for more than a century.

7 Mason was planning a collected edition of his *Poems* which was published in December 1763 (dated 1764). The ode *To a Water-Nymph* had already been printed in Volume 3 of Dodsley's *A Collection of Poems. By Several Hands* in 1748.

8 This allusion remains obscure.

You grow horridly misanthropical: witness your Satires & Comedies.[9] I shall print my innocent Letters on Chivalry forthwith, where there is not a word of ill nature.[10]

Plutarch sends his Love to You, & deserves, I think, to be of your acquaintance.[11]

Remember me to your Neighbours at the Parsonage, & believe me very much Your's

R Hurd.

Endorsed by Richard Hurd, nephew: "Nov 27th 1761".

253 To Sir EDWARD LITTLETON 14 DECEMBER 1761

Text: MS STAFFS RO D1413/1; unpublished.
Addressed: To/Sir Edward Littleton Bart/at his Seat near Lichfield/Staffordshire
Postmarked: LEICESTER

Thurcaston 14. Decr. 1761.

Dear Sir

I have your favour of the 5th. What you say in answer to my last, is kind & satisfactory. I have not a word more to say upon that subject.[1]

You are very obliging in the affair of Sharshill.[2] But, as it certainly will not be worth my taking, so I think You do perfectly right to think of disposing of it in the way You mention. As to Mr Moss, I remember something of him, & believe he behaved himself well in College, but this is all I can say.[3] Mr Bickham is not, as You seem to

9 Mason occasionally published satirical verse but his correspondence indicates that he wrote more than has actually survived. No comedies were published and none have been traced in manuscript.

10 *Letters on Chivalry and Romance* was published in May 1762. (Bowyer, *Paper-Stock Ledger*, 1717–73.) Richard Hurd, nephew, records RH's decision: "I shall print my Letters on Chivalry forthwith", attributing the excerpt to a letter of 7 November 1761. (MS HC, Extracts from Letters to Mr. Mason, from the Rev. Mr. Hurd., p. 4.) It is likely that this is a wrongly dated transcription from this letter.

11 See *ante* To Mason, 28 October 1761, n. 6.

1 RH had written with the request that his brother might be commissioned to supply the liveries required by Littleton as Sheriff of Staffordshire. (See *ante* To Littleton, 22 November 1761.) Littleton's response is not known.

2 Shareshill was a small benefice in the gift of Littleton. (John Ecton, *Thesaurus Rerum Ecclesiasticarum. Being an Account of the Valuations of all the Ecclesiastical Benefices in the several Dioceses in England and Wales*, Second Edition, revised by Browne Willis, 1754.) It had been offered to RH but on his refusing it, it was to be made over to successive Head Masters of Brewood Grammar School (of which Littleton was principal trustee) as a memorial to William Budworth, who had himself been Perpetual Curate of Shareshill. (James Hicks Smith, *Brewood: A Résumé Historical and Topographical*, Second Edition, Revised, Wolverhampton, 1874, pp. 12, 79; *Notes and Collections relating to Brewood*, 1858, p. 105.)

3 Moss (first name unknown) had applied for the position of Head Master of Brewood Grammar School which had fallen vacant by the death of Roger Bromley in 1761. His death and the new vacancy had been advertised in the local papers and the election was fixed for 5 January 1762 at 11.00 a.m. (Staffs. RO, D1416/4/2/1.) Moss, who may have been related to John Moss of Brewood, clerk (Staffs. RO, 475/M/1), had been admitted to Emmanuel in June 1757 and in February 1761 was made B.A. His name remained on the College books until February 1763 but he did not reside in College. (*Commons Accounts Books*, STE. 15. 10, STE. 15. 11.) He was not successful in his application.

have supposed, at Loughborough, where he is not expected till the Spring.[4] I do not certainly know whether he be at present in College. I think your best way will be, to signify to Mr Moss that it will be proper for him to procure a Letter from Mr Hubbard, who was his Tutor, testifying his opinion of him.[5] This Letter, if it be to his advantage, will be of weight with all the Electors. If it be not, You will have the best reason for declining to serve him. It is usual, in such cases, to apply for these Letters. And Mr Hubbard, You may be sure, will express his real opinion. It is not his way to make a compliment of such matters.

As to the affair of the Assize-Sermon, I will tell you what I think of it, with my usual frankness.[6] These things are usual compliments to the Minister of the High-Sheriff's parish. And as Mr Stafford is a very reputable clergyman, & in the chief of your own Preferments, I think You should by all means make him your Chaplain on this occasion.[7] It will do him credit, & is what he will naturally expect.

To say the truth, these public sermons are so much things of course, & so little minded by any body, that there can be no reason for You to go out of the common road. And for myself, tho' I see your kind intention in proposing me, I had much rather decline it. But tho' I tell You my real sentiments plainly, as I would always do on all occasions, & should certainly, in your case, employ Mr Stafford, yet if You continue to think otherwise, You know it is not possible for me to deny You anything. I will certainly preach, if You would have me. But, as I said, my judgment is entirely on the other side. You will determine this affair at your leisure.

I cannot but, again, very much applaud your design in the disposal of Sharshill. It will be a valuable addition to the School, if You can fix a deserving man in it. It will serve to keep him there, which will be a further benefit to the country. In all views, the thought is worthy of You, & will do You much honour.

You will please to present my compliments & best wishes to Lady Littleton, & to be believe me, with all affection, My dear Sir, Your most faithful humble Servt.

R Hurd

254 To Sir EDWARD LITTLETON 23 DECEMBER 1761

Text: MS STAFFS RO D1413/1; unpublished.
Addressed: To/Sir Edward Littleton Bart

Thurcaston 23 Decr 1761

Dear Sir

I wrote to Mr Bickham to inquire the character of Mr Moss, & shall acquaint You with the answer as soon as I receive it.[1]

4 James Bickham, Fellow of Emmanuel, and one of the two tutors allocated to Moss. Bickham had been nominated by the College to the rectory of Loughborough, Leicestershire, on 25 August 1761. (*Order Book*, COL. 14. 2.) He remained in Emmanuel until the end of December. (*Commons Accounts Book*, STE. 15. 10.)

5 Henry Hubbard and Bickham were both officially tutors to Moss, but Hubbard was the senior tutor.

6 As Sheriff of the county Littleton was required to attend the two Assize courts held in late February or March, and July or early August. The proceedings were opened with an Assize-sermon given by the Sheriff's chaplain. (*Somerset Assize Orders 1629–1640*, ed. Thomas G. Barnes, Frome, 1959, Introduction, pp. xiv, xvii.)

7 The Rev. James Stafford is referred to as "clerk" of Penkridge on a Staffordshire lease of 1759. (Staffs. RO, 475/M 5.)

1 See preceding letter, nn. 3 and 4.

Mr Field, who transmitts this Letter to You, is, also, a Candidate for the School of Brewood, & has desired me to signify to You the opinion I have of him.

He is Curate to Mr Bickham at Loughborough, & was bred at St John's College under Dr Rutherforth.[2] I have no doubt of his being extremely well qualified for the Master of a Latin School: And from what I hear of him from others, as well as from the short acquaintance I have had with him myself, since he came into this neighbourhood, I believe his character to be, in all respects, unexceptionable.[3]

I have told Mr Field, that You will be determin'd solely by these considerations in the preference You give to any of the candidates; and he is too reasonable to desire any other recommendation to your favour.

I am, Dear Sir, Your most obedient humble Servant

R Hurd

255 To WILLIAM WARBURTON 25 DECEMBER 1761

Text: *Prelate*, 243.

Thurcaston, December 25th, 1761.

. . .

Though I troubled your Lordship with a letter not long since, yet you will perhaps excuse my appearing before you, at this time, with my Christmas salutations: a good old custom, which shews our forefathers made a right use of the *best tidings* that ever came from heaven; I mean, to increase *good-will towards men*.

Your Lordship will take a guess, from the sermonic cast of this sentence, at my late employment. Though I am not likely to be called upon in this way, I know not what led me to try my hand at a popular sermon or two: I say *popular*, because the subjects, and manner of handling are such, but not of the sort that are proper for my Leicestershire *people*. To what purpose I have taken this trouble, your Lordship may one day understand. For you, who are my example and guide in these exercises, must also be my judge. If you blame, I may learn to write better: if you approve, I shall require no other *Theatre*. But when does your Lordship think to instruct us on this head, in the address to your clergy?[1] Certainly, the common way of sermonizing is most wretched: neither sense, nor eloquence; reason, nor pathos. Even our better models are very defective. I have lately turned over Dr. Clarke's large collection, for the use of my

2 A Thomas Fielde was admitted to St John's College on 5 June 1747 under Dr Rutherforth as "tutor and surety". (Scott-Mayor, *Admissions to St. John's*, ii. 122.) According to published records he became Rector of Eastwick, Hertfordshire, in 1764 and Vicar of Stanstead-Abbots, in the same county, in 1767, dying in 1781. (Scott-Mayor; *Alum. Cantab.*) This, or another Thomas Fielde, was however appointed as Vicar of Brewood and Head Master of Brewood Grammar School in 1762. (J.H. Smith, *Brewood: A Résumé*, 1874, pp. 12, 28.) He was a keen antiquary and published a prospectus for a history of Staffordshire in 1768. The project was never completed and Fielde is said to have emigrated to America with his family in 1770 or 1771. (M.W. Greenslade, 'The Staffordshire Historians', *Collections for a History of Staffordshire*, Fourth Series, Vol.II, 1982, pp. 93–6, 181.)

3 James Bickham had been instituted as rector of Loughborough in the autumn of 1761 (Leics. RO, Sequestration Bond, Induction Certificate (26 August 1761), 1D41/30/189); but no records give any indication of Fielde's employment as his curate.

1 See *ante* To Balguy, 26 July 1761, nn. 5, 6.

parish;[2] and yet with much altering, and many additions, I have been able to pick out no more than eight or ten that I could think passable for that purpose. He is clear and happy enough in the explication of scripture; but miserably cold and lifeless; no invention, no dignity, no force; utterly incapable of enlarging on a plain thought, or of striking out new ones: in short, much less of a genius, than I had supposed him.

'Tis well, you have not my doings before you, while I am taking this liberty with my betters. But, as I said, your Lordship shall one day have it in your power to revenge this flippancy upon me.

Your Lordship has furnished me with a good part of my winter's entertainment, I mean by the books you recommended to me. I have read the Pol. Mem. of *Abbe St. Pierre*.[3] I am much taken with the old man: honest and sensible; full of his projects, and very fond of them; an immortal enemy to the glory of Louis the XIVth, I suppose, in part, from the memory of his disgrace in the Academy, which no Frenchman could ever forget;[4] in short, like our Burnet,[5] of some importance to himself, and a great talker. These, I think, are the outlines of his character. I love him for his generous sentiments, which in a churchman of his communion are the more commendable, and indeed make amends for the Lay-bigotry of M. Crevier.[6]

I have by accident got a sight of this mighty *Fingal*.[7] I believe I mentioned my suspicions of the *Fragments*:[8] they are ten-fold greater of this epic poem. To say nothing of the want of *external evidence*, or, which looks still worse, his shuffling over in such a manner the little evidence he pretends to give us,[9] every page appears to me to afford *internal* evidence of forgery. His very citations of parallel passages *bear* against him.[10] In poems of such rude antiquity, there might be some flashes of genius. But here they are continual, and cloathed in very classical expression. Besides, no images, no sentiments, but what are matched in other writers, or may be accounted for from usages still subsisting, or well known from the story of other nations. In short, nothing but what the enlightened editor can well explain himself. Above all, what are we to think of a long epic poem, disposed, in form, into six books, with a *beginning, middle*,

2 Samuel Clarke, *Sermons on the Following Subjects . . . Published from the Author's Manuscript*, by John Clarke, D.D., 10 vols., 1730–31.

3 *Annales Politiques de Feu Monsieur Charles Irenée Castel, Abbé de St. Pierre, de l'Académie Françoise*, 2 vols., Londres, 1757.

4 Charles Irénée Castel de Saint-Pierre (1658–1743) was an economist and the author of many projects of political and economic reform. He was a member of the Academy from 1695 to 1718 when he was expelled following the publication of his *Discours sur la Polysynodie*, 1718, which was outspokenly critical of Louis XIV's administration. His works had a great influence on Rousseau who left elaborate examinations of some of them.

5 Gilbert Burnet (1643–1715), Bishop of Salisbury. Burnet and the Abbé Saint-Pierre shared an inclination towards religious toleration and a belief in liberty and freedom for the individual.

6 Jean Baptiste Louis Crevier was the author of the *Histoire de l'Université de Paris, 1761. (See ante* To Mason, 28 October 1761.)

7 *Fingal, an Ancient Epic Poem, in Six Books: Together with several other Poems, composed by Ossian the Son of Fingal. Translated from the Galic Language*, By James Macpherson, 1762, published in December 1761. (*Lond. Mag.*)

8 [James Macpherson], *Fragments of Ancient Poetry, Collected in the Highlands of Scotland, and Translated from the Galic or Erse Language*, Edinburgh, 1760.

9 *Fingal* is prefaced by a 16-page 'Dissertation concerning the Antiquity, &c. of the Poems of Ossian the Son of Fingal'.

10 In the commentary to *Fingal* Macpherson draws attention to parallel passages in Homer and Virgil, the Bible, and Milton, Dryden and Pope.

and *end*, and enlivened, in the classic taste, with episodes. Still this is nothing. What are we to think of a work of this length, preserved and handed down to us entire, by *oral tradition*, for 1400 years, without a chasm, or so much as a various reading, I should rather say, *speaking*? Put all this together, and if Fingal be not a forgery, convict.[11] All I have to say is, that the Sophists have a fine time of it. They may write, and lie on, with perfect security. And yet has this prodigy of North-Britain set the world agape. Mr. Gray believes in it.[12] And without doubt this Scotsman may persuade us by the same arts, that Fingal is an original poem, as another employed to prove that Milton was a plagiary.[13] But let *James Macpherson* beware the consequence. *Truth will out*, they say. And then – Qui Bavium non odit, amet *tua carmina*, Maevi.[14]

My dear Lord, excuse this rhapsody, which I write *currente calamo*, and let me hear that your Lordship, Mrs. Warburton, and the dear Boy, are perfectly well. I think to write by this post to Mr. Allen . . .

256 To Sir EDWARD LITTLETON — 1 JANUARY 1762

Text: MS STAFFS RO D1413/1; unpublished.
Addressed: To/Sir Edward Littleton Bart/at Teddesly Park near/Lichfield/Staffordshire
Postmarked: cover missing.

Thurcaston 1. Jan. 1762

Dear Sir

Your favour of the 24th, which is just now come to hand, would receive an answer from the Letter Mr Fielde undertook to convey to You.[1] I have little or nothing to add

11 Doubt as to the authenticity of the Ossian poems lingered into the nineteenth century. The matter was finally settled by a Committee of the Highland Society of Scotland who concluded that Macpherson had been accustomed to "supply chasms, and to give connection, by inserting passages which he did not find, and to add what he conceived to be dignity and delicacy to the original composition, by striking out passages, by softening incidents, by refining the language, in short by changing what he considered as too simple or too rude for a modern ear, and elevating what in his opinion was below the standard of good poetry". (*Report of the Committee of the Highland Society of Scotland, appointed to inquire into the nature and authenticity of the poems of Ossian*. Drawn up . . . by Henry Mackenzie, Edinburgh, 1805, p. 152.)

12 Gray wrote of the *Fragments* that the "external evidence would make one believe these fragments (for so he calls them, tho' nothing can be more entire) counterfeit: but the internal is so strong on the other side, that I am resolved to believe them genuine, spite of the Devil & the Kirk". (Gray, *Correspondence*, Letter 313.) Of *Fingal*, he said, he remained "still in doubt . . . tho' inclining rather to believe them genuine in spite of the World". (Letter 353.)

13 Milton had been charged with plagiarism by the Scotsman, William Lauder (d.1771). Lauder had published five papers in the *Gentleman's Magazine* in 1747 followed by *An Essay on Milton's Use and Imitation of the Moderns, in his Paradise Lost*, 1750, issued at the end of 1749. His charges were refuted by John Douglas, afterwards Bishop of Salisbury, who proved beyond doubt that Lauder had inserted extracts from the Latin version of *Paradise Lost* into the quotations from the little known Latin works that he accused Milton of plagiarizing. (John Douglas, *Milton Vindicated from the Charge of Plagiarism, brought against him by* Mr. *Lauder, and Lauder himself convicted of several forgeries*, 1751.)

14 Virgil, *Eclogues*, iii. 90.

1 See *ante* To Littleton, 23 December 1761.

to what I there said. From the character Mr. Fielde bore at Cambridge, & from his behaviour at Loughborough, as well as from the best judgmt I have been able to form of him myself from the short acquaintance I have had with him, I take him to be a very decent worthy man, & see no reason to question the favorable representation which Dr Darwin made of him.[2]

Upon the whole, tho' You are not to expect a second Mr Budworth, I believe Mr Fielde will be, in all respects, a very creditable Master.[3]

Mr Bickham writes me word, that You have received a Letter from Mr Hubbard concerning Mr Moss, & that the college has also granted him a testimonial.[4] So that I have nothing more to say upon that subject. I have only to wish You all the success in the choice of a Master, which your disinterested pains deserve, & am, with my best wishes to Yourself & Lady Littleton, Dear Sir Edward, Your most affectionate humble Servant

R Hurd.

257 To THOMAS BALGUY — 29 JANUARY 1762

Text: MS BEINECKE MS Vault Shelves, Hurd; printed, *Memoirs*, 84.
Addressed: cover missing.

Thurcaston Jan. 29. 1762

Dear Sir

I know nothing of the Intrigues of the late Bp of London: And now, they are of no concern to any body.[1] Your prediction of him was, I fancy, accomplished somewhat sooner than You imagined. His Successor, You see, is the Bp of Carlisle; to nobody's joy that I know of, except Dr Brown's;[2] & He, I dare say, believes I wish him no joy from it, in which however he is mistaken.

I had the greatest pleasure, as You would have, in the news of Mason's preferments

2 Probably Erasmus Darwin of St John's. Three Darwin brothers matriculated at St John's between 1743 and 1750 but no direct connection between them and Thomas Fielde has been found. Erasmus Darwin went on to study medicine and established a practice at Lichfield in 1756. He had been made a Fellow of the Royal Society in 1761. (*Alum. Cantab.*; *D.N.B.*)

3 Fielde's reputation as Master of Brewood Grammar School has not survived him.

4 No copy of the testimonial has been discovered, nor is there any further information concerning Moss.

1 Thomas Hayter (1702–62), Bishop of London, had died on 9 January 1762. Nothing more is known of the "intrigues".

2 Hayter was succeeded by Richard Osbaldeston (1690–1764), Bishop of Carlisle. He was nominated on 30 January 1762. Osbaldeston had not been very effective as Bishop of Carlisle and on his death in 1764 was described by Thomas Secker as having been "every way unequal" to his station as Bishop of London. (Thomas Bradbury Chandler, *The Life of Samuel Johnson, D.D. The First President of King's College, in New York*, New York, 1824, p. 197.) John Brown had been presented to the living of Newcastle by Osbaldeston in whose gift, as Bishop of Carlisle, it lay. (See *ante* To Warburton, 18 March 1761, nn. 8 and 9; Ecton, *Thesaurus Rerum Ecclesiasticarum*, 1763.)

in the Church of York.[3] I know nothing, yet, of the history of the Precentership: The Residentiary's place was owing to Fred. Montague, for which I honour him.[4]

I think of Hume's history, as You do.[5] – Pray send me your account of Plutarch's Miscellanies.[6] I amuse myself amongst his Lives this winter.

The Letters on Chivalry are in the press.[7] But there is not a word in them for your reading.

Mr Bickham is married, & comes to reside at Loughborough in the Spring, very early.[8] Without doubt, as You say, he will be a good Neighbour; but I am got into a way of living without any, which is much better.

The Bishop of Gloucester is in town &, I hope, in perfect health. At least he seems intent on some new things he is preparing for the Press, & is in good spirits.[9] The family were a little alarm'd for him some time ago, but I believe without reason. Mr Allen, too, is reasonably well.

You do not say a word to me of Fingal.[10] The following Epigram is handed about town on Lord Lyttelton's admiration of it.[11]

Quoth my Lord who so wise is, so thin & so tall,
What's the Iliad or Aeneid, compar'd to Fingal?
The once honour'd classics no more he defends,

3 Mason had been appointed Canon Residentiary and Precentor of York cathedral. The canonry had been promised to him in the previous year on the death of the then incumbent, William Herring. (See *ante* To Mason, 3 May 1761, n. 3.) Herring's death is recorded in the *Gentleman's Magazine* for 8 January though this conflicts with Mason's note in his 'Memorandums or Dates of the Principal events relative to Myself' in which he states that "Dr Fountayne Dean of York made me Canon residentiary of that Cathedral" under the date "Jan 7th 1762". (*Commonplace Book*, p. 101, York Minster Library; *Hurd-Mason Corr.*, p. xxx.) The precentorship fell to him on the resignation of Dr Thomas Newton who was appointed Bishop of Bristol. The warrant for presentation was issued by the king on 22 February. (*John le Neve, Fasti Ecclesiae Anglicanae 1541–1857. IV. York Diocese*, compiled by Joyce M. Horn & David M. Smith, 1975.) According to Gray the canonry was worth "near 200£ a-year" and the precentorship "as much more". (*Correspondence*, Letter 353.)

4 Frederick Montagu was the brother-in-law of John Fountayne (1714–1802), Dean of York. He had been admitted a Fellow-commoner of Trinity College, Cambridge in 1751 and had there made the acquaintance of Gray and Mason.

5 David Hume, *The History of England, from the Invasion of Julius Caesar to the Accession of Henry VII*, 1762. (See *ante* To Mason, 28 October and 27 November 1761.)

6 No work by Plutarch has been specifically identified under this title. RH may, however, be referring to a selection from the *Moralia*, such as the *Apophthegmata Regum et Imperatorum. Apophthegmata Laconica etc.* published in 1741.

7 RH had completed *Letters on Chivalry and Romance* by the end of November 1761. (See *ante* To Mason, 27 November 1761.) A month later Warburton had heard (via Mason) that the *Letters* were already "in the Press" (*Prelate*, p. 247); but printing probably did not begin until February following a delivery of paper recorded in the Bowyer *Paper-Stock Ledger* on 30 January.

8 No other information concerning Bickham's marriage has been discovered. He appears to have left Emmanuel by March 1762, but the Commons Accounts', records for January and February of that year are missing. (*Commons Accounts Book*, STE. 15. 10.)

9 Warburton was working on *The Doctrine of Grace: or, the Office and Operations of the Holy Spirit Vindicated from the Insults of Infidelity, and the Abuses of Fanaticism*. It was published at the end of October 1762. (See *ante* To Warburton, 18 March 1761, n. 3; *Prelate*, p. 247; Bowyer, *Paper-Stock Ledger*.) His arrival in London in mid-January was noted by the *London Chronicle*, 14–16 January, p. 55.

10 *Fingal, an Ancient Epic Poem*. (See *ante* To Warburton, 25 December 1761.)

11 No other references to this epigram have been found.

But gives up old bards, as he gives up old friends:
Prefers new acquaintance in Poetry & Wit,
Macpherson to Homer, Newcastle to Pitt.

I heartily wish the continuance of your <. . .> health, & the recovery, if it may be, of your good Mother's. With compliments to Miss Drake, I am ever, Dear Sir, Your faithful humble Servant

R Hurd

258 To JOHN GREEN 31 JANUARY 1762

Text: MS HC; unpublished.

Copy to the Bp Lincoln (Dr John Green)

My Lord

Relying on the relation I now bear to You, as one of your clergy, & still more perhaps on the honour of having had some share in your acquaintance, I take leave to congratulate with your Lordship on your advancement to the See of Lincoln.[1]

I will not disgust your Lordship by saying the common things on this occasion. Your Lordship knows the worth of them when said the most finely. You will accept it as a better testimony of my regard & duty, that I use the plainer language of your friends, & assure You without a compliment how truly I wish your Lordship every satisfaction in the long & happy enjoyment of your high station.

I am, with great respect, My Lord, Your Lordship's most obedient humble Servant

R Hurd

Thurcaston Jan. 31. 1762

259 To Sir EDWARD LITTLETON 28 FEBRUARY 1762

Text: MS STAFFS RO D1413/1; unpublished.
Addressed: To/Sir Edward Littleton Bart/in New Bond-Street/ London
Postmarked: 3 MR

Thurcaston Feb. 28. 1762

My dear Sir Edward

Your favour of the 20th did not come to hand till last night.

I perceive, that for some reason or other, You do not care to appoint Mr S. your Chaplain.[1] If Mr Mainwaring will charge himself with this office, You will be sure to be well serv'd; & I had rather he did, as I cannot be from home this next month witht some inconvenience.[2] If You find any difficulty in engaging him, You may absolutely

1 John Green (1706–79), Master of Bennet College. Green was nominated to the bishopric of Lincoln on 28 November and consecrated on 28 December 1761. (*Handbook of British Chronology*.) RH had known him probably from the early 1750s (see *ante* To Balguy, [?1753]); and as Bishop of Lincoln he was head of the diocese of which Thurcaston was a part.

1 RH refers to James Stafford and the Assize-sermon. (See *ante* To Littleton, 14 December 1761, nn. 6 and 7.) The Assizes at Stafford had been advertised for Thursday 25 March. (*Lond. Chron.*, 4–6 February 1762, p. 122.)

2 John Mainwaring was Rector of Church Stretton, Shropshire.

depend upon me. Only in that case You must favour me with a line directly, & name the precise time when You would have me wait upon You at Tedgely: For my Leicester Paper does not tell me, when the Assizes are fixed for Stafford.

I rejoyce for your safe arrival in Town, & beg You to present my most faithful services to Lady Littleton.

Dear Sir Edward, Your most affectionate humble Servant

R Hurd

260 To Sir EDWARD LITTLETON 12 MARCH 1762

Text: MS STAFFS RO D1413/1; unpublished.
Addressed: To/Sir Edward Littleton Bart/in New Bond Street/ London
Postmarked: LEICESTER

Thurcaston 12. March. 1762

Dear Sir Edward

I think You never determined righter in your Life, than to take Mr S. for your Chaplain.[1] His being the Minister of the Church, You go to; his being in the most considerable of your own preferments; & his having the honour to be related to your family;[2] All these are such strong reasons for Your choice falling on him, that (unless some very particular reason, indeed, had determined You against him) the appointment of any other must have appeared highly improper.

At the same time I assure You, my dear friend, I esteem it a very obliging mark of your kindness to me, that You made me the first offer. And if I could have brought myself to believe that my acceptance of it would have been, in any degree, for your service or honour, I should certainly not have made two words with You about it. But, as I said at first, these Assize-Sermons are so much things of course, & so little minded by any body, that it was not worth your while to pass over Mr S., who stood so naturally in your way, for the sake of what your partiality to me might induce You to reckon, a better Sermon.

I had seen the Epigram, You sent me on L.L.[3] It is a pleasant one; & the ridicule was well deserved, for his foolish admiration of such a thing, as Fingal. I take it to be a notorious & impudent imposture.

The election of a new member for the county is carrying on here with great heat.[4] But I am so ill with one side, as You know, & have been so little obliged to either, that I have a good pretence for taking no part in it.

I take for granted, You return to town after the Assizes are over. Pray let me hear of You, when You come back, & let me know how the ceremony passed at Stafford.

I desire my best compliments to Lady Littleton & am always, My dear Sir, Your most affectionate humble Servant

R Hurd

1 See *ante* To Littleton, 14 December 1761, nn. 6 and 7.

2 This connection has not been traced.

3 See *ante* To Balguy, 29 January 1762.

4 Edward Smith, the tory member for Leicestershire, elected the previous year, had died on 15 February. He was succeeded by Sir Thomas Cave who was elected without a contest on 25 March 1762. Cave's interests were those of the county gentry and he voted sometimes with and sometimes against the Administration. (*The House of Commons 1754–1790*, ed. Namier and Brooke.)

261 To Sir EDWARD LITTLETON 24 APRIL 1762

Text: MS STAFFS RO D1413/1; unpublished.
Addressed: To/Sir Edward Littleton Bart/in New Bond Street/ London
Postmarked: LEICESTER 26 AP

Thurcaston April. 24. 1762

Dear Sir Edward

I have your kind favour of the 15th, & give You joy of one half of your trouble being over.[1] I much approve your retrenchment of that useless & pernicious expence, You speak of; & as I know You are never likely to court the *mob's applauses*, You will find no inconvenience from this reformation.[2] The Gentlemen of the county will, certainly, owe You their thanks for it.

I am glad to hear that Mr Macro is well & in good spirits. 'Tis true, it would have been an additional pleasure to have understood that he was on good terms, again, with his Father. But we have both of us, I suppose, said enough to him, on this head.

I beg my best compliments to Lady Littleton, & wish You both a safe return, after a great deal of amusement, into Staffordshire. It is very uncertain how long I shall stay here. Otherwise, I should be much tempted to petition for a sight of You in this Solitude. However do me the favour to let me know how I may send a small packet to You from London, one of these days.[3]

Dear Sir Edward, Your most faithful & affectionate Servant

R Hurd

262 To THOMAS BALGUY 26 APRIL 1762

Text: MS BEINECKE MS Vault Shelves, Hurd; printed in part, *Memoirs*, 85.

Thurcaston April. 26. 1762

Dear Sir

As I know You are now at Bath, I would not lose the opportunity of inclosing a line to You under the B. of Gloucester's Cover. I hope You continue as well as when You wrote last, & that the Bath waters will carry You safe thro' your Visitation.[1] I doubt I have no chance of catching You, as I did last year, before You leave Bath. The business of my Inclosure still hangs upon me, indeed the most essential part, that of Leases, which cannot be executed till the Commissioners make their award;[2] And they are

1 Littleton as Sheriff of Staffordshire had to preside over the assizes. They were held twice a year in the Lent vacation and the Trinity vacation. The next session was not until 7 August 1762. (*Lond. Chron.*, 24 June, p. 598.)

2 This allusion remains obscure.

3 *Letters on Chivalry and Romance*. The first copies were delivered to the publisher, Andrew Millar, on 22 May. (Bowyer, *Paper-Stock Ledger*.)

1 No records of Balguy's archidiaconal visitation of 1762 have been traced.

2 RH was in the process of arranging for the enclosure of an area of land known as Anstey Fields. (See *ante* To Balguy, 26 July 1761, n. 8.) His proposal had apparently included an application for the right to "let a Lease of his allotment of Lands for 21 Years". This clause had been queried by his bishop, but it seems from an estimate of the value of the lands drawn up in January 1762, that the proposal was to go forward. (Leics. RO, DE1416/60/1–4.) By this time the commissioners

either very busy, or very dilatory. The most I think I can answer for myself, is, that I shall meet the Bishop at Gloucester. What may become of me after that, I cannot pretend to foresee; Only that it seems pretty certain I shall not be here till after August. However if You pass this way, You may depend on seeing the new Recr of Loughborough, who takes the true way of *settling*, as the word is, by bringing a Wife with him. He will be extremely glad to see You.

Dr Barnard of Eton[3] sent me the other day a new book by that Foster, who wrote a simple thing on Elfrida.[4] This is much better. Considering the subject, he has acquitted himself very notably: & the Subject itself does not misbecome an Usher of a Grammar School. If You have not seen it, it is called, *An Essay on Accent & Quantity &c.* A Dr G. (whom I suppose to be Dr Gally) & the University of Oxford who it seems, have renounced Accents, are not unjustly, but cavalierly treated.[5]

If You happen to have read this learned Treatise, You will be somewhat prepared for my *Letters*;[6] which are on a subject as insignificant, with this disadvantage that it is not set off by the same erudition. Foster's book is the fruit of what Pope calls *Learning's Luxury*;[7] mine, of it's *Idleness*, as You will see one of these days, when You receive a copy of it. Need I give a better reason for it's not being to your Taste?

Tell me about (to use a phrase of little Ralph Warburton when he wants to hear a story of a Cock & a Bull) this new Grammar of Dr Lowth.[8] They say, it outsells Tristram Shandy. But above all, let me have your directions about Plutarch's Miscellaneous works,[9] which I fancy will be more to my taste, than this Dr's Elements.

Dear Sir, Your most faithful humble Servant

R Hurd

had set the value of the property concerned and although final permission for the leases had not yet been granted, work on fencing had apparently already gone ahead at the end of 1761. (Leics. RO, DE1416/61/1–2; see also W.E. Tate, *A Domesday of English enclosure acts and awards*, ed. M.E. Turner, Reading, 1978, pp. 35–38, 154.)

3 Edward Barnard (1717–81), Headmaster of Eton. Barnard had been a Fellow of St John's from 1744 to 1756.

4 John Foster (1731–74) had been a Fellow of King's and was an assistant master at Eton. RH mentions his "fond encomiums" of Mason's *Elfrida* in a letter of 1752 (see *ante* To Mason, 29 October 1752), but nothing printed has survived. He had just published *An Essay on the Different Nature of Accent and Quantity, with their Use and Application in the Pronounciation of the English, Latin, and Greek languages*, Eton, 1762.

5 Henry Gally was the author of *A Dissertation against Pronouncing the Greek Language according to Accents*, published anonymously in 1754. It is first mentioned at p. 12 of Foster's work and recurrent references to the book and "Dr. G." appear thereafter. Foster concludes his essay with criticism of recent "*Oxford* editors" who had been guilty of "suppression of accents". (pp. 226–31.)

6 *Letters on Chivalry and Romance.*

7 *Essay on Man*, ii. 46.

8 [Robert Lowth], *A Short Introduction to English Grammar: with Critical Notes*, 1762. Lowth's grammar was probably the most influential and widely used text-book for the rudimentary instruction of English, produced in the eighteenth century. More than forty editions were printed by 1800. (R.C. Alston, *A Bibliography of the English Language from the Invention of Printing to the Year 1800*, Ilkley, 1974.)

9 See *ante* To Balguy, 29 January 1762, n. 6.

263 To CHARLES YORKE 20 MAY 1762

Text: MS BL Add. 35636, ff. 218–19; unpublished; copy, HC.
Addressed: cover missing.

Dear Sir

I have directed a trifle[a] of mine to be sent to You,[1] but am not so unreasonable to expect You should read, or so much as look into it, till the Vacation bring You some leisure from your important business. And if then You should find anything in it to amuse You for half an hour, it is the utmost I ought in reason to expect from it.

But I should not perhaps have troubled You with a Letter on so slight an occasion, but for the opportunity of paying[b] my sincere compliments to You, at the same time, on your late Promotion;[2] which is both of great dignity in itself, & opens the way to still higher honours, to which your eminent & acknowledged merit so justly entitles You.

If I add one word more, it is only to assure You of the constant respect & gratitude, I owe You, being so much, as I have the honour to be, Dear Sir, Your obliged & devoted humble Servant

R Hurd.

Thurcaston May. 20. 1762

264 To Sir EDWARD LITTLETON 5 JUNE 1762

Text: MS STAFFS RO D1413/1; unpublished.
Addressed: To/Sir Edward Littleton Bart/in New Bond-Street/ London
Postmarked: LEICESTER 7 IV

Dear Sir Edward

I am truly concerned that this epidemical Disorder has fallen upon You. It will be irksome to You to be kept in Town at this season. But a little time, I hope, with Dr Heberden's assistance, will perfectly restore You. Pray let me know by a word or two, how You go on. If writing be troublesome to You, I dare say my Lady herself will do me this honour. I shall be very anxious, till I hear again from You.

It is a real pleasure to me that the Letters, as very a trifle as they are, meet with your approbation.[1] Millar tells me the demand for them is greater, than I could have apprehended. I believe a second edition, but witht alterations, will be published immediately.[2]

1 *Letters on Chivalry and Romance*. William Bowyer noted that 50 copies were delivered to Andrew Millar on 22 May and 200 to [?Richard] Chandler on 24 May. A further 255 copies were distributed between the two booksellers before the end of the month. (Bowyer, *Paper-Stock Ledger*.) Warburton had received a separate copy of the *Letters* "in printg".

2 Yorke had been promoted to Attorney-General and sworn in on 25 January 1762. (MS BL, Add. 36248, f. 2.)

a Copy, HC: ". . . a very trifle . . ."

b Copy, HC: ". . . opportunity of paying You . . ."

1 *Letters on Chivalry and Romance*.

2 William Bowyer had printed 506 copies of the *Letters* (including "the Waste") all of which had been delivered to Andrew Millar and [?Richard] Chandler by the end of May 1762. By the end

I have order'd a copy to be sent to You for Mr Macro, which had been sent sooner if I had known of your being still in London: for I have not hear'd where he lodges.

I heard that Mr Allen was upon a little excursion, & very probably he might take London in his way. But I guess he would not stay long enough there to give You a chance for seeing him. However I shall let him know your kind intentions.

I have been kept longer here than I expected, partly by business, & partly by the want of a Curate. I am now in hopes of procuring one soon from Cambridge, & then I remove directly to Gloucester.[3]

While the Influenza is making such ravages in London, my Neighbours here are running mad with Methodism. God deliver us from these visitations, corporal & spiritual!

My most faithful services attend Lady Littleton, & with my best wishes for your speedy recovery, I am ever, My dear Sir Edward, Your most affectionate & devoted Servant

R Hurd

Thurcaston June. 5. 1762

You judge admirably of the *Letters*, that they would have pleased ordinary readers much better, if they had been filled with Tilting-Matches. – But then they would not have pleased such readers as You.

265 To THOMAS BALGUY 1 JULY 1762

Text: MS BEINECKE MS Vault Shelves, Hurd; printed in part, *Memoirs*, 88.
Addressed: cover missing.

Thurcaston 1. July. 1762

Dear Sir

I have your kind favour of the 5th past, & am so well satisfied with your general approbation of the Trifle, I sent You,[1] as to give You leave to make any objections, You please, to particular parts. The *first* edition went off so quick, that Millar would needs print off a *second* forthwith;[2] tho' I can hardly think the Demand will continue for so mere an amusement. I sent a copy of the *Letters* to Mr T. Warton. I certainly meant no incivility to him, & shall be sorry if he takes it in that light. I had spoke my opinion very plainly & truly, of his *Observations*, in the Letter on Imitation.[3]

of June more paper had been ordered and delivered and a second edition was in the press. On 28 July a delivery of 100 was ready for Millar and a further 662 copies, with the "waste", were delivered on 5 and 17 August. (Bowyer, *Paper-Stock Ledger*.)

3 RH was still without a curate in November 1762 and from July to November had had to rely upon a neighbouring clergyman, "Mr Iliff of Leicester", to officiate in his absence. (See *post* To Littleton, 26 November 1762; *Account Book 1756–63*, Leics. RO, DE1416/83, p. 38.)

1 *Letters on Chivalry and Romance*.

2 See preceding letter, n. 2.

3 Thomas Warton had published *Observations on the Faerie Queene of Spenser* in 1754. RH had referred to it in *A Letter to Mr. Mason; on the Marks of Imitation*, 1757, at pp. 31, 32 and 46 where he alludes to Warton as the "ingenious author of the *Observations on Spenser* (from which fine specimen of his critical talents one is led to expect great things)". His own interpretation of the *Faerie Queene* was, however, opposed to that of Warton. The latter saw the poem as part of a literature emerging from "the depths of Gothic ignorance and barbarity" but still confused

I now set forward immediately for Gloucester.[4] My journey has been delayed by a very kind & unexpected Visit of the Bp of Gloucester, who staid near a fortnight with me, & left me yesterday. He returns to P. P. & then removes to Gloucester next week. I obtained a sight of so much of the *Disc. on the Spirit* as is printed off.[5] Some Sheets came hither to the Bishop. It will be a very fine & useful work. I am particularly taken with the part, that concerns Wesley, tho' the whole abounds with very curious things.[6] If any thing can preserve the clergy in their senses, it must be such an admonition as this. As to those, who are already run mad, they are fit only for Monroe, to whose charitable care indeed Wesley & his Coadjutors commit them.[7]

Mrs Warburton is not yet perfectly recovered.[8] She & Miss Allen are at Weymouth, for the use of the Sea-Water. I hope there is no doubt but that she will follow the Bishop very soon to Gloucester. Mr Allen & the rest of the Family are reasonably well.

You will let me know by a Letter to me under cover to the Bp at Gloucester, that You are well after the fatigue of your Visitation, & that You have received your Italian books safe.

You, as well as I, have lost very much in your not being of our party, this last fortnight.

I am, Dear Sir, Your very affectionate humble Servant

R Hurd

P. S.

It will perhaps be an amusement to You to understand that my quondam friend, Dr Heberden, likes the Letters on Chivalry better than any thing I have ever written.[9]

and irregular. "Upon the whole, and in general", he wrote, "it must be observed, that Spenser's adventures, which are the subject of each single book, have no mutual dependance upon each other, and consequenly [sic] do not contribute to constitute one legitimate poem." (*Observations*, pp. 1, 6.) RH, in opposition to these criticisms, champions the concept of the Gothic and proposes an analysis of Spenser's poem "under the idea, not of a classical but Gothic composition". This, he says, "might go some way towards explaining, perhaps justifying, the general plan and *conduct* of the Faery Queen, which, to classical readers has appeared indefensible". (*Letters on Chivalry and Romance*, pp. 60–1.)

4 RH was away from Thurcaston for "19 Sundays i.e. from the first Sunday in July to the first Sunday in Novr 1762 inclus." (*Account Book 1756–63*, Leics. RO, DE1416/83, p. 38.)

5 *The Doctrine of Grace: or, the Office and Operations of the Holy Spirit* (usually referred to in correspondence as the 'Discourse on the Holy Spirit' which was used as the running title). The early sections of Warburton's text had gone into the printers about November 1761 and the paper for printing had been ordered. (Bowyer, *Paper-Stock Ledger*.) By the end of December 72 pages had been printed off but Warburton was still writing. (*Prelate*, p. 247.) The whole was completed in two volumes by the end of October 1762 and a total of 950 copies were delivered to Andrew Millar commencing on 4 November. (*Paper-Stock Ledger*.)

6 *The Doctrine of Grace* is a revised and enlarged version of an earlier sermon. (See *ante* To Warburton, 18 March 1761, nn. 1 and 3.) Particular emphasis is given to an attack on Methodism which was expanded from an 18-page section on "FANATICS" in the original sermon to more than 200 pages in the revised version.

7 John Monro (1715–91), physician to Bethlehem Hospital and author of *Remarks on Dr Battie's Treatise on Madness*, 1758. Monro had succeeded his father as physician to Bethlehem Hospital; both men enjoyed a high reputation in the treatment of insanity.

8 Gertrude Warburton had been suffering from a "long and obstinate" indisposition for some months. (*Prelate*, p. 248.) Miss Allen was Mary (Molly) the daughter of Philip Allen and cousin to Gertrude. (Boyce, *Benevolent Man*, p. 270.)

9 No explanation has been found for RH's reference to Heberden as his "quondam" friend.

This intelligence I receive from Sir E. Littleton, who has lately been under his hands in Town, where he picked up the fashionable fever, which for some reason or other they call, it seems, the *Influenza*.[10] He is now got into the country, & is much better.

266 To Sir EDWARD LITTLETON 30 AUGUST 1762

Text: MS STAFFS RO D1413/1; unpublished.
Addressed: To/Sir Edward Littleton Bart./at Teddesly Park near/ Lichfield/Staffordshire
Postmarked: postmark missing.

Weymouth Aug. 30. 1762

Dear Sir Edward

I thank You for your kind favour of the 19th of June. Soon after the receipt of it I removed to Gloucester, & am just now arrived at this place. The family here are reasonably well & return to Prior-Park in about a fortnight. Mr Allen expects a visit at that time from my Lord Chancellor, & will have me stay with him till towards the end of the month, for the opportunity of making me known to the great man.[1] One inconvenience however attends this scheme, which is, that I shall not be able to wait upon You at Teddesly before my return into Leicestershire, which must needs be as soon as possible after Michaelmas.[2] My design therefore now is to make a journey on purpose to pay my respects to You & Lady Littleton, as soon as I can get a week or two's leisure for that Purpose.

The Letters, You speak so kindly of, have been better received, than I could expect such a trifle would be.[3] You are right in thinking Dr Heberden's compliment somewhat extraordinary.[4] But I know the reason, & You shall know it, when I have the pleasure to see You.

I rejoyce with You for your having got thro' all the disagreable trouble of your Shrievalty, & hope I may rejoyce with You upon your having got the better, entirely, of your late Indisposition.[5]

10 The term "influenza" gained currency in the 1740s in reports of a contagious fever sweeping over Rome. It came into fashionable use about this time. (*O.E.D.*)

1 Robert Henley (1708?–72), first Earl of Northington, Lord Chancellor, 1761–66. Henley had been M.P. for Bath from 1747 to 1757 and had long been acquainted with Ralph Allen. (*The House of Commons 1754–1790*, ed. Namier and Brooke; Boyce, *Benevolent Man*.)

2 RH had returned to Thurcaston by mid October. He was then away once more for two or three weeks and returned for the winter in November.

3 *Letters on Chivalry and Romance* had been published at the end of May and had proved so popular that a second edition was called for a month later. (See *ante* To Littleton, 5 June 1762, n. 2.) The *Monthly Review* and *Critical Review* wrote warmly about the *Letters* remarking on RH's "new vein of criticism" and the entertaining and agreable manner in which it was explored. (*Monthly Review*, xxvii. 81.) The *Critical Review* concluded with the assurance that the "ingenious writer has, contrary to the usual practice, greatly exceeded the expectations raised by his title-page, and deduced a variety of important critical remarks from a subject seemingly unconsequential". (*Critical Review*, xiii. 475.)

4 This allusion remains obscure, although it seems RH was no longer on friendly terms with Heberden. (See preceding letter, n.9.)

5 As sheriff of Staffordshire Littleton had presided over the second of the twice yearly assizes held

I hear nothing of Mr Macro, but suppose he continues in London. The conduct both of Father & Son <are> is to me wholly unaccountable.[6]

I beg my best compliments to Lady Littleton & am ever, with my warmest good wishes for your health & happiness in all respects, Dear Sir Edward, Your most faithful & affectionate humble Servant

R Hurd

267 To Sir EDWARD LITTLETON 23 SEPTEMBER 1762

Text: MS FOLGER w. a. 57 (9); unpublished.
Addressed: To/Sir Edward Littleton Bart/at Teddesly Park/ near Lichfield./Staffordshire
Postmarked: BATH 25 SE

Dear Sir Edward

As I know the kind part You will take in any instance of my good fortune, I cannot deny myself the pleasure of sending You the earliest notice, that my Lord Chancellor,[1] who is now here with Mr Allen, has this day upon his recommendation given me a Preferment in Yorkshire, void by the promotion of the Bp of Carlisle to the See of London.[2] It is a Sine-Cure of the value of 150 £ a year, & in all respects preferable to the best of his Prebends.[3] I shall stay here a fortnight or three weeks longer, & am then, I suppose, to go down into the North, to take possession.[4] I would not lose a moment in sending You this news & am, with my best compliments to Lady Littleton, Dear Sir Edward, Your most affectionate humble Servant

R Hurd

Prior-Park Sept. 23. 1762

Endorsed: Mr. Hurd. Sepr. 23. 1762/ that the Lord Chancellor at the/ recommendation of Mr. Allen has given/ him a Preferment in Yorkshire of/ 150£ per an: a sine Cure at/ Folkeston near Scarborough

at Stafford and advertised in the *London Chronicle* for Saturday, 7 August 1762. His office had a further five months to run, but the assizes was the last major occasion at which he was obliged to be present. ([Josiah C. Wedgwood], 'The Staffordshire Sheriffs (1086–1912), Escheators etc.' in *Collections for a History of Staffordshire*, 1912.) Littleton had also suffered an attack of "influenza" in June. (See *ante* To Balguy, 1 July 1762).

6 Cox Macro and Edward were still unreconciled after a quarrel in 1761. (See *ante* To Littleton, 6 March 1761.)

1 Robert Henley, Earl of Northington. See preceding letter, n. 1.

2 Richard Osbaldeston, Bishop of Carlisle, had been nominated to the bishopric of London on 30 January 1762. (See *ante* To Balguy, 29 January 1762, n. 2.) His promotion left vacant the sinecure rectory of Folkton, Yorkshire.

3 The prebends of the dioceses of Bristol, Gloucester, Norwich and Rochester were in the gift of the Lord Chancellor. In 1762 they were valued at £200 each except at Rochester where the value was set at £180. (*The Correspondence of King George the Third from 1760 to December 1783*, ed. Sir John Fortescue, 6 vols., 1927–28, i. 33–44.)

4 See *post* To Littleton, 26 November 1762.

268 To CHARLES YORKE 25 SEPTEMBER 1762

Text: MS BL Add. 35636, ff. 272–3; unpublished.
Addressed: cover missing.

Prior-Park Sept. 25. 1762

Dear Sir

I shall take another occasion to acknowledge to You, more particularly, the very great pleasure I received from your ingenious & obliging Letter of the 7th, which met me on my return from Weymouth to this Place.[1] But I could not prevail with myself to defer so long to acquaint You, That my Lord Chancellor, who is here on a visit to Mr Allen, has, upon his kind recommendation, been pleased to nominate me to a very valuable Sine-Cure in Yorkshire, vacant by the promotion of the late Bishop of Carlisle to the See of London;[2] & which, considered in all it's circumstances, is, I believe, among the best things in his Lordship's ecclesiastical Patronage.[3]

Your constant & sollicitous endeavours to serve me, on several occasions, assure me that You will have a satisfaction in hearing this good news from me, which I therefore take the earliest opportunity to communicate to You, & am ever, with the greatest Respect, Dear Sir, Your much Obliged & Obedient Humble Servant

R Hurd

269 To THOMAS WARTON 14 OCTOBER 1762

Text: MS BL Add. 42560, f. 98; unpublished; copy, HC.
Addressed: cover missing.

Thurcaston Oct. 14. 1762

Revd Sir,[1]

On my return the other day to this Place, after an absence of some months, I found your very obliging Present of *Observ. on the F. Queen*; for which I beg You to accept my sincere thanks.[2]

I was always much taken with this Performance. But the many, & curious improvements in this Edition, make it incomparably the best piece of Criticism on Spenser, which the Public has yet seen.[3]

1 Charles Yorke's 8-page letter of 7 September 1762 is preserved at Hartlebury Castle. In it Yorke writes at length about *Letters on Chivalry and Romance* partly in response to particular points raised by RH, and partly to explain his own interpretation of the historical origins of chivalry.
2 See preceding letter.
3 According to Norman Sykes the Lord Chancellor was patron of 676 out of 777 crown benefices, those livings valued at £20 and under in the King's book. (*Edmund Gibson*, p. 109.)

1 Thomas Warton (1728–90). (See *ante* To Balguy, 6 September 1759, n. 4.)
2 *Observations on the Fairy Queen of Spenser. By Thomas Warton, Second Edition, Corrected and Enlarged*, 2 vols., 1762, published on 19 August. (Straus, *Dodsley*, Bibliography.)
3 Warton's *Observations* had been expanded from one volume to two in the second edition. The chapters of general criticism which introduce the work remain largely the same, but there is more detailed analysis of the poem and its sources. Between 1750 and 1758 demand for improved texts of the *Faerie Queene* had precipitated the issue of four new editions of the poem and a reissue of John Hughes' 1715 edition of Spenser's *Works*. (Jewel Wurtsbaugh, *Two Centuries of Spenserian Scholarship (1609–1805)*, 1936, reissued 1970, pp. 59–60, 73–4.) However, few sustained critiques of the poem had yet been published. As a general commentary Hughes' 'An Essay on Allegorical Poetry. With Remarks on the Writings of Mr. Edmund

You have, indeed, taken the only way to penetrate the mysteries of this Poet, I mean by investigating the manners & fictions of Chivalry & Romance; the fountains, from which his characteristic excellencies are derived.[4] And I will not despair of seeing this whole subject fully opened & explained by You one day, if You persist, as I hope You will, in the noble design of giving a history, in form, of the English Poetry.[5]

It is true, a work of this sort requires the Antiquarian, as well as Critic. But You are *both*: And the imputation needs not alarm You. For your Genius will always enable You, as it does the true Poet, *ex fumo dare lucem*:[6] Wheras the mere Antiquarian has no means of breaking thro' the cloud which his own Dullness, rather than his Subject, throws about him.

I wish You all success in the prosecution of your liberal & useful studies, & am, with great regard, Revd Sir, Your much obliged & obedient humble Servant

R Hurd

270 To Sir EDWARD LITTLETON 26 NOVEMBER 1762

Text: MS FOLGER w. a. 57(10); unpublished.
Addressed: To/Sir Edward Littleton Bart/at his Seat near/Lichfield/ Staffordshire
Postmarked: LEICESTER

Thurcaston Novr 26 1762

Dear Sir Edward

I thank You for your kind Letter of Septr 29, which was directed to me at Prior-Park, but overtook me at this place, before I set out for the North. I am now return'd from taking possession of my new Preferment, which I found at last in the further part of the East-Riding of Yorkshire, within about 3 miles of the Sea & ten of Scarborough.[1] It is to the full as good as it was said to be, & a perfect Sine-Cure. There was a mistake about the name. It is not *Fawstone, but Folkton*, & in the patronage of the Osbaldeston family, or, to express myself more properly, in the patronage of the

Spenser' remained the standard text and was heavily leaned upon in subsequent editions. A more detailed textual analysis had been attempted by John Jortin in his *Remarks on Spenser's Poems*, 1734, but this was completely superseded by Warton's learned and more complex *Observations*.

4 Warton's text includes chapters on Spenser's "imitations from old romances" (chap. II), "use and abuse of antient history and mythology" (chap. III), "imitations from Chaucer" (chap. V), and "imitations from Ariosto" (chap. VI).

5 Warton published the first three volumes of *The History of English Poetry, from the Close of the Eleventh to the Commencement of the Eighteenth Century* between 1774 and 1781. A few sheets (88 pages) of a fourth volume were issued but the project was discontinued thereafter, the history having reached the end of the sixteenth century. The three volumes are prefaced by two dissertations, the first of which deals with the 'Origin of Romantic Fiction in Europe'; Section III in Vol. I also introduces early "tales of chivalry" and "metrical romances".

6 Horace, *Ars Poetica*, 143.

1 RH was instituted to Folkton rectory on 2 November 1762 and a mandate to induct was issued the same day. (Borthwick Institute, York, Inst. AB, pp. 198–9.) A marginal note records Folkton as a sinecure.

present Bp of London, who, himself, purchased the perpetual advowson of it.[2] It fell to the crown, for this turn, by the Bp's promotion to the See of London, but will for the future, I suppose, be kept as a valuable morsel for some or other of the family.[3]

I take for granted You are return'd to Teddesly before this. Did You see Mr Macro in London? As I know not where to direct to him I wish, when You write next, You would tell him, as from me, that I now think myself settled here for the rest of the winter, & that if he should find it convenient & agreable to himself to pass any part of it with me, I shall be very glad of his company. My design in this invitation, You see, is to save him the expence of living in London. If he be got back to his Father (which I rather wish) You need say nothing of the matter.[4]

I should now, my dear Sir, with great pleasure run over to You, but that I am still without a Curate; & I have been of late so much obliged to my Neighbours for their assistance that I must not trouble them again so soon without a very pressing occasion.[5] I am in hopes however in no long time to have a Resident Curate,[6] & then the first use I make of my liberty will be to wait upon You.

I am much concernd for the return of Lady Littleton's complaint, to whom I beg leave to present my best wishes.

My dear Sir Edward, Believe me always most truly, Your affectionate & faithful humble Servant

R Hurd

270A To ROBERT HAY DRUMMOND 29 NOVEMBER 1762

See Appendix

2 Richard Osbaldeston had purchased the advowson of Folkton in 1748. (John Bacon, *Liber Regis, vel Thesaurus Rerum Ecclesiasticarum*, 1786, p. 1129.)

3 On any appointment to a bishopric the clergyman nominated was required to relinquish all previous spiritual promotions which became void upon his consecration, in the case of first creation as a bishop, or upon his confirmation, in the case of translation. (Thomas Wood, *An Institute of the Laws of England; or, The Laws of England in their Natural Order, according to Common Use*, 1720, i. 62; for Osbaldeston's promotion to the bishopric of London, see *ante* To Balguy, 29 January 1762, n.2.) Presentation to the benefices thus vacated fell to the Crown and only on a further vacancy (except by promotion to a bishopric) reverted to the patron. By 1778 (four years after RH's creation as Bishop of Lichfield and Coventry) the Folkton sinecure had returned to the Osbaldeston family. (Bacon, *Liber Regis*, p. 1129.)

4 Macro and his father remained unreconciled. No evidence has been discovered to suggest his whereabouts during the winter of 1762–63.

5 In RH's absence from July to November his livings had been served by a "Mr Iliff of Leicester". (*Account Book 1756–63*, Leics. RO, DE1416/83, p. 38.)

6 By the summer of 1763 RH had obtained the services of David Ball of St John's, Cambridge, who was ordained deacon in February 1763.

271 To THOMAS BALGUY 3 DECEMBER 1762

Text: MS BEINECKE MS Vault Shelves, Hurd; printed in part, *Memoirs*, 89.
Addressed: To/The Reverend Dr Balguy/Archdeacon of Winchester/ at Winchester
Postmarked: LEICESTER [?3] DE

Dear Sir

I receiv'd your favour of the 28th of Novr this day, namely Friday, & sit down directly to thank You for it, that I may send away my Letter to morrow morning; the only day in the week when I regularly, & of course, send to Leicester.

I thank You for your kind congratulations, & really think Folkton to be all You say of it.[1] After all deductions whatever, as far as I can at present foresee, it will yield me a full & clear 150£ a year, for the sole trouble of acknowledging the receipt of it to my Receiver. It consists of the great Tythes, with a considerable Glebe. The whole is reasonably let, & the Rents well paid. A mistake in the Presentation gave me an opportunity of passing near a Fortnight with Mason at Aston, & of waiting twice on the ABp of York at Brodsworth near Doncaster, who shewed me wonderful civility.[2] But for this, I am to thank my good Lord of Gloucester, who recommended me to his Grace in his warm way. The ABp has taken Skinner for his Chaplain (who happend to be at Cambridge, when I was there) & has made him Sub-Dean of York.[3] The certain Income, I believe, is not large, but his Grace told me an Estate had fallen in, since he had given it him, which would be worth to him at least 500£. This is some amends for his loss of Wigston's hospital at Leicester,[4] which he had a promise of, but is now likely to miss by the resignation of his Patron, Ld Kenoul, the late Chancellor of the Dutchy of Lancaster.[5]

I had a very obliging Letter from Mr T. Warton, in answer to one of mine, which

1 See *ante* To Littleton, 23 September 1762; To Yorke, 25 September 1762; and To Littleton, 26 November 1762.

2 See *ante*, To Drummond, 29 November 1762.

3 John Skynner (1724–1805) had matriculated at St John's in 1741, was made a Fellow in 1747 and public orator from 1752–6. He was collated as Subdean of York on 2 December 1762 and installed by proxy on 10 December (*John le Neve. Fasti Ecclesiae, York Diocese*, compiled by Horn & Smith, 1975, p. 12.) See *ante* To Mason, 29 October 1752.

4 Wigston's Hospital, Leicester, consisted of "a master, confrater, twelve men, and twelve women; by the rules of the house all single". (John Throsby, *The History and Antiquities of the Ancient Town of Leicester*, Leicester, 1791, p. 305.) According to Throsby the master's place had become "a valuable sinecure since the death of Mr. Jackson [1763], who resided, as the founder intended he should do. He has the renewing of all leases. The value of the master's place cannot easily be ascertained. The confrater has a house also to live in: his place is estimated at 60 or 70l. per annum." (Throsby, p. 306.) The presentation to the living lay in the hands of the "KING, as Duke of *Lancaster*". (Ecton, *Thesaurus*, 1754.)

5 Thomas Hay (1710–87), Viscount Dupplin, ninth Earl of Kinnoull. Hay had been M.P. for Cambridge from 1741 to 1758, Chancellor of the Duchy of Lancaster from 1758, and was Recorder of Cambridge from the same year until his death. He had made known his intention of resigning as Chancellor of the Duchy of Lancaster on 11 November 1762 following the Duke of Devonshire's dismissal as Lord Chamberlain. (Lewis Namier, *England in the Age of the American Revolution*, 1961, p. 369ff; *Letters from George III to Lord Bute 1756–1766*, ed. Romney Sedgwick, 1939, p. 162.) Drummond and Hay were brothers, the Archbishop having taken the name and arms of the Drummond family as heir to a portion of the estates of his great grandfather. (*D.N.B.*)

carried my thanks for his agreable present of the *Observations*.[6] I am exceedingly pleased with this second Ed. of his work, & still more with his project of a history of the English Poetry.[7] On both these accounts, he is very much in the good Graces of the Bp of Gloucester.[8] What he said to me on the subject of my *Letters* shews him to be a very candid & amiable man. He only exceeds a little in his favorable opinion of their author. By the bye, these *Letters* seem to have had the Fate, wch Trifles in our time usually have, I mean to have had the reception which is due to better things. Amongst other compliments I have received one from the Attorney General in a very polite strain, & which should speak him something in earnest, for his Letter consists of 2 or 3 Sheets.[9]

You are too old, & too much of a Philosopher, to read Ariosto, with enthusiasm. The Italian Poets address themselves to a young Imagination, & You & I are, alass, turn'd of forty. Not but Tasso, as You observe, can, upon occasion, touch the affections: & even this weakness we shall outlive one of these days. But if You love the pathetic, read Metastasio, where You will find the tenderness, not to say, the morality & good sense of Euripides.[10] He is w[on]de[r]ful in what Dramatic people call Situations.

You mistake at Winchester the <design> reason of publishing the Bp's new book in 2 Volumes.[11] It was only because, being printed in so small a form, there was not margin enough to allow the Sheets to be bound up in one. But I believe this is the main objection which your brethren of the Chapter will be able to make to it, I mean if they be disposed, & qualified to read it.

I beg my compliments to Miss Drake & shall be glad to see You both in the Spring, on your flight westward; as will also Mr Bickham & Dr Cardale.[12] I am here for the winter, & shall expect the pleasure of hearing of You sometimes from Sheffield.[13]

I am, Dear Sir, Your very affectionate humble Servant

R Hurd

6 *Observations on the Fairy Queen of Spenser*. See *ante* To Warton, 14 October 1762.

7 See *ante* To Warton, 14 October 1762, n. 4.

8 Warburton had written to Balguy himself with a request that when he next saw Warton he should tell him "with what new pleasure I have read his improved edition of his *Observations on the Fairy Queen*, which", he says, "I had formerly read with the highest satisfaction". (John Wooll, *Biographical Memoirs of the late Revd. Joseph Warton, D.D. . . To which are added*, A *Selection from his Works; and a Literary Correspondence between Eminent Persons, reserved by him for publication*, 1806, p. 283; Nichols, *Lit. Anecs*., v. 653.)

9 MS HC, Yorke to RH, 7 September 1762. For RH's acknowledgment see *ante* To Yorke 25 September 1762; his full reply was written on 10 December 1762, see *post* To Yorke. The letter was ten pages on three folded sheets.

10 Pietro Trapassi, known as Metastasio (1698–1782), Italian poet and dramatist. Metastasio's poetry and melodramas were widely known and admired in the eighteenth century. His melodramas, which were designed to be set to music, first appeared in England in the 1730s and an edition of his *Works*, translated by John Hoole, was published in 1767. According to Charles Burney, the "lovers of Italian Poetry, as well as vocal Music . . . regard Metastasio as the primary source of their most exquisite delight in the union of those arts". (*Memoirs of the Life and Writings of the Abate Metastasio*, 1796, Preface, [i]; see also Silvio d'Amico, *Enciclopedia dello Spettacolo*, Rome, 1954–68.)

11 *The Doctrine of Grace*.

12 George Cardale (1715?–69); admitted at St John's, 1734; B.A. 1737–8; M.A. 1741; D.D. 1759; Rector of Wanlip, Leicestershire, 1739–d; Rector of Rothley, 1759–d. (*Alum. Cantab.*; Scott-Mayor, *Admissions to St. John's*, ii. (Part 3) 456.)

13 Balguy's family lived in Sheffield.

272 To WILLIAM WARBURTON 10 DECEMBER 1762

Text: MS BL Add. 4310, f. 220; unpublished.

Thurcaston Decr 10. 1762

My dear Lord

I return the inclosed Letter with many thanks.[1] His Grace is very polite & obliging.

I am exceedingly concernd for poor Mrs Warburton.[2] If the faculty do not find out some way to alleviate . . .[3]

I am now digesting my scattered hints & papers on the Use of Travelling.[4] Your Lordship promised to inquire of Dr Birch for L. Essex's Letter to the E. of Rutland on this subject.[5] Hor. Walpole mentions it, as being refered to in the Bacon Papers.[6] If the book itself could be procured by his means, Millar would take care to send it . . .

273 To CHARLES YORKE 10 DECEMBER 1762

Text: MS BL Add. 35636, ff. 290–3; unpublished; copy, HC.
Addressed: cover missing

Dear Sir

At length I sit down to make my best acknowledgments to You for your most obliging & ingenious Letter of the 7th of September.[1] I should have done it much sooner, but that the taking possession of my new northern preferment, of wch I took the liberty to send You a short account from P. Park,[2] carried me from home, & indeed kept me employed, till the Term, & your Business, commenced together. I then

1 Warburton had written to Archbishop Drummond on 24 November 1762 thanking him for his "goodness" to RH, probably on the occasion of RH's institution to Folkton by Drummond. (Borthwick Institute, Bp. C & P VII.) He had enclosed Drummond's reply with his own letter of 30 November 1762. (*Prelate*, p. 250.)

2 Warburton had written that his wife had "had the most violent and dangerous fit of bilious cholic that can be conceived, insomuch that the excessive pain made her delirious". (*Prelate*, p. 250.)

3 The manuscript is torn across here. Warburton had enclosed the fragment in a note to Thomas Birch to "acquaint [him] with our request" i.e the information that RH required for his *Dialogues on the Uses of Foreign Travel* (see next section). The fragment is the top section of RH's letter, recto and verso. (Warburton to Birch, 13 December 1762, MS BL, Add. 4320, f. 196.)

4 *Dialogues on the Uses of Foreign Travel*, 1764.

5 This letter forms part of *Profitable instructions; describing what speciall observations are to be taken by travellers in all nations, states and countries; pleasant and profitable. By the much admired, Robert, late Earle of Essex. Sir Philip Sidney. And, Secretary Davison*, 1633. Part two has a separate title-page: *Two excellent letters concerning travell: one written by the late Earle of Essex, the other by Sir Philip Sidney*. The letter by Essex is addressed to the Earl of Rutland.

6 [Horace Walpole], A *Catalogue of the Royal and Noble Authors of England, With Lists of their Works*, Strawberry Hill, 1758, i. 137, [in the list of works by Robert Devereaux, Earl of Essex] "'Advice to the Earl of Rutland for his travels;' published at London in 1633, 8vo in a book intituled, 'Profitable instructions, describing what special observations are to be taken by travellers in all nations†." ' [Footnote] "†*Bacon-papers, vol. 2. p. 487*."

1 MS HC.

2 See *ante* To Yorke, 25 September 1762.

thought it but decent to forbear encroaching on your valuable time, till the approaching holidays gave me some assurance of your being enough at leisure to attend to an idle Letter.

The *Letters on Ch. & Rom.*, of wch You do me the honour to speak so kindly, are, as You would see, but the faint Outline of a regular discourse on that amusing subject. If I could have presumed on the public indulgence, or rather if I could have foreseen the indulgence of such a reader, as yourself, to a theme of some curiosity indeed, but of <. . .> little importance, I should have endeavour'd to make it something less undeserving, than I doubt it now is, of your kind notice, & still kinder animadversions.

I was extremely entertained & instructed by your accurate & elegant deduction of the origin of Chivalry & Romance, arising out of your comprehensive ideas of the modern, that is Feudal history. It is very certain that Chivalry, such as we see it represented to us in books of Romance, so much posterior to the date of that famous Institution, took it's colour & character from the impressions made upon the minds of men by the spirit of crusading into the holy Land. Yet I still think that if the seeds of that Spirit had not been plentifully sown, & indeed grown up into some maturity in the feudal times, preceding that event, it could not have been possible for the Western Princes to have given that politic diversion to their turbulent Vassals, You so justly take notice of.[3] In short, there are two distinct periods to be considered in a deduction of the rise & progress of Chivalry: The *first*, The breaking up of the western empire, & the feudal governments introduced on it's ruins, by the northern nations: In this aera, thro' the necessary operation of that new Policy, I suppose the first foundations to be laid, & the remote causes to be found, of what we know by the name of *Chivalry*.[a] The *Second*, when these causes had begun to take effect, was, The undertaking the great enterprize of Crusades against the Saracen armies; which not only concurred with the Spirit of Chivalry, already pullulating in the minds of men, but brought a prodigious increase, & gave a singular force & vigour, to it's operations. In this aera, Chivalry took deep root, & at the same time shot up to it's full height & maturity. So that by this time it was in the state of Virgil's Tree,

"Quae quantum vertice ad auras
Aethereas; tantum radice in Tartara tendit.
Ergo non hyemes illam, non flabra, neque imbres
Convellunt: immota manet, multosque per annos
Multa virûm volvens durando saecula vincit."[4]

This period You have shewn me, I did not enough attend to; & what You say upon it,

3 Yorke had written: "For it has often occurred to me, that the real date of Chivalry (which little concerns your Enquiry) may plausibly be stated thus. The Feudal Government commenced on the breaking of the Western Empire by the incursion of the Nations from the North (that *officina Gentium*). They crumbled into small independent states with regular subordinations of Vassals and their chiefs, who looked up to a Common Sovereign. These chiefs & Lieutenants soon grew formidable to their masters; and, just in the moment of that crisis of European manners & Empire, the Saracens having driven *Christianity* out of the *East* by violence, the Western princes with great craft and policy tuned the warlike Genius of their Feudataries into the spirit of *Crusading*, which would otherwise have preyed upon themselves and their countrymen in the confusions of Civil War."

4 Virgil, *Georgics*, ii. 291–5. RH follows the Delphin text which differs from contemporary and modern texts at l. 294. (. . . multosque nepotes)

a "Chivalry" is underlined twice.

with equal ingenuity & learning, will enable me one day to complete & round[b] my system.[5]

Your other excellent observations I could almost assent to, witht one word of explanation.

I had accounted for the respect paid to the Ladies in the days of Chivalry, from the consideration shewn them by our feudal Ancestors in the law of female Succession.[6] "But I have a doubt," You say, "whether, in fact, the introduction of the female succession into Fiefs was not too late to become an ingredient in this matter. It was received into the Feudal Law, when the Greek & Roman Codes & Pandects grew fashionable in the western world; & was deemed a corruption of the purity & martial genius of it."

Nothing is juster than this account; which, in effect, I subscribe to in p. 41, where I speak of the practice, that obtained *in the strict feudal times, of the Lady being in the power & disposal of her superior Lord.*[7] The truth is, I was there comparing the representation of Homer's manners with those painted by the old Romancers, & had then in my eye the state of things that prevailed when they *wrote*,[c] which was after the law of female succession had taken place. This made me express myself more strongly, & with less exactness, than I should have done on such on occasion. Indeed one main cause of confusion on this subject has been, The want of distinguishing between the state of things in the *early* feudal times, & that wch we find described by Romance-writers, in the *later*; when the Genius of the feudal Law, as You observe, had been much changed & corrupted.[8] And this distinction is not so constantly attended to, as it ought to have been, in the *Letters*.

What You say of "the *Erictho* of Lucan, consulted by S. Pompey, being equal or superior in dignity & horror to anything which the Moderns can produce in Necromancy", I readily believe on your authority; for I have not the Book by me, & it is now a long time since I read that Description.[9] But that, in *general*, the Gothic system of Prodigy, or if You will, the Gothic Machinery, exceeded the Classic, I mean for the purpose of the Poet, You will easily agree with me, if You reflect on the ten-fold darkness, out of which those Phantasms first arose in the barbarous northern nations, & the supernumerary horrors in which they were afterwards drest up[d] by Christian

5 In the third edition of *Letters on Chivalry and Romance* RH incorporated a large part of Yorke's letter in a more condensed and polished form followed by his response, formulated here, with similar improvements. His acknowledgment is to "a learned person, to whom I communicated the substance of my last Letter". (*Moral and Political Dialogues; with Letters on Chivalry and Romance*, Third Edition, 3 vols., 1765, iii. 214–17, 218–20.)

6 *LCR*, pp. 40–1.

7 "And tho', in the strict feudal times, she was supposed to be in the power and disposal of her superior Lord, yet this rigid state of things did not last long." (*LCR*, p. 41.)

8 Yorke had written: "The poets of Romance however, in succeeding times, whether in prose or verse, when they carried back the Scene of Adventure to the Warring of Crusade, gave Grace & variety to their Compositions, by introducing the later Refinements of Gothic manners into the earlier Histories, and mixing the courtesy of elegant Love, with the firmness of Heroic valour, and a zeal for the true Religion."

9 Erichtho was a Thessalian woman famous for her knowledge of poisonous herbs and medicine, and, according to Lucan, for the atrocities she was said to commit on the bodies of the dead and the living. (Lucan, *Pharsalia*, vi. 507ff.)

b Copy HC: ". . . round & complete . . ."

c Copy HC: ". . . state of things when they wrote . . ."

d Copy HC: ". . . were drest up . . ."

Superstition. But this subject, which is but just touched in the *Letters*, was curious enough to deserve a further disquisition: And what You observe from Lucan, shews the necessity of entering into it, if ever I give a more complete & corrected Edition of them.[10]

I cannot but be much pleased with your approbation of my defence of Spenser & the Italian Poets. You speak on this, as You are used to do on other subjects, with a full knowledge of the case, having in your early days, I perceive, been a great Reader of these amusing writers, & even a Translator of Tasso.[11]

On the whole, I am equally honour'd & entertained by your obliging Letter; which lets me see, not only your great kindness for me but what, if I knew You less, I should think more strange, your perfect acquaintance with these lighter studies, & the relish, which, among your more serious & important occupations, You still retain of them. But You are one of those privileged men, who can afford to know more things than are necessary, & to all the learning of your Profession to add the politeness of universal knowledge. This may be an invidious distinction to a man of business, but must necessarily draw upon him the esteem & veneration of all idle scholars. In the number of these, I beg leave to profess myself, with the greatest respect, Dear Sir, Your much obliged & most Obedt humble Servant

R Hurd

Thurcaston Decr 10. 1762

10 This passage on the poetic nature of Gothic "manners" and "superstitions" occurs in Letter VI. It was rewritten for the third edition of *LCR* and retains only the introduction and conclusion of the original letter. (*Moral and Political Dialogues*, 1765, iii. 251–9.) The example of Erichtho from Lucan is given at pp. 251–2. No changes had been incorporated in the second edition of *LCR*.

11 Yorke had written: "I subscribe to every word which you have said of Spenser. His *primary* Idea was unity of Design not of Action, by referring, as you say, every Adventure to one common purpose, obedience to the Appointment of the Fairy Queen. His Remedy for the want of unity of Action was *secondary*, by putting prince Arthurs nose into every thing; & making it all his own (as Dryden says somewhere) when he had spit in the porridge; the effect of which was to give a Languor to the Action & principal character of his poem. This observation of yours was quite new to me, but has in truth unravelled the whole mystery of Spenser's poem, and (as all Criticism ought to do) has for ever settled his true merit with his just Censure." and "As to Ariosto & Tasso, they never were fairly treated by any critic on this side of the Alps, till you wrote. They lived within forty or fifty years of one another; equal in the charm of numbers, Eloquence of the Speakers in their poems, and the fancy of their descriptions; but the *one* being only a Romancer fell with the credit of his own Tribe in prose; the *other* being confest an Epic poet has had better quarter, notwithstanding his Gothic manners; and but for *Boileau's* watch-word of *clinquant* (which you have slighted as it deserved) would have past for Sterling instead of Tinsel. I remember, at Cambridge I read *Ariosto once*, but *Tasso* twice over, and employed myself in translating one of his Episodes."

Appendix

120A To WILLIAM BOWYER **14 FEBRUARY 1752**

Text: *Lit. Anecs.*, ii, 230–1.

Cambridge, Feb. 14, 1752.

You must endeavour, if possible, to get me Mr. Warburton's *Visitation Sermon at Lincoln*, and the *pamphlet against Dr. Webster*.[1] I want them exceedingly, to complete my collection of his smaller tracts. Dr. Chapman, you see, has published an answer to the *Opinion*, of which I shall scarce think it worth my while to take any notice.[2] But would it not be proper to take the opportunity of advertising again the Opinion, that you may try to get off the remainder of the third edition.[3] – I have considered your proposal about Horace, and cannot bate a farthing of what I mentioned in my last. We Authors, you know, have always some excuse to comfort ourselves for our books not selling. One reason at least for the Epistle to Augustus not going off was, I think, Thurlbourn's neglect to advertise it properly when it was published.[4] I happened to be abroad at that time, and he is apt to be very careless. I have lately met with some of my own friends who never observed it in the papers till the other day, when it was advertised more carefully. You say, if you purchased the edition, you should expect to have *the right of the copy absolute*. I suppose you only mean the right of the copy of 750; that is, of this edition. Pray let me have your final answer as soon as possible. What I propose is to have the new edition printed off directly, so as to be finished at the farthest this summer; though I would not publish it till the edition of the Epistle to Augustus be sold off. And, as I am sensible, as you say, of the difference betwixt a

1 *Faith Working by Charity to Christian Edification. A Sermon Preach'd at the last Episcopal Visitation for Confirmation, in the Diocese of Lincoln*, 1738, and *A Vindication of the Author of The Divine Legation of Moses, &c. from the Aspersions of the Country Clergyman's Letter in the Weekly Miscellany of February 24, 1737*, 1738.

2 Thomas Chapman, *A Further Enquiry into the Right of Appeal from the Chancellor, or Vice Chancellor of the University of Cambridge, in Matters of Discipline: in which the Objections of the Author of a late Pamphlet, intitled, The Opinion of an Eminent Lawyer concerning the Right of Appeal, . . . are fully Obviated*, 1752. This pamphlet was advertised in *The Gentleman's Magazine* for February 1752.

3 On 18 February Bowyer paid for further advertisements in the *General Evening Post* and the *London Evening Post*. (*The Bowyer Ledgers. The Printing Accounts of William Bowyer Father and Son Reproduced on Microfiche with a Checklist of Bowyer Printing 1699–1777, a Commentary, Indexes, and Appendixes*, ed. Keith Maslen and John Lancaster, 1991, B564.) This strategy, however, failed to work, and Hurd ordered the destruction of the remaining copies in 1759. (*Lit. Anecs.*, vi, 511.)

4 Only 5s. was spent on advertising for the *Epistola ad Augustum*, compared with £1 14s for the first edition of the *Opinion of an Eminent Lawyer* in April and May 1751. (*Bowyer Ledgers*, ed. Maslen and Lancaster, B487, B544.)

piece of dry criticism and a novel, I should not insist on the payment of the 40*l*. till a year after the time of publication, if that would make any difference. But, if I part with the copy for less than this sum, I think myself obliged in honour to let Mr. Thurlbourne have it, against whom I have no complaint, but that as he grows old he grows lazy.[5] – I have not yet had leisure to look into the new edition of Montesquieu's Book, which is well spoken of here.[6]

I am, Sir, your humble servant, R. Hurd.

146A To WILLIAM BOWYER MID-NOVEMBER 1754

Text: *Lit. Anecs.*, ii, 213.

Brown, the antagonist of Lord Shaftesbury, is now in College, and has taken his Doctor's degree.[1] He preached a Sermon here, which many people commended; it was to prove that Tyranny was productive of Superstition, and Superstition of Tyranny; that Debauchery was the cause of Free-thinking, and Free-thinking of Debauchery. His conclusion was, that the only way of keeping us from being a French province, was to preserve our constitutional liberties, and the purity of our manners.

270A To ROBERT HAY DRUMMOND, ARCHBISHOP OF YORK 29 NOVEMBER 1762

Text: MS Borthwick Institute, Bp C & P VII/151; unpublished.
Addressed: cover missing.

Thurcaston. Novr 29. 1762

My Lord

Being at length return'd to this place from taking possession of Folkton, & supposing your Grace by this time to be in London, I beg leave to make my best acknowledgments to your Grace for your most obliging civilities to me at Broadsworth.[1] The mistakes in my Presentation occasioned some delay, & put me to some trouble.[2] But I had a full compensation for all this in those repeated marks of goodness & condescension, with which your Grace was pleased to honour me.

5 *Q. Horatii Flacci Epistolae ad Pisones, et Augustum* was published at the end of March or in early April 1753. Bowyer did not pay £40 for the right to this edition, and it was a shared printing by Bowyer and Thurlbourn. For a detailed discussion of this issue see Donald D. Eddy, 'Richard Hurd's editions of Horace and the Bowyer Ledgers', *Studies in Bibliography*, xlviii (1995), 167–9.

6 This is probably *Reflections on the Causes of the Rise and Fall of the Roman Empire. Translated from the French of* M. *de Secondat, Baron de Montesquieu . . . In two volumes . . . The second edition. With great Additions and Improvements*, 1752.

1 John Brown proceeded D.D. on 13 November 1754. (C.U.L., Cambridge University Archives, Subscriptions, IV.)

1 Drummond's own mansion was at Brodsworth. (*D.N.B.*)

2 This probably refers to the error in Hurd's testimonial, which was addressed to the Bishop of Durham rather than the Archbishop of York, Hurd believing, when he obtained it, that Folkton was in the diocese of Durham. However, the testimonial is endorsed to the effect that "the

I beg your Grace's acceptance of my sincere thanks, & am, with the most perfect respect & duty, My Lord, Your Grace's much obliged & most obedient humble Servt

R Hurd

Endorsed by Drummond: "Thurcaston Novr. 29. 1762/ Mr Hurd".

Archbishop accepted it, & wd. not give Mr. Hurd the Trouble of getting another". It was dated 4 October 1762 and signed by George Cardale, James Bickham, John Simpson and the Bishop of Lincoln. (Borthwick Institute, Adm. 1762.)

BIBLIOGRAPHICAL LIST OF HURD'S WORKS

1746 Remarks on a late BOOK, Entitled, / AN / ENQUIRY / INTO THE / REJECTION / OF THE / CHRISTIAN MIRACLES / BY THE / HEATHENS. / double rule / LONDON: / Printed for M. COOPER, in *Pater-noster-Row*. / MDCCXLVI. / (Price Sixpence.)

1748 GRATULATIO / *Academiae Cantabrigiensis* / DE REDITU / SERENISSIMI REGIS / GEORGII II. / POST / PACEM & LIBERTATEM / EUROPAE / FELICITER RESTITUTAM / ANNO M.DCC.XLVIII. / [engraving] / *CANTABRIGIAE*, / TYPIS ACADEMICIS EXCUDIT J. BENTHAM. / rule / M.DCC.XLVIII.
2-page poem by RH on the Peace of Aix-la-Chapelle at G1.

1749 Q. HORATII FLACCI / ARS POETICA.[red] / EPISTOLA ad PISONES. / With an English / COMMENTARY[red] / AND / NOTES[red] / LONDON,[red] / Printed by *W. Bowyer*, / And sold by R. DODSLEY in Pall-mall, and / M. COOPER in Paternoster-Row. / MDCCXLIX.[red]

1751 THE / OPINION / OF AN / EMINENT LAWYER, / CONCERNING / The RIGHT of APPEAL / From the Vice-Chancellor of *Cambridge*, to / the SENATE; / Supported by a short historical Account of the / JURISDICTION of the UNIVERSITY. / In Answer to a late Pamphlet, / Intitled, *An Inquiry into the Right of Appeal from / the Chancellor or Vice-Chancellor of the University / of* Cambridge, &c. / rule / [quotation] / rule / *By a* FELLOW *of a* COLLEGE. / double rule / *LONDON*, / Printed, and Sold by M. Cooper, at the *Globe*, in / *Pater-noster-Row*. MDCCLI. / [Price One-Shilling.]

THE / OPINION / OF AN / EMINENT LAWYER, / CONCERNING / The RIGHT of APPEAL / . . . The SECOND EDITION.

THE / OPINION / OF AN / EMINENT LAWYER, / CONCERNING / The RIGHT of APPEAL / . . . The THIRD EDITION.

Q. HORATII FLACCI / EPISTOLA [red] / AD / AUGUSTUM. / With an English / Commentary and Notes.[red] / To which is added, / A DISCOURSE / CONCERNING / POETICAL IMITATION.[red] / rule / By the AUTHOR of the COMMENTARY, &c. / on the Epistle to the Pisos. / rule / LONDON,[red] / Printed for *W. Thurlbourn* in Cambridge. / And sold by *R. Dodsley* in Pall-mall; *J. Beecroft* in Lom- / bard Street; and M. *Cooper* in Paternoster-Row. / short rule / MDCCLI.[red]

1752 *The Mischiefs of Enthusiasm and Bigotry*: / rule / A / SERMON / Preached in / The Cathedral Church of *Norwich*, / AT THE / ASSIZES, / On *Wednesday*, 29 *July*, 1752, / Before the Honourable / Sir THOMAS PARKER, Knt. / Lord Chief Baron of the EXCHEQUER. / AND / Sir MARTIN WRIGHT, Knt. / One of the Justices of the Court of KING'S BENCH. / rule / Published at the Request of / The High Sheriff and Gentlemen of the Grand Jury. / rule / By RICHARD HURD, B.D. / Fellow of EMMANUEL COLLEGE, CAMBRIDGE, / And one of the Preachers at his MAJESTY'S / Chapel of WHITEHALL. / rule / LONDON, / Printed for J. GLEED in Norwich; and sold by JOHN and / JAMES RIVINGTON in St. Paul's Church-Yard, / London; Mr. THURLBOURN at Cambridge; Mr. / CRAYTON, at Ipswich; and Mr. EATON, at Yarmouth. / MDCCLII.

1753 Q. HORATII FLACCI / EPISTOLAE / AD / PISONES, / ET / AUGUSTUM: / With an ENGLISH / COMMENTARY and NOTES. / To which are added / TWO DISSERTATIONS: / THE ONE, / On the PROVINCES of the several Species / of DRAMATIC POETRY; / THE OTHER, / ON POETICAL IMITATION. / rule / IN TWO VOLUMES. / rule / The SECOND EDITION, Corrected and Enlarged. / rule / *LONDON*: / Printed for W. THURLBOURNE, at *Cambridge*; / and sold by R. DODSLEY, in *Pall-mall*; / J. BEECROFT, in *Lombard-street*; and / M. COOPER, in *Pater-noster-Row*. / short rule / MDCCLIII.

A / SERMON / PREACH'D AT / *Trinity Church* in CAMBRIDGE, / March 28. 1753. / Being the Time of / The annual meeting of the Children / educated in the CHARITY-SCHOOLS / of that Town. / rule / By RICHARD HURD, B.D. / Fellow of *Emmanuel* College, / AND / Minister of St. *Andrew's the Little in* CAMBRIDGE. / rule / *Printed by Desire of the Stewards for the said Charity*. / rule / To which is annexed, / A short Account of the Rise, Progress and / Present State of the CHARITY-SCHOOLS. / double rule / *CAMBRIDGE*, / Printed by J. BENTHAM Printer to the University. / short rule / M.DCC.LIII.

1755 ON THE / DELICACY / OF / FRIENDSHIP. / A / SEVENTH DISSERTATION. / Address'd to the / AUTHOR of the SIXTH. / rule / [quotation] / double rule / LONDON: / Printed for M. COOPER, at the Globe in Pater noster Row. / MDCCLV.

1757 A / LETTER / TO / Mr. MASON: / ON THE / MARKS of IMITATION. / rule / [quotation] / double rule / *CAMBRIDGE*; / Printed for W. THURLBOURN & J. WOODYER; and / sold by R. DODSLEY in Pall-mall, J. BEECROFT and / M. COOPER in Pater-noster Row, London. / Short rule / MDCCLVII.

Q. HORATII FLACCI / EPISTOLAE / AD / PISONES, / ET / AUGUSTUM: / With an ENGLISH / COMMENTARY and NOTES. / To which are added, / TWO DISSERTATIONS; / The one, / on the PROVINCES of the DRAMA: / The other, on POETICAL IMITATION: / AND / A LETTER to Mr. MASON. / rule / In TWO VOLUMES. / rule / The THIRD EDITION, Corrected and Enlarged. / rule / *CAMBRIDGE*, / Printed for W. THURLBOURN & J. WOODYER; and / sold by R. DODSLEY in Pall-mall, J. BEECROFT and / M. COOPER in Pater-noster Row, London. / short rule / MDCCLVII.

REMARKS / ON / Mr. DAVID HUME'S Essay / ON THE / Natural History of Religion: / ADDRESSED TO / The Rev. Dr. WARBURTON. / rule / [quotation] / rule / [ornament] / LONDON. / Printed for M. COOPER, in Pater-noster-row. / short rule / MDCCLVII. / [Price One Shilling.]

1759 MORAL and POLITICAL / DIALOGUES: / BEING THE / Substance of several Conversations / BETWEEN / DIVERS EMINENT PERSONS / OF THE / PAST and PRESENT AGE; / DIGESTED by the Parties themselves, / AND / Now FIRST published from the original MSS / WITH / CRITICAL and EXPLANATORY NOTES / By the EDITOR. / rule / [quotation] / double rule / LONDON, / Printed for A. MILLAR, in the *Strand*; and W. THURL- / BORNE and J. WOODYER at *Cambridge*. / MDCCLIX.

1760 MORAL and POLITICAL / DIALOGUES . . . THE SECOND EDITION.

1762 LETTERS / ON / CHIVALRY[red] / AND / ROMANCE.[red] / rule / [quotation] / double rule / *LONDON*:[red] / Printed for A. MILLAR, in the *Strand*; and / W. THURLBOURN and J. WOODYER, in / *Cambridge*. M.DCC.LXII.[red]

LETTERS / ON / CHIVALRY[red] / AND / ROMANCE.[red] . . . THE SECOND EDITION.

1764 DIALOGUES[red] / ON THE / USES / OF / FOREIGN TRAVEL;[red] / Considered as a Part of / An *English* GENTLEMAN'S Education: / BETWEEN / LORD SHAFTESBURY [red] / AND / MR. LOCKE.[red] / By the EDITOR of / *Moral and Political Dialogues*. / rule / [quotation] / double rule / LONDON,[red] / Printed by *W.B.* for A. MILLAR, in the *Strand*; / and W. THURLBOURN and J. / WOODYER, in *Cambridge*. / MDCCLXIV.[red]

DIALOGUES / ON THE / USES / OF / FOREIGN TRAVEL; . . . THE SECOND EDITION.

A / LETTER / TO / The Rev. Dr. THOMAS LELAND, / Fellow of TRINITY COLLEGE, DUBLIN: / IN WHICH / His late DISSERTATION *on the Principles / of Human Eloquence* is criticized; / AND / The Bishop of *GLOUCESTER's Idea of the / nature and character of an inspired language*, / as delivered in his Lordship's *Doctrine of / Grace*, / IS VINDICATED / From ALL the objections of the learned Author of / the DISSERTATION. / double rule / LONDON, / Printed for J. WILKIE, in *St. Paul's Church-Yard*. / MDCCLXIV.

1765 MORAL AND POLITICAL / DIALOGUES; / WITH / LETTERS ON / CHIVALRY AND ROMANCE: / . . . IN THREE VOLUMES. / THE THIRD EDITION.

1766 A / DISSERTATION / ON THE / IDEA / OF / UNIVERSAL POETRY. / [ornament] / LONDON, / printed for A. MILLAR, in The *Strand*. / MDCCLXVI.

Q. HORATII FLACCI / EPISTOLAE / AD / PISONES, / ET / AUGUSTUM: / WITH AN ENGLISH / COMMENTARY AND NOTES: / TO WHICH ARE ADDED / CRITICAL DISSERTATIONS. / . . . IN THREE VOLUMES. / THE FOURTH EDITION, / CORRECTED AND ENLARGED.

1771 MORAL AND POLITICAL / DIALOGUES; / WITH / LETTERS ON / CHIVALRY AND ROMANCE: / . . . IN THREE VOLUMES. / THE FOURTH EDITION.

1772 AN / INTRODUCTION / TO THE STUDY OF THE / PROPHECIES / Concerning the CHRISTIAN CHURCH; / AND, IN PARTICULAR, / Concerning the Church of PAPAL ROME: / IN TWELVE SERMONS, / PREACHED IN LINCOLN'S-INN-CHAPEL, / AT THE LECTURE OF / The Right Reverend WILLIAM WARBURTON / Lord Bishop of GLOUCESTER. / rule / By RICHARD HURD, D.D. / Preacher to the Honourable Society of LINCOLN'S-INN. / rule / [quotation] / double rule / LONDON, / PRINTED BY W. BOWYER AND J. NICHOLS: / FOR T. CADELL, IN THE STRAND. / MDCCLXXII.

AN / INTRODUCTION / TO THE STUDY OF THE / PROPHECIES / . . . THE SECOND EDITION.

SELECT WORKS / OF MR. A. COWLEY; / IN TWO VOLUMES: / With a PREFACE and NOTES by the Editor. / VOLUME THE FIRST [SECOND]. / [engraving] / [quotation] / LONDON, / PRINTED BY W. BOWYER AND J. NICHOLS: / FOR T. CADELL, IN THE STRAND. / MDCCLXXII.

SELECT WORKS / OF MR. A. COWLEY; / . . . THE SECOND EDITION.

1773 DISCORD: / A / SATIRE. / rule / [quotation] / double rule / LONDON, / Printed for J. WOODYER, in *Cambridge*: / Sold by J. BEECROFT, in *Pater-noster-Row*; T. CADELL, in *The Strand*; / S. LEACROFT, *Charing-Cross, London*; / and D. PRINCE, at *Oxford*. / MDCCLXXIII.

AN / INTRODUCTION / TO THE STUDY OF THE / PROPHECIES / . . . THE THIRD EDITION. In two volumes.

1776 A / CHARGE / DELIVERED TO / THE CLERGY / OF THE / Diocese of LICHFIELD and COVENTRY, / At the BISHOP'S Primary Visitation / in 1775 and 1776; / And printed at their request. / double rule / LONDON: MDCCLXXVI.

AN / INTRODUCTION / TO THE STUDY OF THE / PROPHECIES / . . . THE FOURTH EDITION.

MORAL AND POLITICAL / DIALOGUES; / WITH / LETTERS ON / CHIVALRY AND ROMANCE: / . . . IN THREE VOLUMES. / THE FIFTH EDITION.

Q. HORATII FLACCI / EPISTOLAE / AD / PISONES, / ET / AUGUSTUM: / . . . IN THREE VOLUMES. / THE FIFTH EDITION, / CORRECTED AND ENLARGED.

SERMONS / PREACHED AT / LINCOLN'S-INN, / Between the Years 1765 and 1776: / WITH / A LARGER DISCOURSE, / On Christ's *driving the Merchants out of the / Temple*; in which the nature and end of / that famous transaction is explained. / double rule / By RICHARD HURD, D.D. / Lord Bishop of LICHFIELD and COVENTRY; / and late Preacher of LINCOLN'S-INN. / double rule / LONDON, / PRINTED BY W. BOWYER AND J. NICHOLS: / FOR T. CADELL, IN THE STRAND. / MDCCLXXVI.

1777 REMARKS / ON / Mr. DAVID HUME's Essay / ON THE / Natural History of Religion: / . . . A NEW EDITION.

SELECT WORKS / OF MR. A. COWLEY; / IN TWO VOLUMES: / . . . THE THIRD EDITION.

A / SERMON / PREACHED BEFORE / THE RIGHT HONOURABLE / THE HOUSE OF LORDS, / IN THE / ABBEY CHURCH OF WESTMINSTER, / ON FRIDAY, DECEMBER 13, 1776, / BEING / The Day appointed by AUTHORITY for a GENERAL FAST, / on Account of the AMERICAN REBELLION. / BY RICHARD, LORD BISHOP OF / LICHFIELD AND COVENTRY. / LONDON: / PRINTED FOR T. CADELL IN THE STRAND. / MDCCLXXVII.

A / SERMON / PREACHED BEFORE / THE RIGHT HONOURABLE / THE HOUSE OF LORDS, / IN THE / ABBEY CHURCH OF WESTMINSTER, / ON FRIDAY, DECEMBER 13, 1776, / . . . THE SECOND EDITION.

SERMONS / PREACHED AT / LINCOLN'S-INN, / Between the Years 1765 and 1776: / . . . THE SECOND EDITION.

1779 SERMONS / PREACHED AT / LINCOLN'S-INN, / Between the Years 1765 and 1776. / VOLUME THE SECOND. / By RICHARD HURD, D.D. / Lord Bishop of LICHFIELD and COVENTRY, / and late Preacher of LINCOLN'S-INN. / LONDON, / PRINTED BY J. NICHOLS: / FOR T. CADELL, IN THE STRAND. / MDCCLXXIX.

1780 SERMONS / PREACHED AT / LINCOLN'S-INN, / Between the Years 1765 and 1776. / VOLUME THE THIRD. / . . . MDCCLXXX.

1781 A / SERMON / Preached before the / Incorporated SOCIETY / FOR THE / *Propagation of the Gospel in / Foreign Parts*; / AT THEIR / ANNIVERSARY MEETING / IN THE / Parish Church of ST. MARY-LE-BOW, / On FRIDAY *February* 16, 1781. / rule / By the Right Reverend Father in God, / RICHARD Lord Bishop of *Lichfield* and *Coventry*. / double rule / *LONDON*: / Printed by T. HARRISON and S. BROOKE, / in *Warwick-Lane*. / short rule / MDCCLXXXI.

1785 SERMONS / PREACHED AT / LINCOLN'S-INN, / Between the Years 1765 and 1776: / . . . THE THIRD EDITION.
Three volumes; Volumes 2 and 3, "A NEW EDITION".

1786 A / SERMON / PREACHED BEFORE / THE RIGHT HONOURABLE / THE HOUSE OF LORDS, / IN THE / ABBEY CHURCH OF WESTMINSTER, / ON MONDAY, JANUARY 30, 1786, / BEING / The Anniversary of KING CHARLES'S MARTYRDOM. / BY RICHARD, LORD BISHOP OF / WORCESTER. / LONDON: / PRINTED FOR T. CADELL, IN THE STRAND. / MDCCLXXXVI.

1788 AN / INTRODUCTION / TO THE STUDY OF THE / PROPHECIES / . . . THE FIFTH EDITION.

MORAL AND POLITICAL / DIALOGUES; / WITH / LETTERS ON / CHIVALRY AND ROMANCE: / . . . IN THREE VOLUMES. / THE SIXTH EDITION.

THE / WORKS / OF THE / RIGHT REVEREND / WILLIAM WARBURTON, / LORD BISHOP OF GLOUCESTER. / IN SEVEN VOLUMES. / short rule / VOLUME THE FIRST. / short rule / LONDON, / PRINTED BY JOHN NICHOLS: / AND SOLD BY T. CADELL, IN THE STRAND. / MDCCLXXXVIII.

1789 TRACTS, / BY / WARBURTON, / AND A / WARBURTONIAN; / NOT / ADMITTED / INTO THE / COLLECTIONS / OF THEIR / RESPECTIVE WORKS. / short rule / [quotation] / short rule / LONDON: / PRINTED FOR CHARLES DILLY, IN THE POULTRY. / short rule / M,DCC,LXXXIX.

1794 A / DISCOURSE, / BY WAY OF / GENERAL PREFACE / TO THE QUARTO EDITION OF / BISHOP WARBURTON'S WORKS, / CONTAINING SOME ACCOUNT OF THE / LIFE, WRITINGS, AND CHARACTER OF THE AUTHOR. / short rule / LONDON, / PRINTED BY JOHN NICHOLS. / MDCCXCIV.

The following works were published posthumously:

[1808] LETTERS / FROM A / *LATE EMINENT PRELATE* / TO / ONE OF HIS FRIENDS. / double rule / [quotation] / double rule / short double rule / Kidderminster [gothic script] / PRINTED BY GEORGE GOWER. / [the following pasted to title-page] PRINTED FOR T. CADELL AND W. DAVIES, STRAND, / LONDON.

1809 LETTERS / FROM A / *LATE EMINENT PRELATE* / TO / ONE OF HIS FRIENDS. / . . . THE SECOND EDITION.

LETTERS / FROM A / *LATE EMINENT PRELATE* / TO / ONE OF HIS FRIENDS. / . . . THE THIRD EDITION.

1811 THE / WORKS / OF THE / RIGHT HONOURABLE / JOSEPH ADDISON, / A NEW EDITION, / WITH NOTES / BY RICHARD HURD, D.D. / LORD BISHOP OF WORCESTER. / short rule / *IN SIX VOLUMES.* / short double rule / VOL. I. / short double rule / LONDON: / PRINTED FOR T. CADELL AND W. DAVIES, STRAND, / BY J. M'CREERY, BLACK-HORSE-COURT. / short rule / 1811

THE / WORKS / OF / RICHARD HURD, D.D. / LORD BISHOP OF WORCESTER. / IN EIGHT VOLUMES. / VOL. I. / [engraving] / LONDON: / PRINTED FOR T. CADELL AND W. DAVIES, STRAND, / 1811.

BIBLIOGRAPHY

This Bibliography consists solely of those manuscripts and printed works cited in the Introduction and annotation. The manuscripts of Hurd's letters are described on pp. lxxix–lxxx.

Manuscripts

Beinecke Rare Book and Manuscript Library, Yale University

MS Vault Film, Sect. 16
Osborn Files

Bodleian Library, Oxford

Eng. Misc. e. 346 Cox Macro, Personal Account Book 1717–53
MS Don. b. 4. William Bowyer, Paper-stock Ledger, 3 vols., 1717–73 (photostat copy consulted at Cambridge University Library)

Borthwick Institute of Historical Research, York

Adm. 1762 Admission Papers
Bp. C & P VII Bishopthorpe Papers, Robert Drummond
Inst. AB Institution Act Books

British Library

Add. MS 4308 Birch collection
Add. MS 4310 Birch collection
Add. MS 4320 Birch collection
Add. MS 5804 Cole collections
Add. MS 25103 Cox Macro, Album, c.1706–1755
Add. MS 25473 A Catalogue of the Library etc. of Cox Macro, D.D. 1766
Add. MS 32557 Macro correspondence
Add. MS 32563 Mitford notebooks
Add. MS 32729 Official correspondence of the Duke of Newcastle. Home correspondence, 1751
Add. MS 32920 Official correspondence of the Duke of Newcastle. General correspondence, 1762
Add. MS 35590 General correspondence of the 1st Earl of Hardwicke
Add. MS 35598 Correspondence of the 1st Earl of Hardwicke and Thomas Herring, 1736–57
Add. MS 35606 Hardwicke papers
Add. MS 35635 Hardwicke papers
Add. MS 36248 Hardwicke papers
Eg. 1952, 1959 Papers of William Warburton
Middlesex County Records. Calendar of Sessions Books and Orders of Court, January 1729–30 to May 1732 (typescript of MS)

Cambridge University Library

Grace Book iota
Misc. Collect. 36 Journal of Henry Hubbard. Manuscript copy of MS BL, Add. 5852, p. 109ff.
UA, Subscriptions, IV
UA / UP / 1 Lecture proposals 1743–1753

Emmanuel College, Cambridge

BUR. 8. 6 Long Book 1748–1794
COL. 3. 2 Admissions 1719–1797
COL. 9. 1. (A), (B) College Register. William Bennett's Book, 1788
COL. 9. 28 Documents concerning the Ansell case
COL. 14. 2 Order Book 1738–1839
COL. 16. 1 Plate Book 1731–1913
COL. 18. 4 Statuta Collegii Emman: apud Cantabrigiam (copy of 1735 by Henry Hubbard)
SCH. 1. 2 Ash Foundation accounts book 1720–1781
SCH. 1. 11 Whichcot and Sudbury Gift 1719–1765
SCH. 1. 17 Thorpe Exhibition 1720–1866
SCH. 1. 19 List of Fellow-commoners and Terms of Benefactions
STE. 1. 5 Steward's Accounts Book 1744–1759
STE 15. 8 Commons Accounts Book 1731–1753
STE 15. 9 Commons Accounts Book 1731–1753
STE 15. 10 Commons Accounts Book 1753–1776
STE 15. 11 Commons Accounts Book 1753–1776
STE. 24. 1, 3 Chamber Rent Books
TUT. 11. 1 Residence Book 1719–1775
A Catalogue of the Plate in the Possession of Emmanuel College, compiled by Joan M. Stubbings, (typescript), 1970–71.

Gloucester County Record Office

GDR 297A Gloucester diocese visitation records, Liber Cleri

Hartlebury Castle

Commonplace Book, 3 vols.
Dates of some occurrences in my own life
Mem: of my Father's death. & Mother's
Thurcaston: certificate of institution, subscription on institution, certificate of induction
Letters from Frederick Hervey December 1754
Letters from Charles Yorke 1757–1762

Jesus College, Cambridge

COL. 1. 2 College Register

Lambeth Palace Library

VB 1 / 8 Act Book of the Archbishop of Canterbury, 1734–1750

Leicestershire County Record Office

DE 1416 / 5 Thurcaston Parish Register, Marriages 1754–1812, Banns 1754–1823
DE 1416 / 29 Correspondence between John Danvers, Swithland and Rev. Mr. Hurd concerning dispute over timber, 20 August – 2 October 1758

DE 1416 / 60 Correspondence re consent to enclosure and tithe commutation, rector's allotments & their value 1759–1762
DE 1416 / 61 Accounts for fencing of rectory land and Thurcaston school land in Anstey Field November 1761
DE 1416 / 73 Correspondence and memoranda concerning Thurcaston rectory, tithes, etc. 1730–1769
DE 1416 / 83 Account of receipts and expenditure of living 1756–1763; also details of tithe lettings 1757–1766, etc.
DE 1416 / 85 Account of receipts and expenditure, etc. 1762–1775
DE 1416 / 86 Receipts for tax payments, curate's wages, etc. 1757–1804
1 D41 / 30 / 189 James Bickham, rector of Loughborough, sequestration bond, induction certificate

Lincolnshire County Record Office

PD 110 / 43 Presentation deed, North Stoke
SUB VII Subscription Book VII

Norfolk County Record Office

Macro family, Box 1, Temp. no. 2 Miscellaneous genealogical notes
NRS 24379 Deed relating to deposition of William Bullock's personal estate, 1745
Archdeaconry induction register
St Giles, Norwich parish register

Nottingham University Library

PWV / 120 / 75 Portland MSS. Letters from Archbishop Herring to William Herring

Private Collections

Macro Letter-book

Harry Ransom Humanities Research Centre, University of Texas, Austin

Warburton MSS Transcripts of letters to Thomas Balguy 1750–1775

St John's College, Cambridge: Bursary

Buttery Books
DS1.3 Long Book 1752–1758
SB9.8 Platt's Foundation 1675, &c.

St John's College, Cambridge: Library

Powell MSS Lecture notes by Thomas Sympson

Shropshire County Record Office

1952 / 44 Hatton rentals, Kenyon-Slaney collection

Somerset County Record Office

D / D / BS / no.9 Clergy subscription book
D / D / VC / 87 Clergy list
Badgworth parish register
Cloford parish register
Shepton Mallet visitation and marriage registers

Staffordshire County Record Office

D260 / M / E / 27–9 Littleton Day Books 1752–1811
D260 / M / E / 116–9a Littleton Ledgers 1752–1808

D260 / M / E / 126–9a Littleton Banking Books 1750–1812
D260 / M / F / 4 / 11 Law–suit: Littleton v. Hellier
D260 / M / T / 5 / 32 Correspondence relating to the sale of Lord Brooke's estate
D260 / M / T / 5 / 107 Sir Edward Littleton, 3rd bart., will, codicil, inventory; Mrs Littleton, private accompt
D260 / M / T / 5 / 110 Sir Edward Littleton, 4th bart., will and 4 codicils, inventories, etc.
D260 / M / T / 5 / 129 Marriage settlement 1752
D798 / 3 / 1 / 1 Eld correspondence
D1178 / 3 Artist's letter-book (Littleton collection)
D1413 / 2 Littleton correspondence
D1414 / 4 / 2 / 1 Brewood Grammar School
D4014 / 1 / 4 Brewood Parish Register
D4190 / 1 / 2 Pipe Ridware Parish Register 1724–1797
475 / M / 1 Staffordshire lease
475 / M / 5 Staffordshire lease

Staffordshire: William Salt Library

H.M. 296 / 40 Papers relating to a company led by Capt. Robins, 1745
S.M.S. 520–3 Gower correspondence

Suffolk County Record Office

Preston parish register

National Library of Wales

MS 12435E Letters to the Rev. Benjamin Conway and other miscellaneous letters
MS 12502E Pedigrees, genealogical notes, &c.

York Minster Library

Add. MS 25 William Mason Commonplace Book

Primary Printed Sources*

The Academic: Or a Disputation on the State of the University of Cambridge, and the propriety of the regulations made in it, on the 11th day of May, and 26th day of June 1750, 1750

Addison, Joseph, *A Discourse on Ancient and Modern Learning. Now first published from an original manuscript of Mr. Addison's, prepared and corrected by himself*, [First edition, 1734], 1739

———, *A Letter from Italy, to the Right Honourable Charles, Lord Halifax, 1701. Together with the Morning Muse of Alexis . . . By Mr. Congreve, 1695. To which is added the Despairing Lover*, 1709

———, *The Medleys for the Year 1711. To which are prefix'd, The Five Whig-Examiners*, 1712

Albin, J., *A New, Correct, and Much-Improved History of the Isle of Wight from the earliest times . . . to the present period*, 1795

The Ambulator; or, the Stranger's Companion in a Tour round London; within the circuit of twenty-five miles, 1774

* Place of publication London unless otherwise noted.

Ambulator: or, A Pocket Companion in a Tour round London, within the circuit of twenty five miles: describing whatever is most remarkable for antiquity, grandeur, elegance, or rural beauty, Fourth edition, 1792

Annet, Peter, *The Resurrection of Jesus Considered; In answer to the Tryal of the Witnesses: . . . By a Moral Philosopher*, [?1743]

Arnald, Richard, *A Critical Commentary upon the Book of the Wisdom of Solomon; Being a Continuation of Bishop Patrick and Mr. Lowth*, 1744

[Askew, Anthony], *Bibliotheca Askeviana. Sive catalogus librorum rarissimorum Antonii Askew, M.D. Quorum auctio fiet apud S. Baker & G. Leigh . . . 13 Februarii MDCCLXXV*, [1775]

[Atterbury, Francis], *The Rights, Powers, and Priviledges, of an English Convocation, Stated and Vindicated. In Answer to a Late Book of Dr. Wake's, Entituled, The Authority of Christian Princes over their Ecclesiastical Synods asserted, &c.*, 1700

Bacon, John, *Liber Regis, vel Thesaurus Rerum Ecclesiasticarum . . . With an Appendix containing proper directions and precedents relating to presentations, etc.*, 1786

Balguy, John, *Twenty-One Sermons on the following Subjects, (Fifteen of which now first printed.)*, 1749

———, *Twenty Sermons on the following Subjects*, 1750

[Beatniffe, R.], *The Norfolk Tour: or, Traveller's Pocket Companion. Being a concise description and present state of all the noblemens and gentlemens seats, as well as of the principal towns, and other remarkable places, in the county of Norfolk*, London and Norwich, [1772]

[Barker, Mary], *A Welsh Story*, 3 vols., 1798

Bedell, William and James Wadesworth, *The Copies of Certaine Letters which have passed betweene Spaine and England in Matter of Religion concerning the generall motives to the Romane obedience*, 1624

Bickham, George, *The Beauties of Stow: or, a Description of the Pleasant Seat, and Noble Gardens, of the Right Honourable Lord Viscount Cobham*, 1750

Bland, John, *A Grammatical Version, from the original Hebrew; of the Song of Solomon, into English blank verse . . . The whole being a drama, in seven scenes*, 1750

Bowden, Samuel, *Poetical Essays on several occasions*, 2 vols., 1733, 1735

Bower, Archibald, *The History of the Popes, from the Foundation of the See of Rome, to the Present Time*, 7 vols., 1748–66

Bromley, Henry, *A Catalogue of Engraved British Portraits, from Egbert the Great to the present time ... With an appendix, containing the portraits of such foreigners as . . . may claim a place in the British series, 1793*

[Broster, P.], *The Chester Guide: or, an Account of the antient and present State of that City . . . To which is added, a Directory*, Second edition, Chester, 1782

[Brown, John], *An Additional Dialogue of the Dead, between Pericles and Aristides: Being a Sequel to the Dialogue between Pericles and Cosmo*, 1760

———, *Athelstan. A Tragedy. As it is acted at the Theatre Royal in Drury-Lane*, 1756

———, *Barbarossa. A Tragedy. As it is perform'd at the Theatre-Royal in Drury-Lane*, 1755

———, *An Essay on Satire: Occasion'd by the Death of Mr. Pope*, 1745

———, *An Estimate of the Manners and Principles of the Times*, 1757

Burgersdijk, Francis, *Institutionum Logicarum Libri duo, . . . Ex Aristotelis, Keckermanni, aliorumq. praecipuorum Logicorum praeceptis recensitis, nov methodo ac modo formati, atque editi*, 2 vols., Lugd. Bat., 1626

[Burke, Edmund], *A Vindication of Natural Society: or, A View of the Miseries and Evils arising to Mankind from every Species of Artificial Society. In a letter to Lord **** . . . By a Late Noble Writer*, 1756

Burn, Richard, *Ecclesiastical Law*, 2 vols., 1763

Burnet, Gilbert, *An Exposition of the Thirty-nine Articles of the Church of England*, 1699

———, *Bishop Burnet's History of his own Time*, 2 vols., 1724–34

Burney, Charles, *Memoirs of the Life and Writings of the Abate Metastasio. In which are incorporated, translations of his principal letters*, 3 vols., 1796

Butler, Joseph, *The Analogy of Religion, Natural and Revealed, to the Constitution and Course of Nature. To which are added, two brief dissertations*, 1736

———, *Fifteen Sermons preached at the Rolls Chapel upon the following subjects*, 1726

Calmet, Augustin, *Antiquities Sacred and Prophane; or, a Collection of critical Dissertations on the Old and New Testament, translated from the French, by N[icholas]. Tindal*, 1724–7

[Cambridge, Richard Owen], *An Elegy written in an empty Assembly-Room*, 1756

Cantabrigia Depicta. A Concise and Accurate Description of the University and Town of Cambridge, and its Environs. A Particular History of the several Colleges and Public Buildings, their Founders and Benefactors; with an Account of the considerable Improvements which have been lately made throughout the University: Many correct Lists of the University Officers, &c. An invariable Rule for the Beginnings and Endings of the Cambridge terms; and other useful Notes relative to the University. To which is added, An Exact Account of the Several Posts, Coaches, Flys, Stage-Waggons, and other Carriers. Illustrated, Cambridge, [1763]

[Caraccioli, C.], *An Historical Account of Sturbridge, Bury, and the Most Famous Fairs in Europe and America; interspersed with Anecdotes Curious and Entertaining*, Cambridge, [1773]

Carter, Edmund, *The History of the County of Cambridge, from the earliest Account to the present time . . . Also a particular account of the antient and modern Cambridge, with the city of Ely, and the several parishes therein*, Cambridge, 1753

———, *The History of the University of Cambridge, from its Original, to the Year 1753 . . . Together with accurate lists of all the Chancellors, etc.*, 1753

Castel de Saint Pierre, Charles Irenée, *Annales Politiques de Feu Monsieur Irenée Castel*, 2 vols., Londres [?Paris], 1757

[Challoner, Richard], *The Catholick Christian instructed in the Sacraments, Sacrifice, Ceremonies, and Observances of the Church. By way of question and answer*, 1737

Chamberlayne, John, *Magnae Britanniae Notitia: or, the Present State of Great Britain; with diverse Remarks upon the Ancient State thereof, The Thirty-eighth edition of the south part, called England; and the Seventeenth of the north part, called Scotland . . . In two parts*, 1755

Chandler, Samuel, *A Defence of the Prime Ministry and Character of Joseph: In Answer to the Misrepresentations and Calumnies of the late Thomas Morgan, M.D. and Moral Philosopher*, 1743

———, *A Vindication of the History of the Old Testament. In Answer to the Misrepresentations and Calumnies of Thomas Morgan, M.D. and Moral Philosopher*, 1741

Chapman, John, *Popery the Bane of true Letters: a Charge delivered to the clergy of the Archdeaconry of Sudbury, at a Visitation on May 12, 1746*, 1746

Chapman, Thomas, *A Further Inquiry into the Right of Appeal from the Chancellor, or Vice Chancellor of the University of Cambridge, in Matters of Discipline: in which the Objections of the Author of a late Pamphlet, intitled, The Opinion of an Eminent Lawyer concerning the Right of Appeal . . . are fully Obviated*, 1752

[Chapman, Thomas], *An Inquiry into the Right of Appeal from the Chancellor, or Vice Chancellor, of the University of Cambridge, in Matters of Discipline: Addressed to a Fellow of a College*, 1751

Cibber, Colley, *The Character and Conduct of Cicero, Considered, from the history of his life, by the Reverend Dr. Middleton. With occasional essays, and observations upon the most memorable facts and persons during that period*, 1747

Clarke, Samuel, *Sermons on the Following Subjects ... Published from the Author's Manuscript, by John Clarke, D.D.*, 10 vols., 1730–1

[Cockburn, Catharine], *Remarks upon the Principles and Reasonings of Dr. Rutherforth's Essay on the Nature and Obligations of Virtue: In Vindication of the contrary Principles and*

Reasonings, inforced in the Writings of the late Dr. Samuel Clarke. Published by Mr. Warburton with a Preface, 1747

A *Complete Guide to all Persons who have any Trade or Concern with the City of London, and Parts adjacent. Containing, I. The names of all the streets, squares, etc. . . . II. The names and situations of the churches . . . III. An account of all the stage-coaches with the fares of passengers . . . IV. The names and places of abode of the most eminent merchants . . . V. The new rates for carmen . . . VI. Rates of the general post . . . VII. Useful tables . . . VIII. Tables of interest*, [First edition, 1740], Third edition, 1744

A *Complete Guide to all Persons who have any Trade or Concern with the City of London, and Parts adjacent*, etc., 1760

Cooper, Anthony Ashley, Earl of Shaftesbury, *Sensus Communis: An Essay on the Freedom of Wit and Honour. In a Letter to a Friend*, 1709

———, *Soliloquy: or, Advice to an Author*, 1710

A *Copy of the Poll for the Knights of the Shire for the County of Norfolk; taken at Norwich, May 22nd, 1734. Candidates: Sir Edmund Bacon, Bart. William Wodehouse, Esq; the Honourable Robert Coke. William Morden, Esq;*, [Norwich?], 1734

Cowdry, Richard, *A Description of the Pictures, Statues, Busto's, Basso-relievo's, and other curiosities at the Earl of Pembroke's house at Wilton*, 1751

Cowley, Abraham, *Poems: viz. I. Miscellanies. II. The Mistress, or, Love verses. III. Pindarique odes. And IV. Davideis, or, A sacred poem of the troubles of David*, 1656

Crebillon, Claude Prosper Jolyot de, *Tansaï et Neadarne. Histoire japonoise*, 1734 [published as *L'Écumoire, histoire japonoise*, 2 vols., 1735]

———, *Le Sopha, conte moral*, 2 vols., 1742

Crevier, Jean Baptiste Louis, *Histoire de l'université de Paris, depuis son origine jusqu'en l'année 1600*, 7 vols., Paris, 1761

Davila, Enrico Caterino, *Historia delle Guerre Civili di Francia. Nella quale si contengono le operationi di quattro re Francesco II. Carlo IX. Henrico III. & Henrico IIII*, Venice, 1630

———, *The History of the Civil Wars of France, A New Translation . . . By Ellis Farneworth*, 2 vols., 1758

[Delamotte, Peter], *The Weymouth Guide: Exhibiting the Ancient and Present State of Weymouth and Melcombe Regis*, Third edition, Weymouth [1790]

Delany, Patrick, *An Historical Account of the Life and Reign of David King of Israel: Interspersed with various Conjectures, Digressions, and Disquisitions. In which (among other things) Mr. Bayle's Criticisms upon the Conduct and Character of that Prince, are fully considered*, 3 vols., 1740–2

———, *Revelation Examin'd with Candour. Or, a Fair Enquiry into the Sense and Use of the several Revelations expresly declared, or sufficiently implied, to be given to Mankind from the Creation, as they are found in the Bible*, 2 vols., 1732, vol. 3, 1763

Disney, John, *Memoirs of the Life and Writings of Arthur Ashley Sykes, D.D.*, 1785

A *Dissertation on Comedy: in which the Rise and Progress of that Species of the Drama is particularly consider'd and deduc'd from the earliest to the present age. By a student of Oxford*, 1750

Doddridge, Philip, *Letters to and from the Rev. Philip Doddridge, D.D. late of Northampton: published from the originals: with notes explanatory and biographical*, ed. Thomas Stedman, Shrewsbury, 1790

Dodsley, Robert, *A Collection of Poems. By Several Hands*, 3 vols., 1748

———, *The Correspondence of Robert Dodsley 1733–1764*, ed. James E. Tierney, Cambridge, 1988

[Dodwell, Henry], *Christianity not Founded on Argument; and the True Principle of Gospel-Evidence Assigned: In a Letter to a young Gentleman at Oxford*, 1741

Douglas, John, *Milton Vindicated from the Charge of Plagiarism, brought against him by Mr. Lauder, and Lauder himself convicted of several forgeries and gross impositions on the public*, 1751

Earle, John, *Micro-cosmographie. Or, A Peece of the World Discovered; in Essayes and Characters*, 1628

———, [*Micro-cosmographie*] *The World display'd: or, several essays; consisting of the various characters and passions of its principal inhabitants*, 1740

Ecton, John, *Thesaurus Rerum Ecclesiasticarum: Being an Account of the Valuations of all the Ecclesiastical Benefices in the several Dioceses in England and Wales, as they now stand chargeable with, or were lately discharged from, the payment of first-fruits and tenths. To which are added the names of the patrons, and dedications of the churches*, 1742

———, *Thesaurus Rerum Ecclesiasticarum . . . The second edition . . . revised, corrected . . . with numerous additions by Browne Willis, LL.D., 1754*

[Edwards, Thomas], *The Canons of Criticism, and Glossary, Being a Supplement to Mr. Warburton's Edition of Shakespear. Collected from the notes in that celebrated work, The Sixth Edition, with Additions*, 1758

Erskine, Ralph, *A Paraphrase, or large explicatory poem upon the Song of Solomon*, 1742

———, *A Paraphrase, . . . A New edition, revised and corrected*, 1758

An Essay towards a New English Version of the Book of Job, 1756

Fenelon, François de Salingac de la Mothe, *Explication des Maximes des Saints sur la Vie Interieure*, 1697

[Fielding, Sarah], *The Adventures of David Simple: containing an account of his travels through the cities of London and Westminster, in search of a real friend. By a Lady . . . The second edition, revised and corrected. With a Preface by* Henry Fielding, 2 vols., 1744

Fontenelle, Bernard le Bovier de, *Nouveaux Dialogues des Morts*, Paris, 1683

Foster, John, *An Essay on the Different Nature of Accent and Quantity, with their Use and Application in the Pronounciation of the English, Latin, and Greek languages*, Eton, 1762

A Fragment, 1750 [variously attributed to James Bickham, Francis Coventry, and Henry Stebbing]

[Freeman, W. *pseud.*], *A Comparison between the Horace of Corneille and the Roman Father of Mr. Whitehead. In letters on the subject, between W.F. and J. Bromley*, 1750

Fresnoy, Charles Alphonse, du, *De Arte Graphica. The Art of Painting . . . With Remarks. Translated into English, Together with an Original Preface containing a Parallel betwixt Painting and Poetry. By Mr. Dryden. As also a Short Account of the most eminent Painters, both Ancient and Modern, continu'd down to the present times, according to the order of their succession. By another Hand*, 1695

———, *The Art of Painting . . . With Remarks . . . As also a Short Account of the most eminent Painters, both Ancient and Modern: By R.G. Esq; The Second Edition, corrected, and enlarg'd*, 1716

[Gally, Henry], *A Dissertation against Pronouncing the Greek Language according to Accents*, 1754

Garrick, David, *The Letters of David Garrick*, ed. David M. Little and George M. Kahrl, 3 vols., 1963

A General Account of Tunbridge Wells, and its Environs: Historical and Descriptive, 1771

George III, *The Correspondence of King George the Third from 1760 to December 1783*, ed. Sir John Fortescue, 6 vols., 1927–8

———, *Letters from George III to Lord Bute 1756–1766*, ed. Romney Sedgwick, 1939

Giannone, Pietro, *Dell'istoria Civile del Regno di Napoli libri XL*, 4 vols., Naples, 1723

Gill, John, *An Exposition of the Book of Solomon's Song, Commonly called Canticles: Wherein the Authority of it is Established and Vindicated, against Objections both Ancient and Modern; several versions compared with the Original Text; the different Senses, both of Jewish and Christian Interpreters considered; and the Whole opened and explained in proper and useful Observations . . . The Second Edition with Additions*, 1751

[Gilpin, William], *An Essay upon Prints, Containing Remarks upon the Principles of picturesque Beauty, the Different Kinds of Prints, and the Characters of the most noted Masters;*

Illustrated by Criticisms upon particular Pieces; to which are added, Some Cautions that may be useful in collecting Prints, 1768

Gratulatio Academiae Cantabrigiensis De Reditu Serenissimi Regis Georgii II. post pacem & libertatem Europae feliciter restitutem anno M.DCC.XLVIII, Cambridge, 1748

Gray, Thomas, *An Ode on a Distant Prospect of Eton College*, 1747

———, *Odes by Mr. Gray*, 1757

———, *Poems by Mr. Gray*, 1768

———, *Correspondence of Thomas Gray*, ed. Paget Toynbee and Leonard Whibley with Corrections and Additions by H.W. Starr, 3 vols., Oxford, 1935, reprinted with corrections, 1971

Grey, Richard, *An Answer to Mr. Warburton's Remarks on Several occasional Reflections, so far as they concern the Preface to a late edition of the Book of Job; in which the Subject and Design of that Divine Poem are set in a full and clear Light, and some particular Passages in it occasionally explain'd. In a Letter to the reverend Author of the Remarks*, 1744

Grey, Zachary, *A Word or Two of Advice to William Warburton; a Dealer in many Words. By a friend. With an appendix containing a taste of William's spirit of railing*, 1746

Hall, Joseph, *Virgidemiarum, Six Bookes of Satyrs*, 1597–8

———, *Virgidemiarum, Satires in six books*, Oxford, 1753

Hallifax, Samuel, *A Charge delivered to the Clergy at the Primary Visitation of the Diocese of Durham, in the Year MDCCLI; By the Right Reverend Father in God Joseph Butler, LL.D. Then Lord Bishop of that Diocese. The Second Edition. With a Preface, . . . By Samuel, Lord Bishop of Gloucester*, 1786

Harcourt, Edward William, ed., *The Harcourt Papers*, 14 vols., Oxford, [1880–1905]

Harris, John, *Navigantium atque Itinerantium Bibliotheca: Or, A Compleat Collection of Voyages and Travels*, 2 vols., 1705

[Hassell, John], *Tour of the Isle of Wight. The drawings taken and engraved by J. Hassell*, 2 vols., 1790

[Hawarden, Edward], *Charity and Truth: or Catholicks not Uncharitable in Saying, That None are sav'd out of the Catholick Communion. Because the rule is not universal*, Brussels [London], 1728

Heber, Reginald, *An Historical List of Horse-Matches Run and of Plates and Prizes run for in Great Britain and Ireland, in 1753 . . . Vol. III*, 1754

———, *An Historical List of Horse-Matches Run . . . in 1754 . . . Vol. IV*, 1755

[Heely, Joseph], *A Description of Hagley Park. By the Author of Letters on the Beauties of Hagley, Envil, and the Leasowes*, 1777

Historical Manuscripts Commission, Twelfth Report, Appendix, Part IX

[Home, John], *Douglas: A Tragedy. As it is acted at the Theatre-Royal in Covent Garden*, 1757

Horace, *Oeuvres d'Horace, en Latin, Traduites en Francois par M. Dacier, et le P. Sanadon. Avec les Remarques Critiques, Historiques et Geographiques, de l'un & de l'autre*, 8 vols., Amsterdam, 1735

Horne, George, *A Fair, Candid, and Impartial State of the case between Sir Isaac Newton and Mr Hutchinson. In which is shewn, How far a system of Physics is capable of Mathematical Demonstration*, Oxford, 1753

Hume, David, *Four Dissertations. I. The Natural History of Religion. II. Of the Passions. III. Of Tragedy. IV. Of the Standard of Taste*, 1757

———, *The History of England, from the Invasion of Julius Caesar to the Accession of Henry VII*, 2 vols., 1762 [1761–2]

———, *The History of England, under the House of Tudor*, 2 vols., 1759

———, *The Letters of David Hume*, ed. J.Y.T. Greig, 2 vols., Oxford, 1932

Hyde, Edward, Earl of Clarendon, *The History of the Rebellion and Civil Wars in England, Begun in the Year 1641, with the precedent passages and actions that contributed thereto, and the happy end and conclusion thereof by the King's blessed restoration*, 3 vols., Oxford, 1702–4

———, *The Life of Edward Earl of Clarendon, Lord High Chancellor of England, and Chancellor of the University of Oxford. Containing I. An Account of the Chancellor's Life from his birth to the Restoration in 1660. II. A Continuation of the same, and of his History of the Grand Rebellion, from the restoration to his Banishment in 1667*, Oxford, 1759

Ireland, Samuel, *Picturesque Views on the River Thames, from its source in Gloucestershire to the Nore; with Observations on the Public Buildings and other works of art in its vicinity*, 2 vols., 1792, Second edition, 1801–2

Johnson, Samuel, *A Dictionary of the English Language: in which the words are deduced from their originals, and illustrated in their different significations by examples from the best writers*, 2 vols., 1755

———, *Prefaces, Biographical and Critical, to the Works of the English Poets*, 10 vols., 1779–81

———, *London: a Poem, in Imitation of the Third Satire of Juvenal*, 1738

Jones, Henry, *The Earl of Essex. A Tragedy. As it is acted at the Theatre Royal in Covent-Garden*, 1753

Jones, Stephen, *A New Biographical Dictionary: containing a Brief Account of the Lives and Writings of the most eminent persons and remarkable characters in every age and nation . . . Second Edition, Corrected: With considerable Additions*, 1796

Jortin, John, *The Life of Erasmus*, 2 vols., 1758–60

———, *Remarks on Spenser's Poems*, 1734

———, *Six Dissertations upon Different Subjects*, 1755

A Journey from London to Scarborough, in Several Letters from a Gentleman there, to his friend in London . . . with a List of the Nobility, Quality, and Gentry at Scarborough, during the Spaw Season, in the Year 1733, 1734

Kennett, White, *Ecclesiastical Synods and Parliamentary Convocations in the Church of England Historically Stated, and Justly Vindicated from the Misrepresentations of Mr. Atterbury. Part I*, [all published], 1701

Kent's Directory for the year 1759. Containing an Alphabetical List of the Names and Places of Abode of the Directors of Companies, Persons in Publick Business, . . . in the Cities of London and Westminster, and Borough of Southwark, Twenty-sixth edition, 1759

[King, William], *Considerations on the Expediency of Making, and the Manner of Conducting the late Regulations at Cambridge*, 1751

———, *A Key to the Fragment. By Amias Riddinge; B.D. With a Preface. By Peregrine Smyth, Esq*, 1751

Kippis, Andrew, *Biographia Britannica: or, the Lives of the most eminent persons who have flourished in Great Britain and Ireland*, Second edition, 5 vols., 1778–93

Kirby, John, *The Suffolk Traveller: or, A Journey through Suffolk. In which is inserted the true distance in the roads, from Ipswich to every market town in Suffolk . . . By John Kirby, who took an actual survey of the whole county in the years 1732, 1733 and 1734*, Ipswich, 1735

[Lambert, Claude-François], *La Nouvelle Marianne; ou les Memoires de la Baronne de ****, Écrits par Elle-même*, The Hague, 2 vols., 1740

Lauder, William, *An Essay on Milton's Use and Imitation of the Moderns, in his Paradise Lost*, 1750

Le Clerc, John, *Logica: sive, Ars Ratiocinandi*, 2 parts, 1692

A Letter from a Blacksmith, to the Ministers and Elders of the Church of Scotland. In which the Manner of Publick Worship in that Church is considered; its Inconveniences and Defects pointed out; and Methods for removing them humbly proposed, 1759 [variously attributed to John Witherspoon and Henry Home, Lord Kames]

Letters concerning Confessions of Faith, And Subscriptions to Articles of Religion in Protestant Churches; Occasioned by Perusal of the Confessional, 1768 [attributed to Thomas Balguy]

Livy, *Historiarum ab urbe condita libri qui supersunt xxxv. Cum supplementis librorum amissorum a J. Freinshemio concinnatis. Recensuit et notis illustravit J[ean]. B[aptiste]. L[ouis]. Crevier*, Paris, 6 vols., 1735–42

[Lowth, Robert], *A Short Introduction to English Grammar: with Critical Notes*, 1762

Lowth, William, *A Commentary upon the Larger and Lesser Prophets; Being a Continuation of Bishop Patrick*, [published in parts] 1714–25, [First edition, book form] 1727, Third edition, 1730

[Lyttelton, George], *Dialogues of the Dead*, 1760

[Macpherson, James], *Fingal, an Ancient Epic Poem, in six books: Together with several other Poems, composed by Ossian the Son of Fingal. Translated from the Galic Language, by James Macpherson*, 1762

———, *Fragments of Ancient Poetry, Collected in the Highlands of Scotland, and Translated from the Galic or Erse Language*, Edinburgh, 1760

Marchant, John, *The History of the Present Rebellion: Collected from Authentick Memoirs, Letters, and Intelligences, as well private as publick: being a genuine and impartial account*, 1746

Martyn, Thomas, *The English Connoisseur: Containing An Account of whatever is curious in Painting, Sculpture, &c. In the Palaces and Seats of the Nobility and Principal Gentry of England*, 2 vols., 1766

[Maslen, Keith, and John Lancaster, ed.], *The Bowyer Ledgers. The Printing Accounts of William Bowyer Father and Son Reproduced on Microfiche with a Checklist of Bowyer Printing 1699–1777, a Commentary, Indexes, and Appendixes*, 1991

Mason, William, *Caractacus, A Dramatic Poem: Written on the Model of the Ancient Greek Tragedy*, 1759

———, *Elegies*, 1763

———, *Elfrida, A Dramatic Poem. Written on the Model of the Ancient Greek Tragedy*, 1752

———, *The English Garden: a Poem. Book the First*, 1772; *Book the Second*, 1777; *Book the Third*, 1779; *Book the Fourth*, 1781

———, *Musaeus: A Monody to the Memory of Mr. Pope, in Imitation of Milton's Lycidas*, 1747

———, *Ode performed in the Senate-House at Cambridge July 1, 1749. At the Installation of His Grace Thomas Holles Duke of Newcastle Chancellor of the University . . . Set to Music by Mr. Boyce, Composer to His Majesty*, Cambridge, 1749

———, *Odes*, 1756

———, *Poems*, 1764

———, *Poems by William Whitehead, Esq . . . Vol.III. To which are prefixed, Memoirs of his Life and Writings*. By W. Mason, M.A., York, 1788

———, *The Poems of Mr. Gray. To which are prefixed Memoirs of his Life and Writings*, York, 1775

[Mead, Richard], *A Catalogue of Pictures, Consisting of Portraits, Landscapes, Sea-Pieces, Architecture, Flowers, Fruits, Animals, Histories, of the late Richard Mead, M.D. Sold by Auction on March 20, 21, and 22, M.DCC.LIV.*, 1755

Middleton, Conyers, *A Free Inquiry into the Miraculous Powers, which are supposed to have subsisted in the Christian Church, from the earliest ages through several successive centuries*, 1749

———, *Germana quaedam antiquitatis eruditae monumenta quibus romanorum veterum ritus varii tam sacri quam profani, tum graecorum atque aegyptiorum nonnulli illustrantur, romae olim maxima ex parte collecta, ac dissertationibus jam singulis instructa*, 1745

———, *The History of the Life of Marcus Tullius Cicero*, 2 vols., 1741

———, *An Introductory Discourse to a larger Work, designed hereafter to be published, concerning the miraculous Powers, which are supposed to have subsisted in the Christian Church from the earliest Ages, through several successive centuries . . . with a postscript*, 1747

———, *A Letter from Rome, shewing an exact Conformity between Popery and Paganism: or, the Religion of the present Romans to be derived entirely from that of their heathen ancestors*, 1729

———, *A Letter from Rome, shewing an exact Conformity between Popery and Paganism: . . . The Fourth Edition, To which are added, I. A prefatory discourse, containing an answer to . . . the Catholic Christian instructed [Richard Challoner], . . . And II. A postscript*, 1741

Monro, John, *Remarks on Dr Battie's Treatise on Madness*, 1758

Montesquieu, Charles Louis de Secondat, Baron de, *Reflections on the Causes of the Rise and Fall of the Roman Empire. Translated from the French of M. de Secondat, Baron de Montesquieu . . . In two volumes . . . The second edition. With great Additions and Improvements*, 1752

More, Sir Thomas, *The Workes of Sir Thomas More Knyght, sometyme Lorde Chauncellour of England, written by him in the English tonge*, 1557

[Nevile, Thomas], *The Eighteenth Epistle of the First Book of Horace Imitated*, 1756

———, *The First Epode of the Second Book of Horace Imitated*, 1749

———, *The First Satire of the First Book of Horace Imitated*, 1755

———, *Imitations of Horace*, 1758

———, *Remarks on Mr. Mason's Elfrida in Letters to a Friend*, 1752

———, *The Seventeenth Epistle of the First Book of Horace Imitated*, 1755

The New Bath Guide, or, Useful Pocket-Companion; necessary for all persons residing at, or resorting to, this antient and opulent city. Giving an account of its antiquity, and first discovery of its waters, . . . Second edition, with large Additions, Bath, [?1762]

Nichols, John, *The History and Antiquities of the County of Leicester*, 4 vols. in 8 parts, 1795–1811

———, *Illustrations of the Literary History of the Eighteenth Century*, 8 vols., 1817–58

———, *Literary Anecdotes of the Eighteenth Century; comprizing Biographical Memoirs of William Bowyer, Printer . . . and Biographical Anecdotes of a considerable number of eminent writers and ingenious artists*, 9 vols., 1812–16

Otway, Thomas, *The Poet's Complaint of his Muse; or, A Satyr against Libells. A Poem*, 1680

———, *Venice Preserv'd, or, A Plot Discover'd. A Tragedy*, 1682

Outram, William, *De sacrificiis libri duo, quorum altero explicantur omnia Judaeorum, nonnulla gentium profanarum sacrificia; altero sacrificium Christi; utroque ecclesiae catholicae his de rebus sententia contra F. Socinum . . . defenditur*, 1677

[Parr, Samuel, ed.], *Tracts by Warburton, and a Warburtonian; not admitted into the Collections of their Respective Works*, 1789

Paterson, Daniel, *A New and Accurate Description of all the direct and principal Cross Roads in Great Britain*, 1771

Peirce, James, *A Paraphrase and Notes on the Epistles of St. Paul to the Colossians, Philippians, and Hebrews: after the manner of Mr. Locke. To which are annexed several critical dissertations on particular texts of scripture. The second edition . . . With a Paraphrase and Notes on the three last chapters of the Hebrews left unfinish'd by Mr. Peirce; and an Essay to discover the Author of the Epistle and Language in which it was originally written. By Joseph Hallett*, [1733]

Pelloutier, Simon, *Histoire des Celtes, et particulièrement des Gaulois et des Germains, depuis les tems fabuleux jusqu'à la prise de Rome par les Gaulois*, 2 vols., The Hague, 1740

[Pendred, John], *The Earliest Directory of the Book Trade by John Pendred (1785)*, ed. Graham Pollard, The Bibliographical Society, 1955

[Percy, Thomas], *The Song of Solomon, Newly Translated from the Original Hebrew: with a Commentary and Annotations*, 1764

Pitt, Christopher, *The Aeneid of Virgil. Translated by Mr. Pitt*, 2 vols., 1740

Plutarch, *Apophthegmata Regum et Imperatorum. Apophthegmata Laconica. Antiqua Lacedaemoniorum instituta. Apophthegmata Lacaenarum*, 1741

———, *Plutarchi Chaeronensis omnium quae exstant operum . . . Typis Regiis, apud Societatem Graecarum Editionum*, 2 vols., Lut. Paris, 1624

Pope, Alexander, *The Dunciad, in Four Books. Printed according to the complete Copy found in the Year 1742. With the prolegomena of Scriblerus, and notes variorum. To which are added, several notes now first publish'd*, 1743

———, *An Epistle from Mr. Pope, to Dr. Arbuthnot*, 1734 [1735]

———, *An Essay on Criticism*, 1711

———, *An Essay on Man: Being the First Book of Ethic Epistles to H. St. John L. Bolingbroke. With the Commentary and Notes of W. Warburton, A.M.*, 1743 [1744]

———, *The First Epistle of the First Book of Horace Imitated*, 1737

———, *The Iliad of Homer. Translated*, 6 vols., 1715–20

———, *Miscellaneous Poems. By Several Hands. Published by D. Lewis*, 1730 ['Christiani morientis ad Animan. Or, The Christian to his departing Soul', pp. 37–8]

———, *The New Dunciad: As it was found in the Year 1741*, 1742

———, *Satires of Dr. John Donne, Dean of St. Paul's. Done into modern English by Mr. Pope*, 1736

———, *Windsor-Forest. To the Right Honourable George Lord Lansdown*, 1713

———, *The Works of Alexander Pope Esq. In Nine Volumes Complete. With his last Corrections, Additions, and Improvements; as they were delivered to the Editor a little before his Death: Together with the Commentaries and Notes of Mr. Warburton*, 1751

———, Mr. Pope's *Literary Correspondence for thirty years; from 1704 to 1734. Being, a Collection of Letters, which passed between him and several eminent persons*, 5 vols., 1735–7

Priestley, Joseph, *Institutes of Natural and Revealed Religion*, 3 vols., 1772–4

Pyle, Edmund, *Memoirs of a Royal Chaplain, 1729–1763. The Correspondence of Edmund Pyle, D.D. Chaplain in Ordinary to George II with Samuel Kerrich D.D.*, ed. Albert Hartshorne, 1905

[Ramsay, Andrew], *The Life of Francois de Salignac de la Motte Fenelon, Archbishop and Duke of Cambray. [Translated into English by* N. Hooke], 1723

Ray, James, A *Compleat History of the Rebellion, from its first rise in 1745, to its total suppression at the glorious Battle of Culloden, in April 1746*, Manchester, [?1747], York, 1749

Reland, Adrian, *Dissertationum Miscellanearum. Pars prima (-tertia)*, 1706–8

Relhan, Anthony, A *Short History of Brighthelmston. With remarks on its air, and an analysis of its water, particularly of an uncommon mineral one*, 1761

Remarks on the New Tragedy, call'd, The Roman Father. With a word to the author. By a spectator, 1750

Richardson, Samuel, *Pamela: or, Virtue Rewarded. In a series of familiar letters from a beautiful young damsel, to her parents*, 4 vols., 1741–2 [1740–1]

———, *The Correspondence of Samuel Richardson . . . selected from the original manuscripts to which are prefixed, a biographical account of that author, and observations on his writings*, 6 vols., 1804

Robertson, William, *The History of Scotland, During the Reigns of Queen Mary and of King James VI. Till his Accession to the Crown of England. With a review of the Scottish history previous to that period; and an appendix*, 2 vols., 1759

Romaine, William, *The Divine Legation of Moses demonstrated from his having made express mention of, and insisted so much on the doctrine of a future state: whereby* Mr. *Warburton's attempt to demonstrate the divine legation of Moses from his omission of a future state is proved to be absurd, and destructive of all revelation.* A *sermon preached before the University of Oxford at St. Mary's, March 4. 1739*, 1739

Ross, John, *Marci Tullii Ciceronis Epistolarum ad Familiares libri XVI*, 1749

Rousseau, Jean Jacques, *Discours sur l'Origine et les Fondemens de l'Inegalite parmi les Hommes*, Amsterdam, 1755

———, *Lettres de Deux Amans, Habitans d'une petite Ville au pied des Alpes. Recueillies et publiées par J.J. Rousseau*, 6 vols., Amsterdam, 1761 [later published as *Julie, ou la Nouvelle Heloise*]

———, *La Nouvelle Heloise* [see above]

———, *Preface de la Nouvelle Heloise: ou Entretien sur les Romans, entre l'Éditeur et un Homme de Lettres*, 1761

———, *Correspondance Complete de Jean Jacques Rousseau*, ed. R.A. Leigh, 45 vols., Geneva and Oxford, 1965-86

Ruffhead, Owen, *The Life of Alexander Pope, Esq. Compiled from original manuscripts; with a critical essay on his writings and genius*, 1769

Russell, Richard, *A Dissertation on the Use of Sea-Water in the Disease of the Glands. Particularly the scurvy, jaundice, king's-evil, leprosy, and the glandular consumption. Translated from the Latin of Richard Russel, M.D.*, 1752

Rutherforth, Thomas, *A Charge delivered to the Clergy of the Archdeaconry of Essex at a Visitation Jul. X. XI. XII. MDCCLIII*, Cambridge, 1753

———, *An Essay on the Nature and Obligations of Virtue*, Cambridge, 1744

St John, Henry, Viscount Bolingbroke, *Reflections concerning Innate Moral Principles. Written in French by the late Lord Bolingbroke. And translated into English*, 1752

———, *The Works of the late Right Honourable Henry St John, Lord Viscount Bolingbroke. In Five Volumes, complete*, ed. David Mallet, 5 vols., 1754

Salmon, Thomas, *A New Geographical and Historical Grammar: wherein the geographical part is truly modern; and the present state of the several kingdoms of the world is so interspersed as to render the study of geography both entertaining and instructive*, 1749

———, *The Present State of the Universities and of the five adjacent counties of Cambridge, Huntington, Bedford, Buckingham and Oxford. Numb. I . . . which treats of the county and University of Oxford*, [all published], [1743], reissue, 1744

Saunderson, Nicholas, *The Elements of Algebra, in Ten Books . . . To which is prefixed I. The life and character of the author. II. His palpable arithmetic decyphered*, 2 vols., Cambridge, 1740

Scapula, Ioan., *Ioan. Scapulae Lexicon Graeco-Latinum, e probatis auctoribus locupletatum, cum indicibus, et Graeco & Latino, auctis, & correctis*, 2 vols., Lugduni Batavorum, 1652

[Seeley, Benton], *A Description of the Gardens of Lord Viscount Cobham, at Stow in Buckinghamshire*, Northampton, 1744

Serle, J., *A Plan of Mr. Pope's Garden, As it was left at his Death: with a Plan and Perspective View of the Grotto. All taken by J. Serle, his Gardener*, 1745

Shakespeare, William, *The Plays of William Shakespeare . . . With the corrections and illustrations of various commentators, to which are added notes by Samuel Johnson*, 8 vols., 1765

———, *The Works of Shakespeare in Eight Volumes. The genuine text, collated with all the former editions, and then corrected and emended, is here settled; being restored from the blunders of the first editors, and the interpolations of the two last: with a comment and notes, critical and explanatory*, By Mr. Pope and Mr. Warburton, 8 vols., 1747

Shaw, Stebbing, *The History and Antiquities of Staffordshire compiled from the manuscripts of Huntbach, . . . including Erdeswick's Survey of the county, and the approved parts of Dr. Plot's Natural History . . . Illustrated*, 2 vols., 1798–1801

———, *A Tour to the West of England in 1788*, 1789

Sherlock, Thomas, *The Tryal of the Witnesses of the Resurrection of Jesus*, 1729

Short, Thomas, *The Natural, Experimental, and Medicinal History of the Mineral Waters of Derbyshire, Lincolnshire, and Yorkshire, Particularly those of Scarborough*, 1734

Spanheim, Friedrich, *Historia Jobi. Praefixa est tabula chorographica, et index capitum*, 1670

Spelman, Edward, trans., *The Expedition of Cyrus, Translated from Xenophon, with critical and historical notes, by Edward Spelman, Esq;*, 2 vols., 1742

Spon, Jacob, *The History of the City and State of Geneva from its first foundation to this present time*, 1687

———, *Voyage d'Italie, de Dalmatie, de Grece, et du Levant, fait és années 1675 et 1676 par J. Spon . . . et G. Wheler*, 4 vols., Lyon, 1678–1680.

[Squire, Samuel], *The Ancient History of the Hebrews Vindicated: or, Remarks on Part of the Third Volume of the Moral Philosopher, By Theophanes Cantabrigiensis*, Cambridge, 1741

Statuta Academiae Cantabrigiensis, Cambridge, 1785

Sterne, Laurence, *The Life and Opinions of Tristram Shandy, Gentleman*, Vols. I & II, York, 1760, Vols. III – VIII, London, 1761–5

The Student, or the Oxford and Cambridge Monthly Miscellany, [continuation of *The Student, or The Oxford Monthly Miscellany*], Oxford, 1750–1

[Sykes, Arthur Ashley], *An Essay on the Nature, Design, and Origin, of Sacrifices*, 1748

———, *The Principles and Connexion of Natural and Revealed Religion Distinctly Considered*, 1740

Tasso, Torquato, *La Gerusalemme Liberata . . . con le annotationi di Scipion Gentili, e di Giulio Guastavini, et li argomenti de Oratio Ariosti, stampata per Giuseppe Pavoni ad instanza di Bernardo Castello*, Geneva, 1617

Taylor, John, *Elements of the Civil Law*, Cambridge, 1755

[Terrasson, Jean], *Sethos: Histoire ou Vie tirée des Monumens anecdotes de l'Ancienne Egypte. Traduite d'un Manuscrit Grec*, 3 vols., Paris, 1731

———, *The Life of Sethos. Taken from Private Memoirs of the Ancient Egyptians. Translated from a Greek manuscript into French. And now faithfully done into English from the Paris edition; by Mr. [Thomas] Lediard*, 2 vols., 1732

Thomson, James, *The Seasons*, 1744

Throsby, John, *The History and Antiquities of the Ancient Town of Leicester: . . . attempted*, Leicester, 1791

Trapp, Joseph, *The Aeneis of Virgil, Translated into Blank Verse*, 2 vols., 1718–20

———, *The Works of Virgil: Translated into English Blank Verse. With Large Explanatory Notes and Critical Observations*, 1731

Tunstall, James, *Observations on the present Collection of Epistles between Cicero and M. Brutus, representing several evident marks of forgery in those epistles; and the true state of many important particulars in the life and writings of Cicero: In answer to the late pretences of the Reverend Dr. Conyers Middleton*, 1744

An *Universal History from the earliest account of time to the present: compiled from original authors [by G. Sale, G. Psalmanazar, A. Bower, G. Shelvocke, J. Campbell, J. Swinton, etc.] and illustrated with maps*, 7 vols. in 8, 1736–44

———, Second, revised edition, 20 vols., 1747–8

[Van Dyck], *Iconographie ou Vies des Hommes Illustres . . . avec les Portraits peints par le fameux Antoine Van Dyck*, 2 vols., Amsterdam & Leipzig, 1759

Veneer, John, *An Exposition on the Thirty-nine Articles of the Church of England: collected out of the writings of the most celebrated divines of the said Church*, 1725

Vertue, George, *Vertue Note Books*, (The note-books of George Vertue relating to artists and collections in England), ed. Katherine A. Esdaile, the Earl of Ilchester, Sir Henry M. Hake, Walpole Society [vols.18, 20, 22, 24, 26, 30], Oxford, 1930–55

Virgil, *The Works of Virgil, In Latin and English . . . The Aeneid translated by Christopher Pitt, the Eclogues and Georgics, with notes . . . by . . . Joseph Warton. With several observations by Dr Holdsworth, Mr Spence, and others . . .*, 4 vols., 1753

[Voltaire, François Marie Arouet de], *Candide, ou l'Optimisme. Traduit de l'Allemand. De. Mr. le Docteur Ralph*, 1759

———, *An Essay upon the Civil Wars of France, Extracted from curious manuscripts. And also upon the Epick Poetry of the European Nations from Homer down to Milton*, 1727

———, *Histoire de Charles XII. Roi de Suede. par Mr. de V****, Basle [i.e. London?], 1731

———, *Histoire de l'Empire de Russie sous Pierre le Grand, Par l'Auteur de l'histoire de Charles XII*, [Geneva], 2 vols., 1759, 1763

———, *La Ligue; ou Henry le Grand. Poëme épique*, Geneva, 1723 [afterwards entitled *La Henriade*]

———, *Le Siècle de Louis XIV. Publié par M. de Francheville conseiller aulique de sa Majesté, & membre de l'academie roiale des sciences & belles lettres de prusse*, Berlin, 1751

Wake, William, *The Authority of Christian Princes over their Ecclesiastical Synods asserted: with particular respect to the Convocations of the Clergy of the Realm and Church of England*, 1697

———, *The State of the Church and Clergy of England, in their Councils, Synods, Convocations, Conventions, and other Publick Assemblies; Historically Deduced from the Conversion of the Saxons, . . . Occasion'd by a Book, Intituled, The Rights, Powers, and Privileges of an English Convocation, &c.*, 1703

Walpole, Horace, *Anecdotes of Painting in England; with some Account of the principal Artists; and incidental Notes on other Arts; collected by the late Mr. George Vertue; and now digested and published from his original MSS. By Mr. Horace Walpole . . . Second edition, with Additions*, 4 vols., 1782

———, *The Yale Edition of Horace Walpole's Correspondence*, ed. W.S. Lewis, 48 vols., New Haven, 1937–83

Warburton, William, *The Alliance between Church and State, or, the Necessity and Equity of an Established Religion and a Test-law demonstrated, from the Essence and End of Civil Society, upon the fundamental Principles of the Law of Nature and Nations. In Three Parts*, 1736

———, *A Critical and Philosophical Commentary on Mr. Pope's Essay on Man. In which is contain'd a Vindication of the said Essay from the Misrepresentations of Mr. De Resnel, the French Translator, and of Mr. De Crousaz . . . the Commentator*, 1742

———, *A Critical and Philosophical Enquiry into the Causes of Prodigies and Miracles, as related by Historians. With an Essay towards restoring a Method and Purity in History. In which, the Characters of the most celebrated writers of every age, and of the several stages and species of History are occasionally criticized and explained. In two parts*, 1727

———, *The Divine Legation of Moses Demonstrated, on the Principles of a Religious Deist, from the Omission of the Doctrine of a Future State of Reward and Punishment in the Jewish Dispensation. In Six Books*, [Books I–III], 1738, Second edition, 1738, Third edition, 1742, Fourth edition, 2 vols., 1755

———, *The Divine Legation of Moses demonstrated, on the Principles of a Religious Deist . . . The Second Volume, in Two Parts*, [Books IV–VI], 2 vols., 1741, Second edition, 2 vols., 1742, Third edition, 2 vols., 1758, Fourth edition, 3 vols., 1765

———, *The Doctrine of Grace: or, the Office and Operations of the Holy Spirit vindicated from the Insults of Infidelity, and the Abuses of Fanaticism: concluding with some Thoughts (humbly offered to the consideration of the established clergy) with regard to the right method of defending religion against the attacks of either party*, 1763

———, *Faith Working by Charity to Christian Edification. A Sermon Preach'd at the last Episcopal Visitation for Confirmation, in the Diocese of Lincoln*, 1738

———, *Julian. Or a Discourse concerning the Earthquake and Fiery Eruption, which defeated that Emperor's attempt to rebuild the temple at Jerusalem*, 1750

———, *A Letter to the Editor of the Letters on the Spirit of Patriotism, The Idea of a Patriot-King, and The State of Parties, &c., occasioned by the Editor's Advertisement*, 1749

———, *The Principles of Natural and Revealed Religion occasionally opened and explained; in a course of sermons preached before the Honourable Society of Lincoln's Inn*, 2 vols., 1753–4

———, *A Rational Account of the Nature and End of the Sacrament of the Lord's Supper*, 1761

———, *Remarks on several occasional Reflections: In Answer to the Rev. Dr. Middleton, Dr. Pococke, The Master of the Charter House, Dr. Richard Grey, and others. Serving to explain and justify divers passages, in the Divine Legation, objected to by those learned writers. To which is added, A General Review of the Argument of the Divine Legation, as far as it is yet *advanced: wherein is considered the Relation the several parts bear to each other, and to the Whole. Together with an Appendix in Answer to a late Pamphlet entitled*, An Examination of Mr. W——s *second Proposition*, 1744

———, *Remarks on several occasional Reflections: In Answer to the Reverend Doctors Stebbing and Sykes. Serving to explain and justify the two Dissertations in the Divine Legation, concerning the Command to Abraham to offer up his son; and the Nature of the Jewish Theocracy; objected to by those learned Writers. Part II. and last*, 1745

———, *A Sermon preached before . . . the Lords . . . in the Abbey Church, Westminster, on Wednesday, January 30, 1760. Being the day appointed to be observed as the Day of the Martrydom of King Charles I*, 1760

———, *A Supplemental Volume of Bishop Warburton's Works*, 1788

———, *Tracts by Warburton, and a Warburtonian; not admitted into the Collections of their respective Works*, [ed. Samuel Parr], 1789

———, *A Selection from Unpublished Papers of the Right Reverend William Warburton, D.D., By the Rev. Francis Kilvert*, 1841

———, *A View of Lord Bolingbroke's Philosophy; in Four Letters to a Friend. Letters First and Second*, 1754

———, *A View of Lord Bolingbroke's Philosophy; in Four Letters . . . Letter the Third*, 1755

———, *A View of Lord Bolingbroke's Philosophy; in Four Letters . . . Letter the Fourth and Last*, 1755

———, *A Vindication of the Author of the Divine Legation of Moses, &c. From the Aspersions of the Country Clergyman's Letter in the Weekly Miscellany of February 24, 1737*, 1738

———, *The Works of the Right Reverend William Warburton, Lord Bishop of Gloucester. In Seven Volumes*, [ed. Richard Hurd], 7 vols., 1788

———, *Letters from the Reverend Dr. Warburton, Bishop of Gloucester, to the Hon. Charles Yorke, From 1752 to 1770*, The Philanthropic Society, 1812

[Warton, Joseph], *An Essay on the Writings and Genius of Pope*, 1756

———, *Odes on Various Subjects*, 1746

Warton, Thomas, *The History of English Poetry, from the Close of the Eleventh to the Commencement of the Eighteenth Century*, 3 vols., 1774–81

———, *Observations on the Faerie Queene of Spenser*, 1754

———, *Observations on the Fairy Queen of Spenser . . . Second Edition, Corrected and Enlarged*, 2 vols., 1762

———, *Poems. A New edition, with additions*, 1777

[Waterland, Daniel], *Advice to a Young Student. With a Method of Study for the Four First Years*, 1730

Watson, William, *The Clergy-Man's Law: or, The Complete Incumbent, collected from the 39 Articles, canons, proclamations, decrees in chancery and exchequer, as also from all acts of parliament, and common-law cases, relating to the Church and clergy of England; . . . for the benefit of patrons of churches, and the parochial clergy. And will be useful to all students, and practitioners of the law*, 1701

Watts, Isaac, *Logick: Or, The Right Use of Reason in the Enquiry after Truth*, 1725

Wesley, John, *The Letters of the Rev. John Wesley, A.M.*, ed. John Telford, Standard Edition, 8 vols., 1931

West, Gilbert, *Observations on the History and Evidences of the Resurrection of Jesus Christ*, 1747

Weston, William, *An Enquiry into the Rejection of the Christian Miracles by the Heathens. Wherein is shewed, the Low opinion which they had of Miracles in general; and this accounted for from their Situation and Circumstances*, Cambridge, 1746

———, *Observations on some Remarks on a late book, intitled:* An Enquiry into the Rejection of the Christian Miracles by the Heathens, Cambridge, 1747

Whitehead, William, *Ann Boleyn to Henry the Eighth. An Epistle*, 1743

———, *The Danger of Writing Verse: An Epistle*, 1741

———, *An Essay on Ridicule*, 1743
———, *Plays and Poems, By William Whitehead, Esq. . . . In Two Volumes*, [Vols.I and II], 1774
———, *Poems by William Whitehead, Esq. . . . Vol.III. To which are prefixed, Memoirs of his Life and Writings. By W. Mason, M.A.*, York, 1788
———, *The Roman Father, A Tragedy. As it is acted at the Theatre Royal in Drury-Lane*, 1750
Wood, Thomas, *An Institute of the Laws of England; or, The Laws of England in their Natural Order, according to Common Use. Published for the direction of young beginners, or students in the law; and of others that desire to have a general knowledge in our common and statute laws. In four books*, 2 vols., 1720
Worsley, Richard, *The History of the Isle of Wight*, 1781
Worthington, William, *An Essay on the Scheme and Conduct, Procedure and Extent of Man's Redemption . . . To which is annexed, A Dissertation on the Design &c. of the Book of Job*, 1743
Young, Edward, *The Complaint: Or, Night-Thoughts on Life, Death, & Immortality*, 1742–5 [for 1746]
———, *The Brothers. A Tragedy. Acted at the Theatre-Royal in Drury-Lane*, 1753

Newspapers and periodicals

Annual Register
Cambridge Journal
Cambridge University Gazette
Critical Review
Daily Advertiser
General Advertiser
General Evening Post
Gentleman's Magazine
Leicester and Nottingham Journal
London Chronicle
London Evening-Post
London Gazette
London Magazine
Monthly Review
Norwich Gazette
Notes and Queries
Retrospective Review
Universal Chronicle and Westminster Journal

Sale catalogues

Art Sales Catalogues, British Library Print Room, A.1.3/S.C.
Sotheby's, Book Sale Catalogue, 19 November 1903

Secondary Sources*

Books

Alston, Robin, C., *A Bibliography of the English Language from the Invention of Printing to the Year 1800*, Ilkley, 1974
Amico, Silvio d', *Enciclopedia dello Spettacolo*, 11 vols., Rome, 1954–68
Baker, Thomas, *History of the College of St. John the Evangelist*, ed. John E.B. Mayor, 2 vols., Cambridge, 1869
Bannister, A.T., ed. *Diocese of Hereford, Institutions (AD 1539–1900)*, Hereford, 1923
Barnes, Thomas G., ed., *Somerset Assize Orders 1629–1640*, Frome, 1959

* Place of publication London unless otherwise noted

Barr, Bernard and John Ingamells, comps., A *Candidate for Praise. William Mason 1725–97, Precentor of York. Catalogue of an exhibition*, York, 1973

Betham, William, *The Baronetage of England, or the History of the English Baronets, and such Baronets of Scotland, as are of English families; with genealogical tables, and engravings of their armorial bearings*, 5 vols., Ipswich and London, 1801–5

Biographia Dramatica; or, A Companion to the Playhouse: containing Historical and critical Memoirs, and original Anecdotes of British and Irish dramatic Writers, from the commencement of our theatrical exhibitions; among whom are some of the most celebrated actors: . . . Together with an introductory view of the rise and progress of the British stage, compiled by David Erskine Baker, Isaac Reed and Stephen Jones, 3 vols. in 4, 1812

Black, Jeremy, ed. *Britain in the Age of Walpole*, 1984

Boyce, Benjamin, *The Benevolent Man. A Life of Ralph Allen of Bath*, Cambridge, Massachusetts, 1967

[Bryan, Michael], *Bryan's Dictionary of Painters and Engravers*, 1816, New edition revised and enlarged under the supervision of George C. Williamson, 5 vols., 1903–5

Buller, Audley Cecil, *The Life and Works of Heberden . . . Wix Prize at St. Bartholomew's Hospital in 1878*, 1879

Burns, R.M., *The Great Debate on Miracles. From Joseph Glanvill to David Hume*, 1981

Cardwell, Edward, *Synodalia. A Collection of Articles of Religion, Canons and Proceedings of Convocation in the Province of Canterbury from the Year 1547 to the Year 1717*, 2 vols., Oxford, 1842

Chalmers, Alexander, *The General Biographical Dictionary: Containing an Historical and Critical Account of the Lives and Writings of the Most Eminent Persons in every Nation; particularly the British and Irish; from the earliest accounts to the present time. A new edition, revised and enlarged*, 32 vols., 1812–17

Chandler, Thomas Bradbury, *The Life of Samuel Johnson, D.D. The First President of King's College, in New York*, New York, 1824

Clarke, Martin Lowther, *Greek Studies in England 1700–1830*, Cambridge, 1945

C[ockayne], G.E., ed., *The Complete Baronetage. Edited by* G.E.C., 5 vols., 1900–6; *Index . . . Together with an Appendix*, 1909

———, *The Complete Peerage, or a History of the House of Lords and all its members from the Earliest Times, revised and enlarged*, 12 vols., 1910–59

Colley, Linda, *In Defiance of Oligarchy. The Tory Party 1714–60*, Cambridge, 1982

[Collins, Arthur], *Collins's Peerage of England; . . . Greatly Augmented, and Continued to the Present Time, by Sir Egerton Brydges*, 9 vols., 1812

Colvin, Howard, A *Biographical Dictionary of British Architects, 1660–1840*, 1954, new edition, 1978

The Connoisseur Period Guides to the houses, decoration, furnishing and chattels of the classic periods, ed. [Herbert C.] R[alph] Edwards and L[eonard] G.G. Ramsey, 6 vols., 1956–61

Cooper, Charles Henry, *Annals of Cambridge*, 5 vols., Cambridge, 1842–1908

Coxe, William, *Memoirs of the Administration of Henry Pelham, collected from the family papers, and other authentic documents*, 2 vols., 1829

Cradock, Joseph, *Literary and Miscellaneous Memoirs. [With a biographical introduction by J.B. Nichols]*, 4 vols., 1828

Downey, James, *The Eighteenth Century Pulpit. A Study of the Sermons of Butler, Berkeley, Secker, Sterne, Whitefield and Wesley*, Oxford, 1969

Draper, John W., *William Mason. A Study in Eighteenth-Century Culture*, New York, 1924

Dufour, Théophile, *Recherches Bibliographiques sur les Oeuvres Imprimée de J.-J. Rousseau suivies de l'inventaire des papiers de Rousseau conservés a la Bibliothèque de Neuchatel*, [ed. by P. P. Plan], 2 vols., Paris, 1925

Eddy, Donald D., A *Bibliography of John Brown*, New York, 1971

Ellis, Kenneth, *The Post Office in the Eighteenth Century. A Study in Administrative History*, 1958

Esdaile, Mrs Arundell, *The Art of John Michael Rysbrack in Terracotta. Illustrated Catalogue*, Spink & Son Ltd., 1932

Eustace, Katharine, *Michael Rysbrack Sculptor 1694–1770*, City of Bristol Museum and Art Gallery, 1982

Evans, A.W., *Warburton and the Warburtonians. A Study in Some Eighteenth-Century Controversies*, Oxford, 1932

Fallon, John P., *Marks of London Goldsmiths and Silversmiths. Georgian Period (c.1697–1837)*, Newton Abbot, 1972

Forrer, L., comp., *Biographical Dictionary of Medallists, Coin-, Gem-, and Seal-Engravers, Mint-masters, &c., ancient and modern, with references to their works. B.C.500–A.D.1900*, 8 vols., 1904–30

Fosbroke, Thomas Dudley, *An Original History of the City of Gloucester, almost wholly compiled from new materials: including also the original papers of the late R. Bigland*, 1819

Foster, Joseph, *Alumni Oxonienses: the Members of the University of Oxford, 1500–1714: Their Parentage, Birthplace, and Year of Birth, with a Record of their Degrees*, 4 vols., Oxford, 1891–2

———, *Alumni Oxonienses: the Members of the University of Oxford, 1715–1886: Their Parentage, Birthplace, and Year of Birth, with a Record of Their Degrees*, 4 vols., Oxford, 1888

Foxon, D.F., *English Verse 1701–1750. A Catalogue of Separately Printed Poems with notes on contemporary collected editions*, 2 vols., Cambridge, 1975

[Franks, Augustus F.], ed., *Medallic Illustrations of the History of Great Britain and Ireland to the Death of George II. Compiled by Edward Hawkins, . . .* and edited by Augustus W. Franks and Herbert A. Grueber, 2 vols., 1885, reprinted, 1969

Gaskell, Philip, *The First Editions of William Mason*, Cambridge Bibliographical Society Monograph No. 1, 1951

———, *A New Introduction to Bibliography*, Oxford, 1972, corrected edition, 1974

George, M. Dorothy, *London Life in the Eighteenth Century*, 1925, new edition, 1966

[Gray, Thomas], *A Catalogue of a Most Interesting Collection of Manuscripts and Books of the Poet Gray . . . also of various editions of his works . . . Which will be sold by auction, by Messrs. S. Leigh Sotheby & John Wilkinson . . . on August 28th, 1851*, [1851]

Greenwood, David, *William King. Tory and Jacobite*, Oxford, 1969

Griffith, Reginald Harvey, *Alexander Pope: A Bibliography*, University of Texas, Austin, 1 vol. in 2 parts, 1922–7

Grimwade, Arthur G., *London Goldsmiths 1697–1837. Their Marks and Lives from the Original Registers at Goldsmiths' Hall and other Sources*, 1976, Second, revised edition, 1982

[Grove, George], *Grove's Dictionary of Music and Musicians*, ed. Eric Blom, 10 vols., 1966

———, *The New Grove Dictionary of Music and Musicians*, ed. Stanley Sadie, 20 vols., 1980

Gurney, Lieut.-Col. Russell, *History of the Northamptonshire Regiment 1742–1934*, Aldershot, 1935

Hagley, Worcestershire, The Official Guide, Third edition, c.1958

Halkett, Samuel and John Laing, eds., *Dictionary of Anonymous and Pseudonymous English Literature, . . . New and Enlarged Edition*, 9 vols., 1926–62

Handbook of British Chronology, ed. Sir F. Maurice Powicke and E.B. Fryde, Second edition, 1961

Hart, A. Tindal, *The Eighteenth Century Country Parson (circa 1689 to 1830)*, Shrewsbury, 1955

Heberden, William, *Commentaries on the History and Cure of Diseases*, 1802

Henning, Basil Duke, ed., *The House of Commons 1660–1690*, 3 vols., 1983

Hermann, Frank, *Sotheby's. Portrait of an Auction House*, 1980

Hind, Arthur M., *A History of Engraving and Etching*, 1908, Third edition, reprinted, New York, 1963

An Historical and Descriptive Account of the Town & Castle of Warwick; and of the neighbouring Spa of Leamington, [By W.F., i.e. William Field], Warwick, 1815

Holgate, Clifford W. and Herbert Chitty, eds., *Winchester Long Rolls 1723–1812*, Winchester, 1904

Horn, D.B., ed., *British Diplomatic Representatives 1689–1789*, The Royal Historical Society, Camden Third Series, Vol. XLVI, 1932

Jackson, Maj. E.S., *The Inniskilling Dragoons. The Records of an old Heavy Cavalry Regiment*, 1909

Jones, Hugh David, *John Balguy. An English Moralist of the 18th Century*, Leipzig, (Falckenbergs Abhandlungen 2), 1907

Ketton-Cremer, R.W., *Norfolk Portraits*, 1944

———, *Thomas Gray. A Biography*, Cambridge, 1955

Labarre, E.J., *Dictionary and Encyclopaedia of Paper and Paper-making*, Amsterdam, 1937, revised edition, 1952

Lempriere's Classical Dictionary of Proper Names mentioned in Ancient Authors Writ Large, 1788, Third edition, revised and rewritten, 1984

Le Neve, John, *Fasti Ecclesiae Anglicanae, or A Calendar of the Principal Ecclesiastical Dignitaries in England and Wales, Corrected and Continued by T. Duffus Hardy*, 3 vols., Oxford, 1854

———, *Fasti Ecclesiae Anglicanae 1541–1857. III Canterbury, Rochester and Winchester Dioceses*. Compiled by Joyce M. Horn, 1974

———, *Fasti Ecclesiae Anglicanae 1541–1857. IV York Diocese*. Compiled by Joyce M. Horn & David M. Smith, 1975

Lillywhite, Bryant, *London Coffee Houses. A Reference Book of Coffee Houses of the 17, 18 and 19 Centuries*, 1963

[Lincoln's Inn], *The Records of the Honorable Society of Lincoln's Inn. The Black Books*, 5 vols., Lincoln's Inn, 1897–1968

Lippincott, Louise, *Selling Art in Georgian London. The Rise of Arthur Pond*, New Haven, 1983

List of Catalogues of English Book Sales 1676–1900. Now in the British Museum, 1915

Lugt, Fritz, *Repertoire des Catalogues de Ventes Publiques, Intéressant l'Art ou la Curiosité, Première Periode vers 1600–1825*, The Hague, 1938

[MacMichael, William], *The Gold-headed Cane* [Anecdotes of Drs. Radcliffe, Mead, Askew, Pitcairn, Baillie] *By Dr. W.M.*, 1827, A New Edition with an Introduction and Annotations by George C. Peachey, 1923

Mason, William, *The Works of William Mason, M.A. Precentor of York, and Rector of Aston*, 4 vols., 1811

Mayor, J.E.B., ed., *Cambridge under Queen Anne. Illustrated by Memoir of Ambrose Bonwicke and Diaries of Francis Burman and Zacharias von Uffenbach*, Cambridge, 1911

Melville, Lewis, *pseud.*, [i.e. Lewis S. Benjamin], *Brighton: its History, its Follies, and its Fashions . . . With portraits, caricatures, views, etc.*, 1909

Milton, John, *The Prose of John Milton*, ed. J. Max Patrick, 1968

Monk, James Henry, *The Life of Richard Bentley, D.D. Master of Trinity College . . . with an Account of his Writings, and anecdotes of many distinguished characters during the period in which he flourished*, 1830, Second edition . . . corrected, 2 vols., 1833

Munby, A.N.L. and Lenore Coral, *British Book Sale Catalogues, 1676–1800: A Union List*, 1977

[Mussett, P.], *Lists of Deans and Major Canons of Durham 1541–1900*, Durham, 1974

Namier, Lewis, *England in the Age of the American Revolution*, 1961

——— and John Brooke, eds., *The House of Commons 1754–1790*, 3 vols., 1964

New Guide. An Historical and descriptive Account of Warwick and Leamington, Second edition, Warwick, 1822

Notes and Collections relating to Brewood, Staffordshire, Printed for Private Use Only, Wolverhampton, 1858

———, a reissue, with additional material and a supplement, 1860

O'Donoghue, Freeman, *Catalogue of Engraved British Portraits Preserved in the Department of Prints and Drawings in the British Museum*, 6 vols., 1908–25

Palmer, W.M., *William Cole of Milton*, Cambridge, 1935

The Parliamentary History of England, From the Earliest Period to the Year 1803, 36 vols., 1806–20

Pattingham Parish Register 1559–1812, Staffordshire Parish Registers Society, ed. H.R. Thomas, Stafford, 1934

Paulson, Ronald, *Hogarth: His Life, Art, and Times*, 2 vols., New Haven, 1971

Peile, John, comp., *Biographical Register of Christ's College 1505–1905. And of the Earlier Foundation, God's House 1448–1505*, 2 vols., Cambridge, 1910–13

Penkridge Church Register 1575–1735, Staffordshire Parish Registers Society, ed. Norman W. Tildesley, 1945–6

Peters, Marie, *Pitt and Popularity. The Patriot Minister and London Opinion during the Seven Years War*, Oxford, 1980

Pipe Ridware Parish Register, Staffordshire Parish Register Society, ed. F. J. Wrottesley, Exeter, 1905

Plomer, Henry R., *A Dictionary of the Printers and Booksellers who were at work in England, Scotland and Ireland from 1668 to 1725*, 1922

———, *A Dictionary of the Printers and Booksellers who were at work in England, Scotland and Ireland from 1726 to 1775, England by H.R. Plomer, Scotland by G.H. Bushnell, Ireland by E.R.McC. Dix*, 1932

Pope, Alexander, *The Poems of Alexander Pope (Twickenham Edition)*, ed. John Butt, 12 vols., 1939–69

———, *Pope. The Critical Heritage*, ed. John Barnard, 1973

Pruett, John H., *The Parish Clergy under the later Stuarts. The Leicestershire Experience*, University of Illinois Press, 1978

Purnell, Edward K., *Magdalene College*, 1904

Randolph, Herbert, ed., *Life of General Sir Robert Wilson, from Autobiographical Memoirs, Journals, etc.*, 2 vols., 1862

Registrum Regale: A List of I. The Provosts of Eton. II. The Provosts of King's College, Cambridge. III. The Fellows of Eton. IV. 'Alumni Etonenses' . . . With illustrative and biographical notices, Eton, 1847

Report of the Committee of the Highland Society of Scotland, appointed to inquire into the nature and authenticity of the poems of Ossian. Drawn up by Henry Mackenzie, Edinburgh, 1805

Rococo, Art and Design in Hogarth's England, Victoria and Albert Museum, 1984

Rye, Walter, *Norfolk Families*, Norwich, 1911–13

Ryley, Robert M., *William Warburton*, Twayne's English Authors Series, Florida State University, Boston, 1984

Sale, William Merritt, Jr., *Samuel Richardson. A Bibliographical record of his Literary career*, New Haven, 1936

Scarse, Charles E., ed., *Birmingham 120 years Ago. Being a Reprint of an old directory, published in 1777; to which has been added a Streets Directory, a Trades Directory, and a few Notes of Comparison between Birmingham of 1777 and the City of To-day*, Birmingham, 1896

Scott, R.F. and J.E.B. Mayor, *Admissions to the College of St John the Evangelist in the University of Cambridge*, 3 vols., Cambridge, 1893–1931

Sedgwick, Romney, ed., *The House of Commons 1715–1754*, 2 vols., 1970

The Sherborne Register. Fourth Edition. 1550–1950, [ed. B.P. Pick], Winchester, 1950

Smith, James Hicks, *Brewood: A Resumé Historical and Topographical*, Second edition, revised and enlarged, Wolverhampton, 1874

Speck, W.A., *The Butcher. The Duke of Cumberland and the Suppression of the 45*, Oxford, 1981

Spence, Joseph, *Observations, Anecdotes, and Characters of Books and Men collected from conversation*, 1820, ed. James M. Osborn, 2 vols., Oxford, 1966

Stephen, Leslie, *History of English Thought in the Eighteenth Century*, 1876, Third edition, 2 vols., 1902

Stone, George Winchester, ed., *The London Stage 1660–1800. A Calendar of Plays, Entertainments & Afterpieces . . . Part 4: 1747–1776*, 3 vols., Carbondale, 1962

Strange, Hamon le, *Norfolk Official Lists, from the Earliest Period to the Present Day, compiled from original sources*, Norwich, 1890

Straus, Ralph, *Robert Dodsley. Poet, Publisher & Playwright*, 1910

Suffolk Notes from the Year 1729. Compiled from the Files of the "Ipswich Journal", Ipswich, 1883–4

Sykes, Norman, *Church and State in England in the XVIIIth Century*, Cambridge, 1934

———, *Edmund Gibson, Bishop of London, 1669–1748. A Study in Politics & Religion in the Eighteenth Century*, 1926.

Tate, W.E., *A Domesday of English enclosure acts and awards*, ed. M.E. Turner, Reading, 1978

Thieme, Ulrich and Felix Becker, eds., *Allgemeines Lexikon der Bildenen Kunstler*, 34 vols., Leipzig, 1907–47

Tomasson, Katherine and Francis Buist, *Battles of the '45*, 1962

Tucker, Susie I., *Protean Shape. A Study in Eighteenth-century Vocabulary and Usage*, 1967

Venables, Edmund, *Annals of the Church of St. Mary the Great*, Cambridge, 1856

Venn, John and J.A. Venn, comps., *Alumni Cantabrigienses. A Biographical List of all Known Students, Graduates and Holders of Office at the University of Cambridge, From the Earliest Times to 1900*, 10 vols., Cambridge, 1922–54

The Victoria History of the Counties of England. Staffordshire, 1968–

Voltaire, François Marie Arouet de, *Candide*, ed. J.H. Brumfitt, 1969

Waagen, Gustave, *Treasures of Art in Great Britain: Being an Account of the Chief Collections of Paintings, Sculptures, Illuminated MSS, &c. &c.*, [Translated from the German by Lady Eastlake], 3 vols., 1854

The Warwick Guide; containing a concise historical account of the town, and particular descriptions of the Castle, Warwick, Leamington and Coventry, [?1830]

Waterhouse, Ellis, *The Dictionary of British 18th Century Painters in oils and crayons*, 1981

Watson, John Selby, *The Life of William Warburton, D.D. Lord Bishop of Gloucester from 1760 to 1779: With Remarks on his Works*, 1863

Webb, Marjorie, *Michael Rysbrack Sculptor*, 1954

Wheatley, Henry B., *London Past and Present. Its History, Associations, and Traditions*, 3 vols., 1891

Willis, Robert, *The Architectural History of the University of Cambridge, and of the Colleges of Cambridge and Eton*, ed. John Willis Clark, 4 vols., Cambridge, 1886

Winstanley, D.A., *The University of Cambridge in the Eighteenth Century*, Cambridge, 1922, reprinted, 1958

———, *Unreformed Cambridge. A Study of certain Aspects of the University in the Eighteenth Century*, Cambridge, 1935

Woodruff, C.E. and H.J. Cape, *Schola Regia Cantuariensis: A History of Canterbury School. Commonly called the King's School*, 1908

Wooll, John, *Biographical Memoirs of the late Revd. Joseph Warton, D.D. To which are added, A Selection from his Works; and a literary correspondence between eminent persons, reserved by him for publication*, 1806

Wordsworth, Christopher, *Scholae Academicae: Some Account of the Studies at the English Universities in the Eighteenth Century*, Cambridge, 1877

———, *Social Life at the English Universities in the Eighteenth Century*, Cambridge, 1874

Wurtsbaugh, Jewel, *Two Centuries of Spenserian Scholarship (1609–1805)*, 1936, reissued, 1970

Articles

Batey, Mavis, 'William Mason, English Gardener', *Garden History. The Journal of the Garden History Society*, i, 2 (Feb. 1973), pp. 11–25

Blore, G.H., 'An Archdeacon of the 18th Century. Thomas Balguy, D.D., 1716–1795', *Winchester Cathedral Record*, xx (1951), 19–22.

Burne, S.A.H., 'The Staffordshire Campaign of 1745', *Transactions of the North Staffordshire Field Club*, lx (1925–6), 50–76

Eddy, Donald D., 'Richard Hurd's Editions of Horace and the Bowyer Ledgers', *Studies in Bibliography*, xlviii (1995), 148–69

Farr, M.W., 'Sir Edward Littleton's Fox-Hunting Diary 1774–89', *Essays in Staffordshire History Presented to S.A.H. Burne*, ed. M.W. Greenslade, *Collections for a History of Staffordshire*, Fourth Series, vi (1970), 136–70

Fletcher, W.G.D., 'Documents relating to Leicestershire, preserved in the Episcopal Registry at Lincoln', *Associated Architectural Societies' Reports and Papers*, xxii. Part 2 (1894), 227–365

Gascoigne, John, 'Mathematics and Meritocracy: The Emergence of the Cambridge Mathematical Tripos', *Social Studies of Science*, xiv (1984), 547–84

Gomme, Andor, 'Catton Hall Derbyshire', *The Country Seat. Studies in the History of the British Country House*, ed. Howard Colvin and John Harris, 1970

Greenslade, M.W., 'The Staffordshire Historians', *Collections for a History of Staffordshire*, Fourth Series, Staffordshire Record Society, xi (1982)

'Institutions of Shropshire Incumbents', ed. W.G.D.F., *Transactions of the Shropshire Archaeological and Natural History Society*, Fourth Series, Shrewsbury, v (1915), 185–208

Kettle, Ann J., 'The Struggle for the Lichfield Interest 1747–68', *Collections for a History of Staffordshire*, Fourth Series, Staffordshire Record Society, vi (1970), 115–35

King, R.W., 'Italian Influence on English Scholarship and Literature during the "Romantic Revival" ', *Modern Language Review*, xx (1925), 48–63

Livingston, James C., 'Henry Dodwell's *Christianity Not Founded on Argument* 1742 – Revisited', *Journal of Theological Studies*, N.S., xxiii (1971), 466–78

Mack, Maynard, 'Pope's Books: A Biographical Survey with a Finding List', *English Literature in the Age of Disguise*, ed. Maximillian E. Novak, 1977

Morton, E.P. , 'The English Sonnet, 1658–1750', *Modern Language Notes*, Baltimore, xx (1905), 97–8

Oswald, Arthur, 'William Baker of Audlem, Architect', *Collections for a History of Staffordshire*, Staffordshire Record Society, (1950–1), pp. 107–35

Pollard, Graham, 'Changes in the Style of Bookbinding 1550–1830', *The Library*, xi (1956), 71–94

Raines, Robert, 'An Art Collector of Many Parts', *Country Life*, 24 June 1976, pp. 1692–4

———, 'Peter Tillemans, Life and Work, with a List of representative Paintings', *Walpole Society*, xlvii (1978–80), 21–59

Rinaker, Clarissa, 'Thomas Warton. A Biographical and Critical Study', *University of Illinois Studies in Language and Literature*, Vol. II, no. 1., 1916

Robson, K.J.R., 'The S.P. C.K. in Action. Some Episodes from the East Riding of Yorkshire', *The Church Quarterly Review*, xlvi (1955), 266–78

Scarfe, Norman, 'Little Haugh Hall, Suffolk', *Country Life*, 5 June 1958, 1238–41

Seton, Sir Bruce, 'The Orderly Book of Lord Ogilvy's Regiment', *Journal of the Society of Army Historical Research*, ii (Special Number) 1923

Speck, W.A., 'Politics', *The Eighteenth Century*, ed. Pat Rogers, 1978

Sykes, Norman, 'The Duke of Newcastle as Ecclesiastical Minister', *English Historical Review*, lvii (1942), 59–84

Taylor, Stephen, ' "The fac totum in ecclesiastic affairs"? The Duke of Newcastle and the Crown's Ecclesiastical Patronage', *Albion*, xxiv (1992), 409–33

Trappes-Lomax, R., ed., 'Archbishop Blackburn's visitation returns of the diocese of York, 1735', *Publications of the Catholic Record Society*, xxxii (1932), 204–388

Tymms, Samuel, 'Cupola House, Bury St. Edmund's', *Proceedings of the Suffolk Institute of Archaeology, Statistics, and Natural History*, Lowestoft, iii (1863), 375–85

———, 'Little Haugh Hall, Norton', *Proceedings of the Suffolk Institute of Archaeology*, ii (1859), 279–87

Wedgwood, Josiah C., 'Staffordshire Parliamentary History from the Earliest times to the present day . . . In three volumes: Vol. II, Part II (1715 to 1832)', *Collections for a History of Staffordshire*, ed. The William Salt Archaeological Society, 1922

———, 'The Staffordshire Sheriffs (1086–1912), Escheators (1247–1619), and Keepers or Justices of the Peace (1263–1702)', *Collections for a History of Staffordshire*, ed. The William Salt Archaeological Society, 1912, pp. 271–344

Theses

Salter, James L., 'Isaac Maddox and the dioceses of St Asaph and Worcester', M.A. dissertation, University of Birmingham, 1962

Shuler, J. C., 'The pastoral and ecclesiastical administration of the diocese of Durham 1721–71; with particular reference to the archdeaconry of Northumberland', Ph.D. dissertation, University of Durham, 1975

Wain, Kathleen, 'The Financial Affairs of Sir Edward Littleton, 4th Baronet, Landowner of the Teddesley Estate in Staffordshire, 1742–1812', Ph.D. dissertation, Liverpool University, 1975

INDEX

Both the Introduction and Letters, including the notes, have been indexed. References are to page number for the Introduction (lower case roman numerals) and to letter number for the Letters (arabic numerals). In each entry for Hurd's correspondents, letters from RH are indexed under the bold-face subheading "letters to".

Bishops and peers are entered under family names, with cross references from the titles. The entries under London include all references to places within the City of London, the City of Westminster, and the built-up area between them.

Church of England Record Society

COUNCIL AND OFFICERS FOR THE YEAR 1995

Patron
The Right Rev. and Right Hon., the LORD RUNCIE

President
Professor P. COLLINSON, C.B.E., M.A., Ph.D., D.Litt., D.Univ., F.B.A., F.A.H.A., F.R.Hist.S., Trinity College, Cambridge CB2 1TQ

Honorary Vice Presidents
E.G.W. BILL, O.B.E., M.A., D.Litt., F.S.A., F.R.Hist.S.
Professor D.S. BREWER, M.A., Ph.D., Litt.D., F.S.A.

Honorary Secretary
The Rev. G.L. CARTER, M.A., D.Phil., Brasenose College, Oxford OX1 4AJ

Honorary Treasurer
R.A. BURNS, M.A., D.Phil., Department of History, King's College London, The Strand, London WC2R 2LS

Honorary General Editor
S.J.C. TAYLOR, M.A., Ph.D., F.R.Hist.S., Department of History, University of Reading, Whiteknights, Reading RG6 2AA

Other Members of Council
K.C. FINCHAM, B.A., Ph.D., F.R.Hist.S.
C.M. HAYDON, M.A., D.Phil., F.R.Hist.S.
Mrs F.M. HEAL, M.A., Ph.D., F.R.Hist.S.
The Rev. Professor P.B. HINCHLIFF, B.A., Ph.D., M.A., B.D., D.D.
C.J. KITCHING, B.A., Ph.D., F.S.A., F.R.Hist.S.
The Rev. J.D. MALTBY, B.A., Ph.D.
W.J. SHEILS, B.A., Ph.D., F.R.Hist.S.
J.R. WOLFFE, M.A., D.Phil., F.R.Hist.S.

Executive Secretary
Miss M. BARBER, M.A., F.S.A., c/o Lambeth Palace Library, London SE1 7JU

'The object of the Society shall be to advance knowledge of the history of the Church in England, and in particular of the Church of England, from the sixteenth century onwards, by the publication of editions or calendars of primary sources of information.'

Membership of the Church of England Record Society is open to all who are interested in the history of the Church of England. Enquiries should be addressed to the executive Secretary, Miss Melanie Barber, at the above address.

PUBLICATIONS

1. Visitation Articles and Injunctions of the Early Stuart Church. Volume I. Ed. Kenneth Fincham (1994)
2. The Speculum of Archbishop Thomas Secker: The Diocese of Canterbury 1758–1768. Ed. Jeremy Gregory (1995)
3. The Early Letters of Bishop Richard Hurd 1739–1762. Ed. Sarah Brewer (1995)

Forthcoming Publications

The British Delegation and the Synod of Dort. Ed. Anthony Milton

German Conversations. Bishop George Bell, The Church of England and German Protestantism, 1928–1957. Ed. Andrew Chandler

Visitation Articles and Injunctions of the Early Stuart Church. Volume II. Ed. Kenneth Fincham

The Diary of an Oxford Parson: The Reverend John Hill, Vice-Principal of St Edmund Hall, Oxford, 1805–1808, 1820–1855. Ed. Grayson Carter

The 1669 Return of Nonconformist Conventicles. Ed. David Wykes

Anglo-Catholic Communicants' Guilds and Societies in the Late Nineteenth Century. Ed. Jeremy Morris

The Diaries of Bishop Beilby Porteus. Ed. Andrew Robinson

Suggestions for publications should be addressed to Dr Stephen Taylor, General Editor, Church of England Record Society, Department of History, University of Reading, Whiteknights, Reading. RG6 2AA.